BEIJING AND SHANGHAI

BEIJING &

Paul Mooney

Additional Material by
Steven Schwankert & Janet Carmosky

Shanghai

Peter Hibbard

Photography by
Anthony Cassidy & Others

ODYSSEY BOOKS & MAPS

Odyssey Books & Maps is a division of Airphoto International Ltd.
1401 Chung Ying Building, 20–20A Connaught Road West, Sheung Wan, Hong Kong
Tel: (852) 2856 3896; Fax: (852) 3012 1825
E-mail: magnus@odysseypublications.com; www.odysseypublications.com
Follow us on Twitter—www.twitter.com/odysseyguides

Distribution in the USA by W.W. Norton & Company, Inc., 500 Fifth Avenue, New York, NY 10110, USA
Tel: (800) 233 4830; Fax: (800) 458 6515; www.wwnorton.com

Distributed in the United Kingdom and Europe by Cordee Ltd., 11 Jacknell Road, Dodwells Bridge Industrial Estate, Hinckley, Leicestershire LE10 3BS, UK. Tel: (1455) 611 185; info@cordee.co.uk; www.cordee.co.uk

Distribution in Australia by Woodslane Pty Ltd., Unit 7/5 Vuko Place, Warriewood, NSW, 2102, Australia
Tel: (2) 9970 5111; Fax: (2) 9970 5002; www.woodslane.com.au

Beijing & Shanghai—China's Hottest Cities, Third Edition
ISBN: 978-962-217-797-0   Library of Congress Catalog Card Number has been requested.
Copyright © 2013, 2006, 2004 Airphoto International Ltd.

All rights reserved. No part of this book may be translated, reproduced or transmitted in any form or by any means, electronic, mechanical, or otherwise, without the prior permission of the publisher, except for brief passages for inclusion in critical articles or reviews. Although the publisher and authors of this book have made every effort to ensure that all information was correct at the time of going to press, the publisher and authors do not assume and hereby disclaim any liability to any party for any loss (including loss of life) or damage caused by errors, omissions or misleading information.

Grateful acknowledgement is given to the authors and publishers who contributed their copyrighted materials to this guide; all said materials remain the property of their respective copyright owners as indicated. The publisher has made every effort to obtain express permission of all copyright holders and to give proper attribution wherever possible; any omission of credit in whole or in part is unintentional.

Additional photography/illustrations courtesy of Magnus Bartlett xii, 18, 39, 43, 69, 91, 113, 119, 130, 140, 141, 152, 153, 155, 156, 158, 159, 184, 185, 196, 201, 202, 205, 207, 214, 220, 234, 242, 305, 318, 321, 322, 334 (top), 336 (bottom), 342, 356, 361, 375, 381, 383, 386, 392, 400, 409, 433, 453, 455, 456, 466, 470, 471, 472, 473, 481, 487, 493, 494, 504 (bottom), 508, 529, 536, 599, 603, 606; Beijing Wuye Yangguang Graphic Design Ltd. 106 (bottom); Kevin Bishop 4; Alex Cao 106 (top); Anthony Cassidy i, ii–iii, iv, vi, vii, ix, 2, 7, 8, 9, 12, 20–21, 33, 50, 54, 55, 57, 64, 65, 66, 77, 79, 81, 96–97, 103, 104, 105, 112, 125, 134, 166, 184, 194, 212, 213, 235, 243, 246, 265, 308, 309, 333, 343, 364, 371, 374, 380, 389, 402 (top), 403, 406, 410, 469, 475, 488, 497, 499, 521, 533, 698; Cathay Pacific 17; China Guides Series 348–9, 510; China Intercontinental Press 417, 531, 532; China Tourism Press 439; Dong Qing 175; Peter Danford 24–25, 29, 61, 78, 100, 124, 149, 150; Richard Dobson 256; Dragonair 23; Er Dong Qiang 357; Department of Kuomintang Party History, Taipei 366, 367; Hongkong Museum of Art 83; Hanart TZ Gallery 70, 109, 306, 319, 416; Park Hyatt Beijing 224, 226; Peter Hibbard 268, 310, 327, 331, 334 (bottom), 336 (top), 338, 339, 341, 352, 373, 391, 395, 396, 401, 402 (bottom), 405, 414, 422, 425, 427, 429, 430, 431, 434, 435, 437, 452, 450, 454, 456, 461 (bottom), 462–3, 486 (bottom), 500, 504 (top), 505, 524, 534, 535; 538, 539; Oliver Horn 461 (top); HSBC 162, 344, 350; Illustrated London News 52, 84, 94, 163, 218, 236, 240, 249, 258–9, 314–5, 316–7, 376, 440, 514–5, 526; William Lindesay 46–7, 93, 174, 199, 239, 260, 262, 267; Li Suk Woon 221; Sarah Lock 379; Lu Chuan 231, 233; Keith Macgregor 377, 387, 490; Mao Posters 86–7; James Montgomery 245, 346, 418, 496; Paul Mooney 10, 30–31, 180, 181, 182, Ingrid Morejohn 250; Museum of History 502; Michael K. Nichols 486 (top); Shanghai Municipal Archives 520; Shanghai People's Fine Arts Publishing House 326, 393, 413, 428, 517; The Commercial Press Ltd 252; Timeless Image 442; Jeremy Tredinnick 263; US Department of Defense 34; US Naval Historical Centre 464; Voices of Asia 25; John Warner Publications 116–7, 139, 34 ... 26–27, 36–37, 110; Jacky Yip 390, Back co...

Editors: Helen Northey, Ne... ...wai
Maps: Mark Stroud, Cindy ... ..d, Hong Kong
Front cover photographers: ... :.com
Xue Changming (bottom ...

Preceding pages: pa... ...nal carving;
page v: King... ...le of Heaven;
...t: Shanghai.

Foreword

This yin-and-yang guide to Beijing & Shanghai informally celebrates over 34 years of our China Series. Our first guide to "Peking" was published in 1979 followed by Shanghai in 1980. Though little more than a quarter of a century has passed, both Beijing and Shanghai have become the old gentlemen of a pubescent nation. Regardless of their wildly different claims on history, both cities now present a face of youth and ambition in a manner that would have been thought inconceivable in 1979.

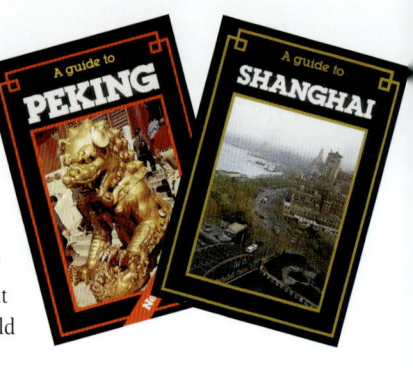

Back then, Beijing was fraught with frustration for many travelers—though it was more than compensated for by the endearing local population. Shanghai, at that time, was redolent with acrid smells and disrepair—but yet again its addictive charm and character was ever-present in one's senses.

Naturally, the China Series has grown up with these cities. Our first guide to Peking by Shann Davies was just 64 pages long. The most recent edition of that guide, by William Lindesay and Wu Qi, suggested the framework for portions of this two-city guide, first published in 2004, and credit must be given to them, as much of their historical descriptions remain valid today. Paul Mooney's considerable knowledge of China's capital, as well as his vast experience in reportage and travel guides, has contributed to the development of the Beijing section ever since. A special note of thanks must be made to all the contributors for providing an insider's view of the capital.

Our original guide to Shanghai was largely written by Lynn Pan, a renowned author who lives in Shanghai. For many years the core material of the Shanghai guide was based on her work along with that of Jill Trew and May Holdsworth. My first contributions appeared in a more recent edition (1995). Since then, the changes in Shanghai have been so great that the Shanghai section of this now-combined guide was started from scratch in 2004, and has been revised for the third time in this new edition.

In addition to the expanded, useful Facts for the Traveler found in the individual Beijing and Shanghai guides, the "Chineasy" language section and the extensive website directory add a further dimension to understanding modern life in these cities. Janet Carmosky's ingenious and idiosyncratic contributions offer an amusing and even somewhat controversial view of life in these metropolises. In deference to the collective authors' wishes, the Beijing and Shanghai sections use American and British spelling conventions respectively. Also, we've included some of the original early guides' photos; their juxtaposition to today's pictures provides a unique insight into the incredible changes these cities have experienced in record time.

—*Peter Hibbard MBE, Shanghai*

Contents

Foreword XII
Introduction XVI
Facts for the Traveler ...13
  Entry and Exit...................................... 13
    Visas 13
    Customs 16
    Air Ticketing and Taxes.................... 16
    Entering and Leaving Beijing............ 17
    Entering and Leaving Shanghai........ 23
  Health 38
  Packing Checklist 40
  Safety and Security 44
  Local Time 45
  Climate... 45
  Sightseeing 51
  Hotels.. 53
  Money 55
  Communications & Media 60
  Useful Websites................................... 65
  A Brief Guide to the Chinese
    Language 72
  Chineasy 74

Beijing 79
  History of Beijing 80
    Under the Ming 81
    Under the Qing 82
    The Coming of the Barbarians........... 83
    Under the Republic 85
    Modernization 85
    Olympic Gold.................................... 88
  Reigns of Ming & Qing Emperors 90
  Getting around Beijing...................... 113

  Beijing Metro..................................... 113
  Taxis and Public Transport 114
Sights in Beijing 125
  Southern Districts......................... 156
  Western Districts........................... 167
  Northern Districts 173
  Museums 173
Sights Around Beijing 182
  The Northwest 183
  The Great Wall............................... 195
  The North 201
  The East 204
  The Southwest................................ 207
  The West 210
Suggested Itineraries for Beijing........ 213
Entertainment & Nightlife 218
  Tea Culture.................................... 218
  Performing Arts............................. 219
  Acrobatics and Puppetry................. 219
  Dance, Music and Film................... 220
  Beijing Opera 220
Food and Eating 234
  Cafe Society 237
Shopping 241
  Places to Shop 242
  Shopping Suggestions 251
Sports, Recreation & Leisure............. 260
Places of Worship 264
  Churches & Others 264

Practical Information
Hotels in Beijing 270
Dining in Beijing 278
Useful Addresses in Beijing 294

Shanghai 308

Shanghai—Yesterday and Today 314
Getting Around Shanghai 326
Sights in Shanghai 342
    Western Heritage 347
    Revolutionary Heritage 363
    Chinese Heritage........................... 375
    Other Places of Interest 393
        The Huangpu River Cruise 393
        Other Sights in Puxi 394
        Sights in Pudong 400
        Other Sights in Pudong 404
    Museums & Exhibition Centres 406
Sights Around Shanghai 423
    Suburban Shanghai 423
        Songjiang District 424
        Qingpu District 429
        Jiading District 434
        Jinshan District 436
        Minhang District 437
        Baoshan District 440
        Fengxian District 441
        Chongming County 441
    Excursions from Shanghai 443
        Water Towns 443
        Resorts 452
        Neighbouring Cities 454
Suggested Itineraries for Shanghai 470
Arts & Entertainment 474
Food and Eating 488
Shopping 498
    High Street Shopping 498
    Markets and Bazaars 503
    Other Shopping Opportunities 507
Sports, Recreation & Leisure 512
    City Parks 516
Churches and Worship 524

Practical Information ... 541

Hotels in Shanghai 541
Dining in Shanghai 553
Useful Addresses in Shanghai 566

Recommended reading ... 583

Index 595

Special topics

Beijing Canned Air 10
A Portrait of Empress
    Dowager Cixi 14
The Anti-Reform Dream Team 34
Imperial Examinations 94
Beijing Rules 101
Beijing Heat 107
Off-Season Beijing:
    The Best Time to Go? 118
Peking Versus Beijing:
    What's in a Name? 121
Hutongs 151
The Pailous 155
The Concubine in the Well 160
Chinese Livess 168
China National Postal
    and Postage Stamp Museum 180
The Garden of Perfection
    and Brightness 190
Chengde: Imperial Resort 205
Saints and Sinners 216
Beijing Nightlife 222
Beijing: A Culture of Walls
    and Lanes 227
Chinese Cinema Today 230
China's Favorite Take-out 238
Dive Beijing 263
Grand Hotel de Pekin 268
East of the Poo 310

THE BUND TO BUBBLING WELL 338
SHANGHAI ARCHITECTURE 357
SHANGHAI'S HISTORY THROUGH
   ITS NAMES 360
THE SONG FAMILY 366
THE SHANGHAI UNDERWORLD 372
NEW HEAVEN—OLD EARTH................... 412
THE PEASANT PAINTERS OF JINSHAN 438
NO SEX PLEASE, WE ARE CHINESE 446
SANCTITY OF THE SANDS 450
YANGPU 458
THE FLOWERS ON THE SEA 484
THE SHANGHAI PERSONA....................... 523
CLASSICS AND CONVERSIONS.................. 534
CHRONOLOGY OF PERIODS IN
   CHINESE HISTORY 594

LITERARY EXCERPTS

GEORGE N. KATES on *A Means of*
   Communication 58
BETTE BAO LORD on *A Matter of*
   Principle.. 71
MARCO POLO on *Seating*
   Arrangements 98
JOHN BLOFELD on *Imperial Eunuchs* .. 136
PU YI on *Bad Omens at his*
   Coronation 138
LAO SHE on *Summer Festivities* 144
WILLIAM LINDESAY on *Being Alone*
   on the Great Wall 198
FRIAR DOMINGO NAVARRETE on *A*
   Seventeenth-Century Prison........... 266
I CHING & CHEN TZU-ANG
   on *Matters of Philosophy*................ 307
ALDOUS HUXLEY
   on *The Social Organism* 323
J. G. BALLARD on *The Fallen Angels* 345
ORVILLE SCHELL
   on *A Visit to the Barber's* 378

ORVILLE SCHELL on *Money Changers*.... 392
SIMONE DE BEAUVOIR on *Class Struggle* 457
VICKI BAUM on *The Roof* 464
PO CHÜ-I on *A Bald, Lazy Man* 468
ANCHEE MIN on *Acting for the Party*..... 476
JAMES LAFAYETTE HUTCHISON
   on *Cocktails at the Club* 478
D. J. ENRIGHT on *Dreaming and Food* ... 491
RICHARD HUGHES on *Shanghai Recalled*.528
RENA KRASNO on *The Restricted Area* .. 530
ODYSSEY 1979 on *Shanghai Nightlife* .. 533
NIEN CHENG on *The Red Guards* 540
LU XUN on *Clutching at Straws*........... 593

MAPS

CHINA—OVERVIEW FOR BEIJING
   & SHANGHAI x
THE OLD CITY, BEIJING........................... 92
BEIJING CITY CENTER 111
BEIJING 122
BEIJING SUBWAY.................................... 126
AROUND BEIJING................................... 132
IMPERIAL PALACE.................................. 135
TEMPLE OF HEAVEN 157
SUMMER PALACE................................... 188
MING TOMBS 200
GRAND CANAL SYSTEMS OF THE SUI,
   SONG & YUAN DYNASTIES 305
SHANGHAI.. 324
SHANGHAI METRO................................. 328
SHANGHAI CITY CENTRE 337
THE FOREIGN SETTLEMENTS
   OF SHANGHAI 348
PUDONG 399
SHANGHAI DISTRICTS............................. 424
SHANGHAI, ZHEJIANG AND JIANGSU 445

INTRODUCTION —*Janet Carmosky*

Anyone who visits China is, by definition, curious. A few weeks of time off, and an adequate stack of hard earned money to spend could take us to luxurious indulgence, exuberant celebration, or serene retreat. China is none of these. We go to China because we want to be surprised, to access the inaccessible, to ponder the opposite, to observe the alternate. We hope to go home understanding more about how the things we've seen fit in the larger scheme of things.

We come to China to observe our reactions to China. Will its otherness perplex, irritate, delight or humble us? Will it be the subtleties or the extremes that touch us most memorably?

Above all, a trip to China exercises our powers of observation and deduction: are we seeing what we think we're seeing? Or something else entirely? Having spent my life since the age of 16 studying China, living in China, doing business in China, raising kids with a Chinese man, and generally explaining China to the west and vice versa, here's my conclusion: as a career China specialist, I'm still surprised by how differently east and west view almost everything. But that's the fun of being in China. Like a well-written mystery, the most revealing answer to the question, "what's going on?" tends to be richly layered, deeply satisfying, and surprising.

As well-traveled as any of us may be, there's still no place quite like China. It's ancient but so incredibly alive; it's constantly changing yet ever true to some immutable definition of Chinese-ness. It has been the most powerful, wealthy, and technologically advanced nation on the earth several times, lost it all, and come back again; down but never out. A powerful and proud nation that cyclically learns from, then shuts out the world beyond its borders, China is simultaneously obsessed with holding the *respect* of the outside world, and utterly unconcerned whether outsiders *understand* it or not.

How could we understand? Two-dimensional descriptions are useless: Rich or poor? Modern or backward? Free or controlled? Spontaneous or structured? Conserving or wasteful? Increasingly egalitarian or increasingly polarized? Based on deep spiritual traditions, or relentlessly crass and commercial? They don't stretch to fit a China-shaped object.

We read about China in the business press—the country's stunning rise to economic, financial, and geopolitical power actually gaining momentum through the global financial crisis. The books about China tend to pull hard to a single pole: strident and sweeping: China is winning, and we have to grasp the magnitude of this development and Do Something. China is falling apart, and we need to Get Out and save ourselves. Fiction and autobiography mine the plentiful veins of tragedy.

If we're lucky, our curiosity will deepen, and urge us to experience China ourselves. Welcome to any Chinese city. We arrive, our senses telegraph frantically: What colors! What sounds! What smells! What rhythm is driving the throng? Is that polite language or an argument? Scanning the hundreds of faces surrounding us, we wonder, where are they going? What are they thinking? Is this ruckus normal or is something going on? It's vast and ancient; loud, in your face but also subtle, complex and deep.

Wait, we think, isn't three-fourths of China's population rural? Do not the roots of Chinese culture reach directly back to mankind's transition from hunter-gatherers, to agricultural settlers, then to urbanization? Could we learn more from a visit to the countryside? The short answer: no. It's not accessible, not navigable. Too subtle. No place for foreign visitors, who would note only that one structure uses a slightly paler tile than its neighbor does, one sign is machine printed while most are hand painted. One intersection appears to be more significant than another. The pace is slow, though conversations begin and end so abruptly. Dwellings behind walls, guarded by dogs. Dusty and half-broken factories and taxi cabs with rusty fenders. That urban-rural income disparity that Hu Jintao and Wen Jiabao were always talking about means, among other things, that if you show up in a village, forget about ATMs or a hotel with a gym, or a decent cup of coffee or much bilingual anything.

Rest assured, if you're curious about China, you'll find plenty to explore by sticking to the cities. At least 30 are considered "major", and all of these are at least moderately user-friendly, with taxi cabs and sidewalks, banks and hotels, Starbuck's and Carrefour, its own unique cultural highlight. To list a very few: Xi'an's terracotta warriors, arguably the world's finest group sculpture; Harbin's ultimate winter carnival; the misty riverside rockscapes of Guilin; the Qing imperial hunting grounds near Shenyang; Hangzhou's West Lake; Xiamen's musical harbor called Gu Lang Yu; Chongqing's pell-mell, smoky, cliff-hanging construction. Each has its landmarks such as a famous train station, river port or pagoda with layers of historical significance; the significant architecture of Russian, Islamic, German, or Buddhist influence.

Hard to plan an itinerary with 30 cities? Pick two, and visit Beijing and Shanghai. They are accessible, energetic, larger than life. Nothing subtle about either place: they are as two symphonies of showy symbolism, yet utterly dissimilar to each other.

Observe how Beijing digs in: blocky, rectangular, and grounded, mostly stone; all hierarchy and tradition. The highways are elevated, eight or ten lane straight lines of brown concrete. Barriers and fences, hidden doors, featureless façades all conspire to leave humans sensing their puny scale, their individual insignificance. The message: China's capital is vast and sufficient unto itself. It rules over all. You may, if permitted, express your gratitude for being here.

Shanghai is architecturally antithetical to Beijing. It strives up and out: vertical, soaring, steel and glass; all ambition, innovation, and experiment, highways flying in outrageous neon-lit curves, lights of countless colors splashed over every surface. Every five steps bring a new doorway, a new shop; every street curves around to surprise with shortcuts or new vistas. The message: Could Shanghai be any more shiny? Any more slick? Isn't this fun? Aren't we clever? Come in, spend some money.

Beijing studies, reads, writes angry rock songs and houses unselfconscious artist colonies. Shanghai engineers, dances, opens commercial art studios, and sells exceedingly polished fashions and furnishings. Beijing is a big loud restaurant under the open stars, with your best mates and draft beer by the pitcher. Shanghai is a den of smoky silence with women who are so accessible, so enticing it just can't be true; cognac and cigars that, while quite good, really should not cost that much. Beijing is proud to be Chinese, while Shanghai is proud to be international.

Beijing and Shanghai are also like rival sisters who secretly wish the other would fall and break her nose. Beijing, host of the 2008 Summer Olympics, began the harangue of preparatory propaganda as early as 1999, during their Olympic bid. In Beijing the exhortation to uphold Olympic spirit with all its competitive, nationalistic undertones is ubiquitous. If Beijing is a symphony, it is by Beethoven. What composer has ever beaten a dead horse with more conviction and force?

In Shanghai, the propaganda machine focused massively on the Shanghai World Expo in 2010. How fitting that the finest in technology, commerce, and quality of life from all over the world should exhibit it this fine city, graceful as a Tchaikovsky ballet, tweedling on, ever so pretty, ever so sweet?

The twin juggernauts are fueled by pride openly and often declared, and an almost taboo, very deep dislike of the other. One has been the capital for 1,000 years, and has come to expect tribute. The taxi driver descended from scholars who had mastered thousands of pages of archaic text, and survived intrigue that would have challenged Machiavelli. Money is easy—it falls from the provinces in the form of taxes. In Beijing, it's all about power.

Everyone is important in Beijing. Never doubt—for Beijingers will readily tell you—they also know people who are even more important. Here's the game in Beijing, in this particular situation: are my important friends more important than your important friends are? Compared to Beijing, Shanghai's power structure is absurdly uncomplicated. All power stems from the Mayor's Office. End of story.

Beijing is the city of ambiguous but ultimately, unquestionably sufficient power. It is huge, built on the scale of the car by a megalomaniac (Kublai Khan, the founding Yuan Dynasty emperor) in the time of horses, indeed in the time when the Yuan

Left: *Girl in minority head gear.*

Dynasty ruled from Korea to Vietnam, Beijing to nearly Vienna. Do not be fooled by the map. If your hotel is only two blocks from the subway stop, it is not walkable. One block may be nearly a long full mile, straight as an arrow, built for the unimpeded speed of imperial chariots.

In Shanghai, by contrast, the eminently walkable streets of Puxi crinkle densely over each other. We can walk the narrow spidery paths streets once strode by the fishermen, craftsmen, factory workers, and financiers that came from the countryside to seek their fortune in traffic with the foreigners. No domain of poet-scholars and diplomats, Shanghai prospered along with shrewd merchants from ingloriously commercial places like Ningbo and Canton; played host to the cunning of barbarian robber barons hailing from London, Baghdad, Boston, Marseilles and Vladivostok.

The city sprang to life late in China's long history: it was in the years after 1840, when Shanghai's river port was ceded to foreign colonial powers. Rich commissions went to the local compradors that assisted the colonials in their trades of textiles, opium, and manufactured goods. The rest of Shanghai—think huddled masses yearning to breathe free, but not getting anywhere close—made do with whatever scraps they could grab. The Japanese occupation in 1937 dammed the river of cash flowing into the pockets of the British, French, Americans and others whose governments held most of the land, so Shanghai's own capitalists grew stronger. The 1949 revolution set off to nationalize industry, so most of Shanghai's capitalists fled, with their equipment, to go build what was then a nasty backwater: Hong Kong. For the Shanghainese who stayed, on they hustled, becoming the industrial engine for the huge segments of the economy. Between 1949 and 1991, perhaps 40 percent of China's industrial output originated from this one city. Obedient as ever, Shanghai shipped 70-some percent of its money made to Beijing as tax revenue.

The Shanghainese have eked out their prosperity by collecting the margin left over when the lion's share of the wealth went elsewhere. Unlike Beijingers, the Shanghainese don't collect tribute, they pay it; and they don't make the rules, they just obey them, carefully, exploiting every shred of common sense or commercial logic they embody.

Deng Xiaoping's last appearance as official head of state was in 1991, in Shanghai. He lowered its rate of tax contribution to Beijing—from a rumored 80 percent to a whispered 18 percent. The city, keeping its own money at last, prospered, and reclaimed its position as China's window to the world. Inevitably, the Shanghainese believe, the city will resume its place as *Asia's wealthiest* financial and commercial center. Yet in perpetuity, it is the capital, Beijing, which presents itself as the most *important Chinese* city. What matters more, the Beijingers ask, the policy that allows

Left: *An old man plays a bamboo flute in the pavilion on the summit of Coal Hill, overlooking the Forbidden City.*

people to make money, or the money those downstream beneficiaries are permitted to make?

In the simplest possible terms, if culture expresses collective values about the distribution of money and power, Shanghai represents money, Beijing represents power, and the feud between them is insight Into the struggle for the nation's soul. They go at it viciously and in secret, ever hoping to grasp an upper hand, humiliate the other for a very nasty, very private split second of historical time. They position against each other endlessly, calculating, who needs who more?

Most visitors develop an immediate preference for one or the other. Being a foreigner can be a very different experience, depending on where you do it. Beijingers think you must be ready for an adventure. Shanghainese think you must have some money. Beijingers think you might be fun to go on a hike in the mountains with, and take to meet their uncle. Shanghainese think you might really enjoy meeting a lovely young relative of theirs in a slinky dress, while you discuss investing in an exciting new business. Beijingers will tell you youíre stupid, insult your nationality, and throw crockery at your head when you owe them money. Shanghainese will tell you that you are the sun, the moon, and the stars, and that the only way you could possibly be better is if you were part Shanghainese, and that it doesn't matter when you pay them back. Then they will assign someone to trail you until you do. Beijingers can never tell you where anything is, even when it's next door, because It makes no difference to them. Shanghainese will fall over each other trying to prove how well they know their city, going out of their way to provide detailed directions so you can go to a place you might like. When you stay in Shanghai, you will meet foreigners who hate Beijing. Too rigid, too slow, too hostile. When you stay in Beijing, you will meet foreigners who hate Shanghai. Too slick, too docile, too manipulative.

As different as they are, they agree on a few things: Our City is the best, that Other City is delusional and no fun at all. Crime, dirt, and social ills are caused by migrant workers, not by Us. Guangzhou, China's third city, is nothing but a rabble rousing blue collar town. Hong Kong? A has-been, a hill of bean counters, and technocrats without a shred of learning or creativity.

Aside from their excessive pride In themselves, what else do Shanghai and Beijing have In common? What universal Chinese traits can we observe in both places? Money mad, boisterous and showy. Calculating and oblique. Grounded in relationships, contextual in all things, never absolute or decisive, guaranteed to change plans in mid stream. Incurably pragmatic, secretly romantic. Constantly, subconsciously, involuntarily calculating their capital in both relationships and cash terms. (Note: Do not ever play cards for money anywhere in China, unless you wish to test your limits of wealth and humility).

Right: *Magic balls.*

8 BEIJING & SHANGHAI

What would Mao think?

Sure, you'll see Beijingers and Shanghainese drinking coffee and speaking English. But fear not—you haven't flown all this way to meet people just like you. Consider that a Christian evangelist named Hong Xiu Chuan once led China into the world's bloodiest civil war—contemporaneous to America's Civil War, the Taiping rebellion sent as many as 20 million to their deaths. Hong, convinced he was the brother of Jesus, exhorted his followers to reconcile themselves to God and Jesus. Who spoke, incidentally, through their numerous, capricious, and often bloodthirsty advisors, relatives and wives. The term "Christian" guaranteed nothing like a familiar value system: why should the kingdom of righteousness look any different than the Imperial court?

We're just different. At the end of a long day, westerners long to go back to the hotel, eat something simple and rest quietly, while the Chinese seem always out, always dining on something novel, always yakking away in groups. How do we explain the Chinese reluctance to reach conclusions, their insatiable appetite for gamesmanship, their flawlessly ambiguous speech; their capacity to be obedient whenever necessary—which is often—anarchic whenever possible—which is not enough for most Chinese people's taste; and inclined to trust—practically nobody, ever.

In Beijing and Shanghai, enjoy using your credit card, your soft bed and fluffy towels, watching well-dressed locals eating at KFC. But don't get too complacent. Watch what happens when you try to force a timetable or explain that anything is "really very simple". Try to win a game of cards. Does the powerhouse city you're visiting run on the same fuel as "back home?"

You're in China. Admit it. It's amazing.

Janet Carmosky, known during her long marriage to Mr. Zhang as Janet Zhang, spent 18 wild years doing business in China, and now, as the New York-based CEO of The China Business Network, *spends her time rediscovering her American side and making China cross-border*

Right: *Admiring the sanctity of the Falun Temple.*

BEIJING'S CANNED AIR —By Paul Mooney

On the evening of January 12, 2013, a thick smog began to envelope Beijing. Skyscrapers and street lights were swallowed by the haze and visibility fell to a under 200 meters—if that far. Citizens stayed close to home or made sure to don face masks if they had to go out, where the air smelled of coal and stung the eyes

The US Embassy reported the hourly peak level of PM2.5—tiny particulate matter than penetrate deep into the lungs—had crept to an unheard of 755 micrograms

The CCTV Headquarters, better known locally as the "walking pants building"

per cubic meter, or "beyond index", and more than 20 times higher the World Health Organization safety levels. The WHO says chronic exposure to particles in the air can increase the risk of developing cardiovascular, respiratory diseases, and lung cancer.

When the reading had hit the already hazardous 500 in 2010, one daring US Embassy official who Tweeted the readings had the temerity to describe the reading as "Crazy Bad," although that politically incorrect distinction soon disappeared.

According to the Environmental Protection Agency, levels from 301 to 500 are considered "hazardous", which means people should avoid outdoor activity. The World Health Organization says a score exceeding 500 to be more than 20 times the level of particulate in the air that is considered safe.

Soon, hospitals were experiencing surges in patients seeking help for respiratory illnesses, with the Beijing's Pediatric Hospital treating 7,000 children a day for respiratory problems. Children were confined to their classrooms and face masks were selling out at Beijing shops.

How did we get here?

Zhou Rong, a climate and energy campaigner at Greenpeace, was quoted by China Dialogue as attributing the phenomenon a perfect storm. For one, a spike in the use of coal during the cold winter months—much of north China uses coal for heat in the winter. Adding to the problem, between the preceding Thursday and Saturday, an inversion layer had formed which prevented pollution from dispersing, resulting in pollution accumulating close to the ground. Then, to top things off, on Friday, pollution from the coal industry in neighboring Shanxi and Inner Mongolia blew into the area, topped off by the arrival Saturday of heavy industry and coal-power pollution from Hebei.

"It was as if someone had put a lid on the city," said China Dialogue.

Yet, the government also has a responsibility for the high levels of pollution in the city.

In a rare interview in the South China Morning Post, Qu Geping, China's first environmental protection chief, put the blame on the country's "economic growth at all costs" mentality and on the political system. Mr. Qu told the newspaper that pollution had run wild for close to four decades as a result of unchecked economic growth under "rule of men," rather than rule of law. "Their rule imposed no checks on power and allowed governments to ignore environmental protection laws and regulations," the Post reported.

The pollution has prompted one wealthy Chinese entrepreneur, Chen Guangbiao, to begin selling "fresh" air in soft drink can, the label embossed with his own likeness and name. Chen, known as a bit of a showman, said the 5RMB earned for each can would go to charity. But his main aim, he said, was to wake up government officials and citizens to the danger.

"If we don't pay attention to environmental protection, in 10 years every one of us will be wearing gas masks and carrying oxygen tanks on the streets," Cheng told ABC News. "By that time, my canned fresh air will be a necessity for household."

Jan 2013, Beijing, pic from www.militaryphotos.net.

Facts for the Traveler
Entry and Exit
Visas

If you are traveling independently, either as a tourist or business visitor, you must obtain a visa before entry in to China. Applications should be made through Chinese embassies or consular offices in your country. If you are entering through Hong Kong visas are easily obtained from various travel agencies, including CITS, CTS and the Foreign Ministry of the People's Republic of China. Visa applications can be processed on the same day in Hong Kong, though if you can wait two or three days the cost is considerably reduced. One to three month tourist visas (L visas) are readily available as well as business visas (F visas) which can be issued for up to one year, including multiple entries. Just one passport photograph and a completed application form are necessary. Generally business visas issued overseas will require an official letter from the official host organization in China, whereas in Hong Kong this regulation can be waived. Tourist visas can only be extended once in Beijing or Shanghai for a maximum period of one month.

Travellers from 45 countries, including the US, the UK and Canada, arriving by air to Beijing and Shanghai in transit to other countries can stay in the localities for 72 hours without a visa. Check the situation with your airline.

Tourists entering China as part of a group may have a document listing members' details on a single group visa prepared by their tour operator and handled by the tour leader or allotted group member. These are valid for the duration of the tour only and the whole group must enter and leave China together. However, some companies ask that you obtain your own visa to give greater flexibility to group participants who may add on optional tours to the beginning or end of standard tour itineraries. This also obviates any difficulties in amending the group visa that would result in a group member being unable to complete the tour.

Border formalities are generally painless and efficient. Those on individual visas receive entry and exit stamps and must complete entry and departure forms. Those on group visas do not receive passport stamps and are not required to complete entry or departure forms. Health declaration forms are issued on the journey to China and should be handed over on arrival. Your passport should be valid for at least six months after your departure from China.

Left: *Exploring the Great Wall is both a cerebral and physical experience.*

A Portrait of Empress Dowager Cixi

Every year, on her birthday, at an auspicious hour, the Empress Dowager would set free 10,000 caged birds. It must have been a spectacular sight to see her and her entourage in the snow-covered grounds of the Summer Palace as she opened cage after cage of exotic and brilliantly coloured birds and then prayed fervently that they would not be recaptured. By doing this, she hoped that Heaven would be good to her in her next life. She did not realize that her eunuchs were waiting on the other side of the hill to resell as many of the birds as they could catch.

Empress Dowager Cixi ca.1890.

Most of what is known about the Court of imperial China concerns the late 19th and early 20th centuries, for it was only then that eyewitness accounts were written. Before that, Court life was meticulously hidden from the curious eyes of outsiders, whether Chinese or foreign.

It was the Empress Dowager Cixi, effective ruler of China from 1861 to 1908, who began, in her 60s, to invite the ladies of the foreign legations to visit her at Court. Moreover, her chief Lady-in-Waiting was Der Ling, daughter of a Manchu official, who had been brought up in France. In Der Ling, Cixi found someone who could bridge Chinese and Western cultures, and explain to her the many puzzling features of Western ways.

In 1903, Mrs Conger, wife of the American Minister to Beijing, persuaded the Empress Dowager to allow her portrait to be painted so that it could be shown at the World Exposition of St Louis. This was a novel idea to the Chinese whose portraits were painted only after death. The American artist Katherine Carl, sister of the Commissioner of Customs in Chefoo, thus became the first foreigner since Marco Polo to stay in the Imperial Palace, and the first foreigner ever to enter the ladies' quarters. The portrait, measuring six foot by four—disappointingly small in Cixi's opinion—is now owned by the US Government and hangs in the Freer Gallery of Art in Washington. Two or three other paintings of the empress were left with her in Beijing.

Miss Carl wrote an account of her unique experience, of her impressions of her surroundings—her surprise at the 85 clocks in the Throne Room, where she painted the portrait—and of the kind and considerate treatment she received from Cixi. But it is only on reading Der Ling's recollections that we see how anxious Cixi was that Miss Carl should not become too well acquainted with Court life. Der Ling was charged to remain constantly with Miss Carl and specifically commanded not to teach the American any Chinese. Cixi was concerned that Miss Carl should not see the eunuchs punished, lest she should consider the Court officials savages.

Cixi's secretiveness pervaded all her dealings with foreigners. A special court language was used when in the presence of foreigners who understood Chinese. On one occasion, entertaining some American ladies at the palace, she invited them to see her private sleeping quarters. Unknown to them, however, the previous day had been spent in totally altering the furnishing and fitting of the bedroom so that her real taste and intimate surroundings remained unknown. Chinese subjects were also traditionally forbidden to look at members of the imperial family. Cixi was greatly surprised to learn from Miss Carl that Queen Victoria, whom she very much admired, took walks and carriage rides in public places where she could be seen by the populace at large.

The Empress Dowager was never alone, for even while sleeping she was attended by eunuchs and ladies-in-waiting who were forbidden to fall asleep. She rose early between 5.30 a.m. and 6.00 a.m. Every morning, with Emperor Guangxu, her adopted son, she would receive her ministers and generals and deal with matters of State. The rest of the day would be given over to diversions. Both Katherine Carl and Der Ling describe walks in the palace grounds, boat trips on the lake and games of dice. There were also theatrical performances of which the empress was particularly fond.

If the day was filled with diversions, the year at the Court was punctuated by festivities. Birthdays, the New Year, weddings, accessions and the seasonal festivals were celebrated with fireworks, day-long performances by eunuchs and Court troupes, presentation of gifts and extravagant banquets at which glittering gold, silver and jade tableware would be heaped with hundreds of delicacies. On these occasions the imperial family and their officials wore their grandest robes and the usual business of the Court was suspended for several days.

Customs

Under a new regulation put into place in 2005, all visitors must fill out a customs declaration form upon entry and departure from China. In Beijing and Shanghai, the forms can be found at counters located just outside the check-in entrance, and must be handed over to a Customs officer before proceeding to check-in.

There is no limit on the amount of foreign currency that can be taken into China. 1.5 liters of alcohol over 12 percent proof, 400 cigarettes (or 100 cigars), unlimited film and medicines for personal use may be taken in free of duty. The carriage of fresh food produce into China is prohibited by health and quarantine regulations. When buying antiques one must remember that only items made after the reign of the Jiaqing Emperor (1820) may legally be exported and all must bear a red wax seal affixed by the Bureau of Cultural Relics. Receipts for large purchases such as legitimate antiques and gold products should be kept in case inspection is required on departure.

Air Ticketing and Taxes

China's air ticket market is somewhat competitive, but is not fully subject to market conditions. Occasionally, government directives will decrease or increase the amount of discount that can be offered on tickets, and price wars break out quickly in times of relative deregulation. A 20 percent discount off the listed fare is usually possible. Look for travel agency advertisements in English-language publications such as *that's Beijing*, *that's Shanghai*, and *City Weekend*. Also, look for international airline special offers by subscribing to the Beijing and Shanghai newsletters of Xianzai.com.

Tickets purchased in China are generally not subject to the restrictions of those bought outside the country. Although buying a ticket at the airport generally means paying full fare, airfares in China do not increase or decrease based upon advanced purchase. They are far more flexible than the non-refundable, non-changeable tickets that are now the norm of international air travel.

Safety on Chinese airlines has improved dramatically over the past 20 years. Once considered unsafe during the early 1980s, China's air fleet is now one of the newest in the world. You're more likely to be on a new Airbus or Boeing aircraft when flying with a Chinese airline than with a US-based carrier. Although service sometimes still lags behind its Asian competitors, such as Singapore Airlines, Dragon Air and Cathay Pacific Airways, Chinese airlines are often a low-cost alternative flying the same routes as their foreign counterparts. Air China should not be confused with China Airlines, a Taiwan-based carrier that has been involved with several serious accidents in recent years.

The airport departure tax is now included as part of your air ticket payment. No separate payment is necessary.

Entering and Leaving Beijing
Air Travel

Air China's main office is located at 15 Xi Chang'an Jie (tel. 400 8100 999 for both domestic and international). Most large hotels have travel desks that offer a computerized reservations service and flight confirmations.

Hong Kong based Dragonair offers seven flights per day to and from Beijing and Cathay Pacific has resumed services. Hong Kong to Beijing is currently the most expensive air route in the world. Air China and China Southern Airlines offer lower fares and less frequent flights, the latter of which has one discount flight between the two cities per day. For a list of airline offices in Beijing please refer to page 294.

For aviation history buffs, the evolution of Beijing's Capital Airport can be seen as some flights taxi to or from their gates. There is one, small, concrete terminal that was the main building during President Richard Nixon's visit to China in 1972. That part of the runway is still used to greet VIPs, and the private planes of multinational executives are often parked there. On the western side of the airport complex is the main terminal used during the 1980s and 1990s. Part of the old airport has been renovated and now handles some domestic flights.

On 1 November 1999, a new airport was opened, increasing capacity and shifting the passenger terminal to allow the renovation of the old terminal in time for the entire complex to handle the flood of visitors expected for the 2008 Olympic Games.

The most common means of transport from Capital Airport to central Beijing is a taxi. For reference, at time of publication, the fare to the China World Trade Center complex cost approximately Rmb 100, including a 10 yuan highway toll that will not appear on the meter. Choose a taxi where the meter is clearly visible to the passenger, instead of being placed down near the gearshift. Make sure the driver starts the meter when driving away, and that the meter is not already running at the time you enter the vehicle. Always ask for receipts for all charges and do not pay until those charges are verified on the printed receipt. There is no charge for baggage.

Three bus lines run from Capital Airport to different areas of Beijing. One of them, the A Line, runs 24 hours. Look for signs inside the airport terminal for

buses—they depart from an area to the right of most of the airport's baggage claims areas. Tickets may be purchased on board each bus at no extra charge, for 16 yuan each. The A Line departs from the right-hand end of the building and stops at the Sanyuan Qiao on the northeast third ring road where one can find a taxi. The final stop is the Aviation Building in Xidan, near the Xidan metro. An Airport Express Line went into operation in 2010, linking Dongzhimen downtown with the airport. The 28km trip takes about 25 minutes, and also links with Terminals 2 and 3. The first train departs from Dongzhimen Station at 6:00am and the last train departs from Dongzhimen Station at 22:30pm. The first train departs from Terminal 3 at 6:21am and the last train departs from Terminal 3 at 22:51pm.

TRAIN TRAVEL

Train travel in China is either the country at its best or its worst. Some people feel that a visit to China that doesn't include at least an overnight rail journey is an incomplete one. For fans, the gentle rocking of the car, the unhurried pace, the rice fields, mountains, and rivers slipping past the window, and interaction with seat and cabin mates, can be the embodiment of travel to a distant destination. For others, riding trains in China can be a nightmare, filled with staring car mates who spit on the floor, stay up all night playing cards and making noise, while English hounds corner the captive tourist to practice their ABCs. Regardless, there may not be a choice—commuter flights are not as common in China as they are in the US, and some shorter routes may be served only by rail or road links, not air.

Beijing can be reached by rail from a handful of international destinations including Moscow, Ulan Bataar, Hanoi and in theory, Pyongyang in North Korea. For train tickets to these places contact 5182 1114 (for all three rail stations). Since July 1997, following China's resumption of sovereignty over Hong Kong, a new service has been running between Kowloon and Beijing. The Beijing-Kowloon train line was specially built and allows express trains to make the more than 2,500-kilometer trip in around 24 hours, it runs on alternating days. In December 2012, the Beijing-Guangzhou Express was opened, this trip takes eight hours! Besides these lines, of course, once in China almost all railway routes lead to Beijing. Beijing and Shanghai are linked to Kazakhstan via Urumqi in China's border Xinjiang region. This railroad is known as the bridge to Europe as it serves as the main cargo transportation route between Ningbo port (in Zhejiang province) and Rotterdam. Numerous luxurious trains, featuring two-berth cabins with private toilet facilities, leave Beijing each evening bound for Shanghai, and super fast trains bringing the cities within a five-

The Temple of Heaven, Beijing: The roof of the Hall of Prayer for Good Harvest is just visible beyond the blue ceramic roof tiles of the Imperial Vault of Heaven, whilst in the foreground are the stone pailous of the Circular Mound.

hour reach were introduced in 2011. Lhasa in Tibet is now in reach of both cities travelling on the highest stretch of rail line in the world.

Train accommodation is available in soft sleeper, hard-sleeper, soft-seat and hard-seat carriage. Sleeper accommodation provides a berth in either a four-bed compartment with door, or a six-bed without a door. All soft sleeper carriages en route to Beijing have air conditioning, as do most hard sleepers. However, be aware that they do not always have heat. Discovering that one's car is not heated during a 14-hour, overnight journey can be a very rude awakening.

Beijing's ticket offices are computerized, as are those in most provincial capitals. This makes ticket purchasing much quicker than it was a few years ago. Food is available on the train and from platforms en route, although quality can vary from decent to inedible. Boilers for hot water exist in every third sleeper carriage.

Incoming trains terminate at either the aging Beijing Station, or the modern Beijing West Station, which opened at the beginning of 1996. Beijing Station serves routes with termini in the north, north-east and south-east, namely the provinces of Heilongjiang, Jilin, Liaoning, Inner Mongolia, most of Ningxia (Yinchuan), Hebei, Tianjin, part of Henan (Luoyang), Shandong, Jiangsu, Anhui, Shanghai, Zhejiang, and parts of Fujian. Beijing West Station serves termini in Xinjiang, Gansu, Qinghai, Sichuan, Chongqing, Yunnan, Guizhou, Guangxi, Shaanxi, part of Shanxi, part of Hunan, Hubei, Jiangxi, part of Fujian and Guangdong.

The Beijing West Rail Station now has an orderly taxi line. However, taxi chaos still reigns outside the Beijing Rail Station and the traffic regulations concerning the setting down and picking up of fares only compounds the situation. Some drivers demand exorbitant fares from baggage-laden arrivals, whether they be foreign or Chinese. If you can walk a few hundred meters away from the station you will be treated more respectfully. Beijing Station is conveniently located on the subway system. Outside the West Railway Station to the east (right) there are a number of bus stops with regular departures to the central part of the city.

Regarding the purchase of tickets for travel out of Beijing, bookings can be made up to four days ahead of departure, but things are changing, with the selling of tickets up to ten days in advance being tested. The concept of roundtrip tickets for rail journeys still has not caught on, so it is advisable to make securing one's return transportation the first order of business upon arrival at your destination.

Both stations have special ticket offices for foreigners. At Beijing Station it is located on the ground floor in a room off the soft sleeper waiting room in the southeast corner of the main hall. At Beijing West Station, the ticket office is on the east side of the first floor. Office hours for both are the same, 5:30am to 10:30pm, and closed for lunch from 12:00pm to 1:00pm daily.

Entering and Leaving Shanghai
Air Travel

More than 25 international airlines serve Shanghai. Although the majority of them serve regional destinations; including frequent flights to Japan, the Philippines, Thailand, Malaysia, Korea, Hong Kong and Macau, Shanghai is well connected to many parts of the globe. Leading European carriers, including British Airways, Virgin, Lufthansa, KLM and Air France, have frequent connections to Europe, whilst major North American airlines, including United Airlines, Northwest Airlines and Air Canada, are all represented. Qantas offers flights to Australasia. China's national carrier, Air China, offers flights to around 30 countries, including numerous flights to Europe and North America. The Shanghai-based China Eastern Airlines also provides a range of international flights. There is a wealth of flights from Hong Kong with Dragonair operating over 100 flights a week on a route that is also operated by Cathay Pacific. Shanghai is approximately two hours from Hong Kong, 11 hours from London and 12 hours from Los Angeles.

Shanghai is comprehensively connected by air to all parts of China. There are usually over 30 flights a day to Beijing with a flying time of around two hours as well as direct flights to as far away places as Lhasa in Tibet. The local carriers, China Eastern Airlines and Shanghai Airlines, are regarded as amongst the best in China. Please refer to page 562 for details of airline offices in Shanghai.

Shanghai is served by two airports. The older and more conveniently located Hongqiao Airport is now largely used for domestic flights. Most international flights and many domestic ones use the Pudong International Airport, which opened in 1999. Both airports have two terminals.

Preceding pages (20–21): *The Forbidden City houses the largest collection of ancient buildings in China.*

Following pages: *A night view of the Bird's Nest.*

The Hongqiao Airport is just 15 kilometers (nine miles) from the center and an inexpensive taxi journey can take less than 20 minutes to cover this distance in good conditions. Within the international arrival halls at Pudong International Airport there are ATMs, money exchange services, numerous hotel desks and a CITS desk. A number of comfortable air conditioned buses run from Pudong to downtown, including ones to the Hongkou Football Stadium (gate 4), Shanghai Railway Station, People's Square, and the city center terminus at 1600 Nanjing Road West, on the corner of Changde Road, as well as to Hongqiao Airport. They depart at intervals of around half an hour. An early morning journey from the city center can take as little as 40 minutes, aided by using the Lupu Bridge that opened in 2003. However, journey times can be a lot longer during rush hour periods, so leave enough time for getting to the airport. The airport is around 40 kilometers (25 miles) from the center of town. Both airports can also be conveniently reached on metro line 2.

The Maglev (magnetic levitation) train made its inaugural journey on New Year's Eve, 2002, just 2.5 years after the inception of the project—with German Chancellor Gerhard Schroeder and Chinese Premier Zhu Rongji on board. The German manufactured train rests on a cushion of magnetism a few millimeters from the track and covers the 31 kilometer (19 mile) journey from the airport to the Longyang Road Metro Station in around eight minutes. The train has an amazing top speed of 430 kilometers (nearly 270 miles) per hour and has been making routine trips to the airport since October 2003. If you have time, take a look at the exhibition hall beneath the station to see how the technology evolved and how it was subsequently applied in Shanghai.

Train Travel

The main Shanghai Railway Station was revamped and given a modern glass and steel face with the turn of the millennium. Same day tickets can be purchased in the main building whilst advance tickets (up to 10 days before departure date) are available in the ticket office to the east of the main building. Queues can be long and it is more convenient to book tickets through hotels or travel agencies. The station is served by metro line 1 and metro line 3. The station's taxi rank is to be found underground in the square to the south of the main building.

The huge South Railway Station, which opened in mid-2006, is also linked to metro line's 1 and 3. Its revolutionary circular design is a world-first. Most trains leaving the station are headed towards Southern China. All regional trains, some of which have two decks of comfortable seating, are air-conditioned and largely smoke

Preceding pages: *China's Olympic National Stadium, aka The Bird's Nest.*

free. There are numerous, convenient, overnight express trains to Beijing with journey times of under 12 hours. A new daytime, all seat, 'bullet' train with a journey time of 10 hours, was introduced in 2007. Bullet trains also travel to the neighbouring cities of Nanjing and Suzhou.

Shanghai is also linked by rail to Hong Kong (Hung Hom Station). This is regarded as an 'international' journey and as of 2003 immigration formalities are now taken care of on the train. This train has deluxe two-berth sleeper cabins in addition to the standard four-berth soft-class and six-berth hard-class. Train K99 departs on alternate days from Shanghai at 12:24pm arriving at 11:53am the next day. It returns from Hong Kong the same afternoon at 3:54pm, in the guise of Train K100, arriving in Shanghai at 4:10pm on the following day.

Above: *The Maglev train, capable of 430 kilometres per hour, links Shanghai to its new airport.*
Following pages: *Beijing's majestic Gate of Heavenly Peace.*

Boat Travel

The only regular international maritime route at present serving Shanghai is from Kobe and Osaka in Japan. There are two weekly departures for Japan operated by the China-Japan International Ferry Company and the Shanghai International Ferry Company. Crossing times are in the region of 40 hours. The long running boats from Hong Kong to Shanghai have been withdrawn from service, although the Hong Kong based Star Cruises do offer occasional luxury cruise packages from Hong Kong that include Shanghai (www.starcruises.com.hk). Boats to and from Japan dock at the Shanghai International Passenger Terminal just to the east of the Bund off Daming Road (E). International cruise liners that call on Shanghai also dock there.

It is possible to arrive or depart from other coastal cities such as Qingdao, Dalian and Xiamen. Most boats dock at the Gongpu Road Passenger Terminal. Many local routes, including passages to Ningbo and Nanjing, have been axed as greatly improved train and highway links have proved much more attractive to passengers. Waterborne services to popular tourist spots such as Putuo Island and Dinghai still operate. Traditionally the Shiliupu Dock, not far from the Bund, has been the major port for regional traffic—but much business has been moved to Wusong Pier on Songbao Road. You are advised to seek information on the current situation from your hotel or CITS should you wish to travel by boat.

Weddings are ostentatious affairs.

LONG-DISTANCE BUS TRAVEL

It is possible to get to Beijing by bus There are numerous daily departures from the Hutie Long Distance Bus Station at 783 Hengfeng Road (tel. 6353 2300), south-west of the Shanghai Railway Station, with journey times of under 15 hours. Many of the long-distance bus stations around town offer services to central and eastern provinces—but some go much further, with journey times of up to 45 hours to get to the Guizhou Autonomous Region. Asia's largest long-distance bus station opened just north-west of the Shanghai Railway Station in mid-2005 with buses traversing the nation. Despite the relative comfort of some of the buses, this form of transport is really for the intrepid traveler. Traveling by bus in the Shanghai region is a different matter and can be a very comfortable alternative to rail travel (*see* pages 443, 454).

Left: *"Loss of the Honourable E.I. Company's War Steamer Madagascar—Captain James Minn Dicey, in a typhoon at the entrance of the Formosa Channel, whilst employed in an expedition against the Chinese, three boats out of four being lost, and fifty-seven of the crew drowned, is respectfully dedicated to his Vice Admiral Sir William Parker G.C.B. Naval Commander in Chief of the fleet on the China Expeditions."—Painted by His Majesty William IV's marine painter W.J. Huggins, based on an original sketch by Captain Dicey, this plate image was engraved by E. Duncan and first published by Mr. Huggins in 1843.*

The Anti-Reform Dream Team
— By Paul Mooney

On the morning of November 15, the seven members of China's new Politburo Standing Committee filed into a room in the Great Hall of the People in a neat row, their places to come to a halt on the floor pre-marked with tape. Their order signaled their place of importance in the new pecking order, although in reality the men are all equals. Each man wore a dark blue suit, white shirt and all but one wore red or maroon ties, and each had the same slicked down, dyed coal black hair that's de rigueur with the country's Communist leadership.

Xi Jinping, No. 1 in the leadership, and the Party's new general secretary, was followed by Li Keqiang, the new premier, Zhang Dejiang, who will oversee Parliament, Yu Zhengsheng, head the Chinese People's Political Consultative Conference, Liu Yunshan, who will be vice president, Wang Qishan, corruption buster, and Zhang Gaoli, economic czar.

Chinese President Xi Jinping, from DoD photo by Erin A. Kirk-Cuomo.

In the opaque world of Chinese politics, little is known about how the all-powerful leading group is chosen, but China watchers say the choice is the result of back-room infighting, old-fashioned negotiation and compromise. In a sharp break with the past two decades, when the Communist Party leadership was dominated by technocrats and engineers, six of the seven members of the new Politburo Standing Committee studied social sciences and the humanities.

The question China watchers immediately began to debate was whether or not the new group of leaders would be closet reformers able to adopt the many measures needed to deal with the countless challenges facing China. If they fail to restructure the economy quickly, China may not be able to survive for much longer.

Although the new leadership boasted different educational backgrounds, most were seen as conservatives, and so there appears to be little hope for far-reaching economic and political reforms, which many agree are needed if the party is to deal with the challenges facing the nation.

And the challenges are many. Cities, towns and villages around China are clogged by pollution, social inequality is on the rise, the educational system is bending under growing strains, rule of law is almost non-existent, ethnic issues are heating up, corruption continues to run rampant, and the economy is in a downturn.

China's new leadership knows it needs to move quickly to restructure how economy works, focusing more on consumption rather than investment and exports. But that would mean lessening the domination of state companies in many industries, something Party conservatives are reluctant to do. Political reform is even more unlikely because party leaders see that as a direct challenge to their control of the government and society.

Minxin Pei, China expert at Claremont McKenna College, says a market economy needs rule of law, which in turn requires "institutional curbs" on government. As these two restrictions on power run against the Party's firm desire to dominate society, the party's hands are tied and China is trapped, says Pei.

18th National Congress of the Communist Party of China. Photo by reporter Tung Fong, Voice of America.

Nicknamed the Water Cube, swimmers at the National Aquatics Center broke 25 world records during the 2008 Olympics. The building has now been internally gutted and an indoor shopping arcade constructed.

The futuristic-looking Grand National Theater with its titanium accented glass dome that is completely surrounded by a man-made lake.

Health

For visits to China's larger cities there are no mandatory vaccination requirements. In recent years the US Consulate in Hong Kong has recommended inoculations against hepatitis A and B, Japanese encephalitis, tetanus, polio, cholera and malaria for travelers to China. In fact, travelers are strongly advised to get the Hepatitis A injection in addition to taking other precautions such as having an immunoglobulin shot before departure. Take the advice of your doctor on these matters. If you are traveling to remote parts of China in the summer months, even more consideration be given to protection.

For maintenance of well-being in China it is highly advisable to pay attention to your daily water intake—whether it be in the stifling height of summer or the dry coldness of the Beijing winter. The public water supplies in Beijing and Shanghai are not potable, though completely safe distilled, and mineral water is widely on sale and provided in hotel rooms. Ice cubes, and for that matter ice-creams, are generally safe to consume—but caution should be exercised in the summer months and when eating outside the well-established hotels and restaurants. Mild stomach upsets are not uncommon. You should take some basic precautions—always peel fruit and avoid seafood in local restaurants during the summer months.

The most common ailments contracted by visitors to China are respiratory tract infections and the common cold. Try and safeguard yourself as much as possible by regulating your room temperature and maintaining your body temperature as best you can. The Chinese are often surprised by how little foreigners wear. Whilst it might be sun-bathing weather for the hardy American or European many Chinese will still be wearing long underwear and will often compliment you on being 'strong' and on having good health, whilst at the same time expressing concern that you will catch cold.

Of more concern in recent times has been the advent of SARS and the Swine flu strain H1N1. On arrival you will notice that heat-seeking detectors will greet you at the airport to test your temperature—and many other strict safeguards have been put in place to protect the public. Past outbreaks of infectious diseases should not obscure the fact that China is a very safe place to visit, but of course you should keep up with the latest health advice in general, just as you would when planning a trip to many other parts of the world. For the latest travel advice, not only on health but on visas and other matters, take a look at the UK Foreign Office site (www.fco.gov.uk/travel) or the site of the US State Department (http://travel.state.gov/china.html). The Australian government site is www.smartraveller.gov.au.

Cigarette poster circa 1930.

For the treatment of minor ailments many of the better hotels have a clinic or a doctor on call. For more serious ailments there are a number of clinics and hospitals in Beijing and Shanghai that come up to Western standards as well as some international medical centers staffed with international doctors and nurses. For consultations and prescriptions payment is made on the spot and most credit cards are accepted. Of course it is essential for all visitors to have adequate insurance coverage to meet with any eventuality. Please refer to our Practical Information sections for details of medical facilities.

The discomforts caused by cigarette smoke have often been remarked on by foreign visitors. However the situation has seen a rapid improvement in recent years as the government has banned smoking in many public places—although a 'no smoking' sign doesn't ensure compliance. Over 320 million Chinese smoke and many do not realize that it's bad for their health. It's still very much part of the culture and being offered a cigarette is just like accepting a handshake in the West—if you don't accept then you may get the cold shoulder.

Smoking is not permitted on tour buses, Chinese international and domestic flights, or on most if not all parts of trains. It is further prohibited in large shopping malls and even in the hotel lobby areas in Beijing. Smoking is also prohibited at most popular tourist sites. Furthermore, dropping litter or cigarette ends at various areas in Beijing and Shanghai can result in an on-the-spot fine.

Packing Checklist

Just about everything you could possibly need can be found in China although getting hold of any required items at any particular time of course cannot be guaranteed. Plan to be self-sufficient by packing an adequate supply of your most essential personal items and accessories. As what is deemed to be 'essential' is highly personal and idiosyncratic, and determined by your needs and habits. Detailed below are a few common items basic to general well-being.

Personal Health and Hygiene

Bring any prescription medicines you know you will need and anything you take regularly for your general health. Taking a basic first-aid kit including antiseptic cream and plasters is a good idea. Outside the winter months you should pack insect repellent—though insect pests are not of great concern in the city centers. You should also pack anti-diarrhoeal tablets and painkillers—especially if you take aspirin as it is not widely available. It is wise to carry sun lotion or sun block outside of the winter months, whereas lip salve is an essential item for visitors to the Beijing area outside of the summer months. If you wear glasses bring along a spare pair as well as your prescription. Soft contact lens solutions are widely available.

Toiletries

A fairly comprehensive range of complimentary toiletries are to be found in all good hotels, including soap, shampoo, tooth paste, shower caps and often a lot more. Moisturizer is usually provided but you are advised to bring your own preferred brand to combat the often harsh dry conditions found in Beijing. Talcum powder, which may be desirable in the humid summer conditions, is not always provided. Wet wipes may come in useful as well. International cosmetics are widely available, but at much higher prices than at home.

Clothing

The Chinese are much more informal than most when it comes to matters of dress. Given the season and the object of your visit, it is best to dress comfortably and appropriately. If you are on business, formal attire may be required for official meetings—whereas much less formal attire would usually be more appropriate when eating with business associates in local restaurants. If you are on a leisure trip formal attire is rarely, if at all, required. There are generally no dress restrictions at tourist sites, including temples. A basic essential is a good pair of flat walking shoes —and an umbrella comes in very useful for not only shelter from the rain, but also from the blistering sun. Umbrellas are readily available at a throwaway cost.

In warm weather, the wearing of short pants and sandals is quite acceptable. During the severe Beijing winter, several layers of thin clothes act as a better insulator than one thick garment—and a hat covering the ears is an essential addition. It can also get very cool in Shanghai, necessitating the wearing of long undergarments. Even when the temperature is heading towards 40°C (102°F) in Beijing or Shanghai it is advisable to keep a light jacket or sweater with you as shopping malls, restaurants, taxis and tour buses can become very cool environments.

Express same day and overnight laundry and dry cleaning services are available in all good hotels. If you wish to travel light and very casually, t-shirts and many casual clothes can be picked from local stores and markets often at less than the cost of hotel laundry services.

Electrical Accessories

The electricity supply is 220 volts and electrical sockets in hotel rooms come in a variety of types—two and three flat pin or three square pin. However, 110 volt two-pin sockets are also found in hotel bathrooms. Ensure that any power adapters you need to bring are suitable for the power supply. All top hotels will have a supply of plug adaptors, but you are advised to bring your own for convenience. Hairdryers are generally provided and clothes irons are either found in rooms or available from housekeeping departments.

Photography

If you use roll film, particularly anything that is not of the snapshot variety, bring all that you need with you. Like all of the latest technologies, digital photography has made a massive impact in China. Many department stores and most ordinary photographic stores carry a huge range of cameras and accessories as well as offering digital services.

The Chinese are photo crazy—though they will rarely take a picture without a human subject in it. The only official restrictions on photography relate to the military and to militarily sensitive areas. In theory this includes bridges, airports and railway stations. The use of still and video cameras at most places is unrestricted. However there are some locations where photography is not permitted and where the 'no photo' signs are far from obvious. Such restrictions generally apply to the interior of some buildings—especially in Beijing. It is highly advisable to carry your camera equipment with you at all times.

Sundry Items

It's a good idea to make a photocopy of your passport and insurance policy and keep them separate from the originals. Also ensure that you have made a separate note of the numbers on your traveler's cheques and have your credit card emergency assistance numbers at hand.

There is no shortage of propriety brands of spirits in the stores of Beijing and Shanghai. If you are a smoker many international brands, and scores of the local variety, are on sale at considerably less cost than in the West. Bring your own favorite brand of cigars with you.

Big, beautiful and bold doors still grace the courtyards, the Forbidden City, 1979.

Luggage

The Chinese air authorities recommend the use of a rigid suitcase in China. If you wish to travel with a soft case, it's an idea to pack some rigid cardboard boxes inside. Apart from reinforcing the case they will provide neat compartments for your clothes and other items—and can be discarded when you leave. Domestic airlines restrict check-in baggage to 20 kilograms (44 pounds) per passenger. Note that current security regulations demand that alcohol be packed inside check-in luggage and international regulations apply as to what can be carried in your hand luggage.

Safety and Security

China is probably the safest destination in Asia. You need not fear walking alone in the small lanes of Beijing or Shanghai, even in the darkness of night, and you are likely to receive a warm and hospitable reception wherever you go. However you should exercise a few basic precautions, just as you would anywhere in the world;

- Leave all valuables you don't need in the hotel safe. Remember that your passport is especially valuable and its loss could ruin your trip. Remember not to inadvertently pack anything valuable, including your passport, travel documents and money in your check-in luggage.
- Always carry details of your hotel address with you. If a hotel card is not available take a piece of stationary from your room.
- Do not wear loose, ostentatious or valuable jewellery (especially necklaces and bracelets) when out sightseeing.
- Make sure small backpacks or bags containing your camera or other essentials are zipped up or locked.
- Carry valuables safely on your person—never put your wallet/purse in your back pocket. It's a good idea to keep a stock of 'small money' in a separate pocket.
- Be wary of strangers who approach you. You may come across 'art students' who want to invite you back to their 'studio' or 'school' that in reality is a commercial gallery. You may also be approached by vendors touting so-called 'antiques', or a range of fake goods from bags to watches and DVD's. It is best to ignore unsolicited advances—should you wish to buy such goods they can be secured at local markets. Also be cautious of people inviting you to take tea or a meal with them.
- Be vigilant if you enter into dealings with street hawkers—some may be professional pickpockets.
- There are fewer beggars here than in most other Asian countries, yet they are becoming increasingly common around tourist sites and on the main streets of Beijing and Shanghai.

Local Time

Amazingly for a country measuring some 4,300 kilometers (over 2,500 miles) from east to west, the whole of China operates completely within one time zone—that is Beijing time—eight hours ahead of GMT and 12–13 hours ahead of EST. Despite a brief flirtation in the past, China does not operate a daylight saving scheme.

Climate

Beijing has four clearly defined seasons. From November to March, winter is usually dry and clear but winds from the northwest can bring temperatures down to –15.5°C (–4°F). In November and the first half of December, the weather is crisp and cool and the cerulean blue of the dawn sky intensifies to the point where it appears like a vast turquoise lens.

As Jim Mann describes it in his book *Beijing Jeep*, there are few weather changes in the world so drastic or dismal as the quick passage from Beijing autumn to Beijing winter. For a stretch of eight to 10 weeks in September and October, Beijing is so sunny and balmy it could be a concrete-covered California. Then, in the first weeks of November, the weather turns cold and the sky increasingly grey. Beijing power plants begin burning dirty, low-grade coal, and the air is so sooty that the city is covered with haze. On bad winter days Beijing can be as frigid as Chicago and as polluted as a nineteenth-century British mill town. Locals describe the early winter sky as 'tall' or 'high' or 'deep'. The best winter clothing is layers of warm garments including thermal underwear, sweaters and coats, in addition to warm boots and fur hats with earflaps. Heating in the hotels can be very fierce, while heating in some public buildings can be inadequate or nonexistent. China follows a system of 'command heating'. North of the Yangzi River the heat in many public buildings and residences is turned on 15 November and turned off 15 March, regardless of the temperature. And in many local apartment buildings, the heat goes on for a few hours in the morning and is turned off during the day to conserve fuel. The Chinese produce good winter clothing such as thick cotton underwear, padded jackets and furs, all at reasonable prices.

Spring usually lasts from mid-March to mid-May and is a good time for a visit, with trees and flowers coming into bloom and the occasional shower to wash the city. Clothing should include a warm coat and sweaters as well as some light-weight clothes, and possibly a raincoat.

Following pages: *Snow covers the Forbidden City.*

Spring is the season for Beijing's notorious dust storms. They don't blow in every year, but when they do you will certainly know it! The atmosphere is filled with a near-pudding of yellow to orange dust from the Gobi Desert that finds its way into everything from sealed closets to your closed mouth. No amount of tree planting seems to be able to reduce the amount or density of the dust. It is also dusty in Beijing whenever it is dry.

Beijing summers are very hot and humid. Temperatures reach 40°C (104°F). Light cotton clothing is recommended. Visitors will often be in places without air-conditioning.

Autumn is the best season in the capital. From September to mid-October it is warm, sunny and dry. There is a wealth of color in the parks, and fruit and flowers in the markets. Dress as you would for autumn in southern Europe or northern California.

Average Temperatures in Bejing

		°C	°F		°C	°F		°C	°F
Average		−4.4	24.1		18.9	66.0		19.1	66.4
High	JAN	1.7	35.1	MAY	25.3	77.5	SEP	25.5	77.9
Low		−9.7	14.5		11.9	53.4		12.2	53.8
Average		−2.1	28.2		23.9	74.5		12.2	53.9
High	FEB	3.8	38.8	JUN	29.6	85.3	OCT	18.7	65.7
Low		−7.2	19.0		17.7	63.9		6.8	44.2
Average		4.7	40.5		25.6	78.1		4.3	39.7
High	MAR	11.0	51.8	JUL	30.3	86.5	NOV	10.0	50.0
Low		−0.9	30.4		21.5	70.7		−0.2	31.6
Average		13.0	55.4		24.0	75.2		−2.5	27.5
High	APR	19.4	66.9	AUG	28.9	84.0	DEC	3.0	37.4
Low		6.5	43.7		19.9	67.8		−7.0	19.4

Average Temperatures in Shanghai

Month	Monthly Average		Average High		Average Low	
	°C	°F	°C	°F	°C	°F
Jan	3.3	37.9	7.8	46.0	0.0	32.0
Feb	4.3	39.7	8.7	47.7	1.0	33.8
Mar	8.3	46.9	13.1	55.6	4.5	40.1
Apr	13.8	56.8	19.1	66.4	9.8	49.6
May	18.9	66.0	24.3	75.7	14.9	58.8
Jun	23.2	73.8	28.1	82.6	19.7	67.5
Jul	27.4	81.3	32.3	90.1	24.0	75.2
Aug	27.5	81.4	32.5	90.5	24.0	75.2
Sep	23.2	73.8	28.2	82.8	19.8	67.6
Oct	17.7	63.9	23.2	73.8	13.7	56.7
Nov	11.7	53.1	17.0	62.6	7.7	45.9
Dec	5.9	42.6	10.9	51.6	2.1	35.8

Although Shanghai doesn't experience the extremes of climate found in Beijing, it has hot sticky summers that force local residents to go around town in their best pyjamas.

The summer generally breaks in early June and is soon followed by the 'plum rain' season when heavy rains can be expected until early July. Between then and the middle of September it's often unbearably humid and hot—with daytime temperatures frequently in the mid to high 30s C (90s–100s F). Autumn is by far the best time to visit the city. October is generally fine and dry with warm days and cooler evenings (20s C, 70s F). November is still a good time to visit. The winters can be very grey, cool and rainy—just like London. Sub-freezing temperatures can be experienced and there is often a cold breeze—though snow is not common. It's often hard to tell when spring arrives as it may be warm for a few days in late February or March, but then go back to feeling like winter again. It can remain relatively cool until the end of May—so anytime up to then is still a good time to visit.

Sightseeing

Many first-time tourists will travel to China as part of a tour group. The significant advantages are the considerable security and convenience afforded, as well as the great value for money that such tours can offer. Most of the worries and concerns associated with independent travel, in a country where getting around on your own can still prove awkward, time-consuming and expensive, can be alleviated. The hassles of queuing for tickets, waiting for transport, wondering where to eat or go and struggling with luggage are banished. An efficiently organized tour can seamlessly take in an extensive number and variety of sights that would be impossible to undertake on your own.

The second option is to travel as a 'freelance independent traveler'—that is the equivalent of traveling on a 'package tour'. There are numerous varieties of packages on offer ranging from single destination room only arrangements to individual tailor-made tours. Of course the final option is to travel on your own—a perfectly feasible arrangement restricted only by your ambition and availability of time and money.

Sightseeing arrangements included on group tours can be fully inclusive or allow room for additional sightseeing options or free time. If you have flexible sightseeing arrangements, or have taken the option to visit sites on your own, you can take two simple actions to radically increase your appreciation, enjoyment and sense of achievement. The first course of action is to ensure that you are the first, or amongst the first, to arrive at the most perennially over-crowded sites. To be one of the first to scale the Great Wall in Beijing or to wander the Yu Gardens in Shanghai in privacy will surely leave you with, as the Chinese say, 'a very deep impression'. The benefits derived from this approach will soon become apparent as the swelling hordes of visitors hard on your heels transform the mood and magic of the occasion to a spectator sport. The other basic tourist avoidance tactic is to approach sites from the opposite direction to the one commonly used by tourist groups. This works well at large sites such as the Forbidden City (most groups enter from the south) and the Summer Palace (most from the east) as well as at many museums and temple complexes.

If you wish to avoid crowds you should be aware that China now has three national holidays, each lasting up to several days, when the transport infrastructure can get overloaded and sites in Beijing and Shanghai become more crowded than usual. The Chinese New Year Holiday in January or February is a colorful and busy

Courtyard, Lamma Temple, Beijing.

time to visit. The other two holidays are at the beginning of May (May Day Holidays) and the beginning of October (National Day Holidays).

Many public parks no longer charge an entrance fee. In general entrance fees to most sites fall in the range of 10 yuan to 30 yuan (between US$1 and US$4) though admission to some larger sites can be over 50 yuan (US$6). Many sites tend to open relatively early (8:00am to 8:30am) with many temples and parks open even earlier than that. Closing times are also relatively early (usually between 4:00pm and 5:00pm) with some sites restricting ticket purchases to one hour before closing.

A Mountain Pass, The Illustrated London News, April 16, 1859.

Hotels

In recent years both Beijing and Shanghai have experienced a massive boom in hotel building, in part inspired by the Beijing Olympics and the Shanghai World Expo 2010, and the growth is set to continue. Deluxe accommodation, catering to the needs of both business and tourist visitors, can now be found across the vast landscapes of these cities (*see* pages 271 and 540).

In Beijing, many downtown hotels are clustered around the main shopping area of Wangfujing (near Tiananmen Square), in the Jianguomenwai area (near the commercial centre and diplomatic area), as well as in the Sanlitun district to the northeast of the centre. However, a number of new hotels have appeared in the northwest of the city in the Haidian district as well as in other suburban locations. Beijing has many fine modern hotels, some of which adopt a classical theme for their decoration and furnishings. In Shanghai, many recent additions to the city's fine hostelries can be found in the heart of Puxi around Nanjing Road as well as in Pudong. Others can be found tucked away in the leafy lanes of the former French Concession. As in Beijing, all of the international hotel chains are represented in the city—often housed in futuristic structures affording fantastic views and superlative service. Shanghai also has a number of historic or villa hotel properties that may fall out of the five-star category—but make interesting places to stay (*see* page 534).

Historically, Shanghai has been the home to some of the finest hotels in Asia and the same holds true today. Of course this is reflected in prices and Shanghai has the most expensive hotel rooms in China. It is standard practice in China to add a 15 percent surcharge to the basic room rate charge and in Beijing a further charge of approximately US$1 per night is added as a city development tax. There is quite a wide variation of pricing within the five-star or deluxe bracket, largely accounted for by the type of management (foreign as opposed to local Chinese) as well as the degree of luxury afforded and location. In general, rack rates for internationally and some locally managed hotels, in Beijing and Shanghai, are in the region of US$200 to US$350 per night. However, some smaller properties and locally managed hotels may have rates well below these levels. Published rack rates may be discounted between 10 percent and 40 percent at particular times and most hotels will offer special deals at holiday times as well as special short-break packages. Discounts are also generally available on the hotels' own websites. Apart from booking through individual hotel websites, there are a number of online agents that can be consulted, including:

Shopping on Nanjing Road, Shanghai.

www.asiahotels.com
www.chinesehotels.net
www.english.ctrip.com
www.elong.net
www.sinohotelguide.com

NOTE: Please be aware that there is an abundance of readily available travel guides that list a selection of hostelries from budget hotels through to the top end. Thus Odyssey Publications' focus is on the needs of the business visitor and traveler who expects to travel and reside in comfort—hotel listings for Beijing (*see* page 270) and Shanghai (*see* page 540) summarise the best hostelries in each city. Whilst most of the properties listed have a five-star designation from China's National Tourism Administration, some are deluxe properties that fall outside the rating system.

Money

Chinese Currency

The Chinese currency is known as *renminbi* (literally translated as the People's Currency). The basic unit is the *yuan* (or *kuai* as it is commonly referred to—just like the British *quid* or American *buck*). The yuan is divided into 10 *jiao* (colloquially called mao). Technically each jiao is further divided into 10 *fen*, however fen coins or notes are now rarely now seen as everything is rounded up or down to the nearest jiao. There are large notes for 100, 50, 20, 10, five, two and one yuan and smaller notes for five, two and one jiao. There are also coins for denominations up to and including one yuan. For notes upwards of five yuan there are now two types of bills in circulation. If you are confused look carefully at the note as they all have numerals and *yuan* or *jiao* printed on them. If you are entering from Hong Kong be aware that the 100 renminbi note looks quite similar to its Hong Kong dollar counterpart. You should also be aware that there are many counterfeit notes in circulation—though these are unlikely to be passed on by legitimate traders.

You can easily check current conversion rates against the Chinese currency online at www.xe.net/ucc. Daily exchange rates and graphs showing the performance of your preferred currency against the yuan for up to the last 120 days can be viewed at www.x-rates.com.

The Shanghai Gold Exchange on the Bund occupies
Shanghai's first modern bank building, completed in 1902.

Foreign Currency, Traveler's Cheques and Credit Cards

Money is most conveniently changed at your hotel's exchange desk. Traveler's cheques are changed at a slightly better rate than cash even though a 0.75 percent service charge is applied to such transactions. The main Chinese banks will also have exchange facilities—though their opening hours are shorter and some banks may be closed at weekends. Unlike in many countries, the hotel rate exactly corresponds to the daily bank rate and there are no other surcharges levied. If you are carrying cash with you ensure that you leave home with clean and crisp notes, as worn or torn specimens may prove impossible to exchange. Most currencies and traveler's cheques are accepted.

When you are changing money always request a supply of smaller denomination notes, 10 yuan and less, as these are useful for buying drinks, snacks and other small items as well as for use at some public toilets. Remember to keep your exchange receipt, as you can change back up to 50 percent of your unused Chinese currency at your exit point. However it is best just to change what you need, as airport banks offering this service can sometimes be closed. If you are traveling on to Hong Kong, renminbi can easily be converted to Hong Kong dollars without the need for such receipts. There are no restrictions on taking foreign currency into or taking renminbi out of China.

American Express cardholders may cash personal cheques for between US$2,000 to US$3,000 over a 21-day period. Most credit and ATM cards can be used to withdraw cash, in local currency, from ATM machines that now seem to be only a few minutes away from wherever you may find yourself in Beijing or Shanghai. Credit cards can be widely used in hotels, upmarket stores as well as many restaurants and bars.

Tipping

Many hospitality industry employees earn a modest basic salary and rely on tipping and other sundry income to maintain their standard of living. This is particularly the case with tour guides and drivers. It is also routine to tip hotel porters. Outside of the hotels and the tourist infrastructure, the matter is not so clear cut. Staff at international standard restaurants and bars may be accustomed to tips–whereas they would be seen as anathema by staff in local restaurants.

Bargaining

In markets and smaller shops, especially those catering to tourists, it is customary to bargain. Don't be hesitant in bargaining—it's a well-established and fun game of strategy and tactics. Bargaining is not just reserved for foreign buyers—the locals go through the same procedures for their purchases, although they will have a better understanding of the basic ground rules and have the advantage of retorting in fluent Chinese.

Do remember that the vendors are trying to earn a living and that they will be unwilling to sell items at a loss. Prices are often displayed on a calculator or written on notepaper, and the initial asking price will often drop dramatically after negotiations have been entered into. At markets try offering half or even less of the initial asking price to start with. If a 'final' price offered is actually or conceived to be still too high politely smile, say thank you and walk away—more often than not your return will be beckoned with a lower price. If you find something that is really special, it's an idea to bargain for an item you do not want and get the lowest possible price before entering into negotiations for the thing that you really want.

Pedestrianized areas are common in both cities.

A Means of Communication

News was always passing, being digested and commented upon; and obviously it kept coming promptly and fresh from its source. This was specially true of the messengers who delivered "chits," the local name for our notes that replaced Western telephone calls. When foreigners were in close relation, such messengers might be on the road constantly. Each chit was entered into a chit-book (I have mine yet); and its receipt was attested, if the master was away from home, by a rubber stamp or else by the ordinary house seal pressed into it. The latter was esteemed more formal and therefore in better taste. If the message was received personally the master might scrawl his initials, foreign fashion, beside his own name. In this way we could nearly always tell quite accurately what had happened to every document.

When only a word of acknowledgement was needed, it was often added in this place. "Would you perhaps like to come picnicking on the lakes next Thursday evening?"—"With pleasure."—"Do you care to see the Devil Dancers tomorrow in the Lama Temple?"—"Drop by my house first!"

These messengers came from other households; they were all known to each other; and they usually sat quietly in the kitchen, chatting and sipping tea while a return message was being devised within. Chits were often frisky; nearly everyone enjoyed the arrangement, not least the messenger himself. Sensing his role, he sat recounting the latest, or hearing our own news; and it never took long for anything of remark to spread over the town. A messenger with five notes to deliver knew by heart who had dined with whom the night before, how it had all gone, and so on, in the whole of his master's circle, by the time he returned home with his chit-book again. Further, since we were all said to have nicknames in these regions, the literal sentences must at times have been somewhat curious. One Westerner, who had a weakness for visiting hostesses just before meal hours, was known simply as the "Want-Food One." There were "Old Virgins" and Great or Small "Very-Verys" (older or younger married women) in numbers.

If that special rupture of the amenities commonly known as a "Peking quarrel" were bubbling, and they often did, the messenger's role would become more active. I do not know whether these altercations sprang from pride confronting pride, since on however small a scale each was sovereign in his own scrap of kingdom; or from exasperation when an adversary of one's own kind began to set bounds, to limit one's power. These were traits that life in courtyards engendered. Even the Chinese were aware of a common temptation to "bolt the door and set oneself up as Emperor."

Here I stumbled upon what must have been a wellspring of classical Chinese intrigue. Especially during love affairs, the messenger had a chance to make so much personal face, which he was not at all loath to seize, that drama sprang into being full-fledged. The household servants were informed: "As she wrote that chit, her amah [maid] told me that she appeared to . . ." etc. This would be relayed within; and although I sternly discouraged such gossip, from time to time the situation would explode if my servants felt that I ought to know something of importance to myself (as they considered it), and therefore to all of us—before I penned my reply. After all they were my small army, and in the world ambush was inevitable. One must be prepared.

Or perhaps some genial party was going forward, perhaps arrangements were being made in fine weather for an excursion to a distant temple; and the preparations—food, crockery, and transportation—were being divided. A message would come, and after domestic consultation I would select a sheet of paper. Finally I would put my envelope into the chit-book, adding on my line the words "Reply herewith." Meanwhile the messenger had kept his own liaison unbroken, sitting comfortably in the kitchen. The oral system worked quite as well, on his level, to keep him in touch with such affairs, as did for us our own writing. Connection was therefore double, and from the Chinese point of view now secure.

George N. Kates, The Years That Were Fat: Peking, 1933–1940 *(Harper, 1952)*

George N. Kates (1895–1990) was an American writer and scholar who rented a house in the Forbidden City in Beijing for seven years during the 1930s. While there he lived as the locals did, following their customs, and became familiar with all the surroundings, language and overall character of Chinese life at that time.

Communications and Media

Telecommunications

China now boasts one of the world's most modern telecommunications systems, and the world's largest mobile telephone market, with more than one billion users. It is also the world's largest Internet market.

A cheaper alternative is to buy an IP (Internet Protocol) card which routes the call through the Internet. Although the call quality can vary, the service is sufficiently standardized to allow normal communication. All you need to do is dial a number prefix and follow instructions that are available in English or Chinese. IP cards are available at Beijing and Shanghai airports, newsstands, telecom shops and a host of convenience stores and small family-run stores. The most reliable cards are issued by China Telecom (prefix 17908), China Unicom (17910) and CNC (17968) come in 50 yuan and 100 yuan denominations. Other IP cards include the Jitong card (prefix 17920). Outside of the airports and larger stores, IP cards can be purchased at huge discounts of at least 50 percent—but you must ask for a lower price before you buy. This makes international calls at least 60 percent cheaper than the standard direct dial rate.

For visitors or business people who would like to remain in touch on the go, inexpensive mobile phones are easily available throughout the country for as little as US$50–100 and can be used with a rechargable SIM card.

Phones used in European and other Asian countries (except Japan) should work in China, and some mobile service providers abroad have roaming agreements with China Mobile or China Unicom, China's two leading service companies. Check with your service provider before leaving for China. GSM phones used in the US (Cingular, for example, is GSM) will also work in China if the phone is tri-band, or can access the GSM 900, 1800, and 1900 frequency networks. Again, ask your service provider before leaving home as to the phone's functionality and service provider's roaming agreements. For around US$30, it is possible to buy a second-hand mobile telephone in Beijing and Shanghai. These can be bought in shops that sell new mobile telephones.

Local mobile telephone numbers in China are available inexpensively. Most newsstands and any store selling mobile phones will have SIM cards, the unique identifiers that give each phone its number, some as low as 30 yuan each. However, the inexpensively priced numbers would not be normally taken by the local population. The cheapest numbers will usually end with a number 4 (which sounds like 'death' in Chinese) whilst numbers ending in 8 (signifying wealth and prosperity) can cost significantly more. If you want a mobile number ending in 8888 expect to

Garden, Forbidden City.

pay well over US$1,000. Prepaid cards are available in denominations of 50 yuan and 100 yuan. When the prepaid amount runs out, simply buy another card and use it to recharge the phone service. Both China Mobile and China Unicom offer recharge instructions in English. Be aware that the two companies' recharge cards are not interchangeable, so be sure to buy the correct card for your service provider. Keep the first card you use to show to vendors when buying further recharge cards. Each recharge card is good for one use. Be assured that your number will not change.

Text messaging is also possible through both companies. Text messages cost 0.10 yuan each, regardless of whether they are domestic or international, if they are sent using a Chinese service provider. Messages can be sent and received by customers roaming on their primary mobile number, but some foreign mobile providers will not deliver messages sent from prepaid accounts in China.

Pay telephones are available but run only on phone cards, not coins. These cards are available from the vendors listed above, but be aware that phone cards are not interchangeable, and that some phones in each city are run by China Telecom, while others are operated by Beijing Telecom and Shanghai Telecom, respectively. It can be a frustrating experience trying to make a call, only to find that the phone card does not work in the phone you are using. One alternative is to use a public phone found at small convenience stores. Off the beaten path, these mom-and-pop purveyors of cold drinks, cigarettes, and snacks often put a large, red phone in front of their establishment, and then base calling price upon a meter reading, which calculates the tariff based on destination and time.

Domestic and international fax services are available at most hotel business centers. Rates vary based on the fax's destination. Some hotels charge a lower rate for faxes to Hong Kong and Macau as they are now technically "domestic" destinations, although the rate is sometimes still higher than a fax to another Chinese city.

China is now the largest Internet market in the world, exceeding 518 million Internet users.

Most hotels—even off-the-beaten-track venues—offer Internet access via both the business center and hotel rooms, which routinely have an ethernet connection that is easy to set up. If you have a problem, the hotel IT staff can help you. Increasingly, hotels are offering WIFI connections in guest rooms as well as in public areas, such as the lobby, restaurants, cafes and bars. Unfortunately, the bigger hotel chains are likely to charge for this service, while smaller hotels offer free Internet access.

Many coffee shops and restaurants in China now offer WIFI, making it easy to get on line in all but very remote locations. In Beijing and Shanghai, free WIFI is available at coffee shop chains, such as Starbucks, Costa, and SPR. In most places this service is free and one may only have to ask the shop for the password. The country is now flooded with WIFI connections, making China arguably one of the most cyber-friendly countries in the world. If you need to get online, just pull out your computer and you're likely to find a connection.

While most Internet sites are available from China, the nation's telecommunications authorities block access to websites dealing with subjects deemed politically sensitive.

Most big hotels offer International Direct Dialling (IDD) to dozens of countries, and domestic long-distance calls. For AT&T USA Direct, call 10811. China has a well-developed postal system. Postcards and letters can be left with the front desk at hotels for postage. Should you have need for other postal or courier services there is no shortage of post offices or international delivery operations in Beijing or Shanghai. Please refer to the Practical Information sections for details.

All international hotels offer business centers providing a full-range of secretarial services. There are also professionally run business centers in Beijing and Shanghai that provide state-of-the-art comunications systems, efficient staff which can be hired as needed, and total flexibility in terms of office rental duration.

ENGLISH-LANGUAGE MEDIA

The availability of English language newspapers and magazines published in China has come a long way since the early 1980s, when the state-run *China Daily* and a few propagandist magazines held a monopoly. The *China Daily*, website: www.chinadaily.com.cn, launched in June 1981, is an official look at what is happening in China. It is published Monday through Saturday, and is available in most hotels and from street news-stands. On Sundays, *China Daily* publishes *Business Weekly*, a round up of the week's Chinese and international business news. Also, on Friday in Beijing, it produces *Beijing Weekend*, a collection of sanitized interviews with Chinese celebrities and listings of cultural events and museum exhibitions. A newcomer to the market is the Global Times [www.globaltimes.cn/], which has adopted more of a sassy take on news about China.

Shanghai has its own English language daily. The *Shanghai Daily* has a daily edition from Monday to Friday, as well as a weekend edition.

Away from the official publications there are now numerous city living magazines that are foreign-run and of the most interest to the visitor. *City Weekend*, *The Beijinger* and *Time Out Beijing* all have good listings of entertainment, events, restaurants, bars, etc in the capital. These magazines are published monthly in English and are available free of charge at numerous bars, restaurants and coffee shops. In Shanghai, there's *City Weekend*, *That's Shanghai*, *Shanghai Talk*, and *Time Out Shanghai*.

Well-known foreign newspapers and magazines, including *The Economist, Time, Newsweek, the International Herald Tribune, The Asian Wall Street Journal* and the *South China Morning Post,* are available at hotels and some larger bookstores.

English-language TV programming is available in all hotels rated four star and above. The channels available may include CNN, CNBC Asia, BBC World, Star World (an Australian-based network owned by Rupert Murdoch's News Corp, which mostly features American programming), HBO, Wow Wow, Star Sports and ESPN (for a wide coverage of live sports including English Premier League football and NBA basketball). There are often Italian, German, French and Japanese channels as well in addition to CCTV 9, Chinese TV's international English language channel.

In Beijing, China Radio International (92 FM) has a current affairs-cum-news magazine broadcast in English every morning from 7:00am to 8:00am followed by Easy Listening FM with an expatriate DJ. Virgin Radio broadcasts in co-operation with CRI, offering international, Asian and Chinese popular music with Chinese and English speaking DJs on 88.5 FM. The Beijing City Government has a new 24-hour English language AM radio station called Radio 774.

The Bund and its fans.

Useful Websites

The Web provides an invaluable resource for learning more about China—whether you are an interested spectator, a serious student, a potential investor, resident, or a past or prospective traveler. Sites come and go all the time so we cannot guarantee that all these sites will be up and running when you hit the button.

For news of what's happening in Beijing and Shanghai, go to **www.cityweekend.com.cn**. or **www.xianzai.com**. Other sites you may find of interest include:

Beijing

www.ebeijing.gov.cn: A basic introduction to the city from the Beijing Municipal Government.

www.bjreview.com.cn: Comment and features from the long-established monthly *Beijing Review*.

www.crienglish.com: Beijing-based China Radio International provides recorded news, features and music as well as a text magazine covering many aspects of modern China.

www.beijingpage.com: Comprehensive Web directory related to Beijing—from tourism and hotels to entertainment, events and more.

Tiananmen Square is a popular spot for group photos as there's space enough for everyone.

www.TheBeijingGuide.com: A well-designed site, steeped in cultural delights, with traditional music, 360° vistas, videos and more including practical information.

Shanghai

www.allaboutsh.com: City guide, news and listings.

www.chinarhyming.com: 'A gallimaufry of random China history and research interests' from Paul French, Shanghai businessman and writer.

Diamond advertisement overshadowing a cultural icon.

http://english.pudong.gov.cn/html/pden/portal/index/index.htm: Comprehensive introduction to Pudong.

www.english.eastday.com: News from The *Shanghai Daily* newspaper.

www.expatsh.com: Useful information if you are planning a move to Shanghai.

www.exploreshanghai.com/metro: Metro map and information.

www.han-yuan.com: Cultural guru, Deke Er's, view of Shanghai and Chinese culture.

www.library.sh.cn/english: Shanghai Library English website.

www.movius.us: Interesting views on Shnghai from US born local writer, Lisa Movius.

www.royalasiaticsociety.org.cn: Home of the Royal Asiatic in China with many interesting events for residents and visitors.

www.shanghai.asiaxpat.com : New, services and listings for expats.

www.shanghaidaily.com: Keep up to date with daily events from Shanghai's leading foreign newspaper.

www.shanghai-ed.com: Practical information on living and working—as well as an historical library and more.

www.shanghai.gov.cn: Practical information from the Shanghai Municipal Government.

www.shanghaiexpat.com: Main website for expat community.

www.shanghaiist.com: Lively news, local information and blog site.

http://shanghaitown.online.sh.cn: news and information from the Shanghai government.

www.smartshanghai.com: 'Webzine' with useful listings and insights.

www.shanghai.talkmagazines.com: Leading city magazine, *Shanghai Talk*, online.
www.thisshanghai.com. Local events and listings website.
www.timeoutshanghai.com: The latest city living guide.
www.urbanatomy.com: successor to city magazine, *That's Shanghai*, website.
www.wangjianshuo.com: Highly successful blog with lots of useful information for visitors.
www.xintiandi.com: All you'd like to know about Shanghai's most chic entertainment district.

Shanghai's Neighbouring Cities
Hangzhou
http://eng.hangzhou.gov.cn/: Informative official government website.
Nanjing
http://english.nanjing.gov.cn: Official government website.
http://nanjing.jiangsu.net: Information on sights and city living in Nanjing.
Suzhou
http://holidayfu.com/suzhou-city-guide: Covers many areas of interest in the city.

General Information
For general news information on China, including Beijing and Shanghai, take a look at the following sites:
www.chinadaily.com.cn: Online version of China's only English daily national newspaper. Features national and business news, as well as weather and sport.
www.china.org.cn/english: Authorized state portal with daily updates of general and business news. Contains topical features and a travel guide section.
www.cnto.org: The official site of the China National Tourism Office—based in the US.
http://english.peopledaily.com.cn: English version of the main Communist Party daily with official views on the economy and politics as well as current headlines, topical features and city weather.
http://www.einnews.com/china/: Part of the European Internet News global network. Extensive general and business news, with links to travel-related sites. This site can only be accessed by paid subscribers.
www.sinolinx.com: A collection of China-related headlines swept from numerous Internet sites.
www.xinhua.org: News from China's official news agency, in Chinese.
www.chinaview.cn: News from China's official news agency, in English.

www.ctrip.com: Probably the best one-stop site for planning independent travel within China, available in English and Chinese.

www.wildwall.com: The best site for the Great Wall and how to visit with the emphasis on conservation.

Business-Related Sites

For the business traveler some of the following sites may be of interest:

www.amcham-shanghai.org: American Chamber of Commerce in Shanghai.

www.austchamshanghai.com: Australian Chamber of Commerce in Shanghai.

www.ccpit.org: Trade and associated matters from the China Council for the Promotion of International Trade.

www.chinabiz.com: China business news from Shanghai-based company.

www.chinabusiness-press.com: Government-approved China business magazine, with links to numerous Chinese companies.

www.chinaonline.com: Business-focused US news site.

www.chinapage.com: Up-to-date business news and information on Chinese companies.

http://www.britishchambershanghai.org/: British Chamber of Commerce in Shanghai.

http://www.sinofile.net/Sinofile/ContentPage.nsf: Multi-sector business news based on a wide range of Chinese press reports—and special business features.

www.sinosource.com: Offers a China business directory.

www.stats.gov.cn/english: Official statistics from the National Bureau of Statistics on all aspects of the economy and society.

Note: Some of these sites may not be accessible in China, so it is best to check these sites before you arrive in the country.

Things Chinese

There are a number of sites that offer an overview of all things Chinese from culture and the arts to entertainment and travel:

www.chinavista.com: A premiere online gateway. Apart from daily news, the site features three main channels—business, travel and culture plus a search engine.

www.china-window.com: Business based—but very informative on arts, culture, history, cuisine and destinations.

www.chineseculture.about.com: Informative and comprehensive guide to the arts, culture and history of China.

www.index-china.com: Covers business and general news with extensive information on many aspects of society and culture. Its travel center has a hotel database and photo gallery.

www.muzi.com: This China portal offers general and business news, features and a search engine. Its 'Gallery' channel contains a large photo resource and 'Chinaroma' has extensive city guides.

www.qi-journal.com: An interesting online magazine related to Chinese culture, philosophy and health. Includes sections on traditional Chinese medicine, Taiji, Qigong and fengshui as well as Chinese history, language and astrology.

LANGUAGE

You can prepare yourself for your visit to China by visiting:

www.mandarintools.com: Advanced site for serious learners, with Chinese software downloads and an online dictionary.

www.chinese-outpost.com/: An introduction to the basics of the Chinese language.

www.zhongwen.com: Learn Chinese online and get an instant translation of your name and its associated meaning.

This work-place graffito is typical of the period when China first started to modernize following the Cultural Revolution.

A Matter of Principle

"I don't understand," I said. "I thought Grandmother died when Mother was a child."
"Whatever gave you that idea?" asked my aunt.
"I don't know. I just assumed...Mother never talks about her. Why?"
"Perhaps she was too ashamed."
"What for?"
"Perhaps you should ask her."
"No, I couldn't, not now, not after all these years. Please, Auntie, you must tell me."
Only then, when I was forty-one, did I learn that once again Grandmother had defied the inviolable mores of Chinese society.

When she failed to have a son, even Grandfather, a 'modern' man who did a wicked turkey trot, could no longer flout tradition. He announced that he would be taking a second wife. Without a word, without a tear, Grandmother packed her bags and walked out of the House of Fang forever.

When I heard this, I gave Grandmother a rousing cheer. It was exactly what I would have done. My aunt shook her head at such foolishness and said, "Do not be so hasty. How can you be certain she did not regret that decision for the rest of her life?"

The idea startled me, but I refused to consider it and, shrugging a shoulder, hastened to declare, "I would not!"

"Silly one, you are an American married to an American, living in a culture and a time where husbands and wives leave one another as indifferently as the wind changes direction. But that was not true for my mother. She was a Chinese married to a Chinese in a culture and a time when marriage had little to do with love and everything to do with life. What kind of life could she have had without a husband, without her children, without a rightful place? Only one of ever-deepening sorrow."

"But she was right to leave. How could she ever again have held her head high if she'd stayed?"

"You ask the wrong question. You should be asking, how could she after she left?"

Bette Bao Lord, *Legacies: A Chinese Mosaic*, Ballantine Books, 1991

Bette Bao Lord, born in China, raised in America, author of the bestselling novel *Spring Moon and wife of a former American ambassador to China*, was resident in Beijing during the "China Spring" of 1989. Lord's unique web of relationships and her sensitive insight have enabled her to observe Chinese life both high and low, Communist and dissident, intellectual and ordinary.

Standard Family, *digital color photograph, 1996 by Beijing-based Wang Jinsong*, A Strange Heaven—Contemporary Chinese Photography.

A Brief Guide to the Chinese Language

Mandarin (*Putonghua* or common speech), designated as the official Chinese language by the Guomindang government in 1912, is historically a dialect of the Beijing area. The Beijing dialect is one of five main dialect groups—another one being Wu that is spoken in the Shanghai region. The differences between the Shanghai and Beijing dialects can be compared to the differences between the English and French languages.

Regardless of the differences in the spoken language it is consoling to find that the written script is uniform throughout China. The only quandary presented is that over 50,000 characters are entered in the largest dictionary. In practice, however, educated people ordinarily use just 4,000 to 5,000 characters. The mammoth 900,000 character *Selected Works of Chairman Mao* is based on a glossary of just over 3,000 different characters.

Each character is a syllable, many of which can stand alone as words. In fact words with one or two syllables account for more than nine out of 10 of those found in the Chinese language. Characters based on pictures formed the basis for the development of the Chinese script. For instance the character for a person (人) is based on a side view of a human being, the character for big or large (大) resembles a man standing legs apart and arms widespread, whilst the character for a tree (木) depicts a tree with roots and branches. Whilst there are only a few hundred such pictographic characters there are many more which build upon them, though an association or indication to form other words. For example, one person behind another person (从) means to come from or follow and one person above two others (众) means a crowd.

The Chinese government introduced the pinyin system in 1958 allowing an approach to the spoken language through the 26 characters of the Roman alphabet and its associated numerals. Around the same time, the written script was 'simplified' with many characters being rewritten in a less complicated arrangement so as to make them easier to learn. The pinyin system enables foreigners to achieve a reasonable level of spoken Chinese without any knowledge of the characters. This approach is also used in primary education as an aid to basic character recognition.

You will encounter pinyin on road signs, some maps and store fronts and in the Western media. You will initially meet with some difficulty in pronouncing Romanized Chinese words, despite the fact that most sounds correspond to usual pronunciation of the letters in English. The exceptions are:

INITIALS
- c   is like the *ts* in 'i*ts*'
- q   is like the *ch* in '*ch*eese'
- x   has no English equivalent, and can best be described as a hissing consonant that lies somewhere between *sh* and *s*. The sound was rendered as *hs* under an earlier transcription system.
- z   is like the *ds* in 'fa*ds*'
- zh is unaspirated, and sounds like the *j* in '*j*ug'.

FINALS
- a   sounds like '*a*h'
- e   is pronounced as in 'h*e*r'
- i   is pronounced as in 'sk*i*' (written as *yi* when not preceded by an initial consonant). However, in *ci, chi, ri, shi, zi* and *zhi*, the sound represented by the final is quite different and is similar to the *ir* in 's*ir*' but without much stressing of the *r* sound
- o   sounds like the *aw* in 'l*aw*'
- u   sounds like the *oo* in '*oo*ze'
- ü   is pronounced as the German *ü* (written as *yu* when not preceded by an initial consonant). The last two finals are usually written simply as *e* and *u*.

FINALS IN COMBINATION
When two or more finals are combined, such as in *hao, jiao* and *liu*, each letter retains its sound value as indicated in the list above, but note the following:
- ai   is like the *ie* in 't*ie*'
- ei   is like the *ay* in 'b*ay*'
- ian is like the *ien* in 'V*ien*na'
- ie   similar to '*ear*'
- ou   is like the *o* in 'c*o*de'
- uai sounds like '*why*'
- uan is like the *uan* in 'ig*uan*a' (except when proceeded by *j, q, x* and *y*; in these cases a *u* following any of these four consonants is in fact *ü* and *uan* is similar to *uen*.)
- ue   is like the *ue* in 'd*ue*t'
- ui   sounds like '*way*'

TONES
A Chinese syllable consists of not only an initial and a final or finals, but also as tone or pitch of the voice when the words are spoken. In *Pinyin* the four basic tones are marked ¯, ´, ˘ and `. These marks are almost never shown in printed form except in language text.

Chineasy
—by The Ginger Griffin

Characters	Pin-Yin	Odyssey-Yin	English
Basics and Greetings			
你好	ní hǎo	knee how	Hello
你好吗	ní hǎo ma?	knee how mah	How are you?
早上好	ní zǎo	knee zow	Good morning
晚上好	wán shàng hǎo	wan shang how	Good evening
晚安	wǎn ān	wan-an	Good night
再见	zài jiàn	z-eye gee-en	Good bye
谢谢	xìe xie	x-ier x-ier	Thank you
是/对	shì/duì	sher/dway	Yes (Is!)
不是/不对	bù shì/ bù duì	boo-sher/boo-dway	No (Is not!)
我是	wǒ shì	w-aw sher	I am
英国人	yīng guó rén	Ying g-woe wren	English
美国人	Měi guó rén	may g-woe wren	American
加拿大人	Jīa ná dà rén	gee-en ah d-ah ren	Canadian
澳大利亚人	Ào dà lì yà rén	ow-dah-lee-yar ren	Australian
我叫....	wǒ jiào	w-aw gee-ow	My name is....
你叫什么名字	ní jiào shénme ming-zi?	knee gee-ow shen-mer míngzi?	What is your name?
几岁了	jǐ suì le?	gee sway ler?	How old are you? (children only)
对不起	duìbùqǐ	d-way boo-chee	Sorry/excuse me
我不懂	wǒ bù dǒng	w-aw boo-dong	I don't understand
可以	ké yǐ	ker-yee	Able/can do
我喜欢中国	wó xǐhuān Zhōngguo	w-aw she-wan zhong g-woe	I like China
很好	hén hǎo	hen how	Very good
马马虎虎	má mǎ hú hǔ	mar-mar who-who	So-so; just OK
不好	bù haǒ	boo how	Not good
在哪	zài nǎr	z-eye n-are	Where?
厕所	cè suǒ	stir-swoe	toilet
男/女	nán/nǔ	nan/new	male/female
入口	rùkǒu	rue k-oh	entrance
出口	chūkǒu	chew k-oh	exit

超市	chāo shì	chow sher	supermarket
药房	yào fáng	yow fang	pharmacy
电话	diànhuà	dee-en hwah	phone
出租车	chūzū chē	chew zoo ch-err	taxi

Necessities—Dining and Shopping

请给我	qíng gěi wǒ	ching gay w-aw	Please give me:
来	lái	lie	bring me:
一杯	yì bēi	ee bay	one cup or glass of:
一瓶	yì píng	ee ping	one bottle of:
啤酒	píjiǔ	pee-gee-you	beer
红葡萄酒	hóng pútáojiǔ	hong poo-tow-gee-you	(dry) red wine
白葡萄酒	bái pútáojiǔ	bye poo-tow-gee-you	(dry) white wine
白兰地	báilándi	bye-lan-dee	brandy
可乐	kělè	ker-ler	cola
矿泉水	kuàngquánshuǐ	kwang-chew'an-shway	mineral water
桔子水	júzishuǐ	jew-zir-shway	orange juice
红茶	hóng chá	hong char	black tea
花茶	huā chá	h-wah char	jasmine tea
咖啡	kāfēi	car-fay	coffee
牛奶	niú nǎi	knee-ou nigh	milk
盐	yán	yan	salt
胡椒粉	hújiāofěn	who-gee-ow-fen	pepper
糖	táng	tang	sugar
酱油	jiàngyóu	gee-ang y-oh	soy sauce
辣酱	làjiàng	l-ah gee-ang	chilli sauce
我要买	wǒ yào mǎi	w-aw y-ow my	I want to buy
有没有	yǒu méi yǒu?	yo-may-yo?	Do you have?
橘子	júzi	jew-zir	tangerine
苹果	píng guǒ	ping g-woe	apple
挑子	táozi	t-ow-zir	peach
香蕉	xiāngjiāo	she-ang gee-ow	banana
冰淇淋	bīngqílín	bing-chee-lin	ice cream
邮票	yóupiào	yo-pee-ow	stamps
明信片	míngxìnpiàn	ming-sin-pee-en	postcard(s)
电池	diànchí	dee-en-chur	battery(ies)
胶卷	jiāojuǎn	gee-ow-jew-an	print film
幻灯片	huàndēngpiàn	hwan-dung-pee-en	slide film

手纸	shǒuzhǐ	show zher	toilet paper
太贵了	tài guì le!	tie-gway ler!	Too expensive!
便宜一点儿	piányi yidiǎnr	pee-en-ee-eed-ee-en	A little cheaper!
太大了	tài dà le	tie d-ah ler	Too big
太小了	tài xiǎo le	tie she-ow ler	Too small
太短了	tài duǎn le	tie d-wan ler	Too short
太长了	tài cháng le	tie chang ler	Too long
我要	wǒ yào	w-aw y-ow	I want (it)
我不要	wǒ bú yào	w-aw boo y-ow	I don't want (it)
再来...个	zài lái....ge	z-eye lie....ger	I'll have (x number) more
多少钱	duōshao qían	d-woe show chee-en	How much money?
对吗？	duì ma	d-way mah	Right?

NUMBERS

零	líng	ling	0
一	yī	ee	1
二	èr	err	2
两	liǎng	lee-ang	2 (both)
三	sān	san	3
四	sì	sir	4
五	wǔ	woo	5
六	liù	lee-oo	6
七	qī	chee	7
八	bā	bah	8
九	jiǔ	gee-oo	9
十	shí	sher	10
十一	shí yī	sher-ee	11
二十	èr shí	err-sher	20
二十五	èr shí wǔ	err-sher-woo	25
一百	yì bǎi	ee buy	100
一千	yì qiān	ee chee-en	1,000
一万	yí wàn	ee wan	10,000

EMERGENCIES

快找人帮忙	Kuài zhǎo rén bāng máng	k-why j-ow wren bang mang	get help quickly
叫警察	jiào jǐng chá	gee-ow jing cha	Call the police
找医生	zhǎo yī shēng	j-ow ee-sheng	Get a doctor

A traditional "Little Emperor".

THE CHINA GUIDE

A Beijing based, American managed travel agency specializing in quality tours with no factory shopping stops.

TheChinaGuide.com features a detailed destination guide and photography by professional photographer Peter Danford (also an Odyssey Publications contributor).

Service, **quality** and a **reasonable price** are our focus. With no commission shopping allowed, our guides focus on your needs. Meals are in local restaurants, our guides are screened and trained by foreigners; there is free bottled water in vehicles and are no hidden costs.

See our recommended itineraries or we can customize a private tour for you. Specialties include sleeping and hiking on the Great Wall, boutique hotel stays at a reasonable price and discount show tickets. We cater to families, children, couples, business travelers, academic groups and have experience providing to people in wheelchairs and those handling adoptions.

Our English speaking travel agents (Western and Chinese) are available to advise you.

www.TheChinaGuide.com

Beijing
Capital City

History of Beijing

Beijing is both an old and a new city—old in its cultural heritage, and new as the capital of the People's Republic of China. Today, a first impression is of fast development in preference to reverence for the past. Even so, many of the buildings here are steeped in the history of China over the last 800 years and it becomes rapidly obvious to any visitor how integral the city's development is to the rise and fall of dynasties, and indeed, to Chinese civilization itself.

Peking Man The story of Beijing starts a long time before recorded history. Fragments of the bones of 'Peking Man', dated to a period about 300,000–500,000 years ago, were discovered at the village of Zhoukoudian, outside the present city (*see* page 208).

Capital of Conquerors During the Zhou (1027–221 BC) and subsequent dynasties, a series of large established settlements grew around Beijing. But as the area was the focus of an unsettled frontier region far from the capital—Chang'an; now Xi'an—and other centers of power further south, it suffered a turbulent history.

For part of the period dominated by the Liao Kingdom (916–1125), the city was a secondary capital enjoying the pretty name (which is still used from time to time) of Yanjing. In the 12th century the 'Golden Tartars' swept down from Manchuria and wrested the city for their own, establishing the State of Jin.

When Kublai became Great Khan of the eastern part of the Mongol empire in 1260, he decided to develop Beijing as his winter capital, calling it 'Dadu', or Great Capital, and took up residence in a palace in what is now Beihai Park.

By the time the Venetian explorer Marco Polo reached Beijing at the end of the 13th century, it was called Khanbaliq, the City of the Khan, and was already one of the world's great metropolises. From his long detailed description of the city, it is clear that Marco Polo was utterly overwhelmed by the size and opulence of the Mongol capital.

Preceding page: *Hall of Prayer for Good Harvests, Temple of Heaven.*
Right: *Over 200,000 workmen labored to build the Forbidden City between 1407 and 1420.*

UNDER THE MING

The Ming Dynasty, founded in 1368 upon the defeat of the Mongols, first established its capital in Nanjing, and on account of its relegation Dadu was renamed 'Beiping' (Northern Peace). With the accession of the dynamic third Ming emperor, Yongle, the dynasty entered a period of vitality and expansion. He re-established Beijing as the capital in 1421, giving the city its modern name, which means Northern Capital, and which Europeans later romanized as 'Peking'.

Much of present-day Beijing was built during the period that immediately followed. In contrast to the unplanned, sprawling cities of the south, traditional concepts of town-planning were employed, and nowhere was this more evident than in the grid layout of Beijing. The foundations of Khanbaliq were, of course, already

there, but they were now extended; walls were built and moats were dug. As Beijing flourished, the city originally established by the Tartars became too small, and in 1553 a new outer wall, or Chinese City, was built to enclose the suburbs that had burgeoned out to the south.

Within the boundaries, a massive building and renovation programme created some of the most striking testimonies to Ming confidence and power. Over 200,000 workmen labored to build the Forbidden City between 1407 and 1420. Though the palace buildings have been restored and rebuilt many times since then, the plan remains essentially the same. The Temple of Heaven (a magnificent example of Ming architecture) and the Temple of Agriculture (which no longer exists) were erected in the Outer City. Mindful of their mortality, the early Ming emperors planned and prepared their own burial grounds in a methodical and grandiose fashion that can be seen at the Ming tombs. Nor was the defence of the realm neglected: the finest sections of the Great Wall to the north of Beijing were constructed during this period.

Under the Qing

For a century after Yongle, stability was maintained in the empire. But weak rulers and corruption eventually fragmented the authority and drained the energies of the state. The last Ming emperor hanged himself on Prospect Hill (Jingshan) behind the Forbidden City in 1644, when rebels were at the city gate.

The Manchus, founders of the Qing ('pure') Dynasty that came to rule China, were descendants of those Tartars who invaded Beijing in the 12th century. This time they were to stay for 267 years.

The Qing were more interested in maintaining the existing capital and administrative systems than in making any radical changes. As they themselves became culturally assimilated (to the extent that they lost their own language), their improvements to Beijing and its environs tended to preserve the styles and techniques of the Ming period. The most interesting contributions the Qing rulers made to their adopted capital were the various summer palaces that they built outside the city.

Notable Qing rulers included Kangxi (reigned 1661–1722), Qianlong (reigned 1736–95) and the Empress Dowager, Cixi (ruled 1861–1908). Kangxi's reign was the longest in Chinese history; he was a contemporary of Louis XIV of France and Peter the Great of Russia (both of whom he had contact with). During the long reigns of Kangxi and Qianlong, China enjoyed peace and prosperity. The 18th-century European ideal of the Chinese nobility as a highly cultured people dressed in gorgeous silks and much given to splendid ceremonies derived from Western travelers' accounts of this land of plenty.

But the ideal was an elaborate façade; the Manchu court had, by the 19th century, become enervated and stagnant. Clinging rigidly to ancient systems of thought and rituals, the ultra-conservative officials rejected all original ideas or innovations as seditious. Attempts by reformers to modernize China were invariably quashed.

The Coming of the Barbarians

The history of the late Qing empire is a sorry account of unsuccessful resistance to Western encroachment from without, and to domestic rebellion from within. The First Opium War (1840–42) pried open China to foreign trade. In a second round of the conflict (1858–60), Beijing was actually captured by Britain and France, whose troops burned down the Old Summer Palace (Yuanmingyuan), and whose representatives established embassies in a Legation Quarter (southeast of the Forbidden City, in the area bounded by Dong Chang'an Jie, Chongwenmennei Dajie and the Inner City wall) over which the Chinese had no jurisdiction. It was this Legation Quarter that the men of 'The Society of the Harmonious Fists', the Boxer rebels, besieged for two months in 1900 in protest against the growing influence of the foreigners.

The State entry of Lord Elgin into Peking, 1860.

Piecemeal reforms, reluctantly conceded by Cixi, came too late. Her grand nephew Puyi, who ascended the throne at the age of six, was the last emperor of China. For some years after the collapse of the Qing, he continued to live in the rear quarters of the Forbidden City, while the front portion was turned into a museum. He was forced to move from the palace in 1924.

UNDER THE REPUBLIC

Following the 1911 Revolution, Beijing became the stage for important events in the development of modern Republican China. On 4 May 1919, Tiananmen Square was the arena of an historic mass demonstration: students and patriots, in what became known as the 'May Fourth Movement', passionately denounced the humiliating terms for China under the newly-signed Treaty of Versailles. It was a show of solidarity that started many Chinese on the road to socialism. In 1928, when the political center of the Republic was moved to the Nationalists' power base at Nanjing, the old name of 'Beiping' was restored to the abandoned capital.

Emerging from its Japanese occupation between 1937 and 1945, the city had to wait another four years before regaining its paramount status. The communists entered Beijing unopposed in January 1949. On 1 October, Chairman Mao Zedong proclaimed the establishment of the People's Republic of China (PRC) from the rostrum of the Gate of Heavenly Peace, and a new era for Beijing, indeed for the whole of China, began.

MODERNIZATION

Since the founding of the PRC, Beijing has become the country's political and cultural center and has experienced many drastic changes. In the spirit of the revolution, many of the city's prominent monuments went the way of the city's walls and were pulled down in the late '50s and '60s. By the late '60s, Beijing was awash with the many political currents of the Cultural Revolution. At the height of this highly charged period, a trip to Tiananmen Square became a requisite pilgrimage for thousands of zealous young Red Guards who journeyed to Beijing from the farthermost reaches of China as a demonstration of their revolutionary ardor and commitment to the cult of Mao.

Political struggles, public purges and mass campaigns rent society for a full decade before popular outrage was vented at what was to become known as the Tiananmen Incident. On 5 April 1976, 100,000 people gathered at Tiananmen Square to protest the removal of memorial wreaths which had been laid at the Monument to the People's Heroes as a tribute to the late Zhou Enlai. This public

Actors in the Chinese drama: A "Boxer". The Illustrated London News, August 18, 1900.

On 1 October 1949, Chairman Mao Zedong proclaimed the establishment of the People's Republic of China from the rostrum of the Gate of Heavenly Peace. Mao Posters.

mourning for the moderate premier is now seen as a turning point in the political tide, a clear denunciation of the last years of Mao's rule and of Jiang Qing, his widow. Within six months, Mao Zedong had died, and subsequently, the 'Gang of Four' and the political structure of the Cultural Revolution were dismantled.

With Deng Xiaoping as its new leader, China embarked on a programme of adapting Maoist thought through a reform movement known as the 'Four Modernizations'—of agriculture, industry, science and technology, and national defense. The result of China's opening to the outside world has been a marked increase of cultural exchanges, joint-venture projects and direct investment from a multitude of foreign sources. International-style hotels and office high-rises now line major thoroughfares. Private enterprise markets are commonplace. The affluence of the middle class Chinese is apparent as more and more families purchase computers, cars and their own apartments.

But with this reform, China has inevitably experienced pangs of growth. Breaking the 'iron rice-bowl' has meant that employment is no longer guaranteed, and so the voices of the discontented and dispossessed have become louder. China today also boasts a huge, nomadic army of 120 million rural employment-seekers who inundate the large cities.

The upside of all of this is the gradual resurgence of a commodity economy geared more or less to consumer demand. Tourists and local residents alike have benefited from a broadening of the service economy to include private taxis, restaurants, guest houses and travel services, although letting out the reins in this regard has in some cases led several years later to the imposition of strict regulations which have finally brought a sense of order to these small scale enterprises.

An upsurge in domestic tourism has also changed the face of the city. The most popular tourist spots are crowded with sightseers from every corner of China. So successful has been the campaign to encourage Chinese people to travel that the railways report running at 140 percent of capacity, and tourist hot spots like the Forbidden City and Temple of Heaven are restricting access to certain centuries-old flights of steps and marble pedestals because they are beginning to be chafed away by vast numbers of well-shod feet, some wearing high heels and steel taps.

Olympic Gold

The 2008 Olympics launched the city into on one of the most ambitious urban makeovers the world has ever seen, running from fast rising urban business districts to the renovation of declining hutongs (Beijing's quaint old alleyways), dramatically changing the layout of a city that has not changed much since imperial times.

Glassy skyscrapers and high-end apartment buildings shot up throughout Beijing, gleaming shopping malls threw open their doors and new ring roads and subway lines were extended to improve transportation. The top names in international architecture began pouring in to compete for huge projects, much to the consternation of Chinese architects, some of whom argued that overseas builders were experimenting with outrageous designs in the ancient capital.

Unfortunately, this makeover has also included the razing of blocks and blocks of hutongs and their signature courtyard houses to make way for new Olympic venues and modern complexes. There are indications now that the Beijing government is working to retain some of the city's wonderful history, naming some hutongs protected sites, remodeling or rebuilding courtyard houses in a few areas. The municipal government even gathered city wall bricks—"borrowed" by Beijing residents decades ago to build their own structures—to reconstruct a small section of the old city wall. Several new NGOs dedicated to the preservation of the city's proud past have also been established. As Beijing moves rapidly into the 21st century, it is hoped that the city will find a comfortable balance between past and present.

In the spirit of the revolution, many of the city's prominent monuments went the way of the city's walls and were pulled down in the late '50s and '60s.

Reigns of Ming and Qing Emperors
Ming Dynasty (1368–1644)

Hongwu	1368–1398
Jianwen	1399–1402
Yongle	1403–1424
Hongxi	1425
Xuande	1426–1435
Zhengtong	1436–1449
Jingtai	1450–1456
Tianshun	1457–1464
Chenghua	1465–1487
Hongzhi	1488–1505
Zhengde	1506–1521
Jiajing	1522–1566
Longqing	1567–1572
Wanli	1573–1620
Taichang	1620
Tianqi	1621–1627
Chongzhen	1628–1644

Qing Dynasty (1644–1911)

Shunzhi	1644–1661
Kangxi	1661–1722
Yongzheng	1723–1735
Qianlong	1736–1795
Jiaqing	1796–1820
Daoguang	1821–1850
Xianfeng	1851–1861
Tongzhi	1862–1874
Guangxu	1875–1908
Xuantong	1909–1912

Dongbianmen, the Gate of the North-East Angle, houses four floors of museum space, including the Red Gate Gallery. Adjacent is the last remaining section of the magnificent Ming Dynasty city wall. The small park here is a nice place for a stroll either early or late in the day, beneath the very wall itself.

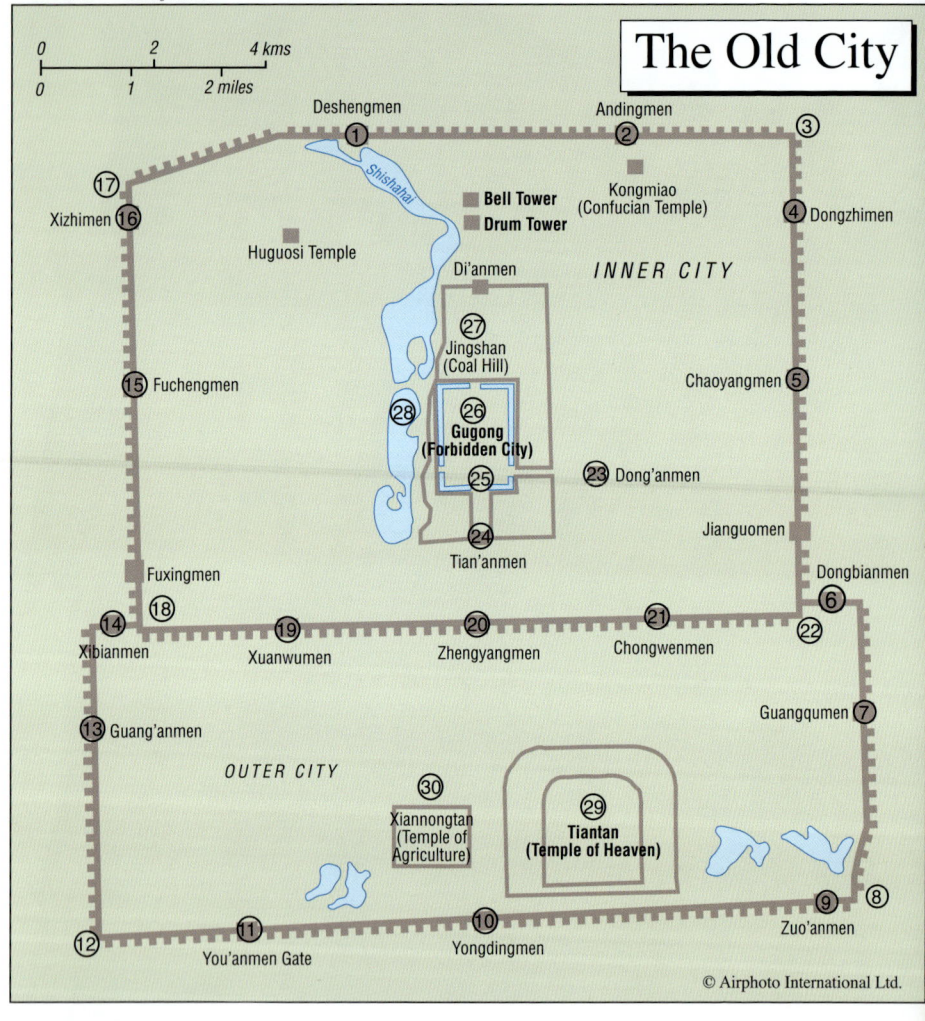

1. The Gate of the Exaltation of Virtue.
2. The Gate of Stable Peace.
3. City Armory Tower.
4. The Gate facing the East.
5. The Gate of the Rising Sun.
6. The Gate of the North-East Angle.
7. The Gate of the Great Canal.
8. Watch Tower.
9. The Left Gate of Peace.
10. The Gate of Eternal Constancy.
11. The Right Gate of Peace.
12. Watch Tower.
13. The Gate of Perfect Repose.
14. The Gate of the Western Angle.
15. The Gate of the Rampart.
16. The Gate facing the West.
17. City Armory Tower.
18. City Armory Tower.
19. The Gate of Military Glory.
20. The Gate facing the South.
21. The Gate of Venerable Wisdom.
22. City Armory Tower.
23. Situation of the Legation Quarters.
24. The Great Pink Gate.
25. Entrance to the Palace.
26. The Imperial Palace.
27. Coal Hill.
28. The Imperial Lakes.
29. The Temple of Heaven.
30. The Temple of Agriculture.

A caravan of camels are led away from You'anmen, circa 1920, see #11 on opposite page.

Imperial Examinations

Northwest of the junction of Jianguomen and the Second Ring Road, in the vicinity of the present Chinese Social Sciences Institute, is the site of the Ming and Qing Examination Hall (Gongyuan). Nothing is left of it now; its existence is recalled only by the streets—Gongyuan Dong Jie and Gongyuan Xi Jie—and a few *hutongs* named after it.

The system of imperial examinations, by which candidates were recruited into the ranks of the civil service, had its origins in the Han Dynasty (206 BC–AD 220). As the government of a united and increasingly less feudal China grew more complex, an established, non hereditary, corps of officials and administrators gradually became the accepted basis of political organization.

Place for competitive examinations at Pekin.
The Illustrated London News, March 8, 1873.

The competitive examinations originally tested competence in a broad range of subjects—economics, philosophy, administration—but by the Ming these had narrowed to a highly formalized syllabus based on interpretations of the Confucian classics. The increasingly orthodox responses demanded by examiners culminated in the very stylized 'eight-legged essay' (*ba gu wen*), a rigid literary form later critics condemned for its tendency to inhibit originality and creative writing.

During the Ming and Qing, examinations were held not only in the capital but also in provincial centers during the autumn. By March, thousands of hopeful candidates would be assembling for the triennial examination in Beijing. For nine days they would be confined in row upon row of tiny cells, being fed meagre meals brought in from outside and closely guarded by invigilators, to scribble away at their 'eight-legged essays' in the hopes of dazzling rewards. Success meant being received by the emperor in one of the sumptuous halls of the Forbidden City and the privilege of joining the ruling elite. Indeed, by 1400, the examination was the only guaranteed means of entry into the imperial service. While the system was not immune to corruption—invigilators were bribed, cribs were smuggled in, sometimes in the form of minute embroidery on the cuffs of a robe—it did furnish scores of talented sons of peasant families with brilliant careers and political advancement.

The ideal of the loyal scholar-official has remained a figure of awe to the Chinese to this day. Stories of their erudition and civilizing influence on warrior-emperors abound. They tell of dutiful ministers who expounded the moral precepts and historical precedents set down by ancient sages, and related them to the political issues of the day. By gentle reminders that an emperor's mandate to rule depended on 'government by righteousness,' they curbed the worst excesses of their arrogant sovereigns.

This system of competitive entry to the civil service came to be adopted by countries outside of China but, by the late 19th century, profound scholarship was no longer an adequate qualification for statesmanship. The debâcle of the Boxer Rebellion in 1900 forced Empress Dowager Cixi to initiate a number of reforms. These included abolishing the imperial examinations in 1905.

Following pages: The Great Wall wends its way across rugged terrain.

Seating Arrangements

When his Majesty holds a grand and public court, those who attend it are seated in the following order. The table of the sovereign is placed on an elevation, and he takes his seat on the northern side, with his face turned towards the south; and next to him, on his left hand, sits the Empress. On his right hand are placed his sons, grandsons, and other persons connected with him by blood, upon seats somewhat lower, so that their heads are on a level with the Emperor's feet. The other princes and the nobility have their places at still lower tables; and the same rules are observed with respect to the females, the wives of the sons, grandsons, and other relatives of the Great Khan being seated on the left hand, at tables in like manner gradually lower; then follow the wives of the nobility and military officers: so that all are seated according to their respective ranks and dignities, in the places assigned to them, and to which they are entitled.

The tables are arranged in such a manner that the Great Khan, sitting on his elevated throne, can overlook the whole. It is not, however, to be understood that all who assemble on such occasions can be accommodated at tables. The greater part of the officers, and even of the nobles, on the contrary, eat, sitting upon carpets, in the halls; and on the outside stand a great multitude of persons who come from different countries, and bring with them many rare curiosities.

In the middle of the hall, where the Great Khan sits at a table, there is a magnificent piece of furniture, made in the form of a square coffer, each side of which is three paces in length, exquisitely carved in figures of animals, and gilt. It is hollow within, for the purpose of receiving a capacious vase, of pure gold, calculated to hold many gallons. On each of its four sides stands a smaller vessel, containing about a hogshead, one of which is filled with mare's milk, another with that of the camel, and so of the others, according to the kinds of beverage in use. Within this buffet are also the cups or flagons belonging to his Majesty, for serving the liquors. Some of them are of beautiful gilt plate. Their size is such that, when filled with wine or other liquor, the quantity would be sufficient for eight or ten men.

Before every two persons who have seats at the tables, one of these flagons is placed, together with a kind of ladle, in the form of a cup with a handle, also of plate; to be used not only for taking the wine out of the flagon, but for lifting it to the head. This is observed as well with respect to the women as the men. The quantity and richness of the plate belonging to his Majesty is quite incredible.

At each door of the grand hall, or of whatever part the Great Khan happens to be in, stand two officers, of a gigantic figure, one on each side, with staves in their hands, for the purpose of preventing persons from touching the threshold with their feet, and obliging them to step beyond it. If by chance any one is guilty of this offence, these janitors take from him his garment, which he must redeem for money; or, when they do not take the garment, they inflict on him such number of blows as they have authority for doing. But, as strangers may be unacquainted with the prohibition, officiers are appointed to introduce and warn them.

The numerous persons who attend at the sideboard of his Majesty, and who serve him with victuals and drink, are all obliged to cover their noses and mouths with handsome veils or cloths of worked silk, in order that his victuals or his wine may not be affected by their breath. When drink is called for by him, and the page in waiting has presented it, he retires three paces and kneels down, upon which the courtiers, and all who are present, in like manner make their prostration. At the same moment all the musical instruments, of which there is a numerous band, begin to play, and continue to do so until he has ceased drinking, when all the company recover their posture. This reverential salutation is made as often as his Majesty drinks. It is unnecessary to say anything of the victuals, because it may well be imagined that their abundance is excessive.

Marco Polo, The Travels of Marco Polo
(Ed. Ronald Latham, Viking Press, 1958)

Marco Polo's (1254–1324) travels are the subject of much debate. He is said to have written about his travels during the years 1296–1299, when he was in Genoa.

Happening Beijing

No one can dispute that changes in the way Beijing looks, feels and acts have been no less than dramatic during the past 20 years. The ancient stage of the capital now presents uncensored scenes of modern life in all its guises and with all its sins and saviours. Throughout Beijing's long history the city has always maintained a distinct and unique identity—one that is perhaps stronger today than ever before.

The following two essays offer an insight into modern Beijing from the perspective of two long-term and celebrated foreign residents. William Lindesay, a British national most noted for his passion of the Great Wall, was the author (with his wife, Wu Qi) of the 1999 Odyssey Guide to Beijing. His essay first appeared as an introduction to that guide.

Kaiser Kuo, an American national, has figured large in the cultural scene of the capital and was formerly a member of the influential Tang Dynasty rockband. His essay has been especially commissioned for this edition.

Beijing Rules —*by William Lindesay*

Beijing is unlike any other city in China, totally unrepresentative in grand capital style, a true center at the edge. Home to one in 100 Chinese, or 12 out of China's 1.3 billions, power emanates over its high walls, through its sentried gates, and from ministerial motorcades as they speed along the city's boulevards.

This notorious officialdom diminishes in direct proportion to distance from the capital, if popular doggerel is anything to go by: 'If you don't go to Beijing, you won't realize how small your local officials are; if you don't go to Shanghai you won't know how small your ideas are; if you don't go to Shenzhen you won't know how small your wallet is, and if you don't go to Hainan you won't realize the bad state of your health.'

But even though Shanghainese have the most radical ideas, Shenzheners the most money and Hainan islanders provide 'exhausting' nightlife, for better or for worse, richer or poorer, Beijing rules them all. And it's been like that for most of the last 900 years.

Conquest dynasties from the north first favored the site for settlement, at the edge of the North East China Plain in the lee of the Yanshan mountains. Jurchens, Quitans, Mongols and Manchus either overran each other or Han rulers to establish, destroy and rebuild, or occupy cities here.

All who came, saw and conquered left their marks, monuments and memories. The Liao (916–1125), made the site their secondary capital, naming it Yanjing; the birds still dart around the eaves of Beijing's ancient buildings every summer.

Special Topic

Left: *The drums are played in the Drum Tower daily at 9.30am, 10.30, 11.30, 13.30, 14.30, 15.30 and 16.50. The Drum Tower was used to keep time for the Imperial court and city.*

Nothing remains from the Jin Dynasty (1115–1234) capital, Zhongdu. Besieged by the invading Mongols for six years, it was finally razed to the ground for the building of Genghis Khan's Dadu. Remains of the Yuan Dynasty city wall, which had impressed Marco Polo, can be seen between the northern legs of the third and fourth ring roads. Buildings, monuments and relics from the Ming and Qing capital of Beijing, being more recent, are relatively abundant.

Yet in today's sprawling Beijing the past is well hidden by the present and future. Cranes and scaffolding are never far, and arriving at the city's new state-of-the-art international airport, or the new monolithic West Railway station, and making the trip into town, it is difficult to see anything of antiquity. Guidebooks, tour brochures and the foreign press tend to portray an image of a benighted populace, dressed in green Mao suits and caps, living in the shadows of quaint pagodas and eaved pavillions. Nothing could be further from the truth.

Be prepared for huge billboards advertising Apple, Nokia and Hennessy Cognac, sparkling-glass fronted skyscrapers, real estate developments, 4-lane expressways and ring roads jammed with traffic. See women flaunting femininity, with the aid of make up, mousse and designer fashions which were frowned upon for decades; see men flashing their fortunes by posing with mobile phones. This is Deng Xiaoping's legacy of reform and opening.

It's all the more remarkable when you realize that many of the other great sites of the city are reminiscent of times when reactionary politics, isolationism and, seemingly, xenophobia were in command.

Mao's portrait still adorns Tiananmen, the Gate of Heavenly Peace, from where he proclaimed the foundation of the People's Republic on 1st October 1949 with a speech and raising of a new flag. Later, in 1966, he received millions of fanatical Red Guards in the square below at the height of his cult status. Fittingly, or unfittingly, depending on one's judgement of history, the late chairman still presides over the raising of the Chinese flag every day. The 'Sentry of the Motherland' march out through the archway under his portrait at dawn, halt the traffic and raise the flag. And 400 meters south is Mao's mausoleum where his remains are on show in a crystal sarcophagus.

Tiananmen is an architectural, and therefore historical interface. Austere, Stalinesque buildings rim the square to the east and west, while to the north lies the largest collection of ancient palacial buildings in the world: the Forbidden City.

The maze of golden-roofed buildings and courtyards was home to every Ming and Qing emperor from 1420 until Pu Yi, the last emperor, left in 1924. In this citadel isolated by a moat and high perimeter walls that no ordinary person saw behind, some 23 emperors, their families, ministers, eunuchs and concubines lived in a world apart from the masses, with emperors believing themselves to possess the mandate of heaven for ruling the vast Middle Kingdom outside.

Mao's portrait still adorns Tiananmen, the Gate of Heavenly Peace.

As if a mile were a foot, Ming emperors regarded their huge empire just like a palace ground which needed a boundary wall for security, and with millions of subjects under their direction ordered the construction of the strongest Great Wall in history through the Yanshan mountains to the north of Beijing. US President Richard Nixon, walking on the Wall in 1972, summed up its magnificence with masterly understatement: 'Yes, it really is a *great* wall.'

China has changed beyond recognition since that Ping-Pong diplomacy brokered between Beijing and Washington in the early 1970s. Perhaps the most remarkable transformation has been in the people. They are one, or rather many, of the great sights of China.

In Beijing's downtown areas a foreign face hardly causes a head to turn, except from those brothers and sisters from outside, the term for migrant workers from labor-exporting provinces such as Sichuan, Anhui and Henan, who flock to the capital to work as construction workers and domestics.

Individualism is the backlash to enforced collectivism that was imposed for so long. More people want to be different, crave to be successful and show it off. The country has suddenly become a land of businessmen, and Beijing has its unfair share. Kickbacks are essential operating costs to grease the palms of obstructive bureaucrats into giving their permission to make things happen.

The economy finds itself somewhere between a semi-dismantled, centrally-planned system, and a semi-constructed, market economy. Many Beijing families are microcosms of the national situation: typically, one spouse sticks with the state employer for the socialist life preserver of an apartment and eligibility to a host of state benefits, while the other will *xia hai*, or plunge into the commercial sea, and try to make a fortune. But another plunge, *xia gang*, into unemployment, has been inflicted on surplus staff by the restructuring of state enterprises.

Money is the hottest topic of conversation. At the advent of Deng's economic reforms in the early 1980s, it was stressed that a good communist did not have to be poor, and to get rich was glorious. Wealth seeking suddenly became

Huge billboard advertisements display what each good rich communist can aspire to have.

politically correct. On the streets these maxims were popularly summarized as *xiang qian kan*, looking ahead and looking at money, quoted in a recent social survey of Beijing urbanites as being the philosophy which best describes their aim in life.

The 90s also saw *zhao le*, or having fun and pleasure seeking, gathering momentum. Now restaurants are everywhere. A walk down a Beijing street is akin to a culinary tour of China. And there are some foreign concessions worth visiting. McDonald's and KFC burst at weekends as Beijing's parents cater to their little emperors' needs, while granny looks on dotingly. Nights are livelier, too. While most of Beijing becomes increasingly addicted to TV, the young, beautiful, rich, curious and bad go out to play. Entertainments range from rock and roll to jazz gigs, from karaoke to song-and-dance-hall action. Some establishments are more than just venues for social intercourse, a chat and a tipple.

Vices which Mao fought ruthlessly for so long to eradicate are now rampant again. Deng opened China's door to the world and gave the people more than

Domestic tourism is huge business throughout China and particularly, of course, in the capital city; a patriot at the Temple of Heaven's Hall of Prayer for Good Harvests.

they ever had. Now departed, the side-effects of his reforms—money worship, hedonism, rising corruption and crime—have been targeted by campaigns to put the good heart back in the nation.

But for all these problems, China today is much more human and relaxed than it was, even a decade ago. As any visitor to Beijing will quickly find out, most Chinese are friendly, flexible and fun loving. And their likes are making China less of a People's and more of a people's republic with each passing day.

BEIJING HEAT —by Kaiser Kuo

Beijing is a hot town? In fact it is, although it's easy to forgive first-time Western visitors their reluctance to dispute that claim. Given the tone of the popular media coverage in the West, it's hardly the impression one might form. For many, Beijing still conjures up powerful and painful images from the not-too-distant past. Even for those aware of China's rapidly rising economic might, conceptions still often focus on political and cultural repression. Sadly, visitors to Beijing who don't take the time to explore beyond "must-see" attractions like the Great Wall and the Forbidden City often come away with the impression of a sprawling city built on an inhuman scale, with imposingly broad boulevards laid out in soulless rectilinear efficiency. The reality is far more complex, and more observant first-time visitors are invariably surprised by the level of sophistication, cosmopolitanism and openness they find. Over the last decade, Beijing has emerged as the unrivaled center of contemporary culture in Greater China, and may well be the most culturally dynamic and creative city in East Asia. The capital is the firmament in which new movements are born. It is home to the most prestigious academies, the best studios, the hippest venues, the most influential media and critics—and to the commercial apparatus that ultimately sustains culture. Anyone who spends time in China comes quickly to the realization that it's not freewheeling, fashionable Shanghai that dominates the Chinese culture scene, but rather gray, dusty Beijing. Proximity to the political center has done more to stimulate than stymie the development of contemporary culture. The weight of authority has emboldened more creative individuals than it has broken.

It's the profusion of culture that ultimately gives the city its sizzle, most conspicuous in Beijing's lively nightlife scene. On any given night, there are rock concerts—Beijing is home to some 400 bands playing every conceivable genre—and art exhibitions, international DJs playing to packed clubs and discos, dance performances, film screenings, plays and fashion shows. The Sanlitun nightlife district alone boasts over a hundred pubs to suit every taste and lifestyle choice. The Party's town has become a real party town, and if it's gotten less Red, it's gotten ever more red-hot.

left: *photos of band Carsick Cars by Tim Franco, copyright 2010 Maybe Mars.*

It is worth exploring why it is that Beijing, and not Shanghai, has become China's unquestioned cultural hothouse. Part of this lies in the makeup of the city's expatriate community. In the first decade of reforms, Beijing was the more open city—home then as now to far more foreigners than Shanghai, and of a type more apt to stay longer, learn Mandarin, and interact with local people. While Shanghai tended to attract foreign business people, it was students, diplomats, journalists and scholars who formed the nucleus of Beijing's expat scene in the 1980s. Through personal contact, this group was critical in exposing young Beijingers to a world of Western culture from which they had long been cut off—the visual arts, film, literature, rock music. Today, some 200,000 foreigners reside in Beijing, and they continue to play an important role as patrons and consumers of Beijing's cultural output.

But the expatriate presence would have made no difference were it not for a more basic affinity Beijingers have toward culture. The traditional arts—painting, calligraphy, poetry, music, drama—have always been more closely tied to officials than to merchants. Traditionally, Chinese intellectuals have regarded themselves as owing a double duty both to governance and to culture, and the modern Beijing cognoscenti still pride themselves on their awareness of culture and feel bound to participate in its creation. In imperial times, cultural sophisticates always gravitated toward the capital, just as the cream of the creative crop makes its way to Beijing today. Rare is the artist who can claim to be somebody unless he's somebody in Beijing—the uncontested proving ground for filmmakers and painters, rock musicians and playwrights alike.

Culinary artists have migrated to Beijing as well, and what was once a gastronomically challenged city has come to eclipse Hong Kong and rival Taipei as the discerning diner's destination of choice. With talented chefs from every far-flung corner of the country, Beijing now offers excellent eateries representing the cuisines of every region of China—Sichuan, Hunan, Canton, and dozens of other regional flavors known only to seasoned gastronomes. As Beijingers have a taste for strongly-spiced food, it's no surprise that the peppery preparations of Sichuan have been particularly well-received, and even Sichuan natives themselves admit that Beijing's Sichuan restaurants do justice to their native cookery. Increasingly cosmopolitan tastes have helped to buoy the selection of international restaurants, too, and native Beijingers often outnumber foreigners in the city's many non-

Chinese restaurants. Nearly every world can now be sampled in Beijing, with new restaurants opening too fast to track.

Beijing is an ancient city that has served as the Middle Kingdom's capital for over 600 years, and its ancient attractions—its palaces and temples, its labyrinthine alleyway neighborhoods and quaintly traditional courtyard homes—remain its principal draw for visitors from abroad, and rightly so. But equally compelling is the dynamism and the dizzying pace of change. Young Beijingers have proven up to the challenges that rapid modernization has brought, stepping with confident alacrity and impressive savvy into the age of wireless technology and the Internet. The stark and often startling contrasts between the very old and the futuristic are part of the quirky charm of Beijing.

Rare is the artist who can claim to be somebody unless he's somebody in Beijing. Great Criticism Series: Pepsi, 1992 by Wang Guangyu, Paris-Pekin.

Beijing punk.

Beijingers themselves are the city's real treasure. Lazy, proud, garrulous, hopelessly addicted to politics and punditry—so the capital's denizens are satirized elsewhere in China, and few Beijingers would really object to the essence of this caricature. The city's full of real characters—wry and sardonic, given to spewing earthy wisdom and potty-mouthed poetry spoken in the musical torrent of gargling 'r' sounds that is the Beijing dialect.

With so much happening in Beijing, choices are difficult for the visitor with limited time. Fortunately, there are excellent English-language magazines offering up-to-date listings of events and venues as well as current pieces on personalities and trends in China. Check out *The Beijinger, City Weekend and Time Out Beijing* —available at many bars, restaurants and hotels around town—to find out what's happening.

Today, with society more open than ever, Beijingers are no longer reliant on expatriates to learn about what's happening in the world beyond. Satellite television, the Internet (to which Chinese have an ease of access that would surprise most westerners) and—for better or for worse—the ubiquity of pirated CDs and DVDs have all brought the world much closer to Beijing. The contemporary arts in China—visual arts, music, film, theater—are passing out of their imitative phase and into their own, finding a confident voice that can be heard loud and clear in hot, happening Beijing.

Getting Around Beijing

Twenty-five years ago the bicycle reigned supreme on Beijing's wide boulevards, save for buses and a few lace-curtained Soviet-made cars. No more. Today, the city is gridlocked with vehicles of every conceivable shape and make, and in one of the world's most populous cities that spells environmental trouble.

Town planners gasped in awe at the pace Beijing built its ring roads (it now has six, with a seventh under construction), but only in heavy traffic did they realize what chaos broke out as vehicles met when they joined and left the highways: the same place is used causing queues to build up around every side road.

Beijing Metro

Beijing's expanding subway system, now equipped with many high-tech comfortable trains, is the best way to get around the capital these days. Currently, Beijing has nine subway lines, including the Light Rail and Airport Express Line. The Light Rail, referred to as Line 13, one led residents to wonder where the other 11 lines were, or where they would go once they're constructed. The No. 2 Line basically follows the Second Ring Road, which follows where Beijing's city walls once stood. For the visitor,

Above: *The No. 2 Line is a user-friendly subway and a good way to avoid the inner-city traffic gridlock.* Left: *The Hall of Prayer for Good Harvests, the Temple of Heaven, was extensively renovated in 2005.*

the subway stops at places such as Jianguomen, the the Central Business District; Yonghe Gong, or the Lama Temple; the Beijing Railway Station, which connects to many cities in northern and southern China; and Qianmen, a historic area south of Tiananmen Square.

The East-West Line connects the eastern and western extremes of the city, from Sihui East to Apple Garden (Pingguoyuan) in the west, near the Fragrant Hills. Along the way, it alights at helpful stops including the World Trade Center (Guo Mao); Jianguomen; Wangfujing, Beijing's best known shopping street; Tiananmen Square, on both the east and west sides of the square; and the Military Museum.

These two lines join in two places: Jianguomen Station and Fuxingmen Station. Passengers may switch between the lines at no additional cost. Signs in English indicate the direction to the other line and distinguish it from the exits.

Tickets are two yuan for any trip; you can purchase a stored-value card that works with both the subway and buses. Trains run every five minutes or so from 5:00am–11:00pm. Platforms are simply bi-directional and station names are posted in both Chinese characters and pinyin on signposts affixed to pillars facing the tracks. Maps on the tunnel wall indicate the name of the next station down the line. Once aboard, announcements are made via a bilingual recording.

With the sharp increase in the number of motor vehicles taking to the streets of Beijing, clogging the arteries and making travel difficult, more and more foreign visitors are taking to the underground, which has expanded its reach in recent years. The subways are fast and easy to use, with station signs and stops announced in both Chinese and English. See our subway map on inside front cover.

TAXIS AND PUBLIC TRANSPORT

The flagfall for all Beijing taxis is 10 yuan, and covers the first four kilometers of any journey. Nowadays fares register in whole yuan denominations.

If you are traveling from the airport to the city by taxi make sure to head for the official taxi station and indeed, at many places and sites where tourists congregate, avoid all unsolicited offers from taxi touts. Please note that an additional charge of 10 yuan is added to the fare to cover the highway toll. On finishing your taxi journey, you should be presented with a printed receipt of the fare. Save the receipt—if you're cheated or lose anything, you'll be able to find the driver with the receipt.

Most Beijing taxi drivers abide by the rules: however, a handful will prey on unsuspecting visitors and relieve them of many times the regular fare. When you embark on a taxi journey ensure that the meter is visible and switched on after you get into the vehicle. If you are not given a receipt please ask for one and don't pay the fare until it has been received. Should you decide to hire a taxi for a day, or part thereof, ensure that you agree on a price before your departure.

Buses are difficult to use because of gross overcrowding, troublesome ticket purchasing and uncertainty of where one should alight. But if you have time to get lost it is worth experiencing the push and shove. (Warning: pickpocketing is rampant on crowded buses and trains so put valuables in a wallet around your neck and inside your clothing!) Buses have conductors to take fares and give change and some buses accept the stored value card that is also good for the subways—you get a small discount if you use the card on the bus. City maps, published annually, are the best source of information on bus and trolleybus routes. They can be bought for about three yuan from roadside newsstands.

Minibuses, charging much higher fares than the public buses since they offer passengers more chance of a seat and choice of places to alight, follow conventional bus routes and have the number of the route they follow posted in their windscreens. Fares are between one and five yuan. From each end of their terminus, minibuses may wait until they are at least half-full before leaving.

The bicycle remains the average Beijinger's main transport: for the environment's sake, the later the masses swap their bike lock keys for ignition keys, the better. Bikes can be hired on an hourly, half-daily, daily, weekly and monthly basis from many hotels geared to taking foreign tourists. Four-star and five-star hotels probably will not have their own but may be able to arrange for rental via the concierge desk. Deposits or leaving behind one's passport are usually required.

If cycling in Beijing, remember that the rule of the road is the Law of the Jungle: survival of the fittest, or in this case, survival of the biggest. Cyclists and pedestrians do not have the right of way, so give yourself plenty of time and room to make turns and street crossings. At intersections, any motorized vehicle turning right on red is not required to stop before the turn. Also be aware that taxis and buses stop quickly and without warning at the side of the road, often without signaling, so stay well clear of both.

The best advice for cyclists new to Beijing roads is to go with the flow. The riders around you will know the game, and if you follow them, they will probably steer you correctly.

The central street in the Chinese Quarter of Peking, photographed by John Thomson, 1879.

GETTING AROUND BEIJING 117

Getting Around Beijing

Off-Season Beijing: The Best Time to Go? —*Steven Schwankert*

Each year, Beijing is blessed with a single time to visit that is superlative to all others: October. Seemingly from the celebration of the founding of the People's Republic on October 1 until its close on Halloween, a post-monsoon high-pressure system keeps the skies clear, the days warm, and the nights crisp and cool, rarely requiring more than a sweater.

Although Beijing occasionally experiences a spring that carries neither the chill of winter nor segues directly into a sweltering summer, it usually seems like only those two dominant seasons are felt here.

Summer, usually the "high" travel season, is in some ways unforgiving. The normally dry air of Beijing gives way to an unseasonable humidity, and there is little shelter from the heat, as most of the city's main attractions are outdoors. This, combined with poor air quality thanks to an increasing number of automobiles, can make the summer a tough time to plan a proper China visit.

When, then?

To truly appreciate Beijing and understand the character of its people and why it has become the city that it is, it must be visited in the off-season, which generally runs from November until April.

There is a reason that most traditional buildings in Beijing, from the Forbidden City to the lowliest courtyard home, face south. Bad things come from the north, namely barbarian armies and cold winter winds. The south gates never did much to keep out the former, but the latter was always a more consistent and formidable enemy.

In winter, the traveler will be rewarded with lower prices. Only the heartiest of domestic travelers will visit during this time, leaving most venues generally empty. While the Great Wall at Badaling is rarely empty, with cold winter winds blowing, walkers who journey to the top of the wall may find themselves momentarily feeling like lonely sentries scanning the hills for invaders.

Residents of Beijing brave winter weather in Tiananmen Square.

Sights in Beijing

Tiananmen Square 天安门广场

The enormous square facing the Gate of Heavenly Peace—Tiananmen—is the heart of modern China. During the centuries of the Qing empire the square did not exist. There were originally buildings on either side of a central thoroughfare leading northwards to the entrance of the Imperial Palace. Gradually cleared during the first half of the 20th century, this huge area, covering about 40 hectares (98 acres), has witnessed both triumphant and traumatic events. Important political demonstrations first took place there during the Republic (1911–49). On 1 October 1949, Chairman Mao proclaimed the establishment of the People's Republic of China from the rostrum of the Gate of Heavenly Peace (*see* page 86). Twenty-seven years later, the Tiananmen Incident—when masses demonstrated their affection for the late premier, Zhou Enlai—heralded the end of the Cultural Revolution, and the downfall of the Gang of Four.

The **Gate of Heavenly Peace** itself is an imposing long red structure with a double roof of yellow tiles on the northern side of the square (*see* page 103). Tourists are allowed to enter the gate and climb to the rostrum from which emperors once handed down edicts. Besides being steeped with historical significance, this rostrum, overlooking the National Museum of China, Tiananmen, and the Great Hall of the People, provides one of the finest views of Beijing. Open from 9:00am to 6:00pm, with the last tickets sold at 5:00pm, it is best to visit as early or late as possible, so one may reflect profoundly upon both the triumphs, and the tragedies, of China's long march from the humiliations of the nineteenth and twentieth centuries towards what seems inevitable super-power status, once again.

Increasing numbers of Beijingers are adopting the car for their personal use, but for now the ubiquitous bicycle still just about rules the daily commute across the urban landscape. In the background, The Gate of Heavenly Peace, Chairman Mao Zedong's portrait hangs below the rostrum.

Left: *Foreigners stroll the shops and restaurants on Gulou Dong Dajie (Drum Tower East Road), an excellent shopping area between the Drum Tower and Nan Luogu Xiang. Unfortunately this area is slated for redevelopment and will be populated by chain stores.*

On either side of the gate's rear portion are two parks. To the east is the **Working People's Cultural Palace**. Over 550 years old, this was an imperial ancestral temple and now contains a park, a library, a gymnasium and other recreational facilities. On the western side is **Zhongshan Park**, dedicated to Dr. Sun Yat-sen, the leader of the 1911 Revolution and founder of modern China.

On the eastern side of Tiananmen Square is the **National Museum of China**.

In the center of the square is the **Monument to the People's Heroes**, an obelisk in memory of those who died for the revolution, with inscriptions by Mao Zedong and Zhou Enlai, as well as a dozen stone carvings.

At the far southern end of the square (beyond Chairman Mao's Memorial Hall, his mausoleum) is **Qianmen**, or Front Gate, a massive double gate which controlled entry to the northern section of the city. Qianmen Dajie, directly to the center-south of the square, underwent a major renovation prior to the Olympics. The result is a disappointing collection of new buildings that are poor representations of the great architecture that once graced much of the area.

GREAT HALL OF THE PEOPLE 人民大会堂
On the western side of the square, this monumental building, completed in 1959, houses the National People's Congress. It may usually be visited on Monday, Wednesday and Friday mornings, however, visits cannot be made when party or state meetings (which naturally take precedence) are scheduled. The 17th Communist Party Congress was convened here in October 2007 and annual sessions of the National People's Congresses are held every March.

The Great Hall of the People is built round a square, very much in the solid 'revolutionary-heroic' mould. It is worth going inside where, even if the decor is not to everyone's taste, the sheer scale of the rooms is breathtaking. From the huge reception room, the *Wanren Dalitang* (Ten-thousand People Assembly Hall) leads off to the west, the banquet wing to the north, and the offices of the standing committees of the national congress to the south. The Assembly Hall is over 3,000 square meters (3,600 square yards), containing more than 9,700 seats on three tiers, all installed with simultaneous interpretation equipment. Overhead, the vaulted ceiling is illuminated by 500 recessed lights radiating outwards from a gleaming red star. Some 500 guests can sit down to dinner in the banquet room, which is half the size of a football field. Gilded columns and brilliant lighting combine to produce a sumptuous if overwhelming effect. In addition to the formal public rooms, the Great Hall has 32 separate reception rooms, named after each province, provincial-level city and autonomous region of China (including one for Taiwan).

Chairman Mao's Memorial Hall 毛主席纪念堂

Standing behind the Monument to the People's Heroes is Chairman Mao's mausoleum. It was built in only one year by teams of volunteers and inaugurated on 9 September 1977, the first anniversary of his death, by his successor to the Communist Party leadership, Chairman Hua Guofeng. This imposing two-tiered edifice resting on a foundation of plum-colored Huangang stone is supported by 44 granite columns and topped by a flat roof of yellow glazed tiles. It bears a striking resemblance to the Lincoln Memorial in Washington, DC.

There are three main halls on the ground floor, one to the north, one to the south, and the Hall of Reverence in between. Entering the first, a vast reception area capable of accommodating over 600 people, the visitor will be confronted by a seated statue of Mao carved in white marble. Behind it hangs a painting of Jingganshan in Jiangxi Province.

Inside the Hall of Reverence, the embalmed body of the late chairman draped with the red flag of the Chinese Communist Party lies in a crystal coffin. The dates '1893–1976' are engraved in gold on a plaque.

Leaving the mausoleum by the south hall, the visitor will see a celebrated poem by the late Mao Zedong inscribed in gold on one of the walls. The walk-through will take less than five minutes, since stopping is not allowed. Security is very strict, and handbags and cameras must be checked in before entry. There is no entrance fee.

A bustling shopping area near the exit of the hall on the south side of the building offers a wide range of new Mao memorabilia. For more valuable Mao souvenirs from the Cultural Revolution, visit the Panjiayuan market.

The Imperial Palace (*Gugong*) 故宫

Center of the Chinese world for nearly 500 years, the Imperial Palace today remains the most complete and best preserved collection of ancient buildings in China. Also called the Purple Forbidden City (*Zijincheng*) for the exclusive nature of the emperors who built and inhabited it, the Palace is a vast complex of halls, pavilions, courtyards and walls. It is within these walls that 24 emperors of two dynasties, aided by their ministers, eunuch guards, concubines and servants, acted out the drama of ruling imperial China from the early Ming in 1420 to the fall of the Qing in 1911.

Gugong, as it is known to the Chinese, is also a masterpiece of architecture. An extraordinary sense of balance is maintained between the buildings and the open spaces they surround. The scale is monumental but never oppressive; the design symmetrical but not repetitive. True to the Chinese predilection for harmony over diversity, the Palace makes use of a single style of building in an awe-inspiring combination of geomantic planning and aesthetic beauty. All the buildings are carefully laid out on a north-to-south axis, but there is no sense of rigidity to them. Like the Louvre or the Taj Mahal, the Forbidden City is a monument that can be visited with pleasure again and again.

Originally built in 1420 by over 200,000 workmen at the direction of the third Ming emperor, Yongle, the Palace was almost burnt to the ground in 1644 during the Manchu takeover. Rebuilt and renovated many times, it nonetheless retains the initial design set down 500 years ago.

The Palace can roughly be divided into three parts. In the foreground are four gates, each of which may look large enough to the first-time visitor to be a palace by itself. Beyond these gates, at the center of the complex, are three principal halls, of monumental size and scope, where the emperors conducted important State ceremonies. In the rear are three lesser halls, still of notable size, and many smaller courts where the emperors and their families and attendants lived.

Occupying an area of over 74 hectares (183 acres), the complex was indeed more like a city than a palace. The visitor entering for the first time may be surprised that each gate and hall leads to yet another, seemingly grander one, at its rear. The effect can be overwhelming and the similarity of design in buildings throughout behoves the visitor to note the special functions of each in order to gain an appreciation for the complexity of the whole. One can, with little imagination, easily understand how the emperors who ruled this Forbidden City could consider themselves at the center of the universe.

It is often stated that there are 9,999 'rooms' in the palace; one room less than the great palace in heaven, which has a perfect 10,000 rooms. Actually, there are many fewer than 9,999 rooms, but there are nearly that number of bays (in Chinese, *jian*). A bay, in Chinese architecture, is defined as the square or rectangular space between four columns. Columns do all the work of supporting the roof in Chinese buildings as no weight is borne by the walls.

The Palace collided with modern culture when the Starbucks coffee chain opened a store within its walls. Local media called the move a slap in the face to Chinese culture (even though the Chinese government had approved the opening) and the store was eventually shut down following a public outcry.

The Forbidden City can be approached from either its south or north gates. Most visitors enter from the meridian gate at the south which provides the greatest dramatic impact. Tickets are sold at both entrances. It would be easy to spend a day exploring the palace—but generally around two hours is enough to cover the main areas of interest. An Accoustiguide recording can be hired giving an introduction to 17 sites. The palace is open from 8:00am to 5:00pm, with entry no later than 4:00pm.

The Palace Gates 午门
By passing through the **Gate of Heavenly Peace** (*Tiananmen*) and the **Upright Gate** (*Duanmen*), one arrives at the imposing **Meridian Gate** (*Wumen*), which is the traditional entrance to the Forbidden City. The horseshoe-shape of the Meridian Gate's massive fortress walls, topped with five towers, seems to draw the visitor submissively forward through the entrance to the inner precincts. This gate was originally used for impressive functions such as reviewing victorious troops and announcing the lunar calendar. Only the emperor himself was permitted to pass through the central opening of the gate.

Beyond this gate lies a courtyard leading to the fourth and final gate, the **Gate of Supreme Harmony** (*Taihemen*), a huge open porch supported by red lacquered pillars. One crosses a stream by one of five marble bridges, beautiful pieces in their own right that are dwarfed by the enormity of the surrounding courtyard and palace walls. Two striking bronze lions guard this entrance, the female with a cub beneath her paw, the male with a ball. They symbolize the power of the emperor and the subservience demanded by him.

Left: *Decorative gate in the Forbidden City protected by two door lions.*

132 Beijing

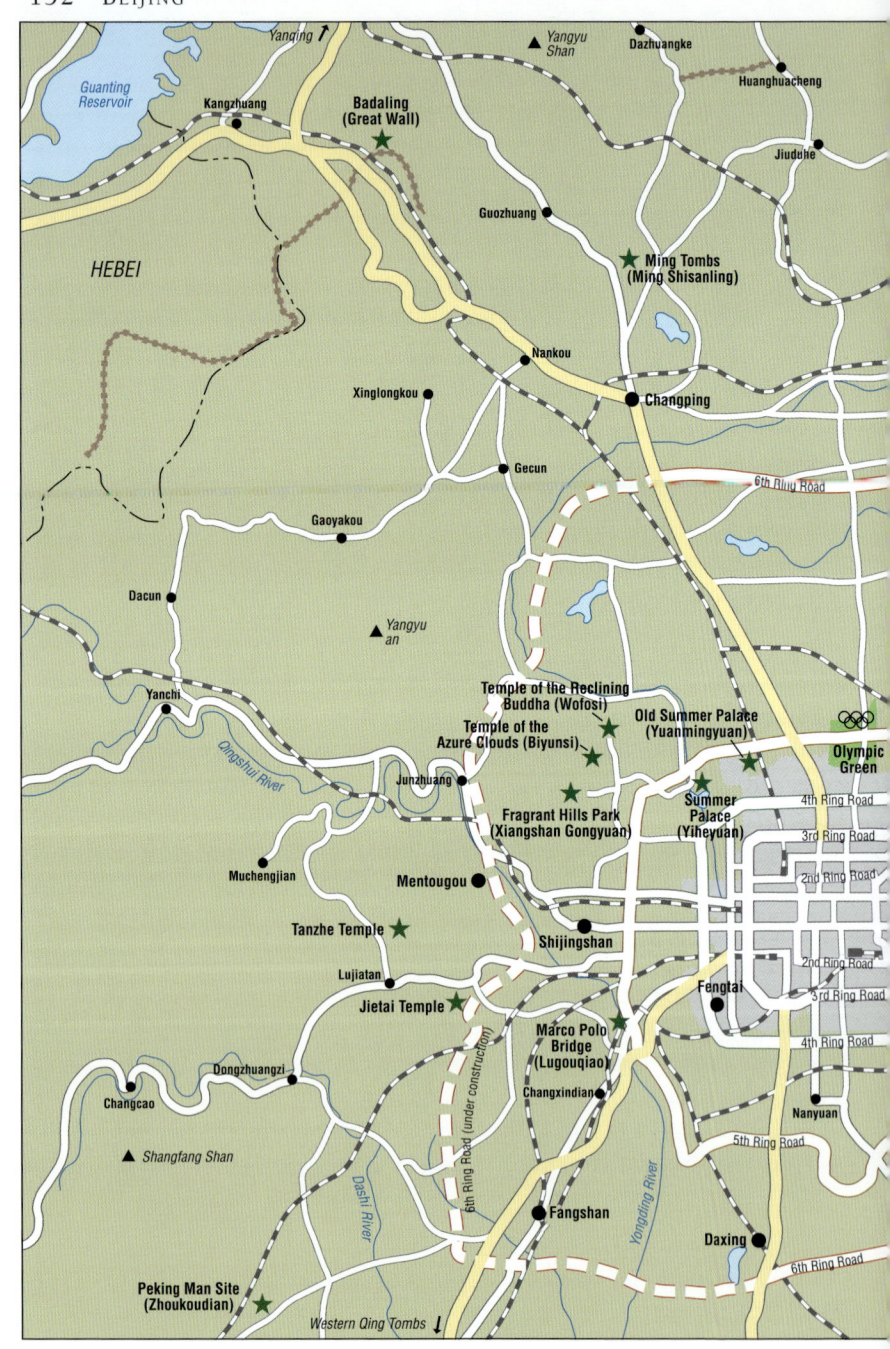

SIGHTS IN BEIJING 133

Sights in Beijing 135

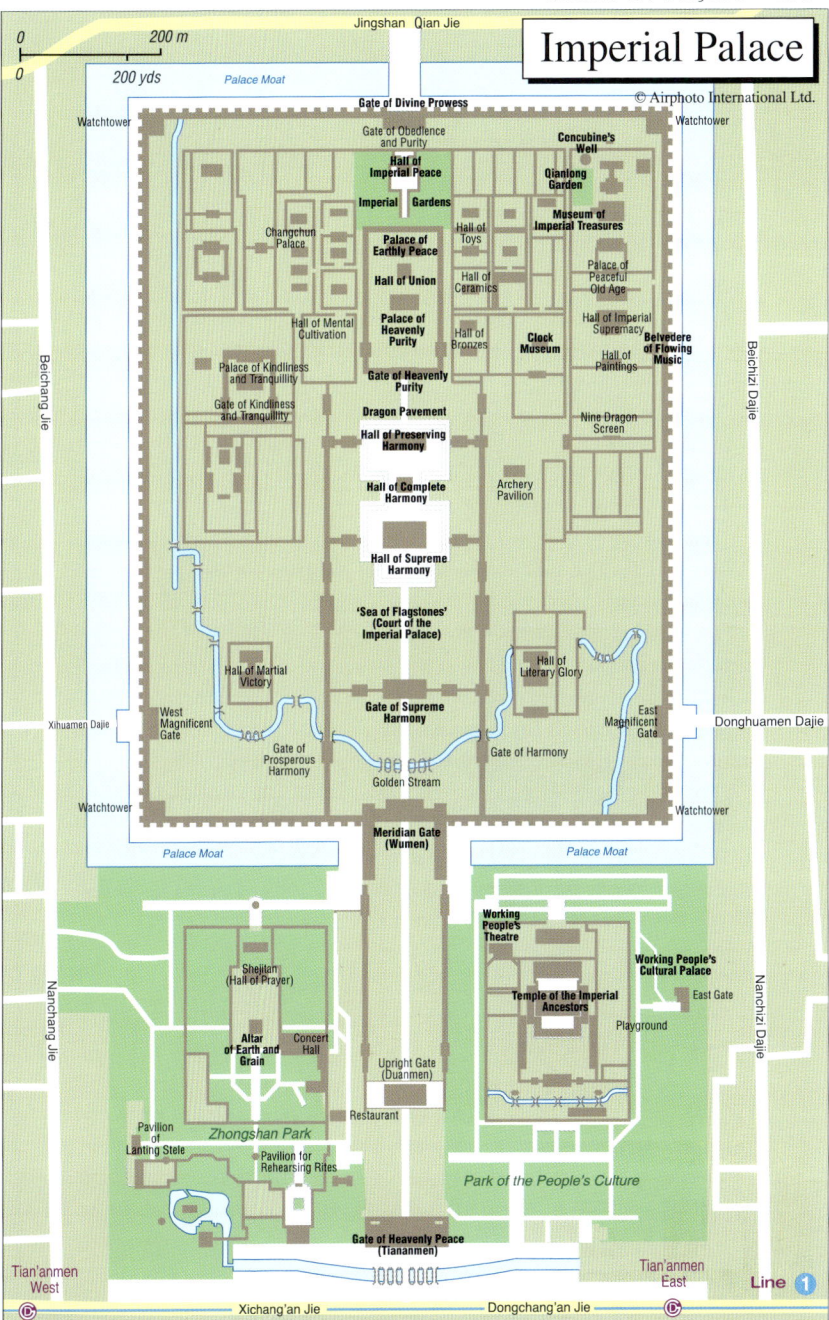

Left: *A bronze ding (cauldron) handle detail*

Imperial Eunuchs

While I was picturing the scene, an unknown voice said quietly:
"In her day there was no electricity. The attendants carried lanterns of scarlet guaze."

I swung around startled. I had been so sure I was alone; the soft, almost feminine voice, emerging unexpectedly from the darkness and seeming like a continuation of my thoughts was disturbing.

"I beg your pardon?"

A shadowy figure, his face barely visible above a dark robe which blended indistinguishably with the night, was standing so close to me that I might have touched his hand. Perceiving he had startled me, he apologized and added:

"I saw you gazing across at the pavilions by the landing-stage. They are beautiful, are they not? But that yellowish light is out of place and garish—like so many things these days."

"Do you mean to say you were here then?"

He laughed, or rather tittered, musically, his voice so feminine that, could I have believed it possible in Peking to encounter a woman walking alone in a solitary place at night, I should certainly have taken him for one. (The Manchu-style gowns of men and women were, even when seen in daylight, not greatly dissimilar.)

"Yes, indeed I was here then. You are a foreigner, but you speak Chinese well. Doubtless you have heard of Tai Chien?"

"The imperial eunuchs? Of course. But they vanished long ago."

"Long as a young man sees things, short enough to one well into the autumn of this life. I was already middle-aged when the Revolution dispersed us. Now I am sixty."

"Were you with them long? In the Imperial Household, I mean?"

"Not long. I was castrated in the seventh year of Kuang Hsü (1882), so I had only twenty-nine years in the Forbidden City. How quickly the time passed!"

"Castrated by your own choice?"

"Why not? It seemed a little thing to give up one pleasure for so many. My parents were poor, yet by suffering that small change I could be sure of an easy life in surroundings of beauty and magnificence; I could aspire to intimate companionship with lovely women unmarred by their fear or distrust of me. I could even hope for *power and wealth of my own. With good fortune and diligence, I might grow more rich and powerful than some of the greatest officials in the empire. How could I foresee the Revolution? That was indeed a misfortune. I have sacrificed my virility and my hope of begetting children for a dream which, passing fleetingly, stopped short and can never return."*

"And so now you come here sometimes in the darkness to recapture an echo of your dream? But how do you live?"

"I manage well. I am a guide—not one of those so-called guides who live by inventing history for foreigners and by making commissions on things they purchase. I have not yet fallen to that. Discriminating Chinese gentlemen arriving from the provinces prefer to obtain their guides through the Palace Eunuchs' Mutual Prosperity Association. Often they have heard my name from their friends and are kind enough to ask specially for my services. I charge highly, for I am able to tell them many things they could scarcely learn from other sources."

After chatting with him longer, I asked if he and his fellow eunuchs were happy in their old age.

"Happy? How could that be? We have no wives, no sons to bear us grandsons and sacrifice at our tombs. We manage to live. We are not often hungry. We dare not ask for happiness."

John Blofield, City of Lingering Splendour: A Frank Account of Old Peking's Exotic Pleasures (Shambhala, 2001)

John Blofield was a bold, spiritual adventurer who, after leaving Cambridge, went out to China in the 1930s and immersed himself in Chan culture and practice. Later in life he studied Tibetan Buddhism and lived in Bangkok. His translations from the Chinese are outstanding and popular while his autobiography makes fascinating reading. In his early 20s, John Blofeld spent what he describes as "three exquisitely happy years" in Peking during the era of the last emperor, when the breathtaking greatness of China's ancient traditions was still everywhere evident. In 1934 it was still possible to travel back in time, to a culture that had remained virtually untouched for thousands of years—and chew Peking Duck with Taoist sages. Blofield is regarded as the foremost translator of the classic work of Huang Po, perhaps one of Zen Buddhism's most brilliant Zen masters. He also wrote a popular translation of the Chinese oracle The I Ching.

BAD OMENS AT HIS CORONATION

Two days after I entered the palace Tzu Hsi (Cixi) died, and on December 2, the "Great Ceremony of Enthronement" took place, a ceremony that I ruined with my crying.

The ceremony took place in the Hall of Supreme Harmony (Tai Ho Tien). Before it began I had to receive the obeisances of the commanders of the palace guard and ministers of the inner court in the Hall of Central Harmony (Chung Ho Tien) and the homage of the leading civilian and military officials. I found all this long and tiresome; it was moreover a very cold day, so when they carried me into the Hall of Supreme Harmony and put me up on the high and enormous throne I could bear it no longer. My father, who was kneeling below the throne and supporting me, told me not to fidget, but I struggled and cried, "I don't like it here. I want to go home. I don't like it here. I want to go home." My father grew so desperate that he was pouring with sweat. As the officials went on kotowing to me my cries grew louder and louder. My father tried to soothe me by saying, "Don't cry, don't cry; it'll soon be finished, it'll soon be finished."

When the ceremony was over the officials asked each other surreptitiously, "How could he say 'It'll soon be finished'? What does it mean, his saying he wanted to go home?" All these discussions took place in a very gloomy atmosphere as if these words had been a bad omen. Some books said that these words were prophetic as within three years the Ching Dynasty was in fact "finished" and the boy who wanted to "go home" did go home, and claimed that the officials had a presentiment of this.

Pu Yi, From Emperor to Citizen, *translated by W J F Jenner*

Aisin-Gioro Pu Yi, *From emperor to citizen : the autobiography of Aisin-Gioro Pu Yi.* Foreign Language Press, 2002. Henry Pu Yi (1906–1967), the last emperor of China, was a member of the Qing Dynasty and a Manchu. He describes with vivid details the events of the 50 years between his ascension to the throne and the last, decadent days of the Qing Dynasty through to the final period of his life as a retiring scholar, citizen of the People's Republic of China and quiet-living resident of Beijing.

Chinese ministers of state (left to right)
Shen Kwei Fen, Tung Hsun *and* Mao Chang Hsi. *Photographed by John Thomson, 1870.*

The Principal Halls

The next courtyard, called the '**Sea of Flagstones**', was designed to accommodate 90,000 people during an imperial ceremony. In its center stands the **Hall of Supreme Harmony** (*Taihe Dian*), the largest and grandest structure in the Palace. Here were held the most solemn of ceremonial occasions, such as celebration of the New Year and the emperor's birthday, or announcing the successful candidates of the imperial examinations. This hall is filled with many treasures, including bronze incense burners, musical chimes made of jade, and a nine-dragon screen behind the throne.

Behind the Hall of Supreme Harmony are the halls of **Complete Harmony** (*Zhonghe Dian*) and **Preserving Harmony** (*Baohe Dian*). In the former, the emperor donned formal regalia before proceeding to the Hall of Supreme Harmony, or performed lesser State functions like inspecting seeds for a new planting. The Hall of Preserving Harmony was used for a time as the site for the highest level of the imperial examinations (*see* page 70). Behind this hall, between the descending staircases, is the '**Dragon Pavement**', an exquisitely carved block of marble said to weigh over 200 tons.

The Hall of Complete Harmony.

The Inner Court 故宫内殿

The three rear halls, the **Palace of Heavenly Purity** (*Qianqing Gong*), the **Hall of Union** (*Jiaotai Dian*) and the **Palace of Earthly Peace** (*Kunning Gong*), were also the site of lesser State functions. During the Ming Dynasty, emperors lived among these buildings, but later the Qing rulers moved to smaller, less formal parts of the Palace. They nevertheless continued to use the Palace of Earthly Peace to consummate their marriages. The last emperor, Puyi, who ascended the throne as a child and formally abdicated in 1912, was allowed to use this chamber on his wedding night. However, intimidated by the color scheme of gaudy red (the traditional color of joy), he fled to his usual quarters.

The east and west sides of the Palace's rear section contain a dizzying succession of smaller courts where the imperial families, concubines and attendants lived, schemed for power and engaged in their many intrigues. In the far northeast corner of the complex, behind the **Palace of Peaceful Old Age** (*Ningshou Gong*), is the famous well down which the Pearl Concubine was cast (*see* page 160). Several of the eastern palaces have been converted into exhibition halls for the collections of the Palace Museum (*see* page 142).

Landscaped with cypress and pine trees that are now hundreds of years old, this is a perfect spot for a rest or a casual stroll.

Two sections in the eastern palaces are worth seeing. One is the **Qianlong Garden**, built for the retirement of the aging emperor (reigned 1736–95). It is a quiet, secluded rock garden with a central pavilion made of fine wood brought from the forests of Sichuan and Yunnan provinces. One of three smaller pavilions was specially constructed for elaborate drinking games with strong Chinese liquor, a favorite pastime of the emperor.

The **Belvedere of Flowing Music** (*Changyin Ge*) is a three-storey theater, the largest in the Palace, and a favorite haunt of the Empress Dowager Cixi. Magnificently carved and painted eaves set off the stage where dramas often depicted Buddhist worthies and Taoist immortals swarming all over the boards, dropping from ceilings and popping out of trap doors. The building opposite, where Cixi watched the dramas, has a rich display of silk costumes, stage properties and scripts used by the imperial troupe. There are also drawings of famous productions of the 60th birthday celebrations of Qianlong and Cixi. The latter affair is said to have continued for 10 consecutive days.

Beyond the rear palaces, by the northern gate of the Palace, are the **Imperial Gardens**. Landscaped with cypress and pine trees that are now hundreds of years old, this is a perfect spot for a rest or a casual stroll.

Before leaving the palace, you might visit an interesting exhibition of palace architecture and construction located in the tower of the **Gate of Divine Prowess**. Here there are blueprints, tools, color schemes, roof tiles and old photographs that are highly informative despite the frustrating absence of labels in any language except Chinese.

A quiet corner in the eastern Palace near Qianlong Garden, 1978.

Tickets for the exhibition are sold in the kiosk on the east side of the courtyard inside the gate. You reach the tower by a long incline once used by the soldiers guarding the palace.

Although the Imperial Palace in its entirety is regarded as a museum of architectural and artistic heritage, there are specific halls and pavilions within it—collectively known as the Palace Museum—which are used as showcases for the cornucopia of treasures in the palace. As the restoration of the Palace is constantly in progress, new areas of exhibits are opened from time to time.

The Historical Art Museum 历史艺术博物馆
Housed in the Hall of Preserving Harmony (*Baohe Dian*), the collection here provides a broad conspectus of Chinese cultural development. Arranged chronologically, the exhibition is in three parts. The first part deals with the period from earliest times to about 4,000 years ago, illustrated by excavated ancient painted pottery, bronzes and sculptures. The fifth to the 13th centuries—the period covered by the second section—saw the emergence of an early modern style of painting as well as significant developments in the art of ivory carving, lacquerware, weaving and calligraphy. The third part of the exhibition shows samples of the arts during the Yuan, Ming and Qing dynasties; of particular interest is the fine porcelain that was produced in this era.

The Hall of Bronzes 故宫青铜器馆
This collection is shown in the Palace of Abstinence (*Zhai Gong*), the Hall of Sincere Solemnity (*Chengsu Dian*) and the Palace of Revered Benevolence (*Jingren Gong*), and includes examples of bronze wine goblets, tripod cooking vessels and pots from the Shang, Zhou, Spring and Autumn and Warring States periods.

The Hall of Toys 清宫玩具陈列室
An odd and delightful assortment of some 80 mechanical toys manufactured in China and Europe (Switzerland, France, England and Germany) in the 18th and 19th centuries is on display in a hall immediately inside (to the south of) the southern gate of the Imperial Garden, to the northeast of the Palace of Earthly Peace. The automatons include a songbird that sings, a conjuror who performs tricks, a smoker who exhales real smoke, and a boy waving a fan, which functioned as an early form of air-conditioning.

The Hall of Ceramics 故宫陶瓷馆
The Palace of Heavenly Favors (*Chengqian Gong*) and the Palace of Eternal Harmony (*Yonghe Gong*) contain Neolithic pottery from the Shang to the Western Zhou dynasties, with examples of Longshan blackware, incized and glazed pottery from

the Han Dynasty on through to the celadon ware of the Yuan, the tri-colored glazes of the Tang and the blue and white of the Ming and Qing dynasties. Many fine examples from the famous imperial kilns of Jingdezhen can be seen.

The Hall of Paintings 故宫书画馆
Scroll paintings and calligraphy are displayed in the Hall of Imperial Supremacy (*Huangji Dian*), the Palace of Peaceful Old Age (*Ningshou Gong*) and galleries on its eastern, western and southern sides. For a few weeks each autumn, during the dry weather, the rarest examples of Chinese visual arts are brought out for public view.

The Museum of Imperial Treasures 故宫瑰宝
This superb hoard of ritual and everyday items used by the Qing Court is displayed in the Hall of Character Cultivation (*Yangxin Dian*) and the Palace of Happy Old Age (*Leshou Gong*). The treasures grouped together in the first hall include silver and gold tableware, jewelled knick-knacks and little Buddhist shrines. The latter, generally made of gold, include one especially made for Emperor Qianlong to preserve a strand of his mother's hair

In the second hall, which contains the gorgeous habiliments and attire worn by emperors, empresses and concubines, there are exquisite pieces of jewelry, hairpins and headdresses as well as Court costumes. One of the most outstanding exhibits is Qianlong's peacock feather-trimmed robe studded with seed pearls and tiny coral beads.

The sybaritic Court amassed a vast number of ornaments and decorative pieces to adorn the palace interior. One kind of curio (which is still popular with collectors today) is the jewelled penjing—artificial miniature potted landscapes composed of precious stones, with leaves and petals carved out of gold, silver and jade—which are shown in the third section.

Note that although the Museum of Imperial Treasures is open 8:30am–4:15pm daily, the ticket office closes at 3:15pm.

The Hall of Clocks and Watches 故宫钟表馆
A small gallery in the Hall of Ancestor Worship, located to the east of the Gate of Heavenly Purity, houses an extraordinary collection of elaborate clocks, both European and Chinese, dating from the 18th and 19th centuries.

Exhibition of Historical Relics from the Qing
Several aspects of imperial life and duties are represented by the relics here in the Palace of Heavenly Purity (*Qianqing Gong*), for example the imperial seals for giving the stamp of royal approval to decrees issued in the emperor's name. There are also musical instruments, more ceremonial and traveling regalia plus weapons and arms.

Summer Festivities

The time to take incense to the temple on Miao Feng Mountain had come again and it was very hot. Sellers of paper fans seemed to have emerged from somewhere all at once with boxes hanging from their arms and strings of jingling bells to attract attention hanging from the boxes.

Many things were for sale in the streets; green apricots were heaped in piles while cherries gleamed redly and brightened your eyes. Swarms of bees swooped over bowls of roses or dates and the agar jellies on porcelain plates had a milky glow. Peddlers of cookies and jellies had their wares arranged with remarkable neatness and spices of every kind and color were also set out on display.

People had changed into brighter and more colorful unpadded garments and the streets were suddenly filled with their colors, as if many rainbows had come down into them. The street cleaners worked faster, going down the road sprinkling water without a pause, but the light dust soon flew around as before and vexed people. There were longish twigs of willow in the slightly dusty air and lightly and delightfully swooping swallows as well which made people feel cheery in spite of themselves. It was the sort of weather that really made you wonder what to do with yourself and everyone yawned great lazy yawns while feeling tired and happy too.

Processions of various kinds set out for the mountains continuously. Lines of people beating on drums and gongs, or carrying baskets on shoulder poles, or waving apricot yellow flags went by one on the heels of another, lending an unusual kind of bustle to the entire city, lending an elusive and yet familiar thrill to the people and lingering sounds and fine dust to the air. Those in the processions and those who watched them all felt a kind of excitement, devoutness, and exuberance.

The hurly-burly of this chaotic world comes from superstition; the only solace the stupid have is self-deception. These colors, these voices, the clouds filling the sky, and the dust in the streets made people energetic and gave them something to do. The mountain goers climbed mountains, the temple goers went to temples, the flower gazers looked at flowers. Those who couldn't do any of these things could still watch the processions from the sidelines and repeat the name of Buddha.

It was so hot it seemed to have roused the old capital from its spring dream. You could find amusements everywhere but everyone wondered what to do. Urged on by the heat, the flowers, grasses, fruit trees, and the joy among the people, all burgeoned together. The newly furbished green willows along the South Lake enticed harmonica-playing youngsters; boys and girls tied their boats up in the shade of the willows or floated among the lotuses. Their mouths sang love songs and they kissed each other with their eyes.

The camellias and peonies in the park sent invitations to poets and elegant gentlemen who now paced back and forth while waving their expensively decorated paper fans. They would sit in front of the red walls or under the pine trees when tired and drink several cups of clear tea, enough to draw out their idle melancholy. They'd steal a glance at the young ladies of wealthy families and at the famous "flowers" of the south and north who strolled by.

Even places which had heretofore been quiet had visitors sent to them by the warm wind and bright sun, just as the butterflies were sent. The peonies of the Ch'ung Hsiao temple, the green rushes at the T'ao Jan pavilion, the mulberry trees and rice paddies at the site of the Zoological and Botanical Gardens, all attracted the sounds of people and the shadows of their parasols. The Altar of Heaven, the Temple of Confucius, and the Lama temple had just a little bustle in the midst of their usual solemnity as well.

Students and those who like short trips went to the Western Hills, the hot springs, and the Summer Palace. They went to sightsee, to run around, to gather things, and to scribble words all over the rocks in the mountains.

Poor people also had somewhere to go: the Hu Kuo temple, the Lu Fu temple, the White Pagoda, and the Temple of Earth. All the flower markets were busier. Fresh cut flowers of every sort were arranged colorfully along the streets and a penny or so could take some beauty back home.

On the mats of the soybean milk vendors fresh pickled vegetables were arranged to look like big flowers topped with fried hot peppers. Eggs were really cheap and the soft yellow egg dumplings for sale made people's mouths water.

T'ien Ch'iao was even more fired up than usual. New mats had been hung for tea sheds, one right next to another. There were clean white tablecloths and entrancing singing girls who waved to the ancient pines above the wall at the Temple of Heaven. The sounds of drums and gongs dragged on for eight or nine hours and the brisk heat of the day made them sound especially light and sharp in a way that struck and disturbed people's hearts.

Literary Excerpt

Dressing up was simple for the girls. One calico frock was all they needed to go out prettily dressed and it revealed every curve of their bodies as well.

Those who liked peace and quiet also had a place to go. You could drop a fishing line at the Chi Shui reservoir, outside the Wan Shou temple, at the kiln pits east of town, or on the marble bridge west of town. The little fishes would bump into the rushes now and then, making them move slightly. When you finished your fishing, the pigshead meat, stewed bean curd, and salted beans you ate with your baigan could make you both satiated and drunk. And afterwards, following the willow-edged bank and carrying fishing pole and little fish, you entered the city at a leisurely pace while treading on the beams of the setting sun.

There was fun, color, excitement, and noise everywhere. The first heat wave of summer was like an incantation that made every place in the city fascinating. The city paid no attention to death, paid no attention to disaster, and paid no attention to poverty. It simply put forth its powers when the time came and hypnotized a million people, and they, as if in a dream, chanted poems in praise of its beauty. It was filthy, beautiful, decadent, bustling, chaotic, idle, lovable; it was the great Peking of early summer.

Lao She, Rickshaw, *(1936), translated by Jean M James*
(University Press of Hawaii, 1979).

Chinese playwright and author of humorous, satiric novels and short stories, Lao She (1899–1966) was born of Manchu descent in Beijing. His father, who was a soldier, died in a street battle during the Boxer uprising. Fatherless since early childhood, Lao She worked his way through Peking Teacher's College. He served as a principal of an elementary school at the age of 17, and later he was a district supervisor. Lao She spent the years from 1924 to 1929 in London, where he taught Chinese at the School of Oriental and African Studies. In 1931 Lao She returned to China and continued to write and teach in various universities. Between the years 1946 and 1949 Lao She lived in the United States on a cultural grant at the invitation from the Department of State. When the People's Republic was established in 1949, Lao She returned to China. He commited suicide in 1966, after being beaten severely by zealous Red Guards.

Juanqinzhai 倦勤摘

The stunning restoration of Juanqinzhai, the former residence of Emperor Qianlong, and one of the most important interiors in the Forbidden City, was completed in 2008 following a five-year effort that cost US$3 million.

The construction of Juanqinzhai, or "the studio of exhaustion from diligent service," and its adjoining gardens and pavilions, was commissioned by Qianlong in 1771 to serve as his retirement home in 1796. The emperor had promised that "if the Heavens blessed him to be on the throne for 60 years," he would step down out of respect so as not to surpass the 61-year reign of his grandfather, Kangxi, China's longest-reigning emperor.

The project, a cooperation between the World Monuments Fund (WMF), an NGO that focuses on historical preservation, and the Palace Museum, was not an easy one. Qianlong was a patron of the arts and he collected some of the best art pieces and techniques during his trips around China, with much of this being used in his retirement home.

Intimidated by the huge task of restoring such an important venue, officials of the Forbidden City hesitated for decades before contacting the WMF for help with the project. Many of the art forms employed in building the original complex had seemingly already disappeared and the team was not sure how to go about restoring or reproducing the quality of the work that was done some 240 years ago. Gradually, however, rare crafts people were discovered throughout China through word of mouth and the media. These artisans were able to either restore the work or create excellent copies of what was beyond repair. Juanqinzhai thus showcases many rare art forms from around China that are on the verge of extinction.

Within the studio, walls and screens are decorated with delicate bamboo marquetry and double-sided silk embroidery, and imperial chairs are covered in embroidered silk. Each piece of furniture had to be researched to establish that it had indeed once been part of the complex—otherwise it would not be put on display.

The emperor, a fan of opera, built an indoor theater in the studio, covering the entire room with silk murals depicting Beijing's verdant hills, palace buildings and exotic fowls. To do this, artists used the perspective of trompe l'oeil, a technique that creates a visual illusion in art that tricks the eye into seeing painted detail as a three-dimensional object. This Western technique was not known in 18th century China, and so it's believed that this work was influenced by the Italian Jesuit Giuseppe Castiglione, an accomplished painter who lived in Beijing at the time.

Qianlong never actually retired to Juanqinzhai. He abdicated the throne in 1795, but remained in his formal abode at Qianqinggong, continuing to wield influence from behind the scenes until he passed away in 1799.

The building is not yet open to the general public, but plans are underway to offer regularly scheduled tours for visitors that can accommodate the fragile and intimate nature of the building's interiors. During this time, a special limited number of tours may be allowed at the discretion of the Palace Museum. Inquiries should be addressed to: Department of Foreign Affairs, The Palace Museum, 4 Jingshan Qianjie, Beijing, China 100009, Fax: +86 (10) 8511 7650.

Prospect Hill (*Jingshan*) 景山公园 (煤山公园)
Just north of the Imperial Palace, the site occupied by Prospect Hill was a private park reserved for the use of the emperor in the Yuan Dynasty (1279–1368). During the Ming (1368–1644), an artificial hill with five peaks was made, utilizing earth excavated when the moat of the Imperial Palace was dug. There is an old but fallacious story that an emperor kept supplies of coal hidden under the hill, hence its other name, Coal Hill (*Meishan*). A pavilion was erected on each peak, and five bronze Buddhas given pride of place in them. Four of the statues were removed by the troops of the Allied Expeditionary Force when they came to Beijing to relieve the Siege of the Legations in 1900. Prospect Hill was opened to the public in 1928. Designated as a park after 1949, and closed during the Cultural Revolution, it can now be visited between 6:00am and 8:00pm.

At the southern approach is the **Gorgeous View Tower** (*Qiwang Lou*). Previously visited by emperors coming to pay their respects at an altar to Confucius, it is now an exhibition venue for displays of paintings, porcelain and calligraphy.

The best view of Beijing is from the **Pavilion of Everlasting Spring** (*Wanchun Ting*) perched on top of the middle peak, which used to be the highest point in the city. Northwards, one can see the Drum and Bell Towers, a traditional feature of old Chinese cities. To the northwest, the two slabs of water of the Shichahai and Beihai Lake are intersected by Di'anmen Dajie. To the south, the golden roofs of the Imperial Palace can be seen stretching into the distance.

On the eastern slope there used to be an old tree (said to be cassia) from which Chongzhen, the last Ming emperor, is supposed to have hanged himself in 1644. According to one version of the incident, the emperor decamped to the hill upon hearing that rebels intent on overthrowing the dynasty had already stormed the city. He had evidently retreated in some disarray: he wore no head-dress, had only one shoe, and the sleeves of his robe were freshly stained with the blood of his consort and two princesses. The story goes that he committed suicide with his own belt. The spot was once marked by a stone tablet. Later emperors in the early Qing, passing this place to go to the Hall of Imperial Longevity behind the hill, were required to alight from their sedan-chairs and proceed past the tablet on foot, perhaps in order to show more

Behai Park.

humility when contemplating the salutary example of an unpopular predecessor. Part of the Hall of Imperial Longevity is now the **Beijing Children's Palace**.

BEIHAI PARK 北海公园

To the west of Prospect Hill is one of the most beautiful places in Beijing. Beihai Park is open from 6:00am to 8:00pm (extended to 9:00pm in the summer), and is a popular place for skating in the winter and boating in the warmer months. There is a jetty on the northern shore, in front of a botanical garden, from which boats can be easily hired. The extraordinarily beautiful lotus blossoms make late summer a favorite time for visitors.

A lake was first dug here during the Jin Dynasty (12th–13th century); a palace, an island—*Qionghua* or *Hortensia*—and pleasure gardens together created a retreat for the Court.

The retreat was refurbished three times during the Yuan Dynasty, and again overhauled in the 15th century by Emperor Yongle, the architect of Beijing. The lake was divided into two: the central and southern lakes to the south, Zhongnanhai, is now reserved for senior members of the Chinese government. Dubbed the 'newForbidden City' by Beijing residents, **Zhongnanhai** contains the villa where Mao Zedong lived and worked. The complex is off-limits to foreigners. The northern part, Beihai, is open to the public. By the south entrance to the park is the **Round City**, which contains the enormous jade bowl, with fine carvings of sea monsters around the outside, that was given to Kublai Khan in 1265. The bowl went missing for several centuries, and was functioning as a pickle vat in a monastery in the northern part of the city until the Qianlong emperor rescued it and brought it here in the 18th century. The carved inscriptions on the bowl date from this time.

The building that stands in the center of the Round City, the **Hall of Receiving Light**, contains a large white jade Buddha image that resembles the statue in the Jade Buddha Temple in Shanghai. It was here that the Guangxu Emperor met with the British ambassador in 1893. Former emperors would rest and change their clothing in the Round City on their way to the palaces in the western suburbs. The Round City is open to visitors from 8:30am to 4:30pm.

QIONGHUA ISLAND 琼华岛
The dominant landmark on Qionghua Island, also called Hortensia Island, is the **White Dagoba**, a Buddhist shrine of Tibetan origin, built in 1651 in honor of the visit of the Dalai Lama to Beijing. Terraces lead down the southern slope, near the bottom of which is the White Dagoba Temple, now known as the **Temple of Everlasting Peace** (*Yongan Si*).

HUTONGS

Beijing's hutongs—back alleys—are where life in the northern capital can be seen at its most traditional. Regularly slated to be torn down and redeveloped for modern housing or commercial real estate, these fascinating little streets form a miniature grid of walled courtyards and passage ways, in between the sweeping boulevards which are the main traffic arteries. Often blessed with picturesque names—Knitting Yarn Hutong, Sea Transport Granary Hutong, Performing Music Hutong, Little Trumpet Hutong and Big Trumpet Hutong—the hutongs are essentially residential areas where the informality of ordinary life can be witnessed. Potted plants nod at the visitor passing by, and a canary in a cage mocks the rare cat that slinks over an old, grey-plastered wall. Old men dawdle with their long-stemmed pipes, and grandma takes the well-padded baby out for a stroll.

There is much debate about the origin of the word hutong. The most convincing argument is that hutong derives from a Mongol word, hotlog, that means 'water well' and suggests a small geographical area of the city that may have been served by a single well. It is likely that during the Yuan dynasty, when the Mongols established their capital Dadu in an area that generally coincides with the limits of the later Ming and Qing capitals, they dug many wells. However as most of the well water was brackish, and eventually proved insufficient for the growing city's needs, canals were dug to supply the city with water from several sources in the western suburbs and link up the Grand Canal to the urban waterway system. In this way the imperial granaries could be filled directly from the barges that transported tribute rice from southern China, whereas transhipment had previously been necessary. The names of some Beijing hutongs have changed several times, and underwent an extensive anti-feudal whitewashing during the Cultural Revolution. One choice example from that period can be rendered in English as 'Red-to-the-end-of-the-Hutong'.

Sometimes a commune donkey-car loaded with vegetables seeks passage along the narrow lanes, and teenagers loaf around joking. The walls are daubed with slogans such as 'Observe Hygiene' and 'Look After Soldiers' Families Well' but the air of perpetual afternoon overpowers propaganda.

While foreign visitors generally find hutongs charming and quaint, many residents are pleased to move into modern apartments when the bulldozer finally arrives. Hutongs often have neither indoor plumbing nor heating, and can be extremely hot in summer. Also, the close quarters shared by numerous families are increasingly at odds with the growing privacy in Chinese life. Zhang Yang's award-winning film *Shower* is an excellent portrayal of hutong family life.

Left: *The alleys near Nan Luogu Xiang, a great part of town to stroll, shop and eat.*

Fangshan Restaurant (*see* page 282), famous for its imperial dishes, is located among the buildings that form the **Hall of Rippling Waves** (*Yilan Tang*), a former palace, at the northern end of the island. Not far from this, to the west, is the **Pavilion for Reading Ancient Texts** (*Yuegu Lou*), which is a storehouse of 495 stone tablets, engraved with calligraphy during the Qianlong period, including samples of writing from 1,500 years ago.

THE NORTHERN SHORE 北岸

Over a period of 30 years, Emperor Qianlong embellished several pavilions, halls and terraces along the northwestern shore of the lake. To commemorate his mother's 80th birthday, he had erected the **Ten-thousand Buddha Tower** (*Wanfo Lou*) at the western end of the cluster of buildings and gardens. Sadly, the little Buddhas have all been stolen.

Nearby, in front of the former Temple of Expounding Fortune (*Chanfu Si*), now the site of a botanical garden, stands the **Iron Screen**, a Yuan-Dynasty wall of volcanic stone carved with strange mythical creatures. A later version, the **Nine-Dragon Screen**, made of glazed tiles in 1417, can be found further east, scaring evil spirits away not from the temple that used to stand behind, but from the Beihai Sports Ground.

Some of the old buildings around Beihai Lake have been converted to modern use; one of the most well-preserved is the **Study of Serenity** (*Jingxin Zhai*) near the northern apex of the lake. This, deservedly called 'a garden within a garden', comprises a quiet walled enclave with a summer house, which now accommodates a literary research institute.

The Empress Dowager Cixi used to go to Beihai for picnics on the lake, and today the park continues to be a favorite with citizens enjoying a snack either from some of the small pavilions serving food, or a full meal at the Fangshan Restaurant.

White Dagoba, a Buddhist shrine of Tibetan origin, built in 1651.

The Drum and Bell Towers (Gu Lou and Zhong Lou) 钟鼓楼

Drum and bell towers are a traditional feature of an old Chinese city. In Beijing they are located to the north of Prospect Hill. The Drum Tower (*Gu Lou*) dates from the Ming period. Rising from a brick podium, the multi-eaved wooden tower is pierced on two sides by six openings. In Imperial times, 24 drums would beat out the night watches; now only one of them remains. The tower has been renovated, and it may be entered and climbed.

Not far north of the Drum Tower is the Bell Tower (Zhonglou).

Not far north of the Drum Tower is the Bell Tower (*Zhong Lou*), a structure 33 meters (108 feet) high. The present tower was constructed of brick in 1747. The copper bell, which replaced an earlier iron bell that is still intact, rang out over the city at seven o'clock every evening until the practice was stopped in 1924. The towers are open every day from 9:00am to 5:00pm.

Song Qingling's Residence 宋庆龄故居

Song Qingling (Soong Ching-ling), born in 1892 in Shanghai, was married to the famous Republican leader, Dr. Sun Yat-sen, and became an active political figure in her own right after his death in 1925. Although initially aligned, through her husband, with the Nationalist Party (*Kuomintang*), whose leader Chiang Kai-shek married her sister Meiling, she eventually split with the right wing and, after spending several years in the Soviet Union, became a supporter of the Communists.

The Chinese accord Song Qingling enormous respect not simply because she held several high offices in the government of the People's Republic; she was also, in a very prominent way, a convert from the 'class enemy', coming as she did from a powerful and wealthy Shanghai family. She remains a figure invoked by women's groups in China, similar to the memory of Eleanor Roosevelt.

Her former residence at 46 Beiheyan, overlooking the Back Lake (*Houhai*), originally belonged to a member of the Qing royal family. Song Qingling occupied it from 1963 to her death in 1981. It may be visited daily between 9:00am and 4:30pm, and provides a relaxing diversion from Beijing's larger sights. The house is enclosed by a lovely garden filled with pine, cypress and flowering shrubs as well as traditional pavilions linked by winding corridors. The Fan Pavilion (*Shanting*) gives a view of the whole garden.

The living quarters have been turned into a modest museum displaying memorabilia of the former occupant's eventful life. Song Qingling was educated at Wesleyan College in Macon, Georgia and the bookshelves contain an impressive collection of English-language books. Take a look at page 366 for an insight into the Song family.

The Mansion of Prince Gong (Gongwangfu) 恭王府

Located at number 17 Qianhai Xijie in the Rear Lakes (*Shichahai*) district, the Mansion of Prince Gong is one of the largest and best preserved prince's mansions in Beijing. Prince Gong was the younger brother of the Xianfeng emperor, whose short rule lasted only 10 years (1851–1861). When Xianfeng died and the young Tongzhi emperor mounted the dragon throne at the age of five, Prince Gong served as regent along with Xianfeng's principal concubine and Tongzhi's mother, the notorious Empress Dowager Cixi. Prince Gong offended Cixi when he had An Dehai, her favorite eunuch, killed. Prince Gong also represented the Chinese government in negotiations with Lord Elgin in 1860, and was a key player in Chinese politics during the troubled decades of the late 19th century.

The mansion is divided into three sections. There is the residence itself, with a large banquet hall now used for evening shows. The spacious garden has several artificial hills made of heaped Lake Taihu stones, grotesquely eroded chunks of limestone that were transported from the Yangzi delta region. Atop one of the hills there is a pagoda that was used for gazing at the moon. There is also a large square fishing pond with an island in its center.

A number of literary scholars in China have suggested that Prince Gong's mansion was the model for the mansion and garden, the Prospect Garden (*Daguan Yuan*), described by Cao Xueqin in *The Dream of the Red Chamber* (Honglou Meng), the 18th century novel generally regarded as China's greatest. Indeed, several details of the mansion correspond with the descriptions in the book, especially the layout of the buildings. In the 1980s, the mansion was rescued from the clutches of the Public Security Bureau, which was using the grounds as a residence for retired officers. It is now fully restored and open to the public every day from 8:30am to 5:00pm.

A modern Prospect Garden was built in the southwest district of the city, based closely on the novel. It was used in the filming of the television series based on the book, and is now open to the public as a park (*see* page 165).

Right: *Pailous viewed from the Round Altar, also known as the Circular Mound.*

The Pailous

To get to the Temple of Confucius and the Former Imperial College, one must pass at least one of the few extant street *pailous* in Beijing. But before modern transport made it necessary to reduce their numbers radically, *pailous* decorated many streets and intersections in Beijing and other cities in northern China. For example, *Xidan* means 'western single' and refers to a single *pailou* that once stood at the intersection of Xi Chang'an Jie and Xidan Bei Dajie, while *Xisi*, literally 'western four', reminds us that there were once four *pailous* at the intersection that is still referred to by that name.

Some scholars trace the origin of the *pailou* to India, where *toranas*, a gateway constructed of two columns (posts) with several decorative crossbeams (lintels), were placed at the entrances to temples. There is a striking resemblance between the stone *toranas* surrounding the large hemispherical stupa at Sanchi, and those at the Round Altar in the Temple of Heaven in Beijing. Later pailous have highly elaborate (and often ungainly) wooden superstructures with manifold roofs, always in odd numbers, and sometimes covered with glazed tiles.

In residential districts, *pailous* were erected to commemorate virtuous women or heroic men. No such *pailous* have survived in Beijing.

Pailous can be seen in the Temple of Confucius, Imperial College, Lama Temple, Beihai Park and the Summer Palace, to mention a few. The marble *pailou* at the entrance to the Ming Tombs, once painted a brilliant red and green, is regarded as probably the finest in China. Today it is often passed unnoticed as it sits to the side of the main road through the tomb area.

Xu Beihong Memorial Museum 徐悲鸿博物馆

This quiet little museum, at 53 Xinjiekou Bei Dajie, is dedicated to the renowned modern Chinese artist Xu Beihong (1895–1953), who is known internationally for his traditional Chinese paintings with brush and ink, primarily of horses, a style that has been widely imitated. Xu, who studied in Europe in the 1920s, also combined classical Western realism with Chinese themes and political messages.

The present museum displays Xu's collection of oil paintings, sketches and watercolors simply but effectively. It is an enjoyable place to visit; hours are 9:00am to 12 noon, 1:00pm to 5:00pm (closed Monday). Tel. 6225 2187.

Southern Districts

The Temple of Heaven (*Tiantan*) 天坛

The Temple of Heaven has been called 'the noblest example of religious architecture in the whole of China'. Begun in 1406, in the reign of Emperor Yongle, it was completed in 1420. The huge site is reached by going south along Qianmen Dajie, following a route traversed by past emperors and their entourages in splendid procession from which the commoner had to avert his eyes.

The emperors came to Tiantan at the winter solstice to offer sacrifices to Heaven—momentous occasions for which the temple's grandeur and simplicity provided a fitting background. The temple's design symbolized certain tenets of their beliefs. The altar and temple buildings are located within a wall which is half-circular to the north, and square to the south. During the Yongle period, annual sacrifices to the earth at the summer solstice were also performed here; the outline of the enclosure represented the imagined shapes of heaven (curved) and earth (square).

Sights in Beijing

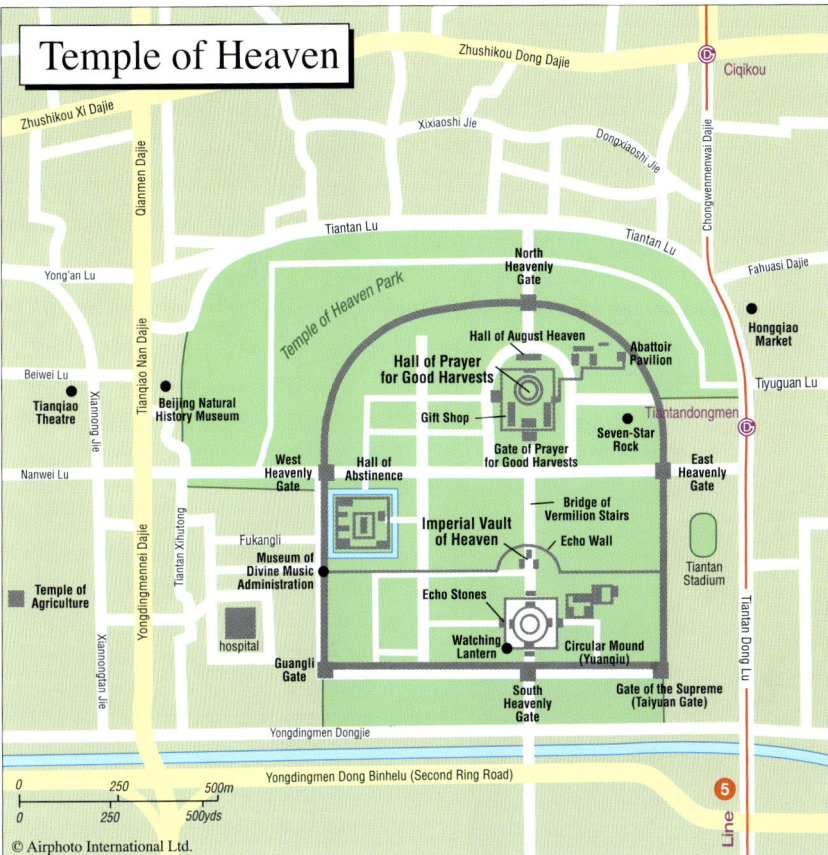

Note that the roof tiles of the **Hall of Prayer for Good Harvests** (see picture page 112) are a deep blue, the color of the sky. Moreover, each of the main structures in the temple has three tiers, making a total of nine, a number in Chinese cosmology representing Heaven. A separate Altar to the Earth (*Ditan*) was later constructed to the north of the city.

From the entrance at West Heavenly Gate, an avenue leads to the **Hall of Abstinence** (*Zhai Gong*). For three days before the rites began, the emperor would have forsworn meat and wine, and the last day of his fast would be spent here. For his safety, the hall was and still is enclosed by a moat, which is currently lacking water.

From the Hall of Abstinence, its just a few minutes walk to the **Museum of Divine Music Administration**.

Left: *The Hall of Abstinence, or Fasting Hall, with its decorative bridges spanning its moat.*

From there visitors can walk up to the **Circular Mound** (*Yuanqiu*), an open altar set on three round marble terraces, built in 1530. The emperor used to come here to commune with Heaven and, interestingly, there is a curious acoustical effect to be heard from the center of the Circular Mound.

Next to the Mound is the **Imperial Vault of Heaven** (*Huangqiong Yu*), a wooden structure roofed with blue tiles and built entirely of wood in 1530. Tablets used in ceremonies held on the mound were stored here. The Imperial Vault is surrounded by a round wall, popularly known as the **Echo** or **Whispering Wall**,

The Imperial Vault of Heaven, a wooden structure roofed with blue tiles and built entirely of wood.

because of its remarkable acoustics. If the round courtyard is relatively quiet—something it has not been in several years due to the rising tide of domestic tourism—two people standing out of earshot at any point along the wall with their heads at approximately the same distance off the ground can hear each other talking.

A second acoustical phenomenon is the '**echo stones**', which refer to the first three rectangular stones at the foot of the staircase that leads up to the Imperial Vault.

The Echo or Whispering Wall.

If you stand on the first stone at the foot of the stairs and clap your hands once, you will hear one echo. If you clap once on the second stone, you will hear two echoes. And a single clap from the third stone will produce three echos. Again, this 'works' only if the courtyard is quiet enough for the vibrations to resonate in peace.

Leaving the Imperial Vault, there is a fine walk along a raised approach called the **Bridge of Vermilion Stairs** to the main building of the park, the magnificent **Hall of Prayer for Good Harvests** (*see* picture next page). This round wooden hall is surmounted by a triple roof covered in blue tiles and crowned with a gilded ball. The walls are resplendently painted in rich colors—red, blue, gold and green. It stands on three marble terraces.

The original Hall of Prayer for Good Harvests was built in 1420, but burned down in 1889 and was later reconstructed. At the time, there were no trees in China tall enough to supply the wood for the four tall columns, and thus these pillars, representing the four seasons and four directions, were imported from Oregon in the US by the American shipping magnate, Robert Dollar. This showpiece of architectural ingenuity, 39 meters (125 feet) high and supported by 28 wooden pillars, stands without the aid of nails. The hall was last used in 1914 by Yuan Shikai, then president of the infant Republic, who had imperial ambitions.

Two rectangular buildings stand in the courtyard before the Hall. The one to the west is a large comprehensive gift shop, while the one to the east now contains a display of the musical instruments, both authentic and reproduction, used in the imperial rituals.

Hall of Prayer for Good Harvests.

Both the Altar and the Hall of Prayer are circular structures enclosed by square courtyards, a design symbolizing the journey from earth to heaven as the supplicant approached the place of worship. Behind the Hall of Prayer for Good Harvests is the **Hall of August Heaven** (*Huangqian Dian*), where many of the objects used in the ceremonies are now exhibited.

None of Beijing's other three altars can compare with the Temple of Heaven, but potentially the finest is the **Altar of the Earth** (*Ditan*), built in 1530, and set in a wooded park in the northeast of the city. The Hall of Abstinence has already been renovated. Some of the buildings of the **Altar of the Sun** (*Ritan*), built in 1531, as well as the altar itself, still exist in a pleasant park near the Friendship Store. The **Altar of the Moon** (*Yuetan*) on the opposite side of the city, also built in 1531, is now the site of a television tower.

The Temple of Heaven grounds open daily at 7:00am and close at dusk.

The Hall of August Heaven seen from the Hall of Prayer for Good Harvest.

The Concubine in the Well

If the walls of the Forbidden City enclosed a dazzling Court presided over by enlightened emperors, they also—down the centuries—hid the innumerable plots, intrigues and betrayals that were played out in the struggles for power. It is said that the Forbidden City is a graveyard of souls; within its tortuous precincts, inexplicable deaths and suspected murders were almost a familiar feature of Court life. There were always, at one time or another, the conflicting interests of pretenders, concubines, eunuchs and ministers to be resolved, especially when questions of succession were involved, or when weak emperors—either because of extreme youth or sheer incompetence—could be manipulated by self-seeking regents and corrupt officials.

The method of exterminating rivals by secret murder was employed with particular frequency, even finesse, by the Manchu Empress Dowager Cixi. This venal and selfish woman, who was supreme ruler of China for nearly half a century (1861–1908), has been regarded with such horror and fascination that, in the popular mind, the facts of her life have become blurred by legend.

As a young woman, Cixi entered the palace as a low-ranking concubine to Emperor Xianfeng (reigned 1851–61). On producing a son, she was promoted to Concubine of the First Grade, and skilfully charmed the emperor until she held him in thrall. On the emperor's death, she continued her scheming to eliminate her rivals and eventually achieved such considerable power that she was in a position to have herself and Empress Ci'an declared as regents during the minority of Emperor Tongzhi, her five year-old son. (Even Ci'an was eventually disposed of, by poison it is rumored, in 1881.) When Tongzhi came of age, Cixi, instead of relinquishing her power, thwarted his attempts to be with his wife and encouraged him in a life of debauchery, which no doubt hastened his death at the age of 18, leaving no heir.

In flagrant defiance of succession laws, Cixi then contrived to put her infant nephew, whom she adopted, on the throne as Emperor Guangxu. She ruled in his name, 'behind a silk screen', until he reached maturity and she ostensibly retired to the Summer Palace in 1889. Nevertheless she continued to meddle in Court affairs. In 1898, in the wake of China's humiliating defeat in the Sino-Japanese War, Guangxu launched the abortive Hundard Days reform movement that was to cost him his freedom. He was kept in semi-captivity by Cixi, who emerged from retirement to assume supreme control of the government once more.

At the height of the chaos following the anti-foreign Boxer Rebellion, the Empress Dowager was to commit one of her most ruthless murders. The date was 15th August 1900. At the time all of Beijing was in alarm as the Allied troops approached to relieve the besieged legation quarter of foreigners. In the Forbidden City, the Empress Dowager made ready to flee to the western city of Xi'an. Donning the dark blue clothes of a peasant woman, Cixi cut her long lacquered nails and dressed her hair in Chinese style. She summoned the young emperor to prepare by torchlight for their immediate departure in three horse-drawn carts.

At the last moment, the Pearl Concubine (*Zhenfei*), who was the emperor's favorite, appeared before Cixi and audaciously proposed that either the emperor be allowed to stay in Beijing or that she be allowed to accompany him to the west. Like the Empress Dowager, who had been a concubine herself, this spirited young woman was not given to showing respect or submission to her superiors. She had frequently interfered with Cixi's plans by giving the emperor contrary advice. Now, it must have appeared to the Empress Dowager, the Pearl Concubine had finally over-reached herself.

According to one account, Cixi lost no time in giving orders to her trusted eunuchs, who swiftly wrapped the concubine in a carpet and carried her off, over the young emperor's objections, to the rear of the palace, where they threw her down a well. Her body was recovered a year later and temporarily buried in a field in the city's western suburbs. Later she was laid to rest in the concubines' grave, near Emperor Guangxu's mausoleum, in the Western Qing Tombs.

The well is still there, inconspicuously marked by a small Chinese plaque, in a tiny courtyard in the northeastern corner of the Imperial Palace, by the Palace of Peaceful Old Age. A few Chinese tourists are usually clustered around it, trying to figure out how the eunuchs could have forced someone down so small an opening.

The final mystery surrounding Cixi was the strange coincidence of her death with that of Emperor Guangxu. It is alleged that Cixi, adamant that the emperor should not outlive her, gave orders from her deathbed for him to be poisoned, but that is just one more sinister intrigue that will never be proved.

This portrait, A Chinese Lady In Red, by an unknown artist is believed to be one of many copies of a portrait painted by Lang Shih Ning *(the Chinese name for Jesuit Father Guiseppe Castiglione). He lived at the Court of Peking for about 50 years before he died in 1766. One such copy held by The Bank of Canton purports the sitter to be Princess Hsiang Fei. Image courtesy of Hongkong & Shanghai Bank.*

The Imperial Cortege on the road. The Illustrated London News, September 15, 1900.

The Source of Law Temple (Fayuan Si) 法院寺

Situated in Fayuan Si Qian Jie off Niu Jie in the Xuanwumen district, this temple is in the southwest quarter of the city. It was built by the Tang emperor, Taizong, in AD 654 in memory of troops killed in a battle with the Koreans and has been restored many times since. Two pagodas used to stand beside the temple, but they were destroyed by fire in the middle of the Tang period. It was at Fayuan Si that the Song Minister Xie Dieshan, brought under guard by Yuan troops to Beijing, chose to starve himself to death rather than submit to the Mongols.

Fayuan Si comprises six courtyards planted with lilac trees. In the past, the temple was obliged to lay on a series of vegetarian banquets every spring for local dignitaries, for it is an age-old Chinese custom to spend a convivial evening wining and dining with crowds of friends on the pretext of admiring the season's new blooms.

The present occupants belong to the Chinese Buddhist Theoretical Institute, and the temple buildings now provide accommodation and classrooms for a number of novice monks. The temple is open daily from 8:30am to 11:00am and 1:30pm to 4:00pm.

Ox Street Mosque (Niu Jie Qingzhen Si) 牛街

Of the 80-odd mosques in Beijing, this one, right in the center of the city's Moslem district, is the largest and oldest—it was built in AD 996 by Nazruddin, son of an Arab priest. The mosque is open daily from 5:00am to 7:00pm.

The exterior gives very little hint that it is other than a temple, but inside the gate there is a hexagonal Tower for Viewing the Moon, serving an Islamic purpose. This structure enables the imam to determine the beginning and end of Ramadan according to sightings of the moon. Grouped round courtyards behind the tower are the main prayer hall with its entrance facing west towards Mecca, a stele pavilion, the minaret from which the muezzin calls believers to prayer, a bath-house and some classrooms. The prayer hall is decorated in bright red and gold, with a section reserved for women behind a screen.

Islam was introduced to China in the Tang Dynasty (618–907) and today the religion is embraced by several minorities in the country as well as the Hui, a more widespread community of ethnic Chinese Moslems, often distinguishable from the Han Chinese only by the faith they profess.

White Clouds Taoist Monastery (Baiyun Guan) 白云观

Located approximately one kilometer south of the Yanjing Hotel on Binhe Lu off Baiyun Lu, the White Clouds Taoist Monastery is one of the most important Taoist temples in China. The first Taoist monastery was built on this spot in the eighth century, but the present incarnation is the result of two overhauls that took place in 1956 and 1981.

The most famous inhabitant of the monastery was the Yuan-dynasty monk, Qiu Chuji, to whom one of the halls is dedicated. The period during which Qiu rebuilt the monastery, around 1230, is regarded as its golden age.

Like all other religious institutions in China, the White Clouds Monastery was hit hard during the Cultural Revolution, but now 100 monks, including young adepts, live on the premises, all of whom belong to the *chuanzhen* sect of Taoism. The monastery is the headquarters of the China Taoist Association, and thus is actively involved in 'foreign affairs'. The monastery performs a number of traditional Taoist ceremonies for a fee, and is crowded with believers and curiosity seekers on the two dozen Taoist holy days every year. In the old days, a grand three-day ritual including horse races in the street took place here during the first lunar month, but this practice has long ceased.

The monastery is laid out on three parallel axes, with the most important structures on the central axis. There is a peaceful courtyard containing an ordination platform that resembles a miniature outdoor stage in the rear section of the western axis. Immediately inside the main gate, there is a stone-lined pond spanned by a bridge with an oversize Chinese coin hanging from it. Good luck is accorded to whoever can hit the giant coin with a coin of the realm. All the profits go to the monastery.

The White Clouds Monastery is open everyday from 8:00am–4:00pm. There is a modest admission charge.

Prospect Garden (*Daguan Yuan*) 大观园

In 1986 a new park, complete with pavilions, ponds, miniature hillocks and piped music, was opened to the public. Located in the southwest corner of the city, this pleasure ground has been built in imitation of the garden meticulously described in the great Chinese classic, *The Dream of the Red Chamber* (Honglou Meng) by Cao Xueqin. As recounted in the novel, the name 'Daguan Yuan' was chosen by Imperial Concubine Yuanchun on a visitation. She wrote:

> Embracing hills and streams, with skill they wrought
> Their work at last is to perfection brought.
> Earth's fairest prospects all are here installed,
> So 'Prospect Garden' let its name be called!
>
> From *The Story of the Stone*, translated by David Hawkes

Although somewhat lacking in authenticity, Daguan Yuan is a pleasant park which draws crowds of local visitors. It served as the setting for a popular television series based on the novel that enjoyed great success in China as well as Hong Kong and other overseas communities.

The Western Yellow Temple, Andingmenwai district, is one of the finest monuments of Lamaism.

The Ancient Observatory (*Guanxiang Tai*) 古观象台

Kublai Khan established an observatory at the southeastern corner of his city and it is still there today. Functioning as part of the more modern Beijing Observatory and Planetarium (which is right at the other end of the city, opposite the Beijing Zoo in the northwest), the Old Observatory is now a museum with a small but superb collection of Ming and Qing astronomical instruments.

Of the instruments that were made from the 15th century onwards only 15 pieces remain, including several made by Jesuit priests—notably Adam Schall and Ferdinand Verbiest—in the 17th century. When these missionaries came to China they proved themselves to be such skilful astronomers that they were put in charge of the observatory. The most famous Jesuit was Matteo Ricci (1552–1610), who, aside from being science tutor to the emperor's son, was also an influential preacher; he left behind hundreds of Catholic churches in the Ming Dynasty.

These instruments were taken to Germany in 1900, as spoils of war after the Allied forces had subdued the Boxer Rebellion, but were returned to China in 1919. Eight of them are displayed on the Observatory terrace atop one of the few remaining sections of the old city wall (the other seven were moved to the Nanjing Observatory in 1931). They include three armillary spheres, a quadrant, a sextant, a celestial globe, a horizon circle and a quadrant altazimuth.

The observatory may be visited from 9:00am–11:30am and 1:00pm–4:30pm but is closed on Mondays and Tuesdays.

Western Districts
The Temple of the White Dagoba (*Baita Si*) 白塔寺

The 48-meter (150 feet) high Yuan Dynasty dagoba, off Fuchengmennei Dajie, dominates they city's northwestern skyline. It is to the west of the White Dagoba in Beihai Park.

Even at the time of completion in 1279 under the supervision of Arniko, a famous Nepalese architect, it was considered one of the gems of the Mongols' new capital. A large monastery was established here by Kublai Khan which was later destroyed, but rebuilt and renamed Miaoying Temple during the Ming Dynasty. A beautiful filigree copper canopy, hung with bells, tops the dagoba.

The temple suffered damage during the Cultural Revolution and in the 1976 earthquake, but it has now been restored. The four existing halls date from the Qing and contain Yuan and Ming Buddhist statues and Tibetan *tankas*. During the restoration Buddhist scriptures and other relics dating from the Qianlong period were discovered.

CHINESE LIVES —Paul Mooney

Foreigners new to China are more often than not very impressed by the big changes they see around the country. They're awed by the glassy high-rise buildings, efficient highways that wind through the mountains of Gansu province, savvy entrepreneurs, innovative artists, the hard work ethic of everyday Chinese, and school kids who go to school at 7am and don't turn out their bedroom lights until their homework is done, often after midnight.

There's no denying that the world now views China in super power terms, in politics, economics, science and military affairs. There's a growing sense that the 21st Century belongs to China.

I have friends who come here from New York, often stopping by San Francisco, Tokyo, or Singapore, places that are much more developed than Beijing or Shanghai, but it's China that they rave about. Why is it that they are so taken by China? To a certain degree it's a question of relativity. Many foreigners, despite all they've read in the international media about China's advances, are still not prepared for what they see after they get off the airplane.

What's most interesting is the impressions foreigners have of the Chinese people.

"The Chinese have a fire in their belly that we Americans no longer have," an old American friend said to me recently. I thought about his comment quite a bit and came to the conclusion that he was right. Pretty much every Chinese person I know—students, farmers, office workers, CEOs, scholars, scientists, maids, prostitutes—has an incredible desire to get ahead.

One might ask, "So what, who doesn't want to get ahead?" But in China it's somehow different. Maybe it's the competition factor. China has 1.3 billion people who are all competing fiercely for a limited number of resources or opportunities. Another possible factor is that after decades of political uncertainty, people are now enjoying opportunities never before available, and they're anxious to take advantage of this while they can.

I sense this fire every day and everywhere in China. My former students from the Chinese University of Communications are all talking about doing graduate study in the United Kingdom or the United States, and they're mainly interested in the top schools. The Shanxi mom and pop who work as cleaners near my house, living in a tiny space under the steps of the office building with their two sons, nudge their 12-year-old son out the door with his English book when they see me walk by. We stand on the sidewalk reviewing his lesson for a few minutes while his mom and dad beam.

I get occasional calls from Chinese I barely know, asking me to be their business partner, and despite the fact that I have no business experience. My family maid of 15 years, a farmer's daughter from Jiangxi, spent half a year's income to get her very bright son into a decent high school (his younger brother was sent back to the village because she couldn't afford to pay for both of them); she works several jobs and six days a week to make a living.

Whatever, the reason, the desire to get ahead is almost an obsession in China. And this might be the crux of the problem. Values seem to have been turned upside down in today's China. While Chinese often pay lip service to nationalism and patriotism. In reality, people seem more concerned about getting more material goods than caring about China. Where is the idealism that so many had in the 1950s and 1960s?

Society considers the guy who owns a gas-guzzling Humvee a folk hero to be emulated while the young woman who uses her own savings to set up an NGO to help the children of AIDS victims is a loser. One gets the sense that if Lei Feng—a legendary soldier known for doing good deeds—turned up today on the streets of Beijing that he would be mocked for not having status and for wanting to help others.

A few years ago, shelves in Chinese book stores were loaded with titles such as The Harvard Girl, The Cambridge Girl, The Yale Boy. Around that time, Zhou Hong, a parent, wrote a book called "I'm Mediocre, I'm Happy", in which he explained that he wasn't going to pressure his daughter to be the Beida or Qinghua girl, references to China's two leading universities. Mr. Zhou was vilified by readers, who accused him of being an irresponsible father and of ruining his daughter's future.

"In America, making your kids happy is the priority and conventional success is secondary", Mr. Zhou told the New York Times. "That idea is not acceptable in China. If your child isn't the best, then he is considered mediocre". Despite his efforts, he confided that his daughter still felt great pressure to excel. "It's not easy for a person to be mediocre in this kind of society", he told the American newspaper.

During the very short-lived Bobo craze of a few years ago, Xinhua News Agency described Bobos as a person who owned a small downtown apartment and drove a fashionable car, while downing cups of cappuccino at Starbucks in between licking ice cream cones at Hagen Daz. They watch hip Iranian movies and have a copy of the latest Marguerite Duras' work by their bedside, the news agency said.

Special Topic

The term bobo, made famous in David Brook's book titled *Bobos in Paradise*, was popular among Chinese because it made having money respectable at a time in China when there were still prejudices against those with capitalist tails.

"The term bobo is popular because it means having both money and culture", Miao Wei, an editor at Sanlian Shenghuo, told me during an interview. But he was not so positive about the trend, writing an article that castigated China's would-be Bobos for being overly interested in Western things: "Italian fashions, a German car, an American MBA". "The only thing Chinese today are interested in preserving is Chinese food," the magazine scoffed.

Miao Wei claimed that the average Chinese person was actually much more bourgeois than bohemian. "We have people with a lot of money, but there's no social consciousness", he complained. "Rich people don't care about the environment, unemployment, rural problems or mine disasters". A writer for Chinese Newsweek also commented on the bobo trend, asking readers "one simple question". "Do you feel John Lennon and the Red Guards are made of the same stuff?".

This same questions popped up when I did a story on "City Magazine", a glossy magazine that reports on China's wrenching social problems in a stylish way. Beautifully illustrated articles on AIDS and stunning photographs of black-faced coal miners are sandwiched between stories about Cartier jewelry and photos of pouting Chinese models posing on the Great Wall in Gucci outfits (Why do they look so unhappy? They're wearing Gucci, aren't they?). The idea, it seems, is to seduce China's wealthy into becoming more caring people.

I asked the City Magazine editors if China's middle class really cared about these social issues. "We're not doing it for fun", said one editor. "We feel if we can make people read these articles, they will care".

Thomas Shao, the president of the successful Modern Media Group that publishes City Magazine, and the most accomplished media tycoon in China, told me that the magazine's target readers are wealthy entrepreneurs, a group he concedes may not yet know it needs a magazine like this. City Magazine aims to address a moral and cultural vacuum in China. While the West has religion and law to guide people in the right direction, Mr. Shao says neither is playing such a role in China.

"There are no binding factors in society" he said. "It's not that people don't want morality. They never learned about it". In one article titled "The World that has Disappeared", one contributor lamented that Chinese no longer revere the

Confucian term junzi, or gentleman, and he complained that China's traditional moral codes are regarded as "impractical nonsense". Chinese traditions, he says, "are like exhibits in a museum".

Mr. Edmond Yu, a former deputy publisher, calls the magazine "a search for a national spirit", "For our generation, the traditions of China collapsed during the Cultural Revolution" he says. "We know nothing about our past, or how China became the country it is today".

The magazine is also very much about Chinese culture—or the increasing lack of it. Stories have focused on lost imperial city gates, the endangered Kunqu opera and the Baiyangdian poet group. The magazine runs featured interviews with Chinese cultural icons such as Ang Li, director of Brokeback Mountain and Lust, Caution, Li Yang, the director of "Blind Shaft", a brutal film about coal miners, and Bei Dao, the contemporary poet. "We're trying to make a cult of Chinese culture" said Mr. Yu.

Things, of course, may be changing. The once vilified Confucius is making an amazing comeback around the country, toddlers are memorizing The Analects at the Confucius Temple, Guo Degang, a well-known performer of traditional comic dialogues, is packing them in at the Tian Qiao Theater, young people are flocking to Christian services on Sundays, college students are doing volunteer work, and all sorts of people are setting up their own NGOs. An article in Business Week titled "China's Spiritual Awakening" described how Chinese business people are showing an increasing interest in Buddhism.

A friend of mine, a very successful business woman, has devoted herself to helping orphans in Qinghai, a disabled migrant worker I met wants to set up a factory and living space for other disabled people who can't find jobs. A seriously handicapped woman who taught herself to read as a child, and who later earned two BA degrees through correspondence courses, has helped countless handicapped kids in her native Dongbei to be able to attend school.

Cynics wonder, however, if the bulk of China's new elite, still caught up in amassing wealth, will take the time to slow down and think seriously about people who are not as well off—or even poetry or films for that matter.

The editors of City Magazine are betting that the post-materialist generation of elite has bought enough and is now ready to do good.

All that's needed, they say, is a gentle nudge to convince them that caring is as fashionable as that Prada bag.

Special Topic

The Five Pagoda Temple (Wuta Si) 五塔寺

In the reign of Ming emperor Yongle (reigned 1403–24) a temple, to be named *Zhenjue Si* (Temple of the True Awakening), was ordered to be built on this site. It was to house a model of the famous ancient Indian Buddhist temple in Bodhgaya that was presented by an Indian monk to the Court. In 1473, in the reign of Emperor Chenghua, a building with five pagodas, based on the Bodhgaya model, was finally constructed here. Ransacked by English and French troops towards the end of the Qing, the temple never recovered its former glory. The five-pagoda building still stands, however, and its stone bas-relief carvings of figures and flowers, which are beautiful and varied, have been preserved. The Five Pagoda Temple is located one kilometer north of the Beijing Zoo in the Haidian district, off Baishiqiao Lu.

The Big Bell Temple (Dazhong Si) 大钟寺

This charming small temple one kilometer east of the Friendship Hotel on the north side of the Third Ring Road was built in 1733. In 1743 a huge bell was brought here, and the temple's name was changed to Dazhong Si. The giant bronze bell is believed to have been cast in the Ming Dynasty, during the reign of Yongle, and is by this reckoning more than 550 years old. Over seven meters (nearly 23 feet) high and weighing 46 tons, it is inscribed with Buddhist scriptures in Chinese characters and is regarded as one of China's national treasures.

The bell is housed in a tower at the back of the temple, in an inner courtyard. Also displayed in the courtyard are some 30 bronze bells from various periods, showing the high degree of skill and workmanship that had been achieved. Many stone steles and statuary can be seen here too. One can go right to the top of the Bell Tower by climbing a spiral staircase.

Beijing Zoo (Beijing Dongwu Yuan) 北京动物园

The zoo is located in the northwest part of the city. Visitors usually go straight to see the giant pandas to the left of the main entrance, but there are many other interesting animals to be seen—among them tigers from the northeast, yaks from Tibet, enormous sea-turtles from China's seas, and lesser-pandas from Sichuan.

The Beijing Zoo has an interesting and unusual history, dating back to the 17th century, when it was a garden belonging to one of the sons of Shunzhi, the first emperor of the Qing Dynasty. In 1747, the Qianlong emperor had it refurbished as a park, and carried out many other substantial repairs on the imperial properties throughout Beijing and in the summer palaces in the western suburbs, in honor of his mother's 60th birthday.

In 1901, the Empress Dowager did another extensive rebuilding job, and used it to house a collection of animals given to her as a gift by a Chinese minister who had acquired them at great cost during a trip to Germany. By the 1930s, most of them had died and were stuffed and put on display in a museum on the grounds. The zoo is open from 7:30am to 6:00pm.

Former Residence of Mei Lanfang 梅兰芳故居

Mei Lanfang (1894–1961) is regarded as one of the Four Great Female Impersonators in the history of the Peking Opera, an art form little understood and not widely appreciated outside of China and Chinese communities abroad. Mei's skill enabled him to perform women's roles more convincingly than any woman, so say the experts.

The courtyard house Mei lived in during his last days is open to the public as a shrine at number 9, Huguosi Jie in the Western district. Mei's studio contains many of his personal possessions, including the intricate embroidered outfits he performed in. There are also videotapes of the great diva's performances to watch.

Unlike the other 'former residences' open to the public in Beijing, Mei's home, a classic example of a Beijing courtyard house, can be enjoyed for its architecture as well.

Northern Districts

Western Yellow Temple (Xihuang Si) 西黄寺

Lammaism, a branch of Buddhism, is celebrated at this temple, which was constructed along with its sibling the Eastern Yellow Temple during the middle 1600s. The Eastern Yellow Temple was destroyed during the Great Leap Forward. Fortunately, the Western Yellow Temple remains, situated in the Andingmenwai district approximately two kilometers north of the Ring Road on Huangsi Lu. It is considered to be one of Beijing's finest monuments of Lammaism. The Western Yellow Temple is open daily from 9:00am to 5:00pm.

Museums

A Beijing museum pass is available for 80 yuan, providing discounted or free entrance to 60 museums in the capital, worth 1,800 yuan in discounts. The pass can be purchased at post offices or by calling the hotlines: 6221 3256, 6221 3275.

Beijing Art Museum 国家美术馆

The Beijing Art Museum, which was established in 1985, occupies the grounds of the Wanshou Temple (Temple of Longevity) which for years had been occupied by the military. The museum is located immediately off Xisanhuanbeilu (the Third West Ring Road) where it crosses over the canal some 500 meters north of the Shangri-La Hotel. Hours are 9:00am to 4:00pm. The museum is closed on Mondays.

The Wanshou Temple dates back to 1577, when Emperor Wanli of the Ming Dynasty erected it on this spot as a library for Buddhist scriptures. In front of the museum runs a canal used by the court of the Qianlong Emperor in the 17th century to travel by barge from the Forbidden City to the summer palaces in the northwestern suburbs. On the occasion of the 70th birthday of Qianlong's mother, 1,000 Buddhist monks stood on the banks of the canal as part of the birthday celebrations taking place in the temple.

Empress Dowager Cixi stayed in the now restored western section of the temple when she broke her journeys to the Summer Palace. She instigated an extensive rebuilding campaign in 1894.

The museum has speciality collections of Ming and Qing textiles, Qing and Republican period paintings, Buddhist art, personal name seals, Ming and Qing ceramics, and Japanese paintings acquired from collections in the formerly Japanese-occupied areas of Manchuria. The collection was assembled in the late 1980s under the aegis of the Beijing Municipal Bureau of Cultural Relics. Opening times are from 9:00am to 4:00pm. Closed on Mondays.

Below: *Main street of outer city, Chien Men, by photographer Osvald Siren (1879–1966). He was regarded as a great authority on Chinese art and architecture. Collaborating with the Ministry of Works circa 1920, he conducted a survey of Peking's city wall. His many photographs (see also pages 93 and 267) were published by Bodley Head, London, in 1924 in the tome* The Walls and Gates of Peking, *which Siren closed with: "How long will they still remain, these wonderfull walls and gates, these silent records of Peking's most beautiful and glorious past?"*

National Museum of China
(Guojia Bowuguan) 国家博物馆

The National Museum of China, erected in 1959, re-opened in 2011 after being extensively renovated. China boasts that this new museum will be the largest art museum in the world, with a large collection of Chinese art dating from Paleolithic times to 1911. The Museum is located at 16 East Chang'an Ave., Dongcheng district.

Lu Xun Museum 鲁迅博物馆

This museum in Fuchengmennei Dajie commemorates one of China's most outstanding writers of the 20th century, Lu Xun (1881–1936), who is also noted for his considerable contribution to the liberal movement in China in the 1920s. (*See* excerpt on page 511).

National Museum of China, Scala, 2011 photography by Dong Qing.

The museum, which abuts Lu Xun's former Beijing residence, displays manuscripts, letters, and pages from his personal diary. Some 13,000 books from his library are also kept in the museum, as well as items of clothing and other memorabilia.

The museum, which is located at 19 Gongmenkou Ertiao, is open from 9:00am to 3:30pm, but is closed on Mondays.

Military Museum of the Chinese People's Revolution 军事博物馆

This is a permanent exhibition of 5,000 items—photographs, directives, military uniforms, and weaponry, including tanks and missiles. There are Eighth Route Army insignias, along with portraits of revolutionary heroes and martyrs—covering the Chinese revolutionary army's 28-year history between 1921 and 1949. The museum is at 9 Fuxing Dajie and is open from 8:30am–5:00pm and closed on Mondays.

China Aviation Museum 空军博物馆

In 1989, the Chinese Air Force opened this huge display of military and civilian aircraft at Datangshan, Changping County, between Shahe and the Changping county seat, approximately 30 kilometers (19 miles) north of the city limits. After passing through Shahe on the road to Changping, make a right turn at the Baige Lu intersection, and watch for the museum on the left. The easiest way to get there is by taxi. Opening hours are 8:00am–5:30pm daily (tel. 6178 4883).

The 140 aeroplanes are displayed as in a used car lot. Many are parked outside in long queues, while some 50 choice specimens are housed in a reinforced concrete structure that pierces the 1 kilometer deep Datangshan (Datang Mountain) with double antiblast doors at both ends. Military buffs will also enjoy the mobile radar equipment and guided missiles.

Reflecting the history of aviation in China, there are specimens from the former Soviet Union, the US and Britain dating back to pre-liberation days, as well as samples of China's own fighting and passenger aircraft.

Exhibits include the 'Ilyushin 12', which was used to gather samples from a mushroom cloud during a Chinese nuclear test (keep your distance); a Chinese helicopter used by Zhou Enlai during an inspection tour; a single-prop plane that buzzed Tiananmen Square during the celebration of China's first National Day (1 October 1949); a two-engine job that Chairman Mao took to Guangzhou once; and a fighter plane that saw action in the Korean War.

Beijing Aviation Museum 北京航空馆

This modest aviation museum sits on the campus of the Beijing University of Aeronautics and Astronautics at 37 Xueyuan Lu in Haidian, with indoor and outdoor exhibitions. The collection includes a wide variety of aircraft, from the P-61 Night Fighter, nicknamed the "Black Widow," to a British Harrier jet and several versions of the MiG fighter jet. Open 8:30am–12pm and 2pm–5pm, except Mondays.

Beijing Museum of Natural History 北京历史博物馆

The museum contains four halls devoted to botany, zoology, paleozoology and paleoanthropology, the latter science—the study of primitive man—being one in which China has contributed much in recent discoveries and research. It is open 8:30am–5:00pm (admission till 4:00pm only), and closed on Mondays. It is located at 126 Tianqiao Road.

The Temple of Confucius (Kong Miao) 孔庙
and the Former Imperial College (Guozijian) 国子监

This site is one of Beijing's most underrated historical places. Serene, small, and rarely crowded, the Confucius Temple is a refuge for travelers shell-shocked by postcard sellers and modern Beijing traffic.

Situated in Beijing's northeast quarter, close to the Lama Temple, the temple dedicated to Confucius was raised in the Yuan Dynasty and housed the ancestral tablets of Confucius and four other sages. Ceremonials and sacrifices were conducted by the prominent scholars of the day and members of the imperial court three times a year, including Confucius' birthday.

Connected to the museum by a side door is the former **Imperial College** (*Guozijian*), first built in 1287 and substantially extended in 1784. The focal point of the former college is the square pavilion, which can be thrown open on all four sides by means of doors and shutters, called the Imperial Schoolroom. It is sited in the middle of a pool and reached by bridges. Here the emperor used to lecture on the Classics to ministers and students. On either side of the structure there used to stand 190 stone tablets engraved with 800,000 words of the *Thirteen Classics*, which took the calligrapher 12 years to transcribe. The tablets have been moved to a courtyard east of the main gate, Taixuemen, and the Imperial College is now the **Capital Library**.

National Gallery of China 美术博物馆

One cannot help but notice the National Gallery of China, a large traditional-style building at the top of Wangfujing. This edifice was constructed in 1959 and is considered one of socialist China's ten best architectural designs. It was entirely refurbished in 1991. The large central building is flanked on either side by long corridors and adjoining wings. Yellow glazed tiles, sloping roofs and upturned eaves lend this building an air of dignity and reserve. There are 14 exhibition rooms and several studios where artists can work.

This gallery holds an increasing number of interesting national and international exhibits and is a good place to discover some of the emerging trends in China's rapidly evolving art world. Many of the works exhibited can be purchased from the artist. Enquiries about how to purchase a painting can be made at the sales shop located in the west wing. The gallery is open everyday 9:00am–5:00pm and tickets can be purchased until 4:00pm.

Poly Art Museum 保利博物馆

This important art museum is situated in the gleaming New Poly Plaza, an all-glass tower facing the Second Ring Road. The museum has a mission of buying Chinese art back from foreign owners and so has made a number of high-profile international purchases. The collection includes ancient bronzes, sculptures, stone carvings and paintings. Some of the most interesting items are the four bronze animal heads that were stolen from the Old Summer Palace by marauding Anglo-French troops during the Second Opium War in 1860. It is located at 9 New Poly Plaza, 1 Chaoyangmen Bei Dajie.

Capital Museum 首都博物馆

Formerly part of the Confucius Temple complex, the Capital Museum moved into this modern building in 2006. The museum has seven floors of exhibits focusing on Beijing's long and rich culture and history. There is a wide array of things on display here: imperial robes, ancient horse fittings, religious items, traditional architecture, and religious artifacts, and folk life and culture. It is located at 16 Fuxingmenwai Dajie.

Beijing Mumingtang Ancient Porcelain Museum 北京沐民堂陶瓷博物馆
This small private museum has an impressive collection of more than 50,000 pieces of porcelain made between the 7th and 20th centuries. The museum is at 1 Huashi Beili Dongqu.

Urban Planning Exhibition Hall 城市计划
The exhibitions here introduce urban planning—past, present and future—in the Chinese capital. Worth seeing is the scale model of the city, the center part actually composed of models of actual buildings, while the outlying areas are shown in photographs on a glass floor. It is located at 20 Qianmen Dong Dajie.

Museum of Ancient Architecture 古代建筑博物馆
The site for this museum is the former Altar of Agriculture, where Qing emperors held ceremonies to mark the lunar equinox. The venue exhibits architectural models representing each of China's dynastic periods. This museum is at 21 Dongjing Lu.

Dashanzi Art District 大山子艺术区
Possibly better known as the 798 Factory, the Dashanzi Art District is housed in an old factory complex in which the plants have been converted into art galleries, cafés, restaurants and shops. This is the place to view China's contemporary art scene. Exhibitions are held regularly and news about the latest events can be found in the various expat magazines. Saturday and Sunday afternoons are the best times to visit. Located at 4 Jiuxianqiao Lu.

China Film Museum 中国电影博物馆
The little-known China Film Museum, which is located in an uber-chic modern building on the outskirts of Beijing, has four screening rooms and IMAX. The museum has a good collection of the great Chinese films minus some controversial movies—some of China's best—that did not make the censor's cut. The excellent presentations include short English summaries.

Sony Explora Science 索尼探索科技
This interactive science and technology museum features some of Sony's latest digital technologies. Exhibits focus on Illusion, Refraction/Reflection, Light/Colors and Sounds. Special exhibits open every two months. It is located inside Chaoyang Park, which has plenty of other activities for children.

Dongbianmen Red Gate Gallery 东边门 红门画廊
Get a taste of both the past and present by visiting the Red Gate Gallery, located in the imposing Dongbianmen Watchtower, Beijing's only remaining tower from the Ming Dynasty. Red Gate shows the works of contemporary Chinese artists. The second and third floors are devoted to the history of the Chongwen District. Brian Wallace, the owner of the Red Gate Gallery, has been involved in the art business in China for some two decades. Situated on Levels 1 & 4, Dongbianmen Watchtower, Chongwenmen.

Nan Luogu Xiang 南锣鼓巷
Nan Luogu Xiang, or South Gong and Drum Lane, which dates back some seven centuries, in recent years has seen row after row of artsy restaurants, coffee shops, bars and boutiques take over the old Beijing houses along this quaint street. Check out Wenyu Nailao (No. 49) for delicious Chinese custard; Plastered 8 (No. 61), a T-shirt shop with amusing Beijing motifs; and the Jindian Consignment Shop (No. 43) for Beijing nostalgia items. What really makes the neighborhood interesting, however, is that it's hedged in by eight of Beijing's most colorful remaining hutongs lined with a number of historical courtyard houses. Wander in any direction and you'll stumble across wonderful architecture. Nan Luogu Xiang is located between Di'anmen Dong Dajie and Gulou Dajie

Nanxincang 南新藏
Nanxincang was where grain was stored for the imperial family and court officials during China's last two dynasties. This site is now Beijing's newest hot spot, home to several art galleries, a teahouse and several bars and restaurants. Cooking is not permitted in the wonderful 600-year-old structures, so the restaurants here are located in the newly-constructed buildings on the site, unfortunately constructed with a dubious traditional look.

Nanxincang—just 10 years junior to the Forbidden City—was one of the more than 300 granaries that existed during imperial days. Grain storage was an exact science in imperial China. The floors were paved with thick bricks and covered with wooden boards sitting on brick shoulders to insulate the grain from the earth's moisture. A raised opening running along the center of the roof, which can still be seen today, used strips of woven bamboo to keep birds from flying in, while at the same time providing sufficient ventilation. The thick walls (1.5m) maintained the room temperature and prevented the grain from getting moldy.

Grain moving along the 3,000 mile long Grand Canal was delivered to the various granaries, of which today Nanxincang is the only surviving one. Nanxincang is on Dongsi Shitiao, one block west of the Second Ring Road.

CHINA NATIONAL POSTAL AND POSTAGE STAMP MUSEUM 中国邮政邮票博物馆

The **China National Postal and Postage Stamp Museum** is a three-floor venue, with postage stamps exhibited on the first floor, the early history of postal services introduced on the second floor, and China's modern postal system on the third floor.

A pre-liberation Post Office in Beijing.

The exhibition begins with the Qing Dynasty (1644–1911). One of the most interesting stamps is the Dowager Jubilee, issued on November 7, 1894 to mark the celebration of the 60th birthday of the notorious Empress Dowager Cixi. The stamp does not carry an image of the Empress Dowager, but rather a drawing of a dragon, likely because it would have been considered improper to put the image of a member of the ruling family on a postage stamp.

The next era on display is the Republic of China (1912–49), featuring stamps with the image of Sun Yat-sen (the founder of the Nationalist Party that overthrew the Qing Dynasty) Nationalist strongman Chiang Kai-shek, and sampans. During the civil war between the Nationalists and the Communists, the 'People's Government', although not the official government of China, printed stamps in the areas that they held. A 1947 stamp celebrates the victory over the Japanese, featuring Communist leaders Mao Zedong and Zhu De. There is also a workers' series printed in February 1949 showing an intellectual, soldier, postal worker and coal miner standing staunchly together in solidarity.

The central hall is primarily dedicated to Chinese culture. The collection includes stamps on historical sites around China—the Forbidden City, Temple of Heaven, Potala Palace, the Summer Palace, and Confucius' hometown. There are also stamps on folk dance, musical instruments, Peking opera, traditional paintings, Buddhism and temples and mosques. Of particular interest is the series on Peking opera, featuring the legendary Mei Lanfang, who performed the huadan, or female role, in opera before women were allowed to perform.

The second floor introduces the history of communications in China, featuring the use of drums, beacon towers and horseback couriers to cover the long distances that separated frontier fortresses in ancient times. In the Ming Dynasty a rudimentary postal system begins to develop, and by the Qing we have a management system governing the courier stations around China. The exhibition traces the birth of the modern postal system in 1896 during the final years of the dynasty, the advances under the postal system of the Republic of China, and the revolutionary period of secret communications instituted by the Communists.

The third floor is dedicated to China's modern postal system. Of special interest is a video about a postal worker in the mountains of Sichuan province, who is shown leading a mail-laden horse up mountain paths, and across snow-covered trails, as he delivers mail to far-flung reaches of the province. The trip took one month back and forth.

The museum is located at Building D, 6 Gongyuan Xijie, Dongcheng District. Open daily 9:00am–4:00pm; closed Mondays.

Letter dated 1978 bears images of Lei Feng, a model soldier; a stamped envelope dated 1910

Sights Around Beijing
The Northwest
The Summer Palace (*Yiheyuan*) 颐和园

To avoid the intense heat of the summer, the imperial court used to leave the Forbidden City and stay in a specially built resort about 11 kilometers (seven miles) northwest of Beijing. Known in the West as the Summer Palace and in China as *Yiheyuan*—the Garden for Cultivating Harmony—the resort encompasses Longevity Hill (*Wanshoushan*) and a series of palaces, pavilions, terraces and covered walks strung out along the northern shore of Kunming Lake. Indeed, the Summer Palace is three-quarters covered by water and Kunming Lake, whose shape and size have been altered many times by successive landscape architects, is central to the overall design of the park. The indefatigable Emperor Qianlong, for one, reconstructed it to resemble the West Lake in Hangzhou in 1751, the year of his mother's 60th birthday (Longevity Hill was named for her).

The Old Summer Palace, known as **Yuanmingyuan** (*see* page 186), was ravaged by Anglo-French troops in 1860. In 1888, the Empress Dowager Cixi diverted funds allocated for improving the navy to the Summer Palace's renovation at a new site. She gave it its present name, Yiheyuan, and retired to its peaceful environs in 1889. Following further destruction in 1900, the Summer Palace was again restored at great expense.

The Summer Palace today is a delightful park, informal and less imposing than the Forbidden City. Much has been restored and the palace is in a fine state of preservation. The palace also borders the entrance to Tsinghua University, one of China's top institutions of higher learning.

Imperial Residences

Directly opposite the **East Palace Gate** (*Donggongmen*), across a large courtyard, is the **Hall of Benevolent Longevity** (*Renshoudian*) where Cixi and her nephew, the nominal Emperor Guangxu, gave audience to their ministers. Behind the courtyard were the private apartments of the imperial household, the **Hall of Jade Ripples** (*Yulantang*). This residence was made even more private when the Empress Dowager had a wall erected on its lake side. Here Guangxu was for 10 years her prisoner, having flouted her authority by giving his support to an ill-fated reform movement in 1898. With him safely under guard (but officially 'chronically ill'), she emerged from 'retirement' to assume control of the government once more.

Cixi's own quarters were in the **Hall of Happy Longevity** (*Leshoutang*), with **Longevity Hill** behind and a pleasant lake view in front. Both sets of private apartments, hers and Guangxu's, contain contemporary Qing furniture. Another part of the compound is the **Court of Virtuous Harmony** (*Deheyuan*), made up of the **Hall for Cultivating Happiness** (*Yiledian*) and a theater, built at the cost of 700,000 taels of silver to commemorate Cixi's 60th birthday. She was inordinately fond of theatricals and *tableaux vivants* and even appeared in them herself. In this theater a water tank had been sunk under the stage in order to provide such touches of verisimilitude as trickling streams and gushing fountains. The building, now renovated as a theater museum, should not be missed. Attendants dressed in Qing-dynasty clothes are on hand to direct visitors to superb exhibitions of theater costumes and stage props. A collection of Cixi's personal possessions is also on display. These include the automobile—the first imported into China—presented by Yuan Shikai, the military commander who was later President of the new Republic for a brief time, silver and gold ware, brushes, garments and perfumes. The Hall for Cultivating Happiness now displays over 200 historical artefacts, among them the four large carved screens inlaid with jade which are considered national treasures.

Kunming Lake's Northern Shore

From the *pailou* (ceremonial arch) on the northern shore of Kunming Lake, the **Cloud-Dispelling Hall** (*Paiyundian*), the **Hall of Virtuous Brilliance** (*Dehuidian*), the **Pavilion of Buddhist Incense** (*Foxiangge*) and the **Temple of the Sea of Wisdom** (*Zhihuihai*) rise straight up the slope of Longevity Hill. Inside the Cloud-Dispelling Hall, where Cixi celebrated her birthdays, are displays of *penjing* (potted miniature landscapes) and artefacts which were almost all tributes from her ministers. The oil painting of the empress was executed by an American for Cixi's 69th birthday (*see* page 183).

The Long Corridor

Following the shoreline of the lake, the Long Corridor—730 meters (2,550 feet) in length—leads from the Hall of Happy Longevity to the ferry pier beside the **Marble Boat**. All along it views of the lake mingle with pictures of birds and flowers, scenes from legends and famous landscapes that have been painted on the beams of the roofed walk (*see* picture on page 127). The Chinese like to compare the promenade with a picture gallery, and say that so beguiling is the beauty that no courting couple can emerge at the other end unbetrothed.

Following page: *Summer Palace, June 1979.*

Summer Palace looking towards Kunming Lake.

SOUTH LAKE ISLE

From beside the Marble Boat (actually made of stone), below the Summer Palace's popular lunch restaurant **Pavilion for Listening to the Orioles**, it is possible to take a ferry across the water to the **South Lake Isle** (*Nanhu Dao*) and the **Dragon King's Temple** (*Longwangmiao*). From Nanhu you can walk across the **Seventeen-Arch Bridge** (*Shiqikongqiao*) back to the entrance.

The Summer Palace is open from 7:00am to 7:00pm (9:00pm in summer). Entrance tickets are sold up until 4:30pm.

Summer Palace seen from Kunming Lake, June 2003.

The Old Summer Palace (*Yuanmingyuan*) 圆明园

Not far from the Yiheyuan is the site of the old Qing Summer Palace, Yuanmingyuan. Little is left of it now except some broken pillars and masonry lying about in a field. There is a museum—the Garden History Exhibition Hall—with a well-arranged display of drawings and models showing the splendor of the palace in its heyday.

The museum is part of a public park, with some shrubs, trees and a few paths for the many citizens of Beijing—who can bicycle here in about half an hour—seeking respite from their urban surroundings.

In the late 1980s, a French consortium of historians and architects reconstructed the maze in concrete. For years there have been plans afoot to rebuild the entire palace as a sort of Qing-style Disneyland. But a conservative faction opposed this idea on the grounds that it was a better lesson for China and the world if this monument of Chinese splendor and foreign imperialist destruction remained in fragments rather than be turned into a commercial spectacle.

Temple of the Reclining Buddha 卧佛寺

This temple, 19 kilometers (12 miles) from the city, is reached by continuing west on the road from the Summer Palace towards the Fragrant Hills, passing Jade Spring Hill with its distinctive twin pagodas.

The Temple of the Reclining Buddha, named after a huge bronze sleeping Buddha at the rear of the temple, is situated in the Beijing Botanical Gardens. Built in the Tang Dynasty, the temple was rebuilt and renamed several times in the Yuan, Ming and Qing dynasties. When you enter the temple you'll walk along a beautiful stone incline that is lined with cypress trees and which will lead you to the triple-arched red gate with yellow and green tiles. As with most Buddhist temples, drum and bell towers flank the first courtyard. In the first hall are the statues of Generals Ha and Heng, who respectively emit white clouds and yellow smoke to repell enemies. In the second hall, you'll find a statue of Maitreya, a red-caped Future Buddha, who is standing admidst the Four Heavenly Kings. These guardians can be seen weilding their distinctive weapons: thunder, wind, rain, and harmony. Weituo, the protector of Buddhism, stands guard at the back of Maitreya. The third hall is dedicated to Sakyamuni, sitting here in peaceful meditation with his hands folded calmly in his lap.

The main attraction here is the Hall of the Reclining Buddha, which houses a bronze statue dating back to the 14th century of a sleeping Sakyamuni surrounded by 12 of his followers. The statue, which extends 5 meters, is covered in a long red robe. There's a hall behind this that displays photos of reclining Buddhas from all over China as well as a very interesting exhibit on how this statue was made. Located in Wofo Si Lu, Beijing Botanical Gardens.

Dajue Temple 大觉寺

This pleasant and secluded temple, which sits at the foot of Yangtai Mountain, was built in 1086 during the Liao Dynasty (916–1125). It was rebuilt in the Ming Dynasty (1428) and was renovated several times in the Qing, when Emperor Qianlong often made retreats here.

The Dajue Temple, or Temple of Great Enlightenment, faces east, unlike Chinese Buddhist temples, which normally face south. This is due to the Khitan (Liao) custom of "turning to the sun." After entering the gate you'll walk over a bridge that spans a small pond filled with turtles and gold fish. As with most Buddhist temples, there is a drum and bell tower on each side of the courtyard.

Around the grounds are several yulan magnolia trees and ginko trees. One yulan magnolia tree on the grounds here is said to have been planted by a monk some 300 years ago. There is also a ginko tree said to date back some 1,000 years.

You will first come to the Hall of Deva Kings (Tianwang Dian), where Milefo, the rotund Future Buddha, is guarded by the Four Heavenly Kings. Weituo, the protecting Buddha, takes his normal defensive pose to the back of Milefo.

The Mahavira Hall, built during the Ming Dynasty, contains images of three Buddhas. The building is constructed of wood, which is rare in temple architecture today, where concrete and bricks are the dominant building materials.

The calligraphy of Qianlong that hangs over the entrance to the next building, Amitabha Hall, proclaims "Change and Quietude are Balanced." At the back of the temple is a wall displaying a diorama made of painted mud.

Beside the last hall is a Liao-era stele that provides the history of the temple. The carving is no longer clear, and the stele is broken in several places, but much of the inscription is still clear.

Take the steps to the right of the stele and go to the next level, where you'll find a large white dagoba, with elaborate dragons, clouds and flowers carved on the base. When you take the steps down, pay attention to the narrow stone gutter that serves as a viaduct for the water flowing down to the pond. You'll next arrive at the nice Minghui Tea House, which is furnished with traditional furniture. A little past here is a decent restaurant that serves Shaoxing cuisine from Zhejiang province—oddly, this is not a vegetarian venue. Turn left here and follow the steps back to the courtyard. There is a simple courtyard style hotel in this area that is open to the public .

The small market outside the temple sells local produce, including pumpkins, peaches, dates, corn, almonds, luva, gourds and pomegranates. You can also purchase long, thick incense sticks.

The Garden of Perfection and Brightness

The ruins of the old Qing Summer Palace, Yuanmingyuan, barely conjure up the former glory of the 'Garden of Gardens'. Yuanmingyuan—the Garden of Perfection and Brightness—was first established by Emperor Yongzheng (reigned 1723–35), although several gardens had existed on this site since the Ming Dynasty.

From the Ming to the early Qing, garden-making gained enormous popularity and the art of taming disordered landscape and yet preserving its 'naturalness' reached the height of sophistication in the reign of Emperor Qianlong.

The northwestern suburbs of Beijing, stretching right up to the Fragrant Hills, must have appeared eminently suitable for exercising this art. The area is a large plain where terrain and natural springs provided ideal conditions for creating the private gardens and lavish resorts that came to be established there. The Fragrant Hills resort palace was one of these; the Garden of Carefree Spring (*Changchunyuan*) was another. In due course the whole area became almost totally the exclusive pleasure grounds of emperors and their kinsmen.

Changchunyuan was more than an imperial garden. Emperor Kangxi had a palace built so that he could administer State affairs there as well as in the Forbidden City. To the north of Changchunyuan was Yuanmingyuan, a private garden bestowed on Prince Yinzhen, Kangxi's fourth son, in 1709. On Yinzhen's accession, he embarked on a massive project to extend and transform Yuanmingyuan into a resort fit for an emperor. The Auspicious Sea (*Fuhai*) was excavated at that time. Water was in fact the dominant theme of the garden and extensively used by landscape artists in designing architectural groupings, scenic spots or formal views. From the time Prince Yinzhen ascended the throne as the Yongzheng Emperor, five successive rulers moved their Court to Yuanmingyuan after each New Year. Except for excursions to Chengde during the summer, they lived in Yuanmingyuan until the winter solstice.

Under Emperor Qianlong, Yuanmingyuan became even more splendid. From his inspection tours of the area around the Yangzi River, the emperor assimilated and then transplanted garden-making ideas and scenery from the south. Altogether 69 'scenes' or 'views' were created in the Summer Palace;

40 of them were recorded by Yongzheng's Court painters Shen Yuan and Tang Dai, and it is from these scrolls that historians have reconstructed a broader picture of this outstanding garden. Descriptions of it have also survived in the correspondence of the Catholic missionaries employed by the Qing Court. One of them, the Jesuit artist Giuseppe Castiglione, was commissioned by Qianlong in 1745 to design the European-style Western Mansions (*Xiyanglou*) that were constructed along the northern wall. It is the ruins of these extraordinary palaces that remain today.

In 1860 when Anglo-French troops captured Beijing, rampaging soldiers, on the orders of Lord Elgin, set fire to Yuanmingyuan. A young captain of the British Royal Engineers, who was later to gain fame as 'Chinese Gordon', wrote after the destruction: '[We] went out, and, after pillaging it, burned the whole place, destroying in a Vandal-like manner most valuable property which would not be replaced for four millions. We got upwards of £48 a-piece prize money before we went out here; and although I have not as much as many, I have done well.

'The people are civil, but I think the grandees hate us, as they must after what we did to the Palace. You can scarcely imagine the beauty and magnificence of the places we burnt. It made one's heart sore to burn them; in fact, these palaces were so large, and we were so pressed for time, that we could not plunder them carefully. Quantities of gold ornaments were burnt, considered as brass. It was wretchedly demoralizing work for an army. Everybody was wild for plunder.'

Thirteen years later an attempt was made to rebuild the palace to mark Empress Dowager Cixi's 40th birthday, but dwindling funds put a full-scale restoration out of the question. It was once again devastated in 1900, this time by the Allied Expeditionary Force which relieved the Siege of the Legations. Over the years the damage was compounded by local peasants scavenging for building materials.

In 1977 maintenance of the ruins of Yuanmingyuan was put in the charge of the Beijing municipal authorities, and a small museum has been set up at the site to show the scale and magnificence of the palace in its day. Despite these efforts at conservation, the area remains a wilderness with a few romantic rococo ruins for children to climb on when families picnic there. Energetic Beijing residents say that the best time to visit Yuanmingyuan is at dawn. To many Chinese it remains a powerful symbol of imperial folly and Western aggression.

Special Topic

Dongyue Temple 东岳庙

Dongyue Temple, Beijing's most unique center of Taoist worship, is dedicated to the Holy Emperor of the Eastern Peak Equal to Heaven, who watches over all the good and bad that people do. He is also in charge of hell.

The temple was constructed between 1314 and 1320, and was once one of the biggest Taoist temples in Beijing. Destroyed by fire, it was built again in the Ming Dynasty.

The entrance is guarded by two door guardians, Generals Heng and Ha, two deities with fierce facial expressions. One is said to be able to project fire from his nose while the other emits a yellow smoke from his mouth.

On the west side of the complex is a large abacus, which is here to remind us that good and bad deeds will be reckoned with some day. Along the sides of the first courtyard are small halls that house the Taoist deities who serve in the 72 departments, and who are responsible for handing out punishments.

Dongyue Temple has many frightening life-size plaster statues that serve in these 72 departments of the afterlife, or who suffer in the 18 Layers of Hell. These various halls exhibit officials giving out punishments, many very grotesque, a sort of Dante's Inferno with Chinese characteristics.

The main courtyard also contains the Hall of Taishan (one of China's five sacred mountains), including statues of the God of Mt. Tai and his senior subordinates.

Despite the very dark ambience of Dongyue Temple, it's one of the best places to observe a traditional temple fair during Chinese New Year. This is one of the few places where you can watch stilt walkers—heavily made-up young children walking on long stilts—and hawkers selling old folk crafts and traditional Beijing snacks. Dongyue Temple is located at 141 Chaoyangmenwai Dajie.

The Temple of Azure Clouds (Biyunsi) 碧云寺

A short way from the Temple of the Sleeping Buddha on the road leading to the Fragrant Hills is one of Beijing's great temples, the Temple of Azure Clouds. A temple has stood here since the Yuan Dynasty. It was restored and extended on two separate occasions by palace eunuchs Yu Jing and Wei Zhongxian, who planned to place their graves in the hill behind (they both failed in their ambition). There are many buildings here, arranged on the side of a hill, and much to see. At the top of the hill is the Diamond Throne Pagoda, an Indian-style stone temple with a spectacular view from its roof. It was built on the lines of the Five Pagoda Temple (*see* page 167) in 1792. Below is the Memorial Hall to Dr. Sun Yat-sen. After his death in 1925 the body of the founder of modern China lay in state in this temple, reposing in a crystal coffin presented by the Soviet Union. His body was moved to Nanjing in 1929 when the mausoleum there had been completed.

To one side of the Memorial Hall is the Luohan Hall, with its four inner courtyards, which was built in the mid-18th century. *Luohan* are the disciples of Buddha, and over 500 gilded wooden statues of these proselytes, each one quite distinct with an individual, and very human, personality, are crammed into this section of the temple complex.

Biyunsi, open between 8:00am and 5:00pm, makes for a particularly delightful excursion in the spring, when the peach and almond trees—both within the temple complex and on the surrounding hillsides—are covered in blossom.

Fragrant Hills Park (*Xiangshan Gongyuan*) 香山公园

Close to the Temple of Azure Clouds, this park is set in a belt of hills northwest of Beijing, about 40 minutes' drive away. The Western Hills, as the area is also called, was long a favorite retreat of the emperors. In the 12th century when it was a royal hunting park, the landscape was considered so picturesque that the hills came to be designated as one of the Eight Great Scenes of Yanjing. With the addition of a resort palace in the reign of *Kangxi*, its attractions further increased until the park reached the peak of its splendor in the 18th century.

Roads fan out from the main east-facing gate. To the left is the Fragrant Hills Hotel, a recent construction. Many of the old beauty spots still remain, however, most notably at the northern end of the park. One can reach this part by entering through the north gate from the direction of the Temple of Azure Clouds. Crossing Spectacles Lake (*Yanjinghu*) one comes to the Study of Self-knowledge (*Jianxinzhai*), a 16th-century garden with a circular pool, enclosed by a rounded wall and promenade and shielded by clumps of trees on three sides. To the south of it are the remains of Zhaomiao, a Tibetan-style temple erected in the Qianlong period, as well as an ornamental archway and a pagoda roofed in yellow glazed tiles, with bells dangling from its eaves. There is now a cable car.

The name 'Fragrant Hills' probably derives from the two slabs of stone—shaped like incense burners—on top of the highest peak at the western extremity of the park. The wisps of mist clinging to the summit resemble puffs of scented smoke coming from the incense burners at the top. But the park is famous above all for its autumn aspect. The blaze of red on the hillsides when the leaves of the Huanglu smoke tree (sometimes referred to as maple) are turning is a sight much celebrated in poetry and painting.

The Great Wall (Changcheng) 长城

The Great Wall, an integral feature of the geography of North China, has captured the imagination of countless people throughout its long history.

The wall was built in a piecemeal fashion over a long period, from the fifth century BC down to the 16th century AD, as a means of defence against raids from northern nomadic tribes. When the empire was unified under Qin Shi Huangdi in 221 BC, a continuous line of fortifications was constructed by joining up the old walls.

'A wall between is a mountain' goes an old saying, and in the hearts of the Chinese, the 'Wall of Ten-thousand Li' (*Wanli Changcheng*) not only protected them from the barbaric Huns (*Xiongnu*). Its significance lay also in separating the familiar, safe patterns of settled agriculture, from the alien pastoral nomadic life of the steppes and deserts beyond.

Historical texts record as many as 300,000 men working for 10 years on the construction of a section of the wall. Stories of the hardship suffered by these conscripted laborers have been passed down, contributing to the image of the Qin emperor as a hated tyrant. Composed partly of earth faced with brick and partly of masonry, Great Walls were built by rulers of 10 dynasties and their defensive works totalled an incredible 25,000 kilometers in length. The most recently built Great Wall, the work of all 16 Ming emperors, totalled 6,300 kilometers. Naturally, the strongest, and therefore best-preserved sections, shielded the dynastic capital, Beijing.

Since the late 1950s, five parts of the wall have been restored. Visitors have traditionally been taken to the section at Badaling, in Nankou Pass, about 70 kilometers (44 miles) from the city, either before or after a visit to the Ming Tombs.

The road to Badaling passes through Juyongguan, or Juyong Pass, where there is a stunning white marble structure, the Cloud Platform, at the foot of a newly reconstructed section of the Great Wall. Built around 1345 during the Yuan Dynasty, it originally served as the base for three pagodas that were destroyed several decades later. A hexagonal archway pierces the platform. The ceiling and walls are covered with wonderful carvings of the Four Heavenly Kings and the texts of Buddhist scriptures in six languages: Nepalese Sanskrit, Tibetan, Phags-pa Mongolian, Uighur, Xi Xia and Han Chinese. Earlier last century, an American traveller called it the 'language archway'.

Badaling is the easy way to visit the wall, in terms of reaching it conveniently or on a tight schedule, via a highway that now whisks visitors there in just over an hour. That said, making it up the wall is not necessarily easy.

The Great Wall, icon of China.

Upon entering the Badaling Wall, One can turn right or left. Left is the easier side, right is much steeper and more challenging. Right also has a better payoff in terms of views.

For those choosing the route to the right, be aware of two things. First, it gets really steep at points. Rest often, and if doing the climb in hot weather, bring plenty of cool water to drink, and a hat for protection from the sun. Second, if you climb all the way to what is called the Eighth Tower, you run into a dead end. After climbing for about an hour to reach it, it can be disheartening. Stop where a path to the right goes towards a cable car, which runs between that part of the wall and the parking lot. Follow the path to the other section of the wall where the climb can resume.

At the tallest part of the Badaling Wall, the visitor can choose to return from whence they came, or to take a different route to the bottom. However, with no signage, a key question arises: is it possible to go down the other way and still make

Back in '78, visitors almost had the Wall to themselves.

it back to the tour bus or other conveyance? The answer is yes, but once you reach the bottom, you'll have to climb back up a bit, go through the tunnel near the wall entrance, and then down into the main parking lot. Admission to the Badaling Great Wall is 45 yuan for April–October and 40 yuan for November–March. Visitors should decline the insurance they will try to sell you at the wall for no apparent reason. If you get a little white ticket along with the turnstile card, hand it back and give the impression that you don't want it, they will refund your two yuan per person.

In 2003 there was a change in regulations forbidding visitors access to unrestored parts of the wall. However, special permits can be secured for the serious hiker. The most convenient way to get off the beaten track is with *Wild Wall* (www.wildwall.com) which offers homestay hiking weekends.

The second most popular section of the Great Wall to have been restored is at Mutianyu, northeast of Beijing in Huairou County. The advantage of visiting this

section is that it is a little less crowded than that at Badaling. Before reaching the wall one has to mount some thousand steps or ride the cable car. This expanse of the wall trails off for more than a mile and one has an unobstructed view in both directions of great lengths of the defense undulating along mountain crests until they fade into the distance. Here there is a much more peaceful atmosphere and one can really get a sense of the Great Wall's history and grandeur as it spans the horizon.

Alternative sites for climbing on the Great Wall are the adjacent sections of Jinshanling and Simatai, approximately 120 kilometers (75 miles) northeast of Beijing. This is wall par excellence and is well worth a full day of your itinerary.

The wall is best visited by taxi, with a driver waiting. Round trips to Badaling and Mutianyu should cost approximately 700 yuan roundtrip. Trips to Jinshanling or Simatai cost approximately 1,000 yuan roundtrip. For visitors to the latter, it is also possible to go first to the Jinshanling section and walk to Simatai, a challenging hike that takes approximately three hours, and be picked up in the Simatai parking lot. Taxi drivers are generally happy to make these trips as they represent easier money than trying to pick up 10 yuan fares all day long. Although a taxi can be hailed on the spot and taken to the Great Wall, it's best to book the night before. Hotel cars will charge more than the above prices for these excursions.

Alone on the Great Wall

Getting initial access to the Great Wall was not too problematical. Taking a long distance bus to Changping, I walked a few kilometres up to a road junction and hitchhiked southwest, then northwest beyond Hengling. Here was a convenient location to join an inner system of ramparts, well to the south of the Ming's main line of the Great Wall some sixty kilometres away. Nevertheless, this was a defensive line of paramount strategy in protecting the capital and as such is built to a scale I had not before witnessed. A fearsome scramble on the broken stone-blocked ramparts and I was climbing high on the snow ridges above the glassy Gaunting Shuiku, one of Beijing's enormous reservoirs. If ever an injection of hope was needed it was now; and the sight of this solid stone dragon, its torso dotted with towers like fins and scales, was exactly that—the greatest Great Wall of China, the stupendous creation of the Ming, dipping and thrusting into the distance across multiple ridges a day's struggle away. I wanted to run fast and free.

First I had to tread slowly, climb, stretch for footholds, jump off the wall, clamber back on, chimney down, balance low for fear of the strong wind blowing me to the ground some six metres below. For the Wall is so steep, its surface rough, loose and slippery with crenellated ramparts, decaying, weather-beaten and earth-shaken. Its overgrown pavement concealed holes where rubble core had been washed away. Beacons and watch-towers rose like derelict ghost houses, for so long the providers of shelter for so many.

An awesome creation. In the afternoon sunshine its light-coloured stone contrasting with the vegetation of the slopes thinned by the approach of winter. It perched like a cardboard cut-out upon mountains, not hills, undeterred by precipices. Cold stone blocks, rectangular lime facing bricks, bound by crumbly mortar, lay chalky white and friable at the side of the parapet, as if left by workmen just days ago. My feet were slipping on the gravel and slush, fingernails full of clay and mortar, palms grazed, knuckles scraped by thorn bush, ankles banged and bruised between boulders and rocks. My lungs gasped for breath on the climbs and teeth chattered in the bitter wind. Ice-cold inhalations stung my nostrils.

Certainly it was a Wonder of the World, arguably the Wonder. For I was aware that the Great Wall was not merely a single view—no more than a person's life is a single day. The Great Pyramid at Cheops had been a brisk scramble

Having a bit of the Great Wall to oneself is now a rare treat experienced by very few of its visitors.

amid the cries for baksheesh. Thebes and its valley of the Kings was a morning's inspection, Pompei a sultry afternoon's walk, the Grand Canyon a day's hiking. But the Great Wall was a wonder of a thousand vistas. A lifetime would be needed just to inspect every remaining rampart from the Warring States to the Qin, from Han to Ming. For when the fever-like fascination of the Great Wall takes hold of the imagination, one is drawn into studying the core millenia of China's wonderful civilisation; uncovering inventions, discovering legends, analysing the xenophobic mind, and paying respect to the labourers of countless generations who devoted their lives, somewhat reluctantly, to its construction. For beneath my feet was the world's longest cemetery. There was blood on every stone. The cannibalistic appetite of the Great Wall, perpetually in need of repair and extension, gave no dispensation from servitude to any Han generation.

William Lindesay OBE, *Alone on the Great Wall*
© Hodder & Stoughton, London. 1989.

The North
The Ming Tombs (*Ming Shisanling*) 明十三陵

The valley of the Ming Tombs lies about 48 kilometers (30 miles) north of Beijing. Thirteen of the 16 Ming emperors are interred here, hence the site's Chinese name, *Ming Shisanling* (The 13 Ming Tombs). The tombs were located in accordance with Chinese geomantic specifications requiring graves to be protected by high ground.

The approach is impressive. The modern road passes by a stone portico with five carved archways. This is the beginning of the imposing route known as the Spirit (or Sacred) Way. Next comes the Great Vermilion Gateway; of its three openings the central entrance was reserved for the coffins of deceased emperors, and all followers were required to dismount at this point. The whole tomb site, to which this gateway was the actual entrance, was of course surrounded by a wall, now gone.

The Spirit Way

The emperor's coffin would have been borne past a stele pavilion, a typical imperial structure with the floating clouds motif repeated on its supporting columns. The procession of mourners would then have filed along the Spirit Way, a funereal guard of honor of six pairs of animals and six pairs of human figures carved from large blocks of stone. The latter, all standing, are statues of scholars, administrators and

Bronze lion, Forbidden City.

warriors. The animals-lions, *xiechi* (a mythical beast), camels, elephants, unicorns, horses-are either standing or crouching. The Spirit Way ends at the Dragon and Phoenix Gate.

In its entirety, this part of the Ming Tombs dates from the 15th century. Beside the road there is now a mass of shrubs and fruit trees. Once across an arched bridge, visitors can then visit the different tombs, scattered round the valley.

A word to the wise: when visiting the Ming Tombs, travelers should manage their expectations. China's emperors lived in spectacular fashion, evident at the Imperial Museum, but they were buried rather simply. Anyone expecting an experience akin to Egypt's Valley of the Kings will be grossly disappointed. A stop at the Ming Tombs is best scheduled at the end of a day trip to the Badaling Great Wall, without making a special trip from Beijing.

Changling

The most important tomb, appropriately, belongs to the great Yongle, the third Ming emperor, who was responsible for building so much of Beijing. He chose this site and had his burial place built on the traditional plan of a walled enclave, enclosing buildings separated by three courtyards, with the tumulus at its head. The tumulus, marked by a stele tower and traditionally referred to as the Precious Fortress (*Baocheng*), has not been excavated, but visitors may see inside the magnificent Hall of Sacrifice. This very fine structure built in 1427 is supported by 32 massive wooden pillars wrought from huge trunks of *nanmu* wood from the extreme southwest of China. The Yongle Emperor was interred in the Changling in 1424. Sixteen royal concubines were buried alive in ancillary graves following a custom that was finally discontinued during the reign of the sixth Ming emperor.

Dingling

The tomb of the Wanli Emperor (reigned 1573–1620) and his two consorts is known as Dingling. Its construction was started in 1584, when Wanli was aged 22, and took six years to complete. It was excavated in 1958, and one may now descend by a modern spiral staircase to the underground tomb behind a stele tower.

The vaulted marble palace, built deep underground so that it is cool in summer and comfortably warm in winter, consists of three burial chambers. At the entrance to the antechamber is a carved marble gateway. The floor is paved with specially made 'golden bricks' which had been fired for 130 days and dipped in tung oil before being laid. The middle chamber contains three marble thrones; in front of each of them are five drumshaped stools for holding offerings and a large glazed pot known as the Ever

A mythical beast stands proud.

Bright Lamp. The lamps would have been filled with oil and lit before the tomb was sealed. The back chamber was the actual repository of the royal coffins. On being opened by the excavation team they were found to be stuffed with some 300 assorted garments. Even more lavish, countless pieces of jewelry, curios and porcelain—stowed in 26 lacquer chests—were also deposited to provide for a luxurious life in the nether world. The regalia and the treasure have all been moved to two small exhibition halls outside. They should not be missed.

The East

The Eastern Qing Tombs (Dongling) 东陵

The site of the Eastern Qing Tombs is over the provincial border, in Hebei, some 121 kilometers (75 miles) east of Beijing (a round trip journey of about four hours by car). The 15 tombs are spread over an area 34 kilometers (21 miles) wide, and built under the lee of Mount Changrui. The choice of this site as the Qing imperial burial ground is attributed to the Shunzhi Emperor, who came upon it when out hunting. He is interred here, together with the Kangxi, Qianlong, Xianfeng and Tongzhi emperors. Other tombs include those of the Empress Dowager Cixi, several less notorious empresses, concubines and royal children, as well as that of Emperor Kangxi's revered teacher.

There are some striking differences between the Ming and Qing tombs. Whereas the Ming created a single 'Spirit Way' (the approach to imperial burial grounds lined with stone animals and officials), the Qing have several shorter ones leading to tumuli which are also on a smaller scale. The Qing stone figures have their hair in the traditional Manchu plait, and while the scholar is shown wearing a string of beads of Buddhist origin, emblematic of the strong lamaistic leanings of the Manchu rulers, the Ming statues are generally depicted carrying Confucian tablets. The animals too differ in style and decoration.

The tombs of the Qianlong Emperor, the Empress Cian and the Empress Dowager Cixi are open to the public. The underground marble vault of Qianlong is particularly impressive: every interior wall and arch is richly carved with images of the Buddha, the Celestial Guardians and with thousands of words of Buddhist scriptures in both Sanskrit and Tibetan. Ornate carving also embellishes Cixi's mausoleum, where one can see the repeated use of such imperial motifs as dragons, phoenixes and clouds. Built over a period of 30 years, the tomb was a subject of great interest to the Empress Dowager, who visited the site several times. Unfortunately both this tomb and that of the Qianlong emperor were broken into by grave robbers in the 1920s, and the fabulous treasures, buried with the view of ensuring a comfortable afterlife, have all disappeared.

Chengde: Imperial Resort 承德避暑山庄

Chengde lies 354 kilometers (220 miles) northeast of Beijing. Formerly known as Jehol, or 'Warm River', this beautiful 18th-century city was the resort of the Manchu emperors of the Qing Dynasty. From 1681 the emperors would escape the scorching Beijing summer and travel north on a two-week journey over the Great Wall to the cool hunting grounds of Jehol. The resort is also called *Bishushanzhuang*: Mountain Lodge for Avoiding Heat.

The wooded river basin in which Chengde lies is surrounded by pleated hills, punctuated at intervals by strange rock formations. Emperor Kangxi created the palace, lakes and parks to blend in with the natural beauty of the site. The palace itself is an appropriately simple building, constructed of *nanmu*, a hard aromatic wood. The audience chamber, the Modest and Responsible Hall, is connected to the other chambers by *lang*, or covered walkways, that wind around the courtyards which are themselves shaded by ancient pines.

Through the palace it is only a few minutes walk to the park and lakes. Emperor Kangxi decreed that 36 beauty spots were to be created in the park. His grandson Qianlong then doubled the number. As you wander beside the lake, there are carefully placed brightly colored bridges which are designed to arouse your curiosity and lure you to one of the beauty spots.

Outside the palace grounds, Emperor Qianlong built eight magnificent temples, seven of which still remain. The eighth, which was built of bronze, was removed by the Japanese during the war. The first to be built was the Temple of Universal Peace (*Puningsi*), in 1775. This was a period in Chinese history of massive annexations, including Tibet and what is now Xinjiang. To integrate and, in some cases, to placate his new subjects, the emperor modelled the temples on their religion and culture. For this reason the *Putuozongshengmiao* is a copy of the Potala at Lhasa in Tibet.

Jehol lost favor with the Qing Court after the unfortunate—and ominous—accident to the Emperor Jiaqing, who was struck dead by lightning there. The summer palace and temples now form part of a public park.

Chengde can be reached in less than five hours by a daily train from Beijing Railway Station.

Visitors may like to round off their excursion to Dongling by calling in at the two small museums that have been established in the sacrificial halls at the tombs of the two empresses, Cixi and Cian. Opening times are from 9:00am to 4:00pm.

Dule Si (Temple of Solitary Joy) 独乐寺

Dule Si, in Jixian County, just north of Tianjin, was built in the 984 during the Tang Dynasty and was later renovated in the Liao Dynasty. The temple is an excellent example of an ancient Chinese wooden temple. Dule Si is still in very good condition, despite its wooden structure and long history.

As you approach the Liao Dynasty temple gate you'll notice two mythical beasts on the east and west corners. Just inside the gate, you'll be welcomed by two menacing-looking door guards, General Heng and General Ha, who are clutching swords in their hands as they protect the Goddess of Mercy. The Kings of Four Directions are depicted on the walls behind them.

The highlight of the temple is the Guanyin Pavilion, which is home to a 16 meter statue of the Goddess of Mercy, believed to be one of the biggest terracotta figures still in existence in China. The statue extends past the second and third floors, almost scratching the octagonal ceiling. Ten small Guanyin heads have been added to the sculpture, which is also known as the Eleven-Faced Guanyin. Each head of this savior deity displays a different aspect of the goddess. The wooden statue was covered with clay, which was combined with egg white and glutinous rice. Also quite interesting here is the colored mural of the 16 arhats, produced in the Yuan Dynasty, which is quite rare in its unique composition, color and style.

Baoen Hall contains a statue of the Maitreya Buddha, surrounded by the almost comic-looking "four mad" Buddhas.

On the east side of the Temple is the Qing Dynasty Villa, where the imperial entourages rested on their way to pay their respects to their ancestors at the Eastern Qing Tombs. There are 28 stele here that were inscribed by Qianlong. About 300 meters south of the temple is the Dule Temple Pagoda, which is more than 1,000 years old. The pagoda was badly damaged during the Tangshan earthquake in 1976. Workers restoring the pagoda discovered a tower inside containing more than 100 ancient artifacts.

Although situated some 80 kilometers from Beijing, this temple is worth a day trip. Located at 41 Wuding Jie, Jixian.

The Southwest
Marco Polo Bridge (Lugouqiao) 芦沟桥

Proceeding southwest from Guang'anmenwai for about 16 kilometers (10 miles), one reaches Lugouqiao, celebrated not only for being Beijing's oldest surviving bridge, but also for the impression it made on Marco Polo, who saw it in 1290 (hence the bridge's Western name). He has left us with a fine description.

Marco Polo Bridge spans the Yongding River. As early as the Warring States period (475–221 BC), the site of the present bridge had been a strategically important river crossing. Initially the crossing was probably made by a wooden bridge or by pontoons. From the Jin Dynasty onwards, when the capital was at Beijing, increased traffic across the river warranted a more permanent bridge, which was completed in 1192. Constructed with careful reference to the river's flow, this solid stone structure resting on 11 arches has withstood weathering for several centuries.

The piers supporting the bridge are specially strong, being reinforced by triangular metal posts which locals used to call 'Swords for Decapitating Dragons' in the belief that evil dragons, seeing these posts, would quietly go away rather than cause mischief for river craft.

On either side of the bridge there is a parapet with 140 columns carved and surmounted with lions. Imperial steles stand at each end; one commemorates the renovation of the bridge in 1698, the other carries a four-character inscription by Emperor Qianlong, 'Bright Moon on Lugou'.

The way things were, visiting a commune, September 1978.

Chuandixia 川底下

One of the most interesting trips outside Beijing is a trip to Chuandixia, a late Ming and early Qing Dynasty village in the mountains of **Mentougou**. Time stopped here some 400 years ago. There are only a dozen or so remaining households of the original 80, and most of the villagers go under the name of Han. The old stone houses are spacious, with red peppers and garlic hanging from the windows and doors, and corn drying on the roofs. The old fashioned windows are glassless. In the winter, which is bitterly cold here, they are covered by several layers of paper. These houses still have the old fashioned brick kang beds that are heated from below. This is where the whole family congregates in the winter.

Peking Man Site 周口店

The village of Zhoukoudian, which can be reached by train from Beijing, used to be notable for its production of lime. In 1929 it achieved worldwide fame with the discovery of the first skulls of Peking Man. The fossil remains of *Homo erectus pekinensis* have been dated to about 600,000–700,000 years ago.

The limestone caves of Zhoukoudian were probably the location of a paleolithic settlement. So far bones of over 40 inhabitants have been unearthed and, with the evidence of other remains, scientists have pieced together a fascinating picture of this early community.

Some of the limestone caves on the northern slope of Dragon Bones Hills (*Longgushan*) to the east of Zhoukoudian may be visited. There is also a comprehensive museum on the evolution of man and the Zhoukoudian culture. Included in the displays are stone implements used by Peking Man and Upper Cave Man (who lived about 50,000 years ago), fossils of animals hunted by them, and evidence that Peking Man used fire. The whereabouts of the original Peking Man fossils, lost during the Second World War while en route to the United States for safekeeping, is still shrouded in mystery. Zhoukoudian is 90 kilometers to the southwest of Beijing. It is best to go with a tour guide as very little information is available in English at the site.

Dabaotai Han Tomb 大堡台汉

Located about 15 kilometers (10 miles) from the city limits in the Fengtai district, the Dabaotai Han-dynasty tomb is a worthwhile half-day outing. Difficult to locate on account of a lack of road signs, the best way to get there is to take a taxi (there is no public transport) to the village of Guogongzhuang and ask the way from there. Dabaotai is about four kilometers (2.5 miles) directly south of the Fengtai Railway Station.

The archeologists who excavated the tomb in 1975 are unable to determine who was buried in this spectacular underground 'wooden palace', but the choice has been narrowed down to one of two princes belonging to the Liu clan who died in approximately 50 BC.

The excellently restored tomb consists of three inner and outer coffins of wood surrounded by a boundary wall built with tens of thousands of square wooden beams. The wall of the tomb was further lined with a boundary wall of heaped beams, and sealed with a thick layer of plaster to keep it dry, which partially explains its excellent state of preservation. The entire tomb, which has been enclosed in a poorly-lit building, is 23.2 meters (80 feet) long, 18 meters (56 feet) wide and 4.7 meters (14.5 feet) deep. The most extraordinary objects on view are the three lacquered chariots and 11 horses that were buried alive with them in a long narrow chamber that stands at the entrance to the tomb. A second tomb containing the remains of the queen consort was plundered and burnt in ancient times and nothing is left of it except the site.

Newly built models of the chariots are on display in a separate hall, and there is a small museum containing some of the burial objects found in the tomb, including jade carvings, miniature wooden burial figures, bronze incense burners and a bronze door decoration in the form of a grotesque beast.

Emperors commissioned only the finest artisans, such as this ornately carved stone attests to.

The West
Western Qing Tombs (Xiling) 西陵

Like the Eastern Qing Tombs (see page 204), the Western Qing Tombs lie a good distance from the capital, some 125 kilometers (78 miles) southwest of the city in Yixian, Hebei Province. Four emperors—Yongzheng, Jiaqing, Daoguang and Guangxu—are buried here, along with nine queens, 76 princes and 57 imperial concubines.

One traditional view holds that Yongzheng (reigned 1723–35), son of the great Kangxi and father of the great Qianlong, chose to be buried apart from his father because he had ascended the throne by devious means, but there is little evidence to support this. In any case, Qianlong decreed that after his own death the tombs of the emperors that came after him should be distributed alternatively between the eastern and western burial grounds. Incidentally, Puyi, the last emperor of the Qing Dynasty was cremated after his death in 1967, and his ashes were placed in the revolutionary cemetery at Babaoshan. In 1995 his casket of ashes was finally taken to Xiling for a simple burial.

Tailing, the tomb of Yongzheng, is the largest tomb in the entire mausoleum complex. It consists of numerous gateways and buildings that were used during the various Buddhist rituals and sacrifices held in the emperor's memory.

The Muling of the Emperor Daoguang (reigned 1821–50) is small in comparison to the Tailing but is more exquisitely constructed. Soon after his ascension to the throne, Daoguang began building his tomb at the eastern burial grounds, as decreed by Qianlong. One year after its completion, however, the underground burial chamber was found to be flooded, and Daoguang, finding this inauspicious, went to the Western Tombs to select a new site for himself. Because Daoguang believed that the flooding in his first tomb had occurred because several dragons had been deprived of their homes, he lavishly decorated his second tomb with carved images of this auspicious creature.

Chongling of Emperor Guangxu (reigned 1875–1908) was left unfinished when the Qing Dynasty fell in 1911, and was only completed four years later. Accompanying Guangxu in a tomb of her own is Zhenfei, known as the 'Pearl Concubine'. Zhenfei was forced down a well in the Imperial Palace (see page 160).

The Temple of the Pool and Wild Mulberry (Tanzhesi) 潭泽寺

Situated in the Western Hills, this Buddhist temple lies 45 kilometers (28 miles) west of Beijing. It is reached by a winding road which passes the Ordination Terrace

Temple (*see* below) and some quite spectacular scenery, especially in the spring when the fruit trees are in blossom. One of the biggest and oldest temples in the Beijing area, Tanzhesi has been completely restored in recent years.

A temple known by various names has existed on this site for 1,600 years. Its present name is derived from the Dragon Pool nearby and from the trees, growing on the hillside, whose leaves were used to feed silkworms. The present structure, laid out on traditional lines, is typical of Ming and Qing architecture. A ceremonial arch or *pailou* (*see* page 155) frames the entrance to a compound of several halls, pavilions and courtyards: there is the **Hall of Abstinence**, the **Ordination Altar** and, at the back of it, the **Hall to Guanyin**, the Goddess of Mercy. The latter is associated with Kublai Khan's daughter, Princess Miaoyan, who entered the nunnery here in the 13th century. Her devotions were performed so assiduously, it is said, that she wore deep marks into the piece of stone on which she stood. Some of the strangely shaped trees within the temple are said to be a thousand years old.

To the right of the Hall of Abstinence is the **Flowing Cup Pavilion** (*Liubeiting*), where dragon-shaped channels feed spring water into the **Dragon Pool**. This water has a special quality which enables objects to float upon the surface easily. On the third day of the third month people used to gather here for the 'purification of the fermented wine'; brimming wine cups were floated down the stream and only when they stopped moving was the wine drunk. Below the temple are beautiful stone stupas built over the burial sites of the temple's monks dating from the Jin, Yuan, Ming and Qing dynasties.

THE ORDINATION TERRACE TEMPLE (*JIETAISI*) 戒台寺

The temple lies in the Western Hills, 33 kilometers (22 miles) from Beijing on the road that leads to the Temple of the Pool and Wild Mulberry. There has been a temple in this mountain cleft for 1,350 years, but it was in the Liao Dynasty (916–1125) that its chief function—the ordination of Buddhist novices—was established when a monk, Fajun, founded an altar here.

The Ordination Altar, in the northeast courtyard, is of white marble and its three tiers are carved with hundreds of figures, some as tall as a meter (just over three feet). Once a year, at midnight, an initiation ceremony was conducted; the novices, having fasted all day, would endure burns from lighted incense sticks upon their tonsured heads.

As the temple was one of his favored rest-stops, the Qing emperor Qianlong handsomely endowed it during his reign, and the present buildings date from this period of expansion and renovation. The ancient pine trees contribute to the temple's peculiar charm. One of them, which sadly no longer survives, is marked with a stone

tablet to the left of the Thousand Buddha Pavilion behind the temple's main hall. In the time of Qianlong this remarkable pine was dubbed the 'Mobile Tree' on account of its ability to shake all over when any one of its branches was pulled.

Temple of the Sea of the Law (Fahaisi) 法海寺

Located approximately two kilometers (1.5 miles) northeast of Moshikou in the Shijingshan district, the Temple of the Sea of the Law can be visited at the same time as its neighbors, the Tanzhesi and Jietaisi.

According to an inscription in the temple, the building was completed in about 1440 by an eunuch in the Court of the Ming Zhengtong Emperor with funds he collected from various officials, lamas, monks, nuns and lay Buddhists. Its design is similar to that of other mountain temples, which are traditionally laid out on three levels.

The finest works of art in the temple are the famous frescos painted on the interior walls of the Main Hall (*Daxiongbaodian*), which stands on the north side of the rearmost courtyard. The paintings date back to the temple's construction, and were executed by some 15 palace painters who are named on a stone tablet found near the temple.

The frescos show groups of emperors, empresses, and religious figures engaged in Buddhist worship as well as the objects of their worship, the bodhisattvas Guanyin (*Avalokitesvara*), Wenshu (*Manjusri*) and Samantahbadra (*Puxian*). Note also the painted mandalas in the three cupolas in the ceiling of this hall. These lively, colorful and wonderfully detailed examples of brush work are important monuments in the history of Chinese painting.

Above: *"Temple of the Sea of the Law."*
Right: *A colorful gateway to the Summer Palace.*

Suggested Itineraries for Beijing

Three full days are a basic minimum for a general introduction to Beijing, but for various reasons many visitors to the city have less time. The following lists are based on a Peking pecking order that begins with the Forbidden City.

One Day Intensive

Hire a taxi for the day. Start at about 7:00am with an early morning meditation at the **Monument to the People's Heroes** in the center of Tiananmen Square. Walk through the **Working People's Cultural Palace** and get to the **Meridian Gate** (*Wumen*), the main entrance of the Forbidden City, at around 8:30am. Spend about four hours in the Forbidden City, following the main north road to the **Palace of Heavenly Purity** and the **Hall of Mental Cultivation**. Then head east to the **Nine Dragon Screen** and north through the various exhibitions to the **Concubine's Well** and out through the **Gate of Divine Prowess**, where your taxi should be waiting for

you. Have a Peking duck lunch at either Hepingmen or at the Bianyifang at 1:00pm, and then spend one and a half hours at the **Temple of Heaven**, walking from north to south. Have your driver let you off at Liulichang for a half hour stroll around the nearby lanes and alleys, and then drive to the **Summer Palace**, arriving there by 4:30pm, when they stop selling tickets. Stroll around the buildings and the lake until the sun begins to set, then go out for a late dinner or dine at your hotel. This is a breathless day, but feasible. Best without jetlag.

Two Days

On day one, visit the **Temple of Heaven** in the morning, followed by a visit to the Hongqiao market to do some shopping for pearls, antiques or jewelry. Don't linger too long and head off for the **Great Wall**, preferably with a packed lunch. Return to the city in the evening and take dinner at Li Family Restaurant, the private home of Professor Li, whose grandfather was the chief of the Imperial Guard for Empress Cixi.

On day two, follow the One Day itinerary above, minus the Temple of Heaven, or add a visit to the **Lama Temple** on the way to the **Summer Palace**.

Three Days

On day one, begin with **Tiananmen Square** and the **Forbidden City** in the morning. Visit the **Temple of Heaven** and **Liulichang** in the afternoon.

On day two, go to the **Great Wall** and **Ming Tombs**, stopping for lunch along the way. Better yet, bring a picnic lunch, as the restaurants in the area can be problematical. On return to town take a Peking Duck dinner at Xiao Wang's Restaurant.

On day three, visit the **Museum of Chinese History** in the early morning. Explore **Beihai Park** and

While at the Temple of Heaven, visit the new Museum of Divine Music, which has a fine collection of ancient court instruments, located to the west of the Hall of Abstinence.

have an alfresco lunch at the snack market near **Qianhai**, across the street from the north gate of the park. After lunch spend the rest of the day in the **Summer Palace**, ideally catching the sunset there, and return to the city for a late dinner.

Four Days

On day one, begin with **Tiananmen Square** and the **Forbidden City** in the morning. After a late lunch, explore **Liulichang** and the surrounding hutongs in the afternoon, working your way back to Tiananmen Square.

On day two, go early to the **Temple of Heaven** and watch the local devotees of the martial arts attaining longevity. Then head for the **Great Wall** and **Ming Tombs**, eating lunch along the way, or better yet, bring a picnic lunch. Eat at a Sichuan restaurant for dinner.

On day three, visit the **National Museum of China** in the early morning. Explore **Beihai Park** and head up to **Wangfujing** for lunch and visit the shops before dinner at the nearby **Donglaishun**, featuring mutton hotpots.

On day four, visit the **Lama Temple**, **Confucian Temple** and **Guozijian** in the morning. Spend the last afternoon and early evening in the **Yuanmingyuan Gardens** (one hour) and **Summer Palace** (Yiheyuan), leaving for dinner after sunset.

Five Days

Follow the four day itinerary, and on day four, add visits to the **Beijing Zoo** (to see the pandas), **Beijing Art Museum**, **Big Bell Temple**, **White Clouds Taoist Temple**, **Old Observatory**, or go out of town for a half day visit to the **Tanzhesi** or **Jietaisi** in the western suburbs.

Another alternative is to make a visit on the afternoon of day three or during day four to the **Arthur Sackler Museum of Art and Archeology** at Beijing University. This museum houses an extraordinary collection of fossils, artifacts and relics discovered by Chinese archeologists

A second alternative is to visit several of the destinations mentioned above on the afternoon of the fourth day, and save the **Summer Palace** and **Yuanmingyuan Gardens** for the afternoon of the fifth day; in the morning, visit the **Temple of the Sleeping Buddha** and the **Temple of Azure Clouds** which lie about 15 minutes by car beyond the Summer Palace. Yet another possibility on the fifth day is to make a second visit to the **Forbidden City**.

SAINTS AND SINNERS —*The Ginger Griffin*

When one thinks of Beijing the thought of sandy beaches doesn't readily spring to mind. However, Beidaihe (*Peitaiho*), one of the most established beach resorts in China, is only a short train journey way.

Like most Chinese resorts Beidaihe was established by the foreign missionary community. Missionaries had little opportunity to vacation in China and apart from Chefoo (*Yantai*), a resort established in the 1860s, most headed for Japan. Towards the end of the 19th century, however, most missions had established their own sanatorium in the Middle Kingdom and vacationing had become a routine pastime. For those in the north, Beidaihe became their 'Jewel of the East.'

Although British archaeologists found evidence of a Han Dynasty fortress at Beidaihe in 1924, the beach and surrounding countryside had long remained undisturbed. However, with an extension of the Tianjin to Shanhaiguan railway in 1893 a handful of foreigners claimed the area for more peaceful purposes and by 1896 around 50 foreign residences had been hastily erected. These could be reached by train from Tianjin within nine hours, though the last six miles had to be covered by donkey or cart.

Most foreign properties were destroyed during the Boxer Rebellion in 1900— including those of the British Minister, Sir Claude MacDonald, and the Inspector General of the Chinese Customs, Sir Robert Hart. Nevertheless, by 1910 Beidaihe had been rebuilt and expanded with dwellings stretching over four miles along the seashore.

Three distinct districts emerged. At West End, dubbed the 'sinners quarter,' Tianjin businessmen built handsome houses, whilst at East Cliff and Rocky Point, the 'saints quarter,' large numbers of more modest missionary dwellings were assembled. The British formed the backbone of the community, though Americans, Germans and Russians were in evidence. In 1905 an association was established to oversee the building and management of Rocky Point, the present-day centre of Beidaihe. The bungalow properties had huge verandas where Indian Army servants presided over after-dinner musical performances. Locals basking in a new-found prosperity delivered over-priced fish, meat and vegetables to the door, with a consummate zeal.

Although Beidaihe's climate and beaches were amongst the best in China, often drawing comparisons with British seaside resorts such as Scarborough and Brighton, the town was slow to adopt modern conveniences. Things began to change in 1918 when improvements, including the installation of electric lighting and the opening of a railway station, attracted more summer visitors. Beidaihe became a convenient weekend destination for Beijing and Tianjin residents who would travel overnight in comfortable berths on trains replete with an excellent Western dining car. The resort also attracted an increasing number of Shanghai residents happy to endure the 55-hour boat journey northwards. Beidaihe also became the summer base for many foreign legations and their diplomatic staff as well as a watering hole for the British-Asiatic fleet.

In the early 1920s Beidaihe's main beach was known as 'black-leg beach,' echoing the fashion for women to wear costumes fitted below the knee accompanied by black stockings. The mid-20s were also black times for Beidaihe as anti-foreign sentiments and threats from bandits and warlords scared away most visitors. Yet with the dawning of the 30s Beidaihe was again in full swing.

In summertime the town would be overrun with women and children. Menfolk were curious by their absence and would join their families only when the obligations of work were lifted. Two large community halls hosted Sunday services, concerts, plays, entertainment and other activities. Life was slow—there were no cars and donkeys provided the most popular means of transport. Mornings were spent on the beach, either canoeing or bathing in the warm waters. Afternoons were reserved for visiting and leisure activities—tennis, cricket, baseball or fishing for sea-bass. Picnics were a popular pastime, whilst locals making dough figurines and toasting popcorn provided amusement for the children—as did a mini-golf course with the last hole laid out like Beijing's Temple of Heaven.

By the mid-1930s the resort had become popular with well-to-do Chinese—swarms of new hotels and stores were opened and electric lighting was installed on the beach. Scanty swimming costumes and cocktail parties were all the rage—much to the scorn of the local missionaries. Like the Russian beauties from Shanghai, who invariably took the Miss Beidaihe title, those years remain the resort's crowning glory.

Entertainment and Nightlife
Tea Culture

Sanwei (tel. 6601 3204), nestled above the bookstore of the same name, and just across Chang'an Avenue from the Minzu Hotel, serves tea all day in a timeless, studio setting. Down in the Qianmen area south of Tiananmen on the third floor of 3 Qianmenxi Dajie there is the **Lao She Tea House** (tel. 6303 6830), named after the author of *Rickshaw Boy*. Tea and snacks are served to the accompaniment of storytelling, cross talking, Peking opera, magic and ballad singing. Book ahead for evening shows between 7:50pm–9:20pm tickets cost 160–180 yuan. It's open from 9:30am to 22:30pm.

If you do not have the time to take a walk in the hutongs, then the next best is the old tea house in the Tianqiao district. In ancient times the Tianqiao neighborhood was the site of a never-ending circus where acrobats, magicians, performers and peddlers of youth elixir would gather and perform. In those days there was a famous group of eight acrobats called "The Eight Eccentrics of Tianqiao". And in this section of town, where the spirit of the eight eccentrics lingers on, is the old **Tianqiao**

Teahouse at Peking, The Illustrated London News, February 23, 1861.

Happy Tea House. The atmosphere of Old Beijing permeates everywhere. The waiters welcome guests in their old-fashioned way and as the lights dim, the show begins with the old custom of throwing hot towels to the audience with unbelievable accuracy. There is no need to master the language to understand the magic performed by an old gentleman garbed in an enormous robe concealing every imaginable trick, the Suzhou-style ballad sang by a beautiful young lady or the antics of the Monkey King who delights and outwits everyone. For the price of admission (10 yuan plus) guests are given copper coins which may be exchanged for a typical Old Beijing dish. These include such delicacies as almond and walnut puddings, rice flour cakes, noodles, sesame seeds buns with cured beef and the Old Beijing favorite, sour bean juice. The tea house (tel. 6301 4630) is on Beiwei Lu in the Xuanwu District, and opens its doors at 6:30pm for the 7:30pm performance.

Performing Arts

Bai tian kan miao, wan shang shui jiao (look at temples during the day and sleep in the evenings) used to sum up Beijing's cultural entertainment scene in the 1980s, but now a mixture of local and imported diversions are on offer in relative abundance every night of the week. Check listings in *Time Out* and *The Beijinger,* the Friday editions of *China Daily* and the fortnightly *City Weekend* for its what's on pages. And remember, the Chinese have been starved of music, dance, theater and movies for so long that a veritable culture-vulture society hovers to swoop down on tickets when they go on sale. So be sure to scan the press for the shows and book fast. If you find a box office is sold out, but still really want a ticket, scalpers usually loiter outside venues touting tickets at small premiums.

Acrobatics and Puppetry

The wonderful talents of Chinese acrobats should not be missed during any stay in China. If it's breakable, valuable, heavy or dangerous then it gets tossed by an acrobat somewhere in Beijing. Most provinces have their own troupes. Sichuan, noted for its short people who lend themselves well to acrobatics, have two troupe performings daily, 5:15pm and 7:15pm at the **Chaoyang Theater** (tel. 6507 2421), at 36 Dongsanhuan Beilu. Admission is 180, 280, 380, 480, 580, 680, 800 yuan. **The China Puppet Theater** (tel. 6424 3698, ext 8004) at Anhua Xili, Chaoyang District, has a show from 10:30am–2:00pm on Saturday and Sunday only. Admission is 50, 80, 180, 280 yuan.

Dance, Music, Film

A mixed bag of Western contemporary ballet, Chinese revolutionary operas and ethnic folk dance can be found in Beijing. The premier **Central Ballet of China** (tel. 6264 7003) performs both Chinese and foreign ballets: in recent years there has been a nostalgic revival of interest in *The Red Detachment of Women* and *The White Haired Girl*, while *Swan Lake* and *Giselle* always pull in the romantics. The troupe may perform at any of several venues, including the **Poly Plaza** (tel. 6500 1188 ext. 5682) located near the Dongsishitiao subway station. For Chinese folk dances try the **Oriental Song and Dance Ensemble** (tel. 6467 3042) playing at various venues. Classical music's main venue is the **Beijing Concert Hall** (tel. 6605 5812) at 1 Beixinhuajie. Chinese and touring foreign orchestras give concerts here.

The wonderful talents of Chinese acrobats should not be missed.

Beijing Opera (Peking Opera)

In the early 1990s it seemed that Beijing opera—a unique blend of acting, singing, dancing, music and acrobatics—was on its deathbed. Movies and video rentals were largely to blame for its demise, and then came along karaoke with what seemed like the final, fatal blow. Only a miracle could save the unique artform from being demoted to a mere tourist attraction. The miracle did come in the form of the genre's megastars: 1994 was the centenary of the birth of Beijing opera's two most famous actors, Mei Lanfang and Zhou Xinfang. Unfortunately, the trend did not last. Beijing opera is now struggling as much as ever, neglected by all but older audiences. The capital's premiere venue, the Zhengyici Theater, Xiheyan Dajie, Xuanwu District was torn down. This venue, originally built as a temple in 1620 during the reign of Wanli, became a theater in 1713. The Lao She Tea House and Tianqiao Acrobatic Theater, 95 Tianqiao Market Street, east end of Beiweilu, Xuanwu District (tel. 6303 6830, 9:30am–22:30pm) both put on shorter shows (*see* pages 218–219). Liyuan

Theater within the Qianmen Hotel (tel. 6301 6688, ext. 8867) has a pick of famous opera scenes, but for a spit and sawdust experience among mainly local opera buffs try the Huguang Huiguan (tel. 6355 3112) at 3 Hufanglu, Xuanwumen. However, performances are not held regularly.

An Iranian-born, British student of Beijing opera, Ghaffar Pourazar, regularly stages performances of Beijing opera in English. For schedules and information, contact him at beijingopera@yahoo.com or www.beijingopera.info.

Beijing opera profoundly affects the costumes and facial make-up of the other regional operas, such as the Cantonese opera.

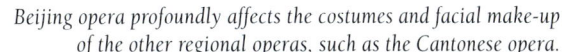

BEIJING NIGHTLIFE —by Paul Mooney

Visitors to Beijing may expect the communist capital to be a bit conservative, but actually, the most exciting nightlife in China can be found right here. Beijing has more bands per square meter than any other city in China, and a plethora of *ku* (cool) bars and clubs are springing up to accommodate the growing demand for nightlife entertainment. After decades of staid Marxism and Maoism, Beijing is rocking on into the night.

JIANGUOMENWAI

Xiu is without a doubt Beijing's hottest nightlife venue. Located on the sixth floor of the Park Hyatt Hotel, Beijing Yintai Centre, 2 Jianguomenwai Dajie, Chaoyang, this roof-top location features a wonderful open air terrace garden bar and separate theme bars in a fusion of traditional and modern pavilions. There's also live music and a dance bar. Before or after visiting Xiu, head upstairs to the **China Bar**, located on the 65th floor, with amazing panoramic views.

The Lan Club Lan is no doubt Beijing's most unique bar and the reason is simple. It's the work of the wildly innovative French designer Philippe Starke. The eclectic design makes one feel like he or she has stumbled into Alice in Wonderland. Lan offers a wide selection of New World and European wines and good cocktails. Lan also features an Oyster Bar, cocktail lounge, cigar divan and 45 private and VIP rooms. The bar is part of a sprawling restaurant with the same name. The individual bathrooms, equipped with a sofa and a swan-faucet sink, are a must see. LG Twin Towers, Building B1 Jianguomenwai Dajie, 4th floor.

Centro, one of the poshest bars in Beijing, proves that not all hotel bars are dull affairs to forget. The place has a bright contemporary design, good signature and classic drinks and real live jazz without the normal musical clichés. The place is packed most nights with visiting businessmen and Beijing's beautiful people. This is definitely a place where you want to arrive dressed to party. The Kerry Center,1 Guanghua Lu.

The **Chocolate Club** is the place where Beijing's Russian crowd parties late at night. Take the escalator down to the underground club where the decor is tacky, the music is techno and loud and the dancing girls are sultry. 19 Ritan Bei Lu, near the northwest corner of Ritan Park.

Finally, there's **Maggie's Bar**, Beijing's worst kept, longest running, inside joke. Go there and find out why. Leave the kids at home. Directly to the right of the south gate of Ritan Park and look for the red neon sign in English.

Sanlitun and Northeastern Beijing

Q Bar is said to mix the best drinks in the entire city, but this should come as no surprise. The bar is owned by Echo, who poured their way up and down the Sanlitun Bar street before opening their own place. The Martinis and Margaritas are excellent. In the summer enjoy yourself on one of Beijing's best rooftop patios. 6th floor, Eastern Hotel.

Apothecary, whose design was inspired by some of New York's coolest bars, offers New Orleans-style bar snacks and vintage cocktails in a sophisticated and intimate atmosphere highlighted by polished blonde woods and warm lighting. This popular venue was established by Leon Lee, a long-time Beijing resident, and Max E. Levy, one of Beijing's better known international chefs. 3rd floor, Nali Huayuan, 81 Sanlitun Beilu.

An art space during the day, **d.lounge**, which has a chic industrial look, with six-meter ceilings and exposed brick walls, transforms itself into a lounge in the evening. Courtyard 4, Gongti Beilu, next to the Ikazay Restaurant.

Bar Blu is one of Beijing's favorite night spots, with two different rooms offering two different types of music spun by imported live DJs. Special programs offered every night—ladies' night, drinks promotions, quiz night. The nice outdoor terrace is also an attraction in the warmer months. 4th and 5th floors, Tongli Studio, Sanlitun Back Street.

The cozy **Bookworm** has become a Beijing institution with its large collection of books and frequent talks by well-known authors from around the world. The venue has three distinct rooms: cafe/bar, restaurant serving European food, and hangout sofa room with new books for sale. There is also a nice roof terrace. The more than 11,000 books are spread throughout the venue. Building 4, Sanlitun South Street, Gongti Beilu.

Paddy O'Shea's has a distinct Irish pub look with its dark brown wood furnishings and high tables and stools. It serves draught Guinness and Kilkenny as well as premium whiskeys. Enjoy rugby or football screenings on one of the five large LCD screens. 28 Dongzhimenwai Dajie, opposite the Canadian Embassy.

The loungy and glamourous **Mesh**, so-named because of it's metal-mesh decor, is on the first floor of The Opposite House, one of Beijing's hippest boutique hotels. The bar, which has a wonderful decor, is the place to watch Beijing's beautiful people while sitting on one of its comfortable sofas. **Punk** is the sister dance club in the basement. 11 Sanlitun Beilu.

Special Topic

Gongti

The sleek **Fubar Peking**, tucked behind a secret door in Stadium Dog, has a sort of speakeasy feel. The bar is known for its inexpensive but great drinks, specialty cocktails and classic jazz. The bar's trademark is the Buddha Cocktail, which is served in a ceramic Buddha. Gongti Dongmen 10–11.

Vic's is a popular dance venue featuring top international DJs spinning hip hop, R & B and top 40 tunes. Inside the north gate of the Workers' Stadium.

Chaoyang Park Area

Wanna see where the diplomatic community and rich, attractive Chinese hangout? Tell your taxi driver to take you to "Chaoyang Gongyuan," Chaoyang Park. The area abutting the western gate of Beijing's largest public park is also among the preferred places to see and be seen. Don't go before 10.30 in the evening. Things get started late and keep going until the early morning. On the west side of the park, highly stylized and very, very cool, is the **World of Suzie Wong**, which may have more in common with the eponymous Richard Mason novel than anyone wants to acknowledge. As one local magazine put it, "get there early to put your feet up on the Ming Dynasty bed." West Gate of Chaoyang Park.

City Weekend called Bling Beijing's "only high-end hip-hop club." This sexy club boasts 26 VIP booths, a Rolls Royce Phantom DJ booth and silver-sequins-lined restrooms. What more can be said? Solana #5–1, No. 6 Chaoyang Park Road, Chaoyang Park

Houhai Area

North of Beihai Park, this once serene and quiet area has two lakes, Houhai and Qianhai, separated by a famous arched stone bridge dating back to the Yuan Dynasty. Once a quiet residential neighborhood most representative of what the capital once was, the banks of the lakes have almost overnight been turned into a new nightlife area with over 50 establishments to be found. This area is definitely worth a visit or two—great setting, and a whole range of different bars, from the trendy to the very relaxed, with plenty of places to sit outside. Take your time to wander and choose too.

China's best live jazz venue, **East Shore Live Jazz Cafe's** floor-to-ceiling windows provide great views of the lake. Sit back and enjoy the music, the view and good drinks. 2nd floor, Building 2, Shichahai Nanyan.

Walking south from the Drum Tower on Di'anmen Avenue, about 30 meters north of the McDonald's (the only one on the street), turn west into Yandai Xiejie, where you'll find a number of small and nondescript bars as well as a string of small shops selling Chinese arts and crafts. Continue on from here until you reach the lake where you'll find more bars, coffee shops and restaurants, many with lakeside seating in the warmer months.

No Name Bar is so named because it had no sign but became famous through word of mouth. The first bar to open in Houhai, the No Name Bar, has moved from its former lakefront spot to the quiter Dajinsi Hutong, a few blocks away. It has a tranquil terrace that is perfect for an alfresco meal or drink during the warmer months.

Another place in this area worth a visit is the new **Lotus Lane**, facing the southwest corner of the lake, where you will find about a dozen more upmarket restaurants, bars and coffee shops. Many of these venues have outside seating along the lake, as well as rooftop tables with lovely views overlooking the lake.

Gulou

About a ten minute walk to the east along Gulou Dong Dajie, on the left side of the street just past the north end of Nan Luogu Xiang, is the **Mao Live House**, where mainly Chinese go to enjoy local metal and punk bands. Set up by Japanese record label *Bad News*, this rock club has an amazing sound system in a warehouse-like space with worn-looking secondhand furniture and inexpensive drinks.111 Gulou Dongdajie.

Yugong Yushan, with its state-of-the-art sound system and voguish design, is without a doubt one of the capital's best spots for live music. West courtyard former site of Duan Qirui Government, 3–2 Zhangzizhong Lu.

Dashanzi

Outside of the main entertainment areas, a few bright spots exist. An old factory in Dashanzi (North of the Lido Hotel between the Fourth Ring road and the airport expressway), Factory 798, has become the trendiest art enclave in Beijing, best described as "Soho-esque". The area hosts a bunch of galleries, studios, exhibition space, design companies, restaurants and bars. The nicest bar here is on the first floor of the trendy and artsy Grace Beijing, a new boutique hotel set up in nicely refurbished old crystal factory. Have a drink in the cozy **Gossip Bar** and mingle with the crowd that makes up this industrially-chic artists' village.

Forbidden City

The **Yin Bar**, the multi-level rooftop venue that overlooks the east side of the Forbidden City, has one of the greatest views of any bar in Beijing. A great place for a drink as the sun sets. The Emperor Hotel, 33 Qihelou Street.

Wangfujing

The swankily dark **Red Moon**, tucked in a corner of the Grand Hyatt Hotel, has a little bit of something for everyone, with decent mixed drinks and premium whiskies, a wine bar, sushi bar and cigar lounge. There's also a live band playing modern music on traditional Chinese instruments. 1st floor, Grand Hyatt Hotel, Beijing Oriental Plaza, 1 Dong Chang'an Jie, Dongcheng.

Haidian

If you're really into music visit D-22, a bar-club that says it's dedicated to discovering and promoting talented young Chinese musicians and artists. The club, located across town in the university district, also brings in leading experimental musicians from around the world to perform here and work together with local musicians. D-22 boasts one of the best sound systems in China. 242 Chengfu Lu, Wudaokou.

For the latest news on nightlife and drinking in Beijing don't miss www.beijingboyce.com, which provides a lot of useful information about where to drink. Sister web site www.grapewallofchina.com is the place to look for news about wine in the capital. Also check out beijingboyce on Twitter for breaking news.

BEIJING: A CULTURE OF WALLS AND LANES —by Paul Mooney

Anyone who has flicked through a book of old black and white photographs of Beijing's former city walls, wandered through one of it's rapidly disappearing old alleyways, or read the personal memoirs of a Beijing resident of a century ago, cannot help but feel nostalgic for those olden days.

Although the bulk of the old capital has been erased over the past six decades, traces of colorful old "Peking" can still be found here if you take the time to scratch the surface a bit. Dongcheng District, with its quaint hutongs and historical sights, is one of Beijing's most interesting areas. A few hours spent exploring the streets will give you a better feel for the city's past. Xicheng District, which abuts Dongcheng, is an eclectic mix of old hutongs, or alleyways, courtyard houses and lakes interspersed with historical sights. In the Chongwen and Xuanwu districts, in the south of Beijing, one can still stumble across small traditional shops, decaying old European architecture, theaters featuring performances by Peking opera stars, comedians and acrobats, or street-side performers doing magic.

The makeup of the city began to change dramatically, however, with the arrival of the Red Army, which marched into Beiping on January 31,1949, on the heels of fleeing Kuomintang (KMT) soldiers. Beijing residents, who had suffered for decades under the control of ruthless warlords, corrupt KMT officials and the brutal Japanese military, welcomed their liberators. However, the new government did not bode well for a city that Edmund N. Bacon mused was "the greatest single work of man on the face of the earth...."

The Communist leadership was made up of staid outsiders who had no sentimental feelings about the ancient capital and no sympathy for modern cities. The government immediately set about transforming their new Red capital from a consumer metropolis to an industrial one. The same Russian experts who dismantled Moscow years earlier helped draw up the urban plan for Beijing as a new industrial hub. The city underwent a wrenching transformation, as ancient structures made way for bland, box-like Soviet style architecture and factories.

No doubt the most traumatic part of the urban renewal was the dismantling of the one thing that was most symbolic of the ancient capital—it's city walls. Anthony Tung has written in *Preserving the World's Great Cities* that the city walls were "unparalleled" and an extraordinary monument of world civilization, likening the structure to the ancient city of Teotihuacan and the great pyramids at Giza.

Liang Sicheng, a University of Pennsylvania-trained architect, who loved traditional Chinese architecture, had been commissioned by the Party to draw up a master plan to save the wall. Chinese urban planners compare his design to Le Corbusier's 1925 Voisin Plan for Paris, although the two plans are diametrically opposed. Le Corbusier wanted to erase the historic center of Paris, while Liang's plan called for cocooning old Beijing within the arms of the city walls as a living museum.

The government had a change of heart however, and opted instead for something more symbolic of the new socialist state. "We'll see a forest of chimneys from here," Chairman Mao Zedong allegedly gushed from atop the city wall, spreading his arms in front of him toward the horizon. Liang was broken-hearted. The city walls thus came tumbling down except for the odd gate or tower to make way for a new ring road and to supply bricks for the construction of the subway and a sprawling underground bomb shelter.

During the Cultural Revolution (1966-1976), rampaging Red Guards destroyed temples and historical sites, anxious to wipe out 'the four olds': old customs, old habits, old culture and old thinking. The city's idyllic courtyard homes were further damaged when new tenants started crowding into these spaces, building small structures inside the yards.

"The half of Beijing that was destroyed in the three decades from 1950 to 1980, constituted one of the single greatest losses of urban architectural culture in the twentieth century", laments Anthony Tung. Belgian Sinologist Simon Leys made a visit to Beijing in 1972 and was shocked when he went off to look for the city's famous gates and found them destroyed. "Peking now appears to be a murdered town," he wrote. "The body is still there, the soul has gone".

Urban spread in recent years continued the demolition of the city's charming hutongs and courtyard houses that escaped earlier attacks. However, patches of this old way of life remain, and the best way to scratch the surface of the city's past—before it disappears forever—is to walk through the remaining, but dwindling, hutongs—which one Chinese writer called "the soul of Beijing". For generations, he continued, people in Beijing have lived in a "culture of lanes".

No one seems to know exactly how many hutongs there are, with estimates running between 1,300 to several thousand. According to one old Beijing saying: "The major ones number 360, small ones are as many as the number of hairs on an ox". In other words, more than one can count.

It is known, however, that hutongs have been around for more than 700 years, dating back to the Yuan Dynasty (1271-1368), when Kublai Khan had his capital at Dadu, the site of present-day Beijing. In fact, the word hutong is believed to have derived from the Mongolian word hong tong, which means water well.

Peek inside a courtyard door and you'll likely see dozens of potted plants, and maybe the morning's vegetable shopping: a long string of entwined garlic bulbs hanging from a wall alongside strands of red peppers. Cabbages, onions, string beans, winter melons and eggplants sit on a windowsill. In the corner is a neat pile of honeycomb-like coal briquettes that are used for cooking and heating the house in the winter.

Architectural details, which can still be seen today, whisper secrets about the former owners of these once grand complexes. In the past, there was a strict hierarchy that dictated the architectural style of one's home. For example, the symbols on the front of a house described the owner's rank and social status. Homes with elaborate Chinese-style gates and spreading eaves were the former residences of imperial officials or wealthy businessmen, while the homes of commoners would have simple square topped gates, known as the "eagle will not alight" gate.

There are either two to four lintels above the doorway of each house that are often carved with auspicious Chinese characters. Common families would have two lintels, wealthy ones four. A typical phrase on lintels will have the characters "ru yi," or "as you wish". Others simply say "revolution". Wealthy homes also have decorative door clasps, cymbal-shaped door knockers, and protective brass wrappings often in the shape of a pomegranate.

The carved stone drums that sit on each side of the door of a courtyard house also indicate something about the status of the family within. Royalty would have dragons, common people artistic designs, and the poor a very small stone. The stones serve two purposes. One, they support the door axle, two, they were decorated to repel evil and attract good fortune. Some of the houses have intricate overhead brick carvings along the walls. Lions were used for the homes of military generals, elephants for civil officials, and plums, orchids and bamboo for scholars.

One good way to gain a leisurely close-up the insides of these houses is by visiting one of the restored homes of well known past residents of the city, many of which have been turned into museums. These houses are also an important part of the city's cultural history. Courtyard houses provided inspiration to scores of artists and writers. For example, the famous writers Lu Xun, Lao She and Mao Dun all lived in Beijing courtyard houses. "Without the hutongs, modern Chinese literature in China would only have been half as significant as it has," wrote one writer. The same can be likely also be said of Chinese art, as famous painters such as Qi Baishi and Xu Beihong also lived in beautiful courtyard houses in the city.

Maybe because of the jarring changes the city has experienced in such a short time, Beijingers are beginning to seek comfort in the things of the past. Photographers wander around the city, looking for those quintessential images of the city's old way of life, hoping to record them before they disappear forever. One group of concerned Beijingers has formed an NGO to protect the hutongs. Meanwhile, famous old shops, are enjoying a new found popularity and people are once again dining at their favorite old Beijing restaurants. Theater-goers are returning to once deserted theaters to watch dramas about the old city, to sing along quietly with Peking opera stars or to laugh at comedians doing xiangsheng, or comic dialogues, a folk art that was on the brink of extinction just a few years ago. Quaint old courtyard houses are being renovated and built anew for use as shops, restaurants, hotels and comfortable modern homes.

To be fair, Beijingers never really abandoned all their traditions. The city's parks remain crowded in the mornings with people practicing martial arts, sword-fighting, taijiquan, or kicking a shuttlecock around (although they are facing growing competition for space from others cutting up the sidewalks doing ballroom dancing and disco routines). Elderly Beijing men still fly their kites, raise crickets, play chess or mahjong on the street, or hang their ornate bird cages from tree branches, much as their ancestors have done for hundreds of years.

A Beijing writer lamented a few years ago that there was no longer any place in the city to hang one's bird cage, a sad reminder of the impact of rapid urbanization. But there are increasing signs that the city is seeking a way to balance tradition and modernity, and that there will be a branch to hang that bird cage on for a few more years to come.

Chinese Cinema Today —by *Paul Mooney*

After the Communists came to power in 1949, the cinema, like other art forms in China, did little more than serve politics, extolling the bigger than life exploits of workers, soldiers and peasant heroes performing miraculous feats in the factory, on the farm or on the battlefield.

That all began to change, however, after the launch of reform and opening up in the mid-1980s, which brought radical changes to the staid film industry. Most important was the arrival of the Fifth Generation of Chinese filmmakers, such as Zhang Yimou, Chen Kaige and Tian Zhuangzhuang, who were among the first graduates of the Beijing Film Academy after it reopened its doors following the Cultural Revolution (1966–1976). These young directors began to turn out non-orthodox films with China's rich past and present as a backdrop. Chen's *Yellow Earth*, with Yang behind the camera, marked the arrival of this group.

Zhang, a former factory worker turned cinematographer turned director, made the classic *Red Sorghum*, and then went on to turn out other hits such as *Raise the Red Lantern, Ju Dou, To Live,* and *Hero,* an ambitious cinematic effort that was nominated for an Oscar in 2003. Chen Kaige made the popular *Farewell My Concubine*, the moving story about the love between two opera performers that spans the period from pre-liberation up to the heady political days of the 1970s.

Gu Changwei's directorial debut, *Peacock* (2003), had none of the flash or gimmicks of recent blockbusters. There were no crouching tigers or hidden dragons, no kung fu hustle. This may help explain why the script for the movie, written by Henan writer Li Qiang, the author of a novel by the same name, gathered dust in directors' offices for some seven years without any takers. Several directors read it, but were ultimately afraid that such a simple story would flop at the box office. The thoughtful Mr. Gu, however, immediately recognized the script's potential and succeeded in turning it into one of the best Chinese films of recent years. Screenings in Beijing sparked emotional memories, by showcasing the collective suffering of the first three decades of Communist rule.

Mr. Gu called his film "a subtle investigation into the human condition" during a period of wrenching change. *Peacock* is the story of an ordinary family struggling to get ahead as China shifts from the post-Cultural Revolution period to the early days of reform. Chinese society is slowly opening up, offering the first glimmers of hope to the people who have survived the previous years of trauma. The artistic two-hour film—shot in a small city in Henan province in the local dialect—moves slowly but forcefully, with long camera shots and short but poignant dialogues. Mr. Gu's cinematography beautifully captures the blues and grays of urban life.

Probably China's finest cinematographer, Mr. Gu has shot films such as *Red Sorghum*, *Judou*, *Farewell My Concubine*, *King of Children* and *In the Heat of the Sun*, working with the best of the big-name directors such as Zhang Yimou, Chen Kaige and Jiang Wen. He spent several years in Hollywood gaining more experience working as a cinematographer on American films.

One prominent trend in China's cinema has been the Fifth Generation's obsession with the production of the Chinese blockbuster, a movement that has resulted in uneven results. Hoping to pull in bigger domestic and international receipts, local film producers have been willing to boost investments in larger projects, such as Chen Kaige's *The Promise* and Zhang Yimou's mega hits *Hero*, and *Curse of the Golden Flower*, the latter a lavish effort set during the Tang Dynasty about a despicable royal family.

The more rebellious Sixth Generation filmmakers, such as Zhang Yuan (*Seventeen Years*, *Beijing Bastards*, *East Palace West Palace*), Jia Zhangke (*Still Life*, *Xiao Wu*, *Unknown Pleasures*, *Platform*) and Wang Xiaoshuai (*The Days*,

Director Lu Chuan on the set of City of Life and Death.

Beijing Bicycle), and Lou Ye (*Suzhou Creek, Summer Palace*) began to grab the spotlight at international film festivals from Paris to Venice to New York in the 1990s, for their individualistic and unromantic portrayals of modern life in China. Many of the Sixth Generation films were shot cheaply, sometimes with hand-held cameras, and they had more of a documentary flavor. More often than not, these films, which focused on the lives of ordinary people and the negative by-product of China's rise, won praise abroad, but were deemed cinema non grata at home.

Working in China's tightly controlled environment, and outside the official cinema mainstream, these directors could not wait for the censors to give a nod to their films—which was unlikely to come anyway—and so they had to rely on themselves. Zhang raised the funds to make *Beijing Bastards* by directing music videos. Wang made *The Days* for a mere $10,000. "Desperate circumstances create principled outlaws," wrote Richard Corliss of Time. "The censors didn't intend this, but by their intransigence they helped spawn a truly independent film culture."

The wrenching transformation brought about by two decades of rapid social and economic change provided a fertile ground for the rise of what became known as the New Documentary Movement. Examples include Li Yang's *Blind Shaft*, a grim story about two ruthless con-men in China's dangerous mining sector, Wang Bing's monumental nine hour documentary *West of the Tracks*, about the slow decline of an industrial complex in Shenyang, and Li Hong's *Out of Phoenix Bridge*, in which the female documentarian depicts the experiences of four young women who leave their rural home, Phoenix Bridge, for the big city to work as maids and street vendors.

A more recent trend has been the appearance of post-Sixth Generation film makers known as dGeneration (d stands for digital), who rolled out very low budget films using digital technology. A prominent member of this movement is Ying Liang, whose films so far have all been set in Sichuan province, each focusing on a tragic character struggling to get by in Sichuan's gritty social millieu. His credits include *Taking Father Home*, *The Other Half* and *Good Cats*, the latter about a young man whose attempt to improve his life, at the behest of an ambitious wife, ends in tragedy. Peng Tao's *Little Moth*, about the very real problem of child exploitation throughout China, focuses on a handicapped girl who is adopted by parents who employ her in their begging business.

Japanese soldiers on the move in a scene from City of Life and Death.

City of Life and Death (2009), a somber movie about the Nanjing massacre of seven decades ago, was a box office hit, with ticket sales given a big boost by biting criticisms on the Internet that the film portrayed Japanese soldiers in too sympathetic a light.

The stunningly-filmed movie tells the story of the occupation of Nanjing by Japanese troops in December 1937, which carried out a brutal massacre over the ensuing six weeks. Known as *Nanjing! Nanjing!* in Chinese, the movie was shot in black and white with hand-held cameras.

A new trend in recent years has been a focus on the lives of everyday Chinese as they attempt to cope with a rapidly changing China. *Bachelor Mountain* is the story of San Liangzi, a jobless logger who has a child-like affection for a young woman named Meizi, who does not return his love. The movie is directed by Yu Guangyi, one of China's leading independent filmmakers and is the third in a series that examines the lives of men facing tough situations in contemporary China.

Buddha Mountain, directed by Li Yu, tells the story of three friends who aimlessly roam around the city of Chengdu, until they find themselves in serious trouble. They then fortunately meet an aging Beijing opera performer, played by Taiwan actress Sylvia Chang, who after a few twists and turns shows them the road to salvation.

Han Jie's absurd comedy-cum-romance *Mr Tree*, which critic Shelly Kraicer described as "a bit of Fellini, a hint of Jia Zhangke," is about Mr. Shu, who escapes his simple village for the big city lights of Changchun, where he unexpectedly finds love. After his marriage, he enters into a mixed state of reality and fantasy that is hilarious.

Food and Eating

Most Chinese restaurants outside China serve Cantonese, Sichuan or Shanghai food. The typical food of Beijing is rather different. Rice is not grown in north China as abundantly as in the south and the staple cereal is wheat. Steamed bread, dumplings and many kinds of noodles form the basis of any Beijing meal. The most commonly eaten vegetables are those of a northern climate—carrots, spinach, turnips, onions, scallions and large white cabbages.

Beijing has adopted and modified various northern cooking techniques—particularly for barbecueing or boiling mutton—which are not a special feature of its cuisine. But the capital's most celebrated dish, famous far beyond the borders of China, is 'Peking duck'.

White-feathered Beijing ducks are raised in the outskirts of the city. One such farm, near Landianchang alongside the Jingmi Irrigation Canal that flows out of Kunming Lake, can be visited on the way to the Summer Palace. For the last two weeks of their life, the ducks are force fed a rich diet of grain and beans. When they reach the kitchen, boiling water is poured over the bird, which is then hung for several

Maxims arrived in Beijing in the early 1980s.

hours to dry. The duck is basted with syrup, and air is pumped into it to separate the skin from the layer of fat underneath, so ensuring that the skin is crisped while the bird cooks on a spit. The skin, which is the delicacy, is eaten with small pancakes, scallions and a thick, salty bean sauce. After slices of meat have been eaten, the rest of the bird is often used to make stock for soup which is served at the end of the meal.

The other famous dish of Beijing is *shuanyangrou*, usually known in English as rinsed mutton. More suitable for winter than summer, cooking is done at the table in boiling stock contained in a charcoal-burning metal pot with a chimney. The diners themselves plunge finely sliced mutton into the stock, then vegetables, beancurd, and vermicelli.

Beijing has a long-established tradition of excellent restaurants which offer the best of China's many regional cuisines. This reputation is still well justified, and first-class restaurants serve food from Sichuan, Shanxi, Shandong, Hunan, Canton and Shanghai.

China has come a long way in recent years in terms of alcoholic beverages. Every province and city has one or more breweries, now turning better brews and more choices, such as new light and dark beers. It's also possible today to get beers from all over the world, and many of them on tap, such as Guiness, Kilkarney, Stella Artois, just to name a few. One of the most popular new trends is Belgian beers in all sorts of different flavors. There are some excellent rice wines, such as Shaoxing. The highly potent Chinese spirit Maotai, made from sorghum, is good for any flagging social occasion and is a great stimulus to speechmaking, but it is an acquired taste. There have also been significant advances in the production of local wines. The two best and most accessible Chinese wines are Grace Vineyard, which is produced in Shanxi province, and Helan Mountain, which comes from Ningxia province in far nortwest China. Decent bottles of these two wines are available for between 60–250 yuan.

Most of the restaurants listed below prepare set banquets for visitors, served in private rooms, which may be preferable for a special occasion or for large groups.

The quantity of food served at a banquet can sometimes be overwhelming—there may be as many as 15 courses. One way to avoid this is, when booking the meal,

Chinese street delicacies!

to stipulate only five or six courses and a low price per head. Banquet prices in Beijing generally range from 50–250 yuan a head, depending on the restaurant. Restaurants tend to close very early in Beijing. Hotel staff are usually very willing to help you book a table.

For a more adventurous dining experience that may be more of a photo opportunity than a culinary one, stroll past the intersection of Wangfujing and Jinyu Hutong where each evening private vendors set up stalls and offer a wide range of specialities that seemed prepared more to shock than delight. Offerings include fried starfish, goat testicles, a wide array of bugs, and much more.

Another restaurant area with a fine view of the Rear Lakes is Lotus Lane at Shichahai, which begins across the street from the north entrance to Beihai Park and extends along the shore of the lake for about 100 meters.

In recent years, countless new restaurants from around China, and the world, have opened in every corner of the city. Some occupy old residences, others are

The China New Year: Woman preparing cakes.
The Illustrated London News, January 12, 1861.

carved out of unused factory space, but most of them provide excellent food for surprisingly low prices. Perhaps the best way to judge a restaurant is whether or not it is crowded with Chinese.

Virtually all international-standard hotels have top-quality Chinese restaurants, although perhaps not as exciting as dining out in a local restaurant. They are particularly safe bets for the visitors staying for just a short while or those with sensitive stomachs. For Cantonese food (prepared under the professional eye of Hong Kong chefs), you could try the **Private Room** (tel. 8567 1838) at Park Hyatt which serves a particularly good *dim sum*; the **Celestial Court** at the St. Regis Hotel (tel. 6460 6688); the **Spring Garden** at the Holiday Inn Lido (tel. 6500 6688); the refined **Shang Palace** at the Shangri-La Hotel (tel. 6831 2211) and **Noble Court** at the Grand Hyatt Beijing (tel. 8518 1234). For those who can take the heat, the Grand Hotel's **Rong Yuan** Sichuan restaurant (tel. 6513 7788) sets tongues ablaze.

Cafe Society

Starbucks, the international coffee franchise, arrived in Beijing in 1999, opening its first location in China at the China World Trade Center. Travelers in need of a "half-caf latté" can get their fix in numerous locations in Beijing, especially on and around Jianguomen Avenue. There are two at the China World Trade Center, one in each tower; one at the Kerry Center, behind the China World and across the street; one next to the Jianguo Hotel, about 200 meters west of the China World; at Cofco Plaza, about 200 meters west of Jianguomen subway station; two at Oriental Plaza, which spans the entire block between Dongdan and Wangfujing; and another at the APM Shopping Center, just directly north of Oriental Plaza. No one ever need visit Tiananmen Square low on caffeine ever again. The Starbucks originally located in the Forbidden City was shut down after nationalistic Chinese complained about the foreign encroachment in one of China's most hallowed imperial sites.

Just north of the Confucian Temple is Wudaoying Hutong, which is home to dozens of small but cozy Western and Chinese restaurants, and cafes, which provides a soothing oasis for locals and travelers.

An excellent newcomer to the Beijing coffee scene is **Costa Coffee**, a British coffee shop chain, which has branches all over Beijing.

China's Favorite Take-out

—*By Steven Schwankert*

Beijingers may prefer the heavier, starchier foods of the north, and Shanghainese have their sweet tooth, but when it comes to dining out or take-away, diners in both cities agree on the pungent, spicy flavors of southwestern China's Sichuan.

Like pizza in the United States and curry in Britain, Sichuan food is the take-away of choice in China's larger cities. Just as Chinese restaurants are somewhat ubiquitous in many foreign countries, Sichuan (sometimes known abroad as Szechwan) restaurants pop up in just about every part of China.

The secret to Sichuan food's success is the spice. Although there are many excellent mild dishes, those with a hearty palate (and even stronger stomach) should try some of the region's hotter fare. Some popular favorites include *mapo doufu* (pock-marked grandmother's tofu: firm tofu cooked in chili oil with minced pork); *gan bian si ji dou* (stir-fried dried green beans with minced pork); *gan bian niu rou si* (strips of dried beef stir-fried with chilies); and *yuxiang qiezi* (fish-flavored eggplant, a spicy aubergine that never really tastes like fish). Instead of rice, consider a Sichuan staple, *dan dan mian*, a thin noodle mixed with chili oil and spring onion.

A special treat is *guoba rousi*, one that can be enjoyed by spice lovers and haters alike. A mild stew of pork slices, mushrooms, carrots, and pea pods is poured over crispy rice cakes, which sizzle as the sauce mixes with the rice. This is a dish to be enjoyed with at least four people lest they be overwhelmed by the sheer quantity of food.

Dining out for Sichuan food is also a social experience, especially if selecting Chongqing hotpot (*Chongqing huoguo*). At a typical hotpot restaurant, guests, sit at specially designed tables with a large hole in the middle, under which is placed a gas burner. Upon ordering, the server will bring a metal cauldron, split down the middle by a divider. On one side of the pot is a lighter-colored soup made from chicken stock. The opposite side is usually reddish in color, essentially a chili oil sauce guaranteed to set the tongue on fire.

Hotpot menus feature a large selection of meats, including beef, mutton, fish, vegetables, tofu, and noodles that will eventually find their way into the pot. Thinly sliced for fast cooking, beef and mutton withstand the boiling better than poultry, and also retain more of their original flavor after being dipped in either broth. Leafy green vegetables such as lettuce (*shengcai*) and cabbage (*baicai*) also work well, as do thin noodles like rice vermicelli (*fensi*).

However, diner beware: eating a meal so hot can cause gastro-intestinal discomfort the following day, which can make sightseeing or traveling a very unpleasant experience, so time your culinary trip to Sichuan appropriately. The night before hiking the Great Wall or flying back to your home country is probably not the best occasion to sample spicy food.

Meal time, 1905. Eating seems to have always been a social activity, whether dining in or out.

CURIOSITY-STREET, PEKIN.—FROM A SKETCH BY OUR SPECIAL ARTIST.—SEE PAGE 147.

Shopping

Chinese consumers are tough. Having cut their teeth mostly before market reforms came into effect, they are demanding, price-conscious, and like to test everything before they buy. Who could blame them? In the old days, after an item was purchased, there were no returns, no exchanges, and no refunds, so if it didn't work, that was your problem.

That said, the Beijing Rule of Shopping, also known in some places as the Moscow Rule of Shopping, still applies: if you see something you want, buy it when you see it. Although selection of goods and quality now is much improved, some items just aren't available everywhere. Even between branches of the same chain store, they may not have the same selection or sizes. If you like it, if you really want it, if it's perfect for your den/Aunt Bertha/Little Tommy, then buy now rather than fret later.

The other Beijing shopping rule of thumb is a cliché, but no less true: you get what you pay for. If you want to buy knock-off designer goods, that's fine, but chances are that if you pay 10 percent of the brand-name store price, it will also only last 10 percent as long before the zipper breaks or the fabric begins to wear.

In this case, do as the locals do: test anything you wish to buy, make sure it works, fits, and looks uniform. If it doesn't look right or work properly, move on.

Ask for a receipt, especially from larger stores. However, if you're buying from a market stall, there's no such thing, so be extra careful when making a selection.

Always bargain, especially in clothes and curio markets. If 100 yuan is the starting price quoted for an article, you should be able to obtain it for between 50 and 70 yuan. However, outlets of Western clothing and luxury goods purveyors will not likely bargain.

If you want to buy more than one of something, first bargain for the single item to establish an acceptable price. Then say you want to buy two or three and negotiate a discount for your multiple purchase.

Bargain in good faith. Unless you're ethnic Chinese and speak Mandarin fluently, you will never get as good a price as a Chinese person. Don't overpay, but at the same time if what your buying represents a good deal over a similar item in your home country, then spend your time doing something other than trying to knock a few yuan off a price.

To get the best deal you need time. Walk away and be reluctant to return. Don't show immediate interest in the item that you really want. Also, cash is king. Most places won't accept credit cards. If they do, they will charge you four percent more

Curiosity street, Pekin. The Illustrated London News, February 16, 1861.

to cover the service charge, and probably won't give you as good a deal because of the processing time required. The retailer also assumes you're not using cash, so you must have lots of money.

One piece of good news for shoppers: China has no sales tax or VAT, although more than one enterprising retailer has attempted to collect that tariff from unsuspecting tourists.

PLACES TO SHOP

Up until the 1990s there were just a couple of main shopping areas, such as Wangfujing and Xidan. Recent development has answered the needs of Beijing's near-14 million population with the construction of shopping centers in all parts of the city that feature prominent department stores.

A popular tourist shopping venue in Beijing is the Friendship Store, a short walk east on Jianguomenwai Avenue from the Jianguomen subway station. Look for the tall brown CITIC bank building. It's next door to that. A one-stop shop for stuffed toy pandas, cloisonné, and simple silk clothing, this is a good place to start for people who don't like shopping. It certainly doesn't offer the best quality in town, but

Wangfujing 2005.

prices are reasonable, staff is helpful if not always fluent in English, and there are Western food outlets there including Starbucks, and several bakeries.

Wangfujing

Beijing's most famous shopping street is Wangfujing. Once called Morrison Street after the Australian-born London Times correspondent who lived at number 98, the street is largely occupied by uninteresting commodity shops and international franchises within modern shopping malls. Of certain interest are: **Beijing Shi Baihuo Dalou** (literally Beijing City 100 Buys Big Building), which though having undergone modernization still carries many local lines and a vast array of goods. Nowhere is the impact of the arrival of Western culture more vividly illustrated than on the ground floor, where Beijing girls have face packs and volunteer for make-up demos offered by the world's biggest cosmetics makers. Elsewhere, check out the redeveloped **Beijing Arts and Crafts Store**, **Lisheng Sports Goods Department Store** and a couple of stores between the aforementioned two specializing in the sale of culinary equipment, a must for foodies who want to prepare authentic Chinese food back home. **Oriental Plaza**, on the corner of Chang'an and Wangfujing, has a number of Chinese and Western restaurants, a wide variety of shops and a modern cinema showing the latest foreign and Chinese films.

Wangfujing 1978.

The Village
Beijing's hippest new shopping area is The Village, which stretches north along the Sanlitun Bar Street. The Village is home to some of the best restaurants in Beijing, and also has excellent shopping for modern goods, include the first Apple Store in Beijing and the largest Adidas Store in the world, as well as dozens of other brand names. There's also a movie theater in the basement.

Xidan
Along with Wangfujing once one of the top shopping streets in Beijing. Extensively redeveloped, the street holds little of interest to the visitor as it is now occupied with characterless malls and international franchises. Around the Xidan crossroads (see the bike jams here during the rush hours), however, there are several wedding photo stores where newly-weds dress up to the nines in Western matrimonial splendor to take romantic portfolios.

Qianmen Area
Dazhalan, meaning "large stockades," is an area of town rarely visited by foreign visitors. During the Ming and Qing Dynasties, Dazhalan was both an entertainment district and a commercial center as shops and entertainment houses were allowed to be built and opened only south of the Qianmen (*men* means gate). Various legends are associated with this interesting old area of the city claiming that several emperors left the Forbidden City disguised as simple merchants to enjoy a night in one of the "song houses" that lined this narrow little neighborhood. Today, it is crowded with visitors from the provinces and therefore gives a foreign visitor a good idea of the colorful street life with stalls selling everything from lighters and fans to fruits, vegetables and clothing.

This area has been an established shopping neighborhood for over 500 years and many traditional stores still survive today. Visit the 400 year-old **Liubiju Pickle Shop** where several dozen porcelain jars stand in rows containing delicacies such as apricot nuts, spicy eggplant, lightly smoked tofu, spicy tofu, soft tofu, pickled cucumber, hot cabbage and other delights. The shop assistants are ready to help and explain, for example, why the apricot kernels are good for one's health, when to eat them and how to prepare them.

Looking for old-fashioned hand-sewn shoes? Visit the **Neiliansheng Shoe Shop** established in 1853. This famous shop was patronized by the Imperial family. It is said that in the old order books one can still find the measurements and preferred colors of generations of members of the Imperial family and their court officials. Hand-sewn cloth shoes are rarely seen on the streets of Beijing today on Chinese feet, but foreigners find them irresistible. The late Chinese leaders Mao Zedong and Zhou Enlai used to buy cotton shoes for distinguished visitors from this store.

The car has replaced the bicycle on the roads of Beijing, as it has in most big cities in China. Consequently, traffic jams and air pollution have become serious problems.

The shop was so important that there was a saying that those wearing shoes made here would be promoted. In fact the name of the shop means "internal promotion". Embroidered ladies satin shoes are very popular. These delicately embroidered shoes carry the auspicious designs of phoenix and dragon, peacock or a pair of mandarin ducks—a symbol of marital fidelity.

The **Ruifuxiang Silk and Cotton Fabric Store** was opened in 1893 and sells a variety of beautiful silk, cotton and woollen fabrics at reasonable prices. Here one can also see the old-fashioned way in which money was sent to the cashier and the change returned to sales lady to be given to the customer. The **Tongrentang Pharmacy** was established in 1669 and is the leading traditional Chinese medicine shop in Beijing. A "resident" doctor is available for consultation and oversees the preparation of remedies, which may be collected after the pharmacists have carefully selected such delicacies as ginseng, dried antlers and seahorses. It is interesting to watch the preparation of these medicines. At the back of the shop there is a whole wall of old medicinal cabinets from where the pharmacists fill the doctor's prescriptions.

The **Yueshengzhai Delicatessen**, located at 3 Qianmen Street, was opened in 1775. It is famous for its braised beef and mutton seasoned and marinated in soy sauce. The famous vegetarian restaurant **Gongdelin** has relocated a few blocks away

A large factory on Liulichang made the original glazed tiles for the Forbidden City.

to No. 2 Qianmen Dong Dajie and offers such vegetarian delicacies as "chicken cutlets in the shape of a lantern", "shrimp" in sesame paste and much more. The menu in itself isinteresting to read for the poetic names given to the various dishes that even a non-vegetarian will enjoy sampling.

On the east side of Qianmen, near the Gate, is the famous, state-owned Quanjude Kaoyadian (Old Duck Restaurant), which has moved back into a brand new building close to its original location. This 150-year old restaurant; chain has unfortunately become increasingly commercial in recent years and is no longer one of the best places to sample a duck dinner. That said, the restaurant usually has long lines snaking outside, so be sure to make a reservation.

Jianguomen

The area along the eastward continuation of Beijing's main thoroughfare of Chang'an Avenue known as Jianguomen is a popular and busy shopping and business district. Five-hundred meters east of Jianguomen subway station is the Friendship Store with Scitech Plaza across the avenue. Silk Street Market (**Xiushui Market**) is farther east towards the China World Trade Center.

Some people may lament that the original Silk Alley—once primarily a place for its namesake product—has been torn down. The new location of the Silk Market, or Xiushui Jie, is a four-story building called 'Silk Street', which sells the same things originally found in Silk Alley, including designer clothing of dubious origin. The name of the game here is inspect, inspect, inspect, and bargain, bargain, bargain. For anyone who still believes that China is a communist country in anything more than name, a morning or afternoon here will change that. Languages that may be heard include Chinese, English, Japanese, French, German, and Russian. Anything that can't be expressed verbally will be done using numbers on paper, calculators, and with fingers. Didn't bring enough local currency? No problem, most currencies are likely accepted by vendors.

Many of the products here are indeed fakes. Some are authentic products that "fell off the truck" and ended up here. Others are factory rejects, which may be perfectly good except for some minor flaw that will be hardly noticeable. Be aware that customs agents in some countries will confiscate counterfeit goods if found, so buyers be warned.

How to decide? If you like the item, test it out. If it passes reasonable muster, then bargain to a point where price is in line with expectations for performance. If that doesn't happen, walk away.

Liulichang

The charming old street known as Liulichang (Glazed Tile Factory) is best known for antiques, books and paintings. It has been completely restored, and the high concentration of shops, many privately owned, make it an attractive place to wander in, even if you do not intend to buy anything.

Liulichang was established over 500 years ago in the Ming Dynasty. Initially it was the site of a large factory which made glazed tiles for the Imperial Palace. Gradually other smaller tradesmen began to cluster around, and at the beginning of the Qing, many booksellers moved there. The area became a meeting place for intellectuals and a prime shopping district for art objects, books, handicrafts and antiques.

In 1949, Liulichang still had over 170 shops, but many were quickly taken over by the state. Inevitably, much of the street was ransacked during the Cultural Revolution. Following large-scale renovation of the traditional architecture, the street reopened in 1984 under the policy that the shops should only sell arts and crafts and cultural objects. The street is a mixture of state-run and privately owned shops. You will be encouraged by owners of the latter to step inside, browse and bargain. Staff in state-run shops have a minimum price for stock so it is acceptable to bargain here as well. Shops that accept credit cards and have the largest amount of English signage will also be the most expensive.

Markets

Beijing has dozens of markets or streets specializing in the wholesale or retail sale of specific commodities. While some are of great interest to the visitor, others are sector vignettes showing the development of the economy.

Many such markets, including the former thriving **Russian Market** at Yabao Lu, along the Second Ring Road north of Jianguomen, have been torn down or slated for demolition to make way for commercial office and retail space.

Antique markets are the best places to browse for a special gift whether the item in question is old or not so old. From bird and cricket cages to antique desks, old Chinese wedding beds or 1920s and 1930s Shanghai calendar girl posters, porcelain, scrolls, calligraphy or costumes—all is to be found in one or the other of the markets. The best known locations for antiques are the **Jinsong Curio Market** and the **Panjiayuan Dirt Market**.

The **Panjiayuan Dirt Market**, south of Jinsong Nanlu—about a ten-minute taxi ride from the China World Hotel, just off the Third Ring Road—is open Saturday and Sunday mornings from dawn. The wheeling and dealing continues into the

Countless, priceless treasures were shamelessly looted by foreigners during their occupation of China following the Opium War of 1856–1860. The Illustrated London News, April 13, 1861.

FRENCH SPOILS FROM CHINA RECENTLY EXHIBITED AT THE PALACE OF THE TUILERIES.—SEE PAGE 339.

afternoon, but some of the best stuff is gone by noon. Mainly in open air, most on offer is of curio-value or fake, but great buys have been made by those in the know. It's one of the few places to buy decent arts and crafts by local artisans. This is a market more for China's recent past than its ancient. The patient and the early can find gems from China's revolutionary history, with sheaves of Cultural Revolution posters and kitsch items to be found. Unlike the **Silk Market**, the atmosphere here is friendly, and prices are generally low. It's more flea market than bazaar. For directions and information (in Chinese only) call 6775 2405.

The **Hongqiao Market** near the east gate of the Temple of Heaven is best known for the contents on its fourth floor where one finds cultured pearls, semi precious stones, coral, silver jewelry and antiques. The **Jinsong Curio Market** is also known

Sundial, Forbidden City.

as Curio City. Located near the Panjiayuan exit from the Third Ring Road it has three floors of shops selling everything from new to antique furniture, rugs, paintings and porcelain.

Temple Fairs

In old Peking, religious rituals at Taoist and Buddhist temples were often accompanied by temple fairs, basically street markets where everything from food to antiques to jewelry was sold by pedlars who set up stands or simply spread their goods on a cloth on the ground. In this century, the fairs gradually shed their religious appurtenances and became purely commercial ventures where the average Beijing citizen could buy things at low prices.

Large fairs took place at five Beijing temples from three to 10 or more days per month. In recent years, these fairs have been revived, although they are held only during the Spring Festival, the lunar New Year, which usually falls in late January or early February. The fairs feature traditional toys and snacks, performances of feats of strength, ballads and opera, and general merchandise. The principal sites for these fairs are: Ditan Park, White Clouds Temple (*Baiyunguan*), Longtanhu Park, Big Bell Temple, former Imperial College (*Guozijian*), and the Drum and Bell Towers. The Dongyue Temple, on Chaowai Street, hosts one of the more authentic and interesting temple fairs in Beijing.

Shopping Suggestions

Antiques

Antiques that can be exported must bear a red seal, although the red seal does not guarantee that an item is necessarily an antique worthy of the name. On the whole, the oldest pieces date from the middle to late Qing period—between 100 and 150 years old. Many pieces sold as antiques may be no more than 50 or 60 years old, but the shop assistants in the state-run stores are generally truthful about the period of any particular item, when asked. The **Yueyatang** in Liulichang is the exception. Here it is possible to purchase much older *objets d'art* such as Ming porcelain, Tang carvings, Zhou coins, and very old paintings and calligraphy.

Most antiques for sale already have a red export seal on them—be sure to keep these on, as you may be required to show the items as well as the receipts to customs on departure. Should you buy antiques which do not have a seal, it is advisable to have one fixed. This involves a visit to the Beijing Arts Objects Clearance Office situated in the compound of the Friendship Store, open 2:00pm–5:00pm on Mondays and Fridays. A small fee per piece is charged.

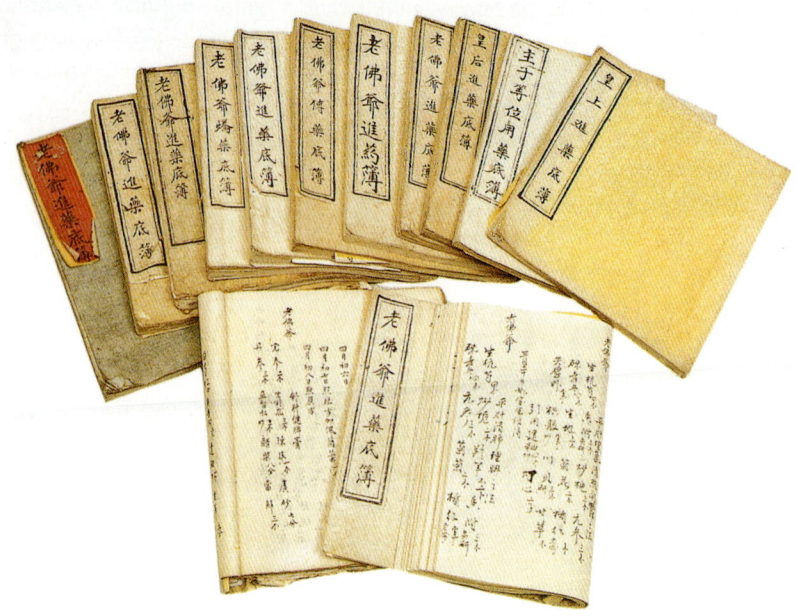

Records of medical prescriptions for Emperor Guangxu and Dowager Empress Cixi, Palace Museum Collection.

The best-known antique shops in Beijing are in Liulichang. **Yunguzhai** at 80 Liulichang East, is famous for its antique ceramics—vases, plates, bowls, bird-feeds and jars, bronzes and stone Buddhist carvings as well as jade and ivory carvings.

On Zhushikou Dajie, just opposite the Fengzeyuan Restaurant, is another shop, the **Zhenyunge**, which has antique porcelain vases, pots and dishes, lacquer boxes, cloisonné, jewelry and miscellaneous objects of interest.

Another shop of particular interest is the **Huaxia Arts and Crafts Store** at 12 Chongwenmennei Daijie. Foreign residents call this store the 'Theater Shop' because of its collections of old Beijing opera gowns and costumes. Although not strictly an antique store, the assortment is fascinating. The first floor has sections selling embroidered linen, old fur coats, carpets and restored pieces of old Chinese furniture. Upstairs are elaborate blue kingfisher-feather hairpins, children's silver pendants, brass ink-boxes and incense burners, Buddhist mantra beads, small old pieces of embroidery and braid and odd pieces of pure kitsch of Chinese, Russian, Japanese and European origin.

Books

All four and five-star hotel bookstores carry a selection of books, guidebooks, and international newspapers and magazines. The third floor of the **Xinhua Bookstore**, at the south end of Wangfujing, has a large selection of English fiction and non-fiction, including a wide array of books on China. **The Foreign Languages Bookstore**, 219 Wangfujing, stocks books in a number of languages printed by Beijing's Foreign Languages Press as well as some foreign paperbacks, guidebooks and news magazines. Art books on many aspects of China's culture and her treasures are handsomely reproduced. Translations of Chinese novels and short stories, both modern and classical, are most reasonably priced, as are dictionaries, booklets and pamphlets on a wide range of subjects.

The Friendship Store once had a large selection of books on China, but has now reduced the size of it's book shop. The best collection of art books in Liulichang is at **Zhaohua Calligraphy and Paintings House**, 4 Liulichang Xijie.

Maps of every province of China can be purchased at the China Cartographic Publishing House on Baizhifang Xijie in Xuanwu District.

The largest bookstore in town is the Beijing Book City on the north side of Chang'an Avenue just east of the Xidan crossroads. Though stocking mainly Chinese books, titles in foreign languages are available on the second and third floors. The store is more user-friendly than most with benches provided for browsers to sit and read. Elsewhere, there is Haidian Book City, actually a congregation of bookstores and a good source of materials for those studying Chinese. Lufthansa Shopping Center, fourth floor, has a very good range of travel and history books.

The most pleasant place to shop for books in Beijing is Liulichang. The large traditional compound on the east side of the intersection of Liulichang Dongjie and South Xinhua Jie called *Haiwang Cun* (Village of the Sea King) has been taken over by the China Bookstore (*Zhongguo Shudian*). The store sells mostly new Chinese books, but there is a large selection of used Chinese, Japanese and Western books in the building lining the east side of the courtyard.

A spacious café-cum-library offering gourmet eats, guest lectures and eclectic literature, **The Bookworm** offers an ideal place to share a drink with friends, have a family meal, or take advantage of the 14,000 English language books that comprise the library. Open daily from 9:00am–1:00am at Yard 4, Sanlitun South Street, Gongti North Road Chaoyang District, Beijing. Tel. 6586 9507; Fax. 6503 2050. Email: books@beijingbookworm.com; www.beijingbookworm.com

Carpets

New Chinese carpets of all sizes, in classical and contemporary designs in wool and silk, may be seen at the **Friendship Store** and at the carpet pavilion in the Round City at the entrance to Beihai Park. **Beijing Arts and Crafts**, 200 Wangfujing, also has a good collection of both Chinese and Central Asian carpets, but prices are high. Prices at **Jinchang**, 118 Liulichang East, or at the Beijing No. 5 Carpet Factory on Xiao Liangmaqiao Lu, are marginally better than at the Friendship Store and Beijing Arts and Crafts. Several stores in the west section of Liulichang sell old carpets, as does the Huaxia Arts and Crafts Store at 12 Chongwenmennei Dajie.

Silk

The **Yuanlong Embroidery Silk Store**, near the north gate of Tiantan Park, has a history of more than 100 years of handling silk and embroidery and offers a tailoring service. The **Beijing Silk Store** at 5 Zhubaoshi in Dazhalan started business in 1840 and also undertakes tailoring orders at reasonable prices.

Showroom of a lantern merchant, Peking, Thomas Allom, 1804–1872.

Furniture

The widest selection of renovated original furniture is available at the **Liangma Antique Furniture Market**, which moved to a new address about 1 kilometer east of the Kempinski Hotel—27 Liangmaqiao Lu, Chaoyang District, 9:30am–6:00pm daily. Tel. 6467 9664. The Friendship Store and department stores such as Lufthansa offer reproduction period furniture. A wide selection is available at the **Huaxia Arts and Crafts Store** (*see* page 63). Plainer Ming-style chests and cupboards with attractive brass fittings, upright chairs and cabinets are to be found at the **Donghuamen Furniture Shop**, 38 Dongsinan Dajie. Most of the pieces here are reasonably old and have been restored in the workshop located behind the store.

Jewelry

Modern and traditional styles of jewelry set with semi-precious stones are for sale in many of Beijing's tourist shops. You may find old pieces of silver in the form of pendants which were traditionally worn by children as good luck charms, small needle-holders which women wore hanging from their jacket-button, pill-boxes, or bells. Chinese skill in cutting and working jade is seen in the artistry or carved figurines, vases and medallions. **Wenfangsibaotang** at 99 Liulichang Xijie has a good selection of jewelry, and **Peiwenxuan** at 37 Liulichang East is a small, charming shop selling attractive jewelry and small trinkets.

Painting and Calligraphy

Fan paintings, embroideries, original old scroll paintings and calligraphy by some of China's master painters are found in the famous **Baoguzhai**, in picturesque premises at 63 Liulichang Xijie.

A favorite shop is **Rongbaozhai** at 19 Liulichang Xijie. Here reproductions of old paintings, rubbings and the works of modern painters may be found. This shop specializes in art materials, and its clients are mostly artists, amateur and professional, who lovingly feel the quality of the reams of handmade paper and discuss the merits of the squirrel-hair brush as opposed to the fox-hair brush. Decorative blocks of ink are for sale as are the various porcelain accoutrements of Chinese painting. Behind the shop are block-printing workshops well worth investigating.

Moyuange, at 61 Liulichang East, is another good shop for paintings. **Beijing-Anhui Sibaotang**, on Liulichang East, is a specialist dealer in the 'four essentials' of Chinese calligraphy: paper, ink, brush and inkstone.

Contemporary Chinese painting, including oil painting, now commands great interest and high prices on the international art market. Regular shows are held at the **Red Gate Gallery** in the Dongbiamen Watch Tower (tel. 6525 1005), the

Wan Fung Art Gallery at 136 Nanchizi Street, east of Tiananmen Square (tel. 6523 3320) and the artists' colony, **798 Space**, 4 Jiuxianqiao Rd, Dashanzi Art District, Chaoyang District (tel. 6438 4862).

PORCELAIN

While wandering about the streets the visitor will find many small local shops stocking cheap, everyday porcelain and pottery, rice bowls, storage pots and small ornaments which are often quite appealing. In Qianmen Dajie, the Hunan Pottery Products Store (No. 99) has tea sets, bowls, plates, vases and ornaments all made in Changsha, capital of Hunan Province. The Jingdezhen Porcelain Shop has products from the principal porcelain center in China, Jingdezhen in Jiangxi Province. The Beijing store is located at 150 Qianmen Dajie, Chongwen District (tel. 6303 2613). Open 9:00am to 6:00pm. Pottery has been made at Jingdezhen since the second

Pavilion of Viewing Scenery, the Summer Palace.

century BC and during the Northern and Southern Dynasties (317–589) its porcelain graced the tables of the imperial court. Both Chinese and Western dinner services are for sale in various designs, including the famous blue and white rice pattern.

SEALS AND INKSTONES

Seals or chops engraved with one's name are a good and useful purchase. While scholars of old paid large sums for rare stones with well-cut characters, visitors can buy cheaper ones at many arts and crafts stores in the city. The cheapest stones, including the carving of your name in both scripts, plus a box, start at about 25 yuan. Most expensive *chicken blood stones* can cost thousands of yuan. Orders can sometimes be fulfilled on the spot in less than 10 minutes. Cutters can transliterate foreign names into Chinese. The cheapest stones, including the carving of your name in both scripts, plus a box, start at about 50 yuan.

A NOTE ON CHINESE ARTS AND CRAFTS

Jade carving is rather expensive but for those who wish to buy some exquisitely carved jade there are several workshops. Be aware that jade is a hard stone, therefore it is very difficult to carve and intricate designs can demand a high price. Cloisonné or enamel-work is an ancient art form peculiar to Beijing, dating back to the 15th century. Price varies from a few yuan to several thousands. It is painted in brilliant colors over thin copper, over which the delicate patterns are laid-out in fine copper wire filled with colored enamel glaze. Papercuts are very popular and are beautifully designed with flowers, birds, figures, and scenes from famous tales and stories. They are particularly popular around Spring Festival when they are used as window and door decorations. This folk art dates back to the Tang Dynasty. There are two styles, the northern style with sharp and forceful lines, and the southern style with delicate and more intricate lines.

Snuff bottles of all kinds of shapes and sizes can be purchased. Some are painted from inside with a tiny brush and a magnifying glass. Those not painted are made of either glass or semi-precious stones. One of the best stores to buy old snuff bottles is found in the Summer Palace, near the Marble Boat. The most spectacular brass pieces one may see around Beijing streets are enormous brass tea pots and brass fondue pots. The most famous brass shop is just off the crossroad of Tianqiao and Qianmen Street. Here you can buy a Mongolian hot pot for around 400 yuan or a giant teapot for 1,500 yuan. Not everything in the shop is for the kitchen, there are brass candlesticks, paperweights, and brush stands.

The British Legation, Peking. The Illustrated London News, March 15, 1873.

Sports, Recreation and Leisure

'Running water never goes stagnant, and a door which is often opened never has a rusty hinge,' sums up the Chinese attitude to the importance of keeping fit. But tradition never took into the account Beijing's increasingly polluted air, especially during the often cloudy summer season.

For vigorous exercising, it is essential to get up and out at dawn before fumes are choking. College campuses always have sports fields and tracks, and being a few hundred meters away from the nearest roads, have cleaner air to breathe. Social joggers can run with **Beijing's Hash House Harriers**. For information on Hash House Harriers see *City Weekend,* available at most coffee shops, as well as hotel lobbies. For a peaceful run make a bid for the Western Hills. The gates of the Summer Palace are open free to dawn patrollers before 6:30am, while a little further out west, Fragrant Hills, for just five yuan admission, is a great place for a jog or a brisk hike up Incense Burner Mountain. Getting there by bicycle could make the outing into a bi-athlon: for longer rides just head northwest. Serious cyclists can find good quality frames, with Japanese Shimano components and accessories, including helmets, at **Giant** bicycle shops, which can be found throughout Beijing.

Join the locals for regular sessions of tai chi exercise, sword dancing, and early morning disco and ballroom dancing in Beijing's parks. Sessions begin at 6:00am and usually are over by 8:00am. The Temple of Heaven offers the entire scope, from simple tai chi exercises to ballroom dancing. Other parks, such as Beihai, Ditan, Ritan and Zhongshan, are also very much alive. One may join in any of the activities, and the local people are very happy to teach guests the various slow but highly beneficial stretching movements and breathing routines.

The great outdoors can take on a special meaning for those with hiking boots.

First class indoor facilities can be found in the leading 5-star hotels around Beijing, all of which have indoor pools. Several luxury hotels offer sports facilities. The **Friendship Hotel** (tel. 6489 8888, ext. 32), within a garden complex, has two swimming pools, one indoor and one outdoor, two tennis courts, a golf driving range, snooker tables and a mini gymnasium. Take a dip in the complex where two dozen world records were set during the 2008 Summer Olympics. Beijing's famous Water Cube has been turned into a water park that features a wave pool, lazy river, spa area and 13 water slides and rides, including the Bullet Bowl, Speed Slide and Tornado. Outdoor swimming in lakes is enjoyed all over Beijing, most notably at Shichahai, outside Song Qingling's former home and on the east shore of Qianhai. These are also famous winter swimming spots where clubmembers from groups such as *Bei Xiong*, Polar Bears, break the ice and enjoy a few minutes chill. However, be aware that this is not the world's cleanest water, and may contain anything from algae to untreated sewage. That doesn't stop many old timers from swimming there each day. Ice skates and sleds can be hired for use on specially-prepared, cordoned-off stretches of ice. The season is usually December and January and is most idyllic on the Summer Palace's Kunming Lake and on Beihai.

The great outdoors can take on a special meaning for those with hiking boots heading out to the wilds of Beijing's Great Wall country.

Golfers fed up with bucket and net practice can have a downtown nine-hole round at the **Beijing Chaoyang Golf Club** (tel. 6500 1149). For a full round, head out to the Ming Tombs. You know you are nearing the **Beijing International Golf Club** (tel. 6076 2288) when local peasants seemingly jump out of the bushes into the path of your car waving bags of the latest cash crop: Dunlop 65s, Penfold Aces and Titleist golf balls—fished from a lake on the course. The opulent **Pine Valley Golf Resort and Country Club** (tel. 8528 8038), some 35 miles west of Beijing, is situated on 1,000 acres of lush green fairways that seem somewhat out of place in the parched surroundings. They include an 18-hole Jack Nicklaus Signature Course and a brand new 27-hold Jack Nicklaus II Links Course, designed by Jack Jr. These challenging courses offer spectacular panoramic views of the nearby mountains and far glimpses of the Great Wall at Badaling. There are two clubhouses, a 5-star boutique hotel, corporate villas, a SPA offering Thai massages, an Equestrian Club, a Pet Hotel and even a helipad. In case you are wondering, club membership in Pine Valley will set you back US$150,000. An alternative, near the airport, is the 36-hole **Beijing Country Golf Club** (tel. 8947 0005).

There are currently more than 30 equestrian clubs in Beijing with a membership of around 4,000 people and a stable of around 1,000 horses. For centuries, in the West, horseback riding has been the sports of the well-to-do. During the late 19th and the early 20th century it was a sport for the foreigners who lived in Beijing. In those days the riding was limited to strong Mongolian ponies. The sport has seen a massive rise in popularity in recent times. The **Zhongxing Equestrian Sports Club** (tel. 8481 5854) is located north of the Xiaoqing River in Chaoyang District. **The Equeeles International Riding Club** (tel. 6432 4946; www.equriding.com) at 91 Shunbai Road, Sunhe Zhen, Shunyi County is also worthwhile.

For watchers, not players, national and international competitions are held at the Worker's Stadium, Capital Gymnasium and Olympic Center: check the English-language press for details. On TV, CCTV 5 is an all-day sports channel.

"The Great Wall is more than history: it is landscape, many landscapes, part of the very geography of north China."—William Lindesay, Images of Asia: The Great Wall, 2003.

DIVE BEIJING —by Steven Schwankert

Landlocked Beijing is better known for its spring dust storms than for anything resembling a white-sand beach. Indeed, the city's most significant bodies of water are all man-made. So who would think to go scuba diving here?

An increasing number of foreign visitors, residents, and local outdoor enthusiasts are taking the plunge at Beijing's three aquariums. In the late 1990s, the push to create aquatic environments in the capital resulted in the opening of the Blue Zoo, a Sino-New Zealand joint venture, at the south end of the Workers' Stadium complex. This was followed by the Taipingyang Aquarium, near the Beijing Television Tower in western Beijing, and finally, the opening of the Beijing Aquarium in the Beijing Zoo complex, the largest of the three with the most diverse selection of aquatic life.

For those who prefer a more interactive experience, both the Blue Zoo and Taipingyang offer dives in their main tanks. Both dives cost approximately 650 yuan and include a one-tank dive and admission to the respective aquarium. Prior scuba experience is not necessary but always recommended.

Dives are accompanied by divemasters, who will demonstrate proper techniques for interacting with the aquarium's inhabitants, including stroking the tails of sleeping sharks. Creatures in either tank are accustomed to being approached by divers, so there is no danger in interacting with them in a manner approved by the divemaster.

For more information on scuba experiences available in and around Beijing: e-mail: steven@sinoscuba.com.

Places of Worship

Although China is officially an atheist country, there are three distinct religious philosophies: Taoism, Confucianism and Buddhism. Although all three have separate origins, Taoism, combined with animistic beliefs of how to keep harmony with the universe, is the only true Chinese religion. Confucianism is a philosophy and Buddhism came from India. They are in fact entwined. Other religions such as Islam, Christianity and Judaism entered China at various times. Islam came to China via the sea merchants who came from Arabia and established their mosques in Guangzhou and other coastal cities, while overland merchants established mosques in north-west China. Christianity first entered China during the seventh century when the Syrians presented Christian scriptures to the Tang Dynasty court at Chang An (*Xi'an*). However, it was not until the 16th century that Jesuit missionary Mateo Ricci set up his base in Guangdong, and eventually made his way up to Beijing where he was presented to the Emperor. Between the 17th and 19th centuries, a large number of Catholic and Protestant missionaries established churches in Beijing and other cities in China. The Catholic missionaries brought with them to China Western science and astronomy.

Churches and other Places of Worship

St. Michael's Catholic Church, A13, Dongjiaominxiang, Dongcheng District, (tel. 6513 5170). Services on Saturdays at 7:00am and on Sundays at 7:00am and 8:00am and 6:00pm.

St. Joseph's Catholic Church, 74 Wangfujing Street, Dongcheng District, (tel. 6524 0634). Services on Saturday at 6:30am and Sundays at 6:30am, 8:00am and 6:00pm.

Northern Cathedral, 33 Xishiku Street, Xicheng District, (tel. 6617 5198). Services every morning at 6:00 am and 7:00am and Sundays at 6:00pm. (Catholic)

St.Mary's Southern Cathedral, 141 West Qianmen Street, Xuanwu District, (tel. 6603 7139). Services every morning at 6:00am and 7:00am and Saturdays at 6:00am and 6:30pm. An English language service is held at 10:00am on Sundays. (Catholic)

Catholic mass is also held at the **Canadian Embassy** (overseas passport holders only) on Saturdays at 5:30pm and at the **British Embassy** (overseas passport holders only) on Sundays at 11:00am.

Chongwenmen Protestant Church, D2, Hougou Hutong, Chongnei Street, Dongcheng District (tel. 6513 3549). Services on Monday, Tuesday, Thursday and Saturday at 7:00pm and Sundays at 8:00am and 10:30am.

Gang Wa Shi, 57 Xisi Nan Lu, Xicheng District, (tel. 6617 6181). Services every Tuesday and Thursday at 7:00pm, every Wednesday and Friday at 8:00am, and Sundays at 7:00am, 8:30am, 10:30am and 7:00pm. (Protestant)

Zhushikou Protestant Church, 129 Qianmennan Dajie, Chongwen District (tel. 6301 6678). Services on Tuesday, Thursday, Friday and Sunday at 8:30am and 10:00am and Wednesdays and Saturdays at 7:00pm.

Judaism has been practised by Jewish traders who have been visiting China for well over 1,500 years. For information on Jewish services in Beijing contact *Kehillat Beijing* through www.sinogogue.org (tel. 6467 2225).

Islam came to China over 1,000 years ago by sea and via the Silk Road. In Beijing there are some 200,000 Moslems or *Hui* (as they are known in China), and 50 mosques for them to worship in. The largest are the **Niu Jie** (Ox Street) **Mosque** (tel. 6303 2564) in the southern part of the city, formerly a Moslem quarter, and the **Dongsi Mosque** (tel. 6525 7824), which dates back to the Mongol or Yuan Dynasty.

Taoism was practised in many monasteries in the city, the majority of which have been closed since 1949. The largest remaining city monastery, the **White Clouds Taoist Monastery**, (*Baiyunguan*) on Binhe Jie, Guang'anmenwai, (tel. 6346 7179 and 6346 3887), also houses the China Taoist Association.

Buddhism came to China around the time of Christ and has had a profound influence on Chinese thought, art, architecture and cuisine. Buddhist temples in the urban and suburban areas are described in the Sights section of this book. Listed here are three places of active worship: **Guangjisi** on Fuchengmennei Dajie, (tel. 6616 0907); **Fayuansi** on Fayuansi Qianjie, (tel. 6303 4171); and the **Yonghegong**, or Lama Temple, 72 Yonghegong Jie, (tel. 6404 9027).

The distant White Dagoba on Qionghua Island stands out from the yellow-tiled rooftops of the Forbidden City.

A Seventeenth-Century Prison

As for the good Government, Quietness and Ease and Cleanliness of the Gaol, I do not question but it exceeds ours in Europe. As soon as we were brought into the First Court we spy'd the Head Gaolor, who sat in great State on his Tribunal-seat; he presently ask'd for the 'mittimus' of the Criminal Judge that had sent us to him. But him we had not yet seen, (for he was still not come to himself after a great Feast he had been at the day before) so one of his Deputies sent us to Prison. Then the Gaolor began to examine us concerning our coming to China, upon what intent it was, what we liv'd upon, &c. We answer'd him with a great deal of freedom and ease, the Consequence whereof was that they put us in through another little Door which was lock'd, and had a porter at it; we went on through a Lane, and they brought us to an Idol Temple. I don't know that in the Prisons in these our Countries there is any Church of God so great, so spacious, so clean, so neat, and so much frequented by the Prisoners as that is. In all the Gaols, Dungeons and Courts of Justice throughout the Empire, they have Temples richly adorn'd, and cleanly, where the Prisoners, and such as have law-suits make their Suits; but, those Wooden and Earthen Images neither hearing nor seeing, they give no Relief to their Suppliants. At Night they turn'd us through another Lesser Door into a Court, and then convey'd us into a great Hall, quite dark and dismal, without any Window and so full of People, that there was hardly room for them to stand; this was call'd the little Prison to distinguish it from the Dungeon which was far enough from thence. Here we continued 40 days, having always Light at night and there was an Overseer who took care no Noise should be made. All Men were wonderful submissive to him, so that there was no roaring, or noise, or quarrelling, but all as hush'd as if it had been the Novice-house of a well govern'd Monastery, which we did not a little admire.

Domingo Fernandez Navarrete
The Travels and Controversies of Friar Domingo Navarrete, 1618–1668 (Vol. 1)
Ed. J. S. Cummins. Cambridge University Press; Published for the Hakluyt Society
at the University Press; 1962

A Dominican missionary, Domingo Fernandez Navarrete (1618–1686) was archbishop of Santo Domingo. His travels took him to Mexico and Manila, the East Indies, Mindoro and Macasar, Macao, Canton, Peking, Malacca, India and Madagascar.

Te Sheng Men (Deshengmen), outer wall of the old city, circa 1920.

Te Sheng Men
View through the inner gate

Grand Hotel de Pekin —*The Ginger Griffin*

The Beijing Hotel is a survivor. Situated close to Tiananmen Square it boasts four linked facades, each reflecting a different era of hospitality. The Grand Hotel Beijing, to the west, opened in 1989. The recently renovated tower to the east was finished in 1974. Sandwiched between is a stately 1950s Russian designed section and an elegant French building dating back to 1920—the former Grand Hotel de Pekin. In pre-War days it proudly stood as the centre of social life in the city and by its own admission was 'the only hotel de luxe in the Far East.'

The original 'Hotel de Pekin', founded in 1882, was located in the old Legation Quarter. Its Swiss manager Chamot and his American wife attained hero status during the 1900 Siege of Peking, providing essential supplies for foreign residents and taking care of hotel guests impounded in the British Legation. Soon after the hotel was sold in 1902 it was moved to its present location. Russo, the new Italian manager, had a reputation for watering down the wine and dodging taxes. Advertised as a 'first class hotel', a 1909 visitor found it nothing but 'a box with worn out sheets and mattresses'.

The property was later purchased by the French Commercial Bank and replaced with the Grand Hotel de Pekin in 1915—an impressive five-storey structure (demolished in 1973). Such was the hotel's success that an extravagant new seven-storey building opened alongside in 1920. The structure towered over a city crowded with single-storied buildings with its stature being compared to that of the Great Wall.

Crucial to the hotel's success was the long serving efforts of its managers. J. Roustan managed the hotel for more than 20 years, overseeing the years of Japanese occupation. The solitary Chinese manager, who gave 48 years service, was a key figure in mediating between foreign management and local employees. Relations were respectful, yet strict. Minor indiscretions, such as using the Otis lifts or the main stairway, would be heavily penalised. Staff were usually recruited though family connections. A veteran worker told me that he earned seven dollars a month in 1923—but the customers of his allotted two restaurant tables proffered dozens more in tips.

This was a handsome income at a time when room and board was five dollars a day and when one dollar could purchase 25 kilograms of flour.

The management had a keen eye for profitability and promotion of their tourist business. Beds and baths were imported from New York, whilst Paris supplied porcelain and silks. The French cuisine was superlative and on opening the hotel boasted the largest and finest wine cellars in China. The fashionable roof garden hosted exotic dances and was the place to feast and delight in the autumn evenings. Afternoon dances to the hotel's classical, and later, jazz orchestras unceasingly attracted Peking's 'smart set'. Unlike hotels in Shanghai, there were relatively few entry restrictions for Chinese patrons—but a suitable status and a bulging wallet were prerequisites. Many deposed Qing Dynasty aristocrats were to be seen here rubbing shoulders with foreign diplomats and businessmen.

Grand balls were arranged and Peking society was invited to 'meet the tourists' and see the latest fashions from Europe for themselves. As one Peking resident put it, "You don't need to make a trip around the world, just remain at home and the world will come to you." Cooks Travel Agency and foreign shopkeepers did a brisk business in the hotel lobby. One American, Helen Burton, amassed a considerable fortune from sales of furs and jewellery in her 'Camels Bell' shop.

Special Topic

Practical Information
Hotels in Beijing

COUNTRY PHONE CODE: 0086 CITY CODE: (0)10

Beijing Asia Jinjiang Hotel
8 Xinzhongxi Street, Gongti Beilu. Tel. 6500 7788
www.bj-asiahotel.com.cn
北京亚洲大酒店 北京朝阳工体北路新中西街8号
A conveniently located hotel in the central business area of Beijing, near the second ring road and embassy district.

Beijing Hotel
33 Dong Chang An Daijie. Tel. 6513 7766
北京饭店 北京东城区东长安街33号
This historic hotel is located next to Tian'anmen Square and the Forbidden City. It is said that the late Chairman Mao used to dance here on the specially sprung ballroom floor of the gilded ballroom. The hotel has hosted such historically important luminaries as Dr. Sun Yat-sen, Premier Zhou Enlai and Ho Chi Minh of Vietnam. The business suites in the newest section offer the latest comfort and in-room technology. Recreational facilities include a bowling alley, swimming pool, gym and tennis court.

Beijing Lu Song Yuan Hotel
22 Banchang Lane, Kuanjie, Dongcheng District
Tel. 6404 0436; www.the-silk-road-com
北京侣松园宾馆 北京东城区宽街板厂胡同22号

Hotel Nikko New Century
6 Shoudutiyuguan Nanlu. Tel. 6849 2001; www.newcenturyhotel.com.cn
北京新世纪日航饭店 北京海淀区首都体育场南路6号
This upgraded hotel is in the west of town close to the zoo and 'Silicon Valley' and is geared up for the business visitor.

Hotel New Otani Chang Fu Gong
26 Jianguomenwai Dajie. Tel. 6512 5555; www.cfgbj.com
北京长富宫饭店 北京朝阳区建国门外大街26号
Opened in 1989, the New Otani Chang Fu Gong is a large-scale business-style hotel, which is located in the embassy and commercial district, a 10-minute car ride from Tiananmen Square. The 500 guest rooms are furnished in Japanese and Chinese traditional design. The decorative Chinese courtyard is a popular relaxation spot with hotel guests.

China World Summit Wing
1 Jianguomenwai Avenue. Tel. 6505 2299
www.shangri-la.com/en/property/beijing/chinaworldsummitwing
国贸大酒店 北京朝阳区建国门外大街1号
With unrivalled views over the historic city centre, China World Summit Wing, Beijing offers a luxurious sanctuary on the upper floors of Beijing's newest landmark—the 330-metre tall China World Tower, which soars 81 floors above the city. This new hotel by Shangri-La Hotels and Resorts comprises 278 guest rooms and suites, four designer restaurants, two bars and a lounge, and four exclusive venues devoted to private dining, one of which will be an observation deck on level 81. The hotel also houses the city's highest spa retreat on level 77, a health club with a Life Fitness-equipped gymnasium, and an indoor infinity swimming pool overlooking the city.

Crowne Plaza Hotel Beijing
48 Wangfujing Dajie. Tel. 5911 9999; www.sixcontinentshotels.com
北京国际艺苑皇冠假日酒店 北京王府井大街48号
Just 10 minutes' stroll from the awe-inspiring Forbidden City, this newly renovated, Holiday Inn hotel places you at the heart of the city's main shopping and business districts. Half of its 382 rooms are non-smoking and the hotel has an art gallery.

Diaoyutai State Guesthouse
2 Fucheng Lu, Haidian District. Tel. 5859 1188
www.chinadyt.com/dythotel/dythotel.htm
钓鱼台国宾馆 北京海淀区阜城路2号
In former times this was the exclusive domain of state and foreign leaders, but this secluded property is now open to all who can afford it.

East, Beijing
22 Jiuxianqiao Road, Chaoyang District. Tel. 8426 0888; www.east-beijing.com
东隅 朝阳区酒仙桥路22号
East, Beijing, sister hotel of the popular Opposite House, is arguably Beijing's hippest new hotel. The hotel is located in the bustling Wangjing area, close to the Beijing Capital International Airport and the Central Business District. Each beautiful room offers an iPod Touch, 37-inch LCD TV, an iHome stereo system and free Wifi. An added plus is the walk-in rain shower and fully-equipped work station. Feasts is an open kitchen that offers an international menu and Hagaki serves modern Japanese cuisine. Check out Xian for an after hours drink.

Grand Hotel Beijing

35 Dong Chang An Dajie. Tel. 6513 7788; www.grandhotelbeijing.com
北京贵宾楼饭店 北京东长安大街35号

This 218 rooms and suites hotel was opened in 1989 and has the best views of the Forbidden City and the Avenue of Eternal Peace. Although it is connected to the western wing of the Beijing Hotel, it is independently managed. The rooms have all the modern conveniences of a five-star hotel. The Imperial Suite is palatial.

Grand Hyatt Beijing

Beijing Oriental Plaza, 1 Dong Chang An Dajie. Tel. 8518 1234; www.hyatt.com
北京东方君悦酒店 北京东长安街1号

The Grand Hyatt Beijing is located in the heart of the sprawling Oriental Plaza complex at the corner of Wangfujing and Chang An Avenue. This 591-room hotel is within 10 minutes walking distance from Tian'anmen Square and the Forbidden City. The rooms are well designed with desks incorporating data-ports for international access. The safe is large enough to store a notebook computer and any valuables. The hotel's health club offers the perfect retreat from the pressures of everyday life with a magnificent resort-type 1,500-square meter swimming pool nestled amongst lush vegetation and a state-of-the-art "Life Fitness" gymnasium.

Great Wall Sheraton

10 North Dongsanhuan, Chaoyang District. Tel. 6590 5566
www.sheratonbeijing.com
北京长城饭店 北京朝阳区东三环北路10号

Located near the Agricultural Exhibition Center, this property has 1,007 rooms, 10 function rooms and a ballroom. The 21st floor restaurant serves Sichuan and Guangdong style food and boasts 37 different types of Chinese tea. The panoramic view of the city and the distant Western Hills is an added bonus to your dining pleasure.

Beijing Hilton

1 Dongfang Road, Dongsanhuan Bei Lu, Chaoyang District
Tel. 5865 5000; www.beijing.hilton.com
北京希尔顿酒店 北京朝阳区东三环北路东方路1号

Beijing Hilton is ideally located along the Third Ring Road within 20 minutes of the international airport. All 340 rooms have the latest technology, including Internet access. The hotel is well known for the quality of its restaurants, including signature restaurant, Louisiana, one of the finest in Beijing.

InterContinental Beijing Hotel
11 Financial Street, Xi Cheng District. Tel. 5852 5888; www.ichotelsgroup.com
金融街洲际酒店 北京西城区金融街11号
The 332 spacious guest rooms and sites are stylish, with a contemporary design and touches of traditional Chinese artistry. The hotel features a 24-hour business center, health and recreational facilities including a spa, an indoor swimming pool, state-of-the-art fitness facilities in an 18-storey atrium setting. The hotel is also conveniently located within minutes of popular tourist sites and major shopping centers.

Jianguo Hotel
5 Jianguomenwai Dajie. Tel. 6500 2233; www.hoteljianguo.com
建国饭店 北京朝阳区建国门外大街5号
Opened in 1982, this hotel is fondly remembered by many "old China hands" for its friendly atmosphere, its well established restaurant (Justine's) and bar (Charlie's) and its beautiful water garden. It is located in the heart of the central business district near the famous Silk Alley, Friendship Store and within walking distance to many embassies and offices. In addition to a fully equipped health club and 24-hour business center, the hotel features excellent room facilities including high-speed Internet connection, voice mail, safety box, tea and coffee making service and international satellite TV programs, plus 24-hour movie and entertainment channels.

Kempinski Hotel
Lufthansa Center, 50 Liangmaqiao Lu. Tel. 6465 3388
www.kempinski-beijing.com
北京凯宾斯基饭店 北京朝阳区亮马桥路50号北京燕莎中心
Situated in the new diplomatic and business district, the Kempinski Hotel is part of the Lufthansa Center, a comprehensive complex with grade A offices, fully serviced apartments, restaurants, bars, medical center, showrooms, airline offices and other services. The rooms are of various shapes and have high-speed internet access, satellite TV and other business features. Located on the premises are Paulaner Brauhaus, Beijing's premier micro-brewery, and Salsa Cabana, one of the city's favorite night spots.

The Kerry Center Hotel
1 Guanghua Lu, Chaoyang District. Tel. 6561 8833; www.shangri-la.com
北京嘉里中心饭店 北京朝阳区光华路1号
This 487-room contemporary hotel belongs to the Shangri-La group. The rooms and suites are in cream and pales tones with an ergonomically designed desk and chair, free 2MB broadband access, separate shower and bath. The Kerry Sports

Fitness Center is one of the finest in the capital city with a 35-meter swimming pool, gym, tennis courts, squash, basketball, volleyball, badminton and jogging and roller skating track.

King Wing Hotel
17 Dongsanhuan Nanlu. Tel. 6766 8866; www.kingwing.com.cn
北京京瑞大饭店 北京东三环南路17号
This hotel has 358 rooms including an entire floor dedicated for special business travellers as well as seven conference halls, each capable of seating over 200. A hot spring feeds the hotel's swimming pool.

Kunlun Hotel Beijing
2, Xinyuan Nanlu, Chaoyang District. Tel. 6590 3388; www.hotelkunlun.com
北京昆仑饭店 北京朝阳区新源南路2号
Situated beside the beautiful Liangma River, a location famous for its embassies, foreign companies, exhibition centers, shopping centers and other deluxe hotels.

Langham Place, Beijing Capital Airport
No. 1 Er Jing Road, Terminal 3, Capital International Airport
Tel. 6457 5555; http://beijingairport.langhamplacehotels.com/
北京首都机场朗豪酒店 二经路1号, 三号航站楼 首都国际机场
Hip and stylish, up-to-the-minute, high-tech hotel. Short ride away from the historical sites, shopping and eateries in downtown Beijing.

Legendale Hotel Beijing
90–92 Jinbao Street, Dongcheng District. Tel: 8511 3388; www.legendalehotel.com
励骏酒店 北京东城区金宝街90-92号
Legendale is conveniently set in the old commercial area of Wangfujing and close to major historic sites, such as. The hotel's architecture is southern European, with rich royal blues, golds and burgundy reds throughout the sprawling structuring, emanating an old-world ambience. The elegant gilded staircase winds upward from the 1st to the top 17th floor, giving the venue a theatre-like feel. A dome-like atrium pulls in a good deal of natural light. Sparkling and ornate Baccarat crystal chandeliers dangle high above the ceilings; an antique Parisian fire place and a 17th century clock are the center pieces in the lobby adding to the loftiness and opulence. The Legendale has 390 rooms and 81 suites and a variety of Chinese and European cuisines.

The Orchid
65 Baochao Hutong, Gulou Dajie, Dongcheng District. Tel. 8404 4818
http://www.theorchidbeijing.com
东城区鼓楼东大街宝炒胡同65号

The Orchid, Beijing best designed new courtyard hotel, is buried down a rundown, tiny alleyway along one of the city's busiest hutongs, or ancient alleyways, and so guests could be forgiven for wondering what they've gotten themselves into. The hotel, in a nicely remodeled courtyard house, is terraced, and offers views of the surrounding ancient hutongs and both the Drum Tower and Bell Tower. There are just 10 rooms, some offering special views, private garden spaces and the premium luxury room boasting its own private roof terrace. This is the place to come to for the real Beijing experience.

The Peninsula Beijing
8 Goldfish Lane. Tel. 6559 2888; www.peninsula.com
王府半岛酒店 北京王府井金鱼胡同8号

The tastily renovated Peninsula Palace is an ideal hotel for business and leisure travelers wishing to stay in downtown Beijing. The glass door entrance opens on to a large lobby with marble staircase. The lobby bar is an ideal place for afternoon tea or pre-dinner cocktail. All new guestrooms have teak or rosewood flooring, comfortable king-size bed and bedside control table for lights, radio and plasma TV. The hotel hosts one of the finest shopping arcades in China, home to many top international designer boutiques. The new concept restaurant Jing has three show kitchens to entertain diners.

Renaissance Beijing Hotel
Air China Plaza, 36 Xiao Yun Lu. Tel. 6468 9999; www.marriott.com
国航万丽酒店 北京朝阳区霄云路36号

Located in the heart of the city—with 212 superbly equipped rooms.

Shangri-La Hotel Beijing
29 Zizhuyuan Lu. Tel. 6841 2211; www.shangri-la.com
北京香格里拉饭店 北京紫竹院路29号

Set amidst charming landscaped gardens, near the financial district and Technology Park (the Silicon Valley of Beijing). It is also close to the State Guest House and historical Summer Palace, providing an excellent base for business and leisure travelers.

CITIC Hotel Beijing Airport
9 Xiao Tianzhu Nanlu, Capital Airport. Tel. 6456 5588; www.sino-swisshotel.com
北京国都大饭店 北京首都机场小天竺南路9号
Located at Beijing Airport with state-of-the-art conference facilities.

St. Regis Hotel
21 Jianguomenwai Dajie. Tel. 6460 6688; www.starwoodhotels.com
北京瑞吉酒店 北京朝阳区建国门外大街21号
This Luxury Collection hotel stands on the grounds of the well-known Beijing International Club, where foreigners who lived in the early 20th century in Beijing used to meet. This boutique hotel has 273 rooms and suites and a butler service extended to all guests. The rooms are spacious with comfortable king-size beds and luxury duvet. The excellent spa, fitness center and the pool are located in the annex and can be reached through the lobby. The turn of the century atmosphere of the Beijing International Club is re-created in the Press Bar, where one can contemplate on the days gone by in comfortable leather armchairs. The lobby Garden Lounge serves afternoon high tea accompanied by a harpist.

State Guest Hotels Presidential Plaza
9 Fuchengmenwai Dajie, Xicheng District
Tel. 6800 5588; www.stateguesthotel.com
国宾酒店 北京阜城门外大街9号
Centrally located in Beijing's western District, close to China's commercial banking institutions, government ministries, high-tech industrial basin, Diaoyutai State Guest House, Beijing Zoo and several shopping centers.

Swissôtel
2 Chaoyangmenbei Dajie. Tel. 6553 2288; www.swissotel.com
北京港澳中心瑞士酒店 北京朝阳门北大街2号
Swissôtel Beijing is situated in Beijing's rapidly developing commercial and diplomatic district, a mere 35-minute drive from the airport, with easy access to downtown Beijing. The hotel offers 423 well-appointed guest rooms and suites featuring the latest in-room technology such as broadband Internet access, smart desk with separate computer data port and IDD telephone with personalized voice mail. Soft colors, elegant fabrics, and special touches, such as a marbled bathroom with separate shower area and tea and coffee making facilities, add to the feeling of "home-away-from-home". The hotel is part of an exclusive complex including 62 fully-serviced apartments, grade-A offices, boutiques and other supporting facilities and services.

Sunworld Dynasty Hotel
50 Wangfujing Dajie. Tel. 6513 8888; www.tianlunhotel.com
北京天伦王朝酒店 北京王府井大街50号
Located in Beijing's busiest commercial area, is in the style of an ancient Chinese Palace. 408 guest rooms and suites.

The Opposite House
The Village House, Building 1, No. 11 Sanlitun Road.
Tel. 6417 6688; www.theoppositehouse.com
瑜舍 北京朝阳区三里屯路11号
Created by renowned Japanese architect Kengo Kuma, this intriguing urban hotel's exterior stuns onlookers with an emerald green glass overlay. Located within the southern sector of the prestigious Village of Sanlitun, this captivating luxury hotel derives its name from a translation of a Chinese word, describing the guesthouse which sits on the opposite side of a traditional Chinese courtyard house where esteemed travelers would be accommodated.

Westin Chaoyang
7 Dong Sanhuan North Road, Chaoyang District. Tel. 5922 8888
金茂威斯汀大饭店 北京朝阳区东三环北路7号
The brand-new Westin Beijing Chaoyang offers contemporary class with 550 spacious guest rooms. Colors are warm with modern furnishings including the Heavenly Bed and rainforest shower, a flat screen interactive television, audio video system and IP telephone.

Grace Beijing
706 Hou Jie No. 1, 798 Art District, Jiu Xian Qiao Lu, 2 Hao Yuan
Tel. 6436 1818; www.yi-house.com/
北京格瑞斯 酒仙桥路二号院 798艺术区术 706后街1号
Grace Beijing is one of Beijing's more interesting concept hotels. The boutique hotel is located on the grounds of the Dashanzi Art District, better known as 798. The red-brick bauhaus structure, which sits in what was once a old crystal factory, has been refurbished to accommodate visitors to Beijing's most popular art district and is complimented by interesting art pieces. On the inside the design has a French colonial and Deco touch. The entrance hall fitted with a lime colored couch and seating, a federal style round table with candles, and contemporary artworks by photographer Marco Berreta. Artwork is also displayed in the rooms, from nostalgic black and white photos to the works of avant-garde artist Chi Peng. The restaurant features Mediterranean cooking.

Dining in Beijing

Beijing as the throne of the feudal past and the crown of the present day new republic has long been a magnet for all kinds of people from all over China. It's also true that the best cooks throughout the country have flocked to the ancient capital since early times. Some were brought here by officials posted to the capital, some hired by wealthy merchants or artists, and some were lured by the city's endless opportunities. They collectively contributed to making Beijing the country's culinary capital. Today you can sample all of China's varied cuisines without ever leaving the city, from humble but good eateries in winding hutongs to extravagant high-end regional restaurants the city's high-rise buildings.

Chinese Cuisine

Beijing offers much more than just Peking duck. The city's traditional cuisine includes an abundance of old dishes, many unknown to outsiders. They may sound intimidating or offensive, but they are unique and worth sampling. Beijing favorites include the following: mung bean pulp sautéed in mutton fat, mustard cabbage, pan-fried 'sausage' with a dipping garlic sauce, pork internal organs and entrails brewed in an aromatic broth with dozens of spices and herbs. Equally interesting are a wide variety of halal foods from the Hui (Chinese speaking Muslims), including stir-fried morsel-sized pasta, boiled tripe (*baodu*), 'roasted' lamb, donkey rolling on the ground (*lvdagun*) and glazed Chinese yam (*tang juanguo*).

Peking Duck

Bianyifang

A2 Chongwenmenwai Dajie, Chongwen District. Tel. 6712 0505
便宜坊 崇文区 崇文门外大街2号甲

The oldest duck house in the capital, Bianyifang opened its doors in the 1500s. The duck is roasted in a closed-door oven referred to as *menlu kaoya*. A whole duck costs 168RMB.

Duck de Chine

1949 The Hidden City Courtyard 4, Gongti Bei Lu, Chaoyang District
Tel. 6539 3683
全鸭季 朝阳区 工体北路1949号 隐匿城市四号院

The duck served at this stylishly rustic-looking duckery is roasted over fruit wood for about an hour and ten minutes—the longer roasting period is said to reduce the oil content. The thin pancakes come in a square bamboo steamer along with a plate of light, crisp and hollow baked breads that can be stuffed with duck and condiments.

The sauce for the duck is a blend of a little hoishin and oyster sauce added to the fermented wheaten sauce—a creation of a perfect sauce that's neither too sweet nor too salty. Side dishes include crispy duck tongue, deep-fried and smothered with a savory garlic topping, and crunchy broccoli with a hint of rice wine flavor.

Li Qun Kaoya Dian
11 Beixiangfeng, Zhengyi Lu, Chongwen District. Tel. 6702 5681
利群烤鸭 崇文区 正义路北翔风11号
Li Qun is situated in a dilapidated courtyard house in a hutong in the old part of Qianmen. Eating at Liqun is like dining in the home of a Beijing friend. Li Qun's ducks are tasty, with the meat moist and the skin crispy.

Xiangmanlou
18 Xinyuan Xi Li Zhong Jie, west of Yuyang Hotel, Chaoyang District
Tel. 6467 4391
香满楼 朝阳区 新源西里中街18号 (鱼阳饭店西侧)
Xiangmanlou is a favorite with Beijing families, who pack the place every night. A whole duck costs 98RMB including condiments.

Beijing

Fu Man Yuan
10 Xinyuan Nan Lu, Chaoyang District. Tel. 6461 8656
福满园 朝阳区 新源南路10号
Fu Man Yuan, Garden Full of Happiness, is an appropriate name for this excellent little eatery. *Hongshao daiyu*, red-cooked ribbon fish, *suanla tudousi*, spicy shredded potatoes, *shao qiezi*, braised eggplant and deep-fried bread served with fermented bean curd are the typical home-style dishes on the menu here.

Jing Wei Lou
181 A Di'anmen Xi Dajie, Xicheng District. Tel. 6617 6514
京味楼 西城区 地安门西大街181号甲
A statue of an old man holding a birdcage, a symbol of old Peking, greets you by the entrance to this eatery, which offers old Beijing favorites as well as Peking ducks roasted in open wood burning oven.

Jiumen Xiaochi
1 Xiaoyou Hutong, Xicheng District. Tel. 6402 5858
九门小吃 西城区 孝友胡同1号
A dozen or so restaurants specializing in old Beijing specialties have re-grouped here under one roof after their original homes were demolished in the historic Qianmen district.

Cantonese

Cantonese cuisine is the most familiar Chinese regional cuisine known outside China. It is relatively refined, generally mild and mellow. Dim sum, pork barbecue, goose, and cured sausages are also one of the best features of this cuisine. Steamed fish in ginger and scallion is the hallmark of Cantonese food.

Lei Garden
3/F, Jinbao Tower, 89 Jinbao Street, Dongcheng District. Tel. 8522 1212
利苑 东城区 金宝街89号 金宝大厦三层
Lei Garden offers authentic Cantonese food with a modern twist. Their innovative baked soft-shell crab is a big hit.

The Private Room
Park Hyatt, Beijing Yintai Centre, 2 Jianguomenwai Dajie, Chaoyang District
Tel. 8567 1234
Chef Lo is a rare caliber chef who received his training in an old Chinese cooking school. He prepares excellent cold appetizers and exquisite main entrées at The Private Room. The restaurant is set on the fifth floor of the Park Hyatt Beijing.

Summer Palace
2/F China World, 1 Jianguomenwai Dajie, Chaoyang District. Tel. 6505 2266
夏宫 朝阳区 建国门外大街1号 国贸饭店2层
The Summer Palace prepares light, delicate and savory Cantonese and Huaiyang delights. Chef Stanley Yuen, who is passionate about tonic cookery, creates dishes that are both flavorful and nutritious by adding appropriate herbal ingredients. The double-boiled chicken soup is arguably one of the best clear soups—it has the complexity of fruit aroma with a long after taste. The venue is designed to evoke 1930s Shanghai.

Guangxi

The food of Guangxi is characterized by the indigenous love for the pungent taste found in fermented sour pickled bamboo shoots.

Jin Fu Yuan
72 Xinjiekou Dong Jie, Xicheng District. Tel. 6616 1893
金福源 西城区 新街口东街72号
Baofan, or steamed rice in an earthenware bowl, is the focus of Jin Fu Yuan. The addition of an aromatic soy sauce (*lushui*) in the rice lends a superb flavor to this dish. Each rice casserole is served with the house-made spicy-sweet-sour pickled-cabbage, making the dish even more baiting. The crushed chillies in a silver container provided on every table are also deliciously hot.

Na Lan
2F, Guangxi Daxia, 26 Huaweili, Panjiayuan, Chaoyang District. Tel. 6779 6688
那兰 朝阳区 潘家园华威里26号 广西大厦2层
Na Lan, an excellent restaurant for Guangxi specialties, serves a wonderful roasted suckling pig, steamed belly pork with seasonal taro, beer stew duck with bamboo shoots and delicious chewy beer bread.

GUIZHOU

Guizhou cuisine is intensely spicy and sour at the same time. The flavor is best exemplified by the sour fish soup. Other dishes are seasoned with crushed fermented chillies known as *zao lajiao*.

Jun Qin Hua
88 Meishuguan Houjie, Dongcheng District. Tel. 6404 7600
君琴花餐厅 东城区 美术馆后街88号
Jun Qin Hua, a small and unassuming restaurant, has the most savory dishes of Guizhou. Whet your palate with *mi doufu* or *juanfen*, rice-based appetizers in a spicy dressing. Also try the *lazi ji*, bite-sized pieces of chicken smothered in cloves of garlic and crushed chilies. Another favorite is potatoes sautéed in Guizhou's seductive zaola chillies.

HUNAN

Hunan province is one of China's chilli belts notorious for its bold and spicy food. Hunanese eat fresh lip numbing peppers as if they were vegetables. Salted black beans and chopped salted chillies are indispensable condiments in this cookery.

The Four Seasons
2F, Minzu Fandian, 51 Fuxingmennei Dajie, Xicheng District. Tel. 6601 4466
四季厅 西城区 复兴门内大街51号 民族饭店二层
The Four Seasons Restaurant, hidden on the second floor of the Minzu Hotel, offers the best Hunan dishes in Beijing. Farm-style stir-fried pork dish fits for bold and spicy food fix, while red-cooked melt-in-your-mouth fatty pork is amazing beyond words. You can't go wrong at a restaurant, where Chef Zhang Haibin, young and enthusiastic, takes his cooking affectionately.

Karaiya Spice House
Bldg. 8, The Village South, 19 Sanlitun Road, Chaoyang District. Tel. 6415 3535
辣屋 朝阳区 三里屯路19号 The Village南区8号楼
Karaiya Spice House is an upscale restaurant serving Hunan dishes with a modern twist. The house Signature Fish is laced with spicy hot chillies, and the Spicy Pepper Diced Rib-eye, studded with dried red chillies, is equally hot and marvelous.

The floor-to-ceiling glassed restaurant with a bar on the second floor is stylishly designed featuring a contemporary interior with a Chinese touch. With plenty of natural sunlight pouring in, Karaiya is a cheerful dining spot.

Imperial Cuisine

Imperial cooking is a haute cuisine that was once served to members of the imperial court. This heritage was preserved by court chefs after the fall of the imperial system and was handed down to future generations.

Fangshan
Inside Beihai Park, East Gate. Tel. 6401 1889
仿膳饭庄 西城区 北海公园内 (东门)

This prestigious restaurant, which opened in 1925, uses recipes from the 19th century Imperial court. Banquets are highly elaborate and expensive—a meal including delicacies such as shark's fin and bird's nest soup can cost over 200 yuan per head. With its magnificent setting, this must surely rank as one of the most splendid dining spots in China.

Pavilion for Listening to the Orioles (Tingliguan)
Inside Summer Palace. Tel. 6288 1955, 6288 1608
听鹂馆 西城区 颐和园内

Set up in attractive rooms round a courtyard in the heart of the Summer Palace, this lunch restaurant is very popular with Western visitors.

Tan

Tan cuisine was created and developed by the ladies of an official called Tan Zongjun, who was posted to Beijing in the Qing Dynasty. Tan cuisine adopts the best cooking styles of several regions, including Anhui, Huaiyang, and Shandong combined with Cantonese, which forms the foundation.

Guoyao Xiaoju
58 Bei Santiao, Jiaodao Kou, Andingmennei Dajie, Dongcheng District
Tel. 6403 1940
国肴小居 安定门内大街 交道口北三条58号

Guoyao Xiaoju is a family-run restaurant with a handful of tables set up in a small courtyard house perched in an old Beijing neighborhood. Fit for an emperor fish maw soup (*nongtang yudu*) is creamy rich and flavorful. "Eggrolls" filled with smoked duck meat and chives are deliciously crunchy, and the dough-drop soup (*geda tang*), an ordinary and unassuming folk staple, was turned into a refined dish in the Tan kitchen.

Rinsed Mutton
Donglaishun
5F, Beijing APM, formerly Sun Dong An, 138 Wangfujing Dajie, Dongcheng District Tel. 6528 0932
东来顺 东城区 王府井大街新东安广场5层
Donglaishun is one of the oldest hotpot establishments in the capital, dating back to 1914, with a flagship located at Xin Dong'an Plaza.

Jubaoyuan
Building 1, Niujie Xili, Xuanwu District. Tel. 8354 5602
聚宝源 宣武区 牛街西里1号商业楼5-2号
Jubaoyuan, in the heart of the Ox Street Muslim area, arguably has the best rinsed mutton. It's served in a traditional brass hot pot heated with charcoal. Come before six in the evening to secure a table, otherwise, expect to queue for at least an hour.

Shandong
Shandong cooking was once ranked as No. 1 among China's eight regional cuisines, known as *Lu Cai*. Prior to 1949, Beijing's dining scene was literally monopolized by Shandong people from the proprietor and manager all the way down to the chefs and dishwashers. Shandong cuisine features banquet dishes using seafood and dried goods such as abalone and sea cucumber, and a wide section of ordinary dishes made with poultry, pork, and vegetables.

Tongheju
71B Yuetan Nanjie, Sanlihe. Tel. 6852 2917
同和居 三里河 月坛南街71号乙
Established in 1822, Tongheju was one of the earliest restaurants specializing in Shandong cuisine in the city, and it remains faithful to its traditional dishes, such as *mushu* pork, a fancy 'squirrel fish' in sweet sauce, braised sea cucumber and diced chicken in sweet wheaten sauce. The famous 'three no sticks" which doesn't stick to your plate, to your chopsticks or to your teeth—is a delicious buttery custard.

Shanghai
Shanghai cuisine is a sub-branch of Zhejiang cuisine, known for its braised-cooking for hours at low temperatures. Steamed buns (*xiaolongbao*) and pan-fried buns (*shengjianbao*) are common snack foods prevalent on Shanghai streets. The famous steamed buns (*xiaolongbao*) originated from Nanxiang, a town close to Shanghai.

Madame Zhu's
B1/F, Bldg D, Vantone Center, 6A Chaoyangmenwai Dajie, Chaoyang District
Tel. 5907 1625

汉舍中国菜馆 朝阳区 朝阳门外大街甲6号 万通中心D座地下1层
The menu at Madam Zhu's Kitchen is a division between Cantonese, Shanghai and Sichuan dishes which come with authenticity and quality, sometimes with a little twist, but no MSG is used. Despite its basement location, the white walls and bright lighting give the venue a pleasant feel. The sofas, cabinets displaying blue and white china, fresh flowers and framed photos hung on the walls give Madame Zhu's a cozy ambience, making diners feel as if they are dining in someone's home, rather than in a restaurant.

Xiao Nanguo
2/F, Jinbao Tower, 89 Jinbao Jie, Dongcheng District. Tel. 8522 1717
小南国 东城区 金宝街89号 金宝大厦2层
Shanghainese living in Beijing say that Xiao Nanguo, or "Little Southern Country," offers the best traditional Shanghainese dishes, such as stir-fried glutinous rice cakes, sweet and sour spareribs, old duck soup, and pan-fried buns. Black is the dominant color of the venue, which has a minimalist look.

Yuan Yuan
16 Tuanjiehu Park (west gate), Dong Sanhuan, Chaoyang District. Tel. 6508 2202
圆苑 朝阳区 东三环 团结湖公园16号 (西门南侧)
Perched in a two-story traditional-looking building beside the west gate of Tuanjiehu Park, this Shanghai chain is best known for its *hongshao rou*, or red cooked meat.

SICHUAN
Sichuan cuisine is notorious for its numbing and spicy flavors. However, it is not true all Sichuan dishes are hot and spicy—smoked tea duck, boiled napa cabbage or dry-fried French beans are among the mild dishes of Sichuan.

Dezhe Xiaoguan
1 Bei Jixiang Hutong, Jiaodaokou Nan Dajie, Dongcheng District. Tel. 6407 8615
得着小馆 东城区 交道口南大街 北吉祥胡同1号
Tucked inside a hutong just off Jiaodaokou Nan Dajie, Dezhe Xiaoguan is a charming courtyard restaurant serving Sichuan dishes from Leshan. *Jiaoma ji* is drenched in a rich clear broth impregnated with the fresh aroma of Sichuan peppercorn, and the spicy-sweet-salty-sour *bobo* dish, are among the fabulous dishes offered here.

The Source
14 Banchang Hutong, Nan Luoguxiang, Kuanjie, Dongcheng District (next to Lu Song Hotel). Tel. 6400 3736
都江源 东城区 南锣鼓巷 宽街 板厂胡同14号

Dining at this traditional siheyuan restaurant, with its hundred-year-old date tree in the middle of the courtyard, is a pleasant and peaceful experience. The Source offers a set meal consisting of several appetizers and hot dishes, all chosen by the chef—the menu is never the same.

TAIWAN
The cuisine of Taiwan is an assimilation of various cuisines from different parts of China with Fujian cooking at its core and some Japanese influence.

Fan Qian Fan Hou
A13 Warehouse Complex, Dongcheng District. Tel. 6409 6978
饭前饭后 东城区 东四十条22号 南新仓国际大厦古仓群A13
Located in an old Ming Dynasty granary, Fan Qian Fan Hou features Taiwanese classic dishes, such as Taiwan sausages, stir-fried vermicelli and *lurou fan*, rice with minced pork topping. The complimentary small dishes of pickled turnip and seaweed-coated peanuts are memorable.

XINJIANG
The spices that are used in flavoring the meat, usually mutton, has converted anti-mutton eaters to loving it. Unlike Chinese food, Xinjiang does not use any soy sauce or cornstarch. Roasting is the most common method in Xinjiang cookery and the dishes are all evolved around mutton and lamb.

Crescent Moon
16 Dongsi Bei Dajie Liu Tiao Hutong, Dongcheng District. Tel. 6400 5281
新疆弯弯月亮维吾尔穆斯林餐厅 东城区 东四北大街六条胡同16号
Crescent Moon is a simple restaurant serving up delicious Xinjiang fare from kebabs to roasted leg of lamb to stir-fried noodles.

Kashgar
60 Pen'er Hutong, Xuanwu District. Tel. 6358 2243
喀什饭庄 新疆维吾尔自治区 喀什地区行政公署驻京办 宣武区 盆儿胡同60号
One of the best Uighur restaurants in town, this government-run eatery is always packed with diners. Baked buns (*sam sa*) have a thin and crispy crust with a tasty lamb filling. *Ququ* are a Uighur-style wonton served in a wholesome broth. The lamb skewers are made with excellent cuts of meat.

YUNNAN
Yunnan cuisine is as diverse as its inhabitants, which include many minorities with different customs and cultures. The characteristics of Yunnan cuisine is a cross between southeast Asian and Han cooking. Yunnan is also known for its wild mushrooms and vegetables.

Dali
67 Xiaojingchang Hutong, Gulou Dongdajie, Dongcheng District. Tel. 8404 1430
大理
Three reasons to dine at Dali: (i) the fantastic Yunnan food served with a southeast Asian twist; (ii) the laid back courtyard house provides a peaceful ambiance, and (iii) a feast of delightful dishes is available at just RMB100/person with no hassle of having to decide what to order from the menu. Wild mushrooms, mozzarella-like goat cheese, kaffir leaves and lemon grass can be expected at Dali.

The Moss
17 Jianhua Lu, Chaoyang District. Tel. 8530 6400. 峡谷 朝阳区 建华路17号
The Moss offers exotic and authentic Yunnan dishes in a home-like setting. The design is also appealing. Formerly a storage area for Russian buyers, it has corrugated ceilings with thick steel girders that provide an industrial look above. Below there is a somewhat distinguished modern touch at ground level. It is furnished with dark wooden bookcases, floor-to-ceiling glass windows, leather chairs and sofas and wooden tables, all romantically accented by flickering candles on the walls.

South Silk Road
North of Workers' Stadium West Gate, Gate 4 (bet. Gongrentiyuchang North Rd. & Gongrentiyuchang South Rd.) Tel. 8580-4287
茶马古道 朝阳区 工人体育场西门
Specializes in the spicy food of Yunnan province, with many minority dishes on the menu.

Yunteng Binguan
Building 7, Huashi Beili, Dongqu, Chongwen District. Tel. 6711 3322
云腾宾馆 崇文区 东区 花市北里7号搂
Despite its faux-jungle-waterfall-décor, this provincial government restaurant is popular for its seasonal vegetables fresh from Yunnan and the authenticity of its cuisine.

Zhejiang
Zhejiang is another regional cuisine blessed with a wide variety of materials from the rich Yangtze River, and the use of yellow wine in cooking, giving it a distinctive flavor which can be characterized as light, winey and palatably sweet.

Din Tai Fung
22 Hujia Yuan, Dongcheng District (northwest of the Yuyang Hotel) Tel. 6462 4502

6F, Shinkong Plaza, 87 Jianguo Lu, Chaoyang District. Tel. 6533 1536
鼎泰丰 东城区 胡家园22号迤北楼
朝阳区 建国路87号 新光天地6楼

Din Tai Fung is one of the few restaurant chains that enjoy a high reputation. The highlight here is their steamed dumplings. Steamed to perfection in bamboo baskets, each dumpling is wrapped in a paper-thin-light flour skin, and always arrives at your table steaming hot. Highly recommended.

Kong Yiji

South Bank of Houhai Shichahai Deshengmen, Xicheng District. Tel. 6618 4917
孔乙己 西城区 德胜门后海什刹海南岸

This restaurant is named after a character in a short story by Lu Xun, one of China's most famous writers of all time. Kong Yiji serves food from the Zhejiang area, including some of the dishes from the short story.

Vegetarian

Most vegetarian restaurants in China make great efforts to make their dishes look and taste like meat, even carving scales onto a "fish". Some of the dishes are so tasty that it's hard to believe that they are primarily made from soy bean products or gluten.

Jingsi Su Shifang

18A, Dafosi Dongjie, Dongcheng District. Tel. 6400 8941
静思素食坊 东城区 大佛寺东街18号甲

A pleasant and quiet small restaurant tucked in a hutong several blocks north of the well-known Sanlian Bookstore. It offers a wide selection of house vegetarian specialties.

King's Joy

2 Wudaoying Hutong Lama Temple Dongcheng District. Tel. 8404 9191
京兆尹 东城区 雍和宫 五道营胡同2号

King's Joy offers vegetarian food, but not the restrictive monastic style, where leeks, onions, garlic, chives and other pungent ingredients are prohibited. Hence, the flavor and fragrance here are bursting and not impeded. The focus here is on health and preservation of the environment. Many of the vegetables come from nearby cooperating organic farms or from far-away Yunnan. Adding to the attraction of the food is the magnificent design of the restaurant, which is the work of Zhang Yonghe, one of China's most famous architects. The restaurant is built in a simple courtyard style with a small outdoor dining area in the rectangle. A mist floats up from the sides of the ground, which combined with the scent of incense wafting over the walls of the Lama Temple just across the street, gives the restaurant a mysterious but alluring feel. Quality like this comes at a price, however. The lowest-priced set meal, which is served in the private dining rooms, runs Rmb 699 per person for a 10-course meal. If you want something simpler, choose a table in one of the open areas or in the Zen-like courtyard, where you can order more reasonably priced meals from the menu.

OTHER RESTAURANTS

My Humble House
1 East Chang'an Ave., Beijing Oriental Plaza Podium Level W3 (west of Grand Hyatt Hotel's entrance). Tel. 8518 8811
China Central Place, 89 Jianguo Lu (On Xidawang Lu) Level 2, Club House, Chaoyang District. Tel. 6530 7770
寒舍 东城区 东长安街1号 东方广场西3号楼
朝阳区 建国路89号 华贸中心
The contemporary feeling at My Humble House is not limited to its décor, but extends to its finely prepared cuisine. The creativity of the chefs is boundless, yet the dishes retain the original flavor of Chinese cuisine. This bold and avant-garde Chinese restaurant will give you a pleasant surprise.

The Red Capital Club
66 Dongsijiutiao, Dongcheng District. Tel. 6401 7150, 8401 8886
新红资俱乐部 东城区 东四九条66号
Serves "Zhongnanhai" cuisine, such as Deng Xiaoping's Chicken and the Marshall's Delight—fiery hot green peppers stuffed with pork and shrimp. The restaurant is in a well-restored old courtyard house, decorated with antiques and 1960s memorabilia. Popular so make a reservation in advance.

Whampoa Club
23A Financial Street, Xicheng District. Tel. 8808 8828
黄浦俱乐部 西城区 金融街23号甲
An artsy and elegant venue set up in a contemporary courtyard house serving beautifully-presented Chinese food with a modern twist.

Wuyutai Neifu Cai
144 Dongzhimennei Dajie, Dongcheng District. Tel. 6401 2238
吴裕泰内府菜 东城区 东直门内大街144号
Located on the lantern-lined street Ghost Street, this restaurant offers a total of 26 dishes that use tea or tea leaves in the process of cooking. Sweet-sour spareribs (*mizhi liangzhai pai*) are served with a glass of Anhui *liu'an guapian* green tea, which

maximizes the taste of the meat. *Jinzhong cha jiuxiang furou*, one square piece of braised belly pork, is simmered in vintage rice wine, soy sauce and crystal sugar to a perfect tenderness that dissolves in your mouth, and is served in a petit pumpkin. *Chahua shuangjun nuomi ya*, a moist and slightly smoky duck breast and sticky rice is paired with a glass of bitter tasting tea, which lifts the flavor.

OTHER ASIAN CUISINE
INDIAN
Taj Pavilion
China Overseas Plaza, North Tower, 2nd Floor, F2–03, NO.8. Guanghua Dong Li, Chaoyang District. Tel. 6505 5866
泰姬楼 朝阳区 建国门外大街 光华东里8号 中海广场北楼2层F2-03
Original Indian food served with friendly service.

JAPANESE
Hatsune
2/F Heqiao Building C, 8A Guanghua Lu, Chaoyang District. Tel. 6581 3939
隐泉日本料理 朝阳区 光华路8号甲 和桥大厦2层
Hatsune's design is unconventional, a fusion of classical with contemporary that is also reflected in its sushi rolls.

Naoki
Naoki Aman at Summer Palace, 15 Gongmen Qian Jie, Summer Palace Tel. 5987 9999.
Naoki, part of Aman at Summer Palace, offers spectacular French accented Japanese dishes, adhering to the *kaiseki* tradition, where dishes are artistically arranged to stimulate the eyes as well as the taste buds. Housed in a beautiful, traditional building.

Yotsuba
2 Xinzhong Jie Xili, Chaoyang District. Tel. 6467 1837
四叶 朝阳区 新源西里中街2号楼旁 (近新东路)
Best to park yourself at the sushi counter where sushi master does his art right in front of you.

MALAYSIAN
Café Sambal
43 Doufuchi Hutong, Jiu Gulou Dajie, Xicheng District. Tel. 6400 4875
西城区 旧鼓楼大街 豆腐池胡同43号
Near the Drum and Bell Towers, this restaurant serves classic Malay food in a laid back, lovely, old courtyard house.

Thai
Purple Haze
Opposite the North Gate of the Workers' Stadium, in the small alley behind the ICBC bank, Chaoyang District. Tel. 6413 0899
紫苏庭 朝阳区 工体北门对面 工商银行后胡同
Reasonably priced Thai food in a cozy and intimate environment.

Tibetan
Tibetan cuisine is unique and evolves around yak meat and barley. Given the climate in the high plateau, where few vegetables grow, barley is the main crop.

Makye Ame
2/F, A11. Xiushui Nanjie, Jianguomenwai, Chaoyang District (directly north of the Friendship Store). Tel. 6506 9616.   朝阳区 建国门外 秀水南街11号甲2层
Dining at Makye Ame is like going to a Tibetan family home. The restaurant is decorated with beautiful Tibetan furnishings. Makye Ame's best dishes are curried potatoes, roasted lamb, grilled mushrooms and beef with pickled carrots.

Vietnamese
Susu
10 Qianliang Hutong Xixiang, Dongcheng District. Tel. 8400 2699
东城区钱粮胡同西巷10号
Susu, Beijing's best Vietnamese restaurant, is set in a charming and beautifully restored courtyard house in a secluded side street off Qianliang Hutong. The fabulous venue and wonderful food combine to provide one of the best dining experiences in the city. The Vietnamese dishes prepared at Susu are wonderfully light, greaseless and with little starch, yet they are very satisfying. Almost every dish is accompanied by a fleet of fresh vegetables and herbs, no easy task and something we appreciate. The menu is the product of ttwo young Vietnamese chefs from Ho Chi Minh City.

International Cuisine
Beijing's international dining scene has undergone revolutionary changes over the past decade, with the arrival of foods and wines from all over the world.

Aria
Aria 2/F, China World Hotel, 1 Jianguomenwai Dajie, Chaoyang District
Tel. 6505 2266 ext.38.   中国大饭店 朝阳区 建国门外大街1号

Cepe
The Ritz Carlton Hotel, 1 Jinchengfang Dong Jie, Xicheng District. Tel. 6601 6666
Many of the dishes at Cepe, one of the finest Italian restaurants in the capital, revolve

around *boletus*—Italian for mushrooms. Cepe also offers creative and stimulating dishes that are light and wonderful. Fantastic wine selection is carefully chosen.

Capital M
3/F, 2 Qianmen Pedestrian Street, Qianmen. Tel. 6702 2727
北京市 前門步行街2号3 楼
A branch of Shanghai's popular M on the Bund, Capital M is located on the newly renovated Qianmen Pedestrian Street, facing the southern end of Tiananmen Square. The rooftop dining area has stuffing views of two ancient towers and the gate of the Forbidden City. The restaurant, which has black-and-white Art Deco tiles, serves delicious contemporary European cuisine.

Grill79
79th Floor, China World Summit Wing
1 Jianguomenwai Dajie, Chaoyang District. Tel. 6505 2299
国贸79 朝阳区建国门外大街1号 国贸大饭店79层
Grill 79, located on the 79th floor of the imposing China World Summit Wing, has the most amazing views of Beijing, looking west to the Forbidden City, and north to the Bird's Nest and Water Cube of Olympic fame. The restaurant serves an excellent David Blackmore heirloom wagyu steak, which chef Ryan Sablan Dadufalza calls the Louis Vuitton of meat.

La Dolce Vita
8 Xin Dong Lu (north), Chaoyang District. Tel. 6468 2894
甜蜜生活 朝阳区 新东路8号
La Dolce Vita is known for its old-fashioned pasta dishes in classic sauces and pizza baked in an open wood fired oven.

Maison Boulud
23 Ch'ianmen, Qianmen Dong Dajie, Dongcheng District. Tel. 6559 9200
布鲁宫 东城区 前门东大街23号
The spectacular food and wine at Maison Boulud, a Michelin-rated restaurant, matches the classic interior of the former American Embassy compound that dates back to the early 1900s. The building is a blend of classic and modern, making this the hottest dining spot for China's noveau riche.

Mercante
4 Fangzhuanchang Hutong, Dongcheng District. Tel. 8402 5098
商贾 东城区 方砖厂胡同4号
This hutong tratoria, which has just eight tables, is known for its excellent home-made pasta, bread and desserts. The restaurants, located in the heart of the hutongs not far from the Drum and Bell Towers, has a quaint rustic look.

Morel's
1–2, No. 5 Building, Xinzhongjie, Chaoyang District. Tel. 6416 8802
莫劳 朝阳区 新中街5号楼1-2号
Belgian beers and grandmother-style mussels and steaks are a big hit at Morel's. Try the Belgian Waffles for dessert.

Mosto
D308 Nali Patio, 81 Sanlitun Beilu, Chaoyang District. Tel. 5208 6030
Mosto, a Latino inspired restaurant with a central open kitchen, serves innovative and contemporary dishes. It is located on the Sanlitun Bar Street between Dongzhimennei and Gongti Beilu.

Sureno
Chaoyang The Opposite House Bldg. 1, 11 Sanlitun Beilu. Tel. 6410 5240
www.surenorestaurant.com; www.surenorestaurant.com
An upscale Mediterranean restaurant that is modestly priced, dishes up light superb meal with the touch of fresh herbs and drenched in rich olive oil.

Temple Restaurant Beijing
23 Shatan Beijie, Dongcheng District. Tel. 8400 2232. 东城区 沙滩北街嵩祝寺23号
After driving down a bustling narrow alleyway, one arrives at the door of the temple entrance, where you're greeted by a man in black, complete with fedora, who will escort you inside. You'll pass under the carved stone gate, walk through the temple hallway, and then pass through a small courtyard peopled by modern sculptures before entering the elegant bar and finally the stunning dining room. The contemporary interior, which stands in contrast to the 600-year-old temple complex outside, is simply elegant. The main room features a skylight and full-length windows that look out over the courtyard. The stunning room, designed by Australian architectural and design firm Hassell, is a model of minimalist design, with white and grey walls and wonderful Danish modern furniture from MatzForm's Twist collection. The complex, which dates back to the Ming dynasty (1368-1644), and which was once an imperial factory that printed Sanskrit sutras and the former home of a Tibetan living Buddha, underwent renovation in 2008, which focused on preserving the many layers of history and keeping as much as possible of the original structures. The restaurant is run by Ignace Lecleir, former general manager of Beijing's Maison Boulud. The simple menu offers rich contemporary European cuisine.

Xiu
2 Jianguomenwai Dajie, Chaoyang District. Tel. 8567 1234
秀 朝阳区 建国门外大街2号

This top-notched roof top garden bar nestled in a stunning contemporary courtyard house offers diners an alfresco terrace barbeque as well as snack boxes with a glass Moet Chandon before dinner. Other exquisitely prepared foods include roast duck roll, spicy chicken wings and calamari rings. There are separate bars for wine and champagne, Martinis and vodka and whiskey, with live music every night. A reservation is a must to secure terrace seating.

CAFES
Café de la Poste
58 Yonghegong Dajie, Dongcheng District. Tel. 6402 7047
云游驿 东城区 雍和宫大街58号
Located not too far from the Lama Temple, Café de la Poste is a place where people come to have a cup of coffee, a beer or just a simple French family meal prepared by chef-cum-owner, Yannick Gauthier.

IFW (International Food Warehouse)
B1/F, Park Life, Yintai Center, 2 Jianguomenwai Dajie, Chaoyang District
Tel. 8567 1568. 朝阳区 建国门外大街2号 北京柏悦酒店地下1层
IFW is a comprehensive all-in-one food court complex offering international cuisine from East to West. The pastries, tarts and cakes are also wonderful.

Kempi Deli
Kempinski Hotel, 50 Liangmaqiao Lu, Chaoyang District. Tel. 6402 7961
朝阳区 亮马桥路50号 凯宾斯基饭店
Attached to the Kempinski hotel, this deli has a nice selection of pastries, doughnuts, tarts and danishes.

L'Atelier
Unit 102, Tower 20, Central Park, 6 Chaoyangmenwai Dajie, Chaoyang District.
Tel. 6597 0724 **讲麦堂** 朝阳区 朝阳门外大街6号 新城国际20号楼102室
The glass counter at L'Atelier is filled with good-looking pastries: plain and chocolate croissants, buttery Palmier, Rhurbarb tarts, scones, apple turnovers, apple tarts, and chocolate cakes, eclairs, lemon cheese cake and meringues. There are also a variety of tasty breads. The cafe is designed simply but with an elegant touch. The white painted walls are adorned with alluring black and white photographs—cracked eggs, dusted dough, whipped cream—expressing the bakery's philosophy that baked goods taste their best taste when everything is fresh. This excellent French cafe has a cheerful atmosphere that makes you want to linger over your coffee and pastry.

Useful Addresses in Beijing

Airlines

Air China
Beijing Booking Office: Room 1537
15/F Jingxin Building, 2A North
Dongsanhuan, Chaoyang District
Hotline: 400 810 0999
www.airchina.com.cn
中国国际航空公司
朝阳区 东三环北路甲2号
京信大厦 15层1537室

All Nippon Airlines (ANA)
2F, Fazhan Daxia
5 Dong Sanhuan Bei Lu
Chaoyang District
Tel. 6513 0888; www.ana.co.jp
全日空航空公司
朝阳区 东三环北路5号 发展大厦2层

British Airways
Rm 210, SCITE Tower
22 Jianguomenwai Dajie
Chaoyang District
Hotline: 8511 5599; www.ba.com
英国航空公司
朝阳区 建国门外大街22号
赛特大厦210室

Air Canada
Rm C201, Office Building Kempinski
Office Building, 50 Liangmaqiao Lu
Chaoyang District
Tel. 400 811 2001
www.aircanada.com
加拿大航空公司
朝阳区 亮马桥路50号
凯宾斯基饭店写字楼C201室

Delta Airlines
1308 China World Office
1 Jianguomenwai Dajie, Chaoyang District
Tel. 6505 3505
Reservations: 40081 40081
www.delta.com
达美航空公司
朝阳区 建国门外大街1号
中国国贸大厦13楼8室

Dragonair
East Tower 28/F, LG Twin Tower
B12 Jianguomenwai Dajie
Chaoyang District
Hotline: 400 888 6628
www.dragonair.com
港龙航空公司
朝阳区 建国门外大街乙12号
双子座大厦东塔28层

Finnair
Rm 204, SC ITE Tower,
22 Jianguomenwai Dajie
Chaoyang District
Tel. 6512 7180; www.finnair.com
芬兰航空公司
朝阳区 建国门外大街22号
赛特大厦204室

Iran Air
Room 701, 7/F, CITIC Building
19 Jianguomenwai Dajie
Chaoyang District
Tel. 6512 4945; www.iranair.com
伊朗航空公司
朝阳区 建国门外大街19号国际大厦
701室

Japan Airlines
15F, Fazhan Daxia
5 Dong Sanhuan Bei Lu
Chaoyang District
Tel 400 888 0808; www.cn.jal.com
日本航空公司
朝阳区 东三环北路5号 发展大厦15层

Korean Air
Rm. 901–903, Hyundai Motor Building
38 Xiaoyun Lu, Chaoyang District
Hotline: 400 658 8888
www.koreanair.com
大韩航空公司
朝阳区 肖云路38号
现代汽车大厦901-903室

Lufthansa German Airlines
S101 Lufthansa Center Office Building
50 Liangmaqiao Lu, Chaoyang District
Tel. 6468 8838; www.lufthansa.com
汉莎航空公司
朝阳区 亮马桥路50号
燕莎中心写字楼S101号

Malaysia Airlines
10/F, Room 1005, China World Tower 2
10/F Tower B, Pacific Century Place A2
Gongti Beilu, Chaoyang District
Tel. 6505 2681
www.malaysiaairlines.com
马来西亚航空公司
朝阳区 工体北路甲2号
盈科中心B座10层

Pakistan International Airlines
Room 617, Tower 1, China World
1 Jianguomenwai Dajie
Chaoyang District
Tel. 6505 1681, 6505 1682
www.piac.com.pk
巴基斯坦国际航空公司
朝阳区 建国门外大街1号
国贸中心6层617室

Qantas Airways
LG Towers, B12 Jianguomenwai Dajie
Chaoyang District
Tel. 6567 9006; www.qantas.com.au
澳洲航空公司
朝阳区 建国门外大街乙12号双子座西塔10层

SAS–Scandinavian Airlines System
Rm 430 Sunflower Tower
37 Maizidian Jie, Chaoyang District
Tel. 8527 6100, Airport: 6453 2550
www.flysas.com
北欧航空公司
朝阳区 麦子店街37号盛福大厦430室

Singapore Airlines
Room 801, China World Tower 2
1 Jianguomenwai Dajie
Chaoyang District
www.singaporeair.com
Tel. 6505 2233
新加坡航空公司
朝阳区 建国门外大街1号
国贸中心2座801室

Thai International
Room 303, West Tower 3 Oriental
Plaza, 1 Dong Chang'an Jie
Dongcheng District
Tel: 8515 0088; Airport: 6459 8899
www.thaiair.com
泰国国际航空公司
东城区 东长安街1号
东方广场西座三办公楼303室

United Airlines
15/F, Jiancheng Guangchang
Sanyuanqiao, Chaoyang District
Tel. 8468 6666; www.united.com
美国联合航空公司
朝阳区三元桥加程广场A座15层

Uzbekistan Airways
Rm 201, CITIC Building
19 Jianguomenwai Dajie
Chaoyang District
Tel. 6500 6442
www.uzbekistan-airways.info/
乌兹别克斯坦航空公司
朝阳区建国门外大街19号国际大厦
201B

Vietnam Airlines
S121 Lufthansa Center Office Building
50 Liangmaqiao Lu, Chaoyang District
www.vietnamairlines.com
Tel. 8454 1196
越南航空公司
朝阳区 亮马桥路50号
凯宾斯基写字楼S121

BANKS

Bank of America
Room 2609 China World Tower 1
1 Jianguomenwai Dajie
Tel. 6505 3508
美国美洲银行
建国门外大街1号国贸中心2609室

Bank of China (Head Office)
1 Fuxingmennei Dajie, Xicheng District
Tel. 6659 6688
中国银行（总行）
西城区 复兴门内大街1号

Bank of China (Beijing Branch)
No. 8 Yabao Road, Asia Pacific Building
Hotline: 95566
中国银行（北京分行）
雅宝路8号亚太大厦1层

Barclay's Bank
Room 2108 Huaren Daxi
8 Jianguomenwai Dajie
Chaoyang District
Tel. 5816 5020
英国巴克莱银行
建国门外大街8号华润大厦2108室

Citibank
G/F Zuozhu Zhongxin, 6 Wudinghou Dajie, Financial Street, Xicheng District
Tel. 5937 6700
花旗银行
西城区 金融街
武定侯大街6号卓著中心一层101

Hongkong and Shanghai Bank
COFCO Plaza, Chang'an Avenue
Tel. 5999 8888
香港汇丰银行
长安街中粮广场大厦A座首层

Royal Bank of Canada
9 Financial Street, 7th Floor
Xicheng District
Tel. 5839 9388
加拿大皇家银行 西城区金融街7层9号

Standard Chartered Bank
12/F, World Finance Center
1 Dongsanhuan Zhong Lu
Chaoyang District
Tel. 5918 8838
渣打银行
朝阳区 东三环中路1号
环球金融中心 东塔渣打大厦12层

EMBASSIES

Afghanistan
8 Dongzhimenwai Dajie, Sanlitun
Tel. 6532 0240
阿富汗 三里屯东直门外大街8号

Australia
21 Dongzhimenwai Dajie, Sanlitun
Tel. 5140 4111
澳大利亚 三里屯东直门外大街21号

Austria
5 Xiushui Nan Jie, Jianguomenwai
Tel. 6532 2061–2
奥地利 建国门外秀水南街5号

Belgium
6 Sanlitun Lu. Tel. 6532 1736–8
比利时 三里屯路6号

Canada
10 Dongzhimenwai Dajie, Sanlitun
Tel. 5139 4000
加拿大 三里屯路东直门外大街19号

Denmark
1 Dongwu Jie, Sanlitun
Tel. 8532 9900
丹麦 三里屯东五街1号

Czech Republic
Ritan Lu and Jianguomenwai
Tel. 8532 9500
捷克 建国门外日坛路2号

Finland
26/F Kerry Center South Building
1 Guanghua Lu, Jianguomenwai
Tel. 8519 8300
芬兰
建国门外光华路1号嘉里中心南楼26层

France
3 Dongsan Jie, Sanlitun
Tel. 8532 8080
法国 三里屯东三街3号

Germany
17 Dongzhimenwai Dajie, Sanlitun
Tel. 8532 9000
德国 三里屯东直门外大街17号

Hungary
10 Dongzhimenwai Dajie, Sanlitun
Tel. 6532 1431
匈牙利 三里屯东直门外大街10号

India
1 Ritan Dong Lu, Jianguomenwai
Tel. 6532 1908, 6532 1856
印度 建国门外日坛东路1号

Israel
17 Tianze Lu, Chaoyang District
Tel. 8532 0500
以色列 朝阳区天泽路17号

Italy
2 Dong'er Jie, Sanlitun
Tel. 8532 7600
意大利 三里屯东二街2号

Japan
7 Ritan Lu
Tel. 6532 2361
日本 建国门外日坛路7号

Royal Embassy of Cambodia
9 Dongzhimenwai Dajie
Tel. 6532 1889
柬埔寨 东直门外大街9号

Kazakhstan
6 Dongliu Jie, Sanlitun
Tel. 6532 6182
哈萨克斯坦 三里屯东六街6号

Korea
4/F China World Trade Center,
1 Jianguomenwai Dajie
Tel. 6532 6774
大韩民国 建国门外大街国贸中心4层

Laos
11 Dongsi Jie, Sanlitun
Tel. 6532 1224
老挝 三里屯东四街11号

Malaysia
2 Liangmaqiao North Street
Tel. 6532 2531
马来西亚 亮马桥北街2号

Mongolia
2 Xiushui Bei Jie
Tel. 6532 1203
蒙古 建国门外秀水北街2号

Myanmar (Burma)
6 Dongzhimenwai Dajie
Tel. 6532 0359; 6532 0412
缅甸 东直门外大街6号

Nepal
1 Xiliu Jie, Sanlitun
Tel. 6532 1795
尼泊尔 三里屯路西六街1号

Netherlands
4 Liangmahe Nan Lu. Tel. 8532 0200
荷兰 亮马河南路4号

New Zealand
1 Ritan Dong'er Jie
Tel. 8532 7000
新西兰 日坛东二街1号

Norway
1 Dongyi Jie, Sanlitun
Tel. 6532 2261-2
挪威 三里屯东一街1号

Pakistan
1 Dongzhimenwai Dajie
Tel. 6532 2504
巴基斯坦 三里屯东直门外大街1号

Philippines
23 Xiushui Bei Jie
Tel. 6532 1872
菲律宾 秀水北街23号

Poland
1 Ritan Lu
Tel. 6532 1235
波兰 日坛路1号

Russian Federation
4 Dongzhimen Beizhongjie
Tel. 6532 2051, 6532 2181
俄罗斯联邦大使馆
东直门内北中街4号

Singapore
1 Xiushui Bei Jie, Jianguomen
Tel. 6532 1115
新加坡 朝阳区建国门外秀水北街1号

Slovak Republic
Ritan Lu and Jianguomenwai
Tel. 6532 1531
斯洛伐克 建国门外日坛路

South Africa
5 Dongzhimenwai Dajie
Tel. 6532 0171
南非 东直门外大街5号

Spain
9 Sanlitun Lu
Tel. 6532 3629, 6532 1986
西班牙 三里屯路9号

Sri Lanka
3 Jianhua Lu, Jianguomenwai
Tel. 6532 1861-2
斯里兰卡 建国门外建华路3号

Sweden
3 Dongzhimenwai Dajie, Sanlitun
Tel. 6532 9790
瑞典 三里屯东直门外大街3号

Switzerland
3 Dongwu Jie, Sanlitun
Tel. 8532 8888
瑞士 三里屯东五街3号

Thailand
40 Guanghua Lu, Jianguomenwai
Tel. 6532 1749
泰国 建国门外光华路40号

United Kingdom
11 Guanghua Lu, Jianguomenwai
Tel. 5192 4000
英国 建国门外光华路11号

USA
55 Anjialo Street, Chaoyang District
Tel. 8531 3000
美国 朝阳区安家楼路55号

Uzbekistan
11 Bei Xiao Jie, Sanlitun
Tel. 6532 6305
乌兹别克斯坦 三里屯北小街11号

Vietnam
32 Guanghua Lu, Jianguomenwai
Tel. 6532 1155, 6532 1125
越南 建国门外光华路32号

Convention and Exhibition Venues

Beijing International Convention Center
8 Beichen Dong Lu. Tel. 8497 3060
北京国际会议中心 北辰东路8号

Exhibition Hall at the China World Trade Center
1 Jianguomenwai Dajie
Tel. 6505 0540
中国会议中心展览馆
建国门外大街1号

China International Exhibition Center
6 Beisanhuan Dong Lu
Chaoyang District
Tel. 8460 0000
中国国际展览中心 北三环东路6号

Medical Care

Beijing has a number of hospitals, emergency clinics, and international medical evacuation offices for foreigners. For emergency assistance in English, 24 hours per day, try either of the following:

Beijing United Family Hospital
2 Jiangtai Lu, Chaoyang District
Tel. 5927 7000
Tel. 5927 7120 (emergency)
和睦家医院 将台路2号
Close to the Lido Hotel in northeastern Beijing, this hospital is operated by international and board certified physicians, dentists, surgeons, and nurses, all of whom are English-speaking.

Beijing International (SOS) Clinic
Beixin Dasha Building C
1 North Road, Xing Fu San Cun
Chaoyang District
Tel. 6462 9199
Tel. 6462 9100 (24-hour clinic)
Tel. 6462 9112 (24-hour emergency)
toll free. 80 0810 01 80; fax. 6462 9111
www.internationalsos.com
国际SOS
幸福三村北街1号 北信京宜大厦C座
The clinic specializes in emergency medicine and medical evacuation, but also offers clinical services to resident expatriates and travelers. The facility is close to Beijing's Sanlitun District. Travelers may wish to consider

purchasing emergency evacuation insurance prior to departing from their home country; it may or may not be covered in other travel insurance policies.

International Medical Center
S106 Lufthansa Center Office Building
50 Liangmaqiao Lu
Tel: 6465 1561
北京国际医疗中心
亮马桥路50号燕莎中心写字楼S106
Twenty-four hour medical facility with doctors speaking numerous languages, including English. Offers dental and pharmaceutical services also.

Beijing Emergency Center
103 Qianmen Xi Dajie. Tel. 6609 8114
北京急救中心 前门西大街103号

Beijing Vista Clinic
1/B, Kerry Center Shopping Mall
1 Guanghua Lu. Tel: 8529 6618
北京维世达诊所
光华路1号嘉里中心地下1层
Friendship Hospital (Youyi Yiyuan)
Tianqiao. Tel. 6301 4411
友谊医院 天桥永安路95号

Hong Kong International Medical Clinic
9/F Hong Kong-Macau Center
2 Chaoyangmen Bei Dajie
Tel. 6553 2288 ext. 2346 (24-hour service) Tel. 6502 3426 (after 9pm)
香港国际医务诊所
朝阳门北大街2号港澳中心写字楼9层

Peking Union Medical College Hospital
Emergency (foreigners' section)
Dongdan, Dongcheng District
Tel. 6529 6114
协和医院
东城区东单王府井师府园1号

Sino-German Polyclinic (Zhong-De zhen suo) A privately run 24-hour ambulance service; performs minor surgery.
B1, Landmark Tower A
8 Dongsanhuan Bei Lu
Tel. 6590 0901
中德诊所 东三环北路8号
亮马大厦 A座 B1

Sino-Japanese Friendship Hospital
North end of Heping Jie
Chaoyang District
Tel. 8420 5566
中日友好医院 朝阳区 和平北街

Travel and Transport

Travel Agencies

Beijing CITS
28 Jianguomenwai Dajie
Tel. 6515 8587
北京中国国际旅行社
建国门外大街28号

China Guide, The
Bldg. 7-1-81
Jianguomenwai Diplomatic Compound
Tel. 8532 2274; Mobile: 159 1074 0785
www.thebeijingguide.com
建外外交公寓7号1单元8层1号房

CITIC Travel Co.
6th Floor, Business Travel Department
International Building, 19 Jianwai Dajie
Tel. 8526 1166
中信旅游
建外大街19号国际大厦6层商务旅行部

CTS Head Office
3 West Chongwenmen Dajie
Tel: 6512 9933
中国旅社总社
北京市崇文门西大街3号

Wild China
Room 801, Oriental Place
9 East Dongfang Road
North Dongsanhuan Road
Chaoyang District
Tel. 6465 6602, fax 6465 1793
Email: info@wildchina.com
www.wildchina.com
Wild China 朝阳区 东三环北路
东方路9号东方国际大厦801室

Visas

Beijing Municipal Public Security Bureau
Aliens' Entry and Exit Administration Office
2 Andingmen East Street
Dongcheng District. Tel. 8402 0101
北京公安局出入境管理局
东城区 安定门东大街2号

Airport

Beijing International Airport
Information. Tel. 6454 1100
北京国际机场

Taxi Supervision Office

Beijing Chuzu Qiche Diaodu Zhongxin Gongsi
14F, Hangtian Xinxi Dalou, 1 Binhe Lu
Heping Li. Tel: 6837 3388
北京出租汽车调度中心公司
和平里 滨河路1号 航天信息大楼14层

Railway

Beijing Railway Station
General Enquiries. Tel. 5101 9999
Foreigners' ticket office is located on the first floor in the Soft Berth Waiting Hall in the southeast corner of the station.
北京火车站

Beijing South Station
Tel. 5186 7999
北京火车南站

Car Rental

Note that foreigners can only drive in China if they have a Chinese driving license. International driving licenses are not recognized.

Yinjian Qiche Zulin Gongsi (Car Rental)
2F, Area 1, 29 Fanzhuang Guyuan, Fengtai District
Tel. 8761 1468
银健汽车租赁公司
丰台区 方庄芳古园1区29号2层

Theaters

Beijing Concert Hall
1 Bei Xinhua Jie. Tel. 6605 7006
北京音乐厅 西城区 北新华街1号

Beijing Hu Guang Guildhall
3 Hufangqiao, Xuanwu District
Tel. 6301 3680
湖广会馆楚畹园 宣武区 虎坊桥3号

Capital Theater
22 Wangfujing Dajie. Tel. 6525 0996
首都剧场 王府井大街22号

Chang'an Grand Theater
7 Jianguomennei Dajie. Tel. 6510 1309
长安大戏院 建国门内大街7号

Chaoyang Theater
36 Dongsanhuan Bei Lu, Hujialou
Tel. 6507 1818
朝阳剧场 呼家楼东三环北路36号

China Children's Art Theater
Beijige Santiao, Jia 23, Dongcheng
Tel. 6513 4121
中国儿童艺术剧院
北京市东城区 北极阁三条甲32号

Chinese Opera Theater
Xisanhuan Bei Lu, Haidianqu
Tel. 6841 9381
中国剧院 海淀区 西三环北路16号

China Opera and Dance Institute
Building 1, No. 23, Tower C.
Fengtai District, South Third Ring Road
Tel. 5975 2020
中国歌剧舞剧院
丰台区 南三环东路23号院 1号楼 C座

Grand National Theater Beijing
No.2 West Chang'an Avenue
Xicheng District
Tel. 6655 0989, (hotline): 6655 0000
国家大剧院 西城区 西长安街2号

Liyuan Theater
Qianmen Hotel, 175 Yongan Lu
Tel. 8315 7297
梨园 永安路175号前门饭店

COURIER AND POST

DHL Sinotrans Ltd
Zuojiazhuang Tel. 800 810 8000 or
Cell: 400 810 8000
18 Ronghua Nan Lu, Yizhuang
Daxing District
中外运－教豪国际航空有限公司
大兴区 亦庄荣华南路18号

FedEx
Hotline: 400 889 1888
E102 Fortune Plaza
7 Dong Sanhuan Zhonglu
Chaoyang District
联邦快递 朝阳区 东三环中路7号

**International Post and
Telecommunications Office**
Jianguomen Bei Dajie
Tel. 6512 8120
国际邮局管 建国门北大街

Post Office
G/F, CITIC Building B
19 Jianguomenwai Dajie
Chaoyang District
Tel. 8526 3119, 8526 3120
Open Monday to Friday only
邮局
国际大厦B座首层 建国门外大街19号

ESSENTIAL TELEPHONE NUMBERS

Fire: 119
Police: 110
Beijing Emergency Center (medical): 120
Beijing directory inquiry
(Chinese language only): 114
International operator: 115
Domestic long distance operator: 113
Domestic long distance inquiry: 116
Time (in Chinese): 117
Weather (in Chinese and English): 121
Tourist Hotline (24 hours): 6513 0828

GRAND CANAL SYSTEMS 305

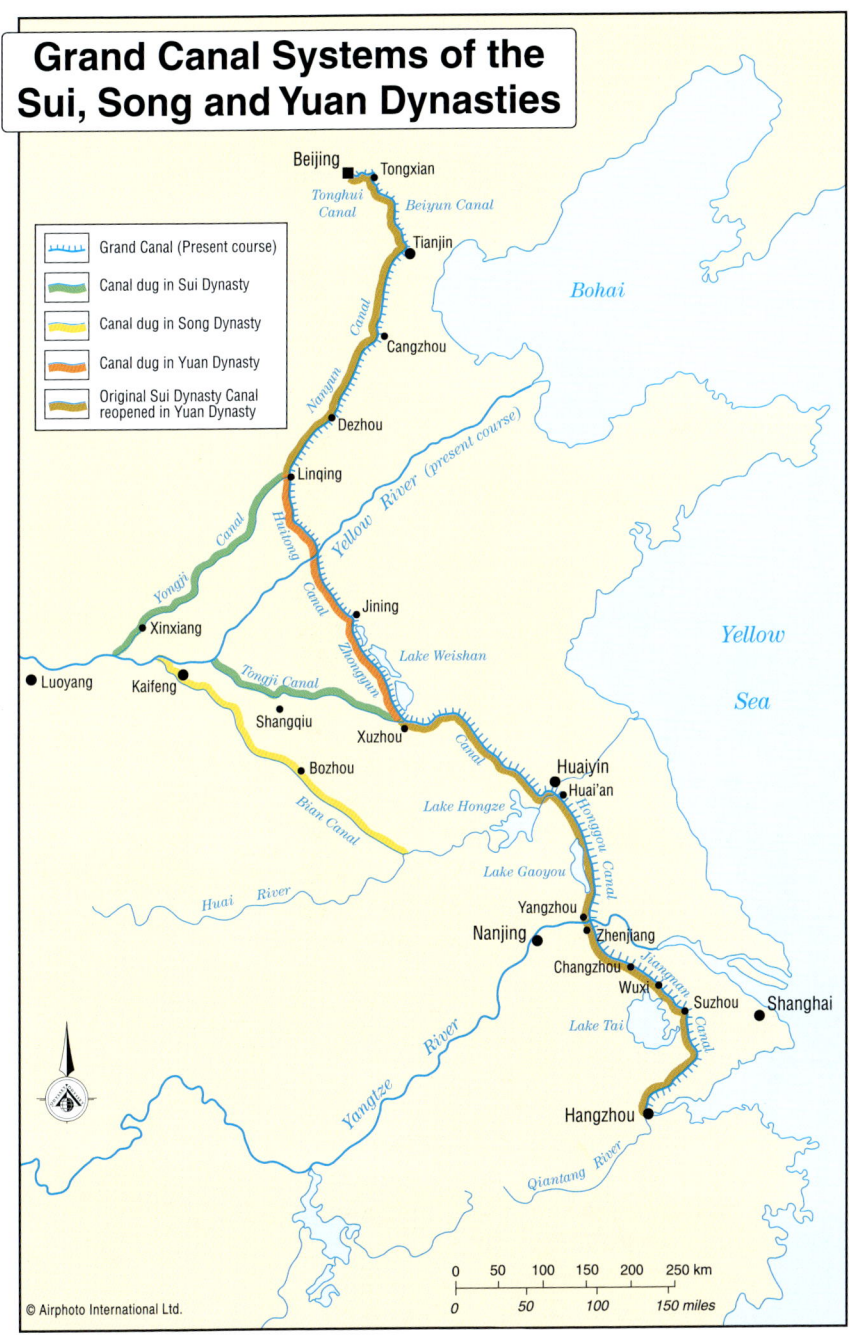

Founders of the Nation in the early days, by Wei Rong 1977, Paris-Pekin.

Matters of Philosophy

Transformation of the Old

The powerful light that has been banished returns
There is movement, but it is not brought about by force
For this reason the transformation of the old becomes easy
The old is discarded and the new is introduced
Both measures accord with the time; therefore
No harm results.

—I Ching

Business Men

Business men boast of their skill and cunning
But in matters of philosophy are like little children.
Bragging to each other of successful depredations
They neglect to consider the ultimate fate of the body.
What should they know of the Master of Dark Truth
Who saw the wide world in a jade cup,
By illumined conception got clear of Heaven and Earth,
On the chariot of Mutation entered the Gate of Immutability?

—Chen Tzu-ang as translated by Arthur Waley

The I Ching; or, Book of Changes. The Richard Wilhelm translation rendered into English by Cary F. Baynes, (Routledge & Kegan Paul Ltd., London 1951). The *I Ching*, written by Fu Hsi, King Wen and the Duke of Chou, represents one of the first efforts of the human mind to place itself in the universe. It has exerted a living influence in China for 3,000 years.

The translation of Chen Tzu-ang's "Business Men" is from *Madly Singing in the Mountains: An Appreciation and Anthology of Arthur Waley* (George Allen & Unwin Ltd., 1970) Edited by Ivan Morris © 1970. Chen Tzu-ang (656–698) was a Tang Dynasty poet. Considered to be an innovator, his verse is oft-described by Chinese as *"Ying"* and is not easily translated into English. Arthur Waley (1889–1966) translated both Chinese and Japanese poetry, yet never came to Asia, and was somewhat of an innovator himself. See page 469 for more of his translation work.

SHANGHAI

East of the Poo—Pootung

Going back to the earliest days of foreign presence in Shanghai in the 1840s Pudong (or Pootung in old speak) was a port of call for many foreign seafarers as their sea-weary opium hulks moored alongside. Given that London was over 100 days away by ship it was no surprise that the crews' rapacious antics endowed the area with a notorious reputation. It is believed that the term 'shanghaied' originates from the activities of a Pudong-based American ship's captain who would drug and kidnap entire ship's crews.

View of Pudong over the Suzhou Creek and the Huangpu River around 1930.

However, Pudong was also renowned for its righteousness as it housed a large Chinese Christian population, including one of the largest communities of Roman Catholics to be found anywhere in China. In one village, a church capable of holding a congregation of 2,000 opened around 1900. A Sailor's Church was established in the 1850s on the site of where the landmark Oriental Pearl TV Tower stands today. Its cemetery, disused after 1904, was the final resting place for over 1,700 sailors who never returned to their home shores.

Pudong is still popularly portrayed as being nothing more than farmland and paddy fields before the opening of China's door in 1978. This was certainly true at the end of the 19th century, when there were just four villages in the area. However, over the following three decades, as Shanghai's industrial revolution surged ahead, tens of thousands of migrants from around China moved in and the four villages were transformed into one mass of housing.

As the following account from *Shanghai by Night & Day*, published by the *Shanghai Mercury* around 1920 portrays Pudong's valuable river frontage and hinterland was crowded with cotton mills, warehouses, factories and wharves. In essence, whilst the stately buildings on and around the Bund housed the headquarters of big business, many of their workplaces occupied the banks on the other side of the river—the Poo as it was then known:

It is by no means an uncommon thing for a great city to be divided into two parts by a river running through it. London proper is so divided from Southwark; and Buda, the great Hungarian city, from Pesth. We have always expected that something of the kind would occur in Shanghai, but comparatively few people know that a beginning has already been made. The International Mill stands out for itself, so do the larger godowns higher up, but the Pootung town—there is one—is modestly hidden from the view of the dwellers on the western side of the river.

A visit to the eastern bank is by no means devoid of interest. As the sampan approaches the jetty, there are some half dozen foreign dwelling houses in a row facing the river, with another building of similar construction on their southern side. The mind instinctively reverts to MARTIN CHUZZLEWIT and EDEN as it surveys the reedy foreshore with its flotsam and jetsam, its posts and puddles. The summer heat of the westerly sun on the front will doubtless be balanced by the cold of the winter's northwesters, and the inhabitants may get what comfort they can from this part, but we hardly think the position an ideal one for family residences.

Near by stands the signal station, with its keeper above, and its marine stores below. A couple of old ship's guns are still in sufficiently good order to give the notices, ever growing in frequency, of incoming mails, but at the back of the shed there is quite a battery of unused muzzle loaders, some dozen or so, not unlike the armament of 'our war ships some forty years ago. We can distinctly remember a visit to the Minotaur not long after she was launched, and seeing similar weapons on board her to the number of a hundred or so.

The cotton mill dwarfs everything near it. Its busy hum is heard all round, but the most interesting event to a visitor who looks on from the outside is the exit of the day shift and the entrance of the night workers. At six sharp the whistle sounds. Three or four men who have evidently been waiting just inside the doorway, are down the steps before two seconds are gone, and then for five minutes the great building empties its living hive. The engines stop, the hum ceases. Out pour the women in a continuous stream four deep. They seem very orderly, and the red-topped Sikh on duty has no need to exert his authority this time. For full five minutes the stream flows on, and one begins to wonder when it will cease. Then, except for a few laggards, the outgoing crowd ceases, and the night shift which has already collected outside enters. These are fresh: they are at the right end of their twelve hours spell to be frisky, and a good many of them apparently are boys. These enter with a rush, a roar, and a scramble, the Sikh after them, doubtless on corrective thoughts intent. The elders follow quietly enough. They stream in twos, threes, and fours, and ere long the respite ends, and toil begins once more.

It is evident that all these crowds need house room. Years ago there were but a couple or three foreign houses in the neighbourhood, one or two of which still remain dilapidated to an extent beyond all but photographic description. But for the teeming hundreds of the mills there has grown up a veritable town with well laid out roads, macadamized and drained after the most approved Municipal model. There are shops, as well as dwelling-houses, and to prove that civilization of the highest sort is not lacking we can bear testimony to the fact that soap is not merely for sale but freely bought. Did we not see two cakes of the "honey" brand disposed of, the one to a coolie who went sniffing at it all along the road, the other to a smutty faced, happy go-lucky youth from Boyd's workshops. There is probably over a mile of well-made road on the Pootung side, a statement that will surprise more than one of our readers. Order is kept by the Sikhs aforesaid, and apparently by a sort of amateur police force on a native model, of which we saw one specimen in a sort of revenue cruiser get-up, truncheon and all. Of course there are Buddhist priests in evidence, notwithstanding the fact that a large proportion of the native population is Catholic.

To the south a little lies the American Cigarette factory, and various godowns occupy sites here and there". Between the little town and the well-known yard of Messrs. Boyd and Co. is the cemetery.

It is, as it should be, neatly kept, for "each in his narrow cell for ever laid" there lie here some 2,000 men, many British, and mostly mariners. The great majority of these have nothing—but the nameless mound which marks their bit of real estate. "Earth to earth, and dust to dust" is literally true of all of them. Not even the lingering record of a slab of stone remains to tell their humble story; they are gone as completely as if they had never existed. Of those whose graves are marked by some lasting token, "erected by his shipmates" is probably the story of the stone in nine cases out of ten; and the impression is burnt in as one visits such mournful spots that if any foreign land has a right to a voice in the affairs of China, that land is Great Britain, who has given with no niggard hand her sons for the good of the world at large.

Adjoining the cemetery is the ever-increasing establishment of Boyd and Co. The sailor dies, the ship is born. There is a rough sort of appropriateness in the proximity of the sailors' resting place and the steam-ships' cradle. The energy of the men who sleep beneath the Pootung turf made possible the energy now being exerted above it. We should be glad to say that the little church where, in the olden days, a hundred of them in little knots came from many a sailing ship "to hear the word of God" was worthy of its watch. But it is not. Dilapidated, dirty, and degraded, its present condition is a disgrace to the religion whose name it bears. Its modest little spire points mutely up to heaven, but who ran raise his eyes in that direction when all his care can scarce avoid the filth that lies below.

But the sun is sinking behind the settlement on the other side. Twilight comes, and on our return we see the Bund in silhouette, and wonder with a great wonder why from the as yet unlighted houses so many chimneys should jut up against the background of the sky. There is the square tower of the Custom house, there is the Cathedral spire rising apparently out of the roof of one of the banks, there is a characteristic touch to two or three other roofs, but for the rest—chimneys, nothing but chimneys, and before we have decided why, the sampan-man wants his fare.

Special Topic

Shanghai—Yesterday and Today

–Lynn Pan and Peter Hibbard

Shanghai has its genesis as China's pre-eminent trading centre in the First Opium War, which ended in 1842 with the defeated Chinese empire agreeing to the opening of five Treaty Ports—Shanghai, Canton (Guangzhou), Ningbo, Fuzhou and Amoy (Xiamen)—to foreign trade and residence. To be a treaty port was to have foreign firms like Jardine Matheson and BAT (British American Tobacco), to have a racecourse, clubs, Sikh policemen, Gilbert and Sullivan at the Amateur Dramatic Club, Lea and Perrin's sauce, and to be visited regularly by British, and occasionally American, gunboats.

In the British and American International Settlement and the French Concession—areas specifically set aside in Shanghai for foreign residence—local administration, from police and sanitation to roads and building regulations, was in foreign hands. The

Preceding pages: *Old and new worlds—Oriental Pearl TV Tower, Pudong and Tai Chi on the Bund.*

Municipal Council, the governing body of the International Settlement, was dominated by a largely British inner circle representing its major business interests. Following the First World War the Council had 5 British, 2 American and 2 Japanese members.

Shanghai became one of the most cosmopolitan cities the world had ever known: the whole gamut of Western and Asian humanity was there, from Jewish tycoons and self-styled White Russian 'countesses' to Annamese gendarmes and Filipino band leaders. One shopped at Hall and Holtz; Lane, Crawford and Company; Laidlaw and Company; and Kelly and Walsh. One read the *North China Daily News*, *Shanghai Times*, *Shanghai Mercury*, *L'Echo de Chine*, *Der Ostasiatische Lloyd*, and the *Shanghai Nippo*. One danced in the chic ballroom of the Cercle Sportif Français or at The Cathay and partied at cabarets like the Casanova, Del Monte and Ciro's.

The city's gaiety and stylishness earned it the name of 'Paris of the Orient'. An English visitor to the city in the inter-war period caught its ambiance nicely when he described a woman he saw sitting alone in a nightclub: dressed all in green, she held a green cigarette between her lips and had a glass of crème de menthe on the table in front of her. On other nights, she would be seen in red velvet, sipping cherry brandy and smoking a rose-coloured cigarette.

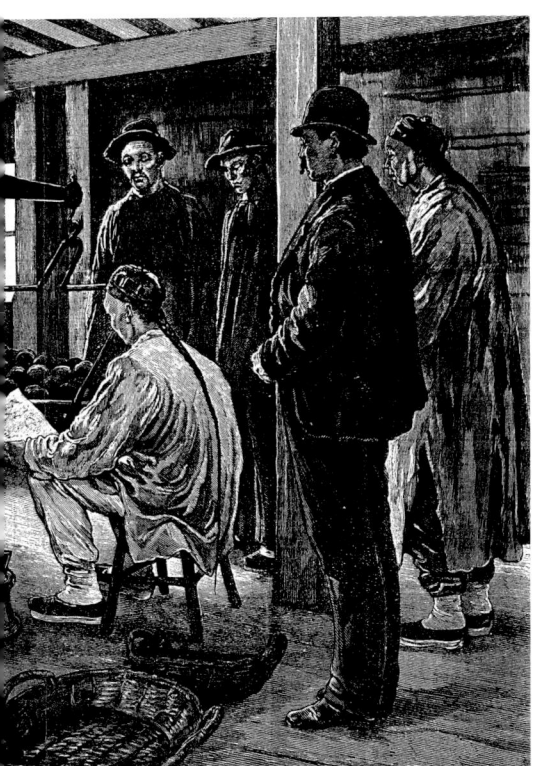

For a long time the Europeans kept Chinese people out of their parks, clubs and homes. Commercially, though, they were on far closer terms, their business transactions channelled through the compradore. Trade and manufacturing grew in leaps and bounds, and Shanghai became the gateway of China—a conduit through which merchandise and ideas were funnelled from the Western world.

Above: *A casual 19th century depiction of the infamous opium trade.*
The Illustrated London News, December 8, 1883.

Laying the foundation-stone of the new Masonic Temple at Shanghai. The Illustrated London News, November 18, 1883.

One of these ideas was Marxism. A burgeoning proletariat, dismal working conditions in the textile factories, the frankly racist attitudes of many of the Europeans, the immunity from Chinese law provided by the self-governing foreign enclaves—all these factors help towards an explanation of why the Chinese Communist Party was founded in Shanghai. The magazine *New Youth*, edited by Chen Duxiu, is a historical reflection of the forum of debate raging in Shanghai at the time, with its discussions of democracy, education, sexual equality and empirical science. Lu Xun, the Chinese Chekhov, first appeared in these pages. This intellectual, political and social movement was brought to Beijing around 1919, and undoubtebly aided China's inexorable move from Confucianism, turmoil and the foreign yoke towards the events that led to the proclamation of the People's Republic of China on October 1, 1949, led by a former assistant librarian at Beijing University—Mao Zedong.

Lu Xun.

When Communism overtook Shanghai in 1949, the city's notorious past was held against it, and the new regime did its best to turn it from what it considered as a Sodom and Gomorrah into a monument to Stalinist central planning. Economically Shanghai was a great success: for years its industrial output and productivity were the highest in the country. With a hundredth of China's population, it accounted for a fourth of the nation's export earnings and a sixth of the national revenue.

The Waving Mao, 1992. *By Shanghai artist Yu Youhan*, Paris Pekin.

Until recently, Shanghai had been starved of investment, Beijing having siphoned off much of its huge earnings. When China began to reform her economic system and opened her doors to the outside world, in the late 1970s, one imagined a resurgence of the entrepreneurial spirit in Shanghai. But this did not quite happen. Shanghai could hardly make the best of the winds of change when it had been left with roads, housing and factories dating back to the 1930s and 1940s. And the more the urban pressures grew, as the streets got more congested and the housing shortage more desperately acute, the more intransigent the general mood became.

For years Shanghai was at cross-purposes with Beijing: once it was too capitalist, then it was too 'leftist'. Its past reputation as a Paradise of Adventurers did not endear it to China's leaders; nor did its association with the Gang of Four, who used it as their base during the Cultural Revolution. Worse still, the Shanghainese are arrogant, and will not be told what to do by anyone, least of all by their masters in Beijing!

Yet, with the passing of the 1980s Shanghai has sprinted towards a new era of development. Since 1991 the city has experienced a frenzy of activity reminiscent of the heady speculative years of the 1930s, when the 'Paris of the East' came of age. Shanghai is again in the advanced throes of a physical, economic and social revolution destined to restore the city's former status as an international centre of trade, finance and commerce.

Ambitious reconstruction programmes are well underway. Numerous spectatcular bridges and tunnels traverse the hectic Huangpu River and many more are planned up to the year 2020. Massive new elevated highways, circling and bisecting the city, have been developed feeding into a modern regional highway network that many Shanghainese claim leads all the way to Tibet. Below ground, core elements of the city's metro system are in place complemented by an efficient overhead light railway. The Pudong International Airport is plugged into the system by way of the world's first commercial magnetic levitation railway. The People's Square, formerly part of the racecourse, has been redeveloped as a home for the city government and new Shanghai Museum; whilst the Bund, one of the most famous waterfronts in the East, has been renovated and enjoys a new lease of life. The outdated fabric of Shanghai, largely untouched since the 1940s, is now eagerly felt, folded and cut by the property speculator and business manager in pursuit of efficiency and profit.

The former main streets of the International Settlement and the French Concession have changed beyond recognition. Coloured and neon lights create avenues of enticement for the wealthier modern Shanghainese, whilst modern buildings arise from the ashes of the past at a hungry speed. Reassuringly the government vows that the best of the old will be preserved. Many remain sceptical.

Pudong seen from the Bund, the hectic Huangpu River carries large vessels towards Zhejiang Province.

Huge tracts of historic housing have been razed in the downtown area and many buildings that have been preserved are often garishly renovated. In the period from 1990 to mid-2003, over 800,000 households were relocated from their old dwellings, robbing the city of some of its fine architectural heritage. In their place huge green areas have been installed and massive high-rise towers have been rapidly assembled.

No where is this more apparent than in the Lujiazui financial district in Pudong where the skyscraper spires of the Oriental Pearl TV Tower, the Jinmao Tower and Shanghai's latest monument to the skies, the astounding 101-storey Shanghai World Financial Centre, stand like huge tentacles of a beast surfacing from the waters of the Huangpu River.

The pressing urgency for the city to get all dressed up for the World Expo 2010 was witnessed by a massive wave of urban gentrification projects. Some major schemes, including that for remodelling the Bund and its neighbouring district, which had had been talked about, or put on hold for years, suddenly sprang to life with a cluttering of mud and metal, and of man and machine. Thousands of buildings, old and not so old, were repainted, washed, manicured and given new faces, often with little respect to their original historical appearance. Shanghai has long been a city of show and face and this holds truer than ever today as it has been 'prettified' like never before.

Strangely, many of the current changes in the city would appear familiar to the 1930s foreign resident returning today. A sense of déjà vu might prevail despite the bodily change the city continues to bear.

The solitude of the night is now broken by a flourishing entertainment industry ranging from all night bowling alleys and discos to ballroom dances, old-time jazz, amateur dramatics staged in Art Deco theatres and grandiose symphony concerts. The gap between rich and poor is manifest, as the Shanghai elite garbed in international designer clothes patronise expensive KTV clubs and consume the best cognac with a passion.

Cartier, on the Bund.

The old cumshaw, or tip, has gained a new acceptance and service charges on basic hotel rates, a practice outlawed by the Nationalists in 1945, have returned. Though coffee shops with European style pastries never fell from fashion, all manner of Western food is back. Gambling fever, spurred by the novelty of the Shanghai Stock Market, molests the most innocent Shanghai citizen—and prostitution, a returned phenomenon in China, has been officially recognised as a fact of life.

The fast-growing foreign business and diplomatic communities frequent their own social and sports clubs. The Hongqiao and Gubei districts, favoured domiciles of foreign capitalists in the 1930s, are jam-packed with luxurious private villas and foreign housing. Massive expatriate villa estates have recently appeared in the Pudong New Area alongside international schools and hypermarkets, golf courses and bars. Property speculation is rife and amongst the stores of Huaihai Road and Nanjing Road can be found a vast array of international goods. On Huaihai Road, the Sincere department store, first seen in Shanghai in 1916, has opened a large new store. Meanwhile the Bund has welcomed the return of foreign occupants. Some people might say that Shanghai hasn't really changed very much at all over the years.

On the Social Organism

I have seen places that were, no doubt, as busy and as thickly populous as the Chinese city in Shanghai, but none that so overwhelmingly impressed me with its business and populousness. In no city, West or East, have I ever had such an impression of dense, rank, richly clotted life. Old Shanghai is Bergson's élan vital in the raw, so to speak, and with the lid off. It is Life itself. Each individual Chinaman has more vitality, you feel, than each individual Indian or European, and the social organism composed of these individuals is therefore more intensely alive than the social organism in India or the West. Or perhaps it is the vitality of the social organism—a vitality accumulated and economized through centuries by ancient habit and tradition. So much life, so carefully canalized, so rapidly and strongly flowing—the spectacle of it inspires something like terror. All this was going on when we were cannibalistic savages. It will still be going on—a little modified, perhaps, by Western science, but not much—long after we in Europe have simply died of fatigue. A thousand years from now the seal-cutters will still be engraving their seals, the ivory workers still sawing and polishing; the tailors will be singing the merits of their cut and cloth, even as they do to-day; the spectacled astrologers will still be conjuring silver out of the pockets of bumpkins and amorous courtesans; there will be a bird market, and eating houses perfumed with delicious cooking, and chemists' shops with bottles full of dried lizards, tigers' whiskers, rhinoceros horns and pickled salamanders; there will be patient jewellers and embroiderers of faultless taste, shops full of marvellous crockery, and furriers who can make elaborate patterns and pictures out of variously coloured fox-skins; and the great black ideographs will still be as perfectly written as they are to-day, or were a thousand years ago, will be thrown on to the red paper with the same apparent recklessness, the same real and assured skill, by a long fine hand as deeply learned in the hieratic gestures of its art as the hand of the man who is writing now. Yes, it will all be there, just as intensely and tenaciously alive as ever—all there a thousand years hence, five thousand, ten. You have only to stroll through old Shanghai to be certain of it. London and Paris offer no such certainty. And even India seems by comparison provisional and precarious.

Aldous Leonard Huxley, Jesting Pilate: An Intellectual Holiday (The Diary of a Journey) (Chatto & Windus, 1926)

Aldous Leonard Huxley (1894–1963) stood apart from the intellectual elite class into which he was born. Even as a small child he was considered different, showing an alertness, an intelligence, what his brother called a superiority. He was respected and loved—not hated—for these abilities, but he drew on that feeling of separateness in writing Brave New World. His mother's death from cancer when he was 14 gave him a sense of the transience of human happiness, and when he was 16 and a student at the prestigious school Eton, an eye illness made him nearly blind. He entered the literary world while he was at Oxford, publishing his first book, a collection of poems, in 1916. Huxley divided his time between London and Europe, mostly Italy, in the 1920s, and travelled around the world in 1925 and 1926, seeing India. In 1937, he emigrated to the United States. Huxley produced 47 books in his long career as a writer.

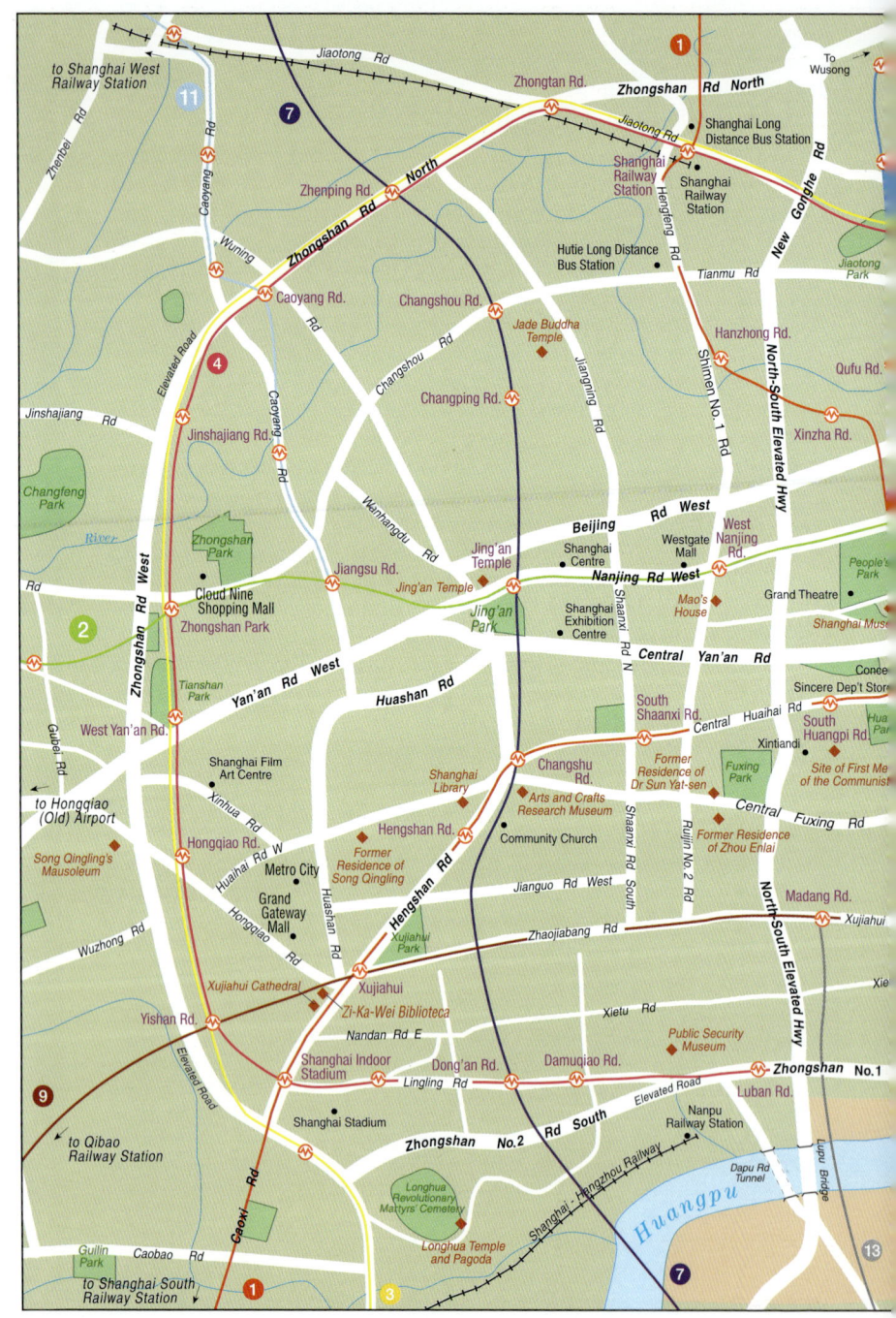

GETTING AROUND SHANGHAI 325

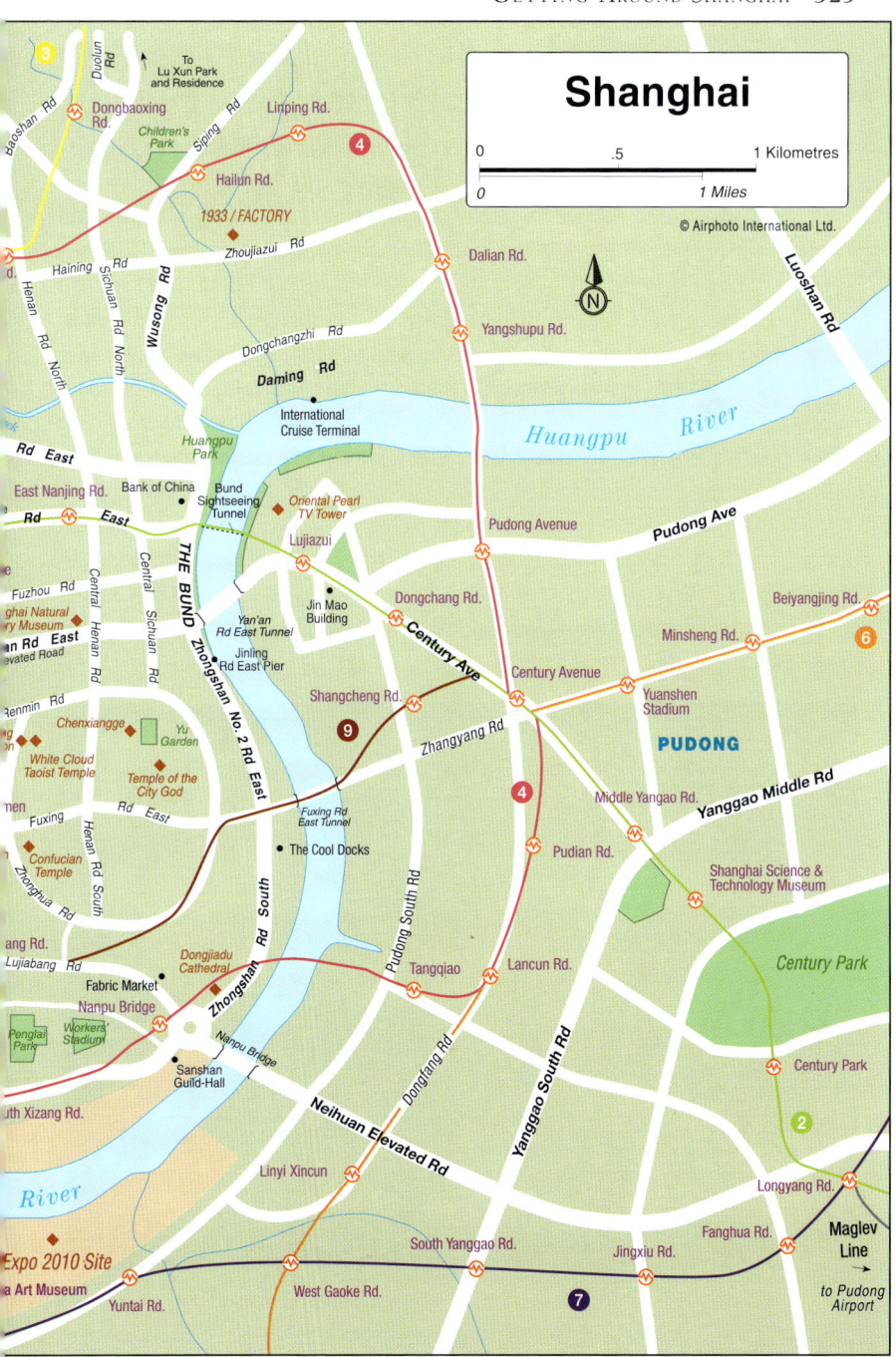

Getting Around Shanghai

Shanghai is a colossus of a city and with the constant, hectic renewal of its districts and transport networks many local people find the city bemusing to navigate. However, saying that, most areas of interest for the visitor have many landmarks, old and new, which make it easy to get around. The main parts of the historic Puxi area (west of the Huangpu River) and the Pudong New Area (east of the river) are laid out on a fairly regular rectangular pattern. However, that all changes when you enter the wizardly warren of lanes in the 'old town,' and to a lesser extent as you wander the meandering plane-tree lined streets in the heart of the former French Concession area. Nevertheless, getting a little lost is all part of the fun—and Shanghai can be one of the most walking-friendly cities in the world. Even if you are in vehicle stuck in slow moving traffic much of Shanghai's beauty and local interest will be easily missed. The real Shanghai resides behind the high walls, wooded entrances and modern shop-fronts. Fine mansions dating back a hundred years, local neighbourhoods in spectacular art deco estates and traditional 'stone-frame door' *shikumen* housing along small lanes and beautiful parks all await those willing to take a short detour from the main roads.

The main parts of the historic Puxi area (west of the Huangpu River) and the Pudong New Area as it looked in 2005.

Even on Shanghai's most modern shopping streets you are never far from the past. And the main attraction is the warm response you are bound to receive from the friendly local people. The only things to watch out for are cyclists and moped riders who take to the pavement as they are banned from many busy roads, and the odd wobbly paving stone.

Getting around the urban area by road has been greatly eased by the massive city highway projects that have materialised since the mid-1990s. The city is now crossed with by an elevated inner ring road and major east-west and north-south highways. Shiny sedans and taxis speeding around the network can often be seen overtaking police cars—something unheard of in many countries. Before 1991, the largely undeveloped Pudong, east of the Huangpu River, was commonly reached by ferry-boat. Today the futuristic Pudong area is easily approached by an ever increasing number of bridges and tunnels, including four tunnels and three spectacular bridges in the central area—the Yangpu, Nanpu and the Lupu and more beyond. However, the system is still far from complete and traffic snarl-ups frequently occur at rush hours.

The real Shanghai resides behind the high walls, wooded entrances and modern shop-fronts.

Most areas of interest however, are found on roads that haven't changed too much in the last 50 years, where traffic trundles at a pedestrian pace at peak periods. In contrast, the Pudong New Area boasts many wide avenues, including the 4.2 kilometre (2.6 mile) long Century Boulevard that is 100 metres (328 feet) wide.

If you are planning to travel a fair amount by taxis or public transport it is well worth investing in a Shanghai Public Transportation Card (Shanghai Jiaotong Ka). They can save a lot of queuing and searching for change. This smart card can be used on the Metro system, most city buses, in taxis and on the local ferry from Pudong to Puxi. They can be purchased for 130 yuan (100 yuan transport credit plus 30 yuan refundable deposit) from all Metro stations as well as at many convenience stores. Collectable souvenir versions cost 140 yuan, including 100 yuan credit, but

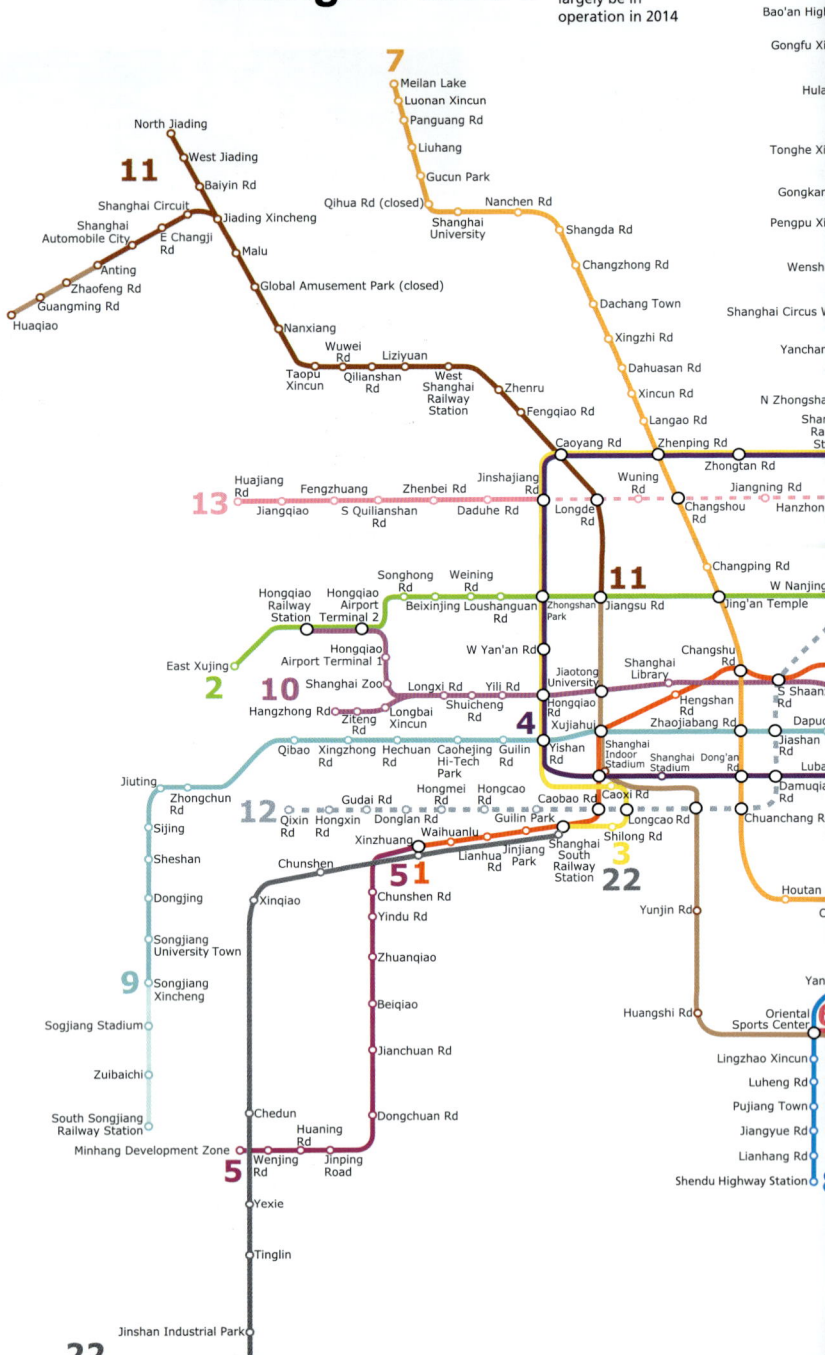

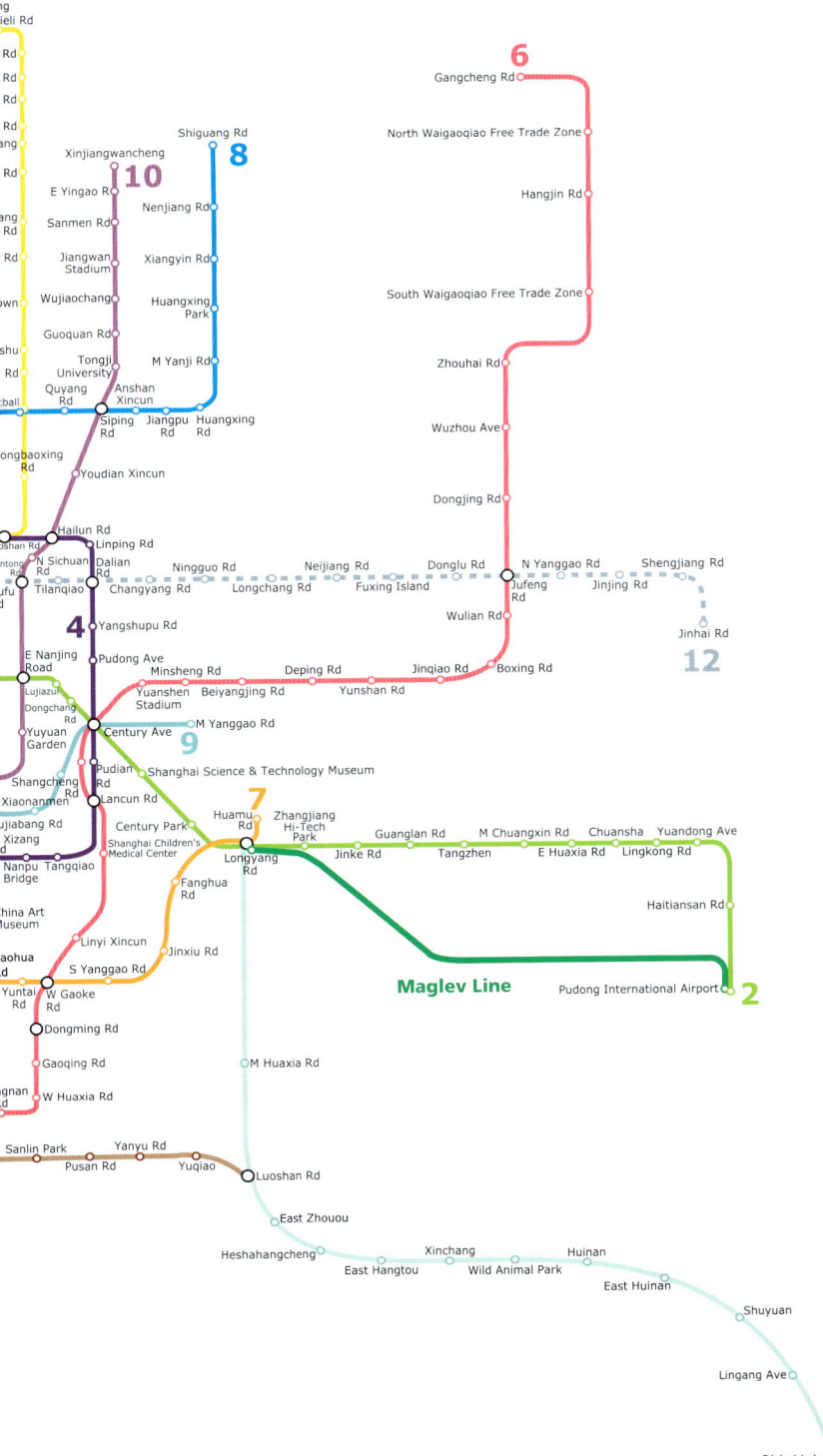

of course no refund. They can be conveniently re-charged at all Metro stations and many convenience stores.

In 2002 the Shanghai Municipal Government, in all its wisdom, decided to make it easier for foreign visitors to get around town by using English on street signs. In fact this move has resulted in some confusion and made life a little more difficult for the visitor—so you should be aware of the situation. Before the change street signs had simplified Chinese characters and a straightforward Pinyin Romanisation (*see* page 72) of them below—usually ending in Lu (road) or Jie (street). Following the change Moganshan Lu, for instance, re-appeared as Moganshan Rd. The Pinyin for the actual street remains the same and Rd. substituted for Lu. Fair enough. However in a minority of instances the Pinyin name of the road has also been changed to English—for instance Xizang Lu now appears as Tibet Rd. and Xianggang Lu as Hong Kong Rd. A special mention should be made of Shaanxi Rd. In Pinyin it should be written as Shanxi Rd., but as there is another street with the same name an extra 'a' has been added to the street sign. However the street's Metro station still is written as 'Shanxi Rd.'.

Some problems have arisen in the uniform application of English for roads that have more than a single name. One of the main shopping streets, for instance, is Central Huaihai Rd on one sign but Huaihai Zhong Rd. on another! Many Shanghai roads are long and broken into various sections—east (dong), west (xi), north (bei) and south (nan). They are now generally seen on street signs as ….Rd. (E) (W) (N) and (S). Some roads also have a middle (zhong) section—now seen as Central ….Rd. or ….Rd. (M). To further complicate matters some roads have an old (lao) and a new (xin) section or a No. 1 (yi) or No. 2 (er) section. You may also see the translation of the word jie as Street. New standardised street signs with a blue background began to be introduced in 2007.

For the sake of consistency, I have used the English version in the text and you should find it easy to convert to Pinyin, if you need to, using the preceding information. Some 'English' maps use the full Pinyin transliteration and are useful if you wish to attempt to ask for directions, whilst others adopt the 'English' approach. You are advised to carry a copy of each kind, if you can find them. Free maps are generally available in hotels, including the Shanghai Official Tourist Map from the Shanghai Municipal Tourism Administration (English approach) and the Shanghai Map from Ossimap (Pinyin approach). Many good hotels also offer excellent folding maps by redBANG. A useful map (Pinyin approach) is also found inside the Shanghai Talk

The former American-designed foreign Y.M.C.A. building from 1928.

magazine. A very good hardcover Shanghai Tourist Map by the Sinomaps Press can be purchased at hotels and bookstores (English approach). One of the best maps, with a comprehensive English index, is to be found within the English edition of the Shanghai Yellow Pages, which is available in some hotel rooms, or in their business centres.

Taxis

Shanghai's taxis are comfortable and plentiful—unless there is a heavy downfall of rain! The Dazhong Taxi Co. is the largest with a huge fleet of VW Santanas and Santana 2000s, and strict codes of conduct for its drivers. Standard taxi fares are 2.40 yuan a kilometre (up to 10 kilometres, and thereafter 3.60 yuan per kilometre), with a flagfall of 14 yuan covering the first three kilometres during the day. Between 11:00pm and 5:00am the flagfall rises to 18 yuan, with corresponding kilometre rates at 3.2 and 4.70 yuan. Receipts are courteously supplied. The cabs of the Dazhong Co. as well as others can be booked over the telephone without charge, and they can also supply limousines or even minibuses on a distance covered basis. Very few drivers speak English, so it is always best to have your destination written in Chinese characters. If you are making a stop on one of the city's long avenues it is customary to state the road intersection at which you wish to alight.

You should note that to reduce the rush-hour crush taxis are not permitted to cross the river by tunnel, other than the one at Fuxing Road, between 8:00am to 9:30pm and 5:00pm to 6:30pm on weekdays. There are no restrictions on Saturdays and Sundays.

Car Hire

For the average visitor the thought alone of the chaotic traffic is enough to put thoughts of hiring a car to the back of the mind. Moreover, car hire is restricted to those in possession of a local driving license, which can only be obtained by foreign residents and those possessing a business visa. For most hiring a car and driver is much the preferred option. If you have a license there are a few agencies around town including Hertz (tel: 6249 7988), Dazhong (tel: 6320 7201) and Angel (tel: 6229 0858).

City Bus

The city bus service is comprehensive and very complicated. Numerous one way streets assure that return routes are wildly different from outward ones, the bus stops are often light-years apart and irregularly placed, and people are packed in like sardines at many times of the day. Nevertheless, if you are in search of a novel experience, a bus journey may just be for you. Modern air-conditioned buses, with LCD screens showing Oriental Pearl TV programmes and advertising, generally cost just two yuan. Stops are announced in English. A couple of bus routes worth considering are the No. 911 and the No. 48. The double-decker 911 allows unparalleled views over the local terrain. Jump on at the terminus near the old west gate (*Lao Xi Men*), Renmin Road, in an interesting old part of town not far from the Yu Garden. The bus travels up Shanghai's classiest shopping street, Central Huaihai Road, through the old French Concession passing the Shanghai Zoo and ending up in a suburban residential district. The No. 48 starts from Pu'an Road, near People's Square, and cuts through some of the most glamorous streets in the old French Concession, including Huashan Road (formerly Avenue Haig) and Xinhua Road (Amherst Avenue), passes a huge Carrefour hypermarket and terminates at the Shanghai Zoo.

BICYCLE

The bicycle remains one of the most convenient ways to get around the city. However, most of the main shopping streets are closed to bikes and many others allow only one-way traffic. Some roads have partitioned bike lanes—but even then motor scooters dodging in and out make the experience less than relaxing. Still,

The bicycle remains one of the most convenient ways to get around the city.

bikes are a good way to explore some of the quieter local neighbourhoods. Some hotels have bike rental facilities and they can be hired from the YMCA bike shop at 485 Yongjia Road (tel: 6472 9325) and from Bohdi Bikes at Room 406, No. 59, Lane 710 Dingxi Road (tel: 3226 0000). Bike theft is rife, but you can leave your bicycle in one of the numerous attended bike parks around the city for a small fee.

Only bicycles, 1978.

Huangpu River Ferry

Whilst not as quite essential as the Star Ferry crossing in Hong Kong, the local ferry from Puxi to Pudong offers a great view of the city and its people. The most convenient crossing is from the pier at of the end of Jinling Road (E). There is also a sightseeing tunnel under the river.

The promenade and docks on the South Bund, opened in 2010, presents a striking visual contrast to the historic architecture in the Bund.

Metro

The Metro (*ditie*) is by far the most efficient way to get around Shanghai–and it is expanding rapidly. It's clean, speedy, inexpensive and relatively easy to navigate. Fares are only three or four yuan to get to most places of interest. Bilingual maps of the metro system are found on station platforms and line plans are placed above the doors inside the trains themselves. Train announcements are in both Chinese and highly audible and discernable English. One other thing to note is the signs on the platforms (in English and Chinese) give the terminus, the following stop and the name of the current station. Don't get confused—the current station is always in larger print. Should you miss your stop simply jump off and cross the platform to return.

Although the trains are efficient they can get very crowded, especially during rush hours and on Sundays. However the situation isn't really that much different from London or New York, though you will find that passengers boarding trains are not so concerned about letting people off first. The Metro also closes operations earlier than in many other major world cities. Of the major lines, line 1 operates from around 5:30am to 11:30pm, line 2 from around 6:30am to 11:00pm and line 3 from around 6:30am to 10:15pm.

The city's first Metro, line 1, commenced operation in December 1994, with 16 stations on its 20.6 kilometre (12.8 mile) track from Xinzhuang Station in the south to Shanghai Railway Station in the north. However a northern extension of the line running up the New Gonghe Road added a further nine stations at the end of 2006. It links the fast growing commercial and residential areas in the southern suburbs with the major commercial and shopping areas in the heart of the city. Line 5, with 11 stations, a southern suburban extension from Xinzhuang serving the Minhang Development Zone opened in late 2003.

Metro line 2 commenced operation in 1999 with 13 stations, starting from Zhongshan Park in the west and running for 19.2 kilometres (12 miles) along the Nanjing Road in Puxi and under the river to its easterly terminus at Zhangjiang Gaoke in Pudong. A western extension with four stations was opened in late 2006 and the line was extended to link Shanghai's two airports in 2010.

Metro line 3, a largely elevated light railway, runs from the northeast of the city and follows the western part of the inner ring road to terminate and the Shanghai South Railway Station. Regular services on the 36-kilometre (22 mile) track with 19 stations started in 2001 and another 16 stations and 15 kilometres (9.3 miles) of track were opened in late 2006. Line 4, a complete circle line crossing to Pudong,

Shanghai can be one of the most walking-friendly cities in the world and strolling the Bund is particularly popular.

came into full operation at the end of 2007. Metro line 6 running south to north in Pudong, line 8 linking Yangpu district with many downtown stops, and part of line 9 linking Xuhui district with Songjiang district also opened around the same time. Line 7 linking the city centre with Baoshan and Putuo districts opened in 2010. The 36 kilometre (22 mile) line 10 with 30 underground stations from the New Jiangwan Town in the north to Hongqiao Airport in the southwest was also opened in 2010. This will indeed be good news for visitors as it will run though most key business and sightseeing areas in the city. Work on lines 11, 12 and 13 are also underway. Line 11 is a massive undertaking expected to cover over 100 kilometres (60 miles) by 2020. The first section of the line opened in 2010. Lines 12 and 13 that will cut a much needed north-south path through the heart of the city will be fully operational in 2014, though a small section of line 13 was in operation for the Expo 2010 only and part of the northern section opened in early 2013. Over 425 kilometres (264 miles) of track were in operation in 2012, carrying some six million passengers daily.

The Maglev connects to Shanghai's Metro Line No. 2 at Longyang Road Station.

GETTING AROUND SHANGHAI 337

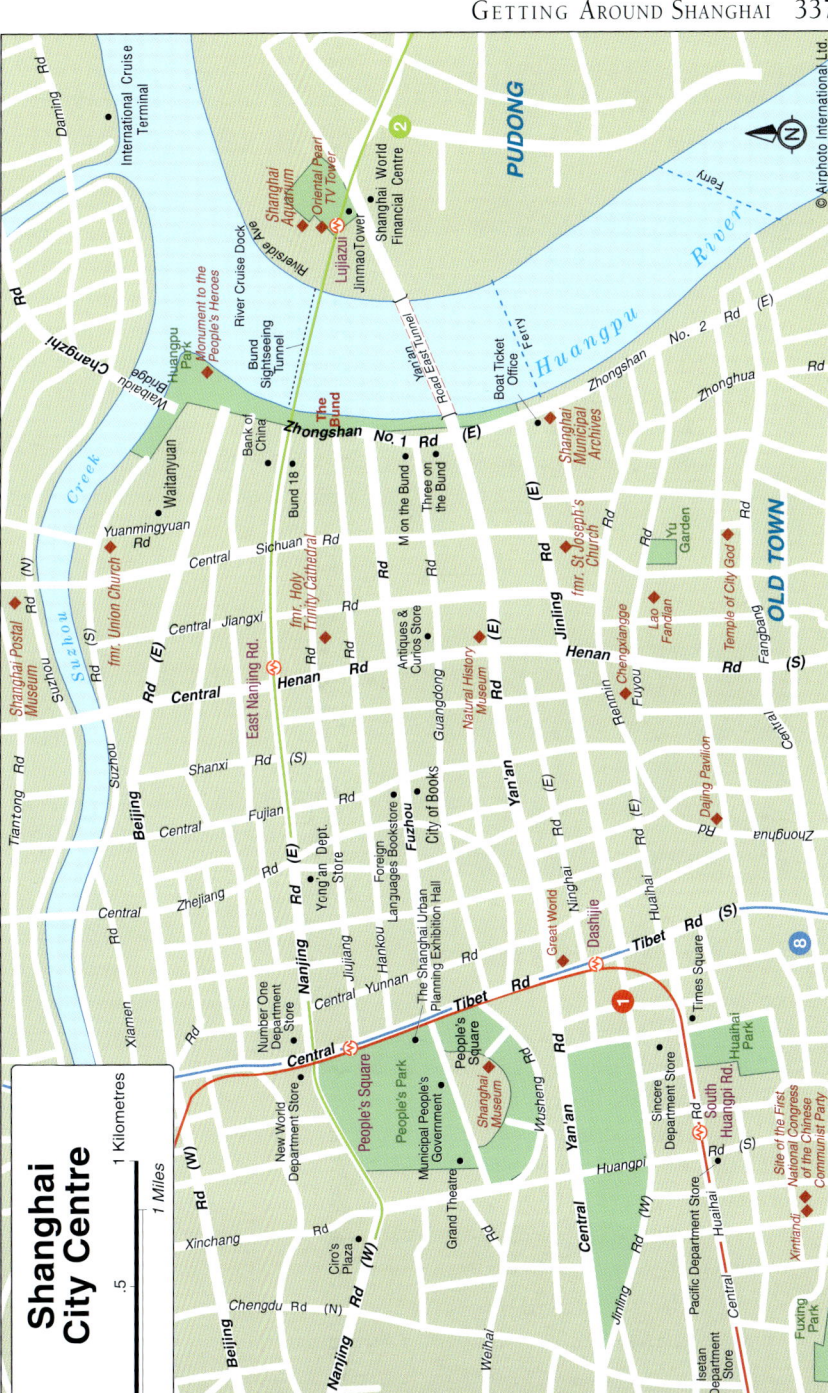

THE BUND TO THE BUBBLING WELL SHANGHAI: STEPS IN THE MAKING OF A MODERN METROPOLIS

—*The Ginger Griffin*

When I first visited Shanghai in 1986 I wasn't too impressed by the way it looked. I didn't come halfway around the globe to see buildings reminiscent of those in London or Liverpool, but came in search of the exoticness of the Orient and few pagodas or temples were in sight. However, I was amazed by the fact that so much of its historic Western-style architecture, albeit neglected or maltreated, had been left in a state of innocent hibernation for so long. Despite the massive and destructive assault on the city's fine 1920s and 1930s architecture over the last two decades so much still remains as testament to the tremendous scale of redevelopment that took place in those years when Sir Victor Sassoon spearheaded the campaign to transform Shanghai into a great international city, with a modern skyline and manners to match. However we have to go back to an earlier age, to that of the 1850s and 1860s, to begin the story of Shanghai's inimitable and rapacious obsession with breakneck speed urban development.

1930s view of today's West Nanjing Road at the junction with North Shaanxi Road.

The British, who had been granted rights to reside and trade in Shanghai following the Opium War (1839-1842) and the signing of the Treaty of Nanking in 1842, settled along the Bund on the muddy foreshore of the Huangpu River. The first official western boundary of the English Settlement, drawn up in 1846, extended three blocks back from the Bund to today's Central Henan Road. By 1848 this boundary had been pushed westwards to today's Central Tibet Road (formerly known as Defence Creek) and bounded by Suzhou Creek to the north and by the Yangkingpang Creek (today's East Yan'an Road) to the south. The British were adamant about keeping their 470-acre area free of Chinese residents. However the dramatic consequences brought upon by the outbreak of the Taiping Rebellion (1851–1864), the world's most bloody civil war, caused them to think again. Swarms of Chinese refugees flooded into the sanctity of the English Settlement and British merchants and their consuls saw the prospect of making very rich rewards. Regulations allowing the Chinese to reside and to rent or buy land in the Settlements were introduced following the election of the newly formed Shanghai Municipal Council in 1854.

While the Bund and its neighbouring streets with their trading houses, banks and social institutions remained a largely British domain, the Settlement area to its west was developed to accommodate the new arrivals. Wooden terraced dwellings, three stories in height, were hastily constructed to pack as many Chinese in as was possible. Adopted from the model of England's northern industrial cities, they were an anathema to the Chinese who would have never have shared an adjoining wall with a neighbour or felt comfortable living on the third floor of a dwelling. Countless Chinese cemeteries and two British racecourses were unceremoniously built over as upwards of half a million Chinese poured into the English and American Settlements (the American Settlement being to the north of the Suzhou Creek). Drinking champagne by the crate was the order of the day and the original English street names were changed to those of Chinese provinces and cities to keep everybody happy. The prevailing sentiment could be summed up in the words of one early British landlord who remarked that 'it is my business to make a fortune with the least possible loss of time, by letting land to the Chinese, and building for them at thirty or forty percent interest. In two or three years at farthest I hope to realize a fortune and get away.'

After inviting the Chinese in, the British devised an escape route from their congested backyard and headed westwards beyond their Settlement boundary. Some of the profits from the building of an all important new racecourse (on the site of today's People's Square) in 1862 went into the construction of the Bubbling Well Road (today's West Nanjing Road) as an extension of the Nanjing Road terminating at the Bubbling Well opposite the Jing'an Temple.

Bubbling Well Road, 1908.

Lined with hundreds of fine mansions and magnificently laid out gardens and parks it had become the most desirable residential area in Shanghai, and indeed was widely regarded as the finest avenue in Asia, by the end of the 19th century. In 1906 land values along the road were reported to be 300 and 400 times over what they had been 25 years earlier. After 1899 the area was incorporated within the International Settlement (an amalgam of the former English and American Settlements formed in 1863) and the Shanghai Municipal Council soon set about widening the road to accommodate Shanghai's booming traffic and later its mad obsession with the motorcar. The Bubbling Well Road had from its inception been the place to show off one's finery on an afternoon's leisure drive, with horses and carts available for hire from the Shanghai Horse Bazaar Company (formerly on the site of the Park Hotel).

In the early years of the 20th century, and particularly after the end of World War I, booming business confidence found expression in a desire to build big and tall. Chinese and foreign money was pouring into the city in the 1920s and property and land values in the International Settlement reached their zenith in 1929 when it was claimed that the saying

'Shanghai Mud, Shanghai Gold,' had never rung so true—values had increased around a thousand percent between 1923 and 1932. The population of the International Settlement, covering just 8.3 square miles, had doubled to around one million between 1910 and 1930. Between 1920 and 1925 no less than seven new buildings were built on the shores of the Bund and a tidal wave of redevelopment was roaring westwards.

By the mid-1930s the remodelled commercial heart of the city stood sleek and tall within the confines of the original Central Henan Road boundary, looking more distinct from its adjoining Chinese district than ever before. Crossing that road one could step from a modern international financial, social and civic centre; with its lofty towers, it's cocktails and canapés, its bow ties and handshakes into a congee of colour, vibrancy and Chinese tradition, of flowing robes, stilettos, soy, syllabic sounds, stateless souls and street children. The recent widening of Central Henan Road, apart from creating a hardened physical boundary, has further distanced those areas in both time and place. The vitally important historical identity of the Bund neighbourhood, with its highly impressive heritage architecture, has been heightened; whilst in a reversal of the previous order the new skyscraper towers to the west appear at first sight to be much more modern and 'international.' However wandering off the main thoroughfares many colourful small streets lined with two-storey 'shop houses' have some how deferred their stay of execution and lanes little more than a metre wide remain hidden just behind the stylish shop facades on East Nanjing Road. Some traditional style shikumen houses on the Fuzhou Road have even been dressed with latticework, red columns and lanterns to evoke a Chinese identity. On the Bund itself one first generation building, that of Russell & Co from 1857, has miraculously survived, but not without mutilation, two massive waves of city redevelopment. Originally known as the 'Stone House' building it is behind the Shiatzy Chen emporium at No. 6, where its garden once was.

During the 1920s and 1930s the Bubbling Well Road was reinvented as a prime, modern commercial and residential district. Motor garages that usually resembled palaces or forts quickly established themselves along the length of the road. One Moorish-inspired building from 1916, formerly the Star Garage that sold Dodge and Hupmobile cars, still stands at 702 West Nanjing Road. Many fine mansions and parks were built over as high-rise apartments, hotels, office buildings and three-storey 'shop-houses' sprung up. As one example, the Chang Su Ho Gardens, the finest gardens and pleasure grounds in the city, were redeveloped into a magnificent housing estate. Much of that development, including a section built by Percy C. Woo, one-time comprador of the National City Bank of New York, still survives on the block where Four Seasons Hotel now stands. Nearby the 10-acre estate of the McBain family, which was taken over by the Hongkong and Shanghai Hotels, Limited in 1923 and converted into the Majestic Hotel, the finest 'boutique' hotel to be found anywhere and favoured by visiting royalty and Hollywood film stars, was demolished in 1933 to make way for the Metropole Gardens ballroom and modern apartments. On a site directly opposite 190 redbrick town houses that were marketed as Shanghai's first community development, including a large clubhouse, survive to this day as the Jing'an Villas (1025 West Nanjing Road). The scheme offered an attractive alternative to modern high-rise living and was hugely profitable. As for the new high-rise apartments nearby, such as the Denis apartments (1930) on the corner of today's Shimen No. 2 Road, they catered for a range of needs and lifestyles; from those of a newly arrived bachelor wanting an affordable studio to those of the well-to-do who wanted a downtown location and a seven or eight room suite that was larger than the average detached residence of the day.

Numerous parallels can be drawn between the recent redevelopment of the road and to that of the early 20th century. The Shanghai Centre, built on a site where two houses built for HSBC managers once stood, was a sign of what was to come when it opened in 1990. The nearby skyscrapers, including those of Plaza 66 and CITIC Square are modern reinventions of the old - they may be of steel and glass, but the nature of their activity has changed little since the 1930s. One can even watch a Hollywood blockbuster at the cinema in Westgate Mall that stands on the site of the Majestic Hotel, which staged Hollywood movies on its lawn 80 years ago. Expensive new high-rise apartments have also made a comeback. The Jing'an district government is promoting an international, and particularly a European, aspect for its fast changing show street. The recent opening of Asia's largest Marks and Spencer's store is just one example of its new face and aspirant cosmopolitanism. And of course the road's long love affair with the motorcar is back as Ferrari, Maserati and Mercedes all keep showrooms there. The name Bubbling Well Road may be long forgotten, but the road's reputation as one of the finest in Asia looks like it is well on the way towards being revived.

Modern high-rise towers on West Nanjing Road tower over the historic Jing'an villas.

Sights in Shanghai

Despite its immediate modern appearance and aspirations, for many foreigners Shanghai conjures up past images and stories of adventure and intrigue. Many of these were probably no exaggeration, for Shanghai was a uniquely progressive, colourful, violent and unforgiving city. In many ways it was the ultimate city-state. For the present-day European visitor Shanghai is a surprising city, for unlike all others in China it feels unexpectedly like home. Even though huge areas of buildings dating back to the early part of the last century have been razed in recent years many European-style living areas have survived—especially in the area that formed the French Concession.

Architecturally Shanghai is one of the most interesting cities in the world with its medley of British, French, Spanish, Russian, Japanese and Chinese styles. Numerous fine mansions set in large estates continue to house the economic and political elites, whist many new buildings employ Western architectural designs or decorative details. In many parts of the city stand the last remnants of Shanghai's traditional form of *shikumen* housing—something of a cross between a British terraced-house and a traditional Chinese courtyard dwelling. Numerous landmark 1930s art deco apartments,

The elegance of the former China United Apartments (1926)
seen here in 1978 (above) provides inspiration in 2005 (right) as the rotunda-topped building,
housing the Radisson Hotel, echoes the architecture of its clock tower.

clubs and commercial buildings have also survived, presenting an indelible reminder of the greatness of this remarkable city, which for most of its career has been at the cutting-edge of modernity.

Shanghai offers a unique arena for sightseeing fashioned by the past presence of Europeans, including its rich and poor Russian and Jewish émigrés; Americans, Japanese and other nationalities as well as its massive indigenous population. And whilst Shanghai is promoting massive new tourist districts and a great array of new attractions, including state-of-the art museums, there are still many reminders of its proud indigenous cultural heritage found in its magnificent temples and traditional gardens.

Whilst the foreign presence in old Shanghai can easily be discerned in its architecture, this belies the fact that the great majority of its grand Western-style buildings and homes were in fact built by Western and Chinese architects for Chinese enterprises and owners. Even in the 1930s the British, French and American populations together only numbered around 20,000 at their height. So when we look at sights in Shanghai we have to consider the unique history and culture of the city. Many of the houses of key revolutionary figures that changed the path of Chinese history are in fact of Western-design, whilst many of the British buildings on the Bund incorporate aspects of Chinese symbolism.

The most opulent building on the Bund can be found at No. 12.

FALLEN ANGELS

He always looked forward to the evening drives through the centre of Shanghai, this electric and lurid city more exciting than any other in the world. As they reached the Bubbling Well Road he pressed his face to the windshield and gazed at the pavements lined with night-clubs and gambling dens, crowded with bar-girls and gangsters and rich beggars with their bodyguards. Crowds of gamblers pushed their way into the jai alai stadiums, blocking the traffic in the Bubbling Well Road. An armoured police van with two Thompson guns mounted in a steel turret above the driver swung in front of the Packard and cleared the pavement. A party of young Chinese women in sequined dresses tripped over a child's coffin decked with paper flowers. Arms linked together, they lurched against the radiator grille of the Packard and swayed past Jim's window, slapping the windshield with their small hands and screaming obscenities. Nearby, along the windows of the Sun Sun department store in the Nanking Road, a party of young European Jews were fighting in and out of the strolling crowds with a gang of older German boys in the swastika armbands of the Graf Zeppelin Club. Chased by the police sirens, they ran through the entrance of the Cathay Theatre, the world's largest cinema, where a crowd of Chinese shopgirls and typists, beggars and pickpockets spilled into the street to watch people arriving for the evening performance. As they stepped from their limousines the women steered their long skirts through the honour guard of fifty hunchbacks in mediaeval costume. Three months earlier, when his parents had taken Jim to the première of The Hunchback of Notre Dame, *there had been two hundred hunchbacks, recruited by the management of the theatre from every back alley in Shanghai. As always, the spectacle outside the theatre far exceeded anything shown on its screen.*

J.G. Ballard, Empire of the Sun *(Simon & Schuster, 1984)*

J, G. Ballard (1930–2009), who was born in Shanghai, was at the forefront of modern British fiction writing for over four decades. After the attack on Pearl Harbor, Ballard and his family were placed in a civilian prison camp. They returned to England in 1946. After two years at Cambridge, where he read medicine, Ballard worked as a copywriter and a Covent Garden porter before going to Canada with the RAF. In 1956 his first short story was published in New Worlds and he took a full-time job on a technical journal, moving on to become assistant editor of a scientific journal, where he stayed until 1961. His writing career began in 1962 when *The Wind from Nowhere* was published—and fittingly ended with the publication of his autobiography *The Miracles of Life—Shanghai to Shepperton* that provides a rich autobiographical account of his life from his childhood and early teenage years to his return to the city in the 1990s

Western Heritage
The Bund
WAITAN 外滩

The Bund, or *Waitan* as it is known in Chinese, is the quintessential Shanghai sight. The word Bund, often mistaken for a German expression, actually derives from the Hindustani word *band* meaning an artificial causeway or embankment. Its row of imposing buildings presents an incredible architectural face representing the domination of foreign, and especially British, business interests in Shanghai before the Second World War. The foreign bosses, known as taipans, controlled the trade and commerce of the great open port from within the confines of its banks, trading houses and other commercial enterprises. Fortunes were made and empires built with an ardour previously unseen in the Far East.

However when the foreigners first arrived in the 1840s it was little more than a muddy towpath. In the 1880s the British-dominated Municipal Council decided to convert it into a public esplanade and connect it to the public gardens that were

The Bund, circa 1927, bustles with activity much like it does so today.
Left: *The Bund, lit up for a past 1st October National Day celebration, throngs with people.*

The Foreign Settlements of Shanghai, 1921. Avenue Edward Vii, today's Yan'an Road (E), marked the division between the French Concession to the south and the International Settlement to the north.

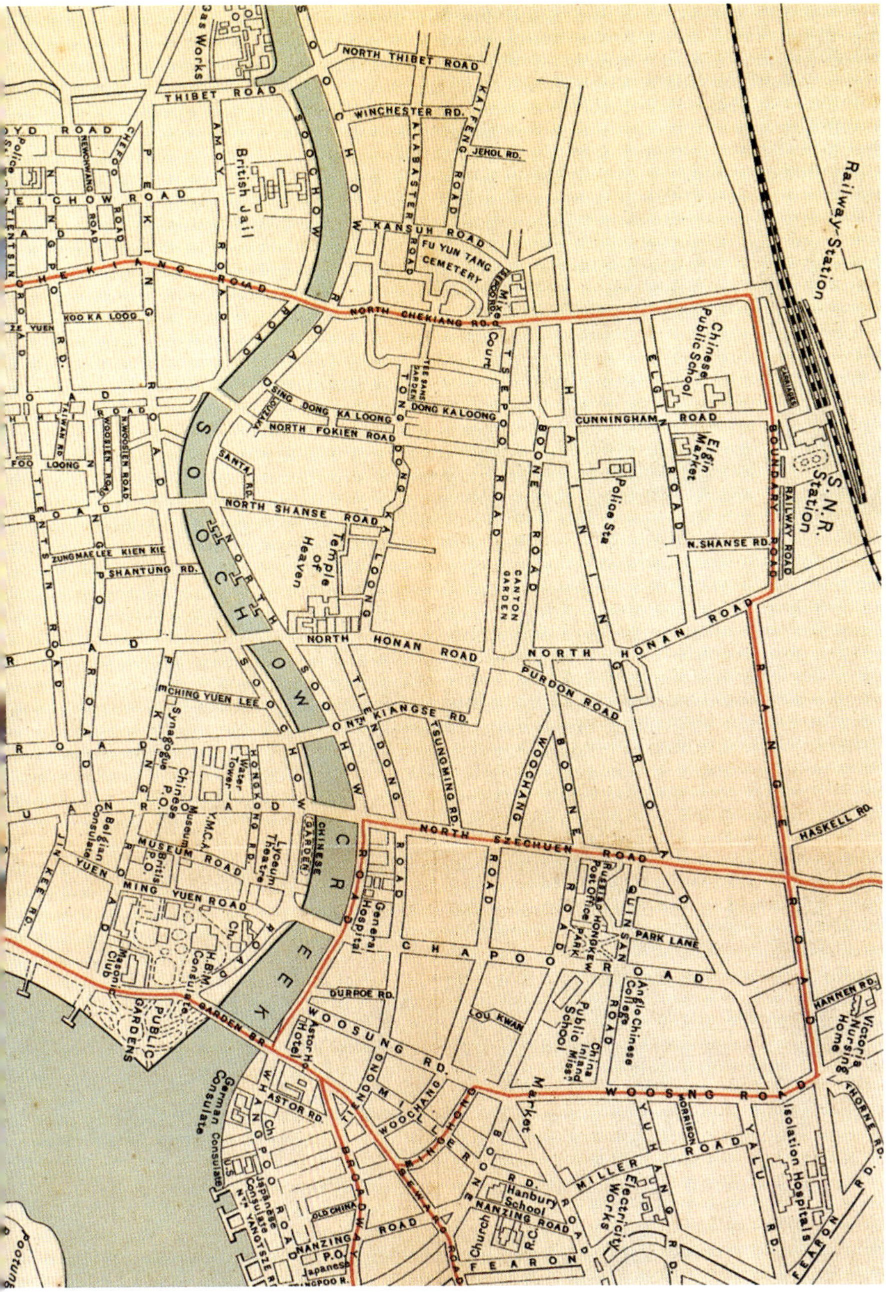
Gas Works
NORTH THIBET ROAD
THIBET ROAD
WINCHESTER RD.
KAIFENG ROAD
JEHOL RD.
ALABASTER ROAD
British Jail
AMOY ROAD
PEKING ROAD
CHEFOO ROAD
NEWCHWANG ROAD
Police Stn
TIENTSIN ROAD
CHEKIANG ROAD
KANSUH ROAD
FU YUN TANG CEMETERY
Mixed Court
NORTH CHEKIANG RD.
KOO KA LOONG
ZE YUEN
Railway Station
Chinese Public School
ELGIN ROAD
CUNNINGHAM ROAD
Elgin Market
SING DONG KA LOONG
DONG KA LOONG
NORTH FOKIEN ROAD
TSEPOO ROAD
BOONE ROAD
HAINING ROAD
BOUNDARY ROAD
S.N.R. Station
RAILWAY ROAD
Police Sta
SANTA RD.
NORTH SHANSE ROAD
N. SHANSE RD.
Temple of Heaven
CANTON GARDEN
FOO LOONG
TAIWAN RD.
WOOSIEN ROAD
N. WOOSIEN ROAD
ZUNGMAELEE
KIEN KIE
SHANTUNG RD.
NORTH SOOCHOW ROAD
SOOCHOW CREEK
NORTH HONAN ROAD
RANGE ROAD
PURDON ROAD
CHING YUEN LEE
Synagogue
Chinese P.O.
Water Tower
HONGKONG RD.
NTH KIANGSE RD.
TIENDONG ROAD
TSUNGMING RD.
WOOCHANG ROAD
HASKELL RD.
NORTH SZECHUEN ROAD
Belgian Consulate
Y.M.C.A.
Museum
British P.O.
MUSEUM ROAD
Lyceum Theatre
CHINESE GARDEN
YUEN MING YUEN ROAD
JINKEE RD.
General Hospital
Russian Post Office
HONGKEW PARK
QUINSAN ROAD
PARK LANE
CHAPOO ROAD
Ch.
H.B.M. Consulate
Masonic Club
PUBLIC GARDENS
GARDEN BR.
DURHOE RD.
Anglo Chinese College
China Inland Mission
Public School
LOU KWAN
HANNEN RD.
Victoria Nursing Home
WOOSUNG RD.
Astor Ho. Hotel
WHANGPOO ROAD
ASTOR RD.
German Consulate
U.S. Consulate
Japanese Consulate
NTH YANGTSZE RD.
OLD CHINA
NANZING P.O.
Japanese
BROADWAY
SEWARD ROAD
MINHONG ROAD
BOONE ROAD
Market
Hanbury School
NANZING ROAD
R.C. Church
FEARON ROAD
MILLER ROAD
Electricity Works
YUHANG ROAD
YALU RD.
MORRISON ROAD
Isolation Hospitals
THORNE RD.
FEARON RD.
Pootung

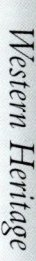

The former Hongkong and Shanghai Bank building was completed in 1923. While the Bund's buildings themselves have seen little outward change during the last 60 years, many of the interiors have been radically altered. Italian marble was originally used in great quantity for the interiors. The bank's interior has been well preserved and today appears much as it does in this photo.

established in 1868. The definition of public used excluded those of local origin. Although the regulations of the International Settlement did indeed forbid Chinese (other than servants and nannies) as well as dogs from the gardens, the infamous sign 'No Dogs or Chinese Allowed' never actually existed. Nannies were prohibited from taking a seat when the town band played. Following growing unrest over the status of the Chinese in the Settlement, they were finally allowed to enter the park in 1928 —though the entrance cost was around that of an average day's labour.

A modest display of photographs of the Bund yesteryear can be found within the small Bund Museum, which is housed in the former Signal Tower built in 1907 and moved about 25 metres (65 feet) from its original site in 1995 as part of a promenade remodelling scheme, near Jinling Road (E). The signal, or semaphore, tower provided an invaluable service to seafarers in old Shanghai by providing 24-hour information for incoming and outgoing ships. The Monument to the People's Heroes, a more modern-day tower structure from the early 1990s, sits at the northern end of the Bund within the former public gardens that are now known as the Huangpu Park.

In the 19th century the buildings on the Bund were only 30 feet from the shores of the Huangpu River. However with city's rapid industrialisation, and increased numbers of motor vehicles to match, the Bund was widened to 120 feet in 1920. The scheme involved the laying of a 55-feet carriageway for trams and fast traffic and one 30-feet wide for slow traffic, as well as car parking ranks and the laying of new lawns along the riverfront. With similar motives the Bund was entirely remodelled in the early 1990s when a mammoth 11-lane highway, part of the city's new inner ring road network, was rolled out along its length and a wide raised promenade built along its foreshore. The promenade soon became an essential destination for sightseers, especially at night when the historic buildings on the Bund and the new glittering towers in Lujiazui on the other side of the river were emblazoned with a vignette of illuminations. The new road totally disconnected the waterfront from its historical context and could only be crossed by way of underpasses. Work on the Bund's biggest and most ambitious remodelling project, in an effort to make it more human again by submerging traffic and creating new public spaces, began in 2008 and was completed at the end of March 2010.

The initial redevelopment of the foreshore in the 1990s was prompted by the need to shore up the city's flood defences. Like Venice, Shanghai is slowly sinking. In fact, the buildings along the Bund, built during the first four decades of the last century, were expected to sink around 12 inches (30 centimetres) after they were completed. Many of then are built on huge concrete rafts underpinned by Oregon pine piles and are literally floating on a mixture 50 per cent silt and 50 per cent water. Temporary steps were installed as the buildings 'settled' over a period of a few years.

The buildings themselves come in a range of architectural styles from neo-Grecian, to English and Italian Renaissance, to art deco. Many of them were the tallest structures in China when they were completed and were constructed using the latest building technologies from England. Remarkably most of the materials used for their construction were imported—including the widespread use of Japanese and Hong Kong granite, Italian marble, British iron, steel and bronze work as well as British sanitary fittings.

All the buildings along the Bund are so-called examples of 'Heritage Architecture'— look out for the (often historically incorrect) plaques outside. However the city has a very ill-defined preservation policy that only refers to the building's exterior face. Although they have experienced little outward change over the last 60 years many of the buildings' interiors have been radically altered. Countless fine marble interiors and elaborate decorative features and fittings have been lost in recent years as attempts to 'modernise' have too often resulted in a disregard for the superior aesthetics of the past.

Soon after Shanghai was opened for business in the early Nineties, the Shanghai Municipal Government announced a scheme to 'Sell off the Bund' expecting foreign occupants to move back to their former premises. The scheme was flawed, as even by the late 1930s most of the buildings were unfit for modern commercial purposes and allowed no room for expansion. A few businesses did return, including the AIA at No. 17, (which as the AUA had been established in Shanghai in 1919) and the ABN Amro Bank (formerly the Netherlands Trading Society) at No. 20. The Bank of China building at No. 23 and the Custom House at No. 13 are the only buildings to remain under the control of their original occupants.

Bund History Museum.

Whilst many of the Bund's occupants still play a vital commercial role, the major headquarters for institutions of finance and commerce are now to be found in the high-rise towers opposite the Bund in Lujiazui. However, such businesses are being encouraged to locate on the waterfront south of the Bund, stretching down to the environs of the World Expo site, an area that has been extensively redeveloped in recent times and dubbed as 'The South Bund'.

With the turn of the millennium and spurred on by the glittering prize of hosting the World Expo 2010, government planners partly shifted their vision of the Bund away from its predisposition as a financial centre to that of its potential as a world-class showcase for the arts, gastronomy, leisure and retail activity. Michelle Garnaut, Hong Kong restaurateur extraordinaire, pre-empted the move by opening M on the Bund atop building No. 5 in 1999. A host of investors, many with Chinese roots, began to take a fresh, hard and cautious look at the buildings that remained up for grabs. The blemished face of the Bund began slowly to take on a distinctly Western look as stylishly chic, cosmopolitan restaurants and international fashion houses took up residence.

Opened in 2003, Three on the Bund was the brainchild of Handel Lee, a Chinese-American entrepreneur. It incorporates the Shanghai Gallery of Art; fine restaurants including Jean Georges, the Whampoa Club, Mercato and New Heights, as well as designer outlets and beauty salons. Bund 18 in the former Chartered Bank Building, built in 1923, was opened as a glamorous multi-level space for dining and shopping in 2004. Magnificent Italian marble columns and facings have been preserved on the ground floor. Here you will Cartier and Zegna, the finest French cuisine at Mr and Mrs and superlative Chinese cuisine at Tan Wai Lou.

The views from the seventh floor rooftop DJ bar, Bar Rouge are breathtaking. (*see* page 553) Bund 18 has set the bench mark for quality and integrity in the restoration and renovation of historic buildings in Shanghai. A Venetian born and trained architect, Mr. Filippo Gabbiani, presided over the two year project.

Other buildings of special interest include the former Shanghai Club at No. 2—a great British bastion that denied membership to women and Chinese—which was completed in 1911. This was the place where mighty business deals were thrashed out over a pink gin at lunch time. Unfortunately its famed Long Bar, which was 110 feet, seven inches long, has long gone. Noel Coward remarked that 'one could see the curvature of the earth along it'. The bar is often rumoured to have been cut in half and removed to Japan during the Second World War—whereas in reality it was cut in half and moved upstairs in the 1950s. The building later housed the International Seaman's Club, and its half remaining Long Bar became a sleazy and dimly lit setting for Shanghai's nefarious pleasures, with the rooms above under the undistinguished management of the East Wind Hotel. The former Long Bar on the ground floor was home to Kentucky Fried Chicken for most of the 1990s. However the building has been restored to grandeur yet again as it now operates as the Waldorf Astoria Shanghai on the Bund, a notable addition to the city's long list of luxury hotels.

The most opulent building on the Bund can be found at No. 12. The former Hongkong and Shanghai Bank building, with two bronze lions at its entrance, was opened in 1923 and is now occupied by the Pudong Development Bank. The bronze lions that rested outside the Shanghai branch were modelled from a design by Henry Poole and were crafted by the renowned company of J. W. Singer & Sons in Somerset, England. They are familiarly known after managers of the bank; Stephen—the roaring one, and Stitt—the acquiescent one. The original lions, often rumoured to have been melted down, are in fact now in the custody of the Shanghai Municipal History Museum (*see* page 355). Faithful replicas now guard the building. Just inside the entrance are fine Italian mosaics of some of the world's greatest cities topped with figures from Greek mythology. Like many buildings on the Bund it was designed the British architect, George Leopold Wilson. Its dome was once covered in gold mosaics—and look out for the banks of loudspeakers above the iconic face of the Custom House clock next door. Previously known as 'Big Ching' the clock once played the chimes of Big Ben, but today it plays a strident digital recording of the Communist anthem 'The East is Red'.

Perhaps the most iconic building on the Bund, which today houses the Fairmont Peace Hotel, is found at No. 20 on the Nanjing Road (E) intersection. Opened by the legendary Sir Victor Sassoon in 1929 as Sassoon House, it incorporated the Cathay Hotel that was regarded as the finest and modern hotel of its time (*see* page 534). It was the 'Claridges of the Far East.' Be sure to take a look at its elaborately decorated eight floor. Another grand hotel, from an earlier period, the Astor House, which described itself as the 'Waldorf Astoria of the Orient' when it opened in 1911 is also

The focus is ostensibly on Shanghai after the foreigners arrived in the 1840s—though there are sympathetic portrayals of aspects of normal Chinese life through a range of dioramas of shops and industries in the 19th century and early 20th century alongside those of foreign life in the Settlement areas. One is reminded that the foreign population of Shanghai was incredibly small compared to the huge outward manifestation of its influence.

All aspects of life from Shanghai's famous cinema industry, to its curious form of criminal justice, its opium houses and its distinctive elements of architectural style are brought to life. There is also a prominent display of old trolley buses, trams, cycles and sedans. Exhibition Hall 3, entitled the 'Metropolis Infested with Foreigners' focuses on the heyday of Shanghai in the 1920s and 1930s. It includes what is said to be one of the precious bronze lions that once lay outside the Hongkong & Shanghai Bank on the Bund—which was often rumoured to have been smelted down by the Japanese in the Second World War. The museum is located in the basement of the Oriental Pearl TV Tower (gate 4) in Lujiazui and is open from 8:00am to 9.00pm.

Former Occupants of the Bund

Address	Original Occupants	Date
No.1	The McBain Building	1915
No.2	The Shanghai Club	1911
No.3	The Union Building	1915
No.5	Nisshin Kissen Kaisha Shipping Co.	1921
No.6	Russell & Co.	1881
No.7	Telegraph Offices	1908
No.9	China Merchants Steam Navigation Co.	1901
No.12	Hong Kong and Shanghai Bank	1923
No.13	The Customs House	1927
No.14	Bank of Communications	1948
No.15	Russo-Chinese Bank	1902
No.16	Bank of Taiwan	1927
No.17	North China Daily News Building	1923
No.18	Chartered Bank of India, Australia and China	1923
No.19	The Palace Hotel	1907
No.20	The Cathay Hotel	1929
No.23	Bank of China	1940s
No.24	Yokohama Specie Bank	1924
No.26	Yangtsze Insurance Association	1916
No.27	Ewo Building (Jardine Matheson)	1922
No.28	The Glen Line Building	1923
No.29	Banque De L'IndoChine	1914
No.32	British Consulate	1873
No.33	British Consular Residence	1882

No.12, the Bund.

Shanghai Architecture

—Tess Johnston & Peter Hibbard

If ever a city's architecture should be called *fin de siècle*, it is Shanghai's. Parts of metropolitan Shanghai resemble a city suspended in 1937, when the Japanese occupied the whole city except for the French Concession and the International Settlement. With the Japanese takeover of these foreign enclaves in December 1941, all Western life—and all building projects— stopped. Foreigners returning to Shanghai after 1945 found themselves to be strangers in a city that was once theirs, with many of their architectural triumphs turned to white elephants.

Since then much of the downtown area has remained unchanged, especially the Bund, though large pockets of modern redevelopment have resulted in the destruction of many pre-war buildings. Somewhat like a dentist pulling teeth, the developers' crane and bulldozer are increasingly crawling over the Shanghai landscape.

Parking has always been at a premium around Custom House.

A remaining example of Shanghai's fast disappearing colonial era architecture.

Shanghai's History Through its Names

When the Chinese want to be literary, or brief, they call Shanghai 'Hu'. The name bespeaks Shanghai's origins as a fishing village, for *hu* is a bamboo fishing device, used during the third century by the people who lived around the Songjiang River (which was subsequently renamed Wusong River, and which forms the upper reaches of the Suzhou Creek). Shanghai is also sometimes known as Chunshen—or Shen for short—because in the third century BC, at the time of the Warring States (475–221 BC), the site on which the city now stands was a fief of the Lord Chunshen, prime minister to the King of the State of Chu. Another name with which Shanghai is associated is Huating. This was a county established in 751, over an area which covers part of present-day Shanghai.

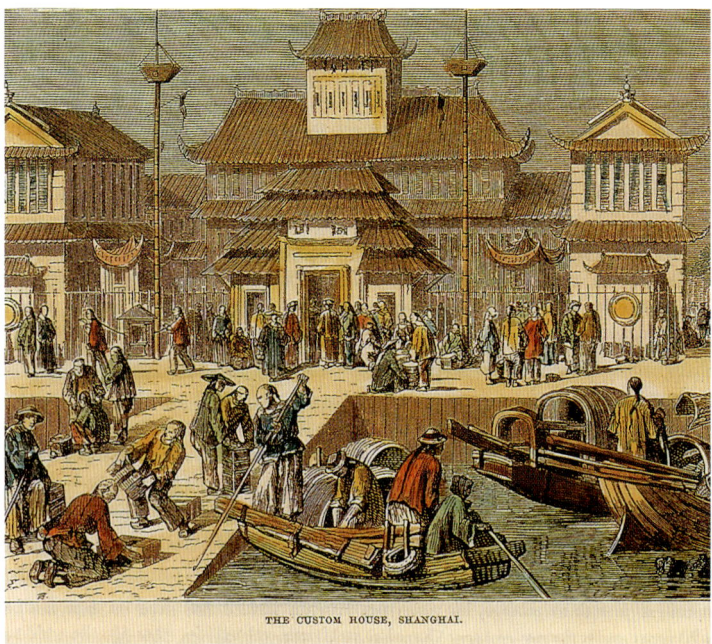

Shanghai's Custom House in the 19th century.

Barge trains on Suzhou Creek, 1978.

Shanghai took its name from the Shanghai River, a tributary, long since gone, of the Songjiang. A township sprang into being on the west bank of the river, as, recognising its natural advantages as a port, junks and ships came to berth there. This was Shanghai, which presently became the largest town in Huating County. In 1292, Shanghai and four other towns in Huating were brought together to form the County of Shanghai. It was at about this time that the Songjiang was renamed the Wusong River.

But today when most Chinese think of Shanghai, they think not so much of the Wusong as of the Huangpu River. Shanghai's qualifications as a deep water port were greatly improved when a canal—forming that part of the Huangpu downstream of Waibaidu Bridge—was dredged and widened in the 14th century. Ships crowded the wharves of Shanghai, and the port itself grew in size and importance, thriving off the trade in cotton and other goods between the coast and the inland provinces on the Yangzi (Yangtze) River.

These were the foundations upon which the Western powers built when, with the opening of Shanghai as a Treaty Port, they came and carved out their enclaves there. The first of the foreign settlements, the British Concession, was bounded on the east along the Huangpu River by the Bund (today's Zhongshan No. 1 Road East), on the west by Yu Ya Ching Road (today's Central Tibet Road), and on the south by the Yangjingbang Creek (which, after it was filled, was named Avenue Edward VII and which is now called Yan'an Road East). The creek separated the British from the French Concession; the latter started from a wedge between the British Concession and the old Chinese city, and then ballooned out to a large area to the southwest of the city. To the north of the Suzhou Creek, in the district known then and now as Hongkou, lay the American Concession. This was later merged with the British Concession to form the International Settlement.

In the British Concession, the streets spread out behind the Bund in a grid. The main thoroughfare, Nanking Road (Nanjing Road), ran westwards from the Bund. The streets parallel to it were named after China's other cities (such as Canton, Fuzhou and Ningbo), while those which ran perpendicular to it (i.e. north-south) were named after the provinces (such as Henan, Sichuan and Zhejiang). There was no mistaking the French Concession, because most of the streets there had French names: Rue Lafayette and Avenue Foch, to name but two. The smartest was Avenue Joffre (today's Huaihai Road), which was to the French Concession what Nanking Road was to the British. All foreign streets were renamed in 1943.

Revolutionary Heritage

Shanghai's unique disposition as a foreign enclave, built on the power of its imperialist overlords and its immunity from Chinese control, provided the perfect context for the most important revolutionary politicians and intellectuals of the 20th century to develop their ideals. Their legacy is still strong in the city as many fascinating museums, often housed in their former western-style homes or offices, have been created.

Site of the First National Congress of the Chinese Communist Party
Zhongguo Gongchandang Chengli Diyici Daibiao Dahuihuizhi 中国共产党成立第一次代表大会会址

This recently renovated and enlarged museum has two sections—the actual site, a small room in the house of one of the delegates, Li Hanjun, is in the second section near the exit at 374 Huangpi Road (S). Buy tickets near the exit and then head around the corner to 76 Xingye Road, past the beautiful stone and brick façade to enter the large upstairs exhibition area, which finely displays the historical context for the founding of the Communist Party. There are a number of fascinating artefacts symbolising the foreign stronghold on the city, including the insignia of the Shanghai Volunteer Corps and the stately chair used by the chairman of the British dominated Shanghai Municipal Council. The nascent revolutionary spirit, unleashed following the student-led May 4th Movement of 1919, culminated in the gathering of Mao and 12 other delegates, as well as two Comintern representatives, here on 23rd July, 1921. A vivid life-like wax diorama immortalises the historic event, with Mao centre-stage. The museum now finds itself curiously closeted amidst Shanghai's trendiest entertainment, eating and shopping area in Xintiandi. It is open from 9:00am to 5:00pm and is close to the Huangpi Road South metro station.

Chairman Mao's Residence
Mao Zedong Jiu Ju 毛泽东旧居

This is in fact one of three houses that Mao used in his early years in Shanghai—but this is the one he frequented most. He lived here with his wife, Yang Kai, their two children and his mother-in-law. The well preserved grey and orange brick shikumen house, where Mao first lived in 1924, features spartanly furnished bedrooms and a large exhibition of photo's, documents and letters of the Great Helmsman. The displays are annotated in English. The house is located at Maoming Road (N), inside Lane 120, not far from the nanjing Road West metro station. It's open on Tuesday to Sunday from 9:00am to 11:30am and from 1:00pm to 4:30pm.

Dr. Sun Yat-Sen's Former Residence
Sun Zhongshan Guju 孙中山故居

Dr. Sun Yat-sen, (1866–1925) the revered father of modern China, was the key figure in the overthrow of the Qing Dynasty in 1911 and the subsequent founding of the Republic of China. He lived here with his wife, China's First Lady, Song Qingling, from 1919 to 1924. She adored the house and remained there until she was forced to move to Hong Kong in 1937. Situated in the former Rue Molière in the French Concession, the modest house with its simple furnishings was the scene for many historic meetings and in the '30s when Madame Sun hosted leading intellectual and political figures from around the globe. George Bernard Shaw paid a visit in February 1933—in famous literary company including Lu Xun and Agnes Smedley. It was also here that Madame Sun's sister, Meiling, was introduced to her future husband, Chiang Kai-shek.

Though the house was gutted by the Japanese in the 1940s, Madame Sun personally ensured that their original treasures were reinstalled. From a fascinating library of over 2,700 titles, to a Suzhou embroidery of a cat with penetrating eyes, a Tang Dynasty pottery horse, beautiful family photo's and a feast of personal items, the residence presents an enchanting record of the lives of two of the most important figures in 20th century history. Recorded commentaries in English are played in the main rooms. The house at 7 Xiangshan Road is open from 9:00am to 4:30pm, except on Saturdays. The nearest metro station is Shanxi Road South.

Former Residence of Madame Song Qingling
Song Qingling Guju 宋庆龄故居

Set in an area of immense historical interest is the house where Song Qingling (Madame Sun Yat-sen) lived for the latter part of her life, from 1948 to 1981. The residence, built in 1920 by a Greek sea captain, contains many personal treasures belonging to China's primary advocate of civil rights and freedom from aggression. The interior has supposedly been kept the way it was during her lifetime—though the wood panelling has received a glossy coat of off-white paint.

In the spacious living room a bookcase in southern Chinese style is indicative of her husband's ancestry, whilst an oil painting, 'The Winter,' tells of her courtship with the Soviet Union as honorary president of the People's Republic of China. The sitting room and adjacent dining room, with French windows opening on to the huge lawn, contain a photographic record of Mao's visit to the house and a large selection of gifts received from foreign dignitaries as well as a silver plate presented to her by her old college in Wellesley, Massachusetts. Unfortunately the upper floor is closed,

Chenyi (陈毅)(1901–1972), born in Sichun, went to study in France in 1919. A founder of the People's Liberation Army and a top military leader, he became the first mayor of post-war Shanghai.

The Chinese are photo crazy—though they will rarely take a picture without a human subject in it.

Chinese Heritage
The Old Town
Shanghai Lao Chengxiang 上海老城乡

The area acquired the name of Shanghai in the 13th century and was walled in the 16th century to repel Japanese pirate attacks. Though the wall has gone it is easy to discern the former native city—it looks like a bulbous egg when you look at a map. It is bounded by Renmin Road to the north and Zhonghua Road to the south. Many visitors are left with the impression that Yu Garden and the neighbouring bazaar are all that there is of the 'Old Town'. This certainly isn't the case as there are many things of interest to the south of this largely tourist district—and they are often ignored by visitors.

With the foreign development of the encompassing city in the 19th century the area remained distinctly Chinese in relation to the international development—and the curious paradox of a Chinatown in a Chinese city emerged. However, the first missionaries and even the first British Consul, Captain George Balfour, were bound to spend their early years within its confines. Its character was further reinforced in the 1990s, with development continuing today, as the central part of the area around Yu Garden reincarnates itself in evermore Chinese style.

The focal point of the old city was the Temple of the City God, Chenghuang Miao, originally built in 1403. The temple hosted numerous festivals and fairground-type activities with entertainers and vendors of all kinds—the forerunner of the modern day bazaar. The Temple of the City God has been restored following years of neglect and prior use as a factory and shop. A gate tower from the city wall, which was demolished after 1911, still survives at the junction of Dajing Road and Zhonghua Road. In the heart of the bazaar area, set in a small lake, the Huxinting Teahouse (*Huxinting Chashi*) has long entertained

Entrance to the Yu Garden Bazaar, 1978.

Presidents and Queens. Translated as the 'Mid-Lake Pavilion Teahouse,' it's more familiarly known as the Willow Pattern Teahouse. Fine selections of teas are served complemented by small plates of sweet and savoury snacks. The teahouse is approached by way of the Bridge of Nine Turnings, zigzagged in nine turns to present the highest form of patriarchal power and to guard against evil spirits unable to turn corners.

Native Tea-Gardens. The Illustrated London News, August 29, 1863.

Yu Garden
Yu Yuan 豫园

Yu Garden, or the Garden of Leisurely Repose, resplendently displays the best of Chinese garden design. It was originally built for the governor of Sichuan province, Pan Yunduan, in the 16th century. Classical Chinese gardens embody much more than flora and fauna, as they were in essence the walled estates of the wealthy and noble—who could imbibe their existence cocooned in a series of interlocking chambers and crafted open spaces. They presented a microcosm of the world.

Space is precious in parts of the Old Town.

Restful water scene surrounding the teahouse in Yu Garden.

The garden has been the scene of many changes and witness to many historic events over the years. With the demise of the original owners, the garden disintegrated, only to be rescued and restored in the middle of the 18th century. At that time an inner garden was added. In 1853 and 1854, the garden's Hall of Heralding Spring was used as the headquarters of the 'Society of Small Swords.' That rebellious group laid siege to the walled city for some 18 months inflicting heavy causalities and wanton destruction. The hall now contains a small museum of the uprising. Since the 1950s the garden has witnessed intermittent restoration, including the placement of an open air theatre built in 1888, but relocated inside in 1985, and further refinements with the dawning of the millennium.

The Yu Garden perfectly demonstrates the sophisticated art of combining several different elements to create a world in miniature—ingeniously mingling pavilions and corridors, hillocks and carefully selected and placed rocks, goldfish-laden lotus ponds, delicate bridges, winding paths, tress and shrubs. Each section of the garden is demarcated by curvaceous white walls crowned with the body and head of a dragon.

The garden contains more than 30 pavilions, and a labyrinth of stairs, corridors and pathways. Standing in front of the Hall of Jade Magnificence (*Yuhuatang*), the Exquisite Jade Rock, with its unusual form and stature is one of the key features in the garden. It was supposedly destined for the imperial park in Beijing, during the reign of Emperor Hui Zong, when by misfortune it came to end up at the bottom of the Huangpu River. It was rescued many centuries later by the original owners of the garden.

Of the restored structures in the garden, the Three Ears of Corn Hall (*Sansuitang*) is the largest. Carved on its doors and windows are rice ears, millet, wheat seedlings, melons and fruit—symbols of plenty. Nearby is the Hall for Viewing the Grand Rockery (*Yangshantang*)—a beautiful two-storey structure with its balustrade overlooking a pond. Upstairs is the Chamber for Gathering the Rain, which derives its name from a 17th-century poem containing the line 'pearl curtains gather the rain from the western mountains in the dusk.'

Near Yu Garden, 1978.

Over the pond leading to the Grand Rockery (*Dajiashan*) is the Corridor for Approaching the Best Scenery. The Grand Rockery, built of 2,000 tonnes of yellow stone quarried from Zhejiang Province, cemented together with rice glue, stands 14 metres (46 feet) high in the heart of the garden. At the foot of the rockery, beside a rivulet, is the Pavilion for Viewing Frolicking Fish (*Yulexie*). Nearby is a 200-year-old wisteria. A gingko tree, reputed to be 400 years old, stands in front of the Ten Thousand Flower Pavilion (*Wanhualou*). Also of note is the Hall of Mildness (*Hexutang*), which contains a century-old set of furniture made of banyan tree roots.

The garden is such a popular spot that actually seeing much of its finery is impossible unless you turn up when it opens at 8:30am. It closes at 5:00pm.

THE DAJING PAVILION
DAJING GE 大境阁

The Dajing Pavilion is the only surviving section of the Ming Dynasty wall that encircled Shanghai before 1911. The three-storey tower originally accommodated archers to repel Japanese pirates, later became the Guangong Temple and today houses an exhibition of the old city of Shanghai. A small model of the old town and a series of Chinese annotated visuals chronicling the area's history can be found on the second floor. It is at 269 Dajing Road and is open from 9:00am to 5:00pm.

CHENXIANGGE NUNNERY
CHENXIANGGE GE 沈香阁

With over twenty nuns in residence this charming temple complex was first established as an estate by Pan Yunduan, by owner of the nearby Yu Garden in the 16th century. It was rebuilt as a temple in the early 19th century and was ignobly converted into a factory workshop during the Cultural Revolution. Restoration began in 1989 and was completed in 1994, with the main structures, the Heavenly King, the Grand and the Guanyin Halls, housing some fine Buddhist sculptures. A single master craftsman was employed to reproduce the statuary. On the surface of a vault over a gilded statue of Buddha can now be found 348 figurines of the Buddhist disciples. It is located at 29 Chenxiangge and is open from 6:00am to 4:00pm.

Lion sculpture.

Left: *The Old Town around Yu Garden provides some of the flavour of Old Shanghai.*

The Jade Buddha Temple
Yufo Si 玉佛寺

The Jade Buddha Temple, dating from 1911, is very much in active use—thanks in no small part to the efforts of the abbot who plastered reverent pictures of Chairman Mao over its bolted doors during the Cultural Revolution. Its role as a Buddhist college was expanded in 2003, with substantial renovations and the opening of the Juequn Hall, at the rear of the complex, to house a display of Buddhist heritage. Funds were secured from numerous paths, including the blessing of cars and their owners, at a minimum of US$500, and the opportunity for patrons to have their names inscribed in the temple at a cost of up to US$12,500.

In many ways the temple has no right to be in eastern China—such decorative splendour is usually restricted to the remote west of the country. Apart from two fine white jade Buddha's from Burma, the main hall houses a grotesquely beautiful mural sculpture. The jade Buddhas were brought to Shanghai in the 1870s. The two metre-high (seven feet) seated Buddha, inlaid with precious stones, is the highlight and is found up a steep flight of stairs. There is a separate charge for entry, shoes must be removed, and photography is, in theory, forbidden. The fine, smaller reclining Buddha is found within one of the temple stores—facing another much cruder manifestation—of which pictures are permitted.

Services are held in the Grand Hall and visitors can pay to summon the monks to pray. The hall is particularly imposing with 20 statues of the Heavenly Kings lining the walls facing a huge central effigy of Sakyamuni—with a mural sculpture depicting Suddhana in search of immortality at the rear.

The temple is high on the list for tour groups and their tour buses snake down the road for most of the day. It's best to get there at opening or after 4:00pm. It is situated in the northwest of town near the railway station at 170 Anyuan Road and is open from 8:00am to 5:00pm.

Jing'an Temple
Jing'an Si 静安寺

A 'temple of tranquility' has existed on this site for around 800 years next to the now defunct Bubbling Well Spring, which used to supply water for the city. Pre-1949, it was run by the notorious Abbott of Bubbling Well Road, a giant of a man with a fabulously rich wife, seven concubines and his own white Russian bodyguard.

Today the temple is again being reconstructed, in Song Dynasty style, on a scale larger than ever. Remnants of the 1880's temple have been torn down and a new

Studying Buddhist scriptures at the Jade Buddha Temple.

reinforced concrete complex has been built—though traditional wood-working methods are being used for the superstructure. Fund-raising is under way for the purchase of a giant two-tonne solid gold Buddha, costing around Rmb 200,000,000 or US$27 million, for the temple's great hall. One of the towers facing the road houses the 3.3 metre (11 foot) Peace Bell, cast in 1999 to signify the advent of the 21st century, and another houses a 2.2 metre (8 foot) cows skin drum. Thirty study rooms with broadband access allow monks to surf the Internet. It's at 1688 Nanjing Road (W), just next to the Jing'an Temple metro station, and is open from 7:30am to 5:00pm.

Zhenru Temple *Zhenru Si* 真如寺

The Zhenru Temple, built in 1320, is to be found on Nanda Jie at Zhenru in the Putuo district to the north-west of the city. Many of the buildings date from the Yuan Dynasty (1279–1368), though there have been several new additions. In recent times a new pagoda has been added and the area around the temple has been given a face-lift. Its great hall is one of the best-preserved wooden structures in the region and the oldest of its type in Shanghai. When the temple was restored in 1963 it was discovered that many of the original craftsmen working on the temple had written their names and their positions on the wooden parts of the structure. The writing is now an important source material for calligraphy students. The temple as a whole is a very fine example of 14th-century architecture and provides much information on ancient construction techniques.

Top: *Xilin Pagoda and Temple;* Left: *Statuary at the Jade Buddha Temple.*

Money Changers

Already estimates put the number of Chinese Kuanye *(cash god) millionaires at 4 to 5 million. And then there were all the* geti hu *(private entrepreneurs) whose capitalist-style businesses formed the backbone of the burgeoning new middle class; the* dakuan *(big bucks) high rollers; the* dahu *(big players) from the stock market; and the* huanqiande *(money changers) in the streets. Each of Nanjing East Road's many money changers had a doorway or arcade entrance from which they worked their 'territory'. As soon as a foreigner appeared on their stretch of the street, they darted out from their hiding places like trout streaking out from under rocks to strike at floating insects. 'Yoooo lika sharnsha manee? OK!' one man dressed in a white, Tom Wolfe-like suit hissed at me as I crossed the Henan Road. Then doing an adept little two-step*

Still enamoured of neon today, though the Sincere Department Store clock glows no more.

beside me as I edged back up onto the sidewalk, he repeated his proposition over and over again, sotto voce, like a mantra. Only seconds after Tom Wolfe broke off contact, another money changer—this one sporting a studied coiffure, a silk windbreaker, and a Marlboro clamped between his nicotine-stained teeth—materialized beside me. Like a pimp, he shadowed me the rest of the way down the block, making his whispered entreaties in the same fractured English. No sooner had he vanished then a third struck. All of these hustlers were part of a Mafia-like syndicate that was doing tens of millions of dollars in black-market currency exchanges. All that I could think was that if any of them dared to ply their trade in Shanghai's streets in 1975, they would have ended up in prison. But in the midst of this neon energy, prisons, especially the idea of political prisoners, seemed utterly remote.

Orville Schell, Mandate of Heaven: A New Generation of Entrepreneurs Dissidents, Bohemians, and Technocrats Lays Claim to China's Future
(Simon & Schuster, 1994)

Other Places of Interest
The Huangpu River Cruise
Huangpu Jiang Youlun 黄浦江游轮

Shanghai's position at the mouth of the life-giving Yangzi River was the prime *raison d'etre* for the conquest of the city by foreign traders. The best way to view Shanghai is from the murky brown mass of water, of one of its tributaries, the Huangpu River. Today its river traffic still presents an amazing display of trading activity—with overloaded smoke-billowing barges vying with modern liners and cargo boats for their livelihoods. River cruises afford a glorious panorama of the majestically enigmatic Bund, the new skyscraper spires of the Pudong New Area, and the coagulation of hectic wharves and shipyards. Day and evening cruises are available. The city takes on a different complexion at night as its face and skyline are dramatically transformed by a cobweb of lights.

Cruises generally take between one to three hours. Many take in the downstream excursion to the Yangpu Bridge (*Yangpu Daqiao*), whilst others include the Nanpu Bridge (*Nanpu Daqiao*). The Nanpu Bridge, with a central span of 423 metres (1,400

Nanpu Bridge is one of the many modern engineering achievements now spanning the Huangpu River.

feet), was opened in 1991 and the Yangpu Bridge, with a central span of 602 metres (1,950 feet), was opened in 1993. Others now extend their itinerary to the spectacular Lupu Bridge (*Lupu Daqiao*), the world's tallest arch bridge at a height of 550 metres (1,800 feet), which was completed in mid-2003. Incidentally, all of these bridges have visitor sidewalks offering great views over the river and the city. The longer cruises travel down as far as Wusong, the former site of a legendary fort, where the Huangpu River collides with the might of the Yangzi. Most of the companies offering river cruises have offices on the waterfront opposite the end of Jingling Road (E). One can also take the short local ferry ride across the river to Pudong from there.

Most companies will revise schedules according to season and demand, so do try to ring ahead. The Huangpu River Tour Company, one of the biggest operators, has departures from No. 127–129 Zhongshan No. 2 Road (E) (tel: 6374 4459, 6329 9992). They offer day and evening cruises, as does the Shanghai Scenery Shipping & Tourism Company (tel: 6356 1932, 6329 3246). On the Pudong side, 30-minute cruises that allow a closer look at the Bund and Pudong embark from the Pearl Cruise Dock, just to the west of the Oriental Pearl TV Tower. There are up to six daytime and two evening departures. The dock is at No. 1 Century Avenue (tel: 5879 1888).

Other Sights in Puxi

Childrens' Palaces
Shaoniangong 少年宫

Shanghai has over 20 childrens' palaces. These are after school activity centres where, apart from training in etiquette and leadership, children aged six to 16 can develop their literary, musical and technical talents. To attend children must gain their teacher's recommendation as well as pass an entrance exam. Many are housed in the palatial buildings of past powerful officials and businessmen. Until recently most visitors would head for the children's palace housed in the magnificent former Kadoorie home, Marble Hall, at 64 Yan'an Road (W). It has now been closed to the public, but the building itself remains open for viewing from Wednesday to Sunday. There are now two options for visitors. The Victorian gothic style mansion built in 1930 for Wang Boqun, and now the Changning District Children's Palace, is the grandest. Wang was the Guomindang Minister of Transportation and the first president of the prestigious Jiatong (Communications) University. It was also used as the base for the cultural section of the British Embassy before 1949. It is at No. 31, Lane 1136 Yuyuan Road. The other is located at 75 Wuxing Road in the Xujiahui area, not far from the Hengshan Road metro station.

Visitors get a chance to see you the young prodigies at work and play and are often treated to some kind of display or performance. Visits are generally restricted to the late afternoon period or all day at weekends. Consult CITS or your hotel concierge for more advice.

Shanghai Public Library
Shanghai Tushuguan 上海图书馆

Located in the heart of the former French Concession, the massive new Shanghai Library was completed in 1996. Its two towers overlook the appropriately named Square's of Wisdom and Knowledge. With over 10 million books and 30 million documents, 24 reading rooms and state-of-the-art electronic equipment, the library ranks amongst the most important in the world. A wide range of foreign language periodicals and books are found on the 4th floor—which is open from 9:00am to 5:00pm. Library cards can be obtained at a nominal cost upon the presentation of your passport. To the side of the library are two large halls that often host interesting exhibitions of art and culture. The library is at 1555 Central Huaihai Road and is open from 8:30am to 8:00pm. The nearest metro station is Hengshan Road.

The Biblioteca.

Reading Room Xujiahui Biblioteca.

ZI-KA-WEI BIBLIOTECA
SHANGHAI TUSHUGUAN XUJIAHUI CHANGSHUGUAN 上海图书馆徐家汇藏书楼

As a part of the Jesuit mission centre in what was then the village of Zi-ka-wei (Shanghainese for Xujiahui), a library was initiated in 1847. Over the years the Jesuits created a centre for science, learning and worship in the area, including the neighbouring St. Ignatius Cathedral and the Shanghai Observatory.

In late 2003 two buildings housing this historically important, and long forbidden, collection were opened to the public. The larger building dating from 1896, and rebuilt in 1931, was originally a residence for priests. It has a reading room allowing access to massive collections of old Shanghai newspapers, magazines and old books. Two wood carvings from the original cathedral adorn its walls. The Wangfung Art Gallery can also be found on the ground floor of the building (tel: 6487 4309).

The adjacent two-storey building, dating to 1867, can only be visited as part of a library tour. It contains a remarkable collection of books on topics ranging from theology to geography, all housed in one of the most atmospheric interiors found in Shanghai. The main room in Gothic style, with two stacks rising from floor to ceiling, is a veritable museum piece in itself. It is located at 80 Caoxi Road North and is open from 9:00am to 5:00pm except on Sundays. Guided tours are available between 2:00pm and 4:00pm on Saturdays. Telephone 6487 4095 ext. 209 to book your place. The biblioteca is adjacent to the number 8 exit of the Xujiahui metro station.

Shanghai Grand Theatre
Shanghai Dajuyuan 上海大剧院
The city's cultural and arts scene has been elevated with the dazzling state-of-the-art Grand Theatre—China's most eloquent statement of its commitment to the arts. It was designed by Jean-Marie Charpentier, who crafted the Bastille Opera in Paris, and is open daily for tours between 8:30am and 11:00am and 1:00pm to 4:00pm. The theatre is located in People's Square at 300 People's Avenue.

Duolun Road
Duolun Lu 多伦路
Some very fine examples of red and grey brick town houses and art deco apartment blocks still survive with impunity in this part of the Hongkou district. The refurbishment of Duolun Street, with its assemblage of historical architecture, was completed in 2002, when it was designated as Shanghai's 'Culture Street.' The architecture is fascinating with mansions, terraces and bungalows abutting the elbow-shaped street. The cultural angle is largely historical as most of the pedestrianised street is taken over with stores selling arts and crafts, antiques and memorabilia and coffee shops and restaurants. In the 1930s the area was the focus for some of China's most famous literary figures including Lu Xun, Mao Dun, Guo Moruo and authors of the League of Leftist Writers. The Jinquan Coin Museum, just off the street and housed in a fine mansion, can be visited for a small entrance fee.

The street is well worth visiting for its ambience, but be sure to shoot off down the quiet local lanes that run off it to see the other side of life. Of special architectural note is a 1924 Moorish creation, by Spanish architect Abelardo Lafuente, which was one of H.H. Kung's (*Kong Xiangxi*) residences at No. 250. He was a powerful figure in the Kuomintang government and married Song Ailing, one of the legendary Song sisters. At No. 57 the Hong De Temple is the only surviving Christian church built to a traditional Chinese design. Built in 1928, it has recently been opened for worship again. The area is close to the Baoxin Road station on metro line 3.

Fuyou Road Mosque
Fuyou Lu Qing Zhen Si 福佑路清真寺
Tucked down an alley not far from the Yu Garden, this small mosque consisting of three interconnecting halls in traditional Chinese style was built in 1870 and reopened in 1979. It's at 378 Fuyou Road and is open from 7:00am to 8:00pm.

Enamoured of neon, 1930. Even the Sincere Department Store's clock glows (see page 392).

Great World
Da Shijie 大世界

On the corner of Central Tibet Road and Yan'an Road (E) the wedding-cake tower of the Great World epitomises Shanghai's gaiety as the 'Paris of the East' in the 1930s. The building which dates from 1915 once housed gambling dens, massage parlours, brothels, dance halls and restaurants that drew every variety of pleasure-seeker and hedonist. Its recent role as a more acceptable centre for amusement was halted in 2003 by a downturn in business—but was thoroughly renovated in 2010.

Small Peach Garden Mosque
Xiao Taoyuan Qing Zhen Si 小桃园清真寺

Translated as the 'small peach garden,' and tucked down a typical Shanghai alley, this mosque remains the focus for the city's growing Muslim population and serves as the headquarters for the Shanghai Islamic Association. This imposing historic building, completed in 1927 and now protected by the Municipal Government, exhibits Western

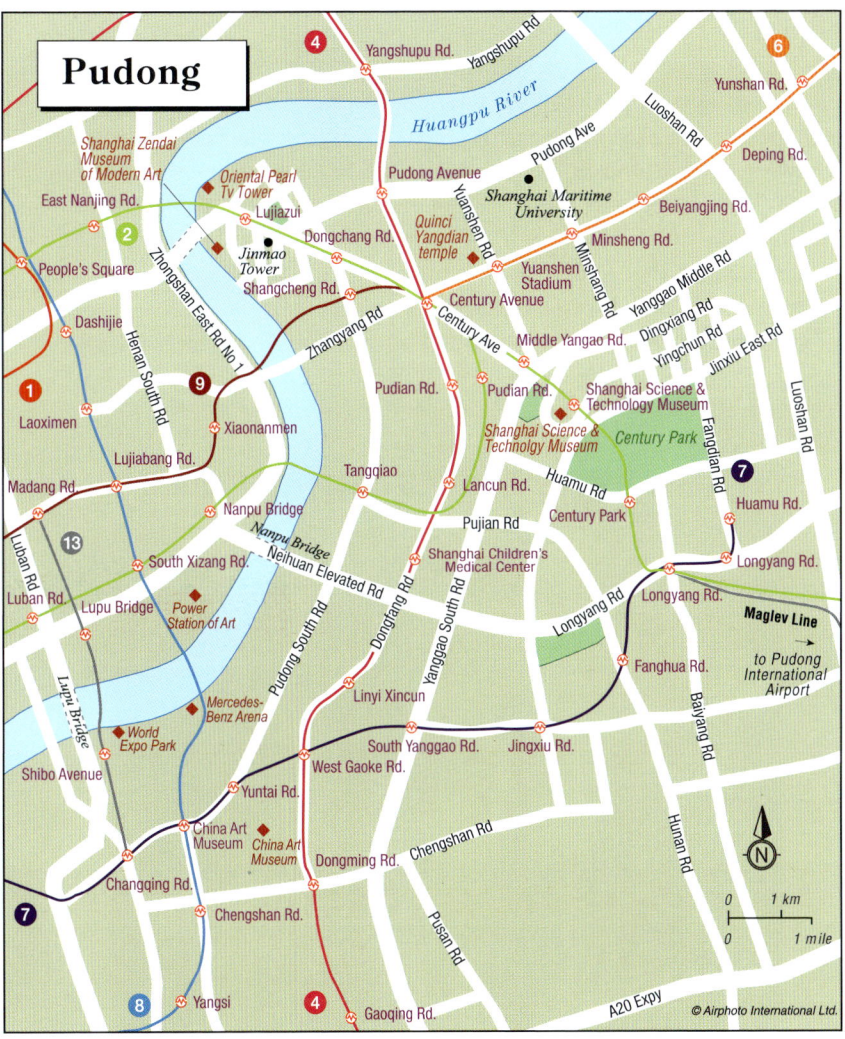

architectural characteristics with Chinese and Islamic adornments. The mosque was seriously damaged during the Cultural Revolution—but has now been restored to its former glory. It is to be found at 52 Xiaotaoyuan Road, off Fuxing Road (E), and is open from 8:00am to 6:00pm.

Sights in Pudong

The local government has huge plans for the development of Pudong as a leisure and tourist destination. Already the huge Century Park and Century Square have been laid out alongside the Shanghai Museum of Science and Technology in the central zone. From the park, the French-designed 100-metre wide Century Avenue extends for five kilometres to join one of the tunnels linking Pudong with Puxi. Three magnificent sculptures are found on the avenue. Just to the east of Century Park the Tomson Golf Club is an international level 18-hole course replete with deluxe residential villas and recreational facilities. To the east of Pudong near the airport the Huaxia Cultural and Tourist Area has been created with the development

of a seaside resort and a cultural park with re-created Ming and Qing Dynasty style palaces and pavilions. However, most of the interesting sights for the visitor are still to be found in the area to the west overlooking the Huangpu River. The Lujiazui area with its modern skyscrapers is an attraction in itself and is easy to reach by metro, the Bund Tourist Tunnel or by local ferry.

Most of the new eye-catching edifices in the Lujiazui area soar high into the sky. However, along the waterfront is the low-rise Shanghai International Convention Centre, incorporating the Oriental Riverside Hotel. Like most of the buildings in the area its design and location incorporates Chinese symbolism and principles of *feng shui*. This flagship development of the Shanghai Municipal Government has two large globes representing pearls, on which there are maps of China and the world. They are placed to each side of the building to represent a bridge between China and the outside world. The building was completed in 1999 in time to host the Fortune 500 forum and was one of the sites of the 2001 APEC ministerial meetings. Nearby the plan of the Shanghai Customs Pudong Building at 153 Lujiazui Road (W) is laid out like the Chinese character for the number eight—a very lucky number signifying prosperity. The design of the Bank of China Tower at 200 Central Yincheng Road is based on an ancient Chinese coin to symbolise wealth and purity.

In the heart of the Lujiazui financial work is underway on creating what is expected to be the world's second highest building with an expected completion date of 2014. The new Shanghai Tower, designed by the American firm Gensler, has an announced height of 632 metres (2073 feet). This comes right on the heels of

Above: *Business as usual on the Huangpu River.*

Left: *From a similar angle in 1978, the Pudong shoreline's buildings barely rose above two stories. Also compare this with today's Pudong New Area (see page 326, 539).*

the completion of the Shanghai World Financial Centre, China's tallest building at 492 metres (1614 feet), in August 2008.

The area along the waterfront around Riverside Avenue has been comprehensively redeveloped with a magnificent new promenade and park areas. Nearby, the huge lawn of the Lujiazui Green, despite signs forbidding entrance, is full of people relaxing on its turf. New attractions, including a curious exhibition complex dedicated to the insect world, have opened nearby. Inside the entrance to the Bund Sightseeing Tunnel, a rather tawdry exhibition of 'Rare Aquatic Animals' is partnered by a fascinating and intriguing exhibition of 'China Sex Culture and Sex Health' (a sister to the museum in Tongli (see page 446). Its erotic exhibits feature anything from mating tortoises to vases adorned with phalluses, and there are special displays on the sexual oppression of women and the formerly taboo matter of homosexuality. The impressive Shanghai Municipal History Museum is in the basement of the Oriental Pearl TV Tower (see page 355).

Oriental Pearl TV Tower dominates Shanghai's skyline.

The Pudong New Area's ambitions are not just tall, but very wide as well. It's neighbouring district of Nanhui was merged administratively with that of Pudong in May 2009 in an effort to create an even larger economic powerhouse to help drive the city's effort to become a major international financial

Xinchang: another side of Pudong.

and shipping centre. Overnight, Pudong expanded its land area from around 533 to 1,210 square kilometres, supporting a population of around 2.7 million people.

THE ORIENTAL PEARL TV TOWER
DONGFANG MINGZHU 东方明珠

The 468-metre (1,535 feet) TV tower is the third tallest in the world and the new symbol of modern Shanghai. It was the first perpendicular icon to arise in the Pudong New Area when it was completed in 1994. Like most other new buildings, symbolism plays a large part in the love it or hate it design. The tower's eleven spheres represent pearls falling from the sky on to a jade plate. There are lofty viewing decks at 263 metres (863 feet) and 350 metres (1,148 feet). In good visibility, which unfortunately Shanghai doesn't encounter too often, great views are afforded across the city and in to the Yangzi River Delta. It can get overwhelmingly busy at the weekends and on holidays.

SHANGHAI WORLD FINANCIAL CENTRE 上海环球金融中心

Built at a cost approaching a billion US dollars, the 101-storey Shanghai World Financial Center, dominates the Pudong skyline. Its design by New York based Kohn Pedersen Fox, often compared to the shape of a bottle opener, takes on many different forms when viewed from different points around the city. It has the highest roof in the world, even though officially it is the second tallest behind the Taipei 101 in Taiwan. The Park Hyatt Shanghai, occupying floors 79 to 93 also claims the accolade of being the world's highest hotel. The building has three observation decks on floors 94, 97 as well as the incredible 'skywalk' observation deck on the 100th floor at a height of 474 metres (1,555 feet).

THE JINMAO BUILDING, JINMAO DASHA 金茂大厦

China's highest building is one of its most attractive, with its design resembling that of a huge glass and steel pagoda. The 88-storey Jinmao is 420.5 metres (1,379 feet) high and its total floor space exceeds that of all the old buildings on the Bund combined. Visitors can ascend to the 88th floor for views not only of the city but also of the spectacularly cavernous atrium of the Grand Hyatt Hotel that occupies the top 33 floors of the building. The viewing platform can be less busy than the one in the nearby TV tower.

The Jinmao Building.

Museums and Exhibition Centres

Shanghai Museum
Shanghai Bowuguan 上海博物馆

This spectacular world-class museum, costing around US$50 million, was opened in 1996. Designed by Shanghai architect Xing Tonghe, this futuristic building with a circular roof with four decorative holders is said to resemble an ancient bronze seen from a distance. Six stone lions and two stone *bixie* (mythical beasts that expel evil) guard the entrance to the museum and the granite walls of the building are decorated with designs found in ancient bronze-ware. The museum has a fine collection of sculptures, furniture, paintings, calligraphy, coins, ceramics, ancient bronzes, jade-ware and minority handicrafts—all housed in state-of-the-art surroundings. The museum is at 201 People's Avenue in People's Square and is open Sunday to Friday from 9:00am to 7:00pm and on Saturdays from 9:00am to 8:00pm.

Bixie, Chinese mythical beasts which became popular during the Western Han Dynasty (206 BC–9 AD) when the living lion began to be imported along the Silk Route of Northwest China, and lions guard the Shanghai Museum.

The China Art Museum 中华艺术馆, Power Station of Art

Following the opening of the China Art Museum, formerly the China Pavilion during World Expo 2010, in October 2012 the Shanghai Art Museum that was housed in the former historic Race Club building on People's Square was closed. The impressive new museum has 27 halls covering around 64,000 square meters. Another huge state-run museum, and the first dedicated to contemporary art, the Power Station of Art opened on the Puxi side of the Expo site at the same time. The China Art Museum has its own dedicated metro stop and the Power Station of Art at Lane 20, Huayuangang Road is close to the South Xizang Road station. Both are open from 9.00am to 5.00pm, Tuesday to Sunday.

Shanghai Urban Planning Exhibition Centre
Shanghai Chengshi Guihua Zhanshiguan 上海城市规划展示馆

The centre is a magnificent showcase of the architectural history of Shanghai—evoking past, present and future through the use of models, dioramas and multimedia. The spacious building houses a huge model of Shanghai envisioned in 2020, covering more than 600 square metres, which can be viewed at eye-level or from above. The second floor reflects on the history of the city, whilst the fourth highlights a series of key projects for the future development of the metropolis. The basement exit contains a rather tepid re-creation of a 1930s street. The exhibition centre is the largest of its kind in the world. It is at 100 People's Avenue to the east of People's Square and is open from 9:00am to 5:00pm (Monday to Thursday) and from 9:00am to 6:00pm (Friday to Sunday).

Museum of Contemporary Art (MoCA) Shanghai
Shanghai Dangdai Yishuguan 上海当代当艺术馆

MoCA, Shanghai's first non-profit and independently-operated contemporary art institution in Shanghai is devoted to both Chinese and international art. It is housed in a magnificent modern glass building in the heart of People's Park and has a coffee shop and restaurant, with terrace, on its top floor. It's open from 10:00am to 6:00pm daily and stays open till 10:00pm on Wednesdays.

Shanghai Natural History Museum
Shanghai Ziran Bowuguan 上海自然博物馆

This magnificent 1927 building was converted to its present use in 1950 and exhibits the same signs of age as its poorly paraded stuffed exhibits. Besides the main hall's impressive display of dinosaur skeletons, the surviving original mosaic floors, woodwork and stained glass windows all remind the visitor of the city's fallen grandeur. An extensive display of invertebrates, fish, mammals, birds and mammals is to be found on the musty upper two floors. The ground floor exhibition plots the development of humankind and includes a room containing a pair of Ming Dynasty mummies found in the Shanghai area. The museum is at 260 Yan'an Road (E) and is open from 9:00am to 5:00pm. The nearest metro station is at Nanjing Road East.

Shanghai Postal History Museum
Shanghai Youzheng Bowuguan 上海邮政博物馆
Opened as the main post office for the former International Settlement in 1924, this imposing building, designed by British architects Stewardson and Spence, continues to operate today. The entrance to the museum is found in its main and magnificently restored transaction hall. Apart from an interesting and comprehensive display encompassing the development of the Imperial postal system, the museum's main attraction is a magnificent roof garden with views across the Suzhou Creek and the Huangpu River. The museum is at 175 South Suzhou Road and is open from 9:00am to 4:00pm (Wed, Thurs, Sat, Sun only).

Shanghai Museum of Science and Technology
Shanghai Kejiguan 上海科技馆
A stunning structure with equally stunning exhibits has made this museum a major attraction for all the family. Hundreds of interactive exhibits wait amongst the various zones one passes though—from the subterranean depths of the earth, to tropical rainforests and space-age technological environs. Allow a whole day for a visit and expect to queue for a while for those 'hands on' (hands off!) exhibits. The complex also houses an IMAX cinema and an IWERKS theatre. Construction of the museum began in December 1996 and was completed in March 2001, at a cost of 1.75 billion yuan. The museum is located in Pudong adjacent to Century Park, at 2000 Century Avenue, and is open from 9:00am to 5:00pm except on Mondays. The museum has its own dedicated metro station.

Shanghai Arts and Crafts Museum (Institute)
Shanghai Gongyi Meishu Bowuguan (Yanjiusuo) 上海工艺美术博物馆(研究所)
Museum-quality arts and crafts exhibits form only a small part of what this destination has to offer. It has been the home of the Shanghai Arts & Crafts Research Institute since 1960, and artisans practising various forms of carving, embroidery and paper-cutting can be seen at work. Many of the works are for sale and there is also an antique store in the basement. The building itself is a fine example of French Renaissances architecture, created in the mid-1920s by celebrated Hungarian architect Laszlo Hudec for Paul Madier, a French silk merchant. Set in one of the most delightful areas of Shanghai, the mansion was faithfully restored in 2002 and is well worth the

visit in itself. It is at 79 Fenyang Road and is open from 9:00am to 4:00pm. The nearest metro station is at Shanxi Road South.

C.Y. TUNG MARITIME MUSEUM
DONG HAO YUN HANGYUN BOWUGUAN
董浩云航运博物馆

This superbly-planned museum, located in one of China's most prestigious universities that began life as the Nan Yang Public School in 1897, opened in early 2003. The museum's namesake, C. Y. Tung, was a Shanghai native turned international shipping tycoon. The university itself has many fine historic buildings set in a delightful campus. The museum occupies a fine redbrick courtyard building that originally opened in 1910 as a boy's dormitory.

Traditional motifs in Chinese art.

The first floor contains the Chinese Maritime History Gallery, plotting China's, often understated maritime history from Neolithic times. Of interest are exhibits highlighting the 'silk and porcelain maritime route' from the Middle Ages and China's leading role in naval architecture and innovation during the early 15th century. In the early Ming Dynasty the renowned Admiral Zheng He commanded fleets and undertook seven great ocean voyages, demonstrating China's marine skills and navigational prowess. The display also reflects Shanghai's importance as a trading port—going back to the eighth century.

Fittingly, Hong Kong Chief Executive Tung Chee-hwa was present at the museum's opening ceremony. The second floor is dedicated to the activities and manifold interests of Mr. Tung, featuring numerous fascinating personal artefacts and ships' memorabilia, including the ship's bell from the ill-fated *Queen Elizabeth*. Tung acquired the old Cunard liner in 1970 only to watch her destroyed by fire in Hong Kong just two years later. Amongst the large collection of family photographs and letters is an invitation from Queen Elizabeth to attend a garden party at Buckingham Palace in 1980 and a White House invitation from Ronald Reagan. Shanghai Jiaotong University is at 1954 Huashan Road, close to Xujiahui metro station. The museum is open from Tuesday to Sunday from 1:30pm to 5:30pm.

Shanghai Banking Museum
Shanghai Shi Yinhang Bowuguan 上海市银行博物馆

The Shanghai Banking Museum was the first such venue of its kind in China and opened in 2000. Within the large display halls tare fascinating artefacts related to banking from the smallest bank note ever issued, to period dioramas of banking institutions, and a 1930s comptometer. Complemented by historic photos and a model with a recorded commentary describing the major, old and new, financial institutions on the Bund and Pudong, the museum offers a fantastic insight into the commercial development of Shanghai. The museum is usually only open to group visitors from Monday to Friday by prior appointment—but individuals can visit on Wednesday afternoons. Groups and individuals should phone ahead (5888 5888 ext. 6701) to check availability. It is located on 7th floor of the Industrial and Commercial Bank of China Building at No. 9 Pudong Avenue, near the Dongchang Road metro station.

Shanghai Museum of Public Security
Shanghai Gong'an Bowuguan 上海公安博物馆

Housed in an impressive seven-storey building located away from the main sights, this museum opened in 1999 and was refurbished in 2003. There are about 3,000 exhibits on display, chronicling the history of the city's public security services going back to the establishment of its first police department in 1854—though the emphasis is on achievements following the founding of the People's Republic in 1949.

The permanent exhibits are arranged on the second to fourth floors, with temporary exhibits staged on the fifth floor. Introductions to the exhibition areas are in English, though all else is in Chinese. However little interpretation is required for many of the artefacts on display—from graphic photos of real life murders to a huge armoury of weapons used by criminals and the security forces.

The second floor focuses on the old days, with a wax model of a red-turbaned Sikh policeman and a reminder of the infamous 'May 30th' incident in 1925 when officers from the Louza Police Station opened fire on a defenceless crowd of students and civilians.

Whistle-blowing traffic assistants police street-corners, admonishing errant pedestrians with shrill blasts.

The third floor records famous criminal cases, aspects of social control and traffic policing, whilst the fourth houses objects from the fire department and an astounding collection of firearms. In fact, the gun collection, with approximately 240 varieties of firearms is reputed to be the largest in the world. It includes many fascinating and ingenious period pieces, including a cigarette case weapon made for Huang Jinrong, a mobster and head of the former French Concession's Chinese detective squad. An ebony pistol that belonged to Dr. Sun Yat-sen is also on display. The museum is at 518 Ruijin Road (S) near the junction with Quxi Road and is open Monday to Saturday from 9:00am to 4:00pm. The sightseeing bus service number 2 from the Shanghai Stadium stops outside.

Sanshan Guild-Hall *Sanshan Huiguan* 三山会馆

Up until the 1920s, guild's were very important associations in regulating the economic and social life of migrant workers living in Shanghai. Sanshan, one of the few surviving guild-halls, was a focus for the Fujian community, having been built in 1909 by a Fujianese fruit merchant. Situated near the Nanpu Bridge, the magnificent courtyard building was restored in 2002 and 2010. Its central feature is an opera stage with an intricately carved roof. The exhibition halls play host to temporary exhibitions from private collections that offer a fascinating insight into the history of Shanghai as well as some more general examples of Chinese arts and crafts. Recent displays have included old Shanghai collectables such as cosmetics, cigarette lighters and cases, furniture and clocks. It is located at 1551 Zhongshan Road (S) and is open from 8:30am to 4:30pm.

Shikumen Open House *Shikumen Shanshiguan* 石库门屋里香

Stone frame door, or *shikumen*, housing has been a key feature of Shanghai architecture for well over a century and is now under threat of almost complete annihilation. Set in the heart of Xintiandi—this fabricated old lane house showcases life in the 1920s and 1930s with its assemblage of Chinese and Western style furniture and artefacts from that period. Apart from seven rooms set out as they may have been, with numerous interesting objects, there is an exhibition area charting the renovation and development of the Xintiandi area itself. It is there that one can get some appreciation of how elements from the past and present have been blended in this historical re-creation of an area that otherwise would have been totally destroyed. The exhibit is at No. 25, Lane 181, Taicang Road and is open from 10:00am to 10:00pm (*see* page 412).

New Heaven—Old Earth —*The Ginger Griffin*

The thing that fascinates Ben Wood most about Shanghai architecture is the thought that foreign architects in the 1920s and 1930s were doing exactly the same things that he is doing today. "It's all happening over again—history is repeating itself," he says. Foreign architects are now engaged with very important projects that are changing the face of Shanghai. In the 1920s and 1930s there was an extraordinary amount of activity by foreign architects who created some of the finest architecture in the world. In those days it was engineered by the scions of Shanghai commerce like the inimitable and wealthy Sir Victor Sassoon—and today Shanghai still conjures up images of a place where anything can be done. Shanghai is a great place for successful architects as their patrons are often billionaires who want to make a name—in much the same way as when Sassoon built Sassoon House, incorporating the Cathay Hotel, in 1929. Such buildings were constructed to glorify a name and consolidate the status of the rich and famous.

Shanghai was an important, if not the most important, city in the world in those days. Whilst the Sassoon dynasty ruled the East, New York was also booming under the aegis of the Rockefellers. Such dynasties changed the face of the world and Ben feels that one of the most incredible things about architecture is the opportunity to leave a legacy behind. The great Chinese American architect, I. M. Pei left China with his family in 1939. In the 1930s his father brought him to Shanghai from their home in Suzhou and, as Ben recounts, it was his view of the magnificent skyscraper Park Hotel that that inspired the youngster to become an architect. Today there are a handful of developers in Shanghai, largely returned overseas Chinese who are not only changing the face of the city but also the culture of China. The construction boom is happening all over again.

Ben first came to China as the architect of a groundbreaking project in Shanghai. His creation of *Xintiandi*, translated as New Heaven on Earth, has established a living legacy backed by a remarkable tale of adventure and innovation. It all started in 1996 with a desire by the Luwan district government to renovate and rejuvenate a large tract of land in the heart of their district in anticipation of the 50th anniversary of communist rule in China. What made the area so special was a French designed shikumen (stone frame door) property that had been the place where the communist party was founded in 1921. Hong Kong-based Shui On Properties, headed by Vincent Lo, was already involved with a couple of projects in Shanghai and landed the contract for the development. Mr. Lo hired an American architectural firm which duly had its master plan approved. However the project just didn't feel right as it lacked a fun element and resembled an office park. So Mr. Lo sent one of his staff around the world to scout for a new architect.

Ben Wood was at his office in Boston, Massachusetts, when he was approached. He had just successfully renovated a large section of the art deco district in South Beach, Miami, that proved to be a huge commercial and cultural success. Ben was given two days notice to get to Hong Kong where he was given a ticket for his first foray into China. Four other architects were also sent to Shanghai to stake a claim on the project. They even stayed at the same hotel but were unaware of each other's presence. Ben landed the assignment and even though he and Mr. Lo were almost complete strangers Mr. Lo remarkably told him the next day that this was a project that was going to change both of their lives.

The past serves the present—Xintiandi.

Ben felt that the unique historic houses in the area had serious cultural value. His desire to save the old buildings was initially met with some scepticism by the board of directors. The timing was everything because it was at that moment in time when that kind of urban fabric was disappearing at an alarming rate. He makes an analogy with the Tuscan hill towns in Italy a century ago. At that time no one wanted to live in their old buildings and no one would have believed that a town like Sienna would one day attract millions of visitors. These traditional Shanghai shikumen houses had been neglected for half a century and were occupied by up to 20 families whereas

Benjamin Wood, architect.

they had been designed to be single family homes. As Ben explains, if it wasn't for the building where the communist party was founded probably none of the old buildings around would have survived at all. However the structures couldn't be saved intact because of earthquake codes, so they were basically demolished and laboriously put back together brick by brick. All the structures and interiors were renewed, but Ben was consummately fanatical about keeping the actual shape of the buildings and the original spatial relationships that form the compelling part of the project.

Shikumen housing is basically an urban adaptation of a traditional courtyard. They are set in *lilongs*, or lanes, similar to the *hutongs* in Beijing. However the Shanghai lilongs are based on a very sturdy and clear hierarchy. They were individual neighbourhoods, each with a name and a strong physical and social identity. The width of their lanes corresponds to a hierarchy of public and private space. Generally, the east-west lanes afforded more privacy than the wider lanes running north-south. Behind the stone-frame door fronting the property would be found a small courtyard and in the house itself there was a hierarchy with small rooms offset by half a level at the back for the servants. In reinventing the Xintiandi area Ben Wood deliberately created European style plazas as collective spaces. Such spaces are alien to Chinese culture and the modern development of Shanghai is typified by huge tracts of 'public' green space that sit idle. Ben maintains that three- and four-storey shikumen properties can achieve the same population density as present-day 30-storey buildings, which have no-man's land green spaces between them. Shanghai's present development is based on a Hong Kong model where tall buildings are surrounded by green and because "that green space belongs to everybody it belongs to nobody—the guy that enjoys it most is the security guard". For Ben that represents the tragic demise of community.

As the area around Xintiandi continues to be developed that sense of community will be reborn in the area. Xintiandi itself houses an exclusive collection of restaurants, stores, entertainment and leisure facilities. It is the first project that made Chinese people feel like that they could do something very Chinese whilst attracting a very fashionable international crowd, including Chinese citizens. The architecture is a fusion between West and East, but it is a very Chinese place and instantly recognisable as Shanghai. It has taken on an international fame like Soho in New York and is known as a place and not as a collection of individual buildings. Xintiandi has developed as a world-class cultural destination. Before World War II the area was part of the French Concession and, as Ben notes, all the terracotta decorations over the stone doors were from Paris. Whilst working on Xintiandi he was also travelling to Paris and came back with photographs of decorations that were precisely replicated in Shanghai in days gone by. He spotted an exact copy of a park bench in the nearby Fuxing Park (former French Park) found outside the Eiffel Tower.

Ben Wood's highly successful formula for Xintiandi has been applied to projects all across China from Chongqing in the west to Hangzhou in the east. The West Lake Xintiandi with its mix of Chinese roof-styles, trellis-covered paths and a high-tech conference centre arose from a formerly quite lakeside location in Hangzhou and has been a huge success.

Ben Wood has also worked with the city of Zhujiajiao in creating Cambridge Watertown near its historic centre in Shanghai's Qingpu district. The city held a competition in the summer of 2003 to select the architectural and development team for what is known as New Zhujiajiao. Normally Ben wouldn't have gone after such a conventional residential project, but in this case he really wanted to demonstrate to the rest of China that "you can do something that is deeply rooted in the Chinese culture". Up until recently the developers of the new towns around Shanghai have focused on borrowing ideas from the West, creating German towns, Dutch towns or American towns. There is massive competition between the districts of Shanghai for fame and fortune with officials behind these projects edging to gain favour with the top party leaders. The creation of a new water town, anywhere in China, has never been attempted before. Linked by a canal to the old town two kilometres away, it will eventually house 200,000 people.

'Ginger Griffin' is Peter Hibbard's nom de plume for writing that has a historical context—especially related to Shanghai. Hibbard also hosts private tours, contracted overseas, in Shanghai under this aegis (www.gingergriffin.com).

Lujiazui Development Showroom
Lujiazui Chenlieshi 陆家嘴陈列室

Set in the south-east corner of Lujiazui Green sits the enigma of a beautiful grey- and red-brick courtyard dwelling. The Chuan, or *Chen Gui Chun*, residence, as it is known, is of a traditional Chinese design with Western features. The house now contains an exhibition of photographs and artefacts that plot the development of this futuristic-looking part of town. It is at 15 Lujiazui Road (E) and is open from 8:30am to 5:00pm.

Shanghai Chinese Painting Academy
Shanghai Zhongguo Huayuan 上海中国画院

Set in the heart of the former French Concession, this modern centre holds temporary exhibitions of contemporary Chinese art on the first floor, where a small but interesting bookstore can also be found. The works of Lin Fengmian are featured on the second floor displaying modern interpretations of classic Chinese scenes and working class studies. The academy is at 197 Yueyang Road and is open from 9:00am to 11:30pm and from 1:00pm to 4:00pm except on Mondays.

Raft of the Medusa, *2000 by Shanghai Artist Hu Jieming from* Paris-Pekin.

Jewish Refugee Museum
Youtai Nanmin Zai Shanghai Jinianguan 犹太难民在上海纪念馆

The former Ohel Moshe Synagogue was built in 1927. It was re-opened in 1992 as a small museum dedicated to Jewish refugees who were forced to leave their homes and livelihoods in other parts of the city for a life of squalor and poverty in a restricted area between 1943 and 1945. The area is often referred to as the 'Hongkew Ghetto', which covers a square mile in the vicinity of the synagogue. The neighbourhood has been designated as a conservation zone by the government and work on renovating the former synagogue and its museum took place in 2007. It's at 62 Changyang Road in the Hongkou district. A small memorial to Shanghai's Jewish refugees can be found nearby in Houshan Park at 118 Houshan Road. For a fascinating account of Jewish life in wartime Shanghai, please refer to page 420. The captivating museum contains

The front cover of the programme of the 21st annual Hanukkah Ball held in the Shanghai Jewish Club in January 1941, less than one year before Pearl Harbour.

numerous period photos and artefacts, including books and furniture. A small memorial to Shanghai's Jewish refugees can be found nearby in Houshan Park at 118 Houshan Road. The museum is at 62 Changyang Road in the Hongkou district and is open Monday to Friday from 9:00am to 11:30am and 1:00pm to 4:00pm. For a fascinating account of Jewish life in wartime Shanghai please refer to page 420.

Shanghai Exhibition Centre Shanghai Zhanlan Zhongxin 上海展览中心

This vast complex at 1333 Nanjing Road (W), opposite the Shanghai Centre, was built in Soviet-baroque style in 1955 and is a copy of one found in Beijing. It is scene to many local and international exhibitions to which entrance can sometimes be gained. The centre also occasionally hosts public exhibitions, which in the past have included ancient treasures from Egypt. The complex has been recently restored to its former magnificence and a fabulously ornate Taiwanese seafood eatery has been installed in one of its side halls.

The site of the exhibition centre was formerly the 26-acre estate of Silas Hardoon. Hardoon, a Sephardic Jew, was one of Shanghai's richest residents before his death in 1931. His wife was Eurasian and they adopted dozens of orphans who were educated in Hebrew, English and Chinese on the grounds.

The Shanghai's Exhibition Centre's Soviet-baroque style, built in 1955, during the celebrations for the 43rd Anniversary of the People's Republic of China (1992).

Shanghai Municipal History Museum
Shanghai Shi Lishi Bowuguan 上海市历史博物馆 (*see* page 355)

Shanghai Museum of Traditional Chinese Medicine
Shanghai Zhongyi Bowuguan 上海中医药博物馆

Located in the Shanghai University of Traditional Chinese Medicine in the Zhangjiang Hi-Tech Park in Pudong, this museum has a large and impressive collection of exhibits and books documenting 5,000 years of Chinese medical history and houses its own herbal garden. It's at 1200 Cailun Road and is open daily, except Sundays, from 9:00am to 4:00pm.

Other Collections

In addition to the private collections on show at the Sanshan Guild Hall there are numerous fascinating private collections, often housed in people's homes, that can be visited by appointment. Collections include theatrical costumes, butterflies, ancient jars, rain flower stones, fans, root sculptures, model boats, miniature musical instruments and teapots. *Private Collections in Shanghai*, a guide published by the Foreign Languages Press, including comprehensive listings with contact details is on sale at the Shanghai Museum and at the Foreign Languages Bookstore in Shanghai.

Primarily located in the traditional industrial areas along the Suzhou Creek and in Yangpu district, there are a growing number of industrial museums in the pipeline. Some such as the Shanghai **Jiangnan Shipbuilding Museum** (600 Luban Road, 6315 1818 ext. 2439), the **China Tobacco Museum** (728 Changyang Road, tel: 6541 9779) and the **Shanghai Waterworks Museum** (803 Yangshupu Road, tel: 6512 6789), are already open. However they may, or may not, be restricted to group bookings at the time of your visit, so it's best to ring ahead to see what the situation is if you wish to visit. For train enthusiasts the **Shanghai Railway Museum** is open to the public from Tuesday to Saturday. It plots the development of the railway in Shanghai from when the British built the first 'illicit' railway in 1875 to the modern day, and there's a simulated ride in a driver's cabin to keep the children entertained. It is located at 200 Tianmu Road (E), where the old railway station, which was bombed by the Japanese in August 1937, stood. The building itself is a replica of the original.

World Expo 2010 Exhibition Area 上海世博会陈列区

Apart from the new art museums the former Expo site, covering an area of around 5.3 square kilometres (two square miles) on both sides of the river is being redeveloped for commercial and cultural use. Some pavilions and facilities have been retained, foremost among them being the impressive multi-function Mercedes-Benz Arena and River Mall, a neighbouring entertainment and shopping complex opened in 2013.

Will's wooden toll bridge over the Suzhou Creek was completed in 1857 and is seen here in 1875.

Sights Around Shanghai

Amongst Shanghai's 17 districts, seven are to be found in the large suburban area surround the city centre—Minhang, Baoshan, Jiading, Jinshan, Songjiang, Qingpu and Fengxian. The suburban area also covers the agricultural part of the Pudong New Area as well as Chongming Island, the only area in Shanghai left holding county status. Roughly half of Shanghai's population lives in these capacious suburbs that cover over 90 per cent of the Shanghai Municipal Area. Whilst agriculture remains economically important to the area, as witnessed by vast areas of paddy fields and fish ponds, light and service industries have blossomed in recent times. Paralleling the transformation of the downtown area since the early 1990s, huge new industrial parks, pristine residential 'new town' developments and new tourist resort and recreational areas have been transplanted onto the landscape, pushing out many remnants of heavy industry. The scale and scope of the redevelopment is grand and comprehensive, adopting architectural and design principles from all over the world.

Suburban Shanghai is full of surprises, with a veritable stack of historical monuments reminding the visitor that the area was well developed long before foreigners ever set foot on Shanghai soil. A few ancient structures have been left untouched, whilst most have been renovated in recent years—often accompanied by the development of a tourism area around them. Inside and beyond the municipal boundary a number of charming small towns, laced with ancient bridges and canals, have also been given a touristic makeover and have become popular spots for day-trippers from Shanghai. Many historically important and scenically endowed cities, in the neighbouring Zhejiang and Jiangsu provinces, are also within easy reach of Shanghai. If you have the time, there are a wealth of interesting and enjoyable places that can be visited offering a completely different experience to that of the city.

Suburban Shanghai
Getting There

Most places of interest are within a one to two hour drive from the city. The most convenient way to get to most of the destinations is to jump on one of the 'no frills' sightseeing buses that depart from the No. 5 entrance to the Shanghai Stadium (Shanghai Tiyuguan) in Xujiahui (666 Tianyaoqiao Road, tel: 6426 5555). It is wise to set off as early as possible as the majority of sights tend to close between 4:00pm to 5:00pm. The bus services generally start at 6:30am or 7:00am, with return buses operating till late afternoon. Another large Shanghai Tourist Bus Centre, the South

Left: *Hui Long Tan Park, Jiading District.*

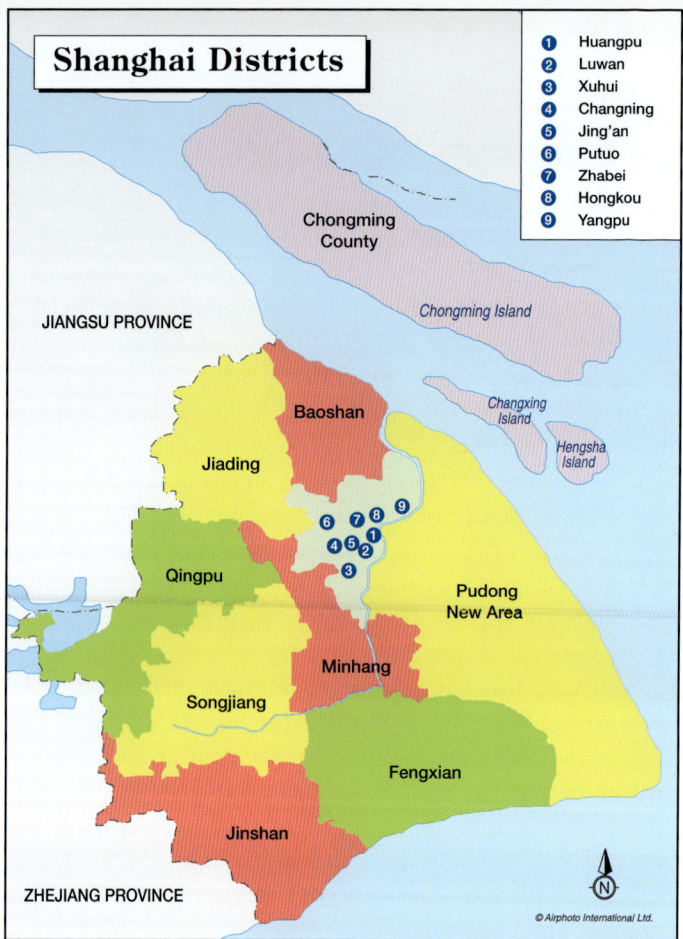

Railway Station branch, is located at No. 666 Shilong Road at the intersection wth Liuzhou Road (tel: 5436 3527). There are also numerous suburban bus services to Songjiang and Qingpu from bus stops around People's Square. Of course personal tours and transport arrangements can be secured at hotel concierge desks and many travel agencies throughout the city.

Songjiang District
Songjiang Qu 松江区

The Songjiang District is interestingly diverse—its flat plains are interspersed with numerous hills and its ancient treasures are to be found amidst the most modern edifices. The district is the scene for a massive 'new town' development, in which an eclectic architectural mix of monumental faux-European style buildings and estates, including a huge new university to the north of the district, are partnered by re-created Ming and Qing Dynasty structures in the south.

Songjiang Town
Songjiang Zhen 松江镇

Most of Songjiang's most famous historical sights are to be found along Zhongshan Road. Part of the west section of the road, known as 'Huating Old Street', has been pedestrianised and enclosed by two large stone pailous. This re-created street was actually completed in 2004 and its main attraction is the **Xilin Temple and Pagoda** (*Xilin Si, Xilin Ta*). The 46.5 metre (153 feet) pagoda was originally built between 1436 and 1449. The brickwork of the seven-storey octagonal structure has survived, though the wooden eaves and other features were replaced when it was last refurbished in 1994. One can climb to the top for views across the town. The pagoda sits in a pristine temple complex, dating back to 1387. The temple was totally destroyed in the Cultural Revolution and was rebuilt in the 1990s in traditional style, washed in ochre colour. It is open 5:00am to 4:00pm.

Further along the street, at 365 Zhongshan Road, the **Songjiang Mosque** (*Songjiang Qingzhensi*), was originally built in the Yuan Dynasty (1314)—making it the oldest in the region. It is also known as the Zhenjiao Mosque or *Yunjian Baisi* (White Crane in the Clouds Mosque). Over the centuries the mosque fell into disrepair and was ravaged many times. Renovation work from 1985 has restored the character of this charming small enclave with its mixture of Chinese and Islamic architecture. The Bangke Gate Tower in front of the Chinese-styled prayer hall is the oldest surviving structure, dating from 1559. The founder of the mosque is interred in an ancient tomb next to the front gate. The mosque remains an important focus for the local Hui Muslim population and is open from 9:00am to 5:00pm.

Above & right: *Xilin Pagoda and Temple.*

Nearby at 64 Renmin Road South is one of the most important classical gardens in the Shanghai area. The renowned **Zuibaichi Garden**, or Drunken Bai Pond, covers five hectares. It was constructed in 1644 and therein the famed Ming Dynasty poet, Dong Qichang, spent many long hours drinking wine and writing verse. The garden was bought and remodelled by Du Dashen, Officer of the Minister of Works, some 100 years later and named in memory of the great Tang Dynasty poet, Bai Juyi. The classical garden he created has largely survived and is now placed within a pleasant and much larger park with a strong European flavour, where plane tree-lined lawns skirt lotus ponds. The garden is open from 7:00am to 4:30pm.

The oldest surviving man-made structure in Shanghai is hidden in the grounds of the Zhongshan Primary School on Zhongshan Road East (No. 43 Xisi Long). The **Toroni Buddhist Sutra Stela** is a 9.3 metre (30 feet) octagonal pillar laden with worn bas-relief and inscriptions, dating back to 859 in the Tang Dynasty. It then stood near the gate of the district, formerly known as Huating, and covered a sea-well. The gatekeeper welcomes visitors during or outside school hours. On the opposite side of the street stands an imposing gate tower at the entrance to the No. 2 Middle School. It was once the entrance to the county offices and the base dates back to 1301. The upper part was destroyed by a typhoon in 1950, but was rebuilt in 1998.

Close-by, the **Square Pagoda Park** (*Fang Ta Yuan*), at 235 Zhongshan Road East, has been skilfully created around Songjiang's best preserved pagoda. The Square Pagoda, built in the period 1068–1094, once stood in the central part of the Huating district in the Song Dynasty. The nine-storey pagoda was restored in the 1970s as the park was created, but unlike many of its age, around 60 per cent of its original wooden structure was preserved. The pagoda stands 48.5 metres (160 feet) high and is open for ascent.

Alongside the pagoda stands the remarkably intact large **Screen Wall** (*Zhao Bi*). Erected in 1370 during the reign of the Ming emperor Hongwu, it is decorated with a massive brick bas-relief. The main feature is a monster known as *Tan*, a homonym of the Chinese word for 'greedy.' It is believed that the beast drowned as it attempted to eat the sun shining on the sea. The screen also features other symbols of human ambition—a carp leaping over the dragon gate as a metaphor for promotion to high office, a lotus blossom growing beside a vase with three lanes suggesting advance by three grades of office, and a monkey jumping to snatch a gold seal hanging from a tree, symbolising the desire to become a prince. The moral is that it doesn't pay to be over-ambitious. The pristine park also features the Song Dynasty Wangxian Bridge—the area's oldest stone bridge, as well as the Qing Tian Fei Palace, moved from downtown Shanghai in 1980. The park is open from 6:00am to 5:00pm.

Zuibaichi Garden.

Songjiang Town is around 40 kilometres (25 miles) southwest of the city centre. **The Shanghai Film Studio** (Shanghai Yinshileyuan, Chendun Zhen, 4915 Beisong Gonglu), is well worth a visit if you are in the district. It's around a 15 minute taxi journey from the town centre. Its estate houses impressive replicas of Shanghai's finest mansions and landmarks, including the Holy Trinity Cathedral, from the 1920s and 1930s. The main stage is a large scale re-creation of Nanjing Road as it was in the 1930s, complete with a working vintage tram. It, like Songjiang Town, can be reached by sightseeing bus from the Shanghai Stadium and is open from 8:30am to 4:30pm.

Sheshan 佘山

The two wooded hills at the core of this area form the basis for this state-recognised resort area incorporating historical sights, scenic spots, amusement parks, tourist attractions and resort hotels—all connected by cable cars. The eastern hill is densely covered with camphor trees and bamboo groves, and has been a recreational area since the Ming Dynasty. In the Qing Dynasty, Emperor Kangxi named the area 'Orchid Bamboo Hill' Shanghai's largest theme park, the Happy Valley Amusement Park, opened there in 2009. The area is located 11 kilometres (7 miles) north of Songjiang Town.

Apart from the holiday villages and golf courses, visitors can now stay in comfort at **Le Meridien She Shan Hotel** (tel: 5779 9999; www.starwoodhotels.com/lemeridien).

From a distance a fortress appears to be perched on top of the 99-metre (325 feet) high west hill. In fact it is the largest Catholic cathedral in East Asia—the magnificent **Basilica of Our Lady** (*Sheshan Tianzhu Jiaotang*). French Jesuits first had a presence on the hill in 1844, and a cathedral was built on its summit in 1871. The present structure was built between 1925 and 1935. Much of its architectural splendour, including the original pulpits, has been preserved, though a niche in the roof which once contained a statue of Madonna and Child was destroyed in the Cultural Revolution and is now replaced with a large cross. The walls inside the basilica are hung with pictures of the Fourteen Stations of the Cross. The basilica is capable of holding 3,000 worshippers. It is the seat of the Bishop of Shanghai and retains a seminary, habited by around 30 priests and sisters, who venture back to their parishes at weekends.

The cathedral closes between 4:30pm and 5:00pm and is not usually open for services, except in May.

The Zhongshan Chapel half way up the hill holds mass on Sunday mornings. Many of the devotees who worship at the church believe that the Virgin Mary appeared on Sheshan in 1980. Admission fees are waived for believers who enter through the 'Quakers Gate' and who are willing to climb to the top of the hill. The **Sheshan Observatory** (*Sheshan Tianwentai*), built by French Jesuits in 1899, is found next to the basilica. Some of the original observation equipment imported from Paris is still in use today. Its museum of astronomy is open from 8:00am to 4:00pm.

Basilica of Our Lady, or Sheshan Tianzhu Jiaotang, *is the largest Catholic cathedral in East Asia and seat to the Bishop of Shanghai.*

The area also takes in the **Huzhu Pagoda** (*Huzhu Ta*), also known as the Pearl Protection Pagoda, on top of Tianma Hill. The pagoda, which was built in 1079, has miraculously survived though the original neighbouring temple was destroyed by Japanese troops in the Second World War. The 20-metre (65 feet) structure is reputed to be the heaviest leaning tower in the world.

QINGPU DISTRICT
QINGPU QU 青浦区

With evidence of human existence going back 6,000 years Qingpu is presumed to have been the birthplace of Shanghai. During the Three Kingdoms Period (220–280), the Qinglong township in Qingpu was an important base for the waterborne forces of Wu Kingdom. During the Tang (618–907) and Song (960–1127) dynasties, the county seat had become a prosperous centre for local and foreign trade. The town came to be known as 'Hangzhou in Miniature' on account of its booming business activities and its magnificent pagodas and temples. Later the area around Qingpu fell from grace and fortune and its temples and shrines gradually disappeared. Today Qingpu is again experiencing a period of renaissance. With its strategic location on the highway from Shanghai to Hangzhou and Suzhou, many light industries have sprung up amidst its rich agricultural territory. The area has also become a popular weekend tourist destination and numerous theme parks and other attractions as well as luxury housing estates and three international standard golf courses have been developed, primarily around Lake Dianshan.

QINGPU TOWN
QINGPU ZHEN 青浦镇

The core of Qingpu town is pleasant and modern. Very little remains to remind the visitor of the past. The oldest surviving structure is around a kilometre from the centre, neglected and almost forgotten in its location down a small residential lane, next to a large factory. The imposing seven-storey brick

Qingpu Museum.

Northern Song Dynasty **Old South Gate Pagoda** (*Lao Nan Men Ta*) is overgrown and its wooden interior rotted long ago. Situated near the old south gate off Qingsong Road locals still venture there to pray.

Located in the centre of the town at 612 Gongyuan Road is the splendidly laid out *Qu Shui Yuan*, or **Garden of Meandering Streams**. The garden was originally a small temple-yard when work started in 1745, but it grew to be one of the finest gardens in Shanghai by the mid-19th century. The garden is composed of 24 scenic sections, infused with a magnificent forest of trees ranging from pines to Chinese wisteria, beautiful pavilions and numerous secluded, irregular shaped courtyards and hillocks. Arranged around two central lakes, with zigzag bridges, rockeries and mammoth rock sculptures, is a maze of water channels giving the garden its name. It is a very popular spot for local people to exercise and practise local operas. The garden is open from 5:30am to 5:30pm.

The highly impressive new US$12 million, butterfly shaped, **Qingpu Museum** (*Qingpu Bowuguan*), is to be found a short distance from the town centre at 1000 Huaqing Road. It houses a rich collection of over 2,000 treasures, of which 500 are featured in two major exhibition halls charting over 8,000 years of the area's history. One focuses on the historical development of water towns in the Shanghai area, whilst the other features some amazing archaeological finds, including numerous Neolithic artefacts that were largely unearthed from 12 local archaeological sites.

Left: *Old South Gate Pagoda*; Above: *Garden of Meandering Streams*.

Qinglong Pagoda and Temple
Qinglong Ta 青龙塔 Qinglong Si 青龙寺
The small town of Qinglong, some 15 kilometres (10 miles) north east of Qingpu town, is set within a sea of rice fields and fish farms. Baode (Award of Morality) Temple was first established here in 743. It was rebuilt and a pagoda added in 821, both adopting the name *Longfu* (Prosperous Fortune). During the Northern Song Dynasty (1041–48) the pagoda was rebuilt yet again, in octagonal form. This impressive brick structure still stands today, leaning slightly with the burden of age. Unfortunately the neighbouring temple was totally destroyed by fire in 1798 and rebuilt in 1834, only to be reduced to rubble again in 1860 at the hands of Taiping rebels. Little attention was paid to the area until 1993 when the temple re-opened. Since then it has grown enormously in size and scale and has a large new guest house for weekend visitors. The temple is open from 6:00am to 6:00pm.

Lake Dianshan
Dianshan Hu 淀山湖
Lake Dianshan is the main attraction for local and a growing number of overseas tourists. It is around 65 kilometres (40 miles) from Shanghai. The lake itself is over 10 times larger than the fabled 'West Lake' in Hangzhou and is filled with carp, mandarin fish, freshwater shrimps and crabs. It covers an area of 62 square kilometres (24 square miles). A huge student study and camping centre called Orient Green Boat has opened, which includes a full-scale model of an aircraft-carrier. For vacationers there is the Sun Island Golf and Hot Spring Resort (tel: 5983 0888) offering a host of recreational activities within its 160 hectare expanse. A favoured attraction for day-trippers is the huge **Grand View Garden** (*Da Guan Yuan*). The garden, which took nine years to complete, is a modern recreation of a classical garden portrayed in *A Dream of Red Mansions*, a popular Chinese novel. Such theme parks are highly attractive to local visitors and despite the lack of authenticity, this garden provides a beautiful environment in which to wander. Fantastic views across the greenery of the garden and the neighbouring lake are afforded by climbing the 47.6 metre (155 feet) **Azure Cloud Pagoda**, in Song Dynasty-style, just outside the entrance to the garden. It was built between 1984 and 1988. A large plum garden and a minority folk village are also nearby.

ZHUJIAJIAO 朱家角

Zhujiajiao came to prominence as an attraction in 2001 when dignitaries from the APEC ministerial meeting in Shanghai came to visit. The heart of the ancient water town was restored for the occasion and many buildings converted to folk museums, depicting a way of life long forgotten. The town with its white-washed houses and a myriad of small canals crossed by 36 ancient stone bridges presents the visitor with an indelible reminder of another age. Most visitors take a Chinese gondola ride through the quaint town and gather on its most famous Ming Dynasty bridge, the *Fangsheng* or 'setting free' bridge, which is the largest five-arched bridge in eastern China. Among the sites is a museum of postal history in a magnificent Ming Dynasty building, a reconstructed traditional pharmacy and a display highlighting the importance of rice to the town's development, again in a magnificent old setting. Not to be missed is the **Zhuxi Garden** (*Zhuxi Yuan*) and the elegant **Temple of the Town God** (*Chenghuangmiao*), which was built in 1763. The town has an English language website—www.zhujiajiao.com. It is located 55 kilometres (35 miles) from Shanghai.

Traditional ways endure because they still work well today.

Jiading District
Jiading Qu 嘉定区

Historically Jiading has a rich cultural heritage, and is noted for producing fine scholars and diplomats. Today, its scholarly activity is manifested in the conglomeration of high-tech industries found within the county. With its attractive natural landscape, Jiading has also evolved as a centre for recreational activity. It boasts three 18-hole golf courses and is home to the Formula 1 Grand Prix, Shanghai's most prestigious annual sporting event that takes place at the 150,000-capacity Shanghai International Circuit.

Fahua Pagoda.

Jiading is around 35 kilometres (20 miles) to the northwest of downtown Shanghai. It can be reached by tourist buses departing form the Shanghai Stadium, or by local buses from near People's Square or on Weihai Road, near the intersection with Yan'an Road (W). The core of the old town still has some remnants of Qing Dynasty times—enhanced by recent mock additions designed to encourage more visitors. The main sites, which are within walking distance of each other, are well worth a look.

The two main halls of the **Confucius Temple** (*Wenmiao*) at 183 Nan Da Jie hosted sacrifices to the great Sage as well as county and prefectural level examinations. The main Dacheng Hall now houses a new statue of Confucius and in its courtyard are small statues of his 72 worthy disciples. The neighbouring Minglun Hall, the former examination hall, is now a museum dedicated to the history of the imperial examination system. The attractive complex sits in a tranquil setting bounded by a large pond and is approached through an entrance containing three magnificent pailous. The main gate features a Yuan Dynasty stone sculpture, an omen for examination success, with carp jumping over the dragon gate. The gates are linked by a balustrade decorated with 72 stone lions. Although most were reconstructed after the Cultural Revolution, those with the smaller heads are original.

Next to the temple is the **Park of Dragons Meeting Pool** (*Hui Long Tan*), which was attractively laid out over 400 years ago and much of it still survives. However,

Garden of Autumn Clouds

it is the nearby **Garden of Autumn Clouds** (*Qiuxia Pu*) that steals the scenic prize. The garden was originally built in 1502 for Gong Hong, the head of the Ministry of Works. The original concept of creating a mountain forest in a city is still evident today, as seemingly expansive areas of water and hills come into view from a succession of vantage points from within the magnificent pavilions, their courtyards and corridors. One of the main buildings inside the garden was the original Temple of the City God for Jiading.

The *Lao Jie* (Old Street), with its re-created Ming Dynasty architecture as well as its small bridges and canals, is the nucleus of a new tourist area. However, some picturesque ancient houses have survived and at its core the **Fahua Pagoda** (*Fahua Ta*) has been magnificently restored (No. 349 Nan Da Jie).

The structure was originally built between 1205 and 1207 and it was not in anyway restored until 1924, when the top of the tower was reinforced with iron. However it wasn't until 1994 that substantial repair work to rectify the heavily listing pagoda was begun, employing the expertise of some of the team who had worked on the Leaning Tower of Pisa. Folklore attributes the tilt to local people digging away at the mortar to extract gold that was mixed in a glutinous rice paste—thus accounting for the building's alternative name of 'gold sand pagoda'. Real treasures—ancient books, coins, statues and jade ware—were unearthed from the base of the pagoda in 1996. The seven-storey structure can be climbed by way of small wooden steps.

Two museums are found within the pagoda compound. One relates to the history of the area, whilst the other is dedicated to Dr. Wellington Koo, China's foremost 20th century diplomat and former Chinese Ambassador to Britain and the USA. Many precious personal items are on display in this charming exhibition. Another interesting small museum, featuring bamboo carving, is found nearby at the Jiading Villa.

Nanxiang Town *Nanxiang Zhen* 南翔镇

Nanxiang, formerly known as Cuoxi, came into being some 1,500 years ago. The town is most noted for its meat-filled steamed dumplings—the one's that Shanghainese and visitors queue up for in the centre of the Yu Garden area in Shanghai. The main attraction is the magnificent **Guyi Garden** (*Guyi Yuan*), which was first laid out in the Ming Dynasty (1368–1644) and later rebuilt in the Qianlong period (1736–1796). It has been renovated and extended since 1949, and now covers an area of 6.5 hectares (16 acres). The garden still retains features of the traditional Chinese garden in its pavilions, lakes, corridors, winding paths and bridges, and it has its own version of the famous marble boat in Beijing's Summer Palace. Known as the United Boat, this is a small pavilion in the shape of a boat built on a stone base in one of the gardens' lakes.

Jinshan District
Jinshan Qu 金山区

Facing the East China Sea and bordering Zhejiang province, Jinshan is Shanghai's largest district. Until recently it was largely identified with agriculture, but a massive petrochemical industry has evolved since 1997. It is also famous for its folk art. Its 'farmers paintings' are in fact a recent art form developed after the Cultural Revolution in an official effort to broaden mass culture. The farmer-artists use vivid colours and draw on the arts of embroidery and paper cutting to produce starkly two-dimensional images with little regard for scale (*see* page 438). Scenes of everyday country life and folk customs and legends are most commonly depicted. The artists can be seen at work in Fengjing Town and at the **Jinshan Academy of Fine Arts** (*Jinshan Nongminhua Meishuxuexiao*), at 318 Jiankang Road in Zhujing Town. Artists at the Academy apply tempera paint mixed with chalk on to rice paper, which is then pasted onto heavier paper. The **Jinshan Museum** (*Jinshan Bowuguan*) can be found nearby at 200 Luoxing Road. It is closed on Mondays and Saturdays.

The **Huayuan Pagoda** (*Huanyuan Ta*) in Songwen Town is well worth visiting as it remains one of the best examples of Ming Dynasty construction techniques and is

Right: Qiabo Canal.

almost completely preserved. In the Yuan Dynasty (1279–1368) the pagoda began life as a Buddhist monastery. The monks there wrote the Huayuan classics in 81 volumes and it was with he proceeds from the sales that the pagoda was built. The wood and brick pagoda, which took four years to build, was completed in 1380.

MINHANG DISTRICT
MINHANG QU 闵行区

The district has undergone dramatic change in recent years. Its Xinzhuang area has become the scene of massive housing developments and the Minhang Development Zone has become the home of numerous multi-national companies. Huge new attractions, including the Silver Seven Star artificial ski-slope, the largest in Asia, and the Tropical Tempest Water Park, have opened in the district. The Minghang District Museum at 255 Xinjian Road (E), near the Xinzhuang metro station features an impressive display of artefacts related Maqiao culture dating back 4,000 years, as well as a collection of over 300 musical instruments tracing the history of Chinese music.

QIBAO 七宝

The ancient town of *Qibao* (Seven Treasures), an important port and transport hub in Ming and Qing Dynasty times, is the main attraction for visitors. It is now swallowed up in urban development, but parts of the area still retain an old world

The Peasant Painters of Jinshan

It all started when a demobbed soldier returned to his native home in Jinshan County. His attention was caught by the way the village women there decorated their kerchiefs, aprons, clothes, pillow cases, hats, shoes and *dudou* ('belly-cloths'). There was something about their sense of colour, and the way they worked the traditional motifs into their craft, which suggested to the soldier that they might, with a little bit of instruction, become good painters. It was only a matter of substituting the needles, cloths, threads and scissors with painting brushes, paints and canvas.

Though some of the women can barely write their own names, they turn out the most wonderful paintings, full of colour, life, and detail. Untutored as painters, the women have nevertheless been working with their fingers—be it spinning, weaving, cutting paper into pictures, doing needlework, making clay toys or decorating their homes—most of their lives. And it proves easy to transfer these skills from one medium into another. The decorative patterns were already there, in the traditional design of local cloth, in the *nianhua* (the New Year pictures) that the Chinese have always liked to hang up, in the lanterns and kites that they have been making for generations. Naive and exuberantly coloured, the pictures demonstrate the country women's love of the decorative, and portray the rustic, everyday concerns of their lives and society.

Because the painters understand so prolifically the roles they embody—as grandmothers and mothers—the scenes depicted are usually domestic ones: weddings, the kitchen, celebrating a newborn baby's first month, ducks and hens, fish and shrimps, crabs and turtles, harvest and markets. Typically a picture shows a village jetty from which a bride is leaving with her dowry. Trumpeters and musicians play. A crowd watches in curiosity. Poignantly, in the backyard, the mother who is about to be parted from her daughter sheds tears.

Another picture shows a woman entering her kitchen with an exaggeratedly large fish in one hand and a cleaver in another. More than half the picture is taken up by the stove, which is decorated with scenes from familiar operas: Liu Hai Teasing the Golden Toad, The Butterfly Lovers and Zhang Fei Challenges Ma Chao.

The attention to detail (a feminine trait?) is charming. In a painting of a fish market, the artist has not neglected to include an abacus, and a couple of steelyards for weighing the fish. Other pictures are elaborations of symmetrical patterns combining naturalistic and abstract fragments.

When the demobilised soldier introduced the paint brush to the country folk of Jinshan, it was the older women, the ones with a lifetime of embroidery and lace-making behind them, who first took it up. But later they were joined by younger women, and now people of all ages paint in Jinshan. Their reputation has grown, so that now their pictures have been exhibited both at home and abroad.

The One-month-old Baby, *a painting depicting one of the happiest days in the life of a grandmother, who is also the painter. Preparations are underway for the celebration—a feast of fish, chicken, and a nourishing soup for the mother.*

charm. The main part of the town has been renovated as a tourist area. On the 'Old Street' (*Nan Da Jie* and *Bei Da Jie*) there are many specialty stores selling crafts and local snacks—including roast lamb and caramelised red bean pies. There, and on a few other small streets, are some interesting small museums and workshops that were opened in late 2003. Amongst them the **Miniature Museum** (*Zhoushi Weidiaoguan*) presents a remarkable display of Zhou Changxing's tiny replicas of everything from furniture and household items to the most intricately carved stones. Nearby, other exhibits include calico weaving, a cricket (insect variety) museum in a magnificent former nobleman's house and a wine distillery.

On a back street the **Qibao Catholic Church** (*Qibao Tianzhu Jiaotang*) is to be found, with a working convent alongside. The church was first built in 1869, but the present structure dates from 1896, with the last changes made in 1929. Gondola rides on the Puhuitang River pass parts of the untouched old town that is well worth exploring on foot. Qibao, some 20 kilometres (13 miles) from Shanghai, can also be reached by taking metro line 1 to its terminus at Xinzhuang and then taking a 20-minute bus ride or a 10-minute taxi ride.

BAOSHAN DISTRICT
BAOSHAN QU 宝山区

The Baoshan District is closely associated with Baoshan Steel, the country's leading steel maker. The district also includes Wusong, famous for its fort from where the British found resistance in 1842, and for its navy base. The area has little in the way

of tourist attractions. The **Shanghai Navy Museum** (*Haijun Shanghai Bolanguan*), found at 68 Tanghou Road, has a lack-lustre display of its naval history in three halls and is only for those seriously interested in the subject. The largest hall contains a collection of missiles, guns and radar equipment—an interesting hall. It is open from 8:30am to 11:30am and from 12:30pm to 5:00pm daily, except Sundays. The Chen Huacheng Memorial Hall, celebrating a national hero during the first Opium War and an Anti-Japanese War memorial hall are to be found in Linjiang Park.

Fengxian District
Fengxian Qu 奉贤区

The Fengxian district, southwest of Shanghai facing the Hangzhou Bay, has recently been developed as a tourism area with the Blue Sea & Golden Sand (*Bihaijinsha*) beach, China's largest man-made beach, as its main attraction. Its sand was transported from Hainan Island, a southern Chinese tropical paradise. An 18-hole golf course has been developed and construction of the Bay Forest Park, featuring Shanghai's largest man-made lake, is well underway. The nearby Fengcheng town has adopted a Spanish style of architecture fashioned on Barcelona.

Chongming County
Chongming Xian 崇明县

Shanghai's most sleepy and inaccessible rural backwater looks set for big changes over the next few years. With bridge and tunnel connections already completed and a metro station due within the next few years Chongming, China's third largest island, faces the challenge of maintaining its ecosystems whilst adapting to the needs of modern development. Massive plans for building China's first 'green city' on the island at Dongtan are currently shelved and so for the time being it remains a haven for bird watchers, cyclists and hikers. Visitors can camp in the Dongping National Forest Park, which covers an area of over 350 hectares. The county also has a local museum housed inside the Chongming Academic Palace. Chongming county also includes the Changxing and Hengsha islands. Chomgming Island can be reached by way of ferry from the Shanghai Wusong Port at No. 251 Songbao Road in Baoshan district (tel: 5657 5500, 5657 6606).

Left: *Chinese First-Class Junk of War*, China and The Illustrated London News, *March 21, 1857.*

Excursions from Shanghai
Water Towns

The modern architectural features of Shanghai are a million miles away from most popular images of China wherein white-washed houses back onto small canals crossed by arched stone bridges. It's not all fantasy—a number of ancient towns around Shanghai in Jiangnan (the area south of the River) have been dressed-up to really match what one would expect. These are generally day-trip destinations and all of their attractions close by 5:00pm. However, there are modestly comfortable hotels in most towns should you wish to see what they are like when the local people reclaim the use of their streets after dusk. The towns charge for entry into their designated tourism and recreational areas which includes admission to their attractions and museums. All offer Chinese-style gondola rides on their small canals—a great way to appreciate the local environment as their former riches were bound to these waterways.

A large number of sightseeing buses depart daily from the Shanghai Stadium (*Shanghai Tiyuguan*)—No. 5 stairs for the neighbouring water towns. There is a metro station at the stadium. Some tickets on offer only cover transportation, while others include entrance fees or include entrance fees and guide services (in Chinese). Buses are also available from the Hongkou Football Stadium (Gate No. 2), 444 East Jiangwan Road. (tel: 5696 3248) and the Yangpu Stadium (front gate), 640 Longchang Road. (tel: 6580 3210). Buses also leave from around People's Square. Tours can also be arranged by local travel agencies including CITS and Jinjiang Tours. Check current information with your hotel concierge. All the towns are within two hours reach of Shanghai.

Zhouzhuang 周庄

Zhouzhuang has been open for visitors the longest and is still the most popular water town, having a grandeur and stature greater than the others. The town has been designated a UNESCO World Heritage Site. Much Ming and Qing Dynasty architecture has survived, including 14 ancient bridges. The most unique is the **Double Bridge** which combines a flat structure with an arched one. The top sights in town include the **Zhang Hall**, a Ming Dynasty family home replete with 70 rooms and a river flowing through it, and the even larger **Shen Hall**. Other highlights include the **Chengxu Taoist Temple** and the Song Dynasty **Quanfu Temple**. Zhouzhuang is about 35 kilometres (22 miles) south of Suzhou, has its own English-language website (www.zhouzhuang.net) and receives more than a million visitors per year.

Zhouzhuang water town, a UNESCO World Heritage Site, is famed for its Ming and Qing Dynasty bridges such as Fu'an Bridge.

Wuzhen 乌镇

Wuzhen opened to tourists in 2001 and is indeed a fine town with its northern part having been converted into a fascinating stretch of museums and workshops. It is easy to imagine how the rich lived in bygone days and there is an exhibition hall of fantastically carved beds to testify to the high art of living. There is also an interesting rice wine distillery amongst its other attractions. In the Song and Qing dynasties Wuzhen produced more successful candidates in the highest imperial examinations than any other town in the region. The Qing Dynasty **Academy of Classical Learning** remains as a reminder of scholarly glories as does the **Former Residence of Mao Dun**, one of China's modern literary giants.

Tongli 同里

Tongli is less than half an hour away from Suzhou and around a 90-minute drive from Shanghai. Visitor numbers have swelled since the town was dressed up for tourists in 2000. Named Tongli in the Tang Dynasty, the town is divided into 15 islets by its maze of small canals that are crossed by 40 ancient bridges. Tongli has a long tradition dating back to the Ming Dynasty of cultivating scholars, officials and artists. Their legacy in the form of their mansions and private gardens still remains, with more than 10 still surviving in their original form. The most famous and revered is the small but magnificent **Tuisi Garden** constructed in the late 20th century. Courtyard houses, some over 500 years old, are still inhabited and many have fine wood panelling and carving. Do venture down the narrow enclosed lanes to have a look—they have a real mediaeval feel. The traditional teahouse is also well worth a visit.

 The Chinese Museum of Sex Culture (*Zhanghua Xing Wenhua Bowuguan*) moved to Tongli from a downtown location in 2004. Its proprietor promotes a healthy awareness of sexuality and its history in Chinese culture. Its eclectic selection of artefacts and images relating to the history of China's sexual mores and practices was established by Professor Liu Dalina and originally opened in 1993. The museum is now housed in a fantastic old red brick school complex with numerous exhibition halls and gardens featuring exotic sculptures. The museums exhibits are annotated in English and there's even a gift shop offering an assortment of erotic souvenirs. Over 2,000 items are on display—from a porcelain prosthetic used by court eunuchs to an illustrated guide to sex for the newly-married, from furniture designed for sexual activity to erotically painted tea cups found in brothels. Many of the artefacts date back thousands of years—and matters from the enslavement of women to homosexual practices are vividly represented. (*see* page 446)

No Sex Please, We're Chinese

—By Paul Mooney

Aged 69 years, Liu Dalin does not appear to be the type of person who would lead a sexual revolution. However, this soft-spoken, bespectacled academic is heading a campaign to teach his fellow Chinese that sex is not a dirty word. So far, it's been an uphill battle.

Liu first became famous in 1992 following the publication of his landmark *Sexual Behaviour in Modern China*, ignoring the advice of colleagues who warned that the topic was too sensitive.

The study of the sexual attitudes of 20,000 Chinese revealed some interesting facts of life. One in three women reported that they had never had an orgasm. While the study discovered that 25 per cent of men and 20 percent of women had premarital sex, disproving the myth of Chinese chastity, it did prove that the Chinese were modest: only 13 per cent of married couples said they ever made love naked.

Liu, dubbed by *Time* magazine the Kinsey of China, went on to write more than 70 books, establishing himself as one of the most eminent experts on sex in the country.

The scholar, who retired as a lecturer at Shanghai University in 1993, began studying journalism in 1949 at Yanjing University, but his studies were interrupted two years later when he enlisted in the People's Liberation Army. After 20 years in the military and a 12-year stint in a factory, Liu was conferred a belated degree in 1982, and took a job editing a sociology journal at Shanghai University. Research related to his job led Liu to focus on marriage and family life, which in turn encouraged him to study sexual relations.

Realising the importance of erotic art and ancient sex paraphernalia for understanding Chinese attitudes toward sex, Liu began building up his own small collection, which he tucked away at home. "I discovered that a lot of Chinese attitudes are influenced by tradition, and that to better understand the present, I would need to better understand the past," he explains. "There are many things that we can learn from our ancestors."

Liu laments the fact that many fine pieces of erotic art were destroyed during the Cultural Revolution (1966–1976), and during anti-pornography campaigns in the 1980s and 1990s. "Anti-pornography should be carried out, but some officials are not very cultured," says Liu. "They don't know what's pornography and what's art. This is frightening."

The substantial collection travelled to six cities around Europe and Asia in 1995 and 1996 before finding its first public home in Shanghai in August 1999, The Museum of Chinese Sex Culture is a joint venture between Liu and the New World Department Store (*see* page 444).

"The purpose of opening the museum was to help Chinese understand the role sex has played in traditional society," explains Liu. "I wanted to clear away the mystery and prejudice surrounding sex in China today and to help Chinese understand more about themselves."

It didn't come as much of a shock that China's first sex museum was forced to close its doors, after being in business for just two years. The surprise was that The Museum of Chinese Sex Culture ever managed to exist at all.

The enterprise appeared to be doomed from the start. Management of the building refused permission for a sign outside the museum, citing government regulations prohibiting the use of the word 'sex' in advertising. Located on the eighth floor in a building located in an alley off Nanjing East Road, few people found the signless museum.

"We had a good reaction from visitors," Liu laments, "but few people knew about us, or where we were."

Ever creative, he opted for a sign in an adjacent department store reading "Exhibition of Chinese Reproductive Culture." Two days later management caught on, and he was forced to take the sign down. Two girls were hired to stand on Nanjing Road handing out brochures, but the second day they were stopped by police, allegedly for littering.

"The law prohibits advertisements for sex products, but we are not a product" argues Liu. "We are a cultural institution."

Pointing to the existence of some 2,000 shops in Shanghai selling sex aids, Liu complained in an interview with the *Shanghai Star* newspaper about his dilemma. "I don't understand why they make such a fuss over one word," he says. "There are more urgent things for them to do."

China was not always so sexually conservative, says Liu, explaining that the country was quite open about sex right up until the Tang Dynasty.

Liu points out that in the early years of Communist rule a lot of progress was made in improving the marriage system and bringing about equality between the sexes. However, by the time of the Cultural Revolution, the party became prudish, with Chinese opting for drab and baggy unisex clothes.

"Individuals were encouraged to be selfless and to work for the revolution and not their own happiness," explains Liu. "Anyone caught indulging in personal enjoyment could be criticised, and even sexual pleasure was restricted."

A cursory glance at the objects on show suggests Liu is correct in saying that Chinese society was more open in ancient times. Works dating back 2,000 years explain techniques for refined sexual intercourse, including the "nine principles of shallowness and one principle of deepness."

Liu points out that during the Eastern Han Dynasty (15–220 A.D), sex education was provided for the children of wealthy families, while ordinary families conducted this mostly "by way of suggestion".

He describes a type of porcelain euphemistically called the "trunk bottom". The piece was usually in the shape of a piece of fruit, boat, or child, and was hidden at the bottom of a girl's dowry trunk. The item has two parts, and when the top is lifted, two naked figures are revealed having sexual intercourse. When a girl was to get married, the mother would take the item and show it to her daughter, suggesting what a husband and wife should do.

Serving the same purpose, dowry scrolls depicting colourful, cartoon-type characters trying different positions for intercourse, were placed among the pieces of dowry for the daughter. The newlyweds would hang it on bed curtains and act out the drawings on their wedding night.

Ancient Chinese culture held that evil spirits were afraid of coitus, and sexual objects came to be used as talismans. "*Bihuo tu*," or "drawings to repel fire," depicting scenes of sexual intercourse, were likewise placed on the roofs of houses to scare away the fire god.

No object is considered too small for display. There are tiny ivory combs used by prostitutes to comb pubic hair, and a porcelain jar decorated with the amorous Lu Dongbin, the patron saint of prostitutes, as well as an ancient chastity belt. Also on display are thick wooden sticks used for punishing prostitutes in brothels, and a 12th century seal used to establish the chastity of girls chosen for the imperial palace: once a girl's virginity was established, the seal was stamped on her buttocks. Small copper coins for use in brothels were given to prostitutes to keep them from saving money to run away.

There are also several naughty pieces. A 17th century porcelain basin shows a man lifting a woman's gown, while a scroll portrays a beautiful naked demon attempting to seduce a monk. A statue of the rotund Laughing Buddha is turned on its side, revealing a man and woman having sex on the normally unseen bottom. An amusing fan shows an innocent painting of a man and woman together in a garden; when it's partially closed, they are caught engaging in a sexual act.

The exhibit on "unusual" sex includes a vase painted with gays "in secret activities", a teapot emblazoned with "two lesbians embracing", and a painting of a woman masturbating.

Using his own savings Liu reopened the museum on at a new location, with two floors and plenty of window space to attract the attention of passersby. "This is a heavy financial burden for me," explains Liu, "but at least I'll be free to run the museum as I like, without any limitations."

Liu says he hopes his museum can teach people to not see sex as something bad, and to help promote a healthy and scientific attitude toward sex.

"When people visit the museum they can see that we had this tradition thousands of years ago, and that there is nothing wrong with it," he says.

Liu's wife is not happy about his avocation, arguing that he's retired and should take it easy. Liu, however, shows no sign of sitting back, explaining that "At my age, the future is not very long."

"I have a responsibility, a duty to society, to save this culture which is being destroyed," he says. "It is important to save this for future generations."

The Museum of Chinese Sex History is located in Tongli (*see* page 444).

Sanctity of the Sands —*The Ginger Griffin*

The revered island of Putuoshan has long been a site of pilgrimage, vested with a Buddhist heritage hailing back to the Tang Dynasty. It lay undisturbed for hundreds of years until the first foreign incursions followed the opening of Shanghai as a Treaty Port. The health concerns of early foreign residents, or *Shanghailanders*, prompted the search for a refuge from the unsanitary city and by the 1850s a few brave individuals had taken up summer residence on the island.

An outbreak of cholera, in the oppressive heat of 1862, alerted *Shanghailanders*, to the need for a sanatorium and a voluntary commission was dispatched to the island. They failed to make any concrete agreements with the residents, but communicated the recuperative benefits of sea-bathing on the island to the Shanghai public.

By the early 1870s the temples hosted over 50 temporarily resident foreigners. Local tensions grew with the influx of foreigners and the priesthood was accused of giving in to

Get away from it all—1930s Shanghai newspaper advert.

the demands of the foreign devils. The situation reached boiling point in 1876 when humiliated priests were forced to submit hefty monetary compensation following a disturbance caused by US Navy visitors. After that staying on the island proved a little more difficult!

The China Merchant Steam Navigation Company was the first to seize upon the commercial possibilities of this new situation, which coincided with a new awareness that the seaside could be fun. They initiated a series of long-weekend summer excursions to the island in 1876. Moored off the island, over-night accommodation and food was provided on the boat. All foreigners travelled saloon class and were segregated from the mass of Chinese pilgrims below. The Chinese would be landed first whilst those above indulged in high-tea before setting off for organised sightseeing.

Such activity continued until the pre-war years, with a boom in the early 1930s prompting Butterfield and Swire to initiate a regular island run. Relations with the priesthood had normalised and visitors were welcome to lodge in the temples, whilst expectant coolies crowded the boat dock with bamboo sedan chairs. The local American Express Company warned passengers not to expect the "gilt and plush comfort of hotels" and to carry only "tinned meats, bread and cheese". Fear still prevailed that the vegetarian enclave would yet again be put out of bounds by the disrespectful deeds of individuals bent on catching themselves a real dinner.

Today there are still two basic classes of visitor—those interested in walking and visiting temples and those content with the beach. The recently refurbished temples are heavily frequented year-round, whilst the golden-sand beaches are only packed with sun-worshippers in the summer.

Special Topic

Luzhi 甪直

Like other ancient and prosperous water towns, Luzhi has a fine assemblage of magnificent former residences including the Xiao residence. It now houses an exhibition of the achievements of a family descendant, the Hong Kong star of screen Xiao Fangfang. More historic exhibitions are to be found in the ancient Baosheng Temple, which includes magnificent stone sculptures dating back over 1,500 years.

Xitang 西塘

Xitang, in Jiashan County, Zhejiang province, is noted for its variety and number of bridges (more than 100) as well as the covered corridors that connect its lanes. Xitang is at the point of convergence of nine rivers that divide the town into eight sections. The town has a more natural feel than many others of its kind.

Resorts

Although many new self-contained holiday resort areas are found around Shanghai, they hold little interest for the short-term visitor. However, there are two contrasting and well-established resort areas near the city that make perfect overnight retreats. **Putuoshan** offers beaches and **Moganshan** offers lush mountain scenery—and they both offer an insight into Chinese history and culture. These areas were the favourites of foreigners resident in Shanghai before the Second World War.

Dried seafood and other goods can be found in the market on Xianghua Street, Putuoshan.

They are now designated tourist zones, which means that a charge is made for entry to each area. They are at their busiest from June to September, and if you travel there at that time it is best to avoid weekends. Out of season they are very quiet, but be sure to bring plenty of warm clothing if you visit in the winter months.

Putuoshan 普陀山

As one of China's four Sacred Buddhist Mountains, the small island of Putuoshan has long been a revered site for pilgrims—who now number more than a million each year. Apart from its temples and shrines, the most famous being **Puji** and **Fayu**, the island also has some fine coastline. There are two main swimming beaches set in attractive bays flanked by fenced European style parks housing tennis courts. A charge is made for entry to bathing beaches. Seafood is the order of the day and what is not eaten is dried and on sale in the charming Xianghua Street market. Outside the main areas of attraction the island remains secluded and calm. The beaches are some of the best around and the terrain is perfect for leisurely walks in the hills or down to non-bathing beaches littered with flotsam and driftwood.

The island can be reached by an overnight ferry (it is suggested that you carry your own food) or by a daytime bus-fast ferry combination that takes around 4.5 hours. Boats depart from the Wusong Pier and tickets can be purchased there, or at the Port Office at No.1 Jinling Road (E) (tel: 6326 0050) near the Bund. In the summer season there are 30-minute flights from Hongqiao airport to nearby Shenjiamen, with a fast boat transfer to Putuoshan. Shenjiamen, itself, is an active fishing port and has a spread of fantastic seafood restaurants along its waterfront. Putuoshan has one four star hotel (**Lu Yuan Resort Hotel**, tel: 580 609 2828) overlooking the beach (*see page 450*).

Moganshan 莫干山

Although a number of hardy foreign missionaries had been taking their summer vacations in Moganshan since 1887, it was not formally established

Tree-lined avenue in Moganshan, summer mountain resort, 1979.

PEAK HOTEL
MOKANSHAN
(The most modern hotel on the mountain)

Situated on a delightful location on the summit of the mountain. Specially planned for Chinese and foreign guests.

Modern Sanitary Equipment
Luxurious Accommodation
Delicious Cuisine
Excellent Service
Reasonable Rates

Rates with foreign meals $6 to $10 per day. Full particulars on application.

Add. 87-88 Mokanshan Tel. 9

as a mountain summer resort until 1898. It had its own foreign resort association and grew to be a favourite summer haunt for not only missionaries, but for wealthy foreign businessmen and China's leading political figures. Chiang Kai-shek spent his honeymoon with Song Meiling here, Du Yuesheng the infamous Green Gang boss had a villa here and Chairman Mao was a frequent visitor. Forgotten for a long time, the resort is enjoying a renaissance thanks to the efforts of Mark Kitto, British entrepreneur turned restaurateur, and with his wife hotel keeper. His compelling account of how this transformation came about and much on Moganshan's history can be found in his excellent book *China Cuckoo* (*see* Recommended Reading page 586). He began with a coffee shop/bar The Moganshan Lodge, (tel. 0572-803 3011, www.moganshanlodge.com) and now offers accommodation at Moganshan House 23, a 1930s stone house featuring six bedrooms (tel. 0572-803 3822 http://moganshanhouse23.com). His success has been followed by others including Naked Retreats, which describes itself as a boutique hotel offering modern comforts in restored old lodges on the mountain (tel. 021-5465 9577 www.nakedretreats.cn). The Radisson Hotel group has renovated two villas to five-star standard, including the one that belonged to Du Yuesheng (tel. 0571-8515 8888 ext. 6848). A number of other villas maintain some of their original features and are available for lodging. The mountain offers good hiking and a great opportunity to relax. To reach Moganshan first travel to Wukang direct by bus, or train to Hangzhou and bus thereafter, and then take the local bus up the mountain.

NEIGHBOURING CITIES

With the rapid development of the region's highway and railway networks getting to other cities of interest in the neighbouring Zhejiang and Jiangsu provinces has never been so convenient. Something that was unthinkable a few years ago, day trips can now be made to Hangzhou, Nanjing and Suzhou—the three major regional destinations. Travelling by train is the most comfortable and speedy way to get to these cities and there are numerous daily departures, from very early morning till late night. From the main Shanghai Railway Station Suzhou can now be reached in little over half an hour, Wuxi in less than an hour and Nanjing in a little over two hours. Most trains for Hangzhou depart from the Shanghai South Railway Station with journey times upwards of 80 minutes. There are of course slower trains if you wish to take in more of the scenery on the way and perhaps stay overnight in one of the cities, all of which have excellent accommodation facilities.

The cities can also be reached by bus, with a number of buses departing form the Shanghai Stadium. Jinjiang Tours (Tel. 6472 0354) offers tours to Hangzhou and Suzhou in the company of an English-speaking guide. Daily pick-ups are made from the Ritz-Carlton, the Renaissance Yantgze and the Jinjiang hotels.

Of course Hangzhou is fabled for its West Lake and its tree plantations, Suzhou for its magnificent classical gardens, and Nanjing is renowned as the former capital of the Nationalist government and the resting place of its founder, Dr. Sun Yat-sen, as well as witness to the horrific 'rape of Nanking' in 1937. For online references to these cities please *see* page 65).

Lingyin Pagoda, Hangzhou.

Class Struggle

The class struggle remains a living actuality in Shanghai. While I was there an exhibit was on at the Palace of Culture; the theme was the history of the workers' movement: on display were yellowed photographs, newspaper clippings, personal letters alluding to the riots, to the blood-bath repressions. These memories, and a great many more, blaze in the Shanghai worker's mind. It is they who represent Chinese Communism's most extreme left wing: they are impatient of the lingering vestiges of capitalism, are urging the government to shorten the transitional period. There is nothing more farfetched than to suggest, as does Guillain, that Shanghai is a city full of counterrevolutionaries; the mysterious Communist friend who obligingly whispered in his ear that "we've got the backing of only 20 per cent of the population here" sounds like a first cousin of those Western fallen angels several specimens of whom I had the privilege to meet, and whose wishful thinking I was able to judge. No: Shanghai is rather the city where the workers' demands are the most adamantly revolutionary and the most pressing; less well paid than heavy-industry workers, discontent surely does exist among the Shanghai proletariat; but it is just as sure that they have no eagerness to return to the old regime: to the contrary, their complaint is that socialization is not moving ahead fast enough. Contemplate the propaganda posters plastered on walls and decide whether the class struggle is not a heated issue; in Peking, these are fairly mild cartoons: of, for example, a profiteer, green about the gills, staggering under the weight of the sack of money on his back. In Shanghai the pictures are realistic and violent. A soldier has his rifle trained on a counterrevolutionary who, surrounded by an angry crowd, slithers up out of his hiding place in a sewer.

Simone de Beauvoir, The Long March (Gallimard, 1957. Eng. Trans 1958)

Philosopher, novelist and essayist, Simone de Beauvoir (1908–1986) was born in France. A lifelong companion of Jean-Paul Sartre, Beauvoir was concerned with the safety of factory workers, abortion rights for women, the rights of the elderly, and the social status of women. She attended the Sorbonne University in Paris and became a professor there, teaching from 1941 to 1943. The publication of *Le Deuxieme Sex*, Vol 2 (The Second Sex) in 1949 will always remain a watershed moment in the history of feminist thought. Beauvoir hopped between fiction and non-fiction, philosophy and essays, but throughout all ran her defining vein of existentialist thought and an awareness of "the other". Despite being initially dismissed by philosophers and academics, *Time* magazine named *The Second Sex* one of its top 10 non-fiction books of the 20th century, while *Life* magazine named Beauvoir one of the top 100 most influential people of the millennium.

Literary Excerpt

Left: *Suzhou waterway.*

YANGPU: PAST, PRESENT AND FUTURE —THE ENGINE OF SHANGHAI

Yangpu, a district of Shanghai has seen many evolutions of identity and has its sights firmly on the future. Name, population, and the very landscape have altered immensely across the passage of time. Yet Yangpu's raison d'etre over the centuries has remained; producing essential elements of the economic structure that turns the wheels of Shanghai.

Yangshupu, Yangtszepoo, Yangpu, as it has been known since 1949, is said to have taken its name from a small tributary of the Huangpu River. A literal translation from Chinese characters reads 'poplar bank', suggesting that originally Yangpu's silted soil saw poplar tree-lined riverbanks. Today Yangpu is one of Shanghai's 17 districts. Located south of Baoshan, Huangpu River forms the southern and eastern borders and Hongkou the west. The current land area of Yangpu Qu (district) was last designated in 1997; its southern edge less than five kilometres from the Bund.

Originally situated along the bank of the Huangpu River, close to the Wusong and Yangtze River mouths, the area was subject to flooding and large silt deposits that changed the course of the rivers and the land alongside. Maps and early accounts indicate settlements, walled villages and temples. By the 15th century canals and additional waterways were built to ease the effect of flooding in the area between the Yangtze, Wusong and Huangpu Rivers. Records further show that the mouth of the Huangpu was dredged and the banks shored, providing groundmass for the expansive era of the Ming Dynasty.

During the late Ming Dynasty the area flourished. Villages sprung up along the banks of the river in response to thriving agricultural, textile and banking industries as well as other areas of trade associated with its proximity to inland access (canals and waterways) and the sea routes available through the China Sea. This early economic success established Yangpu's progressive history of producing essential elements of the engine that was to drive the rapid progress of Shanghai.

In the early 19th century, the strategic position of the Yangtze River delta saw Shanghai benefit from burgeoning global trade. The First Opium War, resulting in the 1842 Treaty of Nanking and the settlement of the treaty ports and extraterritorial status, firmly established Shanghai. The 1863 amalgamation (and 1899 extension) of the British and American Settlements into the International Settlement bears witness to the early urbanisation of the Yangpu district.

Following the incorporation of Yangpu's southern areas into the International settlement the district began to emerge as an industrial one. During the 1860s a number of wharves were created on Huangpu's east and west banks. By 1893 a Germany company built the first oil wharf, followed by a second one, the following year, in Yangpu. The British set up the Shanghai Waterworks Company in 1880 with the construction of the waterworks in Yangpu completed in 1883. This was the first modern waterworks in China. Yangpu's location, outside of the walled Chinese City, partly in and partly outside of the International settlement, promoted another first for the district and for China when, in 1882, the first modern paper mill, initially known as Paper Mill Company, was set up by three Chinese partners. Yangpu's proximity to the river fostered the next major industry: shipping. With the launch of the Shanghai Engineering Shipbuilding and Dock Company in 1896, shipbuilding, wharf and dock companies were to proliferate in the locale. Textile mills were soon to follow.

Shanghai's rapid progress in the early 20th century can be linked to its foreign concessions and to the entrepreneurial nature of the migrating Chinese that flocked to the eastern territories for industrial entrepreneurship and employment. The Yangshupu Power Plant, Yangshupu Gas Works, Zhabei Power Plant, Zhabei Waterworks, new cotton and wool mills, clusters of printing and paper factories, and an electric-wares factory were just some of the results of the first two decades of the new century.

Yangpu was now to Shanghai as Shanghai was to China: the birthplace of modern industry.

Sun Yat-sen's vision of industrialisation and of turning Shanghai into a major port began with the Greater Shanghai Plan of 1929. Wujiaochang, the north-eastern corner of Yangpu, was chosen as the centre of the Greater Shanghai Plan. As the seat of municipal government roads and services were laid out and the core buildings of a municipality designed and built. The town hall, museum, library, stadium, hospital and education facilities were completed and stand as a reminder of the first modern urban planning scheme in China. While the plan was never fully realised it is a concrete dedication to Yangpu's directorial position and economic importance.

Change abounded again when the area was subject to heavy bombing from the Japanese. Yangpu fell to the Japanese in 1937; the International Settlement fell in 1941. After 1949 many of Yangpu's industries were moved to state control and their industrial base broadened to encompass the demands of a new age.

Contemporary Yangpu is again the seat of change. Prior to 1949 the area was home to nine major universities. Since the opening of China, and in particular since the 1990's, these important education institutions have expanded to new campuses. Old infrastructure works have been turned into research facilities and house newly created museums recording the history of Yangpu's industries. Urban renewal has taken place in some of the old factories and warehouses with creative industries being encouraged. Poor, low-level housing continues to be cleared to make way for modern, energy-efficient housing. In consideration of the residential environment factories and works have been moved further from the city, while parks and efforts to clean up the many canals sees a new era of greening the city.

With the emphasis now on education, research and development, culture, urban renewal, residential and commercial harmony, and safeguarding the ever-changing environment, Yangpu is once again evolving to provide the fuel for the engine of Shanghai.

Michelle Blumenthal

Following pages: *Strolling the Bund has long been a popular pastime, and it remains so today.*

EXCURSIONS FROM SHANGHAI   461

Above: *Moving the former Garden Bridge away for repair in 2008.*
Below: *Where the river bends—view over the Lujiazui district in Pudong.*

The Roof

The roof garden of the Shanghai Hotel was always crowded at tea-time. Half of it was covered by an awning of the rust-brown colour of Chinese sails, and a large number of tables were under gaily-coloured umbrellas outside the shade of it in a rectangle round a fountain which somewhat cooled the air. The trees and vines in large Chinese oil vessels looked faded, although they were regularly sprinkled with water. Even the floor, tiled with large flat tiles, was wet and gleaming, for it too was sprinkled with water hourly during the summer to temper the heat. Attentive little Chinese waiters hung about the tables with iced drinks and fragrant hot tea for the residents of the British Concession. A string quartet was playing from somewhere unseen in a thin pizzicato which was entirely drowned by the confused burble of talk.

Four American businessmen, shrewd, gray-haired and alert, with their tall highballs in front of them:

"If we get it now it will be more serious than in '32. America can't just fold her arms and look on."

"What the Japanese want is the Monroe Doctrine for Asia. Asia for the Asiatics. Even this they have to copy from us."

Battle of Pootung Point, Shanghai 1937.

"And we'll have the world market flooded with Japanese-dumped goods. And what about all the American capital that's been sunk in China? And what about the oil? If Japan puts China in her pocket who's going to buy our cotton?"

"America's bound to protect her citizens on land and sea, and the Chamber of Commerce will look to it."

"Yes, but we're told that those who do business in foreign countries do so at their own risk."

"The neutrality act—"

"The democratic countries have got to stand together against Japanese Fascism or else go under."

"There's only one thing to do—to make as much money as you can as fast as you can and then beat it for the States."

"That's what we all say, and yet we've been in this infernal hole for thirty years"

"My wife couldn't exist now without six servants."

Two Chinese compradores, one in European dress, the other with an unusually well-cut sleeveless jacket over his long silk robe:

"I always say, better a dog in peace than a man in war."

"The mayor of Peking was bought. He let the Japanese march in without defending the town. He simply opened the city gates."

"It makes no difference. The North was Japanese long ago. It only means the legalization of smuggling through the gap in the North."

"The only question is: can we do better business with the Japanese or against them? Whoever gives me milk is my mother."

"Let us forget these little unpleasantnesses. A man for whom I was able to do an insignificant service has sent me a mandarin fish, and my cook is an artist in cooking it with brown sauce. May I have the pleasure of your company tonight . . ."

Another group, intellectuals, white people, Chinese, a young Siamese, a Norwegian woman with red dyed hair:

"Unless opium is suppressed, China cannot be saved. It is a terrible, ineradicable national vice."

"Like booze in America. Don't forget Prohibition. It only means driving up the price and the consumption."

"Alcohol makes people stupid, and drunkards go home and slaughter their wives. Opium makes you wise and benevolent."

"They say it has an erotic influence."

"Nonsense. It makes you impotent."

"I smoke eight pipes a night, and my hands are steady. You smoke forty cigarettes and your hands shake."

"The anti-opium office does a lot of good. So one hears at least."

"Certainly. They chop the heads off fifty incurables now and again. They give them opium before they do it—to make their death pleasanter."

Four slender and elegant Chinese women under the awning, eating iced fruit:

"Sleeves are going to be worn shorter, my tailor has copied Anna May Wong's"

```
KY.4395E.
BATTLE OF CHINA'S "STALINGRAD".
Changteh, China... The ground was rocking with the
thunder of battle when "newsreel" WONG made this
strikingly dramatic photo during the battle of
CHANGTEH, strategic City in the heart of China's
Rice Bowl. Changteh changed hands four times in
forty days and the slaughter was appaling. The
battle ended in defeat for the Japanese - their
worst defeat of the war in China. These Chinese
troops are American trained.
              4. Keystone.477745.
```

The original caption for this dramatic press photo by the celebrated Chinese war-photographer "Newsreel" Wong.

"Green silk with a bamboo spray of clipped velvet all the way down, at Sincere's sale, a real bargain."
"If my husband brought a concubine into the house I would shoot him."
"The American method. Did you hear Professor Cheifong lecture? It appears that free love is the only system possible for modern people."
"What we need is missionaries for birth-control propaganda."
Two Chinese fanatics sitting over their fine porcelain cups of jasmine tea:
"China is united for the first time. A united China is unconquerable."
"Four hundred million people. We will build walls of our bodies against the Japanese. A beginning has been made."
"We have the people and the patience. In five hundred years China will be the best country in the world. And how short a time is five hundred years!"
"That is so. Ten thousand years of life, my friend!"
"Thank you, honored first-born. Ten thousand years of blessings and contentment"

The burble of voices, noise and scraps of conversations: they say that Mei Lan Fang has grown old. The New York Stock Exchange has weakened. Whoever wins this war, one thing is certain—we whites can only lose. Better the Japanese than Communists. It is the end of extraterritoriality. What's India going to live on if we cannot export any more opium? Never again shall China be treated as if it were a colony. China—what a hopeless mess! China—what a marvelous country! . . .

Optimists, pessimists, Westerns, Easterns, men, women. Europeans, Americans, Orientals. Courage and cowardice. Idealism and greed. Enmity and love. People of every sort and colour and tendency. Voices, noise, laughter, tristesse, tea, whisky. The full orchestra of every description of humanity: that was teatime on the roof garden of the Shanghai Hotel.

Vicki Baum, Shanghai '37 (Doubleday, Doran & Co., 1939)

Austrian popular novelist Vicki Baum (1888–1960) was born in Vienna and first began her writing career contributing stories to magazines and doing occasional editorial work. Her first big success was 1929's *Grand Hotel*, which became a bestseller and was later made into a play and movie. In the 1930s Baum emigrated with her family to the United States and became a screenwriter in Hollywood. Her popular books were banned in Hitler's Germany. Baum often depicted powerful, self-reliant women caught up in the social and economic turbulence of 20th-century Europe or the US.

On His Baldness

At dawn I sighed to see my hairs fall; At dusk I sighed to see my hairs fall.
For I dreaded the time when the last lock should go . . .
They are all gone and I do not mind at all!
I have done with that cumbrous washing and getting dry;
My tiresome comb for ever is laid aside. Best of all, when the weather is hot and wet,
To have no top-knot weighing down on one's head!
I put aside my messy cloth wrap; I have got rid of my dusty tasselled fringe.
In a silver jar I have stored a cold stream, on my bald pate I trickle a ladle full.
Like one baptized with the Water of Buddha's Law,
I sit and receive this cool, cleansing joy. Now I know why the priest who seeks Repose.
Frees his heart by first shaving his head.

'Lazy Man's Song'

I could have a job, but am too lazy to choose it;
I have got land, but am too lazy to farm it.
My house leaks; I am too lazy to mend it. My clothes are torn; I am too lazy to darn them.
I have got wine, but I am too lazy to drink; So it's just the same as if my cup were empty.
I have got a lute, but am too lazy to play; So it's just the same as if it had no strings.
My family tells me there is no more steamed rice;
I want to cook, but am too lazy to grind. My friends and relatives write me long letters;
I should like to read them, but they're such a bother to open.
I have always been told that Hsi Shu-yeh. Passed his whole life in absolute idleness.
But he played his lute and sometimes worked at his forge;
So even he was not so lazy as I.

Po Chu-I, The Life and Times of Po Chu-I, 772–846 A.D, 701–762
A.D. Translated by Arthur Waley, Allen & Unwin, 1949

Po Chü-i (772–846), a poet and a government official, was one of the great writers of the Chinese Tang Dynasty. He was born at T'ai-yuan in Shanxi, settling later at Ch'ang-an near the north-west frontier. He held the post of palace librarian and several provincial governorships. He was banished a number of times for arguing against government policies. In 832 he retired to the Hsiang-shan monastery a few miles from Lo-yan. He wrote more than 3,000 poems, brief, topical verses expressed in very simple, clear language.

Right: *The beauty of age captured in the warmth of a smile.*

Suggested Itineraries for Shanghai
—*The Ginger Griffin*

Walk 1—The Foreigner

Begin the day in Lujiazui, the heart of the new financial and commercial district to the east of the Huangpu River. Start early, no later than 8:00am, and begin with a stroll along the new promenade in front of the Oriental Riverside and Shangri-La hotels. From here you will have a great panoramic view of the old buildings on the Bund opposite. If there's good light this is the best time for photos across the river. Work your way to the **Oriental Pearl TV Tower** where you can ascend up to the 263-metre viewing level for great views if the weather is fine. Otherwise pay a visit to the **Shanghai Municipal History Museum** in the basement for a solid introduction to the modern history of Shanghai.

Next transport yourself across the river to the Bund itself. You have three options—you can take the **Bund Tourist Tunnel** to near Beijing Road (E) or the metro to Nanjing Road East—or walk along the promenade to take the local ferry from Dongchang Road. The first two options will take you near to the north end of the Bund, the latter to the south. The area around the **Monument to the People's Heroes** at the north end of the Bund is a good spot to take photos looking downstream and across the river to the skyscrapers in Lujiazui. Cross the Suzhou Creek by the Garden Bridge (*Waibaidu*) that was built in 1907 and have a look at the wood-panelled lobby of the **Pujiang Hotel** (formerly Astor House Hotel) from 1911 and the ballroom at the back that hosted China's first stock exchange in the early 1990s. Coming back across the bridge, take a diversion by turning right onto Suzhou Road (S) and left onto

This, and following three pages: *The interior of the Peace Hotel, circa 1978, appears much as it would have when Sir Victor Sassoon established the hotel in 1929 as the Cathay Hotel.*

Huqiu Road and Hong Kong Road to see some impressive 1920s and 1930s buildings that were once occupied by mission societies, banking guilds and a host of others. Back on the Bund be sure not to miss the former Cathay Hotel (now the **Fairmont Peace Hotel**) at No. 20 (*see* pages 352, 534, 542) and the former building of the **Hongkong and Shanghai Bank** (now the Pudong Development Bank) at No. 12. Note that photography is not allowed in the magnificently decorated banking hall. Magnificent views are afforded from the rooftop of the Fairmont Peace Hotel and there are various options for lunch

in the hotel. For a continental set lunch head for the open terrace of M on the Bund (entrance at 20 Guangdong Road, 7th floor), which again has spectacular views. Other options for lunch include anything from the finest French cuisine to Shanghai nouvelle cuisine at Three on the Bund or Bund 18.

Walk off lunch by venturing up Nanjing Road (E)—China's historic number one shopping street which has for the most part been pedestrianised. Carry on across Central Tibet Road to Nanjing Road (W). At No. 170 you will find the **Park Hotel**, which was built in 1934, and remained Asia's tallest building for more than half a century. It overlooks **People's Park** and **People's Square**. In the square you can visit the world-class **Shanghai Museum** or trace the city's past and future development at the **Shanghai Urban Planning Exhibition Hall**. Otherwise just sit and watch the pigeons and people in the square, pay a visit to the tranquil People's Park or walk to the charming bird and pet market on Jiangyin Road at the north-west corner of the square. People's Square is at the intersection of metro lines 1, 2 and 8 so you might wish to transport yourself back to your domicile from there or jump a train to embark on a mystery tour of the city.

Get more out of your walk around the Bund area by picking up a copy of Peter Hibbard's book, *The Bund Shanghai: China Faces West*. Odyssey, 2007.

Walk 2—The Native

Start early, again no later than 8:30am, to arrive at the **Yu Garden** before the crowds arrive. After exploring the gardens take a look around the bazaar area. If you are there on Saturday or Sunday take a look at the antique market on Central Fangbang Road and be prepared to bargain hard for any desirables (there will be many!). Even if it's not the weekend, stroll westwards up the street, also titled 'Old Street', to take tea and snacks at the **Old Shanghai Teahouse** at No. 385. Don't do what most tourists do by heading back to the centre of the tourist area, but carry on walking westwards on the same road crossing Henan Road (S). Just a short walk up you will see the ochre-coloured building of the new part of the **Ci Xiu Monastery** at 593 Central Fangbang Road. Take a sharp right just past the entrance onto Zhenling Street (it's actually a small lane) where you will find the older part of this complex as well as many curious local residents. Carry on a little further and take a left turn on to Dajing Road. Apart from a few magnificent buildings, which are to be preserved, the area west of the intersection of Dajing Road and Luxaingyuan Road was flattened in 2007. Try deviating off Dajing Road southwards to Wanzhu Jie, to see what is left. Carry on westwards to the intersection with Zhonghua Road, where you will find the **White Cloud Taoist Temple** and **Dajing Pavilion**, and evidence of where the old city wall once stood. Take a left to re-join Central Fangbang Road where you will find a multi-storied market selling mobile phones, second-hand computers and all sorts of electrical devices on the corner. Continue up the road until Tibet Road (S), cross it and then continue westwards on Zizhong Road or Liuhekou Road. At the first intersection you will find the popular **Dongtai Road Antiques Market** where you might want to lighten your wallet. Proceed westwards around the huge lake in **Taipingqiao Park** to arrive at Shanghai's latest hotspot—**Xintiandi**—where old houses have been converted into an upmarket dining and entertainment district. There are numerous options for lunch here (which may be a little of a late one by now). It's a trifle quiet in the daytime, but the visit will give you some idea of the place that is packed with party-goers at night should you wish to return.

On the question of parties you could pay a visit to the **Site of the First Communist Party Meeting** and/or the **Shikumen Open House**, which are both in the complex, to catch up on history. From Xintiandi take a turn south down Madan Road until you reach Central Fuxing Road. As *Rue Lafayette*, this was one of the most beautiful residential streets in the former French Concession and it still holds lots of charm. Continue west on Central Fuxing Road to the major intersection with Chongqing Road (S) where you will find the entrance to **Fuxing Park** (the former French Park) opposite. Walk through the park to its northwest exit on Sinan Road. The immediate vicinity has been designated as a conservation zone and there are many fine restored architectural gems around. Take a look at the seaside art deco architecture that sits next to the former St Nicolas Orthodox Church (1933) directly across Sinan Road on the corner Gaolan Road. On Sinan Road itself, just to the left of the park exit, you will find the delightful **Former Residence of Dr. Sun Yat-sen**. Pay a visit if you have time (it closes at 4:30pm). Carry on south on Sinan Road for a short distance to get back onto Central Fuxing Road and then turn right. At the next intersection turn left into Ruijin No. 2 Road where a little further on you will find the entrance to the magnificent grounds of

the **Ruijin Guest House** at No. 118. It was former estate of the Morriss family, who owned Asia's leading English language newspaper, the North-China Daily News, until it was closed in 1951.

As an alternative, on leaving Xintiandi, you could take a north turn on Huangpi Road (S) and stroll up to Central Huaihai Road (the former *Avenue Joffre*) if you want to do some high street shopping.

And don't forget to pack copies of both English and Chinese maps of Shanghai before you venture out! For exclusive group and corporate custom-made tours with the accent on old Shanghai, contact The Ginger Griffin at hibbard@gingergriffin.com.

Arts and Entertainment

Shanghai has been an important hub for arts and entertainment for more than 150 years. A British initiated amateur dramatic club was formed as early as 1850, the city fostered the early career of Dame Margot Fonteyne and in the 1930s it had the most modern art deco theatres playing the latest screen hits from Hollywood as well as those featuring legendary Chinese stars such as Hu Die, also known as Butterfly Wu. Though subdued and bridled after 1949, the city's cultural and entertainment industries have again taken centre stage. Shanghai has an exciting diversity of evening entertainment, ranging from classical and jazz concerts to state-of-the-art pulsating discos and clubs; from Italian and local opera to KTV and beauty pageants. Many famous pre-war theatres have survived, including the Majestic, the Lyceum, the Nanking and the Cathay. Although their interiors have been remoulded they are still in use today for arts and cinema presentations.

An important addition to the arts scene has been the advent of the stunning **Shanghai Grand Theatre**, which opened in 1998. It's the home of the Shanghai Broadcasting Symphony Orchestra as well as the National Ballet of China. Its 1,800 seat main hall has played host to Broadway and West End musicals such as *Les Miserables* and *Cats* as well as to a milieu of artists including Luciano Pavarotti and Placido Domingo. Performances by foreign opera and ballet companies are always sell-out affairs even though the best tickets may cost in excess of US$300. The theatre is at 300 People's Avenue on People's Square and the box office telephone numbers are 6372 8701/02.

Shanghai is also home to the world-renowned Shanghai Symphony Orchestra. The orchestra performed on the soundtrack of Ang Lee's masterful movie, *Crouching Tiger, Hidden Dragon*, for which Tan Dun won an Oscar for the score. The orchestra played regularly at the **Shanghai Concert Hall** until the end of 2002. This historic building, with its fine acoustics, was originally the Nanking Theatre built in 1930. It was miraculously relocated in its entirety some 65 metres (215 feet) away from its original site in 2003—the year marking the orchestra's 125th anniversary. It is again open for concerts. and is now home to **Club Shanghai**, a Michelin pedigree restaurant with fine French dining.

However the Shanghai Symphony Orchestra has migrated to its new home at the landmark butterfly-shaped **Shanghai Oriental Arts Centre** in Pudong which staged its first performance on New Year's Eve 2004. At a cost US$120 million, it is Shanghai's first purpose built performance venue. Designed by French architect Paul Andreu, who also designed the Grande Arche de la Defense in Paris and the Beijing Opera House, it houses a 2,000-seat concert hall and a 1,000-seat opera house.

Right: *Nanjing Road.*

Acting for the Party

The Film Studio was a palace of displayed slogans. It was surrounded by dark-red maple trees. The leaves were like joined hands. They blocked my view. The studio walls were painted white with red slogans written on them. 'Long live Chairman Mao's revolutionary arts' policy!' 'Salute to our greatest standard-bearer, Comrade Jiang Ching!'

I presented a sealed official letter to the studio security guard. He told me to wait as he went inside. A few minutes later a man and a woman appeared in a hallway. They threw themselves at me enthusiastically. The man introduced himself as Sound of Rain, the head of the studio acting department, the woman as Soviet Wong, his assistant. They picked up my luggage and asked me to follow them into the studio.

We passed through a series of gates. The sun was shining through the maple leaves. The leaves were spreading their pinkish rays on to the dustless pavement. The workers walking underneath the maple trees were covered in reddish light. They greeted us with flattery.

Sound of Rain had a pumpkin head with fat cheeks sagging on the sides. Soviet Wong had a face of an ancient beauty. She had slanting eyes, a long nose, a cherry-shaped mouth and extremely fine skin. She was about forty. It was the way she moved, her elegance drew me in. She spoke perfect Mandarin. She had a silky voice. Sound of Rain spoke of Soviet Wong. He said that she was a graduate from the Shanghai Film Acting School in the fifties and was an extremely talented actress. Sound of Rain said that I should be proud that I would have more than one instructor. Sound of Rain said it was Madam Mao Comrade Jiang Ching's order. Soviet Wong said that she was very happy to receive the assignment of being in charge of teaching me. I asked what I would be learning. She said I would be taking intensive classes in politics and acting. I asked if she would do any acting with us. She went silent. Her lips tightened and her head lowered. A lump of hair fell on her face. Her steps slowed down. The Revolution's needs are my needs, she said stiffly. Her resentment spat out between her teeth. She looked clearly unhappy. Flinging back her hair, she quickly sped up to catch Sound of Rain. Her graceful back bent slightly to the right side. She pretended to be very happy. She must be as durable as bamboo—capable of bending in all directions in the wind. I walked carefully, watching my own steps.

Soviet Wong walked half a step behind Sound of Rain, never overtaking him or lagging behind him one step. They both wore blue Mao jackets with collars buttoned tightly to the neck. They nodded, Sound of Rain first, then Soviet Wong, at the workers who passed by. They paid the workers full-scale smiles. The smile made me nervous although it was the most admired smile in the country. It was the smile that Mao had been promoting with the slogan, 'One must treat one's comrades with the warmth of spring.' Lu at Red Fire Farm was an expert at that type of smile.

Finally, we arrived at an abandoned studio set. It was the size of a stadium engulfed by foot-high weeds. As we made a sharp turn, a single little blue house appeared in front of me. It was an old house with a cement sink on the ground. Wild plants climbed around the sink. This is where you girls stay, said Soviet Wong. This used to be an old film set, Sound of Rain explained. There are more living quarters behind the house. It was built as a horse shed for films. We had it converted into a living space for the boys chosen. Twenty-five of you are assigned to live and work in this area. You will be guarded. No visits to or from families except the second Sunday morning of the month. Anyone who breaks the rules will be eliminated. We want no outside influence. Absolutely none, Soviet Wong echoed. My thoughts turned to Yan.

What about letters? I asked. What's so urgent about writing letters? Soviet Wong suddenly turned to me, suspicion rising in her voice. Her long thin eyebrows twisted into a knot in the middle. I reacted quickly to this sign of danger. I said, Oh, nothing, I was just asking.

She did not believe me. I could tell that she went on with her own thinking. You have dark circles under your eyes, which shows that you don't sleep well. What's your problem? We hope your promise to the party was not a fake one. She turned to Sound of Rain and said, We must take preventative measures against possible calamities.

I was offended but I knew not to show my feelings. The engine of my brain sped up to its limit. Nothing is more urgent than the assignment I have been given, I said, trying to sound sincere. It might be my late Mao study habit that causes the dark circles around my eyes. She asked, Why don't you tell us the name of the person you would like to write to so we can check to make sure that it is good for you to keep the correspondence?

Anchee Min, Red Azalea (Pantheon Books, 1994)

Anchee Min (1957–), born in Shanghai, now lives in California. In addition to being a creative writer, she is also a noted painter, musician and photographer. At the age of 17, Min was sent to work at a collective farm. Three years later she was discovered by a talent scout and joined Madame Mao's Shanghai Film Studio. After the death of Chairman Mao in 1976, Min and other supporters of Madame Mao were politically discredited. Min was demoted to a menial position at the film studio, working 14-hour days as a set hand. For eight years she worked as a set clerk and in 1984, she was accepted to the Chicago Institute of Arts. When the Institute found out that she couldn't speak any English, they sent her to the University of Illinois for lessons. Writing about her experiences growing up formed part of her regular English class assignments and late led to the publication of *Red Azalea*, her personal memoir. In 1990, Min graduated from the Chicago Institute of Arts with a B.F.A. and M.F.A. in Fine Arts.

Cocktails at the Club

The Columbia Country Club was at least two miles beyond the point where in 1917 Shanghai ended and the farmland began. For many years increasing numbers of Chinese has been moving into the city, the only place where they were safe from kidnapping, bandits and official squeeze. They were pushing into the foreign settlement, buying up real estate and either driving the foreigners into the new apartment buildings springing up or pushing them farther out into the country. As a consequence a moderately sized American community had built up around the club.

I discovered a difference in attitude of the Americans I had known of old, most of them from small communities, the majority from the South. Drinking had been looked at askance and the young ones were told off when they were hitting it up too heavily. But times had changed. I sat on the veranda with a group of old friends and acquaintances watching the sunset across the tennis courts. By the time the sun had died down tables overflowed the veranda onto the lawn and until after nine Chinese boys were rushing back and forth at full speed to the musical clink of ice-cubes in tall glasses.

I was put up for the American Club in the foreign business section. At noontime the bar was packed from twelve to one, and after lunch until two every chair and sofa in the library was filled with sprawling figure fast asleep. Between seven and eight the bar came to life again, roared with talk and laughter for an hour or so, ceased and again went into a coma awaiting the following noon.

The viewpoint of the American in China had switched to almost the opposite from what it had been in pioneer days. This settled existence of a few rounds of drinks at noon, a few more rounds after the office, followed by a few more before dinner, added to the mixed array that always went with the almost nightly exchange of dinner parties, answered a question that had been stirring around in my mind since my return from the North. The Americans had been going through a minor evolution of casting off homesick small-town inhibitions. Gradually they had adapted themselves to the drinking habits of the English.

Adapting the British sophisticated attitude towards drinking as part of their daily routine, the Americans had developed, as a natural sequence, the British comfortable attitude towards life in general, the habit of "muddlin' through."

The former Shanghai Club, now the Waldorf Astoria Shanghai on the Bund

Business ups and downs should be taken comfortably. If things were bad now, maskee—cheerio—sooner or later they would pick up. Time would see to that. One always "muddled through" somehow and if one had managed to get along all okay with the old tried and true methods, why bother oneself to go out of one's way trying to change things. As one of my fellows in business was wont to say when an argument arose, "Peace be with you, brother. Peace be with you."

This was one reason why, as far as I could see, the Western foreigner was turning over gradually to the Chinese the running of his business, spending less time traveling and more at the office, acting chiefly as adviser and getting information second-hand by reading reports and writing letters instead of keeping up direct contacts.

This partly explained, too, the discussions over extra-territoriality at a time when bandits, communists and war lords had the country severed into bits, making central governmental control utterly impossible.

James Lafayette Hutchison, China Hand.
(Boston: Lothrop, Lee and Shepard, 1936)

Another important large-scale venue is to be found within the **Shanghai Centre** (tel: 6279 8663) at 1376 Nanjing Rd (W). The centre was Shanghai's first city within a city, completed in 1990 and rising like Atlantis with its high rise offices, apartments and hotel rooms. The 991-seat Shanghai Centre Theatre hosts all manner of shows. Past performances have included the Vienna Boys Chorus, La Grande Opera, Harry Connick Jr. and The Chieftains. Yet another capacious concert hall was added to the city's tally with the opening of a magnificent new 780-seat hall on the beautiful grounds of the **Shanghai Conservatory of Music** at 20 Fenyang Road in September 2003 (tel: 800 820 4800 or 6437 0137). Weekly orchestral recitals are also held at 8:00pm on Sundays in the lobby of the **Jing'an Hotel** at 370 Huashan Road (tel: 6248 1888). The art deco building was originally known as the Haig Apartments. The **Jinjiang Hotel** also hosts regular classical recitals on Sunday afternoons in its Grand Hall (at 59 Maoming Road (S), tel: 6258 2582 ext. 9222). The seriously chic Glamour Bar at **M on the Bund** hosts regular literary, cultural and musical events and is home to the internationally renowned Shanghai International Literary Festival that is staged every March (tel: 6350 9988). The **Shanghai International Arts Festival** in September and October features a range of musical presentations, drama's and lots of free street activities.

Shanghai has scores of professional performing companies and art troupes in everything from local (*Kunju*) and Peking opera to modern and classical dance to farce and acrobatics. The drama scene has also made a serious comeback with historical Chinese and Western classics staged alongside contemporary dramas that probe the cultural dilemmas posed by modern Chinese society, as well as experimental theatre. Most plays are in Chinese, but there has been a recent move towards staging more plays in English. The main venue is at the impressive **Shanghai Dramatic Arts Centre** at 288 Anfu Road (tel: 6473 0123, 6473 4567). It hosted a production of *The Merchant of Venice* by the UK's Royal Shakespeare Company in 2002. The historic **Majestic Theatre** (*Meiqi*), at 66 Jiangning Road (5404 1120, 6361 3061) also regularly stages drama—and some performances are held at the recently modernised art deco **Lyceum Theatre** (Lanxin) at 57 Maoming Road (S) (tel: 6256 4631) The Lyceum when it was built in 1931 was home to the Amateur Dramatic Club which was founded in 1867. International amateur dramatic theatre returned to the Lyceum with the a production of Gilbert & Sullivan's Pirates of Penzance in April 2005—some 64 years after it was last staged there.

For a real thrill and dazzling spectacle of sound, colour and movement a visit to see Beijing Opera should not be missed. Even though it's not Beijing, the **Shanghai Yifu Theatre**, is dedicated to carrying on the tradition of this fine, yet declining art form. Its performances are meant for an appreciative local public and are much purer than tourist shows in Beijing itself. The theatre is at 701 Fuzhou Road (tel: 6351 4668). In listening to Chinese opera the foreign ear must first get acquainted with the use of a high falsetto voice before the richness of melodic invention, the drama of the music and the rigorous artistry of the performers can be appreciated. The local Kunju opera, originating from Kunshan, a small town 60 kilometres (37 miles) west of the city, is also witnessing a revival. This opera's intriguing plots often revolve around unrequited love, involving a Shakespearean cast of scholars, sidekicks, lusty maids and fools. Performances are held on Saturdays at the **Kunju Opera House** at 9 Shaoxing Road (tel: 6437 1012) and more infrequently at the Majestic Theatre. Folklore shows designed with the visitor in mind are staged in the Yu Garden area at a purpose-built, traditional-styled theatre. The **Yu Yuan Stage** also hosts local opera accompanied by local snacks (tel: 5358 0421).

A visit to an acrobatic show is the most popular staged event for visitors to Shanghai. And so it should be! More adroit or daring displays of poise, contortion, dexterity, grace and sheer strength are hard to find. The world famous Shanghai Acrobatic Troupe is now based at the futuristic and permanent **Shanghai Circus World** (Shanghai Maxicheng) at 2266 New Gonghe Road (tel: 5665 6622, 6652 2395). This state-of-the-art complex has a gold-globed structure capable of seating 1,600 as its centrepiece. Opened in 1999, it contains a large animal house with horses, elephants, lions, tigers, chimps, and pandas as well as a shopping and dining area. The circus was opened with a series of new programmes performed by the world-renowned Shanghai Acrobatic Troupe. The troupe now divides its performances between here and the **Shanghai Centre Theatre**—with two shows each week at each location. Acrobatic shows are also regularly staged in a 600-seat side hall of the **Shanghai Grand Theatre** (largely booked though hotels or major travel agencies).

The Shanghai Acrobatic Troupe.

The Shanghai New Acrobatic Circus also hosts regular performances in the **Yunfeng Theatre** at 1700 Beijing Road (W) (tel: 6322 1208). Overseas visitors form the majority of the audience at all acrobatic shows. Tickets for many of Shanghai's top performing arts' events can be obtained from the Shanghai Cultural Information & Booking Centre at 272 Fengxian Road (tel: 6217 2426), next to the Majestic Theatre. Tickets can also be booked online at www.culture.sh.cn/English.

There has been quite a revolution in cinema-going in recent years, despite the flagging native film industry and the ready availability of the latest films on counterfeit DVDs (often before their general release in some countries). The cinema has played no small part in China's recent history, and during the 1930s the film companies in Shanghai were deeply infiltrated by the Communists. Besides, if a certain little starlet called Lan Ping, one day to be so famous as Jiangqing, had been more successful in Shanghai, she might not have taken off for the Communist base in Yanan and caught the eye of Mao Zedong. And there is no knowing what might have happened to China if there had been no Madame Mao to urge it towards ever loftier revolutionary heights. Even as China's first lady, she remained starry-eyed about Hollywood, which was part of a dream she once had in Shanghai where, as an unknown, she had sat spellbound through *Camille*, *Queen Christina* and other Greta Garbo classics.

Whilst many theatres continue to show Chinese movies—with period pieces and ever-popular kung fu classics, a new breed of international cinema halls has appeared. China is also relaxing its restriction on the import of foreign blockbusters—resulting in a wide range of foreign films on show in many of its theatres that are increasingly shown in English with Chinese subtitles. State-of-the-art cinema facilities are found in the stunning **Kodak Cinema World** in Xujiahui (tel: 6426 8181 ext. 598), the **UME International Cineplex** (tel: 6373 3333) in the north block of Xintiandi and **Studio City** (tel: 6218 2137) on the 10th floor of Westgate Mall at 1038 Nanjing Road (E). **The Shanghai Film Art Centre**, next to the Crowne Plaza Hotel on Xinhua Road (tel: 6280 4088), also has five international movie theatres. Two magnificent former art deco cinema houses have recently been brought back to life as multiplex movie theatres. The Cathay Theatre (opened in 1932, tel: 6280 4088) at 870 Central Huaihai Road, at the junction with Maoming Road (S) features three screens. For one of the best cinema going experiences in the city head for the spectacular **Grand Cinema** (opened in 1933, tel: 6327 3399, 6327 4260) at 216 Nanjing Road (W) on People's Square, which now features six auditoria ranging from a home-like movie theatre with 25 seats to a main auditorium with over 1500 seats. Just around the corner at 500 Central Tibet Road another famous 1930s picture house, the **Metropol**, albeit in a completely new building, has reopened (6361 6078 ext. 808).

The visual arts scene has also assumed a new importance with the Shanghai Biennale, hosted at the Power Station of Art and numerous intriguing historic spaces in 2012. Shanghai's latest hip cultural and arts district 'Tianzifang' (the name of an ancient Chinese painter) can be found on Taiking Road, near what was the southern boundary of the French Concession. Its meandering lanes and traditional 1920s shikumen (stone frame gate) architecture have been converted into a mini Amsterdam crammed with fashion houses, design shops, art studios and galleries, cafés and restaurants. The development first began along Lane 210 but has now been extended to cover much of the block with another main entrance at Lane 248. Private landlords have rented out their former residences to allow this vibrant organic growth that is very much international in character.

The city's main art district runs along the middle parts of the Suzhou Creek. Numerous old factories and warehouses now accommodate art and design studios and galleries. The main centre is at **M50** (50 Moganshan Road). Artists began moving into its empty warehouses in 2004 and the complex now houses over 60 galleries, architects' offices and associated enterprises. More art spaces and galleries have opened in the more distant Yangpu district, again occupying converted factories and warehouses.

Also, absolutely, not to be missed is a visit to **1933** and complex on Shajing Road in Hongkou District just behind the Kowloon hotel. 1933 occupies one of the most stunning art deco buildings in Shanghai—that of the former Shanghai Municipal Council Abattoir—and it together with neighbouring buildings has been converted to incorporate a range of creative, art, retail spaces. The complex also offers great dining opportunities. For lovers of contemporary art the **Zendai Museum of Modern Art** in the Zendai Plaza at Lane 199, Fangdian Road, Pudong, is another destination worth searching out. The museum also hosts concerts and lectures.

Other upcoming city hotspots where art is melded with entertainment and dining include The **Cool Docks** and **Red Town**. The Cool Docks at 505 Zhongshan Road (S), near Fuxing Road (E), feature an ambient mix of historic residential and industrial architecture; whilst Red Town, at 570 Huaihai Road (W) centred around the Shanghai Sculpture Space, has evolved from the skeleton of an old steel works.

Shanghai was Asia's capital of jazz in the 1920s and 1930s, Legends such at the Paul Whiteman Orchestra visited and Whitey Smith's Orchestra, the best in China, played at the best hotels. **The Peninsula Shanghai** has reintroduced the tea-dance, which they started in 1914, to the city. Top-note jazz with international artists is a regular feature at a few other top hotels, notably the **Portman Ritz-Carlton**, the

The Flowers on the Sea

A 19th-century novel by Han Bangqing, *The Singsong Girls of Shanghai*, begins with a prologue in which the author dreams he is walking on a sea bobbing with flowers. The meaning of this will not be lost on the average Chinese reader, for Shanghai translates as Above-the-Sea and 'flower' is a euphemism for a prostitute.

Prostitution was one of Shanghai's established institutions. The singsong houses (some of which remain standing in Shantou Lu and Fuzhou Lu, though long turned to other uses) had names like the House of Sure Satisfaction and the Hall of Beauties inscribed in red on the glass lanterns outside their doors. The high-class ones would have a strip of red paper posted on the door with the courtesan's name on it. Stepping inside, the patron found himself in a parlour with little rooms partitioned off it. The sound of music might reach his ears—for the girls were entertainers as well as prostitutes—as servant girls appeared to welcome him with tea and bowls of nuts and sweetmeats. A meal would be laid out, with waiters scurrying to bring the caller bowls of cooked dishes and cups of warmed wine.

Next, a pipe would be offered. Lying on a lacquered divan, the patron would watch as his favourite courtesan heated his opium, rolling the paste into a pellet and roasting it over a flame.

With its maidservants, 'aunties' (madams), drinking parties and regular customers, the Shanghai singsong houses had a domestic feel to them. To call them whorehouses would be to do them a disservice. Some of them were select establishments, frequented only by the well-heeled. The most select were the *shuyu*, or 'storytellers' residences', so named because many singsong girls had begun their careers as teahouse balladeers.

The higher the grade of a courtesan, the more one paid for her company. Among the most expensive were the *qing guanren*, the virgin courtesans. They were a kind of apprentice, to deflower whom was the privilege of only the very rich. Summoned to a party or an assignation, these girls made their way through the crush of Shanghai's alleys by riding on the shoulders of their ponces.

Whatever her rank, it was the dream of every singsong girl—who knew only too well how transient were her bloom and beauty—to become the principal wife of her patron. Sadly, the dream seldom came true, for while a man was happy enough to take his favourite singsong girl as a concubine, he demurred at making her his wife.

Tobacco advertisement, 1920s.

Hilton, the **Four Seasons**, the **JW Marriott** and **The Westin**. There are also some great small local clubs, including the **Cotton Club** at 8 Fuxing Road (W) that is Shanghai's longest running club, the **House of Blues and Jazz** at 60 Fuzhou Road (near the Bund) and the **JZ Club** at 1111 Central Huaihai Road, as well as **CJW** (Cigars, Jazz, Wine) and the Brown Sugar Club in Xintiandi.

Other aspects of the lifestyle that lent Shanghai the sobriquet 'Paris of the East' in the 1930s have also been

The famous Peace Hotel Jazz Band, 1986.

revived. Nowhere is this more evident than in Shanghai's glittering parade of nightspots. There's all manner of bars and clubs ranging from those suitable for a first date to sleazy watering holes full of Asian businessmen to state-of-the-art clubs, with big-name international DJs, patronised by the young nouveau-riche (Chinese and foreign) and all-night karaoke bars. There has been an explosion in the number

The Paramount Ballroom is open again.

of private bars and clubs and many involve foreign investment and management. The Paramount Ballroom at 638 Huashan Road, originally opened in 1933, is again back in action but with a much more conservative disposition.

Shanghai's main bar and restaurant district can be found around one of the Consulate districts in the former French Concession—on Hengshan Road, Yueyang Road, Dongping Road, Fenyang Road, Dongping Road, Taojiang Road, Hengshan Road and Wulumuqi Road (S). Favoured hangouts for foreign residents in the area include the legendary **O'Malley's Irish Pub** (47 Taojiang Road) that serves up Guinness on tap and live Irish folk music, as does the nearby **Blarney Stone** (5 Dongping Road). For those looking for a British style environment head for **Sasha's** that is housed in a mansion formerly belonging to the legendary Song family (11 Dongping Road). Nearby the voluminous Paulaner Brahaus (150 Fenyang Road) brews its own German ale on its stately premises. The German enterprise also has branches on the waterfront promenade in Pudong, as well as in Xintiandi. Xintiandi also has a host of music clubs, including **LUNA**, and a number of bars large and small, the **dr bar** established by Ben Wood, the district's distinguished architect, falling into the latter category. Top international DJs are frequent visitors to the city playing to mixed crowds of locals and a fast growing crowd of foreign twenty-somethings in search of fame and fortune. A few bars still survive in what were recognised nightlife districts until recent times. Some are still found near the Portman Ritz-Carlton Hotel on Tongren Road, Fengxian Road and on Maoming Road (S) near Yongjia Road. A host of lively and popular bars are also to be found on Julu Road near Changshu Road.

Nanjing Road (E), as a typhoon approaches Shanghai.

There are a number of very stylish bars on the Bund including **Bar Rouge** atop **Bund 18** and **The Glamour Bar** (and terrace at M on the Bund above) have great views across the Huangpu River to Pudong. Another fine view over the river with the Bund buildings in the foreground is afforded from the **Captain's Bar** at 20 Fuzhou Road. For a completely different view of Shanghai, where water dominates over buildings, the **VUE Bar** at the Hyatt on the Bund offers the most spectacular of Pudong from 'where the river bends.' **Cloud 9** on the 87th floor of the Grand Hyatt in Pudong is the place for views beyond the Bund and the **789 Nanjing Lu Bar** atop Le Royal Meridien Hotel offers panoramic views of the city from its heart, near People's Square.

You can keep up to date with what's going on and where, by picking up copies of the *Shanghai Daily*, *City Weekend*, *That's Shanghai* and *Shanghai Talk* when in town. Take a look at the website listings on page 65 for details on how to get the city run down online.

Food and Eating

On the culinary front, Shanghai offers all that one might expect of an emerging international metropolis—and the choice is expanding just as fast as the city itself. Wave after wave of culinary inspirations hit Shanghai, some of the more recent ones being Brazil steak-houses, Australian BBQ, Taiwanese cuisine and fiery Hunan food. Whilst a wealth of world-class cuisine is available, there are also many poor imitators relying on opulent and sumptuous surroundings rather than on the quality of the food and service. Shanghai has thousands of restaurants and the locals delight in eating out. The hosting of banquets or taking friends out for dinner is often a grand affair—and of course the host pays the, usually mighty, bill.

There is no shortage of the fresh ingredients in the area, and imported fresh produce is jetted in around the clock. Shanghai is amply supplied with freshwater and sea fish and shellfish—eel, carp, shrimp and most celebrated of all the *dazha xie,* or the Shanghai hairy crab, that is in season from late September to November. The majority of these crabs are consumed by overseas Chinese and foreigners living in the city. The surrounding fertile countryside provides the city with an abundance of fresh vegetables—French beans, peas, Chinese leaves, cabbage, carrots, potatoes, celery and a number of delicious greens not encountered in the West. One only has to look at one of the large fresh produce markets to see that the variety of produce on offer is bewildering; for instance, more than six different varieties of mushroom are commonly available. Likewise, the huge hypermarkets and supermarkets operated by British, French, American, German, Thai, Japanese, as well as, local Chinese display an astounding mix of Asian and Western fresh and packaged food products.

Such a culinary milieu, combined with the attraction of Shanghai for people from all over China, has resulted in a wide range of regional cuisines being represented in the city. Local Shanghai cuisine is invariably sweet and can be comparatively oily. Popular local dishes include *shizi tou* (lion's head meatballs) served in a gravy and *hong shao rou* (slow-braised pork). Many restaurants serving regional cuisines often add more than a touch of Shanghai flavour. Foreign restaurateurs have also been quick to move in, with just about every favoured foreign cuisine being found somewhere around town. The range of culinary fare on offer is reflected in prices with good meals including drinks, to be had for less than 20 yuan, in a local restaurant to upwards of 250 yuan in an international one.

Apart from the superlative cuisine on offer in the top hotels, including the **Hyatt's**, the **Four Seasons**, the **Pudong Shangri-La**, the **Ritz-Carlton**, **The Westin**, the **Fairmont Peace Hotel**, the **Waldorf Astoria Shanghai on the Bund**, and **The Peninsula Shanghai**, many restaurants of note can be found within the confines of the former French Concession. The largest cluster is to be found around the Hengshan Road, the former Avenue Petain, as highlighted in our section on bars (*see* page 486). The most extravagant restaurants, such as the **Yongfoo Elite**, are housed in spectacular old villas with prices to match. Fine dining can be an expensive pastime in Shanghai. The historic buildings on the Bund also house many fine restaurants and for many a meal at **M on the Bund**, or one of the other top-notch establishments found there, is an essential part of a visit to the city. For more details of dining on the Bund (*see* page 558).

Historic architecture also plays a significant role in Shanghai's most stylish eating and entertainment area at **Xintiandi**, which opened in 2001. This is Shanghai's answer to London's Covent Garden or New York's Soho. Old or 're-created' buildings featuring stylishly modern interior designs, decorations and equipment play host to a dazzling array of restaurants specialising in French, American, German, British, Brazilian, Italian, Japanese, Chinese, Taiwanese and Hong Kong cuisine. They display the full international dimension of the development of popular restaurants such as the stylish **T8** and the Italian extravaganza presented at **Va Bene**. There are many tables outside the eateries that fill up at night-times. The aforementioned **Tianzifang** on Taikang Road has emerged as one of Shanghai's most popular areas to eat. Unlike at Xintiandi its bistros, bars and cafés are housed in an authentic shikumen residential district that bleeds with character and history. The historic **Cool Docks** district has also emerged as a popular entertainment and dining area.

Markets brim with fresh fruit and vegetables while faces brim with smiles.

As exemplified in Xintiandi and numerous other developments, there is a move towards merging eating with recreation and shopping. Huge food courts or food streets, offering a blend of Asian and international cuisine have become highly fashionable in many of the new shopping malls that often have cinemas and amusements as well. The food areas are generally found in the basements or on the upper floors of these shopping centres. Take a look at our shopping chapter on page 498. A large food square has appeared in **Xujiahui**, around the Orient Shopping Centre, which apart from offering various regional cuisines, serves up anything from Italian to Japanese. Another recently opened food square, '**Holiday Mall**,' is to be found on the southern section of Sichuan Road (N) where it meets Tiendong Road in the Zhabei district.

Other recognised eating areas around town include the **Hongmei Pedestrian Leisure Street** in Changning District—a very long narrow pedestrian street which also features outside dining. It runs between Hongmei Road and Hongxu Road, south of the elevated Yan'an Road (W). The street is in the Gubei area, which is a popular residential domicile for foreigners including many Taiwanese and Japanese. The international flavour of the area is reflected in the cuisine—Indonesian, French, Japanese and much more. Two huge food plazas in the same district, on Shuicheng Road, near the intersection with Hongqiao Road, are also very popular destinations.

Dianxin *time in the oldest tea house in the Chinese city.*

DREAMING AND FOOD

I would like to be that elderly Chinese gentleman.
He wears a gold watch with a gold bracelet,
But a shirt without sleeves or tie.
He has good luck moles on his face, but is not disfigured with fortune.
His wife resembles him, but is still a handsome woman,
She has never bound her feet or her belly.
Some of the party are his children, it seems,
And some his grandchildren;
No generation appears to intimidate another.
He is interested in people, without wanting to convert them or pervert them.
He eats with gusto, but not with lust;
And he drinks, but is not drunk.
He is content with his age, which has always suited him.
When he discusses a dish with the pretty waitress,
It is the dish he discusses, not the waitress.
The table-cloth is not so clean as to show indifference,
Not so dirty as to signify a lack of manners.
He proposes to pay the bill but knows he will not be allowed to.
He walks to the door like a man who doesn't fret about being respected,
    since he is;
A daughter or granddaughter opens the door for him,
And he thanks her.
It has been a satisfying evening. Tomorrow
Will be a satisfying morning. In between he will sleep satisfactorily.
I guess that for him it is peace in his time.
It would be agreeable to be this Chinese gentleman.

D. J. Enright, Dreaming in the Shanghai Restaurant

Poet, novelist and critic, Dennis Joseph Enright (1920–2002) was born in Warwickshire (UK). He taught overseas—mainly in south Asian universities from 1947 to 1970—before returning to England to work as an editor and director of a publishing house, and accept an Honorary Professorship of Warwick University. Part of a group of poets that became known as "*The Movement*" in the 1950s, his own poetry was straightforward, sometimes ironic and almost in the style of light verse, often dealing with themes of inequality, and filled with wit, compassion and self-mockery.

Not far away the **Xianxia Road**, around the intersection with Anlong Road, has a wide and excellent range of large and small eateries—again well patronised by locals in the know. There is also a cluster of international eateries further down the Xianxia Road near the Sheraton Grand Hotel.

The road running up from the north entrance of Fuxing Park (the former French Park) presents a scene of London or Paris. Beautifully restored art deco apartments and traditional 'stone-framed' door houses line a pedestrianised street complete with palm trees and outside seating. The **Yandang Road** was more romantically known as the Route Voyon by its old French residents. With its neon lights and distinctive Chinese flavour, **Zhapu Road**, just over the bridge, north of the Bund is worth exploring if you are in search of local fare. **Yunnan Road** (S) between Jinling Road (E) and Yan'an Road (E) also has a wide range of local eateries and is a popular night time destination. A number of local Muslim restaurants, largely operated by Uygurs from Xinjiang, are also found nearby in the Zhejiang Road (S) and Yunnan Road (S) district.

The **Shanghai Art Museum** on Nanjing Road (W) has an interesting café on two levels around a stair case adorned by horse head figures, reminiscent of the days when it was the British-run Race club. Its roof space is occupied by **Kathleen's** 5, serving Continental food and fine views. The nearby **Ciro's Plaza**, at No. 388 Nanjing Road (W), adopted its name from a famous 1930s nightclub that once stood there also has a range of eateries. A little further up the road at No. 445 the **Gongdelin Vegetarian Restaurant** serves up incredibly skilful and tasty re-created meat and fish dishes. Meilongzhen at Lane 2, 1081 Nanjing Road (W) is popular with tourists and locals alike for Sichuan-inspired Shanghainese cuisine within an historic setting. International eateries can be found nearby on **Wujiang Road**. With the recent upgrading of the area around the Four Seasons Hotel, **Dagu Road** has emerged as a modern and fashionable place to eat and drink. Apart from great Mediterranean food at **Haya's** (No. 415), there's everything from pizzas to chicken tikka on offer here. And there's a bonus in that the western part of the street still has some local eateries, as well as a large fresh produce market that is well worth strolling around. A whole range of restaurants can be found in the major commercial and retail buildings in this district, many on upper floors, or at basement level. **West Gate Mall** at No. 1038 Nanjing Road (W) has a food court and good dining options upstairs, including **Crystal Jade**, a branch of the popular Hong Kong-style dim sum eatery.

Snacks

If you are feeling peckish or looking for a light meal you won't have to walk too far in the downtown area to feast on local or foreign favourites. Although most locals are rice-eaters, Shanghai has a large number of noodle shops and outlets selling local dumplings, the most popular being *sheng jian*, (pan fried meat dumplings) and *xiao long bao* (steamed meat dumplings). The most famous dumpling shop in town selling **Nanxiang steamed dumplings** near the entrance to the Yu Garden. You can't miss it —just look for a small shop with long queues. The nearby **Lubolang Restaurant** (Green Wave Pavilion) also conjures up a fine range of dumplings—especially the crab-filled variety. Another favourite often sold at the front of food stores and restaurants is *zongzi*—sweet or savoury glutinous rice parcels wrapped in bamboo leaves. Try them and many other specialities at **Shendacheng**, 636 Nanjing Road (W). Up the road at No. 805 is another local favourite, **Wangjiasha**, which serves deep-fried noodles and great dumplings. It's a very busy place and you have to purchase vouchers first and, like at most speciality eateries, be prepared to queue. The **Shanghai Qiaojiashan Restaurant** at 336 Xiangyang Road (S) is also a popular venue for its glutinous rice cakes and snacks. The delicious Taiwanese dumplings served up at Din Tai Fung in Xintiandi come internationally acclaimed. Hygiene restrictions severely limit street

*An eclectic mix of Chinese and Western styles on
Nanjing Road (E) grace both sides of the pedestrian thoroughfare.*

food markets—though you will see Xinjiang people barbequing lamb kebabs (*yang rou chuanr*) and baking flat breads (*da bing*) on the streets.

The Shanghainese have a notoriously sweet tooth and the city carries on its European tradition in the form of cake shops—said to number more than 2,000. A small custard tart or *dan ta*, is a popular local favourite. Coffee shops have never fallen from favour and despite the arrival of **Starbucks**, **Costa Coffee** and **The Coffee Bean**, independent and often eclectic cafés rule the roost. There are plenty of foreign and local-managed cafes around town. Be warned—expect to pay between US$3 and US$5 for a cup of coffee. A long established branch of **Kaisiling's**, serving up Western food, coffee and cakes can be found at No. 1133 Nanjing Road (W). Good bakeries can be found in most shopping malls and larger supermarkets. **85 °C**, a Taiwanese chain of cake shops, with reasonably priced coffee and an interesting selection of cakes and pastries, including English-style scones, has become a hot local favourite.

All large shopping areas have branches of **McDonalds**, **Burger King** and **Kentucky Fried Chicken**. Apart from the American model they offer some items modified for local tastes. There are a number of other international fast food operations including **Subway** sandwiches, the incredibly popular **Pizza Hut**, **Dunkin' Donut** as well as branches of **Häagen-Dazs** ice-cream. And if you are in search of a deli sandwich or some healthy western salads and snacks head for a branch of **Slice**, the brainchild of famed Australian chef David Laris, (one is conveniently located at Times Square, 99 Central Huaihai Road). Other Western-style establishments include **Element Fresh**, with branches at the Super Brand Mall in Lujiazui and at the Shanghai Centre at 1376 Nanjing Road (W), amongst others, and **Wagas**. Wagas has over ten branches around town with two central Puxi locations at 69 Wujiang Road and CITIC Square, 1168 Nanjing Road (W). There are also numerous **Subway** sandwich outlets around the city, including one at the Oriental Pearl TV Tower.

Above: *Charlie Chaplin, one of few foreign film stars whose work was acceptable in the 1970s.*

Sandwiches (often of the inferior kind) and a large range of snack foods and drinks are also available on just about every street corner. Shanghai has witnessed an amazing boom in 24-hour convenience stores—there are now over 5,000, including **Alldays**, **Buddies**, **C-Store**, **Kedi and Lawsons**' outlets all over the city. Most stores have a selection of hot snacks including tea-eggs, five-spiced eggs, fish balls on sticks and local pastries.

Drinks

Chinese tea is often, but not necessarily, provided with Chinese meals. The most common type is jasmine tea (*moli hua cha*), but you should try the famous Longjing (Dragon Well) green tea from neighbouring city of Hangzhou. Though there are not as many traditional teahouses as there are branches of Starbucks around town. Some parks, including the beautiful Guilin Park, still have them and some new re-creations have appeared, especially in the area around the Yu Garden. The most famed and established teahouse, the Huxinting, is set in the heart of the area (*see* page 496). Along the nearby Old Street, otherwise known as Central Fangbang Road, a few old-style Shanghai teahouses have recently appeared. The most revered is the **Old Shanghai Teahouse and Museum** at No. 385. The building is littered with memorabilia, photos, wall posters, old maps and even an old working gramophone. Other teahouses along the street include the **Chunfeng Deyi** at No. 337 and **Nora** at No. 452. Another unique environment to take tea or coffee is the **Old China Hand Reading Room** at 27 Shaoxing Road, complete with a library and many museum pieces.

Beer is routinely imbibed with Chinese meals and other wines and spirits make an appearance at banquets. Many locally produced beers, all of the lager type, are brewed with foreign assistance. Reeb (beer spelled backwards) is the most established, using Swedish know-how. In recent years the Japanese influence has gained a stronghold and the Suntory joint-venture has been the most pervasive. Other locally produced Japanese beers include Asahi and Kirin. Joint-venture Budweiser is another local favourite, as is China's number one selling beer, Tsingtao. Local beers are often cheaper to buy in stores than locally produced mineral water.

The Chinese group together all alcoholic products with the term '*jiu*'. One of the most popular drinks is a strong liquor known as '*bai jiu*,' or whit spirit. It is a sorghum-based clear spirit traditionally used for toasts at banquets. *Maotai* is regarded as the finest specimen and commands a high price. The finest Cognacs are also very popular with China's new status-seekers.

Visitors should try some warmed Shaoxing rice wine produced near Shanghai. A lighter form of rice wine, that tastes a little like a home-made potato or elderflower wine, is available from September to March. It comes in large plastic bottles and is simply known as 'mi jiu' (rice wine). Traditional Chinese grape wines are rather sweet by Western standards, though the 'China Red' is a palatable Madeira-like drink.

Visitors should try some warmed Shaoxing rice wine produced near Shanghai. A lighter form of rice wine, that tastes a little like a home-made potato or elderflower wine, is available from September to March. It comes in large plastic bottles and is known simple as 'mi jiu' (rice wine). Traditional Chinese grape wines are rather sweet by Western standards, though the 'China Red' is a palatable Madeira-like drink. Foreign involvement with the industry is becoming widespread with successful recent ventures including the Grace Vineyards in Shanxi and the Sella & Mosca and the Huadong Wineries in Qingdao. Some of China's most palatable and best value table wines are produced in Xinjiang. With French assistance the Lou Lan Winery in Turfan has cultivated particularly good Cabernet and Sauvignon vintages. The most popular brands of variable quality table wines are Great Wall, Dynasty and Dragon Seal.

Sample a Huadong Chardonnay if you can. The Shanghai Shenma Vinery Company produces a perfectly acceptable method champenoise called Imperial Brut.

A huge range of soft and still drinks are available at even the smallest convenience stores. They include Western brands such as Coke and Sprite as well as many local concoctions, from Hainan Island coconut juice to milk tea with pearls of jelly.

The restaurant scene is in a constant state of flux, so be sure to pick up some of the free city living magazines when in town to keep up with what's hot or not. For a selection of fine restaurants please refer to page 558.

Above: *Roasted nuts and seeds, a popular street snack.*
Left: *The Huxinting Teahouse in the Yu Gardens complex was visited by Queen Elizabeth II during her visit to China in 1986.*

Shopping

Shanghai is experiencing a massive retail revolution. Ultra-modern stores, mega-malls and hypermarkets have sprung up all over the city—often sat next to local shopping areas that not only offer a striking visual, but also a remarkable commercial contrast. Shopping cities, with integral recreation and amusement facilities and food courts, are very much in vogue. Designer stores are found in abundance, where the price of a simple handbag may be more than most people's annual salary. Ostentatious showrooms proffer modern Western lifestyles in anything from brocaded French period furniture to Bentley cars. With China's entry to the WTO, tariffs are falling for imported goods, though prices are still far higher than in the West for most products.

However away from the international shopping arena, in local stores and in the city's bustling markets there is plenty to interest the visitor. Shanghai remains a shopping nirvana with a wealth of great value gifts and souvenirs, as well the promise of many fun-filled hours. Do remember that bargaining is *de rigueur* in many local stores and all private markets. Even if objects have a marked price, which is not that common, you should still bargain. Prices are generally fixed in malls and larger stores. See page 57 for advice on bargaining.

High Street Shopping

On the face of it Shanghai's main shopping streets look just like their counterparts in any big Western city. However look beyond the international store fronts and delve into its specialist stores to experience a uniquely different shopping experience. Shopping hours are generally from 10:00am to 10:00pm.

Nanjing Road

In the Chinese mind Shanghai and shopping are synonymous. The millions that descend on Shanghai from all around China will all find their way to Nanjing Road, China's number one shopping street. The main shopping section extends beyond five kilometres (three miles) from the Bund to Jing'an Temple. Known as the 'Great White Way' in the '30s, on account of its things Occidental, it housed China's first department stores and exclusive shops and depicted a modernity hitherto unknown in China. The road is divided

Nanjing Road (W) at People's Square.

into two sections—Nanjing Road (W) used to be known as Bubbling Well Road and now houses some of China's classiest shopping malls and office towers. The main part, Nanjing Road (E), which runs up from the waterfront has largely been pedestrianised and public squares have been installed. It's a great place to stroll, window shop, and rub shoulders with hordes of Chinese pilgrims.

Nanjing Road (E) is famous for its department stores, many of which have a long historic association. The **Number One Department Store**, one of the largest in China, on the corner with Tibet Road, remains one of Shanghai's liveliest and busiest stores. Originally known as the Sun Department Store, it was built in 1936. Its 3,000 or so sales staff deal with about 200,000 customers per day and many more at holiday periods. The six-level store is crammed with high quality domestic and imported goods. Nearby, the famous Wing On Department Store, built in 1918, is showing signs of its former grandeur. Following a recent US$24 million renovation that included the removal of its ugly exterior glass cladding, revealing its original

features, it is now operated by **Yongan**. A restaurant serving Macanese cuisine on its upper two floors has a roof terrace that is open in comfortable weather.

Where the Nanjing Road (E) crosses Central Tibet Road it becomes Nanjing Road (W). The **New World Shopping Mall**, capable of handling 200,000 visitors a day was opened there in 2004. Nearby on Central Tibet Road, **Raffles City** offers a host of shopping and eating opportunities as well an IMAX theatre. The western part of Nanjing Road has some of the most palatial shopping malls in the city. The most prestigious ones are west of Shimen No. 1 Road. They are all located on the northern side of the street. Even though there are modern store fronts on the other side of the road many of them hide whole blocks of traditional *shikumen* housing down small lanes and art deco apartment blocks—it is well worth taking a peek.

Some old lanes still survive off the southern section of Shimen No. 1 Road, near the West Nanjing Road metro stop. In pre-liberation days it was known as the 'road of underwear, curios and other curiosities' and its lacy offerings were found in the best Parisian lingerie shops. Today it doesn't have too much in the way of export garments, but it is an interesting street to stroll along. You could even take lunch at the Four Seasons Hotel, on the corner with Weihai Road—it has one of best and most reasonably priced buffet lunches in the city.

The **Westgate Mall** (*Meilongzhen*) rests on the corner of Nanhui Road featuring seven floors of shopping in its **Isetan Department Store** as well as a massive and excellent basement food court, a **Watsons** drug store and scores of other outlets. Continuing west there are two other huge upmarket malls **CITIC Square** (*Zhongxin Taifu Guangchang*) at No. 1166 and **Plaza 66** (*Henglong Guangchang*) at No. 1266. All manner of designer labels make their mark in these malls—Alfred Dunhill, Lagerfeld, Givenchy, Max Mara, Hugo Boss, Prada, Versace and many more. There are numerous food outlets as well with a large Lu Lu Shanghai cuisine restaurant in Plaza 66 and a Starbuck's in CITIC Square.

Shopping after dark on Nanjing Road.

Next door at No. 1376 is the **Shanghai Centre**—the first and largest multi-use commercial centre and expatriate haven in the city, built at a cost of US$195 million by Japanese and US interests. It contains the Ritz-Carlton Hotel, luxury apartments, offices, an exhibition hall, a theatre, tailor and fashion shops, the City Supermarket and a host of airline offices. The are also many fine restaurants including Palladio, on of the best Italian restaurants in China, Tony Roma's and Element Fresh. Further up the road a lively shopping area has developed around the Jing'an Temple. **City Plaza** at No. 1618 has a fine international supermarket in its basement, as well as a good selection of shops and food outlets.

The Nanjing Road is served by four Metro stops—from east to west, Nanjing Road (E) People's Square, Nanjing Road (W) and Jing'an Temple.

CENTRAL HUAIHAI ROAD

The former Avenue Joffre, the classiest avenue in the heart of the old French Concession, grew up in the 1920s and formerly hosted a large Russian population. It still retains its shopping supremacy as today's Central Huaihai Road. The main shopping area is on the middle section of the road from Central Tibet Road in the east to Xiangyang Road in the west. Much old world dignified charm remains amidst some of the most modern shopping plaza's, boutiques and stores in China.

A huge LCD screen adorns the walls of **Times Square** at No. 99 and inside there's upmarket fashion shopping at Lane Crawford and Maison Mode. Other upmarket stores on the street include the French-based **Printemps**, the Malaysia-based **Parksons** and Japanese-based **Isetan**. All offer a range of goods out of reach of most of the crowds that stroll within. The more affordable **Pacific Department Store** can be found in the Shui On Plaza near the Huangpi Road (S) metro stop. Nearby the old French Municipal Council Building has been converted into a shopping mall and forms part of the **Shanghai Central Plaza**. **Cybermart** at No. 282 is a great place to pick up computer, camera and phone accessories.

Off Central Huaihai Road on Maoming Road (S), opposite the Okura Garden Hotel, there is a stretch of luxury shops known as the '**Promenade on Maoming Road**', which includes tailors and designer brands spearheaded by a branch of the famous Hong Kong based **Shanghai Tang** that opened in 2003. A little further down the street another upmarket centre for international brands and designer labels is found in the **Jinjiang Dickson Centre** at 400 Changle Road. A whole range of top designer labels vie for attention here including Tommy Hilfiger, Versace and Ralph Lauren. An array of smaller boutiques and classy shops run along the Changle Road to the west of the complex.

Another block up, the Shaanxi Road (S), has a large number of good local boutiques and a great selection of shoe shops—many of them displaying copies of the latest European and American designs at a modicum of their native cost. The nearby Ruijin No. 2 Road is also a great place to browse for fashion and gift items. Nanchang Road, the former Route Valon, running parallel to Central Huaihai Road, east towards Fuxing Park, is one of the city's most interesting shopping streets. Classy boutiques and bijou eateries inhabit its classical and art deco buildings. The main shopping section of Central Huaihai Road is served by two metro stops—Huangpi Road (S) and Shanxi Road (S), (Shaanxi Road (S) on the street signs).

XUJIAHUI

The area, formerly on the western fringe of the French Concession and noted for its Jesuit heritage, has emerged as a top shopping and commercial district since the mid-1990s. A cluster of huge malls are to found at the Zhaojiabang Road intersection, namely the **Grand Gateway**, the **Orient**, the **No. 6**, and the **Huijin** department stores. Again the stores are laden with consumer products of all descriptions and offer numerous opportunities for recreation and eating. The area's digital plazas, including Metro City, are great places to pick up the latest high-tech gadget or computer—and there are some bargains around. A large underground mall is also found inside the Xujiahui metro stop.

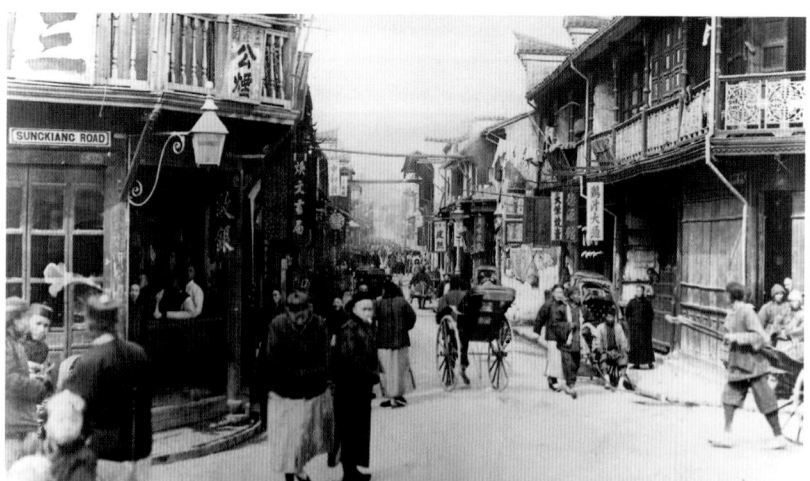

Shops on Sungkiang Road, circa 1900, included a tobacconist, bookstore and noodle shop among others.

Sichuan Road (N)
Historically North Sichuan Road (N) was where the locals went for their high street shopping and that remains largely true today. However its local character has been massively transformed by the recent demolition of much of its 1920s and 1930s shop houses and residential terraces. However some very fine examples of red and grey brick town houses and art deco apartment blocks still survive, especially towards the Lu Xun Park area. The road is still festooned with ladies fashion outlets and is still well worth strolling. It can be reached by metro line 3—alight at the Dongbaoxin Road Station.

Pudong
Keeping up with its grand ambitions the Pudong New Area has some of the largest stores in Asia. On the intersection of Zhangyang Road and Laoshan Road are two magnificent mega-malls, **Times Square** (*Shidai Guangchang*) and the Japanese invested **Next Age** (*Ba Bai Ban*). The latter claims to be the largest in Asia, and second only to Macy's in New York. Right in the centre of the Lujiazui area the Thai-invested **Super Brand Mall** opened in 2002, and apart from its basement hypermarket it has become a popular place to shop, eat and spend the day.

Markets and Bazaars
No trip to Shanghai is complete without a foray into its world of antiques and curios. Given the city's unique heritage and pedigree, a treasure trove of antiques are regularly on show in her antique markets. The contents of block after block of houses that have been demolished spill on to an ever competitive market. Antique hunting has become a serious pastime for growing numbers of local people. That takes in everything from porcelain, jade, embroideries, and calligraphy, to old watches and cameras, furniture, door handles and Mao badges. Most dealers, despite there often modest appearance, are very astute and aware of the market value of their wares. Quoted prices can often appear absurdly high as they often ignore the actual value, history or beauty of the object. With regard to furniture note that it is the type of wood that largely determines the price—mahogany is especially highly valued. Try offering around one quarter of the asking price to start with in the markets. There are still bargains to be had.

The most well-known antique market, the **Fuyou Road** market, is heavily patronised by locals at the weekends and has hundreds of stall-holders on its four levels. An astounding display of antiques and knick-knacks is on offer. It retains its former name but is now found at 457 Fangbang Road, close to the Yu Garden. The market is partially open through the week, but comes alive on Saturdays and Sundays. It begins to wake at between 8:00am and 9:00am and though it is officially open until 5:00pm many vendors start to pack up around 3:30pm. The area is also renowned for its 'ghost market' or '*guishi*', which takes place on the street outside the market on Saturday and at the nearby Renmin Road and Central Fangbang Road intersection on Sundays. Dealers will gather here to collect pieces that will be sold at great multiples of the selling price on their own stalls, or in their shops. It is well worth getting a taxi to the area if you have an eye for a bargain, but be there no later than 6:00am.

Sunday Market outside Yunzhou Curio City.

Art expressed through sculpted and engraved stone.

Situated just to the east of the Taipingqiao Park near Tibet Road South, the **Dongtai Road** antiques market parades a huge display of antiques, curios and artefacts. Many of the items can be found across China—but this is a good place to hunt for fragments of Shanghai's past— from maps and postcards to art deco furniture and period lighting. The area is also known as 'Cricket Street.' Don't miss the **Jueye Fang Craft Market**, an indoor arcade, located at No. 60–62. The market is open from around 9:00am until 4:00pm or 5:00pm daily.

Another large antique market is to be found in the basement of the **Hua Bao Building** nearby at 265 Fangbang Road in the Yu Garden shopping complex. It is open daily from 8:30am to 9:00pm. This market is more tourist-oriented than the others around town, but has some beautiful pieces on offer. Another large market in the heart of the city just off Nanjing Road (E) can be found at No. 188 Central Zhejiang Road. The **Yunzhou Curio City** at 88 Damuqiao Road in Xuihi district, with its six floors crammed with curios, paintings and antiques, is little visited by foreigners. However this is a great place to wander, especially at weekends when vendors set up street stalls around the building, and a must visit destination for those collectors seeking old currency, medals and postcards.

Shanghai's bird and flower markets are also fascinating places to explore. They not only sell birds and flowers, but also other pets and fauna, as well as antiques, curios and arts and crafts The most interesting one, the Jingwen Flower Market that used to be housed in the former building of the 'Canidrome,' a huge greyhound racing auditorium in pre-liberation days, has unfortunately been demolished. The largest surviving market, the **Hongqiao Flower Market** can be found at 718 Hongjing Road, near Hongsong Road, to the west of the city, Although it has diminished in size due to the encroachment of modern buildings, a most charming bird and flower market is to be found in **Jiangyin Road**. Set in an area with small lanes amidst 1920s and 1930s housing, just west of the Shanghai Art Museum off People's Square, it's a must visit destination if you are nearby. You can also take refreshments in the attractive concealed courtyard of the Youth Hostel at No. 57. In Pudong, there is another interesting market, tucked away in a residential area, known as **Pudian Wu Cheng**, which can be approached from 280 Pudian Road between Pudong Road (S) and Nanquan Road.

Not having heard that it was knocked down in 2006, visitors still flock to the former site of Shanghai's most famous fake clothes and accessories market on Xianyang Road. In that knowledge touts still prey on white faces with the words, 'bag, watch, DVD'. As do the more aggressive touts lining the streets around where many of the fashion stalls have moved to in Qipu Road. Just a few years ago this was a bustling local fashion street crowded on a small road amidst a vast and atmospheric 1920s residential district. The last edition of this guide noted that it was

Canine chic.

'little visited by foreigners'. Not any more—most of the historic housing has been knocked down and the over-widened street is now lined with vast, and ugly, market malls. Despite the inhospitable environment, this is one of the favoured the places to shop for clothes and accessories for many locals, foreign residents and visitors. Pickpockets abound—so beware! The **Qipu Road Fashion Market** extends for over half a mile (one kilometre), along Qipu Road all the way from Henan Road (N) to Zhejiang Road (N), north of the Suzhou Creek. The market can be walked to from the northern end of the Bund—cross the Creek, walk along Suzhou Road (N), take a right at a Jiangxi Road (N) and then turn left on to Qipu Road. The major fashion plazas include the Qipu Qinghaung at No. 168, the Xinqipu at No. 179–183, the Xingpu at No. 258 and the Chaofeijie at No. 268. Another large market (the **Yatai Xinyang Fashion and Gift Market**) that opened in the wake of the closure is to be found, of all places, underground alongside the metro station for the Science and Technology Museum in Pudong. Many of the traders from the Xiangyang market can now be found at the **Taobao Market** occupying the first three floors of a high-rise a at 580 Nanjing Road (W) near Chengdu Road (N).

Close to the Nanpu Bridge, the former **Dongjiadu Fabric Market**, Shanghai's largest, has been resurrected as the **South Bund Fabric Market** in new premises nearby at 399 Lujiabang Road, near Nancang Street, close to the magnificent Dongjiadu Cathedral. There are around 240 stalls offering a fantastic range of fabrics, from cashmere to Thai Silk and its open from 8:00am to 6:00pm, daily. The **Qingfang Market**, near the East China Normal University, also offers a wide range of clothing as well as household fabrics. Local tailors can be found to make garments in both areas, though it can be an unpredictable and time consuming process. On the other hand it's amazing what can successfully be pieced together in less for than 24 hours for far less than off the peg in the West. If you are in search of yarns and silk threads the best place to go is the northern (not so touristy) section of the **Yu Garden Bazaar** off Renmin Road.

For those looking for pearls, even though it's a little way out of the centre, the **Hong Qiao New World Pearl Market** on the corner of Hongmei Road and Hongqiao Road has become an attraction for locals and visitors alike—and its open till 10:00pm. There's another large pearl market on the third floor of **First Asia Jewelry Plaza** at 288 Fuyou Road in the Old Town.

Yu Garden Bazaar
Yu Yuan Shangcheng 豫园商城

If modern Shanghai seems all too familiar—head for the bustling and jostling 'China town' area around the Yu Garden. Although the 'native city' of Shanghai has been in existence for over 2,000 years its significance has never been greater than in the present-day. Little is left from the early days, but the ever-expanding bazaar area has been splendidly stocked with replicant Ming and Qing Dynasty style Chinese architecture containing stores and small shops offering a feast of Chinese handicrafts, local food, fashions and copy goods. The bazaar area is a bustling and colourful attraction in its own right drawing in hundreds of thousands of visitors each day and over one million during holiday and festival times. Be prepared to bargain and politely refuse unsolicited offers to view 'art galleries' or 'antiques.'

The area has a number of speciality stores where one can pick up unusual gifts ranging from vegetable carving sets to intricately crafted paper-cuts of the city skyline. You will find shops specialising in chopsticks, umbrellas, walking sticks, musical instruments, pottery, lanterns and much more. There are two large purpose-arts and crafts department stores in the area.

Some interesting shops are still to be found to the south of the main bazaar area on Central Fangbang Road—also titled **Shanghai Old Street** (*Shanghai Lao Jie*), Over 800-metres (2,600 feet) of two-storey shops and dwellings were renovated with the dawning of the millennium, but most have already been demolished in favour of modern multi-storeys with 'Chinese characteristics.' However, the western section of the street, running up to Henan Road (S) still partly survives with its curio shops and teahouses. Also look out for the few surviving old residential areas that are largely located to the north of the street.

Other Shopping Opportunities

Antiques

A number of large and small antique stores have appeared around town in response to the growing demand for past treasures, in part inspired by the massive influx of foreigners and overseas Chinese into the city. Anything from antique furniture to fine porcelain is to be found in abundance, and usually with an abundant price tag too. Large antique stores and warehouses are found in the Hongqiao area to the west of the city. The **Haikun Business Centre** at 1426 Hongqiao Road has a fine selection of Ming and Qing Dynasty furniture. **G E Antiques** at No. 8 Huqingping Highway also has a fine selection of antique furnishings and they offer worldwide delivery. Other

Sadly, this painting and calligraphy shop, thriving in 1979, no longer exists.

areas to hunt for antiques and curios include the **Longhua Tourist and Shopping City** in the southwest suburbs, adjacent to the Longhua Pagoda and the restored **Duolun Road** in the Hongkou district (*see* page 401).

In the central area, the **Shanghai Lyceum Jewellery and Antique Store**, a well established and certified business, has an outlet just opposite the Jinjiang Hotel at 398 Changle Road. It deals in a wide range of treasures ranging from porcelain and ink stones to paintings and clocks. The **Shanghai Antiques and Curios Store** at 192–240 Guangdong Road, which has been dealing in antiques for over a century, has been recently enlarged and sells items ranging from wood carving and furniture to jade, porcelain, paintings and embroideries. Another fine store, the **Yi Hai Tang**, is to be found at 340 Huashan Road. The area around Lane 210 Taikang Road is also well worth a look—it even has a shop specialising in vintage photographic equipment.

Specialist Stores

There are a number of stores around the city that offer items that are distinctly Chinese and make great gifts. For arts and crafts items take a look in the **Arts and Crafts Commercial Building** at 190–208 Nanjing Road (W) or the **Shanghai Arts and Crafts Museum (Institute)** at 79 Fenyang Road (*see* page 408). The **Shanghai Friendship Store** at 1188 Changshou Road also has a large selection of arts and crafts items. It also has a smaller branch selling handicrafts, jade and antique porcelain on the west side of the Jing'an Temple at 9 Huashan Road. Fine pottery can be purchased at the famed **Jingdezhen** outlet at 1185 Nanjing Road (W). A large stock of beautiful pottery, including the revered violet-sand pottery, from the nearby town of Yixing, is on offer at the **Tiehuaxuan Pottery Shop** in the Yu Garden bazaar. Another interesting store in which to look for small gifts is the **Wangxingji Fan Store** at 155 Tibet Road (S). The **Shanghai Philatelic Corporation** outlet at 18 Sichuan Road (N), opposite the main post office, is not only for dedicated philatelists. Its a great place to pick up mementos and gifts, including colourful covers, cards and albums. Although not strictly a store, those in search of precious mementos of Shanghai's revolutionary history should pay a visit to the **Shanghai Propaganda Art Centre** at Room BOC, President Mansion, 868 Huashan Road. It's a little difficult to find, so be sure to ring ahead (6211 1845, 1390 1841 246). Over 3,000 original posters, as well as old maps and other printed materials, are to be found on the premises. Most are for sale.

BOOKSTORES

Many superior hotels have small bookstores containing guides and illustrated books. Other interesting book stores are to be found within the city's museums, with the **Shanghai Museum** outlet boasting a fantastic selection of titles amongst its other offerings. The nearby Urban Planning Exhibition Hall also has a variety of bookstores. The city's literary scene has been enriched with the opening of a number of Hong Kong based Charterhouse bookstores. They are located in the basement of Times Square at 99 Central Huaihai Road, on the 6th floor of the Super Brand Mall in Lujiazui and at the Shanghai Centre (Shop 202B), 1367 Nanjing Road (W). **Garden Books** at 325 Changle Road, near the intersection with Shaanxi Road (S), also have a great collection of imported books, as well as a decent coffee shop. It is open from 10:00am to 10:00pm (tel: 5404 8729 or 5404 8728).

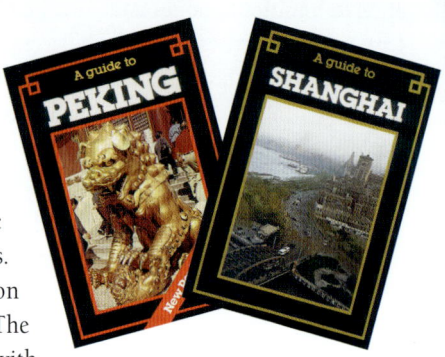

Our own Chinese Guides were first published in the USA in 1979.

The major government-run bookstores are concentrated on Fuzhou Road, amongst a cavalcade of arts and stationary stores, east of Central Tibet Road. At No. 465 **Shanghai's City of Books** is a mega-store of non-stop action, with a foreign language section on the seventh floor. Probably of most interest for the visitor is the **Shanghai Foreign Languages Bookstore** at No. 390, which features some bilingual books and Chinese language learning materials on the first floor as well as a large selection of foreign language books and periodicals on the fourth. Shanghai Book Traders, an outlet of Shanghai Foreign Languages Bookstore, has an interesting store at No. 50 Hongqiao Road in Xujiahui. It takes orders for a wide range of foreign language newspapers and periodicals (tel: 6487 3787). The **Xinhua Book Store** at No. 345 Nanjing Road (E) is also worth a visit.

The Shanghai Book Traders Used Books Bookstore at 36 Shanxi Road (S) has an eclectic assortment of foreign titles. Further places to look for second hand or antiquarian books, in English as well as in Chinese, are the antique market in the **Jubaolou** on Central Fangbang Road (weekends) and the Sunday book market within the grounds of the **Confucian Temple** on Wenmiao Road. **The Old China Hand Reading Room** at 27 Shaoxing Road has an interesting library, seated amongst an impressive collection of antique furniture and artefacts.

It serves up drinks and snacks, hosts recitals and readings and sells some fascinating books on old Shanghai—mainly by the renowned writer/historian Tess Johnston and her partner Deke Erh, who owns this unique venue.

Essentials

Photography

Digital camera services are widespread throughout the city. For those seeking professional digital and print photo services **Fuji** (tel: 6248 5895) has an outlet in a compound at No. 459 Wulumuqi Road, with an entrance just to the north of the Shanghai Hotel. **Guanlong** also provides higher quality photo processing and has a large store conveniently located at No 390 Nanjing Road (E). For the photo enthusiast the **Xingguan Photography Equipment Building** at the corner of Xietu Road and Luban Road has six floors stacked with cameras and accessories, old and new. For those in search of a new digital camera, the digital malls in the centre of Xujiahui provide a one-stop solution.

Medicines

Shanghai is crowded with pharmacies selling Western and Chinese medicines, but that doesn't mean it is easy to find a plain old aspirin tablet. Those interested in holistic and alternative medicine will find traditional pharmacies fascinating places to visit. Remedies, from time honoured recipes, are concocted from a myriad of natural plant and animal ingredients that are generally stored in giant cupboards. Traditionally patients would take the dry mixture home to infuse, but now many stores will do this for them. If you have need to get some Chinese medicines, or are just curious, pay a visit to the Caitongde Store at 450 Nanjing Road (E) or the Leiyunshang Store at 719 Nanjing Road (W). For Western medicines head for the Shanghai No. 1 Pharmacy at 616 Nanjing Road (E). Watsons, the Hong Kong based drug store, has outlets all over the city with some convenient ones located at Westgate Mall, 1038 Nanjing Road (W), the Kerry Everbright City, 218 Tianmu Road and 787 Central Huaihai Road.

Sports, Recreation and Leisure

A fitness craze has swept the city in recent years with numerous gyms and fitness facilities appearing to cater to the growing tide of affluent Shanghainese and a fast growing foreign resident population. Many of these are foreign managed and offer comparable facilities to those found anywhere in the world. Most of the big hotels have extensive and high quality fitness and sports facilities with swimming pools, steam baths, jacuzzis, saunas, gymnasiums and massage services as well as tennis and squash courts, billiards rooms and bowling alleys. The most popular city fitness centres include the **Kerry Centre Gym** at the Shanghai Kerry Centre, 1515 Nanjing Road (W) (tel: 5306 6000) and **Fitness First at Plaza** 66 (tel: 6288 0152) in the basement of the super mall at 1266 Nanjing Road (W) (tel: 6288 0152) A **Clark Hatch Fitness Centre** can be found at the Radisson Blu Xing Guo Hotel (tel: 6212 9988 ext. 3000).

As Shanghai is a city synonymous with business it is not surprising that an extensive number of golf courses have sprouted up around the city to cater to the recreational, residential and social needs of their wealthy and well-connected members. It always helps to know somebody to gain admission to the best clubs. The **Shanghai International Golf and Country Club** at Zhujiajiao in Qingpu County (tel: 5972 8111) was the first golf course to open in the city for more than 40 years. Located 50 kilometres (30 miles) west of the city this Sino-Japanese-US venture has an 18 hole, par–72 championship course designed by Robert Trent Jones. The club also offers six all-weather tennis courts, a swimming pool and a cycle path. The clubhouse, built in 19th century British colonial style, features a Japanese restaurant, sauna, pro shop and bar. This is a members-only club, with entrance fees running from about US$50,000 for individuals to US$100,000 for corporations. However short-term visitors to Shanghai staying at the Sheraton Grand Tai Ping Yang Hotel, as well as members' guests, can make use of the hotel's corporate membership privileges.

There are numerous other options to play golf on world-class courses around Shanghai. Two of the most conveniently located clubs are the **Tomson Golf Club** in Pudong, to the east, and the **Tianma Country Golf Club** set amongst the beautiful hills of Sheshan to the west of Shanghai. The Tomson Golf Club (tel: 5833 8888) is an 18-hole championship course designed by Shunsuke Kato and features, like most clubs, a wide range of five-star attendant sports and fitness facilities. The Tianma Country Golf Club boasts a world-class 27-hole championship course as well as Californian-style residential villas and excellent recreational facilities. The acclaimed **Silport Golf and Country Club** (tel: 0512 5748 1111) designed by Bobby J. Martin, has a 27-hole facility with distinct southern Chinese landscape features, and is located on the shores of Lake Dianshan at Kunshan in Jiangsu province. It is home to the Volvo China Open. **The Sun Island International Club** (tel: 5983 0888) at Shenxiang in Qingpu district is an 18-hole facility designed by Nelson Wright Haworth with 30-bay driving and greens located in a lake. For those just looking to practice their swing there's no need to go out of town as the **East Asia Golf Club** on Jianguo Road (W) (tel: 6433 1198) has a two-storey practice driving range as well as a good tennis facility.

Tennis is another sport that Shanghai has taken to heart. There are fine clubs and public facilities around town. The **Shanghai Racquet Club**, (tel: 2201 0808) at 555 Jinfeng Road, Huacao Town in the Minhang district, offers six indoor courts and seven outdoor courts managed by the Van Der Meer Tennis University. The **Xianxia Tennis Centre** (tel: 6262 6720), located at 1885 Hongqiao Road offers five courts that are illuminated for night play. Conveniently located at 516 Hengshan Road inside the Regal International East Asia Hotel, the **Shanghai International Tennis Centre** boasts two indoor and eight outdoor courts as well as a range of other sports facilities. The **Pudong Tennis Centre** (tel: 5281 5850) inside the Yuansheng Stadium at 9 Yushan Road has 10 indoor courts each equipped with state-of-the-art roofs that can be opened for outdoor play. More basic public outdoor courts are to be found at 1380 Central Fuxing Road (tel: 6431 1846) and on the grounds of the Shanghai Stadium in the Xuhui district.

The city is also making a hit on the world tennis map and has in recent years hosted the Heineken Open and Tennis Masters Series matches that have seen the likes of Philopousis, Aggassi and Kournakova grace the town. Shanghai's status as an international sporting arena was given a massive boost with the completion of a Formula 1 track at Anting in Jiading district, which opened for Grand Prix racing in 2004. However the main spectator sport unquestionably remains football (soccer) and Shanghai's Shenghua football team is one of the best in the land. Football is played at the **Shanghai Hongkou Stadium**, 444 Dong Jiang Wan Road (tel: 6540 0009), in the Hongkou district and at the landmark 80,000-seat **Shanghai Stadium** at 666 Tianyaoqiao Road (tel: 6426 6666), in the Xuhui District. Tickets can often be purchased through hotel concierge desks as well as at the grounds. You can also check out the Chinese Baseball League action by visiting the **Shanghai Sports Palace** (tel: 6265 3338) at 1860 Daduhe Road.

Paper-hunt at Shanghai. The Illustrated London News, April 12, 1873.

Recreation in Shanghai

For more active pursuits an array of participatory sports centres, amusement and theme parks have appeared offering everything from go-karting to bunjee jumping alongside regular fun rides. Tenpin bowling has taken off in a big way around the city and there are over 200 centres, with many of them open 24-hours. For horse riding enthusiasts, visit the **Huihuang Horse Riding Ranch** (tel: 5084 8898) at 517 Xinhua Road to the west of the city or the **Shanghai Equestrian Centre** (tel: 5976 3306) in Qingpu district. For a thrill **DISC KART Indoor Karting** at 326 Macau Road (tel: 6277 5641) is one of Asia's best tracks and it even has a trackside pub and café. For scuba diving the **Aquaria 21** complex (tel: 13701764231) in Changfeng Park is the place to go. For more family-oriented aquatic pleasures head for **Dino Beach** (tel: 6478 3333) in the Minhang district which has Asia's largest wave park. The **Jinjiang Amusement Park** (tel: 6436 4956) on line 1 of the metro in Minhang district was opened in the 1980s but has recently added more thrilling physical challenges. The **Shanghai Celebrity Park** (tel: 5833 4588) near the Yangpu Bridge in Pudong has the city's largest roller skating arena, a karting track and an indoor pool. For a touch of the American dream, the **American Dreamland Park** (tel: 5959 8686) in Jiading district gives a Chinese interpretation of the USA from Main Street to the Wild West. Shanghai's own real Disneyland opens in Pudong in 2014.

City Parks

The greening of Shanghai has been a major feature of city planning in recent years. Huge new green areas and parks have been rolled out across the face of the city. In the city centre these parks have often been created on land formerly occupied by housing from the early part of the last century. A huge new finger of green around Yan'an Road, the Yanzhong Greenbelt, near the People's Square was a heavily populated area until the end of the 1990s. In an area between Dagu Road and Jinling Road (E) alone, nearly 5,000 residents were moved out to make way for the new open space and lake that opened in 2001. The park is popular with early morning joggers. Thankfully not all parks are on such a monumental scale. At the beginning of 2004 it was estimated that there was seven metres of green space per capita as opposed to only 0.16 square metres 50 years ago.

However one thing that most parks share in common is that walking is not allowed on the grass - despite the massive abundance of it. Still, the city parks are not only great places for recreation but also for amusement and relaxation. They are alive with fascinating activity daylong. In fact one of the best times to visit is in the early morning, around 6:00am when groups of people assemble to exercise or practice shadow boxing or sword exercises. Parks often open before their advertised

The Yu Gardens complex lies in the heart of the Old Chinese Town.

opening times. During the daytime groups, largely of elder-folk, will gather to play Chinese chess, mah-jong and cards and some come to write poems on the concrete paths using brushes loaded with plain water.

CENTURY PARK, SHIJI GONGYUAN 世纪公园

This huge park and lake covering around 350 acres (140 hectares) in Pudong was completed to herald the dawning of the new millennium. It was designed by British consultants and its lake has been the scene for international boating events. Many visitors hire a tandem or a four-wheel bike to navigate the site, though electric buggies also cover the terrain. The park still looks immature and desolate in many sections, but it's just the place for the serious jogger. It's open from 7:00am to 6:00pm and can be reached by metro line 2.

CHANGFENG PARK, CHANGFENG GONGYUAN 长风公园

This large park across the road from the East China Normal University was opened in 1959 and inspired by the Summer Palace in Beijing. It has a large lake and hills scattered with pines and bamboo. The park is also home to Aquaria 21, a New Zealand designed aquarium with a South American theme that offers diving lessons and a swim with the sharks. The park is at 25 Daduhe Road in Putuo district and is open from 5:00am to 6:30pm.

Daning-Lingshi Park, Daning-Lingshi Gongyuan 大宁灵石公园

Work started on this new park in 2000 and it was opened two years later. Covering 680,000 square metres, with huge open spaces, wooded hillocks, lakes and a large floral avenue leading to what looks like the Arc de Triomphe in Paris it has a deliberately European flavour—though some time will be needed before it reaches maturity. It is already a favourite photographic venue for brides-to-be. The west entrance is located on the corner of Yuncheng Road and Guangzhong Road (W). The park is open from 8:00am to 5:00pm. To the east, at No. 1688 Guangzhong Road (W), is the smaller peaceful retreat of the more established **Guangzhong Park**. It is open from 6:00am to 6:00pm.

Fuxing Park, Fuxing Gongyuan 复兴公园

The former Koukaza Park (French Park) is one of the most attractive and popular parks in the city. Its attraction has been enhanced through a recent renovation by a Canadian landscape architect that brings back it French flavour. Visit at the weekend when many locals congregate come to enjoy themselves. One of the few parks to have a lawn open to the public.

Gongqing Forest Park, Gongqing Senlin Gongyuan 共青森林公园

Fronting the shores of the Huangpu River to the north of the city this park with its huge expanse of woodland, lakes and children's amusements, is a great place for an escape from the city and its manicured park districts.

Guangqi Park, Guangqi Gongyuan 光启公园

The memory of one of China's first converts to Christianity is celebrated in this attractive small park at 17 Nandan Road, near the former St. Ignatius Cathedral, in Xujiahui. Known in the English world as Paul Xu (1562–1633), his family name lives on in the name of the district (Xujiahui means Xu family meeting place). The park is on the sight of his tomb and features a newly built statue of the man and an exhibition hall.

Guilin Park, Guilin Gongyuan 桂林公园

This magnificent Chinese-styled garden with 'western characteristics' was laid out in 1931 and completed in 1934. It was built for the infamous Huang Jinrong, or 'Pockmarked Huang', who was a feared Green Gang boss as well chief of Chinese detectives for the French police. After 1937 it was ravaged by Japanese and Guomindang forces but was restored in the 1950s and 1980s. There are numerous immaculate gardens within gardens, all bounded by an elegant dragon-wall. There are two charming tea-houses within the grounds. In sharp contrast the **Kangjian Pleasure**

Park, just opposite, offers the chance to kick a football or take a boat ride on its lake. It's at 128 Guilin Road and is open from 7:00am to 5:00pm.

Xujiahui Park and Hengshan Park
Xujiahui Gongyuan and Hengshan Gongyuan 徐家汇公园　衡山公园

Whilst some old housing is to be found to the east of the park and an old mansion has been converted to an upmarket restaurant to the north, water and greenery now cover this expanse of ground that used to be a rubber tyre factory. The park was styled with the collaboration of a Canadian organisation and opened in 2003. A tall factory smokestack stands as an epitaph to its former use. Nearby, on the corner of Hengshan and Wanping Road is to be found the more established Hengshan Park. It's a quiet, small park with a European flavour and a central lawn. The parks are close to Xujiahui and Hengshan Road metro stations.

Huaihai Park, Huaihai Gongyuan 淮海公园

Established in the 1950s, this park was remodelled, expanded and reopened in 1998. Originally on the site of a Qing Dynasty graveyard, today it is very much alive with office-workers and shoppers taking a break in a beautifully landscaped area, flauntingly rich with flora and fauna. It is set amongst the expensive department stores at 177 Central Huaihai Road. The park has a well-known English corner promoted by the *Shanghai Daily* newspaper. The nearest metro station is Huangpi Road South.

Jing'an Park, Jing'an Gongyuan 静安公园

The remoulded Jing'an Park, built on the site of the Bubbling Well Cemetery, one of the largest foreign resting places of old, provides a quiet haven in a busy part of the city. It has a large central lawn and lake for viewing, restaurants and a metro stop in its heart. The centrepiece is an inner garden—the eight scene garden—which recreates long lost sights that used to exist in and around the Jing'an Temple. The park, accredited with 5 stars by the Shanghai Landscaping Administration Bureau, is open from 5:00am to 10:00pm. It's at 1649 Nanjing Road (W), next to the Jing'an Temple metro station.

Longhua Revolutionary Martyrs' Cemetery 龙华烈士陵园

Despite the sombre nature of the area's history the park, containing monuments and memorials to the revolutionary heroes who died there, is one of the most attractive and peaceful places in Shanghai. It is huge in scale, littered with colossal sculptures and huge areas of grass which can be walked upon, as well as marvellous flower beds and fountains. Its main entrance is at 180 Longhua Road West (*see* page 370).

Lu Xun Park, Lu Xun Gongyuan 鲁迅公园

This large park was established in 1905 and was formerly known as Hongkou Park. It is an area that was formerly occupied by many Japanese residents. The park has a large boating lake and an amusement park, and contains Lu Xun's Tomb and Museum (*see* page 369). The park hosts a very popular chrysanthemum show every autumn. It's at 146 Dongjiangwan Road and is open from 6:00am to 6:00pm. It can be reached on metro line 3 alighting at the Hongkou Football Stadium.

People's Park and People's Square
Renmin Gongyuan Renmin Gongyuan 人民公园 人民广场

The People's Park to the north and the People's Square to the south occupy the site of the former horse-racing ground. Before 1949 the area was also used for sports—cricket, baseball and football. The verdant park, with a large lake and many mature trees was first laid out in 1951. A recent addition to the park in the form of a hopelessly misplaced Moorish building housing the Barbarossa restaurant and bar sits aside the lake. The People's Square now houses Shanghai's new civic centre, but still has many green areas and is a very popular place for locals to stroll, romance and feed the pigeons.

People's Park, 1950s.

Shanghai Botanical Gardens
Shanghai Zhiwuyuan 上海植物园

These magnificent gardens, established in the middle of the 1970s are the largest such attraction within a city in China, with over 3,500 plant species on display including bamboo groves, pine forests and a fine orchid garden. A huge 5,000 square-metre greenhouse, housing over 2,000 tropical plants was added in 2001 and plans are underway to further enlarge the gardens. The gardens are a great place to take a picnic on the grass. They are located in the south-western suburbs of the city at 1111 Longwu Road and are open from 8:00am to 6:00pm.

The former Shanghai Recreation Ground and Race Course was transformed into People's Park in the 1950s.

Shanghai Zoo
Shanghai Dongwuyuan 上海动物园

Before 1949 the zoo site was the British created Hungjao Golf Course and it still retains many large areas of green open spaces reminiscent of the lush English countryside. For many years after liberation it remained a park but the site was converted to a zoo in 1981. The 70 hectare (173 acre site) houses over 380 species of animals and birds, including of course the Giant Panda. The zoo is open from 7:00am to 5:00pm and is at 2381 Hongqiao Road.

Shaoxing Park 绍兴公园

A small, but delightful neighbourhood park set amidst an area of 1920s and 1930s preserved architecture on Shaoxing Road (no. 62). It was specifically designed for the elder generation—many of whom can be seen exercising and having fun in the mornings and evenings.

Taipingqiao Park, Taipingqiao Gongyuan 太平桥公园

In tandem with the massive redevelopment of an old neighbourhood into Shanghai's trendiest eating and recreational area at Xintiandi a new park was added to the east of the development. The park contains the city centre's largest lake, covering 12,000 square-metres. The area is particularly attractive at night and is near the Huangpi Road (S) metro station.

Zhabei Park, Zhabei Gongyuan 闸北公园

A huge golden teapot sits at the entrance to this attractive park on the corner of New Gonghe Road and Luochuan Road (W). An annual tea festival has been held in the park since 1994. In an enclosed lake area tame cranes accept minnows from the locals and people can be seen fishing with bamboo rods. The park dates back to 1913 when it was used as a cemetery for a revolutionary martyr named Song Jiaoren, who was assassinated following the overthrow of the Qing Dynasty. The park was rebuilt after being destroyed in the Cultural Revolution and opened in 1981. Song's statue is in the park, which is open from 6:00am to 6:00pm.

Zhongshan Park, Zhongshan Gongyuan 中山公园

Lying to the west of the city and built in 1914, this park was known to Shanghai's local residents as Caofeng Park and to its foreign residents as Jessfield Park. However ordinary Chinese were not permitted to enter until 1928. A church in the park was the seat of the Bishop of Shanghai in days gone-by and a corner of the park was formerly occupied by St. John's University, Shanghai's first university. The park is great for recreational purposes as its large grassed areas are open to the public. The park also has a large amusement park for kids. It's at 780 Changning Road, near line 2 and line 3 metro stops, and is open from 6:00am to 5:00pm.

The Shanghai Persona

It has long been a cliché that the cleverest people in China come from Shanghai, but when the British Consul-General asked the mayor of Shanghai if this generalization was true, the answer he got was, 'No, the cleverest people come to Shanghai'.

The mayor has a point: Shanghai is a melting pot. Even the most Shanghainese of Shanghai families have come not all that long ago from somewhere else. The Shanghainese has something of many regions in China. Yet, for all that he/she is of 'motley' stock, the Shanghainese has a distinct identity.

But the Shanghainese have not always had the same image. In the second half of the 19th century, they compared unfavourably with the Cantonese, whose city was the first port in China to be opened to foreign trade, and who were thus the first people to gain any familiarity with Western ways. This was how three Europeans wrote of the people of Shanghai when they arrived at the port in the mid-1800s: 'The natives of this part of China appear as nearly devoid of intellect as is compatible with the existence of human conformation. In this respect, as in their lighter complexion and manner of dressing (especially in the particular of wearing shoes and stockings, and long gowns instead of jackets), the Shanghai Chinese differ from the brisk and handy natives of the South.'

The love of dress has persisted, but the rest of the image has changed with time. As the foreigner and native found a common interest in the pursuit of profit in the foreign concessions, it began to be felt that the Shanghainese were almost too clever. Several lasting traits, many of them exemplified by the compradore, were initiated during this period. A bent for money-making and an admiration of things Western became part of the Shanghai persona.

A unique creation of Shanghai was true biculturalism, something no other Chinese community, not even Hong Kong, has succeeded in producing. Before the Communist revolution locked China into her own culture, there grew up in Shanghai a class of people who could truly take on the manners and thinking of another culture without the debasement of their own. This is again happening today, particularly among the younger Shanghainese.

Most things in China reach their apogee in Shanghai—capitalism in the pre-revolution period, Gang-of-Fourism during the Cultural Revolution. It is no wonder the Shanghainese think themselves special—they have dictated fashion to China for decades and continue to do so. How all this will affect business and social relations with the new foreign adventurer and entrepreneur—only time will tell.

Churches and Worship

Anyone interested in discovering how many Shanghainese spend their Sunday would find a visit to a church very instructive. It can be a moving experience to witness the faithful resuming an aspect of their lives which had so long been denied to them. A number of Protestant and Catholic churches have re-opened in recent years that have also seen the rejuvenation of numerous temples and mosques. The information below will give you a guide to some church services around the city. Many of the churches are also buildings of great historical interest and can often be visited outside of the regular service times. For places of Taoist, Buddhist and Islamic worship please refer to individual entries in the Index.

Catholic Churches

Christ the King Catholic Church (Tianzhutang Shanghai Jiaoqu Junwangtang), 361 Julu Road, (tel: 6256 6442). A modern church centre with services at 8:30am on Sundays. The church is often publicised as holding English services, though it no longer does and callers will be redirected to St. Peter's Church nearby.

Datian Road Catholic Church (Datian Lu Tianzhutang), 370 Datian Road. Services held at 8:30am on Sundays. This impressive church lies tucked away from view for most of the week amongst an unassuming assemblage of old houses, unknown to most foreign residents (and Chinese for that matter) in the city. It was originally St. Theresa's Irish Catholic Church in days long gone-by.

Dongjiadu Cathedral (Dongjiadu Tianzhutang), 185 Dongjiadu Road, (tel: 6378 7214). Mass is held every morning at 7:00am Shanghai's oldest and one of its most beautiful places of worship was established by Jesuit missionaries, headed by Bishop Besco, with building work taking four years from the laying of its corner stone in 1849. It once housed an unusual organ made of bamboo pipes. Located to the south-east of the original walled city, the magnificent Spanish Baroque style façade and interior have been meticulously restored in recent years. The bas-relief on the upper sections of the walls adopt traditional Chinese emblems and the bell tower still houses all four original bells.

St. Peter's Catholic Church (Boduolutang), 270 Chongqing Road (S), (tel: 6467 8282). The church is located at the intersection with Hefei Road and re-opened in 1992. English services which are highly popular with the resident foreign community, are held at 5:00pm on Saturdays and at 10:00am on Sundays.

Xujiahui Cathedral (Xujiahui Tianzhutang), 158 Puxi Road, (tel: 6464 8896). There are daily morning services starting between 5:30am and 7:00am with an 8:00am service added on Sundays. The cathedral is one of the major landmarks in Shanghai. The former St. Ignatius Cathedral was at the core of the Jesuit missionary area founded there in the 1840s. The present building was completed in 1910 and has the capacity to hold a 3,000 congregation. Its spires reach a height of nearly 57 metres (187 feet).

PROTESTANT CHURCHES

All Saints Church (Zhusheng Tang) 425 Central Fuxing Road, (tel: 6385 0906). Services are held each Sunday at 7:30am, 9:30am and 7:00pm. This was originally an American Episcopal church built in 1925. It's a charming church with oak-beamed vaulted ceilings.

Shanghai Community Church (Guoji Libaitang), 53 Hengshan Road, (tel: 6437 6576). Services are held at 7:30am, 10:00am and 7:00pm on Sundays. This was originally the American Community Church, on which work started in 1925—though the grounds and buildings are demonstrably English. It is a non-denominational church and translation machines are sometimes used for services.

Shanghai Grace Church (Huai'en Tang), 375 Shaanxi Road (N), (tel: 6253 9394). Services are held on Saturday and Sunday mornings at 9:00am and at 7:00pm on Sundays. The church is unusual in that it was completed in 1941 as the city came under Japanese occupation. It was reopened on Christmas day in 1980 and can accommodate over 1,000 people.

Dongjiadu Cathedral—Shanghai's oldest surviving place of Christian worship.

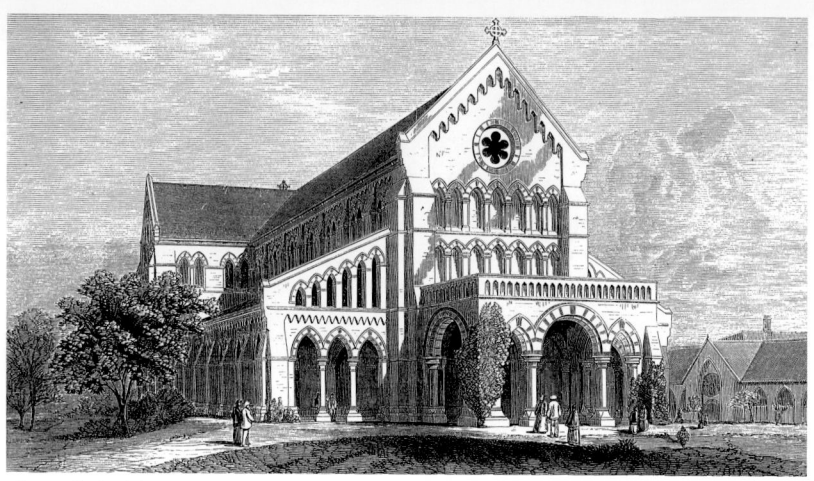
The Cathedral (Trinity Church), Shanghai. The Illustrated London News, March 10, 1877.

St. Joseph's Church (Sichuan Nan Lu Jiaotang), 36 Sichuan Road (S), (tel: 6328 0293). The church is open for worship on Saturdays and Sundays from 6:00am to 7:00am. This magnificent building dates back to 1860 and also around it was the first school for the education of foreign girls in the 19th century. It continues to operate as a day school for local children.

Kunshan Church (Jingling Jiaotang), 135 Kunshan Road, (tel: 5539 1720). This magnificent church in the Hongkou district was built in 1923 and holds services at 8:00am on Sundays.

Mu'en Church (Mu'en Tang), 316 Central Tibet Road, (tel: 6322 5069).This church has services from 7:30am on Sundays as well as weekday services. Formerly known as the Moore Methodist Church, it was established in 1887 and rebuilt in 1931 to seat over 1,000 worshippers. The latter design was by Laszlo Hudec, Shanghai's most famous architect. Charlie Song, the patriarch of the legendary Song family was pastor in the days when Dr. Sun Yat-sen was found amongst the congregation. In more recent times the church hosted the consecration of two new bishops in 1988—the first occurrence in over 30 years—and has also hosted the American evangelist Billy Graham.

Zhabei Church (Jidujiao Zhabeitang), 8 Baotong Road, (tel: 5662 9409). Sunday services are held at 7:30am and 9:30am. This lively church is just north of the railway station and was reopened in 1982.

The former **Holy Trinity Cathedral** that occupies most of the block bounded by Jiangxi, Jiujiang, Hankou and Central Henan Roads re-opened for worship in 2013, following a long and careful restoration designed to bring it back to how it was in the late 1920s—the period when it was last refurbished. The restoration stands out as being one of the city's greatest achievements in historic preservation. The first Episcopal church in Shanghai was built on the site in 1847, but the church building we see today, based on the designs of Sir Gilbert Scott, one of England's most celebrated architects, was completed in 1869. It became the cathedral for the Diocese of North China in 1875 and its bell tower was added in 1893. Its spire, destroyed in the Cultural Revolution, was rebuilt as part of the project.

Disused Churches

The former **Union Church** is to be found on Suzhou Road (S) just before the intersection with Yuanmingyuan Road near the north end of the Bund. This was the former home to the Shanghai Boy's Brigade and was open to all denominations. The church was originally organised by one of China's most prominent missionaries—the Rev. Dr. Medhurst and later presided over by another famous man of faith, the Rev. C.E. Darwent. The main part of the church, in early English style, was built in 1884. Despite being in ruins and further damaged by fire in early 2007, the church building, using salvaged material, was being entirely rebuilt in 2010. It is unlikely to reopen for worship, but is expected to have some civic function.

The Jewish Community

Shanghai's Jewish community is again beginning to swell and whilst the former synagogues are used for other purposes, a new Jewish Community Centre has been established in the Hongqiao area. Shabbat Services are held at 6:30pm on Fridays and at 10:00am on Saturdays. For further information contact Rabbi Shalom Greenberg on 6278 0225 or visit the website www.chinajewish.org. Dinner and lunch are provided, in a communal setting, immediately following services. A Chabad Jewish Centre has also been established in Pudong (tel: 5878 2008).

With regard to the former synagogues the Ohel Rachel Synagogue at 500 Shaanxi Road (N) is overgrown with ivy and is used as a book repository. A guard at the gate prevents visitors from getting close—though President Clinton did manage a visit in 1998, it has been occasionally opened to the Jewish community, particularly during the World Expo period, with a view to its return to sacred use. The smaller Ohel Moshe Synagogue has been converted into the Jewish Refugee Museum, located in the Hongkou district (*see* pages 417, 421).

For details of tours of Jewish Shanghai visit www.shanghai-jews.com.

Other Religious Edifices

There are a few architectural treasures that once were places of worship, but more latterly have been home to restaurants and bars. In the Hongkou district, where around 20,000 Japanese lived at the time of the Second World War, a magnificently decorated former Japanese Buddhist shrine sits hidden away at 8 Zhapu Road. Grand, ornate Russian Orthodox Church architecture can be seen at the former Mission Church at 55 Xinle Road and the former St. Nicolas Church at 16 Gaolan Road.

SHANGHAI RECALLED —by Richard Hughes

It is impossible for the visitor to spend a dull day in Shanghai. I lived there in 1940, made regular visits when I was based in Peking as a reporter in 1956–57, and made another brief return after the passage of a further 16 years in 1973.

There have of course been many changes in life and living. For the locals, it is a far better city. Gone today are the 1940 battalions of deformed and diseased beggars and the armies of child street-walkers. Gone are the terrible factories of forced child-labour. Gone are the hundreds of frozen corpses in the backalleys each winter.

The ghosts of the western traders have been driven out of the old Shanghai Club by a huge Budda-like statue of the late Chairman Mao. The Club, now called the Dongfeng (East Wind), serves as a stopover hostelry for Chinese travellers. My old memories ached to discover that the celerbrated Long Bar (110 feet) had been divided into three sections, over which icecream and peanuts were available for non-member children and women, previously banned from the premises. The once sacrosanct smoking room, opposite the Long Bar, where honourable members dozed after a heavy tiffin draped under copies of The Times from London, is now a communal overnight dormitory, with rolled mattresses and dangling underwear.

The old Cathay Hotel is now the Peace Hotel. The old racecourse—already a park and a people's square in 1956—is the roof of the largest and deepest air-raid shelter in Shanghai, following underground the winding course of the city's most famous shopping street, Nanjing Road. Broadway Mansions—now Shanghai Mansions—has the most efficient elevator service in China; from its lofty roof, one can salute furtively the ancient abandoned British Consulate, which is now a store and a handsome restaurant for the Seamen's Club.

Not even veteran Party cadres could recall the sinister names of Delmonte's or Farren's—former gambling casinos, now schools for dramatic and theatrical training. 'Do you remember "Demon" Hyde, the tough San Francisco boss of Delmonte's in the forties?' No-one does. . .

Laundry hangs in public from the verandahs of millionaire residences which have survived along the former Avenue Joffre in the old French Concession—now converted into worker's tenements. The street once called 'Bloody Alley' is eminently respectable now; once it was a notorious street-walkers' beat. The old French Club was 'closed for repairs' when I squinted at it in 1973, but now has been reopened as the Jinjiang Club, with an indoor swimming pool, bowling alley and billiard rooms, a huge ballroom, and high-class French cuisine in the restaurant. It is intended primarily to cater for tourists but local people come for dinner and evening swimming. They can even play mahjong there—forbidden elsewhere in China.

One of my favourite eating places in Shanghai was the Xinya Restaurant in Nanjing Road. I used to go there regularly. The name in English has been removed from the door, but I had not forgotten the number—719.

There was, I thought, little change inside the crowded two floors of the restaurant. The same diners—mostly family groups—were still eating noisily, gaily, comfortably, abundantly. The same stout barman—it seemed to me—was pouring the same lively Tsingtao beer into the same glass mugs. And there was the same rich enduring fragrance of good Chinese cooking.

'The food is the same,' I was assured by an old waiter, who unbelievably remembered me after 16 years. He eyed me sharply when I asked for a whisky. He brought me a half empty bottle of White Horse, and with difficulty prised open its long-sealed and semi-embalmed stopper.

'This will cost you more than the dinner,' he warned me, lifting the familiar silver egg-cup measure. 'We don't get any more whisky now. The price is fixed.'

He was right. The dinner—luscious prawns, bird's nest soup and tender beef with oyster sauce—cost me maybe US$1. The two straight whiskies cost more than US$2. Just before I left, my friend looked swiftly around, then, interposing his body between my cubicle and the cashier, poured me a third whisky—on the honourable house! We smiled together.

You can't tip waiters in China now. But he could tip me—in Shanghai. There's no place like it.

A menu from the Red House restaurant, one of few foreign eateries in the city in 1978.

Journalist Richard Hughes, now immortalised as Craw in Le Carré's bestseller **The Honourable Schoolboy**, left his native Australia for Asia in 1940. One of the best-known pressmen in the Far East, his career as a correspondent spanned over 40 years. Other books written by Hughes include **Hong Kong: Borrowed Place—Borrowed Time** and **Foreign Devil: Thirty Years of Reporting in the Far East**.

This essay originally appeared in the first edition of the *Odyssey Guide to Shanghai* (1979).

THE RESTRICTED AREA

Last week I received a letter from Heinz, who lives in the Restricted Area (ghetto) in Honkew. I had met Heinz at a friend's party when European Jewish refugees still moved freely in Shanghai. He is a quiet, pleasant, nice-looking boy, unfortunately the only member of his family to escape the Nazis. At the time he was only 15 years old.

Heinz begged me to come and visit him since he was refused a permit to leave the area in which European Jewish refugees are confined, whereas outsiders like me are free to go in and out. I did want to see Heinz very much indeed but dreaded the demeaning experience of bowing low to Japanee sentries on Garden Bridge and, possibly, being roughed up by them. I pleaded with Mama to accompany me and after some resistance she agreed because she too is very fond of Heinz and very sorry for all the misery he has to endure. In fact, last winter she worried so much about his freezing in an unheated room that she ferreted out an almost new leather fur-lined coat for him, which he wore during that day and used as a cover at night. He is a fine looking boy with smooth clear skin and regular features and he does look very manly in his brown coat.

Mama and I set off to Honkew carrying a paper bag full of groceries, among which was a jar of sesame-seed butter, of which Heinz is particularly fond and which many people use instead of real butter (difficult to get even in the black market).

We crossed the Garden Bridge by tram without undue incidents. The tram halted in front of the Japanese guards, all passengers bowed and the bayonet-clasping soldiers waved us on with their free hand. Mama and I looked at each other with deep relief.

When we arrived at Hongkew, we saw that barbed wire barricades had been erected around the Restricted Area with several control points left open for entry and exit. These gates are policed by armed Japanese guards and the auxilary force, the Pao Chia. In Hongkew the responsibility of the Pao Chia is to enforce strict curfew regulations, check passes, and keep order. It is headed by a German-Jewish "director" who has some 3,500 refugees under his command but, of course, the real power is in the hands of the Japanese, who hold a very tight rein over the entire auxiliary force.

Heinz waited for us some 20 yards away from the gate. He was very excited to see us and is very attached to my mother, who always treats him with great kindness. How he must suffer to be here in such awful circumstances with no family at all. However, he never complains and always acts pleasant, smiling rather shyly. Poor, poor boy!

Heinz explained to us that within the ghetto itself people are more or less left to their own devices but serious problems arise when applications are submitted for exit permits. Although Papa had somehow managed to send Heinz the "Certificate of Employment" required by the Japanese, the response to Heinz's attempts to leave the ghetto to work outside was a resounding and humiliating slap on the face.

"I will not try again," Heinz told us. "I really cannot go through this once more!" Mama and I sympathized with his attitude.

The refugees are segregated in 40 square blocks of crumbling buildings (some four blocks wide and 12 blocks deep). The streets—or rather narrow lanes—are strewn with rubble and refuse. Most houses have no toilets nor kitchens for families who live crowded together in single rooms. Tenants are forced to use outside toilets, buy drinking water from street vendors, go to the few public baths, and cook in the lanes or on flat roofs using Japanese "hibachi" stoves. Needless to say there is no heating in winter. In view of all this, Mama and I were not surprised that Heinz did not invite us to visit his room, which he described as "tiny, stifling in summer and freezing in winter, with missing windowpanes and a warped door that never closes." There are two canvas camp beds side by side, one for Heinz and one for an ailing old man.

Fortunately, they do have a toilet in the hal l (for 12 lodgers) as well as a sink with running cold water—a luxury! Both Heinz and his room-mate receive one free meal a day distributed by the Jewish "Kitchen Fund". Only children are given an additional evening supper. With so many horrible diseases in Shanghai, Mama

The Shanghai Jewish Chronicle, English edition. Its counterpart was the longest running German-language Jewish newspaper in Shanghai (1939–49)—founded by editor Ossie Levin.

worries what will happen to the refugees who are undernourished and not resistant to illness.

Still, in spite of all the tensions and insufficient resources, the refugees did succeed in organizing a functioning community—the Gemeinde. Committees regulate the distributioon of dry foods, clothing, medical supplies (bought at black market prices from Japanese and Chinese sources). Many miniature lending libraries have been set up where books in German, Yiddish, Polish, and English are available. Three daily German newspapers are published, as well as one in Polish and Yiddish, on paper whose quality varies from poor to deplorable, according to what is available. An enthusiastic theater company has been formed, as well as an operetta group which plans to initiate the coming season with The Gypsy Baron. There is an outstanding symphony orchestra that always performs to a full house. Hospitals have been set up in ramshackle buildings and refugee doctors have founded the Association of European Doctors. Every effort is being made to provide children with adequate education: English is the medium of instruction while Hebrew is taught in special classes. There is even an ORT School with pupils aged 14 to 60 who attend free-of-charge six months courses in carpentry, electricity, and mechanics. Most of the tools they use are manufactured by the students themselves and some of their products are sold to raise funds for the school.

Published by China Intercontinental Press, 2001.

> Rena Krasno, Strangers Always, A Jewish Family in Wartime Shanghai.
> Pacific View Press Berkeley. © 1992, Rena Krasno.
> Reprinted with kind permission from Rena Krasno.

Shanghai Nightlife

Nightlife for the foreign visitor here, as in the rest of China, is very limited. In sharp contrast to the old image of Shanghai as Sin City, there are now no nightclubs, cabarets or big dance halls. Many local restaurants stop taking orders around 7.30 p.m., and the hotels finish only a little later but hotel cafés stay open until around midnight. The former French Club near the Jinjiang Hotel—considered the most chic of all the pre-1949 clubs—has recently been reopened to foreigners as the Jinjiang Club. For an entrance fee of only a few yuan visitors can use the Club's surprisingly extensive facilities—swimming pool, Western restaurant, bowling alley, games rooms and even pinball machines.

Odyssey Guide, 1979

Advertising on Nanjing Road.

Classics and Conversions
—Boarding in Shanghai —*The Ginger Griffin*

Shanghai boasts some of the finest modern hotels in China, if not Asia, just as it did in its hey-day in the 1930s. Fortuitously many of the hotels built in the earlier part of the last century continue to function. Most of them still retain their original architectural exterior and whilst many interiors have been robbed of their former glory some have survived. Shanghai offers an unparalleled range of places to lodge in an historic setting—not only in its established hotels but also in some classic houses that have since been converted to hostelries.

When the Cathay Hotel opened in 1929 it was regarded as the best hotel in the Far East. Shanghai's Bund-side art deco icon operated as the north wing of the Peace Hotel from 1956 until April 2007, when it was closed to be reopened as the Fairmont Peace Hotel in

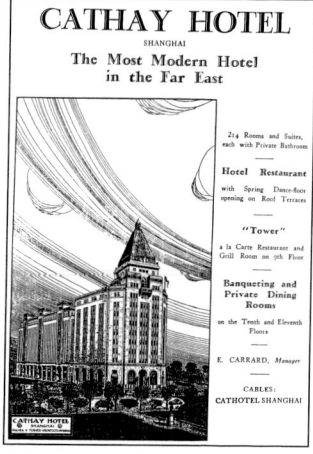

Advertisement for Sir Victor Sassoon's Cathay Hotel, now the Fairmont Peace Hotel.

2010. The Cathay Hotel embodied the personal vision of Sir Victor Sassoon who, having moved the opium enriched family fortune from Bombay, set out to transform Shanghai into a modern cosmopolitan city with a spectacular new skyline. The hotel was practically built around an arsenal of Lalique lights imported from Paris. Then, as now, the eighth floor was the main public area and an extravagant Chinese grill-room was fashioned in 1933. The dragon, representing the emperor, assumes a central position in the design of the restaurant's ceiling panels—which were adopted from door panels in The Forbidden City. The eighth floor also housed the main dining room and ballroom. It provided the setting for Sir Victor's eccentric fancy dress parties where he could often be seen yielding a whip or cane at his circus and school parties.

The south building of the Peace Hotel was originally the Palace Hotel, fully completed in 1909 to a locally interpreted Victorian Renaissance design. With 110 guest rooms, all with baths, it was the largest and most commodious of its time. During the 1930s the Tea Lounge, with its 18th century style decor, attracted the elite of Shanghai and was simply referred to as the 'Shanghai Rendezvous'. Its features are still there to see in the former ground floor restaurant. Plans to demolish the hotel in 1939 were suspended as the city fell under greater Japanese control and it became part of the Peace Hotel in 1965. It reopened as the Swatch Art Peace Hotel for invited guest artists in 2010.

At the north end of the Bund, just over Suzhou Creek, the Astor House (Pujiang) Hotel is Shanghai's oldest hostelry. It was first established in 1858 by P. F. Richards and although the current management like to play on the Richard's Hotel theme, he only actually only owned the premises for three years. The present building is actually composed of two sections dating from 1893 and from 1911. Again, it was the best and largest hotel in China, advertising itself as the 'Waldorf Astoria of the Far East,' with over 200 spacious rooms and host to the rich and famous including King George of England, the Aga Khan and Wallis Simpson. Nine spacious deluxe rooms were added in 2004 and it is now classed as a three star hotel. Many of the original fittings remain and the management has done a great job in restoring, rather than destroying, the hotel. The hotel also has one room, No. 103, which retains its rich dark-wood panelling and fittings endowing it as the oldest hotel room in Shanghai. It is one of the most atmospheric and eclectic hotels in China.

Next door to the Astor House Hotel is the monolithic art deco Broadway Mansions, originally opened in 1934 as a residential hotel for bachelors, which is today a popular tourist hotel. Another art deco spectacle, the Metropole Hotel on Fuzhou Road, was built with commercial visitors in mind and opened in 1932. Whilst the Metropole's appearance resembled that of a New York skyscraper—another of Sir Victor Sassoon's interests, the Cathay Mansions, wore a very British face. The Gothic inspired building was opened in 1929. Besides containing 280 rooms and apartment suites, there were private dining rooms, lounges and a commanding roof garden. It was a popular home for the foreign regiments based in the city. After 1949 the hotel was one of only two Shanghai hostelries allowed to receive foreign guests. Its ultimate 'friendship' visitor was the late Richard Nixon who stayed there during his historic 1972 visit. The hotel has been renovated to five-star standard and is now known as the Old Jinjiang Hotel.

Another landmark art deco hotel is to be found just opposite People's Park on Nanjing Road (W). More at home in Manhattan, the three and a half million dollar, 22-storey Park Hotel was the tallest structure between London and Tokyo when it opened in 1934—and it remained that way for over half a century. Shanghai's most celebrated architect, the Hungarian Laszlo Hudec, was commissioned to design this epitaph to international modernity and native enterprise. The Sky Terrace on the 14th floor hosted parties in flamboyant fashion graced by the highest Chinese officials, including members of the legendary Song family. Nearby the Pacific Hotel started life as the China United Assurance office and residential building when it opened in 1926. It was designed by an American architect, Mr Elliot Hazzard, and bears a passing similarity to the White House in Washington.

Most of Shanghai's hotels were conceived and built by foreign interests. However, two notable art deco hotels have survived that were built by the Chinese themselves. The New Asia Hotel decided to break away from the prevailing standards of Chinese hotels by barring mah-jong, women of ill-fame and opium. Opened in 1934 and situated on Tiendong and North Sichuan Road (N), it was a favourite lunchtime haunt for Shanghai's diplomatic circle. The New Yangtsze Hotel (now the Langham Yangtze Boutique, Shanghai) on Hankou Road, which opened in 1933, was unusual in style and decoration. Its walls were painted yellow and blue and its rooms were furnished in a cocktail of 21 modernistic styles. The hotel's dining room and ballroom, patterned on Chinese restaurants found in Europe, hosted a Honolulu dance band!

The interesting architecture of Broadway Mansions.

After 1949 some of Shanghai's mansions, set in walled areas of parkland, were converted to villa hotels to entertain high-level dignitaries including Chairman Mao. Some are now open to the public. The Ruijin Guest House on Ruijin No. 2 Road was formerly the huge estate of H. E. Morriss. Morriss' father owned Shanghai's leading English language newspaper, the *North China Daily News* and was a key figure in the city's horse-racing establishment. There are numerous architecturally magnificent villas here that not only offer rooms, but also a variety of food and drink delights. A few blocks away an annex to the hotel is to be found in the Tai Yuan Villa complex. Its centrepiece is a magnificent French mansion with nine guest rooms. It is familiarly known as the 'Marshall Residence,' as it is where General George Marshall stayed following the Second World War as he attempted to negotiate a truce between the Communists and Nationalists.

Another fine mansion, this time in English style, can be found inside the grounds of the Butterfield & Swire Company property allocated for its China manager—previously known as 'Hazelwood', but often referred to as 'The Palace' by Shanghai's foreign public. It was designed by the famous Welsh architect Clough Williams-Ellis, who oversaw the construction from the UK and never actually visited Shanghai. The building, set in fine grounds, is now part of the Radisson Plaza Xing Guo Hotel.

Other fine villa hotels, set in secluded parks and woodland, are to be found in the Hongqiao area near the Shanghai Zoo. The Hongqiao State Guest House incorporates many old residences that were once owned by the elite of Shanghai's business circles as does the nearby the Xijiao Guesthouse. Their settings are very reminiscent of the English countryside.

Though not part of an estate, one of Shanghai's most eclectic buildings was converted to a hotel in 2002. A fairytale-like architectural foible that was once the home of British shipping magnate, Eric Moller, stands on the corner of Shaanxi Road (S) and Yan'an Road (W). Rumours abound that the castle-like building was based on a dream his daughter had. The building, completed in 1936, was until recently used by the Communist Youth League. It has been 'restored' in a typically ostentatious Shanghai fashion. Some art deco apartment buildings have also been converted to hotels, namely the Hengshan Hotel (formerly the Picardie Apartments) on Hengshan Road and the Jing'an Guesthouse (formerly Haig Court) on Huashan Road.

There are also a few small establishments that come close to being described as a 'bed and breakfast.' The Old House Inn located down a quiet lane at 351 Huashan Road, with its 12 comfortable bedrooms and contemporary restaurant, has become a favourite for those looking for an alternative to the five-star experience. No. 9

at Lane 355 Jianguo Road (W) offers five bedrooms in a superb art deco family home. Another guesthouse in a converted 1920s property (the Ling Long Hotel) can be found at 939 Yan'an Road (W). On a grander scale, a number of upmarket boutique hotels have opened up in historic properties around the city. Leading the pack in terms of opulence and sophistication is the Mansion Hotel in the former French Concession. Another great addition to what, for sure, is going to be a growing inventory of 'heritage' hotels is the Bund Garden Shanghai in the former Deanery of the Holy Trinity Cathedral. Jia Shanghai, located in a 1925 apartment block, has become a hip place to stay in the city centre at 931 Nanjing Road (W). It's a sister to the renowned Jia in Hong Kong. Encouragingly, some large art deco buildings near the Bund have been converted into hotels recently. The Villas Hotel is housed in a beautiful office building, formerly occupied by The Commercial Press, at 306 Guangdong Road and the Motel 268 occupies over 200 rooms of the former premises of the Shanghai Commercial Savings Bank at 50 Ningbo Road. However, none can match the grandeur of The Waldorf Astoria Club, one of two buildings of the Waldorf Astoria Shanghai on the Bund, which now occupies the premises of the legendary Shanghai Club.

Eric Moller's fantasy home is now a hotel.

Right: *Historically Shanghai has been the home to some of the finest hotels in Asia and the same holds true today. Shangri-La Hotel, Pudong.*

THE RED GUARDS

The streets were in a ferment of activity. Groups of Red Guards were explaining to clusters of onlookers the meaning and purpose of the Cultural Revolution. Other Red Guards were stopping buses, distributing leaflets, lecturing the passengers, and punishing those whose clothes they disapproved of. Most bicycles had red cards bearing Mao's quotations on the handlebars; riders of the few without them were stopped and given warning. On the sidewalks, the Red Guards led the people to shout slogans. Each group of Red Guards was accompanied by drums and gongs and large reproductions of Mao's portrait mounted on stands. At many street corners, loudspeakers were blaring revolutionary songs at intervals. In my proletarian outfit of old shirt and wide trousers, I blended with the scene and attracted no special attention. I walked steadily in the direction of the bank.

Suddenly I was startled to see the group of Red Guards right in front of me seize a pretty young woman. While one Red Guard held her, another removed her shoes and a third one cut the legs of her slacks open. The Red Guards were shouting, "Why do you wear shoes with pointed toes? Why do you wear slacks with narrow legs?"

"I'm a worker! I'm not a member of the capitalist class! Let me go!" The girl was struggling and protesting.

In the struggle, the Red Guards removed her slacks altogether, much to the amusement of the crowd that had gathered to watch the scene. The onlookers were laughing and jeering. One of the Red Guards slapped the girl's face to stop her from struggling. She sat on the dusty ground and buried her face in her arms. Between sobs she murmured, "I'm not a member of the capitalist class!"

Nien Cheng, Life and Death in Shanghai *(Grafton Books, 1986)*

Nien Cheng (1915–2009) was educated at Yenching University in Beijing and the London School of Economics. She was married to Dr. K'ang Chi Cheng, a diplomat of the Nationalist Government. In 1949, Dr. Cheng became the General Manager of Shell International Petroleum Company's Shanghai Office. Nien Cheng also joined the Shell Office as Advisor to Management. During the Cultural Revolution, Chinese employees of foreign firms were accused of being unpatriotic and Nien Cheng was held in solitary confinement for more than six years. In 1973, she was released from prison, and declared innocent of any wrongdoing in 1978. Nien Cheng left China in 1980, and from 1981 to 1983 lived in Ottawa, Canada. In 1983 she emigrated to the United States.

Practical Information
Hotels in Shanghai

Country Phone Code: 0086 City Code: (0)21

In recent years Shanghai has experienced a boom in hotel building and with the World Expo in 2010, and the city's desire to overtake Hong Kong as Asia's leading exhibition and convention destination, the growth is set to continue. Deluxe accommodation, catering for the needs of both business and tourist visitors, can now be found across the city. The following list of hotels, in alphabetical order, is divided into those located in Puxi (the more established area to the west of the Huangpu River) and those in the Pudong area (east of the river).

Puxi

Andaz Shanghai 上海安达仕酒店 上海嵩山路88号
88 Songshan Road. Tel. 2310 1234
http://shanghai.andaz.hyatt.com/hyatt/hotels-shanghai-andaz/index.jsp?null
The super chic Andaz is the first of the Hyatt's new collection of contemporary, boutique-inspired hotels in Asia, set in trendy Xintiandi. 307 spacious guest rooms, an all-day patisserie and Hai Pai, its signature restaurant offering a combination of French bistro and Shanghainese brasserie, as well as 11 event venues.

Astor House Hotel 浦江饭店 黄浦路15号
15 Huangpu Road. Tel. 6324 6388; www.pujianghotel.com
Once the finest in Asia the Astor House Hotel has reinvented itself as three star hotel recently. However, its small number of excellently appointed modern rooms and its historic grand 'celebrity rooms,' with original art deco furniture, put it in a class of its own. You can even have breakfast in the restored ballroom, which housed the Shanghai Stock Exchange for most part of the 1990s.

Banyan Tree Shanghai On The Bund 上海外滩悦榕庄 上海海平路19号
119 Haiping Road. Tel. 2509 1188
www.banyantree.com/en/shanghai_on_the_bund/
Positioned on the banks of Huangpu River in Hongkou this 130-room urban resort features luxurious accommodation, its legendary Spa, warm Asian hospitality and a rooftop bar.

Bund Garden Shanghai 上海外滩花园 上海汉口路200号
200 Hankou Road. Tel. 6329 8800
Occupying the Deanery of the former Holy Trinity this heritage hotel has just nine guest rooms. It features a garden and patio overlooking the former Cathedral and the Cathedral Boys School (where the late J. G. Ballard author of Empire of the Sun was taught).

Four Seasons Hotel 四季酒店 上海威海路500号
500 Weihai Road. Tel. 6256 8888; www.fourseasons.com
Conveniently located in the heart of town within walking distance of Nanjing Road (W) and Central Huaihai Road, the Four Seasons has 439 spacious guest rooms and suites. Superb dining options include an all day Asian/Italian restaurant, a Cantonese and Shanghainese restaurant, one of the city's best steak houses and an excellent lobby buffet. The 37th floor lounge offers excellent live jazz.

Gran Melia Hotel Shanghai 上海新天哈瓦那大酒店 上海录家嘴环路1288号
1288 Lujiazui Ring Road. Tel. 3867 8888
http://www.gran-melia-shanghai.com/en/index.html
The first Gran Melia property in China, located in the Lujiazui financial district features 686 rooms, Spanish and Italian cuisine, as well as Cuban cabaret.

Hengshan Moller Villa Hotel 衡山马勒别墅饭店 上海陕西南路30号
30 Shaanxi Road (S). Tel. 6247 8881; www.mollervilla.com
Occupying one of Shanghai's most eclectic historic buildings, this recently converted hotel offers individually decorated rooms and suites. The fairy tale castle-like structure was previously owned by a British shipping magnate named Eric Moller and completed in 1936. Today it is partnered by a new wing and managed by the local Hengshan Group.

Hilton Shanghai 上海静安希尔顿酒店 上海华山路250号
250 Huashan Road. Tel. 6248 0000; www.hilton.com
The 43-storey Hilton is conveniently located in the former French Concession near to Jing'an Temple and has 772 rooms. The hotel is noted for its range and quality of food in its 10 food and beverage outlets. Besides the Atrium Café—a most attractive 24-hour coffee shop with natural lighting and a garden setting—the hotel also offers Sichuanese, Cantonese, Shanghainese, Japanese and Italian cuisine. It has the most comprehensive spa in the city with its own bar serving healthy food and drinks.

Hongqiao State Guest Hotel 虹桥国营宾馆 上海虹桥路1591号
1591 Hongqiao Road. Tel. 6219 8855
Set in massive and beautifully landscaped grounds near the conference district in Hongqiao, this long established hotel was remodelled in 2002. It offers a full range of facilities for the business traveller.

Howard Johnson Plaza Hotel 古象大酒店 上海九江路595号
595 Jiujiang Road. Tel. 3313 4888; www.hojo.china.com
This impressive hotel, a recent addition to the five star line-up, opened in July 2003, with 360 rooms, magnificent health club facilities and sizeable meeting and function spaces. The cuisine encompasses Mediterranean, Californian and traditional Chinese. It is situated in the heart of the city close to the Nanjing Road (E) pedestrian area.

Huating Hotel and Towers 华亭酒店 上海漕溪北路1200号
1200 Caoxi Road (N). Tel. 6439 1000; www.huating-hotel.com
Located opposite the Shanghai Football Stadium in the west of the city, the property was previously operated by the Sheraton and is now managed by the Jinjiang Corporation. It has 770 spacious rooms and suites and a wide selection of recreational and fitness facilities as well as restaurants offering international, Asian, Cantonese and Shanghainese cuisines.

Hyatt On the Bund 上海外滩茂悦大酒店 黄浦路199号
199 Huangpu Road Tel: 6393 1234; http://shanghai.bund.hyatt.com
Opened in the second-half of 2007 this new Grand Hyatt with its great location and unsurpassed views over the Bund and the Huangpu River, as well its superb appointments and facilities, is sure to set new standards for the city. It has 631 guest rooms, including 52 suites ranging in size from 42 to 300 square metres.

Hotel Indigo Shanghai on the Bund 上海外滩英迪格酒店 中山东二路585号
585 Zhongshan No. 2 Road (E). Tel. 3302 9999; www.shanghai.hotelindigo.com
In the trendy Cool Dock area along the historic waterfront the Hotel Indigo offers individually stylish rooms and CHAR, a rooftop bar and restaurant, as well as a state-of -the-art gym.

Jia Shanghai 家上海 南京西路931号
931 Nanjing Road (W) Tel. 6217 9000; www.jiashanghai.com
Located in one of Shanghai's earliest 1920s apartment blocks in the heart of the city, the exclusive Jia Shanghai offers 55 rooms and suites, all with kitchenettes

and Bisazza tiled bathrooms. The smallest studio is 35 square metres in size—and for that special indulgence a 160 square metre penthouse suite is there to tempt. Houses the impressive Issimo Italian Restaurant.

Jinjiang Hotel 锦江大酒店 上海茂名南路59号
59 Maoming Road (S). Tel. 6258 2582; www.jinjianghotelshanghai.com
Located near the corner of Central Huaihai Road, the main Tudor style high-rise building was opened in 1929 as Cathay Mansions—part of the luxury Cathay Estate owned by Sir Victor Sassoon. It was here that President Nixon stayed when the historic Shanghai Communiqué was signed in February 1972. The building has undergone a thorough renovation and has a vast array of high-class shops and restaurants adjacent.

Jinjiang Tower 新锦江大酒店 上海长乐路161号
161 Changle Road. Tel. 6415 1188; www.jjtcn.com
This 42-storey hotel, which was completed in 1990, has 632 rooms and suites and a host of restaurants, including the Blue Heaven Revolving Restaurant and other facilities for recreation and business. The hotel prides itself on the number of high ranking overseas government officials that have stayed.

JW Marriott Hotel Shanghai At Tomorrow Square 明天金威万豪酒店 上海南京西路399号
399 Nanjing Road (W). Tel. 5359 4959; www.marriott.com
This imposing addition to the misogyny on People's Square is housed in a slender tower topped with four crab-like pincers. It features 342 exquisitely appointed rooms on 24 floors as well as numerous executive apartments. The building is packed with Chinese and Western eateries and recreation facilities, including indoor and outdoor pools. Excellent jazz is performed in the JW's Lounge. The hotel opened in October 2003.

Lapis Casa Boutique Hotel 太仓路68号
68 Taicang Road. Tel. 5382 1600; www.lapiscasahotel.com
Modest 18 room old Shanghai-styled residence close to the trendy Xintiandi area. Its furnishings and fittings are all available for purchase.

Le Royal Meridien Shanghai 世茂皇家艾美酒店 南京东路798号
789 Nanjing Road (E). Tel. 3318 9999
www.starwoodhotels.com/lemeridien/royalshanghai

Stylishly ultra-modern and centrally located near People's Square, Le Royal Meridien boasts over 750 rooms in a landmark 66-storey building. The hotel has an extensive range of fine dining opportunities, with breath taking views from its popular bar on the top floor.

Mansion Hotel 首席公馆酒店 新乐路82号
82 Xinle Road. Tel. 5403 9888; www.chinamansionhotel.com
Claiming to be the first the first heritage property to be converted into a five-star hotel, the Mansion has the air of an exclusive club. The house was originally built in 1932 and was home to members of the infamous Green Gang mobsters in the 1930s. Set in the heart of the former French Concession with 32 luxury rooms and suites and a fantastic rooftop terrace for dining.

Okura Garden Hotel Shanghai 花园酒店 上海茂名南路58号
58 Maoming Road (S). Tel. 6415 1111; www.gardenhotelshanghai.com
A modern 34-storey hotel arises from the former French Club (Cercle Sportif Française) that was built in 1926. The Japan-based Okura Hotels group did a fine job in restoring many parts of the original building, where can be found meeting and banquet rooms and the magnificent ballroom, which is crowned with one of the finest examples of Tiffany glass to be found anywhere in the world. The hotel is located in the city's most prestigious shopping and business district. It offers 500 tastefully decorated rooms as well as fine dining and superb service.

Old House Inn 老时光酒店 华山路351弄16 号
16, Lane 351, Huashan Road. Tel. 6248 6118; www.oldhouse.cn
A charming 12-room guesthouse, tucked away in an alley. All rooms are different, with wooden floors and furniture styled after the Ming Dynasty (1368–1644) and 21st-century amenities. The inn is just around the corner from the Hilton hotel.

Fairmont Peace Hotel 上海费尔蒙和平饭店 上海南京东路20号
20 Nanjing Road (E). Tel.6321 6888; www.fairmont.com/peacehotel
Opened as the Cathay Hotel in 1929, one of the finest and most modern hotels in the world. Following three years of renovation, it reopened under Fairmont management as the Fairmont Peace Hotel in mid-2010. Features over 270 deluxe guestrooms and suites and six restaurants and lounges, including the historic Peace Hall on the eighth floor.

Pudi Boutique Hotel 璞邸精品酒店 雁荡路99号
99 Yandang Road. Tel. 5158 5888; www.boutiquehotel.cc
In terms of individuality, style and sophistication Pudi is probably the pick of the current crop of fashionable small hotels springing up in the city. Conveniently located near Fuxing Park, it offers 52 spacious rooms and suites and a rooftop restaurant reserved for guests and selected members.

Radisson Blu Hotel Shanghai New World 上海新世界丽笙大酒店 上海南京西路88号
88 Nanjing Road (W). Tel: 6359 9999
www.radissonblu.com/newworldhotel-shanghai
In a prime position flanking the People's Square to the north this new high-rise Radisson opened in mid-2005. It adjoins the 10-storey New World shopping emporium and has 520 rooms including 82 suites, as well as a Presidential Suite. Its revolving restaurant can be found on the 45th floor and its bar on the 47th.

Radisson Blu Xing Guo Hotel Shanghai 上海兴国丽笙大酒店 上海兴国路78号
78 Xing Guo Road. Tel. 6212 9998; www.radissonblu.com/plazaxingguo-shanghai
The modern high-rise Radisson sits inside a 15-acre estate full of beautiful gardens and historic houses. The hotel's 190 rooms, including 40 suites, are luxurious, contemporary and designed with the business traveller in mind. The hotel has excellent meeting facilities, including a 45-seat cinema. The No. 1 Building, built in 1934, was regarded as one of the best mansions in Shanghai and was built by the influential Swire family.

Regal International East Asia Hotel 富豪环球国际大酒店 上海衡山路516号
516 Hengshan Road. Tel. 6415 5588; www.regal-eastasia.com
The hotel is set in the prestigious diplomatic district on beautiful Hengshan Road, a street noted for its eateries and bars. There are over 300 rooms and a range of excellent Chinese and Western dining options. The hotel also houses the Shanghai International Tennis Centre.

Renaissance Yangtze Shanghai Hotel 阳子江万豪大酒店 上海延安西路2099号
2099 Yan'an Road (W). Tel. 6275 0000; www.renaissance-shanghai.com
The hotel was completely refurbished in 2002 to luxury standards. It is well known for elegant facilities and services, including advanced meeting and banquet facilities, a state-of-the-art health club, cosy functional guest rooms, two modern business centres and extensive dining and entertainment choices. It hosts the largest and most popular Oktoberfest in China each year. The hotel has 544 rooms and suites on its 33 floors.

Shanghai JC Mandarin 上海锦沧文华大酒店 上海南京西路1225号
1225 Nanjing Road (W). Tel. 6279 1888; www.jcmandarin.com
Located in the heart of the city opposite the shopping malls, the JC Mandarin is one of Shanghai's most established hotels, managed by Meritus Hotels and Resorts of Singapore. It has 510 rooms on its 30 floors with 27 individually-styled suites. There is an excellent all-day buffet in the Tatler's Restaurant and Lounge, and the Park Lane Café has outdoor as well as indoor seating.

Shanghai Marriott Hotel Hongqiao 上海万豪虹桥大酒店 上海虹桥路2270号
2270 Hongqiao Road. Tel. 6237 6000; www.marriott.com
Situated in the heart of the Hongqiao business area, all 315 rooms and suites are specifically designed with the business visitor in mind. Food outlets include a steakhouse, an American bar, a gourmet shop and an international café. The hotel has indoor and outdoor pools and tennis courts.

Sheraton Grand Tai Ping Yang Hotel 喜来登豪华太平洋大酒店 上海遵义南路5号
5 Zunyi Road (S). Tel. 6275 8888; www.sheratongrand-shanghai.com
This property was formerly occupied by the Westin Hotel and features 496 elegant guest rooms, including five luxuriously-appointed specialty suites and four floors of uniquely-designed Club Level rooms and suites. It boasts 10 restaurants, lounges and bars. Its Chelsea Bar, an English-style pub, has the most extensive selection of imported beers in the city and its delicatessen is one of the best stocked. The hotel also has impressive conference facilities.

Shanghai Xijiao Guest House 上海西郊宾馆 上海虹桥路1921号
1921 Hongqiao Road. Tel. 6219 8800; fax. 6433 6641
www.sh-xijiaoguesthouse.com
The Xijiao Guest House is located on quiet Hongqiao Road, near the Hongqiao Airport and Shanghai Zoo. The grounds of this villa hotel incorporates woodland and rivers. In this setting there are 140 guest rooms and suites. Queen Elizabeth II and the Japanese Emperor Akihito have stayed here in the past.

The Langham Xintiandi Shanghai 上海新天地朗廷酒店 上海马当路99号
99 Madang Road. Tel. 2330 2288; http://xintiandi.langhamhotels.com/
This 357-room hotel set in the heart of Xintiandi offers afternoon tiffin, Shanghainese and Cantonese cuisine, an expansive multi-purpose space and spa.

The Langham, Yangtze Boutique, Shanghai 上海朗廷阳子精品酒店 汉口路740号
740 Hankou Road. Tel. 6080 0800
http://yangtzeboutique.langhamhotels.com/en/index.html
The opening of the Langham Yangtze in May 2009 marked the re-birth of a 1930s hotel institution. Its fabulous Art Deco building was opened in 1933 as 'The New Yangtsze Hotel' and featured a Chinese restaurant modeled on a London establishment. Announcing itself a boutique hotel, it is one that stands out in Shanghai with 96 rooms and suites each designed to recapture the glamour and grandeur of the era when Shanghai was famed as the 'Paris of the East'. The hotel features four sensational restaurants, including T'ang Court—the newest sister of the two Michelin Star restaurant in Hong Kong, Ciao Dining Room.

The Longemont Shanghai 上海龙之梦丽晶大酒店 延安西路1116号
1116 Yan'an Road (W) Tel. 6115 9988; www.thelongemonthotels.com
Formerly The Regent Shanghai the Longemont contains 511 luxurious contemporary rooms its 53-storey landmark building. The Longemont is a notable addition to the Shanghai hotel scene. It comes with all that one would expect of a five star hotel including an outdoor tennis court and comfortable club lounge.

The Peninsula Shanghai 上海半岛酒店 中山东一路 32号
32 Zhongshan No. 1 Road (E) (The Bund)
Tel. 2327 2888; www.peninsula.com/Shanghai/en/default.aspx
The legendary Peninsula Hotel Group returns to the city of its roots with the finest property in the city at a prime location on the Bund that was originally part of the grounds of the British Consulate. The hotel comes with you would expect from the brand—a fleet of Rolls-Royces, including a 1934 vintage Phantom II, a large luxury shopping arcade, a grand ballroom and 235 voluminous and impeccably fitted Art Deco inspired rooms and suites.

The Portman Ritz-Carlton Hotel 上海波特曼丽嘉酒店 上海南京西路1376号上海中心
Shanghai Centre, 1376 Nanjing Road (W). Tel. 6279 8888; www.ritzcarlton.com
The 564-room Portman Ritz-Carlton occupies a prime position on Nanjing Road (W). Services and facilities include six restaurants and lounges serving Chinese, Italian, Japanese and Western favourites. An extensive health club with swimming pool, gym, indoor tennis court, and squash and racquetball courts is featured alongside a 24-hour business centre. Jazz is played nightly in The Ritz-Carlton Bar, which has one of Shanghai's largest collections of cigars and malt whiskies.

The PuLi Hotel & Spa 璞丽酒店 常德路1号
1 Changde Road. Tel. 3203 9999; www.thepuli.com
Bills itself as the first luxury hotel of its kind in the city by bringing the concept of an urban resort to Shanghai, the Puli has all the facilities a businessman would expect of a five star hotel, as well as a whole floor devoted to well being operated by award-winning Anantara Spa Group. Features 209 luxury rooms and suites with a great location next to Jing'an Park.

The Waldorf Astoria Shanghai on the Bund 上海外滩华尔道夫酒店 中山东一路2号
2 Zhongshan No. 1 Road (E). (The Bund); www.waldorfastoria.com
The hotel features two connecting buildings, with The Waldorf Astoria Club offering 20 luxury suites, housed in the former premises of the legendary Shanghai Club, A further 249 rooms and suites are located in a new tower to its rear. Features three restaurants, two lounges and a revival of the famous Long Bar.

The Westin Shanghai 上海威斯汀大饭店 上海河南中路88号
88 Central Henan Road. Tel. 6335 1888; www.westin.com/shanghai
The Westin Shanghai enjoys a fantastic location near the Bund, in the Bund Centre. The hotel's 301 rooms on 26 floors offer world-class luxury. It has fine international, Asian and Italian restaurants and international jazz at its Niche Bar. Legendary scene for Sunday brunch.

URBN Hotel URBN酒店 胶州路183号
183 Jiaozhou Road. Tel. 5153 4600; www.urbnhotels.com
URBN has become a hot and hip boutique hotel and lays claims to be the first carbon neutral hotel in China. Features 26 designer rooms by architect Raefer H. Wallis who converted this downtown post office building into a parcel of chic. Situated the heart of the city just a few minutes walk from the Jing'an Temple—a tempting alternative to the city's monolithic and monotone hotels.

88 Xintiandi 88 新天地 上海黄陂南路380号
380 Huangpi Road (S). Tel. 5383 8833; www.88xintiandi.com
This exclusive boutique hotel is best described as an executive residence that caters to long as well as short term guests. The 53 hand-crafted suites in five distinct layouts all have kitchen facilities. They also have state-of-the-art equipment for the business executive, including high-speed broadband Internet access, a full-size desk and a complete compliment of secretarial support services. The hotel is found in the south block of the prestigious Xintiandi development with fantastic views across the Taipingqiao Park and the city.

Pudong

Courtyard by Marriott Pudong 浦东万豪大酒店 上海东方路838号
838 Dongfang Road. Tel. 6886 7886; www.marriott.com
Within easy walking distance of the Oriental Pearl Tower, this hotel is designed for the executive on the move, with 218 rooms featuring a full range of business amenities. The hotel features two executive floors with an exclusive executive lounge as well as seven meeting rooms and a grand ballroom. Excellent dining options are on offer at the Spices Cafe and the Hua Mei Garden.

Grand Hyatt Hotel Shanghai 上海金茂君悦大酒店 上海世纪大道88号金茂大厦
Jinmao Building, 88 Century Avenue. Tel. 5049 1234; www.shanghai.hyatt.com
Located on the 53rd to 87th floors of one of the most striking buildings in the world, the Grand Hyatt is also the highest hotel in the world. It has a spectacular 33-storey central atrium and its 555 rooms and suites are the most spacious in Shanghai. There is a wealth of fitness facilities and a huge range of dining and entertainment venues on offer, including some of the most spacious in best Japanese and Italian food and steaks in the city. The hotel also has a very impressive three floors of flexible space for meetings and conferences, including two ballrooms.

InterContinental Pudong Shanghai上海新亚汤臣洲际大酒店 上海张扬路777号
777 Zhangyang Road. Tel. 5831 8888; www.shanghai.intercontinental.com
Ideally situated in the heart of the Lujiazui, Shanghai's new financial and business district, the InterContinental Pudong Shanghai features 400 guest rooms and suites with two ballrooms and 16 multi-sized function rooms. It was formerly the Shanghai New Asia Tomson Hotel. The hotel has a large recreation centre and has exclusive access to Tomson Golf, a champion 18-hole golf course, which is just a 15 minute drive away.

Jumeirah Himalayas Hotel 卓美亚喜玛拉雅酒店 上海梅花路1108号
1108 Meihua Road. Tel. 3858 0888
www.jumeirah.com/Hotels-and Resorts/Reiseziele/Shanghai/Jumeirah-Himalayas-Hotel/
The Jumeirah Group's Asia Pacific award winning debut hotel, blends tradition with contemporary vision, featuring spacious feng shui designed rooms and state of the art technology.

Mandarin Oriental Pudong 上海浦东文华东方酒店 上海浦东南路111号
111 Pudong Road (S). Tel. 2082 9888
http://www.mandarinoriental.com/shanghai/
Sitting on the Lujiazui waterfront this ultra-stylish luxury hotel, with service that would be expected from the brand, features 318 spacious rooms, 44 suites, worldwide cuisine in six restaurants and bars, a grand ballroom, a spa and stunning views.

Oriental Riverside Hotel Shanghai 东方滨江大酒店 上海滨江大道2727号
2727 Riverside Avenue. Tel. 5037 0000; www.showhotel.com/china
As part of the Shanghai International Convention Centre complex this luxuriously appointed hotel has a great riverside location overlooking the Bund. The 259 rooms and suites are large. The hotel's grand ballroom can accommodate 3,000 people and a wide range of Chinese and Western food outlets are found in the hotel.

Park Hyatt Shanghai 上海柏悦酒店 世纪大道100号
100 Century Avenue. Tel. 6888 1234; www.shanghai.park.hyatt.com
Excelling its neighbour, the Grand Hyatt, in height and in standards the Park Hyatt boasts the highest hotel facilities in the World being housed on the 79th to 93rd floors of the magnificent and eerily chic Shanghai World Financial Centre in the heart of Pudong's business district. 174 luxury rooms and suites all with views over the Huangpu River and Pudong.

Pudong Shangri-La, Shanghai 浦东香格里拉大酒店 上海富城路33号
33 Fucheng Road. Tel. 6882 8888; www.shangri-la.com
This sumptuous hotel has 606 very spacious rooms and suites in its original building affording fantastic views. Japanese and Chinese cuisine is on offer as well as international cuisine in the fine Lobby Lounge. B.A.T.S, the basement bar, is one of the most popular venues for live music in Pudong. The hotel also offers a wide range of first-class leisure and meeting facilities. 36-storey wing containing 375 rooms is replete with a range of trend-setting designer restaurants and bars, another Ballroom, a highly recommended spa and a glassed-in outdoor swimming pool.

Purple Mountain Hotel 紫金山大酒店 上海东方路778号
778 Dongfang Road. Tel. 6886 8888; www.purplemountainhotel.com
The hotel is located on a main intersection, home to some of the largest stores in Asia in the heart of the Lujiazui Financial and Trade Zone in Pudong. The hotel has more than 400 tastefully decorated guestrooms, many offering spectacular views, and is equipped with modern business and conference facilities. The hotel is a 30-minute drive away from Pudong International Airport or Hongqiao Airport.

Renaissance Shanghai Pudong Hotel 上海淳大万豪酒店 上海长柳路100号
100 Changliu Road. Tel. 3871 4888; www.marriott.com
A Marriott Hotel featuring 375 rooms on 27 floors and a brasserie with an open kitchen and 24-hour buffet. Cantonese and Shanghainese cuisine is on offer as well as a French gourmet shop. The hotel also has extensive meeting facilities and services.

Sofitel Jin Jiang Oriental Pudong 滨江索妃特大酒店 上海延高南路889号
889 Yangao Road (S). Tel. 5050 4888; www.accorhotels-asia.com
This 549-room, 47-storey hotel, provides a variety of accommodation styles to suit any need. It is prominently located nearby the magnificent Nanpu Bridge spanning the Huangpu River and offers breathtaking views of Shanghai. The hotel features extensive meeting and sports facilities and offers Shanghainese, Cantonese and international cuisine.

The Hongta Hotel 上海瑞吉红塔大酒店 上海东方路889号
889 Dongfang Road. Tel. 5050 4567
www.starwoodhotels.com/luxury/property/overview/index.html?propertyID=1365
With its distinctive modern design and the largest standard guest rooms in Shanghai and 24-hour butler service, the former St. Regis Hotel is in a class of its own. It offers fine Chinese and international dining, including some of the best Italian food in town at Danieli's as well as comprehensive convention and fitness facilities. Situated in the heart of Shanghai's financial district, the hotel has received numerous international accolades.

The Ritz-Carlton Shanghai, Pudong 上海浦东丽思卡尔顿酒店 世纪大道8号
Shanghai ifc, 8 Century Avenue.
Tel. 2020 1888; www.ritzcarlton.com/shanghaipudong
This stunning luxury hotel, occupying the top 18 floors of the 58-storey ifc, phase one, in the heart of Lujiazui, opened in mid-2010. Features huge guest rooms and suites with splashes of art deco, overlooking the Bund and the city, with fine Italian, Chinese and Asian cuisine, a hip jazz bar and FLAIR, a rooftop lifestyle lounge.

Dining in Shanghai
The Bund

Bund 18
18 Zhongshan No. 1 Road (E)
外滩18号 上海中山东一路18号
Tan Wai Lou 滩外楼中餐厅 Tel. 6339 1188
Mr and Mrs Bund. Tel. 6323 9898
Shanghai's latest triumph on the Bund is sizzling with style—from the contemporary Chinese creative themes of the Tan Wai Lou, presided over by master chef Zhi-Hai Tou—to the ornate richness of the rooftop Bar Rouge. Taking over the space originally inhabited by Sens & Bund is the fabulous modern French eatery in fabulously modern surroundings created by culinary genius Paul Pairet, formerly of Jade 36 at the Pudong Shangri-La. The menu offers a monster selection of over 200 family-style dishes and 32 wines, dispensed from sleek wine machines, by the glass.

M on the Bund
Floor 7, 20 Guangdong Road. Tel. 6350 9988
米氏餐厅 上海广东路20号7楼
Sister restaurant to the renowned M at the Fringe in Hong Kong (now closed) and the latest addition to the M group, Capital M in Beijing, this classy eatery is considered by many to be the one of the best in town—in no small part for its unbeatable location affording a spectacular waterfront view from its terrace. M on the Bund has received more awards and honours than any other independent restaurant in Shanghai and has become the rendezvous for roaming glitterati, statesmen and royalty. The accent is Mediterranean, the décor stylishly retro-1930s and M's fabulous and sexy sixth-floor Glamour Bar is the place to go for cocktails and Sunday afternoon recitals.

Three on the Bund
3 Zhongshan Road No. 1 (E)
Jean Georges 乔治法国餐厅 Tel. 6321 7733; Mercato 意大利餐厅 Tel. 6321 9922
New Heights 新视角 Tel. 6321 0909; Whampoa Club 黄浦会 Tel. 6339 1188
外滩3号 上海中山东一路3号
The 90 year-old neo-classical building is now home to a collection of world-class restaurants. Not the least of these is Jean Georges, just the second restaurant in the world to carry the name of renowned chef Jean-Georges Vongerichten; modern French cuisine, prepared in peerless style, with the best local and imported ingredients. He also inspired Mercato an Italian restaurant in a relaxed, yet sophisticated rustic chic

interior designed by Neri & Hu. Jereme Leung, one of Asia's youngest Master Chefs transforms traditional Shanghai recipes at the classy Whampoa Club. New Heights on the top floor is an unfussy restaurant and bar with great Asian and Western cuisine and fantastic views over the river.

The historic former Russell and Co. property at 6 Bund is now home to Japanese and French restaurants as well as **The Martini Bar**. The House of Roosevelt housed in the former Jardine & Matheson building at No. 27 has a cavernous wine cellar and a roof top restaurant, as well as a cosy courtyard eatery.

Chinese Cuisine
Shanghainese
Club Jin Mao
Floor 86, Jinmao Building, 88 Century Boulevard, Pudong
Tel. 5049 1234 ext. 8688
金茂俱乐部 上海世界大道88号 上海金茂君悦大酒店86楼
With fantastic panoramic views of Shanghai, the city's best chefs and the most exclusive Shanghainese food to be found, the Club Jin Mao sets the benchmark in its creation of fine local cuisine.

Lu Bo Lang
115 Yuyuan Road. Tel. 6328 0602
露波廊 上海豫园路115号
This is one of Shanghai's most famous and popular local cuisine establishments. It has an atmospheric location at the heart of the Yu Garden bazaar area and serves up a full range of Shanghai snacks and favourites. The walls are lined with pictures of prominent dignitaries who have visited the restaurant.

Lu Lu
Floor 5, Plaza 66, 1266 Nanjing Road (W). Tel. 6288 1179
露露 上海南京西路1266号
There are four branches of this ever-busy eatery around town. This one is centrally located in one of Shanghai's classiest shopping malls and is a good place to experience luscious Shanghai cuisine and to capture the beat of Shanghai life.

Meilongzhen
Lane 1081, No. 22 Nanjing Road (W). Tel. 6253 5353
梅龙镇酒家 上海南京西路1081弄22号
Located in the heart of town and set in a faded red-brick mansion, Meilongzhen has been delivering fine cuisine since 1938. The interior has an old world imperial flavour, with Chinese lanterns and wood-panelling. This is a popular spot for visiting tourists as well as local people.

Old Station Restaurant
201 Caoxi Road North. Tel. 6427 2233
上海老站 漕溪北路201号
Located in an a former convent opposite the Xujiahui Cathedral and replete with a train carriage for dining on its lawn, the authentic period setting is hard to match Serves up fairly routine Shanghai fare—but well worth a visit for the experience if you are nearby.

The 7
1110 Central Huaihai Road. Tel. 6415 8158 ext. 77102
7 上海淮海中路1110号
Stylish Shanghai cuisine served in one of the most atmospheric period settings in the city. The small dining rooms occupy a 1920s mansion, formerly known as Hanray, which was at one point owned by Du Yuesheng, the infamous boss of The Green Gang. Downstairs there is a bar, a sumptuous stained glass and wood-panelled cigar lounge, a patio and a lawn.

The Chinoise Story
Shanghai, 59 Maoming Road (S). Tel. 6445 1717
锦庐 茂名南路59号锦江饭店
Distinctive dining in an Art Deco distinctive setting that was home to The National City Bank of New York before WWII. Shanghai and Chinese inspired food that wanders into the realms of the Mediterranean.

The Grape
55 Xinle Road. Tel. 5404 0486
葡萄园酒家 上海新乐路55号
The Grape is a long standing favourite of many long-term foreign residents as well as a popular eatery for local families. The simple, but well cooked and presented, food is consistently satisfying and inexpensive.

The Yongfoo Elite
200 Yongfu Road. Tel. 5466 2727
永福会 上海永福路200号
The Yongfoo Elite sits in the heart of Shanghai's former French Concession amidst leafy avenues populated by consular and government elites. Its magnificent garden villa, which once housed the British Consulate, today administers the finest hospitality, classic Shanghai gourmet cuisine, wine, cocktails and live music. It's wonderfully eclectic and stylish setting attracts celebrities from Hong Kong and Hollywood. A totally unique establishment.

Xin Ji Shi
Unit 4, Building 9, Lane 169, Taicang Road. Tel. 6336 4746
新吉士 上海太仓路169弄9号
With a chic, minimalist re-interpretation of old Shanghai style, Xin Ji Shi offers a welcome change in terms of atmosphere and value from it's neighbours in the fashionable Xintiandi area.

1221
1221 Yan'an Road (W). Tel. 6213 6585, 6213 2441
上海延安西路1221号
A long established destination for those in search of authentic local cuisine in sophisticated surroundings, without the fuss associated with many newer establishments.

Cantonese
Canton Restaurant
Grand Hyatt Hotel, 55/F Jin Mao Tower, 88 Century Boulevard, Pudong
Tel. 5049 1234 ext 8890
粤珍轩 上海世界大道88号 上海金茂君悦大酒店55楼
Spectacular views from the 55th floor of the Jin Mao building complement a spectacular range of Cantonese cuisine, including numerous dim sum delights, in a luxuriant contemporary Chinese setting.

Crystal Jade
Unit 12A/B, Floor 2, House 6-7, South Block, Xintiandi, Lane 123 Xinye Road
Tel. 6385 8752
翡翠酒家 上海新月路123弄 新天地南里6-7号2楼
Located in a shopping mall and cinema complex in the south block of Xintiandi,

the Crystal Jade serves up good value dim sum and congee alongside its reliable main menu. This is one of the best of its kind in town and is highly popular with Cantonese and Hong Kong clients

Li Palace
Floor 4, Radisson Plaza Xing Guo Hotel, 78 Xing Guo Road
Tel. 6212 9998 ext. 3400
丽宫中餐厅 上海兴国路78号 兴国宾馆
Set in spacious and attractive grounds on the fringe of the former French Concession, the Li Palace is one of Shanghai's most elegant Cantonese eateries. The restaurant also features Shanghainese specialities and dim sum favourites.

Noble House Restaurant
Building 1, No. 46 Anting Road. Tel. 6433 3666
名轩是 上海安定路46号
Set in an old Spanish-style villa, all the Cantonese classics are on offer alongside a selection of Shanghainese cuisine. The restaurant prides itself on the freshness of its ingredients and its international award winning chef.

Shang Palace
Floor 2, Pudong Shangri-La Hotel, 33 Fucheng Road. Tel. 6882 8888
香宫 上海浦东富城路33号 香格里拉大酒店
Exquisitely refined setting and service for first-class Cantonese food in the superb Shangri-La Hotel, Pudong.

Si Ji Xuan
Floor 2, Four Seasons Hotel Shanghai, 500 Weihai Road. Tel. 6256 8888 ext 1280
四季园 上海威海路500号 四季酒店
Si Ji Xuan serves up fine traditional Cantonese dishes and Shanghainese specialties in a singularly sophisticated setting. Fresh seafood is high up on the menu, and the Sunday lunch presents an astounding display of dim sum delicacies.

Zen
House 2, South Block, Xintiandi, Lane 123, Xingyue Road. Tel. 6385 6385
采蝶轩 上海新月路123弄 新天地南里2号
With a futuristic setting, fine dim sum and other Cantonese favourites as well as some inventive regional cuisine Zen is one of the coolest places in town.

Sunya
719 Nanjing Road (E). Tel. 6322 4393
新雅 上海南京东路719号
Sunya is simply the most celebrated Cantonese eatery in town with a history going back to 1928. The original interiors have long since been replaced by glittering chandeliers, but the quality of the food remains true to its heritage.

Chinese Regional Cuisines
Di Shui Dong (Hunanese cuisine)
Floor 2, 56 Maoming Road (S). Tel. 6253 2689
滴水洞 上海茂名南路56号
This eatery (and branches) with its brand of super-spicy fare and joyfully noisy patrons make it a hot favourite. The restaurant is famous for its delicious cumin and chilli-coated spare ribs.

Din Tai Fung (Taiwanese cuisine)
Unit 11A, House 6, 2F, Lane 123, Xingye Road. Tel. 6385 8378
鼎泰丰 兴业路123弄新天地南里6号楼2楼11A
A later reincarnation of a restaurant named by the New York Times as one of the 10 best restaurants in the world in 1993 this Taiwanese dumpling house continues to please both the pockets and palates of locals and visitors alike.

Fwu Luh Pavilion (Yangzhou cuisine)
603B, Grand Gateway, 1 Hongqiao Road. Tel. 6407 9898
福碌居 上海虹桥路1号
Even though this restaurant is tucked away in a shopping mall in Xujiahui, its stylish interior and superior service are from ordinary—and it has prices to match. Yangzhou cooking doesn't use heavy seasoning and this is the place to try the artistically prepared dim sum treats.

Oriental House (Chaozhou Cuisine)
Hotel InterContinental Pudong Shanghai, 777 Zhangyang Road
上海新亚汤臣洲际大酒店 张扬路777号
Tel. 5831 8888 ext. 3261
This restaurant specializes in Chaozhou cuisine—but serves up a mixture of Cantonese, Shanghai, and Sichuan as well. Excellent dim sum and buffet at lunchtimes.

South Beauty (Sichuan)
881 Central Yan'an Road. Tel. 6247 5878, 6247 6682
俏江南 延安中路881号
There are a few other branches of this popular and chic Sichuan style restaurant around the city, but this one with its outdoor terrace, its fiery food and its heritage setting tops the list.

Vegetarian

Gongdelin
445 Nanjing Road (W). Tel. 6327 0218
功德林 上海南京西路445号
Established for over 80 years and with a Buddhist heritage still evident in its classic Chinese decoration, Gongdelin serves up some of the most creative vegetarian fare to be found in the form of meat and fish dishes totally free of animal flesh.

Jendow
2787 Longhua Road. Tel. 6457 2299 and 151 Yuyuan Road. Tel. 5168 8077
人道素菜 龙华路2787号 愚园路151号
If you are visiting the Longhua Pagoda area allow an hour or more to indulge in the largest and most inventive range of vegetarian food on offer in the city. Though much of the mock meat fare is based on Chinese cuisine there are influences stretching across the Continents. Hundreds of delicious offerings in a buffet-style restaurant that opens for lunch and dinner only. A real find.

Western

Continental-Fusion

Art 50
Floor 50, Novotel Atlantis Hotel, 728 Pudong Avenue. Tel. 5036 6666
旋转50餐厅 上海浦东路728号
Fine fusion cuisine is on offer in this revolving restaurant which completes one rotation in 90 minutes allowing one to view the contemporary art on view inside and a panorama of Shanghai outside.

Colours
118 Ruijin No. 2 Road. Tel. 5466 5577
上海七彩餐厅 上海瑞金二路118号

Set in the delightful grounds of the Ruijin Guesthouse, with a broad terrace running from a contemporarily reinvented old villa, Colours serves up inventive quality fusion cuisine. The décor is cool and minimalist and its bar also serves up a fine selection of cocktails.

Jade on 36
Floor 36 Pudong Shangri-La Hotel, 33 Fucheng Road. Tel. 6882 3636
浦东香格里拉大酒店 富城路33号
Choose from a range of colour coded set menus for one of the most sensational culinary treats in the city. And all within a vibrant Chinese avant-garde interior.

Haya's Mediterranean Cuisine
415 Dagu Road. Tel. 6295 9511
哈雅地中海餐厅 大沽路415号
Large factory-canteen style space serving up the clean and creamy flavours of the Mediterranean, with Israeli overtures. The place for a Greek feast—wonderful tasting pitas, falafel, hummus, kebabs, salads, fresh lemonade and much more in hearty sized portions.

Luna
Unit 1, House 16, Lane 169, Taicang Road, Xintiandi. Tel. 6336 1717
路娜 上海太仓路169弄16号
Luna occupies a large historic property in Xintiandi and is on two floors, including a cafe with outdoor seating, a restaurant gallery and a music bar. Luna serves some of the best Mediterranean food in town.

Sasha's
House 11, 9 Dongping Road. Tel. 6474 6167
萨莎 上海东平路9号11号
The former residence of TV Soong, a member of one of the most intriguing and influential families in modern Chinese history, has been reinstated as one of China's most authentic bars with a fine continental restaurant upstairs. The large garden area is the perfect venue for summer barbeques.

T8
House 8, North Block, Xintiandi, Lane 181 Taicang Road. Tel. 6355 8999
T8 上海太仓路181弄 新天地北里8号
Voted as one of the best restaurants in the world by Conde Nast Traveller. The combination of a fantastic environment, creative continental cuisine and superb

service blend to make this restaurant an extra-special venue for a light lunch or a sophisticated dinner.

The Stage at The Westin
The Westin Hotel 1st floor, 88 Central Henan Road. Tel. 6335 0577 ext. 7350
威斯汀舞台餐厅 河南中路88号
The Westin's voluptuous Sunday buffet, with free flowing champagne and chilled delights from all parts of the globe, has become a Shanghai institution of the highest order. It's essential to book—do so before you leave home if your visit is short.

French
Allure
Floor 11, Le Royal Meridien Hotel, 789 Nanjing Road (E). Tel. 3318 9999 ext. 7022
艾露餐厅 世茂皇家艾美酒店 南京东路798号
Le Royal Meridien Shanghai's signature restaurant offers fine southern French and Mediterranean dining under the directorship of Michael Wendling, a master student of 3-star Michelin chef George Blanc. The business lunches are particularly good value.

Club Shanghai
Floor 4, Shanghai Concert Hall, 523 Yan'an Road (E). Tel. 5383 9989
漾乐会 上海延安东路523号上海音乐厅
Located in the restored former Nanking Theatre, Club Shanghai is Shanghai's latest fine-dining French restaurant. Designer and owner Lily Ho lavished US$2.5 million on its interior. Chef Stefan Stiller has a Michelin-star pedigree and sommelier Daniel Chia, was previously cellar master of Singapore's Raffles Hotel.

Two of the city's finest French restaurants are found at Bund 18 (Mr and Mrs Bund) and Three on the Bund (Jean Georges)—see page 553.

Italian
Cucina
Floor 56, Grand Hyatt Hotel, Jin Mao Building, 88 Century Boulevard, Pudong
Tel. 5830 3338
意庐意大利餐厅 上海世界大道88号 上海金茂君悦大酒店56楼
On offer here is not only one of the best views in Shanghai, but also some of the finest Italian food in the city. The restaurant also offers great value for money given the setting and high standards of service.

Danieli's
Floor 39, The Hongta Hotel, 889 Dongfang Road, Pudong. Tel. 5050 4567
丹尼艾丽丝意大利餐厅 上海东方路889号 上海瑞吉红塔大酒店39楼
Commanding fantastic views from the top of the St. Regis Hotel, superbly inventive Italian food flows from the large open kitchen presided over by chef Luca Cesarini.

Issimo
Floor 2, Jia, 931 Nanjing Road (W). Tel. 6287 9009
南京西路931号
Located within the trendy Jia Hotel this traditional Italian style restaurant serves up hearty and well-prepared food in a modern and comfortable environment. Conjures up extremely good value and satisfying lunches.

Leonardo's
Floor 1, Hilton Hotel, 250 Hunashan Road. Tel. 6248 7777 ext. 1850
李奥纳多 上海华山路250号 上海静安希尔顿酒店
Upholding the Hilton's fine reputation for dining, the elegant décor, setting and service at this popular restaurant is complemented by a fine wine list.

Palladio
The Portman Ritz-Carlton Hotel, 1376 Nanjing Road (W). Tel. 6279 8888
帕兰朵 上海南京西路1376号 上海波特曼丽嘉酒店
This is one of the best Italian restaurants in Shanghai and possibly in the entire country. The restaurant is noted for its personal service and presents perfect antipasto, an enticing range of pasta dishes, and excellent meat and fish courses.

Prego
Level 2, The Westin Hotel, 88 Central Henan Road, Tel. 6335 1888
帕戈餐厅 上海河南中路88号 上海威斯汀大饭店
This restaurant comes with a real Italian passion—in mood, décor and management. The deserts are exemplary and the selection of grappa on offer is unsurpassed in China.

Va Bene
House 7. North Block, Lane 181, Taicang Road, Xintiandi. Tel. 6311 2211
意大利餐厅 上海太仓路181弄 新天地北里7号
Set in an ultra-stylishly restored shikumen house in fashionable Xintiandi, Va Bene perpares a range of Tuscan delights, including authentic pizzas and the freshest of seafood platters

Other Western Establishments

KABB (American)
House 5, North Block, Lane 181 Taicang Road, Xintiandi. Tel. 3307 0798
凯文印度餐厅 上海太仓路181弄 新天地北里5号
Straightforward and substantial American food in a stylish environment. KABB also features an impressive wine list.

Le Garçon Chinois
No. 3, Lane 9, Hengshan Road. Tel. 6445 7970
乐加尔松 上海衡山路9弄3号
Occupying a restored 1920s house down a quiet alleyway in one of the city's more popular eating and bar areas Le Garçon Chinois offers lovingly prepared Spanish and continental food in a cosy and classy environment.

Malone's American Café (American)
255 Tongren Road. Tel. 6247 2400
马龙 上海同仁路255号
One of Shanghai's most established Western institutions, this American-style bar and restaurant serves a feast of American classics and some Asian favourites as well.

MAYA
2/F Shanghai Grand Plaza, Club House, Julu Road. Tel. 6289 6889
玛雅 上海巨鹿路568号
Tucked away in a modern housing development Maya serves up very hip Mexican food in a lively and sophisticated environment full of Yucatan influences.

O'Malley's (Irish)
42 Taojiang Road. Tel. 6474 4533
欧玛莉 上海桃江路42号
Housed in a late 19th century house, O'Malley's pub is a home away from home for many foreign residents. Apart from its Irish beers and music it serves up hearty Irish food, including Irish stew. The garden is a great place to take a leisurely meal.

Paulaner Brauhaus (German)
150 Fenyang Road. Tel. 6474 5700
宝来纳西餐厅 上海汾阳路150号
A sister to the Ambrosia Japanese restaurant next door, the mansion is the setting for fine home-brewed ales as well as traditional German fare and festivities. The restaurant has a Filipino band. Other branches are to be found in Xintiandi and on the promenade in Lujiazui.

The Steak House

Floor 2, Four Seasons Hotel, 500 Weihai Road. Tel. 6256 8888
牛排餐厅 上海威海路500号 四季酒店

An elegantly designed interior and the best aged steaks, including fine Australian lamb, partnered by an excellent wine list make this one of the best in town. The seafood is also excellent.

Vargas Grill

Floor 3, 18 Dongping Road. Tel. 6437 0136
东平路18号3楼

Local celebrity and chef Eduardo Vargas's signature venue serves up great steaks, fish and burgers and almost anything else, including desserts, all cooked on gas or charcoal grills.

INDIAN, NEPALESE AND THAI

Kaveen's Kitchen

Floor 2, 231 Huashan Road. Tel. 6248 2777
正宗印度餐厅 上海华山路231号

This intimate family run restaurant with masses of Indian character, opposite the Hilton, has some of the best North Indian food in town. Buffets are served on Tuesdays and Thursdays.

Irene's Thai

263 Tongren Road. Tel. 6247 3579
泰式餐厅 上海同仁路263号

Highly authentic Thai food in a richly decorated and comfortable environment. Shanghai's most established Thai eatery has all you can eat offers at weekends and live Thai music on some evenings.

Nepali Kitchen

178 Xinle Road. Tel. 5404 5077
尼泊尔餐厅 上海新乐路178号

With Nepalese management and staff, cushions for seats and some incredible curries, this small restaurant is a highly popular destination for those in search of subtly spicy flavours.

Tandoor
59 Maoming Road (S). Tel. 6258 2582 ext. 9301, 6472 5494
印度餐厅 上海茂名南路59号
Shanghai's longest established and most sophisticated Indian restaurant offers fabulous surroundings and service for an Indian feast.

JAPANESE
Ambrosia
150 Fenyang Road. Tel. 6431 3935
仙炙轩 上海汾阳路150号
Set in the heart of the former French Concession near the consular district, Ambrosia offers an architectural as well as a culinary tour. Its graceful 1930s French villa was built in 1919 by the renowned American architect R.A. Curry—the spiral staircase is an interesting feature as are all the dining rooms named after the gods. Japanese and Korean cuisine is cooked on smoke-free grills.

Shintori Null-2
803 Julu Road. Tel. 5404 5252
This uniqueness of this Japanese restaurant derives not only from its creatively modern menu, but also from its spacious and breathtakingly minimalist interior. Modelled by the Japanese architect, Sakae Miura, an old movie theatre building has been converted into one of the most dramatic stages on which to eat in China.

Wuninosachi
169 Xinle Road. Tel. 5403 0303
海之幸称 上海新乐路169号
The Xinle Road restaurant is the most intimate of the three operated by the owners in Shanghai. If you book in advance there is an extremely good value all you can eat and drink menu, including sushi and sashimi.

Yamazato
Floor 2, Okura Garden Hotel, 58 Maoming Road (S). Tel. 6415 1111 ext. 5216
上海茂名南路58号 花园酒店
Top-quality Japanese cuisine, including Shanghai's only tempura bar set in one of Shanghai's top hotels—Japanese managed of course. The fare is traditional and hearty.

Useful Addresses in Shanghai

Airlines

Aeroflot Russian Airlines
Suite 203, West Tower, Shanghai Centre
1376 Nanjing Road (W)
Tel. 6279 8033
俄罗斯航空公司
上海南京西路1376号上海商城

Air Canada
Rm 3901, United Plaza
1468 Nanjing Road (W)
Tel. 6279 2999
加拿大航空公司
上海南京西路1468号中欣大厦

Air China
Rm.101B Changfeng Centre
1088 Yan'an Raod (W)
Tel. 4008 100 999, 5239 7227
6433 3355
中国航空公司
上海延安西路1088号长峰中心

Air France
Rm 3901, Ciro's Plaza
388 Nanjing Road (W)
Tel. 4008 808 808, 6334 5633
法国航空公司
上海南京西路388号仙乐斯

Air Macau
Rm 104, Equatorial Hotel
65 Yan'an Road (W). Tel. 6248 1110
澳门航空公司
上海延安西路65号贵都大酒店

Air New Zealand
Rm.1208-1209, CITIC Square, 1168
Nanjing Road (W). Tel. 5292 8755
新西兰航空
上海南京西路1168号中信泰富广场

Alitalia
Rm.3607, The Centre,
989 Changle Road. Tel. 6103 1133
意大利航空公司
上海长乐路989号近乌鲁木齐中路

All Nippon Airways
2/F East Tower, Shanghai Centre
1376 Nanjing Road (W)
Tel. 5696 2525, 800 820 1122
全日本航空株式会社
上海南京西路1376号上海商城

American Airlines
Suite 2513-15, Ocean Tower
550 Yan'an Road (E)
Tel. 6351 3386
美国航空公司
上海延安东路550号海洋大厦

Asiana Airlines
2/F Rainbow Hotel, 2000 Yan'an Road
(W) Tel. 400-650-8000
韩业航空公司 上海延安西路2000号

Austrian Airlines
Rm 2904, Raffles City
268 Central Tibet Road. Tel. 6340 3411
奥地利航空公司
上海西藏中路268号来福士广场

British Airways
Rm.703, Central Plaza
227 North Huangpi Road
Tel. 1080 0744 0031, 1080 0440 0031
英国航空公司 上海黃陂北路227号

China Eastern Airlines
200 Yan'an Road (W)
Tel. 6247 2255 (International)
6247 5953 (Domestic)
中国东方航空公司
上海延安西路200号

Continental Airlines
Rm 1905 World Trade Tower
500 Guangdong Road
Tel. 6362 1387
美国大陆航空
上海广东路500号世界贸易大厦

Dragonair
Rm 2101–2104
138 Central Huaihai Road
Tel. 6375 6375, 400 8810 288
港龙航空公司
上海淮海中路138号上海大厦

Emirates
Rm 1905, United Plaza
1468 Nanjing Road (W). Tel. 3222 9999
阿联酋国际航空
上海南京西路1468号中欣大厦

Eva Airways
Rm 3801, Raffles City
268 Central Tibet Road. Tel. 6360 0007
台湾长荣航空公司
上海西藏中路268号来福士广场

Finnair
Rm.2406, 24/F CITIC Square, 1168
Nanjing Road (W). Tel. 5292 9400
芬兰航空公司
上海南京西路1168号中信泰富广场

Japan Airlines
Rm 435, Plaza 66
1266 Nanjing Road (W)
Tel. 6288 3000
日本航空公司
上海南京西路1266号陆陆商场

KLM Royal Dutch Airlines
Rm 3901, Ciro's Plaza
388 Nanjing Road (W)
Tel. 400 880 8222
荷兰皇家航空公司
上海南京西路388号仙乐斯广场

Korean Air
Rm 1009–10, Maxdo Centre
8 Xingyi Road
Tel. 5208 2080, 5208 2081
大韩航空公司
上海兴义路8号万都中心

Lufthansa
Unit 14-21, 3/F, Bldg 1
Corporate Avenue, 222 Hubin Road
Tel. 5352 4999
德国汉莎航空公司
上海湖滨路222号企业天地1号

Malaysia Airlines
Suite 560, East Tower, Shanghai
Centre, 1376 Nanjing Road (W)
Tel 6279 8607
马来西亚航空公司
上海南京西路1376号上海商城东峰

Northwest Airlines
Rm 1007, Kerry Centre
1515 Nanjing Road (W)
Tel. 5298 5368
美国西北航空公司
上海南京西路1515号嘉里中心

Philippine Airlines
Suite 735A, Shanghai Centre
1376 Nanjing Road (W)
Tel. 6279-8765
菲律宾航空公司
上海南京西路1376号上海商城

Qatar Airways
Rm 3703-04, Raffles City,
268 Central Tibet Road. Tel: 2320 7555
卡塔尔航空公司
上海西藏中路268号来福士广场

Qantas
32/F, K Wah Centre,
1010 Central Huaihai Road
Tel. 800 819 0089, 6145 0188
澳大利亚澳洲航空公司
上海淮海中路1010号嘉华中心

Royal Brunei Airlines
Rm 302–306, Kerry Centre
1515 Nanjing Road (W). Tel. 5298 6688
文淶皇家航空公司
上海南京西路1515号嘉里中心

Royal Nepal Airlines
Rm 405, Building B
1 Wanhangdu Road. Tel. 3214 0717
尼泊尔航空公司 上海万航渡路1号

Shanghai Airlines
212 Jiangning Road. Tel. 800 620 8888
上海航空公司 上海江宁路212号

Scandinavian Airlines
Suite 3901, Nanzheng Plaza 580
Nanjing Road (W). Tel. 5228 5001
北欧航空公司
上海南京西路580号3901室

Singapore Airlines
Rm 1106–10, Tower 1, Plaza 66
1266 Nanjing Road (W)
Tel. 6288 7999
新加坡航空公司
上海南京西路1266号恒隆广场

Swiss International Airlines
Rm 2602, Westgate Tower
1038 Nanjing Road (W)
Tel. 6218 6810
瑞士国际航空公司
上海南京西路1038号

Thai Airways
Rm 2302, 23/F, Chong Hing Finance
Centre, 288 Nanjing Road (W)
Tel. 5298-5555
泰国航空公司
上海南京西路288号创兴金融中心

Turkish Airlines
Suite 211, West Tower, Shanghai Centre
1376 Nanjing Road (W). Tel. 3222 0022
土耳其航空公司
上海南京西路1376号上海商城西翼

United Airlines
Rm 3301, 33/F, Shanghai Central Plaza
381 Central Huaihai Road
Tel. 3311 4568, 3311 4567
美国联合航空公司
上海淮海中路381号中环广场

Virgin Atlantic Airways
Suite 221, 12 Zhongshan No.1 Road (E)
The Bund
Tel. 5353 4600, 5353 4605
维珍航空公司 上海中山东一路12号

BANKS

ABN AMRO
25/F Azia Centre
1233 Lujiazui Ring Road
Tel. 2893 9600
ABN银行
上海浦东区陆家嘴环路1233号汇亚大厦

American Express
455 East Tower, Shanghai Centre
1376 Nanjing Road (W)
Tel. 6279 7072
美国运通国际股份有限公司
上海南京西路1376号上海商城东翼

Australia and New Zealand Banking Group Limited
39/F HSBC Tower
1000 Lujiazui Ring Road
Tel. 6841 0111
澳大利亚新西兰银行
上海浦东区陆家嘴环路1000号汇丰大厦

Bank of America
17/F Azia Centre
1233 Lujiazui Ring Road. Tel. 6160 8888
美国银行
上海浦东区陆家嘴环路1233号汇亚大厦

Bank of China (Shanghai Main Branch)
23 Zhongshan No. 1 Road (E)
Tel. 6329 1979
中国银行 (上海分行) 中山东一路23号

Bank of East Asia
1/F Bank of China Tower
200 Central Yincheng Road
Tel. 6888 0333
东亚银行
上海银城中路200号中银大厦

The Bank of Tokyo Mitsubishi
HSBC Tower, 20/F
101 Yincheng Road (E)
Tel. 6841 1515
日本东京三菱银行
上海银城东路101号汇丰大厦

Barclay's Bank
651 Shanghai Centre
1376 Nanjing Road (W). Tel. 6279 8279
柏克莱银行
上海南京西路1376号上海商城东峰

BNP Paribus Shanghai Branch
10/F, China Merchants Tower
161 Lujiazui Road (E). Tel. 5879 7725
法国银行
上海陆家嘴东路161号 招商局大厦10楼

CITIC Industrial Bank
61 Nanjing Road (E)
Tel. 6350 6350
法国银行 上海南京东路61号

Citibank
20/F Marine Tower, 1 Pudong Avenue
Tel. 5879 1200
美国花旗银行
上海浦东大道1号中国船舶大厦20楼

Credit Lyonnais
36/F China Merchants Tower
161 Lujiazui Road (E)
Tel. 5887 0770; fax: 5887 7036

法国里昂信贷银行上海分行
上海陆家嘴东路161号 招商局大厦36楼

**The Hongkong and
Shanghai Banking Corporation**
34/F HSBC Tower
101 Yincheng Road (E)
Tel. 6841 1888
香港上海汇丰银行
上海银城东路101号汇丰大厦34楼

ING Bank
37/F HSBC Tower
101 Yincheng Road (E)
Tel. 6841 3355
ING银行
上海银城东路101号汇丰大厦37楼

JP Morgan Chase
31/F HSBC Tower
101 Yincheng Road (E).
Tel. 6841 1828
JP摩根大通银行
上海银城东路101号汇丰大厦31楼

National Bank of Canada
Suite 665A, East Tower
Shanghai Centre
1376 Nanjing Road (W)
Tel. 6279 8102
加拿大银行
上海南京西路1376号
上海商城东翼665A室

Royal Bank of Scotland
Rm 2701, Jin Mao Tower
88 Century Avenue. Tel. 5099 0688
苏格兰银行
上海浦东区世纪大道2701号金茂大厦

Standard Chartered Bank
G/F & 2/F, Standard Chartered Tower
201 Century Avenue. Tel. 3851 8000
渣打银行
上海浦东区世纪大道201号

CONSULATES

Argentina
402, Sun Plaza, 88 Xianxia Road
Tel. 6278 0300
阿根廷领事馆 上海仙霞路88号

Australia
22/F CITIC Square
1168 Nanjing Road (W)
Tel. 5292 5500
澳大利领事馆 上海南京西路1168号

Austria
1375 Central Huaihai Road
Tel. 6474 0278
澳地利领事馆 上海淮海中路1375号

Belgium
127 Wuyi Road
Tel. 6437 6579, 6437 6628
比利时驻领事馆 上海武夷路127号

Brazil
10/F, 1375 Central Huaihai Road
Tel. 6437 0110
巴西驻领事馆 上海淮海中路1375号

Cambodia
Rm 901, 400 Hankou Road
Tel. 6361-8690
柬埔寨领事馆 上海漢口路400号

Canada
Suite 604, West Tower, Shanghai Centre
1376 Nanjing Road (W)
Tel. 6279 8400
加拿大领事馆 上海南京西路1376号

Chile
Rm 305A, Equatorial Hotel
65 Yan'an Road (W). Tel. 6249 8000
智利领事馆
上海延安西路65号305A室

Cuba
501, New Town Mansion
55 Loushanguan Road. Tel. 6275 3078
古巴领事馆
上海娄山關路55号501室

Czech Republic
Suite 12B, Qihua Tower
1375 Central Huaihai Road
Tel. 6471 2420
捷克共和国领事馆
上海淮海中路1375号12B室

Denmark
Rm 701, Shanghai International Trade Centre, 2200 Yan'an Road (W)
Tel. 6209 0500
丹麦领事馆
上海延安西路2200号701室

Finland
Rm 2501–2505, 1168 Nanjing Road (W)
Tel. 5292 9900
芬兰驻领事馆 上海南京西路1168号

France
2/F, 689 Guangdong Road
Tel. 6341 1057, 6341 1055
法国领事馆 上海广东路689号

Germany
81 Yongfu Road
Tel. 6433 6951
德国领事馆 上海永福路81号

Hungary
Rm 2811, Haitong Securities Tower
689 Guangdong Road
Tel. 6341 0564, 6341 0764
匈牙利共和国驻领事馆
上海广东路689号海通证券大厦

India
Rm 1008 Shanghai International Trade
Centre, 2200 Yan'an Road (W)
Tel. 6275 8885
印度领事馆
上海延安西路2200号上海國貿中心

Iran
17 Fuxing Road (W). Tel. 6433 2997
伊朗领事馆 上海复兴路17号

Ireland
Suite 700 A, Shanghai Centre
1376 Nanjing Road (W)
Tel. 6279 8729
爱以兰领事馆 上海南京西路1376号

Israel
7/F, New Town Mansion
55 Loushanguan Road. Tel. 6209 8008
以色列领事馆 上海娄山關路55号

Italy
19/F, 989 Changle Road
Tel. 5407 5588
意大利驻领事馆 上海长乐路989号

Japan
8 Wanshan Road. Tel. 5257 4766
日本领事馆
上海万山路8号近兴义路

Republic of Korea
60 Wanshan Road
Tel. 6295 5000, 6259 2639
大韩民国领事馆
上海万山路60号

Malaysia
Units 01 & 04, 9/F, Bldg B
Dawning Centre, 500 Hongbaoshi Road
Tel. 6090 0360
马来西亚领事馆
上海红宝石路500号

Mexico
10/F, Bldg A, 500 Hongbaoshi Road
Tel. 6125 0220
墨西哥驻领事馆
上海红宝石路500号

Netherlands
4/F, Sun Plaza, East Tower
88 Xianxia Road
Tel. 6209-9076
荷兰领事馆 上海仙霞路88号4楼

New Zealand
Rm.1605–1607A, The Centre
989 Changle Road. Tel. 5407 5858
新西兰领事馆
上海长乐路989号世纪商贸广场

Norway
Rm 321, 12 Zhongshan No. 1 Road (E)
Tel. 6323 9988
挪威领事馆 上海中山一路12号

Peru
Rm 2705, Kerry Centre
1515 Nanjing Road (W)
Tel. 5298 5900
秘鲁领事馆 上海南京西路1515号

Philippines
Suite 368, Shanghai Centre
1376 Nanjing Road (W)
Tel. 6279 8337
菲律领事馆 上海南京西路1376号

Poland
618 Jianguo Road (W)
Tel. 6433 9288
波兰领事馆 上海建国西路618号

Portugal
16/F, C–D, 567 Weihai Road
Tel. 6288 6767
葡萄牙驻上海总领事馆
上海威海路567号晶采世纪大厦

Russia
20 Huangpu Road
Tel. 6324 2682
俄罗斯独联体领事馆
上海黄埔路20号

Singapore
89 Wanshan Road
Tel. 6278 5566
新加坡领事馆
上海万山路89号

Spain
Rm 303, 12 Zhongshan No. 1 Road (E)
Tel. 6321-3543
西班牙领事馆 上海中山一路12号

Sweden
Rm 1521-1541, 381 Central Huaihai
Road. Tel. 5359 9610
瑞典领事馆 上海淮海中路381号

Switzerland
22/F, Bldg A, 319 Xianxia Road
Tel. 6270 0519
瑞士驻领事馆 上海仙霞路319号

Thailand
7 Zhongshan No. 1 Road (E)
Tel. 6323 4095
泰国领事馆 上海中山一路7号

Turkey
Floor 13, Qihua Tower
1375 Central Huaihai Road
Tel. 6474 6838
土耳其领事馆 上海淮海中路1375号

United Kingdom
Suite 301–302 Shanghai Centre
1376 Nanjing Road (W)
Tel. 6279 7650
英国领事馆 上海南京西路1376号

USA
1469 Central Huaihai Road
Tel. 6433 6880
美国领事馆 上海淮海中路1469号

Yugoslavia
Rm 302, No. 1, Lane 60
Ronghua Avenue (W). Tel. 6208 7412
南斯领事馆
上海榮華西道60弄1号里昂花園

CONVENTION AND EXHIBITION VENUES

All the top hotels in Shanghai have excellent facilities for meetings, conventions and exhibitions. Shanghai also has a growing number of world-class dedicated facilities.

Shanghai Everbright Exhibition Centre
66 Caobao Road
Tel. 6475 3288
上海光大会展中心 上海漕北路66号

Shanghai Exhibition Centre
1000 Central Yan'an Road
Tel. 6279 0279
上海展览中心 上海延安中路1000号

Shanghai International Exhibition Centre
88 Loushanguan Road
Tel. 6275 5800
上海国际展览馆 上海婁山關路88号

Shanghai Mart
2299 Yan'an Road (W)
Tel. 6236 6888
上海世贸商城 上海延安西路2299号

Shanghai New International Exhibition Centre
2345 Longyang Road, Pudong
Tel. 2890 6666
上海新国际展览中心
上海浦东龙阳路234号

Business Addresses

American Chamber of Commerce
Rm 568, Shanghai Centre, 1376 Nanjing Road West. Tel. 6279 7119
上海美国商
上海南京西路1376号上海商城

British Chamber of Commerce
5/F Marks and Spencer Building, 863 Nanjing Road (W)
Tel. 6218 5022
英国商会
上海南京西路863号马莎百货大楼

AustCham (Australian Camber of Commerce in Shanghai)
Rm. 6709, Apollo Building, 1440 Central Yan'an Road
Tel. 6248 8301
中国澳大利亚商会
延安中路1440号阿波罗大厦6709室

China Council for the Promotion of International Trade, Shanghai Sub-Council
28 Jinling Road (W)
Tel. 5306 0228
中国国际贸易促进委员会上海市分会
上海金陵西路28号

European Chamber of Commerce in China
Rm 2204, Shui On Plaza
333 Central Huaihai Road
Tel. 6385 2023
中国区盟商会
上海淮海中路333号瑞安广场

Shanghai Foreign Economic Relations and Trade Commission (SMERT)
Hongqiao Plaza, 55 Loushanguan Road
Tel. 6275 2200
上海市对外经济贸易委员会
上海娄山關路55号新虹橋大廈

Shanghai Pudong New Area Administration
141 Pudong Avenue
Tel. 5878 8388
上海市浦东新区管理委员会
上海浦东大道141号

Medical Care

There are a number of hospitals designated for the treatment of foreigners in Shanghai. These have superior wards and private rooms, with staff geared to working with foreign patients and able to communicate in English. Routine consultations are usually dealt with through the hospitals—but there are now dedicated medical and dental clinics open in the city. Some hotels will have their own clinics; for relief from routine ailments, doctors can usually be swiftly summoned to your hotel room.

Hospitals

Huashan Hospital
Floors 15 and 16, New Building
12 Central Wulumuqi Road
Tel. 6248 9999 ext. 2531, 6248 3986
华山医院 上海乌鲁木齐中路12号

Huadong Hospital
221 Yan'an Road (W)
Tel. 6248 3180 ext. 30106
华东医院 上海延安西路221号

Renai International Patient Centre
133 Caoxi Road (N). Tel. 5489 3781
仁爱国际患者中心 上海漕溪路133号

Ruijin Hospital
197 Ruijin No. 2 Road
Tel. 6437 0045 ext. 668101
瑞金医院 上海瑞金二路197号

Shanghai East International Medical Centre
551 Pudong Road (S), Pudong
Tel. 5879 9999
上海东方国际医院 上海浦东南路551号

Shanghai Medical University Children's Hospital
Floor 3, 183 Fenglin Road
Tel. 6403 7254
上海医科大学儿科医院
上海枫林路183号3楼

Shanghai No. 1 People's Hospital International Medical Care Centre
585 Jiulong Road. Tel. 6324 3852
上海市第一人民医院国际医疗保健中心
上海九龍路585号

CLINICS

Arrail Dental
Room 204, Lippo Plaza
222 Central Huaihai Road
Tel. 5396.6538
瑞尔齿科
上海淮海中路222号力寶广场204室

DDS Dental Care
B1-05 Evergo Tower, 1325 Central Huaihai Road
Tel. 5465 2678, 5465 5766
上海缔矢口腔门诊部 迪迪爱斯齿科
上海桃江路1号二楼

Tokushikai Dental
386 Dagu Road
Tel. 6340 0270, 6340 0290
德真会齿科
上海大沽路386号

World Link Shanghai Centre Clinic
Suite 203, Shanghai Centre West Tower
1376 Nanjing Road (W)
Tel. 6279.7688
瑞新国际医疗中心
上海南京西路1376号
上海商城西翼203室

Worldlink Jinqiao Medical And Dental Centre
51 Hongfeng Road
Tel. 5032 8288
瑞新医科及齿科中心
上海红枫路51号

SHOPPING
ANTIQUES, ARTS AND CRAFTS

Changqingteng
Unit 7, House 1, Lane 181, Taicang Road
North Block, Xintiandi
长青藤
上海太倉路181弄新天地北里1号

Chuangxin Old Arts and Crafts Store
1297 Central Huaihai Road
创新古玩店 上海淮海中路1297号

Ding Jin Antique Shop
701 Central Huaihai Road
鼎金古玩商店 上海淮海中路701号

Hualian Commercial Building
634 Nanjing Road (E)
华联商厦 上海南京东路634号

Guohua Porcelain Store
550 Nanjing Road (E)
国华瓷器商店 上海南京东路550号

Old Town Embroidery Shop
21 New Yuyuan Road
南市刺绣商店 上海豫园新路21号

Old Town Handicraft Store
21 Yicheng Road
南市工艺品商店 上海邑城路21号

Shaanxi Old Ware Store
557 Central Yan'an Road
陕西旧货店 上海延安中路557号

Shanghai Antiques and Curios Store
192–240 Guangdong Road
上海文物商店
上海广东路192-240号

Shanghai Art Treasure Palace
409 Changzhi Road (E)
上海艺术珍宝宫 上海长治东路409号

Shanghai Arts and Crafts Jewellery and Jade Ware Store
438 Nanjing Road (E)
上海市珠宝玉器商店
上海南京东路438号

Shanghai Jingdezhen Porcelain Store
1175 Nanjing Road (W)
上海景德镇艺术瓷器服务部
上海南京西路1175号

Shanghai Lyceum Jewellery and Antique Store
398 Changle Road
宝馨珠宝文物商行 上海长乐路398号

Shanghai Philatelic Company
244 Nanjing Road (E)
上海股票公司 上海南京东路244号
698 Nanjing Road (W)
上海南京西路698号

Tiehuaxuan Pottery Shop
68 Yuyuan Road
铁画轩紫砂陶瓷店 上海豫园路68号

Wang Sin Kee (Wang Xingji) Fan Shop
782 Nanjing Road (E)
王星记扇庄 上海南京东路782号

Wanli Walking Stick Shop
Yu Garden Bazaar
万里手杖店 上海豫园商场

Yuhua Arts and Crafts Store
929–935 Central Huaihai Road
玉华工艺商店
上海淮海中路929-935号

Yuyuan Arts and Crafts Company
Hua Bao Building, 265 Central Fangbang Road.
豫园商城工艺品公司
上海方便中路265号

Zhang Xiaoquan Scissors Shop
490 Nanjing Road (E)
张小泉剪刀店 上海南京东路490号

Bookstores

Garden Books
325 Changle Road
韬奋西文书局
上海长乐路325号 近陕西南路

SBT Bookstore
50 Hongqiao Road.
上海外文书店 上海虹桥路50号

Shanghai Book Traders Used Books Bookstore
36 Shanxi Road (S)
上海外文图书公司 上海山西南路36号

Shanghai Foreign Languages Bookstore
390 Fuzhou Road
上海外文书店 上海福州路390号

Shanghai's City of Books
465 Fuzhou Road
上海书城 上海福州路465号

Shanghai Museum Bookstore
201 People's Avenue
上海博物馆书店 上海人民大道201号

Xinhua Bookstore
345 Nanjing Road (E)
新华书店 上海南京东路345号

Shopping Malls and Department Stores

CITIC Square
1168 Nanjing Road (W).
中信泰富港场 上海南京西路1168号

Cloud Nine Shopping Mall
1018 Changning Road
龙之梦购物中心 长宁路1018号

Friendship Store
1118 Changshou Road
上海友谊商店 长寿路1118号

Grand Gateway
1 Hongqiao Road.
港威 上海虹桥路1号

Hongqiao Friendship Shopping Centre
6 Zunyi Road.
虹桥友谊商城 上海遵义路6号

International Shopping Centre
527 Central Huaihai Road
国际百货中心 上海淮海中路527号

Jinjiang Dickson Shopping Centre
400 Changle Road
锦光迪生中心 上海长乐路400号

Marks & Spencer
863 Nanjing Road (W)
马莎百货大楼
上海南京西路863号

New World Department Store
2 Nanjing Road (W)
新世界百货公司 上海南京西路2号

Next Age Department Store
501 Zhangyang Road
八佰伴新世界商厦 上海張扬路501号

Oriental Department Store
8 Caoxi Road (N)
东方商店中心 上海漕溪北路8号

Pacific Department Store
太平洋百货公司
333 Central Huaihai Road
上海淮海中路333号
932 Hengshan Road
上海衡山路932号

218 Tianmu Road (W)
上海天目西路218号

Parksons
918 Central Huaihai Road
百盛商店 上海淮海中路918号

Plaza 66
1266 Nanjing Road (W)
恒隆商场 上海南京西路1266号

Printemps Department Store
939 Central Huaihai Road
巴黎春天百货 上海淮海中路939号

Raffles City
288 Central Tibet Road
来福士广场 上海西藏中路268号

Shanghai No.1 Department Store
830 Nanjing Road (E)
上海第一百货商店 上海南京东路830号

Superbrand Mall
168 Lujiazui Road (W)
正大百货商店 上海陆家嘴西路168号

Times Square
99 Central Huaihai Road
大上海时代广场 上海淮海中路99号

Times Square Pudong
500 Zhangyang Road
浦东时代广场 上海張揚路500号

Westgate Mall
1038 Nanjing Road (W)
梅龙镇广场 上海南京西路1038号

Yuyuan Department Store
84 Yuyuan Road
豫园商城 上海豫园路84号

Supermarkets

Carrefour
家乐福超市
268 Shuicheng Road (S)
上海水城南路268号
20 Wuning Road 上海武宁路20号
Cloud Nine Shopping Mall
1018 Changning Road
龙之梦购物中心 长宁路1018号

City Shop
城市超市
Shanghai Centre
1376 Nanjing Road (W)
上海南京西路1376号上海商城
B1/F, 618 Xujiahui Road
徐家汇路618号B1层

City'super
LG2/F, ifc Mall, 8 Century Avenue
上海世纪大道8号 国金中心商场地下2楼

EK-chor Lotus Supercentre
Superbrand Mall
168 Lujiazui Road (W)
易初莲花超市 上海陆家嘴西路168号

Health Spas

Banyan Tree Spa
The Westin Hotel Shanghai
88 Central Henan Road. Tel. 6335 1888
上海悦榕 Spa
威斯汀大飯店 河南中路88号

Bund 5 Spa Oasis
5 on the Bund, 5 Zhongshan
No. 1 Road (E) The Bund
Tel. 6321 9135, 6321 9176
上海中山东一路5号外滩五号

Dragonfly Retreat 悠庭保健会所
Numerous outlets around the city including:
20 Donghu Road. Tel. 5405 0008
徐汇区东湖路20号
Shanghai Kerry Centre
1515 Nanjing Road (W). Tel. 6279 4625
南京西路1515号嘉里中心
458 Dagu Road. Tel. 6327 1193
大沽路458号

Evian Spa
2F, No. 3 The Bund. Tel. 6323 3355
依云水疗 外滩3号

Travel and Transport
Travel Agencies and Bodies

Shanghai Municipal Tourism Administration
Huating Guest House
2525 Zhongshan Road (W)
Tel. 6439 1818 ext. 2702
上海市旅游事务管理局
上海中山西路2525号華亭賓館

Shanghai Tourist Information and Service Centre
Main Office: Rm 410–414
2525 Zhongshan Road (W)
Tel. 6439 8947, 6481 0977
上海市旅游咨询服务中心
上海中山西路2525号

China Travel Service Shanghai
881 Central Yan'an Road
Tel. 6247 8888
上海市中国旅行社
上海延安中路881号

China Youth Travel Service Shanghai
2 Hengshan Road
Tel. 6247 8888
上海中国青年旅行社 上海衡山路2号

Shanghai China International Travel Service
1277 Beijing Road (W)
Tel. 6289 8899
上海中国旅行社股份有限公司
上海北京西路1277号

Shanghai Huating Overseas Tourist Company
4/F, 503 Wulumuqi Road (N)
Tel. 6248 5470
上海华亭海外旅游公司
上海乌鲁木齐北路503号

Shanghai Jinjiang Tourist Company
191 Changle Road. Tel. 6472 0354,
6466 2828, ext. 231, 232
上海锦江旅游有限公司
上海长乐路191号

Shanghai Public Security Bureau
Exit-Entry Administration Bureau
1500 Minsheng Road, Pudong
Tel. 2895 1900
上海市出入境管理局
上海浦东民生路1500号

Train Stations

Shanghai Railway Station
303 Moling Road
Tel. 6317 9090, 9510 5123
800 820 7890 (tickets)
上海火车站 上海秣陵路303号

Shanghai South Railway Station
Humin Road
Tel. 6317 6060
上海南站 上海沪闵路

Bus Stations

Shanghai Sightseeing Bus Station
666 Tianyaoqiao Road
(Shanghai Stadium)
Tel. 6426 5555
上海旅游集散站
上海天钥桥路666号 近零陵路

Shanghai Long Distance Central Bus Station
North Square Shanghai Railway Station,
1662 Zhongxing Road
Tel. 6605 0000
上海长途客运总站
上海中兴路1662号铁路 上海站北广场

Hutie Long Distance Bus Station
783 Hengfeng Road. Tel. 6353 2300
上海沪铁长途客运站
上海恒丰路783号

Shanghai Hutai Bus Station
1015 Zhongshan Road (N)
Tel. 5652 8400
沪太客运站
中山北路1015号 近沪太路

Shanghai South Bus Station
399 Laohumin Road. Tel. 5435 3535
上海南站
上海老沪闵路399号

Sea Travel

Shanghai Port International Cruise Terminal
800 East Road (E); Tel. 6595-2299
上海港国际客运中心
上海虹口区东大名路800号

The Japan-China International Ferry Company
18/F, 908 Daming Road (E)
Tel. 6325 7642
上海中日国际渡轮
上海东大名路908号

The Shanghai International Ferry Company
15/F, 908 Daming Road (E)
Tel. 6595 8666
上海国际渡轮 上海东大名路908号

Taxi Companies

Baisha Company Tel. 96840
Dazhong Company Tel. 96822
Haibo Company Tel. 96965
Jinjiang Company Tel. 96961

Museums and Theatres

China Art Museum
161 Shangnan Road
中华艺术馆
上海浦东新区上南路161号

Shanghai Municipal History Museum
Gate 4, Oriental Pearl TV Tower
1 Century Avenue
上海市历史博物馆
上海浦东世纪大道1号

Shanghai Museum
201 People's Avenue
上海博物馆 上海人民大道201号

Shanghai Museum of
Science and Technology
2000 Century Avenue
上海科技博物馆
上海浦东世纪大道2000号

Shanghai Natural History Museum
260 Yan'an Road (E)
上海自然博物馆　上海延安东路260号

Lyceum Theatre
57 Maoming Road (S)
Tel. 6217 8530, 6256 5544
兰心大戏院　上海茂名南路57号

Majestic Theatre
66 Jiangning Road
Tel. 6217 4409
美琪大戏院　上海江宁路66号

Mercedes-Benz Arena
1200 Century Avenue
Tel. 3899 6688
梅赛德斯-奔驰文化中心
上海世博大道1200号

Power Station of Art
Lane 20, Huayuangang Road
Tel. 3127 8535
上海黄浦区 花园港路20弄, 近苗江路

Shanghai Centre Theatre
1376 Nanjing Road (W)
Tel. 6279 8663
上海商城戏院　上海南京西路1376号

Shanghai Circus World
2266 New Gonghe Road
Tel. 5665 6622, 6652 2395
上海马戏城　上海共和新路2266号

Shanghai Conservatory of Music
20 Fenyang Road
Tel. 80 0820 4800, 6437 0137
上海音乐院　上海汾阳路20号

Shanghai Concert Hall
523 Yan'an Road (E)
Tel. 5386 6666, 6386 2836
上海音乐厅
上海延安东路523号 近龙门路

Shanghai Dramatic Arts Centre
288 Anfu Road
Tel. 6473 4567
上海话剧中心美术院
上海安福路288号

Shanghai Grand Theatre
300 People's Avenue
Tel. 6372 8701, 6372 8702
上海大剧院　上海人民大道300号

Shanghai Oriental Arts Centre
425 Dingxing Road
Tel. 6217 2426, 6217 3055
东方艺术中心　上海丁香路425号

Yifu Theatre
701 Fuzhou Road. Tel. 6351 4668
逸夫舞台　上海福州路701号

POST AND TELECOMMUNICATIONS

Shanghai Central Post Office
359 Tiantong Road
上海市邮政局　上海天潼路359号
Shanghai Telecommunications Building
(Service Office)
1122 Yan'an Road (E)

上海电信大楼营业处
上海延安东路1122号

Shanghai Telegraph Office (main branch)
30 Nanjing Road (E)
上海市电报局（总局）
上海南京东路30号

Post offices with
English speaking staff are found at:
212 Xinhua Road
上海新华路212号
1337 Central Huaihai Road
上海淮海中路1337号
Shanghai Centre, 1376 Nanjing Road (W)
上海南京西路1376号上海商城

Courier Services

DHL-SINOTRANS
303 Jinian Road. Tel. 80 0810 8000
敦豪国际航空快件有限公司
上海纪念路303号

Federal Express
10/F Antena Building, 107 Zunyi Road
Tel. 6275 0808
联邦快递有限公司
上海安泰大厦遵义路107号

UPS
Rm 1318–1338 Shanghai Central Plaza
381 Central Huaihai Road
Tel. 8008 208 388
UPS快件有限公司
上海淮海中路381号上海商场

Useful Telephone Numbers

American Express Travel Related Services Tel. 6279 8082
Tourist Information (English) Tel. 6439 8947
Tourist Hotline Tel. 6439 0630
Shanghai Travel Information Service Centre Tel. 6439 8096
Hongqiao Airport Information Tel. 6268 8918–2 (English)
Pudong International Airport Information 3848 4500–2 (English)
Boat Enquiries Tel. 6326 0050
Boat Schedules and Tickets Tel. 6326 1261
Bus Enquiries Tel. 5663 0203
Train Enquiries Tel. 6317 9090
Metro Enquiries Tel. 6318 9000
Maglev Enquiries Tel. 2890 7776/7
Police Tel. 110
Police (English) Tel. 6357-6666
Fire Tel. 119
Ambulance Tel. 120
International SOS Tel. 6295-0099
Beijing International SOS Tel. (010) 6462-9100
International Call Operator (English) Tel. 10810
IDD Code Enquiry (English) Tel. 106
Directory Enquiries Tel. 114
Time Tel. 117
Weather Forecast (English) Tel. 121
Five-day Forecast (English) Tel. 969222

RECOMMENDED READING—BEIJING

Reading up on Beijing, both modern and ancient, is like visiting the city itself: it is tough to find a place to start. Oxford University Press in Hong Kong has done a great deed by having made available some affordable hardback and paperback reprints of several classic works in English about Beijing. A good start is *Old Peking: City of the Ruler of the World* (OUP, Hong Kong, 1997), an anthology of writing on the capital by former New Zealand ambassador to Beijing, Chris Elder. Three indispensable titles that describe the city as it was from the 1920s to 1940s are the highly detailed *In Search of Old Peking* by Arlington and Lewisohn; the more prosaic and evocative *Peking* by Juliet Bredon; and the apotheosis of life in Old Peking, George Kates' *The Years That Were Fat: Peking 1933–1940* (see excerpt page 58). Also in the Oxford series is Reginald Fleming Johnston's *Twilight in the Forbidden City*. Written in the 1920s after the fall of imperial China, Johnston served as the English tutor and tennis teacher of Puyi, the last emperor of the Qing Dynasty. The book served as partial basis for the script of Bernardo Bertolucci's 1986 Academy Award-winning film, *The Last Emperor*. The density of modern Chinese history is prodigiously covered in Jonathan Spence's *The Search for Modern China* (W.W. Norton & Co., 2001). For Spence, widely considered today's most readable China scholar, modern Chinese history begins in 1644! Guaranteed to weigh down your carry-on luggage, this book is perhaps best read prior to arrival in China. Jonathon D. Spence's *Treason by the Book* (Penguin, 2002) and *The Chan's Great Continent* (W.W. Norton & Co., 1998) are also informative.

Foreign journalists working in China have written a bevy of new books introducing contemporary China. Philip Pan of the Washington Post wrote *Out of Mao's Shadow: The Struggle for the Soul of a New China* (Picador USA, 2009), which describes the struggle "for the soul of the world's most populous nation" between a "venal party-state" and "a ragtag collection of lawyers, journalists, entrepreneurs, artists, hustlers, and dreamers striving to build a more tolerant, open, and democratic China." *Factory Girls: From Village to City in a Changing China* (Spiegel & Grau, August 4, 2009) by Leslie T. Chang, former correspondent for the Asian Wall Street Journal, tells the story of several young migrant women who leave the farm to chase their dreams in the big city. John Pomfret, also of the Washington Post, tells the story of modern China by following the lives of his Chinese classmates from the 1980s in *Chinese Lessons: Five Classmates and the Story of the New China* (Holt Paperbacks,

2007). Meanwhile, two other journalists wrote about modern China while driving through the cities and countryside. In *Country Driving* Peter Hessler describes the changes of the past 15 years in China through the eyes of the people he meets along the way. Meanwhile, Rob Gifford *China Road: A Journey into the Future of a Rising Power* (Random House, 2008) drives from Shanghai to the Kazakhstan border, along the way meeting with truck drivers, merchants, hermits and prostitutes.

For a view of modern business in China and Beijing, former *Los Angeles Times* bureau chief Jim Mann's *Beijing Jeep: A Case Study of Western Business in China* (Westview Press, 1997) remains the classic cautionary tale. Although some of the circumstances have since changed, many of the challenges experienced by the automotive executives in the book are still in effect. An excellent but not Beijing-specific look at business in China is Joe Studwell's *The China Dream: The Quest for the Last Great Untapped Market on Earth* (Grove Press, 2003), a penetrating look at China's current economic reality. For an intriguing inside look at the wild world of business in China consider *One Billion Customers: Lessons from the Front Lines of China Business* by James McGregor (Free Press, 2005) and, Tim Clissold's *Mr. China: A memoir* (Collins, 2006). An academic but sometimes humorous look at East meeting West can be found in *Golden Arches East* (Stanford University Press, 1998). A sociological survey of the acceptance of McDonald's in five Asian countries and territories (the Chinese mainland, Hong Kong, Taiwan, Japan, and South Korea), the book shows how the hamburger chain has morphed from an American fast food purveyor into, as one Beijing customer put it, 'a high-class foreign restaurant like this.'

Eileen Wen Mooney's *Beijing Eats* (China Population Publishing House, Beijing 2009) provides an introduction to China's major cuisines and lists 140 Chinese restaurants to sample in Beijing, complete with suggested dishes to sample.

A number of attractive coffee-table books published about the capital include Leong Ka Tai's photographic essay, *Beijing* (Times Editions, Singapore), with a text by Frank Ching; and the earlier *Peking: A Tale of Three Cities* by Nigel Cameron, with memorable photographs from the 1960s by Brian Blake (Weatherhill). Nigel Cameron's *Barbarians and Mandarins: Thirteen Centuries of Western Travellers in China* (Oxford University Press, 1999) is also highly recommended.

Two personal accounts of the old days are David Kidd, *Peking Story: The Last Days of Old China* (New York Review of Books, 2003) and John Blofeld's *City of Lingering Splendour: A Frank Account of Old Peking's Exotic Pleasures* (Shambhala,

2001). Three further literary accounts in the Hong Kong Oxford reprint series are Osbert Sitwell's *(1996) Escape with Me!*, Harold Acton's (1984) *Peonies and Ponies*, and the surprisingly insightful *Superficial Journey through Tokyo and Peking*, by Peter Quennell (1995). Rachel DeWoskin's, *Foreign Babes in Beijing: Behind the Scenes of a New China* (W.W. Norton & Co., 2005) is a diaristic account that provides some interesting insights into Chinese pop culture. The Last Days of Old Beijing: Life in the Vanishing Backstreets of a City Transformed (Walker & Company, 2009) Michael Meyers chronicles the spread of urban planning as it transforms an old hutong part of the city, where he lived for two years.

For a foreigner's view of post revolutionary China and the Cultural Revolution, Sidney Rittenberg's *The Man Who Stayed Behind* (Duke University Press, 2001) is a first-hand account of the turmoil that set the stage for China's transformation from communist monolith to capitalist giant. Rittenberg is one of the few foreigners ever to attain high rank within the Chinese communist party.

The end of the Qing Dynasty is graphically portrayed in two autobiographies and a memoir—*Two Years in The Forbidden City* by Der Ling (University Press of the Pacific, 2001), a Manchu princess who was a lady-in-waiting to the Empress Dowager Cixi; *From Emperor to Citizen* (Beijing Foreign Languages Press, 1964) by the last emperor, Puyi; and *With the Empress Dowager of China* by Katherine A. Carl (Kegan Paul, 1998). Marina Warner's biography of the Empress Dowager, *The Dragon Empress* (Weidenfeld & Nicolson, 1972), is particularly entertaining. Sterling Seagrave's *Dragon Lady: The Life and Legend of the Last Empress of China* (Vintage Books, 1993) has an alternative take on Cixi, opining that much of her infamy was fabricated at the time of her reign by unscrupulous foreigners. The Forbidden City is described in great detail, accompanied by reproductions of contemporary paintings and copperplate etchings, in *The Architecture of the Forbidden City* (Joint Publishing), currently available only with a Chinese text. An excellent account of the Qing Dynasty can be found in *China Marches West, The Qing Conquest of Central Eurasia* by Peter C. Perdue (Belknap/Harvard, 2005). For a valuable read on the history of China's war on foreigners, refer to Diana Preston's *The Boxer Rebellion: China's War on Foreigners, 1900* (Constable & Robinson, 2002).

Those interested in reading some of China's classical novels will enjoy *Dream of the Red Chamber* by the 18th-century novelist Cao Xueqin—translated as *The Story of the Stone* by David Hawkes and John Minford (five volumes, Viking, 1982) or as *A Dream of Red Mansions* (three volumes, Acacia Press, 2001), rendered into English by Yang Hsien-yi and Gladys Yang. A garden featured in the novel—*Daguanyuan*—has been recreated as a park in the southwest of Beijing (see page 165). Life in prerevolutionary China is vividly portrayed in *Rickshaw: The Novel of Luotuo Xiangzi* by Lao She (University Press of Hawaii, 1979) (*see* excerpt page 144), and *Family* by Ba Jin (Cheng & Tsui, 1992)—both well worth reading. *The Selected Stories of Lu Xun*, China's most influential 20th-century writer, is translated by Yang Hsien-yi and Gladys Yang (Beijing Foreign Languages Press, 2000) (*see* excerpt page 511). Two wonderful titles that treat the customs and folkways of Old Peking are *Festivals in Classic China* (Princeton University Press, 1975), translated and annotated by Derk Bodde, and the utterly charming *The Adventures of Wu: The Life Cycle of a Peking Man* (Princeton University Press, 1983) by H. Y. Lowe, a Chinese journalist of the 1930s. A contemporary poet and writer of fiction who has been hailed as a new voice in the post-Cultural Revolution literary scene is Beijing-born Zhao Zhenkai (pen-name Bei Dao), whose collection of short stories, *Waves*, has been translated by Bonnie S. McDougall and Susette Ternent Cooke (The Chinese University Press, Hong Kong, 1985). *Seeds of Fire: Chinese Voices of Conscience*, edited by Geremie Barmé and John Minford, is an anthology of writings-poetry, essays and extracts from novels—representing the new 'literature of conscience' (Noonday Press, 1990). *Riddles of Belief ... and Love: A Story* (Dog Ear Publishing, 2010), by Lin Zhe, A powerful story of a family that ranges across the entire length of China, to California and back again, to the War against the Japanese to the fearsome post-Liberation political movements culminating in the madness of the Cultural Revolution.

For a good picture of life in the foreign community in Beijing in the 1920s read Ann Bridge's novel *Peking Picnic* (Vintage Books, 1975). Oxford University Press's *A Photographer in Old Peking* is a beautiful 1994 volume of rare black-and-white photographs taken between 1933 and 1946, interspersed with an evocative account of people and places by the photographer Hedda Morrison. Another treasure of black and-white photography is *Foreigners Within the Gates—The Legations at Peking* (Oxford University Press, 1993), by Michael J. Moser and Yeone Wei-chih Moser, which reveals the expat lifestyle just before the turn of the 20th century and follows the demise of those quarters to the present. The tale of a great eccentric is told by historian Hugh Trevor-Roper in *Hermit of Peking: The Hidden Life of Sir Edmund Backhouse* (Transatlantic Publications, 1993). Compiled by Asia Art Archive for the eponymous art exhibition, the catalogue *Paris-Pekin* (Chinese Century, 2002) is a thought-provoking anthology of contemporary Chinese art.

Hong Kong University Press published a comprehensive book on *The Ming Tombs*, written by Anne Paludan in 1981, which remains an excellent read. For those with a special interest in the subject, Elizabeth Halston's *Peking Opera* (Oxford University Press, 1983) is one of the best books in English. A concise paperback on the subject appeared in 1981 in *Beijing-Peking Opera and Mei Lanfang: a Guide to China's Traditional Theatre and the Arts of its Great Master* by Wu Zuguang, Huang Zuolin and Mei Shaowu (New World Press, 1981). *Mei Lanfang—Leader of the Pear Garden* by A. C. Scott is written with much absorbing background (Hong Kong University Press, 1959). For general histories of China, two little known gems are *A Short History of the Chinese People* (Dover Publications, 2002) by L. Carrington Goodrich, which brings the reader up to the early 20th century, and Stephen Haw's, *A Traveller's History of China* (Interlink Publishing Group, 2002). Slightly longer is Jacques Gernet's *A History of Chinese Civilization* (Cambridge, 1982).

RECOMMENDED READING—SHANGHAI

With addictive purpose, Shanghai has long captured the imagination of writers—of fact and fiction and a mash of both that this intoxicating city inimically inculcates in the veins of its residents, visitors, onlookers and dreamers. The city's allure is no less dimmed today as a flurry of new books on Shanghai's past, present and future, as well as a flood of historical reprints have appeared. And it's encouraging to see that much of this new impetus emanates from the hearts and hands of many modern Shanghailanders who have made the city their home. The most exciting recent development has been the advent of Earnshaw Books (www.earnshawbooks.com), publisher of many must-read reprints and valuable new editions. Long time Shanghai resident Graham Earnshaw; former Reuters Bureau Chief in China, entrepreneur, writer, Renaissance man and burgeoning media mogul is the man behind the venture. Amongst the reprints are *All About Shanghai and Environs*, a classic 1934 guidebook with a new Foreword by Peter Hibbard, *Shanghai's Schemozzle* featuring images of the advent of the Sino-Japanese war by celebrated Russian cartoonist Sapajou and *Foreign Devils in the Flowery Kingdom* by legendary Shanghai journalist and advertising man Carl Crow, with a new Foreword by Paul French. New editions include *Tales of Old Shanghai* by Graham Earnshaw, *Old Shanghai Clubs and Associations*, an extraordinary insight into treaty port social life by Nenad Djordovic, and *Peace at the Cathay*, a history of the Peace Hotel by Peter Hibbard. New editions are appearing thick and fast, so keep an eye on the website. All are highly recommended.

Even longer-term Shanghai resident and local celebrity Tess Johnston, who founded the Old China Hand Press with her partner Deke Erh in the early 1990s, has published some twenty magnificently illustrated books on the architecture and culture of old Shanghai. Amongst their recent stunning offerings are *Frenchtown Shanghai* (2000), *A Last Look: Western Architecture in Old Shanghai* (2004) and *Shanghai Art Deco* (2006). The Old China Hand Press has also published two absorbing books by Betty Barr, who grew up and spent most of her life in Shanghai, and her Shanghainese husband George Wang: *Shanghai Boy Shanghai Girl—Lives in Parallel* (2002) and *Between Two Worlds—Lessons Learned in Shanghai* (2004). Johnston has also edited a collection letters of a small town American girl in *Missy's China, Letters from Hangzhou 1934–1937* (2008) and edited the memoirs of Diana Hutchins Angulo, a privileged American in *Peking Sun Shanghai Moon, Images From a Past Era* (2008)—both of which give valuable first-hand experiences of life in old Shanghai. (See www.han-yuan.com/zhongguotong/main-chubanshe.htm) Old China Hand Press publications can be purchased at the Old China Hand Reading Room at 27 Shaoxing Road in Shanghai (tel: 6473 2526) as well as in bookstores and hotels around town.

Lynn Pan (Pan Ling), one of the most important and outstanding contemporary writers on Shanghai's history and on much beyond, is again living in the city of her birth. Her recent book *Shanghai Style—Art and Design Between the Wars* (Joint Publishing Co. (HK) 2008) offers an extraordinary insight into the rich cultural milieu of Twenties and Thirties Shanghai. Her *In Search of Old Shanghai* (Joint Publishing Co. (HK) 1982), an early companion guide, remains a valuable resource today. Amongst many other works, Pan is author of the seminal *Old Shanghai—Gangsters in Paradise* (Heinemann Asia, 1984), a reconstruction of the life and times of Du Yuesheng, Shanghai's legendary secret-society chief and mobster. Her compelling personal voyage in rediscovering her family history is wonderfully portrayed in *Tracing it Home—A Chinese Voyage* (Kodansha International, 1993).

Paul French, another Shanghai based businessman, China analyst and author, joined the Shanghai history literati with the publication of *Carl Crow—A Tough Old China Hand* (Hong Kong University Press, 2006), the fascinating story of a remarkable man, living through and making remarkable times. He is also the editor of *Carl Crow—The Long Road Back to China—The Burma Road Wartime Diaries* (Earnshaw Books, 2009). His *Through the Looking Glass—China's Foreign Journalists from Opium Wars to Mao*, (Hong Kong University Press, 2009) is a groundbreaking survey of foreign journalism in China with much to say about Shanghai. Keep an eye out for French's upcoming works that will explore the significance of Shanghai's old street names and expose the colourful life of American Gracie Gale, Shanghai's most infamous foreign lady of the night.

Other recent publications of note by foreigners living in Shanghai include Anne Warr's comprehensive survey *Shanghai Architecture* (Watermark Press, 2007, 2010), Peter Hibbard's *The Bund Shanghai: China Faces West*. (Odyssey, Hong Kong, 2007) and Greg Girards's haunting visual essay *Phantom Shanghai* (Magneta, Toronto, 2007). And last, but not least, Mark Kitto who left Shanghai to live in the nearby mountain retreat of Moganshan has produced a beautifully crafted and totally absorbing book about his extraordinary life in China that should have wide appeal: *China Cuckoo—How I Lost a Fortune and Found a Life in China* (Constable, London, 2009).

Many works from visitors and onlookers in the post-Mao era contain general, or more particular, histories on the fate of Shanghai after it was established as a treaty port. A highly readable historical chronicle of pre-liberation Shanghai can be found in Stella Dong's *Shanghai, The Rise and Fall of a Decadent City* (Harper Collins, 2000). Harriet Sergeant paints a colourful picture of foreign life in the 1920s and 1930s in *Shanghai* (Jonathan Cape, 1991) and an interesting recollection of Shanghai from the 1920s to the 1950s can be found within the pages of *Last Moments of World* (Norton, 1981) by Margaret Gaan. An excellent historical anthology, including literary excerpts from writers as diverse as Lu Xun and Osbert Sitwell, are carefully blended together in Barbara Baker's *Shanghai—Electric and Lurid City* (Oxford University Press, 1998). Pamela Yatsko's *New Shanghai—The Rocky Rebirth of the City* (John Wiley & Sons, 2003) offers starkly real insight in into the cultural and economic milieu of modern Shanghai. Orville Schell's *Mandate of Heaven* (Simon & Schuster, 1994) remains as an absorbing view of China's, and hip Shanghai's, future with its new generation of entrepreneurs, dissidents, bohemians and technocrats (see page 399).

On a more erudite level Betty Peh-T'i Wei's Shanghai, *Crucible of Modern China* (Oxford University Press, 1990) gives a comprehensive overview of Shanghai history. Two scholarly, but eminently readable, books stand out in giving an insight into culture and society in old Shanghai from two radically different perspectives. Sterling Seagrave's *The Soong Dynasty* (Harper & Row, 1985) is packed with riveting historical detail on Shanghai's most famous and powerful family. In sharp contrast

Robert Bicker's outstanding *Empire Made Me: An Englishman Adrift in Shanghai* (Allen Lane, London, 2003) views the city through the life, times and tragedy of an ordinary British policeman. For a finely written historical novel based around the life of a British Imperial Customs Inspector don't miss Christopher New's *Shanghai* (Soho Press, 2002). Frances Wood's *No Dogs and Not Many Chinese.* (John Murray, 1998) also provides an essential account of Shanghai as a treaty port. Jeffrey N. Wasserstrom's *Global Shanghai 1850–1910—A History in Fragments* (Routledge, 2009) includes 'snapshot' essays at intervals of 25 years that reflect upon Shanghai's long-standing status as a global city as it gears up for the World Expo 2010. For those interested in urban history and architecture Edward Denison and Guang Yu Ren's *Building Shanghai: The Story of China's Gateway* (Wiley-Academy, 2006) is a fine, well-researched work, telling the remarkable story of the making and re-making of a great city, replete with many interesting archive images. In *World Cities Shanghai*, (Wiley-Academy, 2002) Alan Balfour and Zheng Shiling also do a fine job in reflecting on Shanghai's urban history as well as profiling some impressive modern architectural schemes created by both Chinese and foreigners.

A few other books with serious academic intent may appeal to those wanting to learn more about Shanghai's unique urban culture. Gail Hershatter's *Dangerous Pleasures* (University of California, 1999) provides a wholesome account of prostitution and modernity in twentieth century Shanghai. *Shanghai Modern* (Harvard University Press, 1999) by Leo Ou-fan Lee focuses on the construction of Shanghai's popular urban culture through its media and entertainment industries in the 1930s. A fascinating discourse on Shanghai's vices and political mores is to be found in *Policing Shanghai 1927–1937* (University of California Press, 1995) by Frederic Wakeman, Jr.

For those interested in the Jewish historical legacy in Shanghai, be it from the perspective of the long entrenched and wealthy British Sephardic Jews to the stateless refugees from Central Europe housed in the city during World War II there is a growing body of literature on offer. An absolutely splendid tale of the fate of a wealthy Jewish family in Shanghai between the two world wars is masterfully recounted in George Spunt's *A Place in Time* (G. P. Putnam's Sons, New York, 1968). For an admirable and comprehensive account of the Sephardic Jews in Shanghai grab a copy of Maisie J. Meyer's *From the Rivers of Babylon to the Whangpoo, A Century of Sephardic Jewish Life in Shanghai.* (University Press of America, Inc., New York, 2003). Marcia Reynders Ristaino's *Port of Last Resort—The Diaspora Communities of Shanghai* (Stanford University Press, 2001) is an intricately researched account of both the Jewish and Russian communities in the city that brushes away many stereotypical views. Local interest in the history of the Jewish community has resulted in the publication of *The Jews in Shanghai* (Shanghai Pictorial Publishing House, 1995). Rena Krasno provides a exceptional and moving first-hand narrative of Jewish life in her *Strangers Always, A Jewish Family in Wartime Shanghai* (Pacific View Press, 1992) (see page 530).

Other books on wartime Shanghai worth looking out for include Bernard Wasserstein's *Secret War in Shanghai* (Profile Books, 1998), an outstanding expose of intrigue and espionage—and *Bridge House Survivor* by Henry F. Pringle (Earnshaw Books, 2009) a harrowing first-hand account of internment and torture in Shanghai's infamous Bridge House prison. *Flight From China* (The Macmillan Company, New York, 1946) by Edna Lee Booker, a popular 'girl journalist' in the city presents a vivid first-hand account of life before and during the Japanese occupation, particularly with regards to the immediate after effects of Pearl Harbour on foreigners. Most of the book was actually written by her husband as she and their children had been evacuated from the city in 1940. Of course, *Empire of the Sun* (Grafton Books, 1985) by the late J. G. Ballard still remains essential reading. For an account of what happened over the following years, Noel Barber's *The Fall of Shanghai—The Communist Takeover in 1949* (Macmillan, 1979), which draws extensively on interviews with those who lived through the period, comes highly recommended. The episode is vividly brought to life by Sam Tata's photographs and Ian McLacklan's text in *Shanghai 1949—The End of an Era* (B. T. Batsford, 1981). Like Ballard's book, Lawrence Earl's *Yangtse Incident* (George G. Harrap, 1950) was also made into a movie, telling of the adventures of the British frigate H.M.S. Amethyst that was held hostage on the great river in 1949. Two books offer fascinating insights into fate of foreigners caught up in Communist Shanghai during the early 1950s. *The Communist Conquest of Shanghai* (Twin Circle Publishing Co. and Crestwood Books, Inc., 1970) written by Paolo Alberto Rossi, the Italian Consul General at Shanghai from 1948 to 1952 tells of the new order from a political perspective. A more personal account can be found in *Stateless in Shanghai* (Earnshaw Books, 2009) by Liliane Willens that chronicles her time growing up in city from the 1930s to early 1950s, before moving to the US.

Neil Hunter, a teacher in Shanghai during the tumultuous 1960s, brings alive those times in his *Shanghai Journal—An Eyewitness Account of the Cultural Revolution* (Praeger, 1969, reissued by Oxford University Press, 1988). For what those years meant to one Shanghai inhabitant, a strong, courageous woman incarcerated in one of the city's prisons during the height of the Cultural Revolution, read Nien Cheng's gripping and incisive account of *Life and Death in Shanghai* (Grafton Books, 1986). *Anchee Min's Red Azalea—Life and Love in China* (Victor Gollancz, 1993) is an intensely moving, sensual and quite different kind of autobiography of a model member of the Red Guard who has to endure the harsh conditions of the communal farm and who is then plucked by one of Madame Mao's associates to become a star of the Chinese propaganda film industry in Shanghai (see page 476).

In the world of Chinese fiction search out copies of translations of works by Lu Xun, Mao Dun and Zhang Ailing (Eileen Chang)—China's most celebrated 20th century literary figures. Chang, the extraordinary doyenne of Shanghai literature whose novel *Lust, Caution* (translated by Julia Lovell, Anchor Books, New York, 2007) was immortalised in celluloid by Ang Lee. Also take a look at *Love in a Fallen City*, stories and novellas from the 1940's, translated by Karen Kingsbury and Eileen Chang, (New York Review Books, 2006). From the pen of Mao Dun, *Midnight* (Cheng & Tsui Company, 2000), a great novel depicting life in cosmopolitan, capitalist and corrupt Shanghai in the 1930s, is an essential read. A number of Lu Xun's fine literary and poetic works, including *Diary of a Madman and Other Stories, Selected Stories of Lu Xun and Wild Grass*, are available in English editions.

Some translations of Chinese classic texts can be found, alongside a large range of locally produced pictorial books on Shanghai old and new, in bookstores around the city itself. The following pictorials, featuring English and Chinese text, are well worth looking for—*Shanghai Longtang*, (Shanghai People's Fine Arts Publishing House, 1997), a look at the fast disappearing community housing form that is unique to the city; *Survey of Shanghai 1840s–1940s* (Shanghai People's Fine Arts Publishing House, 1993) and *Tracing Back the Excellent Architecture of Modern Times in Shanghai* (Shanghai Municipal Bureau of Housing and Land Resources, 2001). A seminal work on the early history of the International Settlement, *A Short History of Shanghai* by F. L. Hawks Pott, originally published by Kelly & Walsh in 1928, has also been reproduced locally and is available in such stores.

Other vintage books on Shanghai history worth searching for online or in second-hand bookstores include *Yellow Creek—The Story of Shanghai* by Brigadier J. V. Davidson-Houston (Putnam, London, 1962), *Shanghai Century* by Captain W. J. Moore (Arthur H. Stockwell, Devon. c.1950) and *The Shanghai Problem* (Stanford University Press, 1937) by W. C. Johnstone that gives a good history of the development of the foreign and Chinese areas of Shanghai, with particular regard to their governance.

CLUTCHING AT STRAWS

High on the Venerable Schoolmaster Gao's list of gripes was the gall of the man who had edited A General Textbook of Chinese History *in not taking the classroom teacher into account when putting this text together. Though some of it did tally with* Liaofan's Shorter History, *there were large chunks that didn't, so that it was impossible to weave the two books together into any kind of coherent lecture. The Venerable Schoolmaster Gao glanced at a slip of paper that had been left in the textbook, and his smouldering resentment against the teacher who had quit halfway through the course was fanned into a full blaze, for the note read:* Begin at Chapter Eight—The Rise and Fall of the Eastern Jin Dyansty [317–420]. *If that clod hadn't already finished lecturing on the Three Kingdoms Period [220–65], Gao himself wouldn't have had nearly so much difficulty preparing. He knew the Three Kingdoms Period up one side and down the other:* The Triple Oath of the Peach Garden, Kong Ming Borrows Arrows, Zhou Yü Thrice Angered, Huang Zhong Beheads Xia Houyuan at Dingjun Mountain, *and any number of other such incidents.* [1]

And if it had only been some later period—let's say the Tang Dynasty [618–907]— well, then you had material like Qin Qiong Sells His Horse.[2] *Yes, he could have told stories like that in a pretty entertaining way, too. But no! It couldn't be the Three Kingdoms or the Tang, it had to be that damned Eastern Jin right in between! Once more, Gao sighed in exasperation; and once more too, he made a dive for* Liaofan's Shorter History.

[1] *All of these episodes are contained in the popular historical novel* Romance of the Three Kingdoms. *In a Western setting, a character like Gao might consider familiarity with Dickens'* Tale of Two Cities *and Hugo's* Ninety-three *sufficient qualification for offering a course on the French Revolution.*

[2] *Qin Qiong was a military hero who helped the first Tang emperor found the new dynasty. Again, Gao's knowledge is derived from popular fiction.*

Lu Xun, The Venerable Schoolmaster Gao, *translated by William A Lyell*

Lu Xun (or Lu Hsün) (1881–1936) is called the father of modern Chinese literature. His first story "A Madman's Diary" is considered the first story written in Modern Chinese. Lu Xun chose to begin writing the way people talk. Lu Xun is a pen name. His real name was Zhou Shuren. Lu Xun wrote stories, poetry, essays, literary criticism and literary history. His stories were published in literary journals of the time and were then collected and published as books. He has three volumes of short stories.

For more on Lu Xun see pages 175, 369.

C

Cai Yuanpei's Former Residence 369
Calligraphy, Beijing 255
Cao Xueqin 154, 165
Caofeng Park *see* Zhongshan Park
Capital Museum 177
Capital Library 177
Car hire/rental, Shanghai 332
Carl, Katherine 14, 15, 185
Carpets, Beijing 252, 254
Cassia Ma 372
Castiglione, Guiseppe 162, 191
Cathay Hotel 353
Chamber for Gathering the Rain 381
Changning District Children's Palace 394
Changling 203
Changping County 175, 176
Chaoyang Park 224
Charpentier, Jean-Marie 397
Chefu 14
Chen Duxiu 318
Chengde 205
Chengdu 3
Chenghuang Miao *see* Temple of the City God
Chenxiangge Nunnery 383
Chenyi 365
Chekiang 121
Chiang Kai-shek 153, 367, 372, 453, 454
Chien Men 174
Childrens' Palaces 394
China Aviation Museum 175
China Council for the Promotion of International Trade 68
China National Tourism Authority 67
China Tobacco Museum 419
Chinese Buddhist Theoretical Institute 164
Chinese Maritime History Gallery 409
Chit 58–59
Chong Ming 441

Chu, State of 360
Chuan residence 416
Chuandixia 208
Chungking 121
Chunshen, Lord 360
Ci Xui Monastery 384
Circular Mound 158 *see also* Round Altar
City Bus, Shanghai 332, 333
City Worker's Club 221
Cixi *see* Empresses
Cloud Platform 195
Coal Hill (Prospect Hill) 148
Communications & services 60, 61, 62
Concubine's Well 160–161, 213
Confucius 176, 367
   Confucius Temple *see* Temples
Continental Terrace 370
Cook, Thomas 358
Court of Imperial China 14
Court of Virtuous Harmony 184
Coward, Noel 353, 358
Culture xvi–8,
Cultural Revolution 320, 358, 359
Custom House 353, 356, 360

D

Da bing 494
Dabaotai Han Tomb 208–209
Dadu 80, 102
Daguanyuan *see* Prospect Garden
Dalian 32
Dalin, Professor Liu 417
Dan ta 494
Dashanzi Art District 178
Deng Xiaoping 5, 88, 102, 104, 105
Deng Yingchao 368
Der Ling 14, 15
Dicey, Captain James Minn 33
Dinghai 32

Dingling 203
Dollar, Robert 159
Domingo, Placido 474
Dongbianmen Red Gate Gallery 179
Dong Biwu 368
Dong Chiang'an Jie 83
Dong Qichang (Ming dynasty poet) 426
Dong Yue Temple 192
Double Bridge 443
Dragon Bones Hills 208
Dragon Pavement 140
Dragon Pool 211
Drum and Bell Towers, The 153
Du Dashen 426
Du Yuesheng 372, 373, 454
Duncan, E. 32
Dule Si 206
Duolun Road 397, 594
Dynasties
   Autumn 142
   Five Dynasties 594
   Han 94, 143, 195, 199, 208, 216
   Jin 80, 102, 149, 207, 211
   Liao 80, 101, 211
   Ming 129, 142, 143, 148, 151, 167, 172, 199, 211, 251, 428, 435, 436
   Northern Song 432
   Qianlong 174, 175, 435
   Qin 199
   Qing 142, 143, 211, 428
   Spring 142
   Tang 143, 164, 251, 257, 264, 426
   Three Kingdoms 429
   Southern 256
   Warring States 142
   Western Zhou 142
   Yuan 102, 142, 143, 148, 151, 152, 192, 211
   Zhou 251

E

Echo stones 158
Echo Wall 158
Eight-legged essay 95
Elgin, Lord 83, 191
Elizabeth I 169
Emperors
   Chenghua 172
   Chongzhen 148
   Guangxu 183, 210
   Hui Zong 381
   Jiaqing 16, 205
   Kangxi 82, 90, 190, 192, 205, 206, 210, 427
   Kublai Khan 3, 80, 98, 99, 150, 167
   Puyi 85, 140, 210
   Qianlong 82, 141, 143, 152, 174, 183, 190, 191, 205, 206, 207, 210, 211
   Qin 195
   Qin Shi Huangdi 195
   Shunzhi 172
   Taizong 164
   Tongzhi 206
   Wanli 174
   Yongle 130, 150, 156, 172
   Yongzheng 190
   Zhengtong 212
Empresses
   Ci'an 160, 206
   Cixi 14–15, 82, 85, 95, 141, 152, 174, 206
      Birthday 183, 184, 191
      Contributions to the arts 174
      Portrait 14
      Summer Palace *see* Architecture
   Wu 367
Eunuchs
   An Dehai 154
   Palace Eunuchs' Mutual Prosperity Association 137

Wei Zhongxian 192
Yu Jing 192
Everbright Lamp 203
Exhibition of Historical Relics from the Qing 143
Exquisite Jade Rock, The 381

F

Fa Zang Jiang Si 384
Fengtai 89
Feng shui 69
Film Museum 178
First National Congress of the Chinese Communist Party, Site of the 363
Fonteyne, Dame Margot 474
Football 513
Forbidden City 129–135, 140–143, 148, 214, 215
Foreign Ministry of the People's Republic of China 13

Formula 1 Grand Prix 513
Four Heavenly Kings 195
Four Modernizations 88
Fragrant Hills 114, 190, 193
French Concession 320, 340, 342, 372, 373, 415
Furniture, Beijing 255
Fuxing Park 415, 492
Fuyou Road 503
Fuyou Road Mosque 397

G

Gang of Four 88, 125, 320, 523
Gates
    City 82
    Deshengmen 267
    Dong'anmen 183
    Dragon and Phoenix Gate 203
    East Palace Gate 183
    Gate of Devine Prowess 141, 213
    Gate of Heavenly Peace *see* Tiananmen
    Gate of Heavenly Purity 143
    Meridian 131, 213
    Palace 131
    Qianmen 128
    Taixuemen Gate 176
    Tiananmen 85, 102, 125, 131
    Upright Gate 131
Garbo, Greta 482
Gardens
    Apple Garden 114
    Eight Scene Garden 519
    Garden for Cultivating Harmony 51, 83, 183
    Garden of Autumn Clouds 435
    Garden of Carefree Spring 190
    Garden of Meandering Streams 431
    Grand View Garden 432
    Guyi Garden 436
    Imperial Gardens 141

A 'Little Emperor' tries for size the throne.

Prospect Garden 154, 165, 580
Purple Bamboo Garden 178
Qianlong Garden 141
Study of Self Knowledge 193
Tuisi Garden 444
Yu Garden 375, 376, 380, 381, 401, 495
Zhuxi Garden 433
Zuibaichi Garden 426
Genghis Khan 102
Getihu 88
Gobi Desert 48
God of Land 431
Gold Sand Pagoda *see* Pagodas, Fahua
Golden Tartars 80
Gong Hong 435
Gong, Prince 154
Gongpu Road Passenger Terminal 32
Gongyuan Dong Jie 94
Gongyuan Xi Jie 94
Gorgeous View Tower 148
Grand Canal 305
Grand Rockery 383
Great Vermilion Gateway 201
Great Wall 51, 82, 101, 107, 118, 195–199, 214
Great White Way 498
Great World 398
Green Gang 372, 453, 518
Guangzhou 8
Gugong *see* Imperial Palace
Guilin 3, 495
Guomindang Government 72
Guo Moruo 397

H

Haidian District 53, 89
Halls
    Abbot's Hall 387
    Chairman Mao's Memorial Hall 129
    Cloud-Dispelling Hall 184

Da Cheng Hall 385
Devajara Hall 387
Examination Hall, Ming & Qing 94
Garden History Exhibition Hall 186
Grand Hall(s) 383, 388
Great Hall of the People 125, 128, 174
Guanyin Hall 383
Hall for Cultivating Happiness 184
Hall for Viewing the Grand Rockery 381
Hall of Abstinance 157, 211
Hall of August Heaven 159
Hall of Benevolent Longevity 183
Hall of Bronzes 142
Hall of Ceramics 142
Hall of Character Cultivation 143
Hall of Clocks and Watches 143
Hall of Complete Harmony 140

Sophora japonica L., *this 500 year old decidious tree, of the bean family, shades a peaceful courtyard at the Museum of Divine Music Administration, see also pages 157 and 214.*

Hall of Happy Longevity 184
Hall of Heralding Spring 381
Hall of Imperial Supremacy 143
Hall of Imperial Longevity 148
Hall of Jade Magnificence 381
Hall of Jade Ripples 183
Hall of Mental Cultivation 213
Hall of Mildness 383
Hall of Paintings 143
Hall of Prayer for Good Harvests viii, 156, 158, 159
Hall of Preserving Harmony 140, 142
Hall of Receiving Light 150
Hall of Rippling Waves 152
Hall of Sacrifice 203
Hall of Sincere Solemnity 142
Hall of Supreme Harmony 140
Hall of Toys 142
Hall of Virtuous Brilliance 184
Hall of Union 140
Hall to Guanyin 211
Juequn Hall 388
Luohan Hall 192
Mahavira Hall 387
Maitreya Hall 387
Sanshan Guild Hall 411, 419
Shen Hall 443
Sutras Keeping Hall 387
Ten-thousand People Assembly Hall 128
Three Ears of Corn Hall 381
Three Sages Hall 387
Zhang Hall 443
Hangzhou 28, 183
Hangzhou Bay 441
Harbin 3
Hardoon, Silas 417
Hart, Sir Robert 216
Hawkes, David 165
Heavenly King(s) 383, 388

Heavenly Teachers 384
Holidays 52, 176
Hongkew Ghetto 417
Hongkew 530
Hongkong & Shanghai Bank building 350, 353
Hongkou 361
Hongmei Pedestrian Leisure Street 492
Hong shao rou 489
Houhai 225
Hsiang Fei, Princess 162
Hu Die 474
Hua Bao Building 504
Huaihai Road, Central 362, 501
Huanglu smoke tree 193
Huang Jinrong 411, 518
Huangpu Park 351
Huangpu River Ferry 334
Huating County 360
Huaxia Cultural and Tourist Area 394
Huayuan classics 437
Huggins, W.J. 32
Hunan 108
Huns 195
Hutongs 89

I

International Ferry Company 32
International Settlement 320, 351, 357, 361
Ilyshun 176
Imperial College 176, 177
Imperial Palace 14–15, 102, 129, 184
Imperial Residences 183
Imperial schoolroom 177
Imperial Vault of Heaven 158
Inkstones 257
Iron rice bowl 88
Iron Screen 152

J

Jardine Matheson 314
Jehol see Chengde
Jessfield Park see Zhongshan Park
Jewelry, Beijing 255
Jiangnan Shipbuilding Museum 419
Jiang Qing 88, 367, 482
Jianguomen 113, 247
Jianguomenwei 53
Jie 330
Jing'an Hotel 481
Jingshan 82
Jinmao Building 321, 403
Jinshan Academy of Fine Arts 436
Jinshanling 197
Jitong 60

K

Kadoorie family 394
Kadoorie, Lady Laura 368
Kadoorie, Sir Elly 368
Kaiser Kuo 101
Kangjian Pleasure Park 518
Karting 516
Khanbaliq 80, 81
King Sebastian 169
Kong Miao see Confucius
Kong Xiangxi see Kung, Dr. H.H.
Kuang Hsü 136
Kublai Khan 3, 80, 98, 99, 150, 167, 211
Kung, Dr. H.H. 367, 401
Kunju Opera 397, 481
Kunju Opera House 481
Kunming Lake 184

L

La Grande Opera 474
Lake Dianshan 429, 432
Lang Shih Ning 162
Lan Ping see Jiang Qing

League of Leftist Writers 397
Lee, Ang 474
Legacies, A Chinese Mosaic 71
Legation quarter 83, 190
Leshoutang see Hall of Happy Longevity
Li Yan'e 368
Liangmahe 244
Library of Congress 178
Lin Fengmian 416
Liu Dalin, Professor 446–449
Liulichang 214, 248
Long Corridor, The 184
Longevity Hill 183, 184
Longfu 432
Longhua Park 370
Longhua Revolutionary Martyrs' Cemetery 370–371, 519
Louis XIV 82
Louza Police Station 410
Lu 330
Lu Dongbin 448
Lu Xun 318, 369, 397, 593
Lu Xun Museum 175
Lu Xun Park 370, 520
Lujiazui 354
    Lujiazui Development Showroom 416
    Lujiazui Green 401, 416
Lupu Bridge 28, 327, 394

M

MacDonald, Sir Claude 216
Maglev see Trains
Malraux, André 372
Mann, Jim 45
Mao Chang Hsi 139
Mao Dun 397, 444
Mao, Madame see Jiang Qing
Mao's Residence, Chairman 363
Mao Zedong 85, 88, 125, 128, 129, 150, 246, 318, 363, 368, 369, 370, 482

Marble Boat 184
Marble House *see* Shanghai Municipal Palace
Marco Polo Bridge 207
Marcos, Imelda 367
Markets, Beijing 248–251
Markets 503, 504, 505
May 30th Incident 410
May Fourth Movement 85, 369
Media
   Der Ostasiatische Lloyd 315
   English Language Media 28, 63–67, 110, 487
   North China Daily News 315
   Shanghai Mercury, 315
   Shanghai Times 315
   L'Echo de Chine 315
   New Youth 318
   Shanghai Nippo 315
   Xinhua 67
Medicines 511
Mei Lanfang 173, 220, 369
Metro, Shanghai 335–336
Middle Kingdom 109
Mi jiu 497
Miaoyan, Princess 211
Ming *see* Dynasties
Ming Tombs 201, 214
Minhang Development Zone 336
Ministry of Foreign Trade 67
Misczek, Janos 378
Moganshan 453, 454
Möller, Eric 538
Monkey King 219
Monument to the People's Heroes 128, 213
Moore, Roger 131
Morriss, H. E. 487
Mountain Lodge for Avoiding Heat 205

Museums
   Arthur Sackler Museum of Art and Archaeology 215
   Aviation Museum 175, 176
   Beijing Art Museum 89, 174
   Bund Historical Museum 351
   Capital Museum 177
   Chinese Museum of Sex Culture 444, 446–449
   Contemporary Art 407, 408
   C.Y. Tung Maritime Museum 409
   Garden History Exhibition Hall *see* Halls
   Historical Art Museum 142
   Jewish Refugee Museum 417
   Jinquan Coin Museum 397
   Lu Xun Museum 176
   Lu Xun Museum, Mausoleum and Residence, Shanghai 369
   Military Museum of the Chinese People's Revolution 175
   Miniature Museum 440
   Museum of Chinese Traditional Medicine 511
   Museum of Divine Music Administration 214
   Museum of Imperial Treasures 143
   Museum of Natural History 176
   Old Shanghai Teahouse and Museum *see* Teahouses
   Postal History Museum 180–181, 408
   Qingpu Town Museum 429
   Shanghai Art Museum 407, 486, 492
   Shanghai Arts and Crafts Museum 408
   Shanghai Banking Museum 410
   Shanghai Municipal History Museum 355, 401
   Shanghai Museum 406, 509
   Shanghai Museum of Science and Technology 394, 408

Beijing's Old Observatory at the intersection of the Second Ring Road with Jianguomenwai Dajie.

Shanghai Museum of Public Security 410–411
Shanghai Natural History Museum 407
Shanghai Navy Museum 440
Xu Beihong Memorial Museum 156
Mutianyu 197

N

Nanjing Road 28, 53, 498, 499
Nan Luogu Xiang 179
Nanjing Observatory 167
Nanpu Bridge 327, 393
Nanxiang steamed dumplings 493
Nanxincang 179
National Ballet of China 474
National Bureau of Statistics 68
National Gallery of China 177
Natural History Museum 176
Nationalists 85
Nationalities Cultural Palace 178
Nehru 368
Nightsoil Queen *see* Cassia Ma
Nine Dragon Screen 152, 213
Ningbo 5, 19, 32

Nixon, Richard 104
North East China Plain 101

O

Ohel Moshe Synagogue 417
Old Observatory, The 167
Old Summer Palace, The 183, 184
Old Town, The (Shanghai) 375, 377
Orchid Bamboo Hill 428
Ordination Altar 211
Orient Green Boat 432
Oriental Pearl TV Tower 321, 354, 403
Ox Street Mosque 164

P

Pagodas
   Azure Cloud Pagoda 432
   Diamond Throne Pagoda 192
   Fahua Pagoda 435
   Huayuan Pagoda 437
   Huzhu Pagoda 429
   Longhua Pagoda 385–387
   Pearl Protection Pagoda *see* Huzhu Pagoda

Qinglong Pagoda 432, *see also* Temples
Square Pagoda 426
Xilin Pagoda 391, 425, *see also* Temples
Painting, Beijing 255
Palaces
    Palace of Abstinence 142 *see also* Halls
    Palace of Earthly Peace 140
    Palace of Eternal Harmony 142
    Palace of Happy Old Age 143
    Palace of Heavenly Favors 142
    Palace of Heavenly Purity 140, 143, 213
    Palace of Peaceful Old Age 140, 143
    Palace of Revered Benevolence 142
Pan Yunduan 383
Pao Chia 420
Park of Dragons Meeting Pool 434
Parker, Vice Admiral Sir William 33
Pavilions
    Dajing Pavilion, The 383
    Fan Pavilion 153
    Flowing Cup Pavilion 211
    Pavilion for Listening to the Orioles 184
    Pavilion for Reading Ancient Texts 152
    Pavilion for Viewing Frolicking Fish 383
    Pavilion of Buddhist Incense 184
    Ten-thousand Flower Pavilion 382
Peace Bell 391
Peace Hotel 353 *see also* Cathay Hotel
Peace Hotel Jazz Band 483
Pearl Concubine *see* Zhenfei
Peking Man 80, 208
Peter the Great 82
People's Square 320
People's Liberation Army 365
Pingguoyuan *see* Gardens, Apple
Pockmarked Huang *see* Huang Jinrong
Poly Art Museum 177
Polo, Marco 14, 207
Poly Plaza 220
Pope Gregory XIII 169

Porcelain, Beijing 178, 256
Portman, John 355
Prospect Garden 165
Prospect Hill *see* Coal Hill
Precious Fortress 203
Pudong 399, 503, 546
Puhuitang River 440
Pure Land Sect 384
Putuoshan 452

Q

Qianmen 244
Qibao 437
Qibao Catholic Church 440
Qin Qiong 593
Qing Bang *see* Green Gang
Qing Tian Fei Palace 426
Qing Tombs, Eastern 206
Qing Tombs, Western 210
Qinglong *see* Padodas, *see* Temples
Qionghua Island 150
Qiu Chuji (Yuan-dynasty monk) 164
Quanzhen Sect 384
Queen Elizabeth 409

R

Reagan, Ronald 409
Ricci, Matteo 167, 264
Roosevelt, Eleanor 153
Round Altar 155 *see also* Circular Mound
Round City 150
Roustan, J. 269

S

St. Ignatius Cathedral 395
St. John's University 521
Sakyamuni 388
Sanlitun 223
Sassoon, Sir Victor 168, 353, 368, 412
Schall, Adam (Jesuit priest) 167

Schroeder, German Chancellor Gerhard 28
Scott Road 370
Scotus, John Duns 395
Screen Wall 426
Sea of Flagstones 140
Seals 257
Seventeen-Arch Bridge 184
Shang 142
Shanghai Acrobatic Troupe 481
Shanghai Arts & Crafts Museum 408
Shanghai Biennale 407, 483
Shanghai Broadcasting Symphony Orchestra 474
Shanghai Centre 474
Shanghai Chinese Painting Academy 416
Shanghai Circus World 482
Shanghai Club 479
Shanghai Concert Hall 474
Shanghai Conservatory of Music 480
Shanghai Dramatic Arts Centre 480
Shanghai Film Art Centre 482
Shanghai Film Studio 427
Shanghai Islamic Association 398
Shanghai Municipal Palace 394
Shanghai Municipal Tourism Administration 330
Shanghai Observatory 395
Shanghai Ocean Aquarium 403
Shanghai Public Library 395
Shanghai Railway Museum 419
Shanghai Symphony Orchestra 474
Shanghai Taoist Association and Institute 384
Shanghai Tourist Information and Service Centre 66
Shanghai Urban Planning Exhibition Centre 407
Shanghai Waterworks Museum 419
Shanghai Wild Animal Park 404
Shanghai Zoo 521

Shen Kwei Fen *139*
Shen Yuan (court painter) 191
sheng jian 493
Sheshan 427, 428
Sheshan Observatory 429
Shikumen 342, 500
 Shikumen Open House 411
Shizi tou 489
Sichuan Road (N) 502
Signal Tower 351
Silk, Beijing 254 *see also* Xuishui Market
Silver Seven Star 437
Simatai 197
Siren, Osvald 174
Sky and Cloud Reflection Pool 385
Small Peach Garden Mosque 398
Small Swords Society 381, 385
Small Swords Uprising 371
Snow, Edgar 368
Song Ailing 397
Song, Charlie 366
Song Meiling 454
Song Qingling 153, 365, 366, 369
 Song Qingling, Former Residence of Madame 365
 Song Qingling's Mausoleum 368
Songjiang Mosque 424
Sony Explora Science 178
South Lake Isle 184
Spectacles Lake 192
Spirit Way, The 201
Square Pagoda Park 426, *see also* Pagodas
Stalin 368
Study of Serenity 152
Study of Self Knowledge *see* Gardens
Summer Palace, The 183, 214, 215
Sun Yat-sen, Dr. 128, 153, 192, 193, 365, 366, 411, 455
 Sun Yat-sen's Former Residence, Dr. 365
Suzhu Creek 420–421

T

Taikang Road Art Street 486
Tan 426
Tan Dun (composer) 474
Tang Dai (court painter) 191
Tang Dynasty (rock band) 101
Taxis, Shanghai 332
Tea
    Longjing (Dragon Well) 495
    moli hua cha 495
Teahouses
    Chunfeng Deyi 495
    Huxinting 375, 376, 380, 495
    Lao She 218, 220
    Mid-lake Pavilion Teahouse *see* Huxinting Teahouse
    Nora 495
    Old China Hand Reading Room 495
    Old Shanghai Teahouse and Museum 495
    Tianqiao Happy Tea House 218, 220
    WIllow Pattern Teahouse 376 *see also* Huxinting Teahouse
    Zhabei Park annual tea festival 522
Temple Fairs 251

Temples
    Baode (Award of Morality) Temple 432
    Baosheng Temple 444
    Chengxu Taoist Temple 443
    Confucian Temple 176, 215, 434
    Dragon King's Temple 184
    Fayu Temple 452
    Five Pagoda Temple 172, 192
    Guangong Temple 383
    Hong De Temple 397
    Jade Buddha Temple 388, 389, 390
    Jing'an Temple 388, 391, 498, 519
    Lamma Temple 58, 113, 177, 214, 215
    Longhua Temple 385–387
    Miaoying Temple 167
    Nanshan Temple 440
    Ordination Terrace Temple, The 211
    Puji Temple 452
    Source of Law Temple, The 164
    Temple of Agriculture 82
    Temple of Azure Clouds 192, 215
    Temple of Everlasting Peace 150
    Temple of Heaven 82, 88, 156–159, 164, 214, 215
    Temple of Longevity 89, 174
    Temple of Solitary Joy 206

Temple of the City God 375
Temple of the Pool and Wild Mulberry 210–211
Temple of the Sea of the Law 212
Temple of the Sea of Wisdom 184
Temple of the Sleeping Buddha 187, 215
Temple of the Town God 358, 433
Temple of the White Dagoba 150, 167, 172
Temple of Universal Peace 205
Qinglong Temple 432, *see also* Pagodas
Qingpu County Temple 432
Quanfu Temple 443
Wenmiao Confucian Temple 385
Western Yellow Temple 173
Xilin Temple 391, 425, *see also* Pagodas
Zhaomiao 193
Zhenru Temple 391
Terracotta warriors 3, 175
Theaters
   Belvedere of Flowing Music 141
   Cathay 474, 486
   Chaoyang Theater 219
   Cherry Lane Movies 230
   China Puppet Theater, The 219
   Grand Theater 397
   IMAX 500
   IWERKS 408
   Lao She Tea House 220
   Liyuan Theater 220
   Lyceum 474, 480
   Majestic 474, 480, 481
   Nanking 474
   Shanghai Centre 474, 481
   Shanghai Grand 397, 474, 481
   Shanghai Yifu 480
   Tianqiao Happy Tea House 220 *see also* Teahouses
   Yu Yuan Stage 481
   Yunfeng Theatre 481
   Zhengyici Theater 220
Thirteen Classics, The 176
Tiananmen Square 125, 214
Tientsin 121
Tongli 444
Toroni Buddhist Sutra Stela 426
Tower for Viewing the Moon 164
Traditional Chinese Medicines *see* Medicines
Trains 19, 28–29
   Beijing Station 22
   Beijing West Railway Station 114
Tropical Tempest Water Park 437
Tsinghua University 183
Tung, C. Y. 409
Tung Chee-hwa 409
Tung Hsun 139

U

Urban Planning Exhibition Hall 178
UNESCO World Heritage Site 443
Union Building 353
United Boat 436
Uygur 493

V

Verbiest, Ferdinand (Jesuit priest) 167
Vienna Boys Chorus 474

W

Wade Giles 121
Waibadu Bridge 360
Wall of Ten-thousand Li 195
Wanli 174
Wang Boqun 394
Wang Guangyu 109
Wangfujing 243

Left: *Overlooking Chongwenmen Dongdajie, the Ming City Wall Relics Park, the Wall back-lit by a setting sun, see also page 91.*

Wangfung Art Gallery 395
Wangxian Bridge 426
War
   Anti-Japanese War of Resistance 174
   Boxer Rebellion 95
   Japanese occupation of Shanghai 5, 85
   Korean War 177
   Opium Wars 83
   Revolutions
      1911 85
      1949 5
      Revolutionary Wars, First and Second 174
   Third Civil War 49, 174
West Lake 432
White Dagoba 150 see also Temples
White Terror 370
White Clouds Taoist Temple 384
White Crane in the Clouds Mosque 425
Whispering Wall see Echo Wall
William IV 33
Wilson, George Leopold (architect) 353
Wisdom and Knowledge, Square's of 395
Working People's Cultural Palace 128, 213
World Expo 419
Wood, Ben 412, 413

X

Xianfeng 154, 160
Xiao Fangfang 444
xiao long bao 493
Xidan 244
Xie Dieshan (Song Minister) 164
Xiushui Market 247
Xing Tonghe 406
Xintiandi 411, 412, 413, 414, 415, 487, 489
Xu Beihong 156
Xujiahui 502

Y

Yang Liwei (astronaut) 311
Yang rou chuanr 493
Yangpu Bridge 327, 394
Yinzhen, Prince 190
Yu Gardens 496, 507, 517
Yu Yuan Stage see Theaters
Yuan Shikai 159
Yuanchun, Imperial Concubine 165
Yuanmingyuan see Old Summer Palace
Yunjian Baisi see Zhenjiao Mosque

Z

Zhang Yang 151
Zhapu Road 493
Zhejiang 121
Zhenfei 140, 161
Zheng He, Admiral 409
Zhenjiao Mosque 425
Zhongnanhai 150
Zhongshan Chapel 429
Zhongshan Park 128, 522
Zhou Changxing 440
Zhou 142
Zhou Enlai 88, 125, 128, 176, 177, 368, 369
Zhou Enlai, Former Residence of 368
Zhou Shuren 593 see also Lu Xun
Zhou Xinfang 220
Zhu Rongji 28
Zhujiajiao 433
Zi-Ka-Wei Biblioteca 395